Digital Photograp...
ALL-IN-ONE DESK REF...
FOR
DUMMIES
3RD EDITION

W9-BPK-223 Cheat Sheet

Front of a Digital Camera

- Microphone
- Optical viewfinder
- Shutter release
- Control buttons
- Shooting mode dial
- Electronic flash
- Focus-assist light
- Lens cover
- Zoom lens
- Battery compartment
- Docking port
- Tripod socket

Back of a Digital Camera

- Indicator LEDs
- Optical viewfinder
- Mode dial
- Control button
- Power
- Shutter release
- Zoom
- File-save LED
- USB port
- LCD panel
- Memory card slot
- Display control
- Cursor pad
- Set/Execute button
- Picture review
- Print/e-mail photos

For Dummies: Bestselling Book Series for Beginners

Digital Photography
ALL-IN-ONE DESK REFERENCE
FOR
DUMMIES 3RD EDITION

Cheat Sheet

Faker's Guide to Digital Photography Lingo

You don't have to be the only quiet one in the room when the topic turns to digital photography. Here are some hot topics and terms to toss out when you want to sound like you live on the bleeding edge of technology.

Term	What It Means
Aperture priority	A camera control that lets you choose the lens opening, letting the camera's exposure meter automatically determine the appropriate shutter speed.
Calibration	Zeroing in components of your computer system (such as your monitor) to provide color that matches the original.
CCD, CMOS	Two kinds of computer chips used as sensors to capture images in digital cameras.
Compact Flash, Secure Digital, xD, Memory Stick	The four competing types of removable storage for digital cameras.
Compression	A way of using software to squeeze an image down to a smaller, more manageable size. If you want to seem really cool, use the terms *lossless compression* (which doesn't discard any information during the squishing process) and *lossy compression* (which does throw away some image information but makes smaller files).
Depth of field	How much of your image is in focus at one time.
Digicam	A cool term for a digital camera.
Dye-sub	A kind of printer that produces extra-good hard copies of digital images.
Interpolation	A process by which software pulls pixels out of thin air to produce an image with higher resolution. (Actually, it calculates the pixels based on those that already exist.)
ISO	Shorthand for the speed equivalent of a digital sensor when compared to traditional film sensitivity, such as ISO 100 or ISO 200. (ISO is the *International Organization for Standardization*. To earn extra awe, point out that ISO is not an acronym but comes from the Greek word *isos,* meaning "equal.")
JPEG	An image file format used by most digital cameras to make images really small so more of them will fit in the camera. JPEG uses *lossy compression*.
Megapixel	One million pixels; a measurement of the resolution of your camera's sensor.
ppi	Picture elements (pixels) per inch; the more the better, especially when it comes time to make a print.
RGB	Red/green/blue: the primary colors of light used by your digital camera to capture images.
Resample	To change the size of an image by recalculating the pixels.
Resolution	How sharp your camera, monitor, or scanner is.
Shutter priority	A camera control that lets you set the length of the instant of time used to take the picture (the shorter the better when it comes to freezing action) and lets the camera's exposure meter automatically determine the proper lens setting.

Wiley, the Wiley Publishing logo, For Dummies, the Dummies Man logo, the For Dummies Bestselling Book Series logo and all related trade dress are trademarks or registered trademarks of John Wiley & Sons, Inc. and/or its affiliates. All other trademarks are property of their respective owners.

Copyright © 2006 Wiley Publishing, Inc. All rights reserved.
Item 3743-1.
For more information about Wiley Publishing, call 1-800-762-2974.

For Dummies: Bestselling Book Series for Beginners

Digital Photography
ALL-IN-ONE DESK REFERENCE
FOR
DUMMIES®
3RD EDITION

by David D. Busch

Wiley Publishing, Inc.

Digital Photography All-in-One Desk Reference For Dummies,® 3rd Edition

Published by
Wiley Publishing, Inc.
111 River Street
Hoboken, NJ 07030-5774
www.wiley.com

Copyright © 2006 by Wiley Publishing, Inc., Indianapolis, Indiana

Published by Wiley Publishing, Inc., Indianapolis, Indiana

Published simultaneously in Canada

No part of this publication may be reproduced, stored in a retrieval system or transmitted in any form or by any means, electronic, mechanical, photocopying, recording, scanning or otherwise, except as permitted under Sections 107 or 108 of the 1976 United States Copyright Act, without either the prior written permission of the Publisher, or authorization through payment of the appropriate per-copy fee to the Copyright Clearance Center, 222 Rosewood Drive, Danvers, MA 01923, (978) 750-8400, fax (978) 646-8600. Requests to the Publisher for permission should be addressed to the Legal Department, Wiley Publishing, Inc., 10475 Crosspoint Blvd., Indianapolis, IN 46256, (317) 572-3447, fax (317) 572-4355, or online at http://www.wiley.com/go/permissions.

Trademarks: Wiley, the Wiley Publishing logo, For Dummies, the Dummies Man logo, A Reference for the Rest of Us!, The Dummies Way, Dummies Daily, The Fun and Easy Way, Dummies.com, and related trade dress are trademarks or registered trademarks of John Wiley & Sons, Inc. and/or its affiliates in the United States and other countries, and may not be used without written permission. All other trademarks are the property of their respective owners. Wiley Publishing, Inc., is not associated with any product or vendor mentioned in this book.

LIMIT OF LIABILITY/DISCLAIMER OF WARRANTY: THE PUBLISHER AND THE AUTHOR MAKE NO REPRESENTATIONS OR WARRANTIES WITH RESPECT TO THE ACCURACY OR COMPLETENESS OF THE CONTENTS OF THIS WORK AND SPECIFICALLY DISCLAIM ALL WARRANTIES, INCLUDING WITHOUT LIMITATION WARRANTIES OF FITNESS FOR A PARTICULAR PURPOSE. NO WARRANTY MAY BE CREATED OR EXTENDED BY SALES OR PROMOTIONAL MATERIALS. THE ADVICE AND STRATEGIES CONTAINED HEREIN MAY NOT BE SUITABLE FOR EVERY SITUATION. THIS WORK IS SOLD WITH THE UNDERSTANDING THAT THE PUBLISHER IS NOT ENGAGED IN RENDERING LEGAL, ACCOUNTING, OR OTHER PROFESSIONAL SERVICES. IF PROFESSIONAL ASSISTANCE IS REQUIRED, THE SERVICES OF A COMPETENT PROFESSIONAL PERSON SHOULD BE SOUGHT. NEITHER THE PUBLISHER NOR THE AUTHOR SHALL BE LIABLE FOR DAMAGES ARISING HEREFROM. THE FACT THAT AN ORGANIZATION OR WEBSITE IS REFERRED TO IN THIS WORK AS A CITATION AND/OR A POTENTIAL SOURCE OF FURTHER INFORMATION DOES NOT MEAN THAT THE AUTHOR OR THE PUBLISHER ENDORSES THE INFORMATION THE ORGANIZATION OR WEBSITE MAY PROVIDE OR RECOMMENDATIONS IT MAY MAKE. FURTHER, READERS SHOULD BE AWARE THAT INTERNET WEBSITES LISTED IN THIS WORK MAY HAVE CHANGED OR DISAPPEARED BETWEEN WHEN THIS WORK WAS WRITTEN AND WHEN IT IS READ.

For general information on our other products and services, please contact our Customer Care Department within the U.S. at 800-762-2974, outside the U.S. at 317-572-3993, or fax 317-572-4002.

For technical support, please visit www.wiley.com/techsupport.

Wiley also publishes its books in a variety of electronic formats. Some content that appears in print may not be available in electronic books.

Library of Congress Control Number: 2006926472

ISBN-13: 978-0-470-03743-0

ISBN-10: 0-470-03743-1

Manufactured in the United States of America

10 9 8 7 6 5 4 3 2 1

3K/TR/QY/QW/IN

WILEY

About the Author

As a roving photojournalist for more than 20 years, **David D. Busch** illustrated his books, magazine articles, and newspaper reports with award-winning images. He's operated his own commercial studio, suffocated in formal dress while shooting weddings-for-hire, and shot sports for a daily newspaper and Upstate New York college. His photos have been published in magazines as diverse as *Scientific American* and *Petersen's PhotoGraphic,* and his articles have appeared in *Popular Photography & Imaging, The Rangefinder, The Professional Photographer,* and hundreds of other publications. He's currently reviewing digital cameras for CNet and *Computer Shopper.*

When About.com named its top five books on Beginning Digital Photography, occupying the #1 and #2 slots were the last edition of this book, *Digital Photography All-in-One Desk Reference For Dummies,* and Busch's *Mastering Digital Photography.* During the past year, he's had as many as five of his books listed in the Top 20 of Amazon.com's Digital Photography Best Seller list — simultaneously! Busch's 90 other books published since 1983 include best-sellers like *Digital SLR Cameras & Photography For Dummies,* and four books in Wiley's Digital Field Guide series, with topics ranging from travel photography to guidebooks for the Nikon D50, D70s, and D200 cameras.

Busch earned top category honors in the Computer Press Awards the first two years they were given (for *Sorry About The Explosion* and *Secrets of MacWrite, MacPaint and MacDraw*), and later served as Master of Ceremonies for the awards.

Dedication

I dedicate this book, as always, to Cathy.

Author's Acknowledgments

Thanks to Wiley Publishing for the continued innovation that has helped keep this book fresh and up-to-date, and, now, in full color at a price anyone can afford. Key personnel include Steve Hayes, Senior Acquisitions Editor; Kim Darosett, Project Editor; and Andy Hollandbeck, Copy Editor.

Technical Editor Michael D. Sullivan added a great deal to this book in addition to checking all the text for technical accuracy. A veteran photographer (in the military sense of the word!), he began his photo career in high school where he first learned the craft and amazed his classmates by having Monday morning coverage of Saturday's big game pictured on the school bulletin board. Sullivan pursued his interest in photography into the U.S. Navy, graduating in the top ten of his photo school class. Following Navy photo assignments in Bermuda and Arizona, he earned a BA degree from West Virginia Wesleyan College.

He became publicity coordinator for Eastman Kodak Company's largest division where he directed the press introduction of the company's major consumer products and guided their continuing promotion. Following a 25-year stint with Kodak, Sullivan pursued a second career with a PR agency as a writer-photographer covering technical imaging subjects and producing articles that appeared in leading trade publications. In recent years, Sullivan has used his imaging expertise as a Technical Editor specializing in digital imaging and photographic subjects for top selling books.

Publisher's Acknowledgments

We're proud of this book; please send us your comments through our online registration form located at www.dummies.com/register/.

Some of the people who helped bring this book to market include the following:

Acquisitions, Editorial, and Media Development

Project Editor: Kim Darosett

Senior Acquisitions Editor: Steve Hayes

Copy Editor: Andy Hollandbeck

Technical Editor: Michael Sullivan

Editorial Manager: Leah Cameron

Media Development Manager: Laura VanWinkle

Editorial Assistant: Amanda Foxworth

Sr. Editorial Assistant: Cherie Case

Cartoons: Rich Tennant (www.the5thwave.com)

Composition Services

Project Coordinator: Jennifer Theriot

Layout and Graphics: Denny Hager, Barbara Moore, Melanee Prendergast, Heather Ryan, Ronald Terry

Proofreaders: John Greenough, Leeann Harney, Ethel M. Winslow

Indexer: Lynnzee Elze

Publishing and Editorial for Technology Dummies

  Richard Swadley, Vice President and Executive Group Publisher

  Andy Cummings, Vice President and Publisher

  Mary Bednarek, Executive Acquisitions Director

  Mary C. Corder, Editorial Director

Publishing for Consumer Dummies

  Diane Graves Steele, Vice President and Publisher

  Joyce Pepple, Acquisitions Director

Composition Services

  Gerry Fahey, Vice President of Production Services

  Debbie Stailey, Director of Composition Services

Contents at a Glance

Table of Contents

Introduction

The future of photography is in your hands, and it's becoming all digital! Not since the 19th century, when photographers had to be artisan, craftsperson, artist, chemist, and public relations expert rolled into one, has so much of the photographic process been entirely in the control of the person taking the picture. Now you can compose and view the exact picture you're going to take by using your camera's full liquid crystal display (LCD) screen. Review the picture an instant after pressing the shutter. If your computer is nearby, you can upload it seconds later, view a super-large version on your display, crop it, enhance it, and then make your own sparkling full-color print — all within minutes!

When you go digital, you never need to buy film or wait while your photos are processed in a lab. You decide which images to print and how large to make them. You can display your digital photographic work framed on your wall or displayed proudly over your fireplace. You can make wallet-size photos, send copies to friends in e-mail, or create an online gallery that can be viewed by relatives and colleagues over the Web.

And if alchemy is in your blood, you can transform the simplest picture into a digital masterpiece by using an image editor. Correct your photos, delete your ex-brother-in-law from a family portrait, or transplant the Eiffel Tower to the seashore.

Digital photography gives you the power to take pictures on a whim or to create careful professional-quality work that others might be willing to pay for. The choices are all yours, and digital photography puts all the power in your hands. All you need is a little information about how to choose and use your tools and how to put them to work. That's what you'll find within the pages of this thick, comprehensive, all-in-one guidebook.

The most exciting aspect of digital photography is how rapidly the technology is changing to bring you new capabilities and features that you can use to improve your pictures. Today, digital cameras with 4-megapixel (mp) or less resolution are difficult to find except in photo-capable cell phones — and some cell phones offer 10-megapixel or more resolution! Even the leanest digital camera you're likely to find in stores will have 5–6 megapixels of resolution. I've tested models in this range that cost less than $150! You'll find 7-megapixel and 9-megapixel cameras for $500 or so, and even 10-megapixel models are widely available for quite a bit less than $1,000. Digital single-lens reflex cameras (dSLRs) with interchangeable lenses are available from companies like Nikon, Canon, Olympus, and Sony if you're willing to pay top dollar.

Adobe Photoshop has bumped up the image editing ante with lots of new capabilities of interest to digital photographers, and even inexpensive applications like Adobe Photoshop Elements have more features than you could find in the most powerful image editor four or five years ago. Your new hardware and software tools make working with digital images easier while giving you important new capabilities.

About This Book

This book, now in its third edition and freshly enhanced with full-color images throughout, has been updated to include all the latest technology and gadgets available to the digital photographer. It is written for the person who has a good grasp of using a computer and navigating an operating system and has at least a cursory knowledge of the operation of a digital camera. It would help if you had some familiarity with an image editor, such as Corel Paint Shop Pro, Corel Photo Paint, or Adobe's Photoshop or Photoshop Elements. It is intended to be a comprehensive reference book that you can read cover to cover or reach for when you're looking for specific information about a particular task.

Wherever I can, I sneak in a useful tip or an interesting technique to help you put digital photography to work for your project needs.

If you have some knowledge of conventional photography, this book will help you fine-tune your capabilities. If you know very little about photography, there's help for you here, too. One large chunk of the book — Book IV — is devoted to tips on the most popular genres of photography, from close-up and sports photography to travel photography and shooting for publication. Check out the helpful section on getting the best composition. If you're puzzled over what equipment to buy, look to the sections on choosing cameras, photo accessories, and related equipment, such as printers and scanners.

There's a new book in this edition especially for you digital single-lens reflex (dSLR) users, although you'll find that another book of mine, *Digital SLR Cameras & Photography For Dummies,* goes into more detail on the special features of these more advanced cameras.

What's in This Book

This book is broken down into minibooks, each covering a general topic. Each minibook comprises chapters, each covering a more specific topic under the general one. Each chapter is then divided into sections, and some of those sections have subsections. I'm sure you get the picture.

You can read the book from front to back, or you can dive right into the mini-book or chapter of your choice. Either way works just fine. Any time a concept is mentioned that isn't covered in depth in that chapter, you'll find a cross-reference to another book and chapter where you'll find all the details. If you're looking for something specific, check out either the Table of Contents or the index.

The Cheat Sheet at the beginning of the book provides helpful information you'll use often. Tear it out, tape it to your monitor, and don't forget to say, "Thanks." (You're welcome.)

And finally, you get pictures. Lots of them. Many of these pictures illustrate good photo techniques as well as traps to avoid. You'll find examples of the kinds of pictures you can take right away and maybe a few that you'll want to strive to equal or exceed.

This book contains eight minibooks. The following sections offer a quick synopsis of what each book contains.

Book I: Digital Photography Overview

This section is your digital photography short course, providing all the information on a variety of topics that you really need to know to get started. Each of the six chapters is an overview of topics covered in depth later in the book. You'll find the essentials of good digital photography, equipment basics, and how to acquire digital pictures. Buzz through the quickie introduction into some of the ways you can edit or restore a photo electronically and take a look at how you can store and organize your digital photos. Then, if you're interested in what's involved in selecting a printer or scanner, you'll find all the basic information summarized for you in an easy-to-understand way.

Book II: Building Your Digital Photography Studio

This book helps you choose the right camera, whether it's your first digital camera or the one you're dreaming about as a replacement for your current model. You'll read all the facts on resolution, lens settings, storage, and accessories. One chapter shows you the requirements for setting up a PC for digital photography. The good news is that you probably already have everything you need in your computer. I'll give you some advice on recommended upgrades that can make your system work even better with digital images.

You'll also discover your options for getting pictures from your camera into your digital darkroom. And, if you want to get the most from your pictures, you'll want to read up on how to add a scanner and printer, too.

Book III: Using Digital SLRs

This book provides a concise overview of the tools and capabilities you'll find in the latest digital SLR cameras. You find out why these cameras can do things that their non-SLR counterparts cannot and how to use those features to improve your photography.

Book IV: Taking Great Pictures

This is the meat of the book for veteran and aspiring photographers alike. Each of the six chapters is devoted to a different kind of photography. You'll see the basic rules for composing great photos — and when to break them. You'll discover the secrets of close-up photography and how to make pleasing portraits of individuals and groups.

Whether shooting for publication is part of your job description or just a goal, you'll find tips on how to take publishable photos and how to market them. I also include chapters on sports and action photography as well tips on travel photography.

Book V: Basics of Image Editing

This book is your introduction to image editing, providing general tips on what you can — and can't — do with popular image editors such as Paint Shop Pro, Corel PhotoPaint, PhotoImpact, or Adobe Photoshop and Photoshop Elements. You'll see the capabilities of these programs, discovering the full range of tools at your disposal.

The book winds up with a chapter that compares and contrasts the most popular image editors so you can choose which image editing program you really need (or whether you might even benefit from owning two!).

Book VI: Editing with Photoshop and Photoshop Elements

This book goes into a little more detail on the use of the two most popular image editing programs: Adobe Photoshop (favored by professionals) and Adobe Photoshop Elements (an inexpensive younger sibling that has lots of power but is still easy to use). You discover the power of making selections, brush away problems in your digital photos, correct your colors, and apply special effects with filters.

Although this book is not a complete guide to Photoshop, you'll find lots of good information you can use right away to try out your digital photo editing muscles. (For tons of in-depth coverage, read *Photoshop CS2 All-in-One Desk Reference For Dummies,* by Barbara Obermeier [Wiley].)

Book VII: Restoring Old Photos

Continue your study of Photoshop and Photoshop Elements with this book, which shows you how to restore old photos and make some common repairs to your digital images. Read chapters on scanning in print images, tips for working with slides and negatives, and some common fixes for vintage photos.

Book VIII: Printing and Sharing Your Digital Images

Your digital photos are going to be so good that you won't be able to keep them to yourself. This book provides more information on printing your photos and shows you ways to share your pictures over the Internet. You'll become more comfortable with your printer's capabilities, discovering all the things that you can do with photos online, whether it's showcasing your pictures among your friends and colleagues or making photo greeting cards, T-shirts, or other gift items.

Conventions Used in This Book

Digital photography knows no operating system limits. All digital cameras and many software applications work equally well on a PC and a Macintosh. To that end, this book is cross-platform. Understandably, some differences do crop up, particularly in the chapters that deal with image editing. In this book, Windows commands are given first, followed by Mac commands, like this:

Press Enter (or Return on the Mac) to begin a new line.

Occasionally, text will be specific to one platform or another. Commands listed often involve using the keyboard along with the mouse — for example, "Press Shift while dragging with the Rectangular Marquee tool to create a square," or "Alt+click (Option+click) the eyeball to redisplay all layers."

When you see a command arrow (⇨) in the text, it indicates that you should select a command from the menu bar. For example, "Choose Edit⇨Define Custom Shape" means to click the Edit menu and then choose the Define Custom Shape option.

Although this book was written based on the latest digital cameras and the newest software (such as Print Shop Pro and Photoshop), if you're still bouncing around with earlier versions, you can still glean valuable info. You might just have to poke around a little more to find a tool or option that has moved — and of course, the topics covering new features won't be applicable. But hey, seeing the cool new features might just be the impetus you need to go out and upgrade!

Icons Used in This Book

While perusing this book, you'll notice some icons in the margins beckoning you for your attention. Don't ignore them; embrace them! These icons point out fun, useful, and memorable tidbits about digital photography, plus facts you'd be unwise to ignore.

This icon indicates information that will make your digital photography experience easier. It also gives you an icebreaker at your next cocktail party. Whipping out, "Did you know that many digital cameras can focus down to within an inch of an object?" is bound to make you the center of conversation.

This icon is a reminder of things that I want to *gently* re-emphasize. Or I might be pointing out things that I want you to take note of in your future digital photography excursions.

The little bomb icon is a red flag. Heed these warnings, or else your camera or image editor might show its ugly side.

This icon points out info you don't necessarily need to know. If you're interested in getting more technical, however, you'll find such information interesting.

Where to Go from Here

If you want your voice to be heard, you can contact the publisher of the *For Dummies* books by visiting www.dummies.com, by sending an e-mail to customer@wiley.com, or by sending snail mail to Wiley Publishing, Inc., 10475 Crosspoint Boulevard, Indianapolis, IN 46256.

And, of course, the very next place to go is to the section of this book that covers your favorite topic. Go ahead and dive right in.

Book I
Digital Photography Overview

The 5th Wave   By Rich Tennant

THE GLACIER MOVEMENT PROJECT UPDATES THEIR WEB SITE

Camera ready? Wait a minute, hold it. Ready? Wait for the action... steady...steady... not yet...eeeasy. Hold it. Okay, stay focused. Ready? Not yet...steeeady...eeeasy...

1 f you're shifting your digital photographic pursuits into high gear and want to hit the ground running, this minibook is your fast track to pixel proficiency. You can consider the six chapters in this overview both a quickie course in digital photography concepts as well as a preview of what you can discover in the rest of the book. All the basics are here, so you can begin taking, sharing, and printing great photos right away. When you want to find out more, you can follow the cross references in this book to discover the in-depth coverage you'll find in the other sections.

This minibook outlines the essentials of good photography and shows you how to decide which digital equipment will do the best job for you. You'll discover the best ways to acquire digital pictures — whether you choose to use a camera or scanner — and find out the fundamentals of editing and restoring photos with image editors like Photoshop, Photoshop Elements, and Paint Shop Pro. If you want to share and preserve your digital images, you'll find tips on managing, archiving, and printing your photos, as well as discover the best ways to post them online for others to enjoy.

Chapter 1: The Essentials of Good Digital Photography

In This Chapter

- ✓ **Choosing equipment**
- ✓ **Making great digital photos**
- ✓ **Converting other photos to digital format**
- ✓ **Making hard-copy prints**

*I*n 1888, George Eastman began promoting the first hand-held Kodak camera with the slogan, "You press the button, we do the rest." His idea was to make the film camera as convenient as the pencil. However, the film king's dream didn't really come true until the invention of the digital camera.

Certainly, conventional photography has long been as simple as pressing a button, but the "we do the rest" part — taking the film to a photo lab, deciding what size and kind of prints to make, and then waiting for the results — is a *lot* less convenient than using a pencil.

Digital photography has finally put the entire process of making pictures in the hands of the person holding the camera. You press the button, and you can do as much of the rest *yourself* as you're comfortable with. If all you want to do is point and shoot, you can do that. If you want to get more involved in the picture-taking and picture-making process, digital photography gives you the tools for that, too.

You compose the picture through the viewfinder (as always), but now, you can preview the exact photograph that you're going to take on a bright LCD (liquid crystal display) screen on the back of your camera. After snapping a shot, you can instantly review the photos you've taken and erase the bad pictures on the spot or "mark" the ones you want to print.

You don't need to remember to stop and buy film. Your digital film is almost infinitely reusable. You don't have to drop off your digital film for finishing: It's "processed" instantly and ready for viewing or printing using your own inexpensive color printer. No more sifting through stacks of prints of marginal images. *You* decide which images to print and whether to make them 4 x 6 inches or 5 x 7 inches or some other size. You can print them at home inexpensively or take a tiny digital memory card to a nearby retailer and have even more inexpensive prints made for you in minutes by an in-store digital print lab.

On the other hand, if you want to have full control over your photos, digital photography gives you that, too, to a degree that has never before been possible. Perhaps your images aren't exactly right or could benefit from a little cropping or other improvements. You can fix bad color, remove your ex-brother-in-law from a family photo, or adjust the borders of an image to focus on the most interesting subject matter. All you need is an image editor, such as Photoshop or Photoshop Elements.

This chapter provides an overview of the sorts of things you find out how to do in this book. I cover each topic in more detail later on in a minibook and chapter of its own. I'll keep the repetition to a minimum; the chapters in Book I are intended to offer an introduction to topics that are explored more deeply elsewhere in the book.

Knowing What Equipment You Need

I realize that you might not be curled up with this book in one hand and a digital camera in the other. You might already have a digital camera, and you purchased this book to find out exactly what you can do with it. You'll find the tips and information you need throughout this volume.

However, I'm guessing that some of you haven't taken the plunge yet. You're ready to stop being a hold-out and want to join the digital camera revolution. So you bought this book to find out more about digital photography before spending your hard-earned money on the equipment you need. Good plan!

After all, there are so many choices available that it's easy to buy a camera that's not quite right for the kind of pictures you want to take. All digital cameras do a good job with general picture-taking for family activities, travel, informal portraits, and other kinds of shots. But some are better than others for taking close-up photos, sports action pictures, or photos indoors where a wide view is needed.

So, you'd like some of your questions answered before you buy: Can a camera I can afford do the things I need to do? Can a computer fumble-fingers like me really do digital photography? What's the best camera to buy? Will I be able to expand my camera's capabilities if I find I need more advanced features?

Or, perhaps you are a digital camera veteran who is already thinking of upgrading. You, too, need some advice about equipment, which you can find in this book.

Choosing a digital camera that's right for you can be tricky because a lot more goes into your selection than simply the specifications. Two cameras with identical specs can perform quite differently. One may exceed your expectations, while the other one frustrates the heck out of you. I explore some of the subtleties of camera selection in Book I, Chapter 2.

The digital camera world has changed dramatically since I wrote the first edition of this book. I warned readers against trying to do serious photography with cheap Web cams or low-end 1-megapixel cameras. Today, some camera phones have a lot more resolution than that, and even the lowest priced digital cameras (in the $100–$200 range), have 4 megapixels (millions of pixels of information). They are more likely to have at least 5 to 6 megapixels of resolution. They feature automatic exposure, a color LCD viewing screen for previewing or reviewing your photos, and removable storage, so you can take out your digital film card when it's full and replace it with a new one to keep shooting. Most have a 3X zoom lens, so you can magnify an image without moving forward, which is invaluable when you want to take pictures of different subjects from one spot.

Those minimum specs give you everything you need to take great photos. After all, the photographer, not the camera, produces the best images. I once wrote an article for a photo magazine in which I presented photos of the same subjects, side-by-side, taken with an inexpensive point-and-shoot film camera and a full-blown professional system that cost 100 times as much. After both sets of photos had been subjected to the vagaries of halftone reproduction, it was difficult to tell them apart.

Spending a lot on a digital camera buys you a few new capabilities, like better zooms, enhanced resolution, or a more sophisticated built-in flash. If you have a full-featured model, you can find lots of information in this book on how to get the most from your camera's capabilities. But this book also contains workarounds for those who own more modest equipment.

You can find digital cameras suitable for the most exotic of photographic pursuits, such as the underwater set-up shown in Figure 1-1. It's a waterproof case for a Canon PowerShot digital camera. It provides full access to all your camera's controls while letting you photograph those colorful coral reefs in Tahiti at depths of up to 100 feet!

Figure 1-1: This waterproof case can take your digital photography to new depths!

Minimum and Maximum Specs

For most of this book, I assume you have a digital camera with at least 4 megapixels of resolution. (If you don't understand resolution right now, see Book I, Chapter 2, for an explanation.) Such cameras are becoming harder to find; it's likely that 5 and 6 megapixels will become the minimum resolution for new cameras introduced during the lifespan of this book.

A camera with a 4-megapixel sensor corresponds to about 2300 x 1700 pixels, which is enough detail to give you decent 6-x-8-inch prints or larger at 200 dpi printer resolution. A 4-megapixel camera also can capture enough information to allow some cropping, especially if you plan to use the image on a Web page, where high resolution isn't necessary.

However, if you happen to have an older camera with less resolution, you can still do plenty of things. You can prepare images for dynamite Web pages and make sparkling 4-x-5-inch prints. One of my favorite cameras is an ancient 3.3 megapixel Nikon CoolPix 995 that is excellent for close-up photos, and I use it from time to time to take pictures for eBay auctions.

Cameras with up to 6 megapixels or more of resolution have dipped down into the inexpensive camera range (under $200), and if you have a little more to spend, you can find point-and-shoot cameras with 10 megapixels of resolution for only a few hundred dollars more. Digital single lens reflex (dSLR) cameras, which boast faster operation and interchangeable lenses, offer around 6 to 8 megapixels of detail in the sub-$1,000 price range, and 10 to 12 megapixels (and more) if you're willing to pay at least $1,500 for your camera. (You can read more about dSLRs in Book III.)

Extensive coverage of digital SLR cameras is new to this latest edition, but very little in this book actually requires a dSLR to achieve. Those of you with these high-end cameras should still find lots to like in this book; one of my goals has been to present pro-level techniques in ways that can help anyone. If you have a digital SLR like the one shown in Figure 1-2, you'll find these techniques especially useful. If you want to find out even more about these cameras, I recommend my book, *Digital SLR Cameras & Photography For Dummies,* from Wiley Publishing.

If you own a more sophisticated camera, whether it's a digital SLR or an advanced non-SLR camera, there are lots of additional capabilities at your fingertips. You can make tack-sharp 8-x-10-inch prints (and even larger prints if your printer supports them or if you take your digital files to your retailer). You can crop out the center of an image and still have sharpness to spare. Your camera will have loads of automated features, such as automatic bracketing (taking several exposures at different settings to make sure one is ideal) or a very long zoom lens (to reach way out and capture distant objects). Your camera may be able to take time-lapse photos and stitch images together to create panoramas.

Although I seem to focus on the number of pixels a camera has, other considerations, such as the range of the zoom lens, may also be important to you. Even the least expensive cameras may have a 2:1 to 3:1 zoom, which can magnify an image 2X and 3X (respectively). Better cameras have 4:1 or longer zooms, up to 12:1 or more. Digital SLRs offer the best zoom capabilities of all: You can remove one lens and swap it for another with a longer range or with wider or longer perspectives. Your camera probably has *macro,* or close-up, capability, which lets you grab images from inches away from your subject. Book IV, Chapter 2 is devoted to close-up techniques.

Most of the other components (such as the amount and type of memory storage, manual/automatic exposure and focusing options, built-in flash capability, and so on) can vary widely. You can find discussions of these in Book I, Chapter 2.

One thing I avoid in this book is mentioning the names of specific camera models, except as a matter of interest from time to time. It's more likely that I'll mention 10- or 8- or 5-megapixel models in a generic sense. You won't find extensive discussions in this book about the relative merits of the latest Nikon or Canon cameras or other references that will be hopelessly outdated in a few months. (Those of you reading this in 2008 with your $500 12-megapixel cameras should refrain from laughing as you encounter some of my quaint advice.)

Figure 1-2: Digital SLR cameras allow you to remove one lens and replace it with another one with different capabilities.

Taking Great Digital Shots

So, when you have a camera in hand, what do you need to know to take great digital photos? In this section, I discuss the knowledge that needs to reside in your brain (or be otherwise available) to take great pictures.

Understand how your camera works

No digital photography book can tell you how to turn on your camera, how to adjust the auto-exposure settings, or how to use your model's self-timer to take a picture with you in it (although Wiley Publishing's *Digital Field Guide* series does offer editions for specific camera models). Those are things best found in your camera's instruction manual. Read it. I promise that the information you seek is in there; it may just be hard to find. The instructions for one of my own digital cameras were so cryptic that I found myself creating a cheat sheet with lists of steps, such as, "To turn off the auto-sharpening feature, press the Menu button, then. . . ."

Some of the techniques in this book call for using a specific exposure mode or lens setting. I may ask you to switch to your camera's close-up mode to take photos a few inches from your subject. You may need to use your camera's built-in flash. Learn how to do these now so that you can add some simple but effective tools to your shooting repertoire.

Know some photography fundamentals

Certainly, you can point your camera and snap off a picture that may turn out great. Some prize-winning shots were taken in an instant as a fast-breaking news event unfolded without warning. Amateur photographers took more than a few of those photos, such as the famous Pulitzer Prize winner of a woman falling from a burning hotel, captured by a 26-year-old Georgia Tech student. However, whatever part instinct and luck take in the production of great pictures, a little knowledge can be much more important.

✦ If you know a little about composition, you can nudge your images into a more pleasing arrangement. (See Book IV, Chapter 1, for a full course in photographic composition.)

✦ Understanding how focus can make parts of your image sharp or blurry gives you the freedom to use focus selectively to isolate or emphasize subjects (Book IV, Chapter 2).

✦ Some background in how shutter speeds can freeze action can improve your sports photography (Book IV, Chapter 5).

✦ And you don't need to become an expert in lighting effects, but understanding how light works can improve your people pictures (Book IV, Chapter 3).

Find out how to use an image editor

In digital photography, the pseudo-snap of an electronic shutter is only the beginning. You can do lots of things after the shot to improve your photo — or transform it into an entirely new one. Simple image editors enable you to crop pictures, fix bad color, or remove defects, such as those glaring red eyes found in many flash photos. However, you can find even more creative freedom in more-advanced image editors that let you do anything from eliminating trees that appear to grow out of your subject's head to bringing seriously damaged photos back to life. If you want to polish your reputation as an all-around digital photographer, plan on developing at least a modicum of skill with a decent image editing program. You'll find general information on a broad range of image editors in Book V, and specifics on Adobe Photoshop and Photoshop Elements in Book VI.

Master a scanner

Digital photographers don't *have* to own a scanner, but you don't *have* to own a camera bag or an extra digital film card, either. Like other digital accessories, a scanner provides you with some supplemental techniques that let your scanner complement or substitute for your digital camera. For example, if you have a large stock of images that originated on film and now exist only as prints or negatives, a scanner can help you convert them to digital format. A scanner also can be used for producing close-up images of relatively flat three-dimensional objects, such as coins. A scanner can grab pictures of very small objects (less than 1 x 1 inch) that are difficult to capture with a digital camera.

The exact kind of scanner you have isn't important, as long as it's a flatbed model, like the one shown in Figure 1-3. I explain the differences between the major types of flatbeds and how their capabilities diverge (that is, some scanners can be used to scan three-dimensional objects, whereas others can't) in Book II, Chapter 4.

Figure 1-3: This scanner's novel design lets you view the photo through the glass while it is being scanned.

Making Any Photo Digital

In this book, you can also find out how to transform any photo you happen to have into a digital image. Scanners are one way to do this: Slap an existing photo down on the scanning bed and scan it into your image editor, and you have a digital image that's the equal of anything you might capture with your digital camera — except it's likely to have dust spots!

Or, drop off your film at your local photo lab and request a Photo CD or Picture CD along with (or instead of) your prints. These CDs can be produced from slide film, too, or even from stacks of existing prints. What you receive for your money is a scan of your images, perfect for manipulating in your image editor and printing on your own color printer. You don't even need to own a scanner: Your photo lab does all the work for you.

Another option is using a local or mail-order service that processes your film and puts the finished images on the Internet. You can download your photos to your computer or make them available for viewing by family, friends, and colleagues on a Web page. What could be easier? You can find more information on this topic in Book VIII, Chapter 2.

Printing Your Final Pictures

The final piece of the digital photography puzzle is the hard-copy print. You may create photos electronically, view them on your computer, post them on your Web site, and send them to others as e-mail, but nothing beats having a stack of prints to pass around or an enlargement to hang over the fireplace.

So, in Book I, Chapter 6, you can find basic information on making prints, and you can find more advanced advice in Book VIII. The good news is that the equipment you need is inexpensive and easy to use. A photo-quality inkjet printer can set you back $100 or so. It probably plugs directly into a USB port on your computer and requires little or no setup. Making the prints can be a point-and-click operation. A variety of printers can do the job for you. The one shown in Figure 1-4 can produce prints directly from your digital camera or storage media, with no computer required at all!

The bad news, if it can be called that, is that the cost of materials can seem a little high. You can pay $1.00 or more just for the paper and ink for a single 8-x-10-inch print. However, I show you some money-saving tips in Book VIII, Chapter 1. The best news is that you don't make a print of every single photo you take. You can view your prints on your computer display and make hard copies of only the very best. From that angle, making your own prints isn't expensive at all. You're printing only the pictures you want, and in the long run, probably paying a lot less overall than you used to spend on those prints that wound up in a shoebox.

Figure 1-4: Plug a memory card into the slot on this printer, choose an image on the built-in LCD, and you can make a print without using a computer.

Chapter 2: Basics of Equipment

In This Chapter

- ✔ Choosing the best camera
- ✔ Looking at resolution
- ✔ Examining camera categories
- ✔ Checking out basic camera features

Choosing a digital camera isn't a once-in-a-lifetime thing any more than buying a car, choosing a computer system, or purchasing a television would be. Your goal should be to select the digital camera that can do the job you want today and for the foreseeable future but not for the rest of your life. Odds are, you'll be making the decision all over again two or three years down the road, when prices have dropped even further and new features are available.

So, you want to choose wisely now, while planning to make future upgrades. In that sense, purchasing a digital camera is more like buying a television than a computer system. Most computers can be easily upgraded to add features or improve performance. You can increase the amount of memory, substitute a DVD burner for an older CD-ROM drive, and perhaps even double or triple the speed with a new processor.

Digital cameras aren't easily overhauled. You're pretty much stuck with the sensor and storage system built into the camera on the day you purchased it. If you don't have a digital SLR with interchangeable lenses, you're more or less married to the lens that comes attached to your camera. You can certainly enhance your camera with add-ons, such as lens attachments, additional removable storage, or a better external electronic flash unit. But, essentially, no matter how much digital cameras improve over the next few years, yours will stay the same. Just as you wouldn't purchase a 45-inch conventional projection TV now if you're going to need a 42-inch HDTV set next year, you want a digital camera that's ready for everything you plan to throw at it.

This chapter is an overview of what to look for when choosing the digital camera that's best for you, whether you're a well-heeled amateur who changes cameras as often as many of us change clothes, or you're a frugal buyer who wants a camera that will do the job for two or three years. You find out the basics of the features that you need to evaluate before you lay down your cash. In Book II, I go into more detail as you build your digital studio, starting with a detailed look at cameras and features in Book II, Chapter 1.

Deciding What You Need

What's the best car on the market? It's hard to say without knowing your driving plans, isn't it? Will you be making a 40-mile commute on crowded freeways every day? You might find that a 40-miles-per-gallon econobox suits your needs. Do you have six kids to transport? Plan on driving off-road? Need to impress the country club set? Will you be running in road rallies during the weekends? You can see why the automotive world has so many options.

The same holds true in the digital camera realm. Some kinds of cameras do some kinds of things better or more easily. Although you can use workarounds to get great sports photos or close-ups with cameras that aren't particularly suited to those situations, you're better off carefully defining your expectations before you purchase a camera.

Unfortunately, price isn't the best indicator. If you want to take lots of different kinds of pictures, you can't just buy the most expensive camera and figure that it has every feature you can possibly need. It's more likely that you'll end up with a camera that's so complicated you'll spend more time trying to figure out how to access a feature than actually taking the photo. I've used digital cameras that forced me to access a menu, press several buttons, and then turn a dial just to be able to manually focus.

In the following sections, I discuss some of the things you need to consider before you begin to narrow your choice to a particular category or brand of digital camera.

How much resolution do you need?

Digital cameras are often categorized simply by the amount of detail they can capture, measured by the number of pixels available in the sensor, regardless of their other features. While the resolution of the camera may be 3000 x 2000 pixels (or some other figure), they're advertised only by the total number of pixels they can grab. Thus, they're classified as 5-megapixel, 6-megapixel, or 9-megapixel cameras, as if that resolution figure is the only measure of the camera's value. I can almost visualize digital cameras on shelves with unit pricing stickers like you find at a supermarket. Hmmm . . .

one camera offers 8000 pixels per $1.00, whereas this other one gives you 12,000 pixels per $1.00. The second one is clearly a better deal!

In practice, the resolution you require depends a lot on what you plan to do with the photos you take. Do you plan on making excellent 8-x-10-inch or larger prints? If so, you need a camera with a minimum of 5 to 6 megapixels. Is it likely you'll crop a small section out of the center of an image and make a 5-x-7-inch print out of that? You'll need one of those high-resolution cameras, too. You may be able to see the difference between the left photo in Figure 2-1, taken with a 6-megapixel camera, and the version to the right, taken seconds later at a 3.3 megapixel resolution. (Both images have been cropped so you can see fine detail in the brickwork of the structure.). But, given the loss of detail that occurs any time a photo is reproduced for the printed page, you might *not* see much difference. In that case, wouldn't the 6-megapixel camera be overkill?

Book I
Chapter 2

Basics of Equipment

Figure 2-1: A 6-megapixel image (left) provides more detail than the 3.3 megapixel version (right) — or does it?

Do most of the photos you take end up in digital presentations viewed on your computer screen? Are you creating newsletters or other desktop publications? Will you rarely make prints larger than 4 x 6 inches? A camera with 5 to 6 megapixels will probably do the job for you. With the money you would have spent on pixels, you can invest in a camera with a better zoom lens or more digital film (so that you can take more vacation pictures).

Perhaps you'll be taking pictures of things you plan to sell on eBay. Figure 2-2 shows a photo I took for an eBay auction when I began unloading my beloved older film cameras so I could buy new digital equipment. This photo was resized to 600 pixels wide so that people who viewed the auction page could download the photo quickly, so virtually any digital camera, from 2 megapixels on up, would have done the job. Or, you might be setting up a Web page of your own with lots of individual photos. A camera with as few as 4 to 5 megapixels might have plenty of resolution for that application. You can find tiny digital cameras in this range that slip in a pocket and are always available for a quick snapshot. There really are times when less is more.

Figure 2-2: Photos used in eBay auctions, such as this one of a classic film camera, rarely need to be wider than 600 pixels, so the lowest resolution digital cameras can do the job.

As you decide the amount of resolution you need, remember that digital cameras are downwardly compatible. A higher resolution camera has shooting modes at lower resolutions, so your 8-megapixel camera can take 4-megapixel photos if you need them, which saves space on your digital film and hard drive when the extra resolution isn't required. If 90 percent of your photos require only 4 megapixels of resolution, but a solid 10 percent could benefit from a bit more pixel-grabbing capability, seriously consider getting a higher-res model. I look at resolution in more depth in Book II, Chapter 1.

Do you plan to manipulate your photos?

Many digital photographers don't want to mess with image editing programs. All they want to do is take pictures and either make prints or view them in digital albums on-screen. They see the need to spend extra time with an image as a drawback and find tasks such as cropping or correcting colors to be a needless waste of time. Such snap-shooters fall into two broad categories. Many are amateurs with little interest in photography itself; their interest is in the pictures that capture memories of vacations or document their little ones as they grow up. Others are business professionals who use photographs as a means to an end and who want the process to be as fast and as simple as possible. If you were a real estate agent preparing an online database of homes for sale, would you want to spend a lot of time editing hundreds of photos of your listings?

On the other hand, others take great joy from the ability to edit their photos, using image manipulation as a creative outlet or, at the very least, a means to perfect their photographic vision as they tweak the image to look exactly as they planned.

If you belong in the latter camp, you'll want a camera with lots of features and lots of options so that you can get sharp images worthy of your image-editing efforts. But if all you want are pictures, consider a basic point-and-shoot digital camera.

Are you a photo hobbyist?

If photography was in your life long before you considered buying a digital camera, you'll want all the manual features you can get, a powerful zoom lens to give you a variety of perspectives, and compatibility with as many add-on gadgets as possible. In fact, you probably want a digital SLR. Dedicated photo hobbyists talk about the importance of composition, darkroom skills, and the photographer's eye. But I haven't met one yet who didn't think that a bit of technology, properly applied, couldn't make a good photo even better.

Photo hobbyists tend to spend a lot on their pastime and understand and value all those features that others seldom use. If you're an avid amateur photographer, don't try to scrimp when the time comes to buy your digital camera. You'll regret it later.

How often do you plan to upgrade?

If you don't intend to replace your digital camera for a long time, consider spending a little more now on a camera that will avoid the shadow of obsolescence a little longer. On the other hand, if you know you'll buy a new camera next year, go ahead and buy one that suits your needs today. Tomorrow will take care of itself.

Believe it or not, you can purchase a digital camera for the long term if you opt for more than a basic model. For example, you can use a 6- to 7-megapixel digital camera with a zoom lens and a standard removable storage system, such as CompactFlash, for most applications for a long time to come. Such a camera has enough resolution for good-looking 5-x-7-inch and 8-x-10-inch photos and is versatile enough to take a broad range of pictures. Unless your needs change drastically, a good digital camera in that range can serve you well for two or more years.

If you find yourself yearning to take different kinds of photos and are constantly upgrading your expectations, however, you'll probably want to upgrade cameras more frequently. Digital cameras are adding features at reduced prices at an amazing rate. When I wrote my first digital photography book in 1995, a 6-megapixel SLR digital camera could cost as much as a new car. By the turn of the century, 6-megapixel dSLRs were available for $5,000; today, they cost $800 or less.

If you can afford it, you might want to upgrade every year or two. Even if you can do that, it's wise to take your upgrade plans into account when buying today. You'll want to use the accessories you buy now with your new camera. Or, if your pocketbook has restrictions, you might want to scale back your expectations today so that you can afford to dump your current camera when you upgrade.

Defining Camera Categories

Digital cameras fall into several overlapping categories, which are usually defined by the number of pixels they can capture plus some other features, such as lens type, availability of manual controls, add-on accessories, and other features. Specifications that define a category change over time. Point-and-shoot cameras once had 640 x 480 to 1024 x 768 resolution (less than a megapixel). Today, even the most basic cameras have 4 megapixels or more of resolution. However, the categories themselves have remained fairly constant in terms of types of snap-shooters or photographers they attract.

Web cams/phone cams

This book more or less ignores Web cams and cell phone cameras. They're not toys, but they're not digital cameras within the scope of this book. Web cams are low-cost (often less than $30) TV cameras that can supply low-resolution (640-x-480 or 320-x-200/240-pixel), full-motion images that can be transmitted over the Internet, put on Web pages, or attached to e-mails. Most can also capture low-resolution still images.

These cameras frequently have no removable storage, no controls, and lenses that don't zoom and may not even have a facility for changing focus. Only a few years ago, they made a good first camera for kids or a spare digital camera, but today that function is more likely to be found in the cell phones that virtually every person in the country seems to carry constantly. I have one in my Nokia cell phone, shown in Figure 2-3, and I find it useful for sending photos to family members along with a text message on the order of "Is this what you wanted me to pick up on the way home?" They can also be handy for note-taking (say, to document the various steps of a science experiment). However, most Web and phone cams aren't flexible enough for serious digital photography. That may change during the life of this book, however; at least one vendor has introduced a cell phone camera with 10 megapixels of resolution.

Figure 2-3: Web cams and phone cams are fun, but they aren't ready for prime time.

Point-and-shoot models

Point-and-shoot digital cameras cost about $200 and can do anything a simple film camera can do. Most have 4- to 6-megapixel resolution, a built-in flash, some sort of removable storage (although the memory card is probably an optional purchase), and a 3:1 zoom that provides a little magnification. Expect automatic exposure and no manual controls. Figure 2-4 shows an innovative two-lens point-and-shoot model.

Figure 2-4: A typical point-and-shoot camera will have basic features, including a 3X zoom lens — and a few have two lenses, like this model.

Intermediate models

Intermediate digital cameras are priced in the $200 to $500 range, and cameras in this category are the most widely used. As such, they have the best compromise of features to suit most consumer needs.

Look for 6- to 10-megapixel resolution; a 5:1 zoom lens; and at least a few special options, such as different exposure modes, close-up focusing, or manual controls. Figure 2-5 shows a selection of intermediate-level digital cameras.

Figure 2-5: Intermediate digital cameras offer more features, such as longer zoom lenses or ultra-compact size.

Advanced consumer models

In the $500 to $600 price range, you can find digital cameras aimed at those who want some special features, extra resolution, or a longer zoom lens. Many of these, like the one shown in Figure 2-6, provide *two* LCD viewfinders: the traditional back panel display and a second, "electronic viewfinder" (or EVF) inside the camera that provides a dimmer, but still SLR-like view. These are 6- to 10-megapixel models with 6:1 to 12:1 zooms (or better) and plenty of add-on accessories, such as wide-angle and telephoto attachments, filters, external flash units, and more.

You can also find lots of optional exposure modes, customizable settings, and other (potentially confusing) features. Advanced consumer cameras usually require a session or two with the instruction manual to master all their capabilities, but they have few limitations.

Figure 2-6: Advanced consumer models may offer both a back-panel
LCD and a second EVF display seen through a viewing window.

Prosumer dSLR models

Prosumer digital SLR cameras (see Figure 2-7) are the models that photo buffs
and even a few professional photographers favor. The avid photographer
doesn't countenance much in the way of compromises and is willing to spend
the $600 to $1,800 sticker price for these cameras in order to get the advanced
features. Pros find them useful as backup cameras, even if most aren't quite
rugged enough to take the beating that professional equipment is subjected to.

Prosumer dSLR cameras feature interchangeable lenses and are prized for
their ultra-fast response. Such cameras have virtually no shutter lag (the
delay between when you press the shutter release all the way and when the
picture is actually taken) and can crank out 3 to 5 pictures per second for
action sequence photography. They can be purchased just as a camera body
alone (in case you already own compatible lenses, perhaps for an older film
camera) or in a kit that includes an inexpensive but serviceable zoom in the
18mm–55mm or 18mm–70mm range.

Expect a minimum of 6 to 10 million pixels to shoot with, plus a lot of extra
weight to lug around compared to point-and-shoot cameras. All controls and
features of a prosumer digital SLR match or beat those found on conventional
film cameras. You get automatic and manual focus, multiple automated
exposure modes, plus manual shutter speed and lens opening settings if you

want them. The key differences between high-priced prosumer digital SLR cameras and professional digital SLR cameras is resolution (pro models have 12 to 16 megapixels or more), speed (pro cameras can usually snap off digital pictures at a 5 to 8 pictures-per-second clip; prosumer models may be limited to 3 pictures per second), and ruggedness.

Figure 2-7: Prosumer digital SLR cameras offer interchangeable lenses and other advanced features.

Professional models

Pro digital cameras still cost $3,000 and up and have both the pedigree and features to match. These high-end models are the equal of their film camera counterparts in every way, and, indeed, some vendors are already phasing out their film camera production. If you can't do it with one of these, it can't be done.

You'll find 12- to 22-megapixel sensors in these cameras, although the highest-resolution cameras are currently found in the so-called "medium format" digital SLR arena, where cameras start out at $10,000! You can fit standard interchangeable lenses to them while retaining all the sophisticated autoexposure and autofocus modes originally introduced in their film camera counterparts. As I mention earlier, one feature pros demand is speed. If you use a pro camera, you'll see just how this speed is applied.

With lesser cameras, there is often a tiny time lag while the autofocus system locks in; with pro cameras, this interval is hard to detect.

With a pro camera, such as the one shown in Figure 2-8, you can usually snap off pictures as quickly as you can press the shutter release, or else trigger the *motor drive* continuous shot mode. You may be able to snap off 5 to 8 pictures per second for as long as you like, or at least until the storage media fills up. That can be a long time, because pro digital cameras usually accept humongous storage options, such as 4GB (or larger) memory cards.

Some pro dSLR cameras (as well as prosumer models) with interchangeable lenses boost the effective magnification of your lenses as well, because the sensors are smaller than the nominal 24-x-36mm 35mm film frame. A 35mm lens or zoom setting has the same field of view as a normal lens on a film camera. A 105mm portrait lens becomes a longer telephoto. However, some of the latest professional cameras have a true 24-x-36mm sensor and can use lenses at their marked focal lengths.

You can read more about the advantages and challenges of using a digital SLR in Book III.

Figure 2-8: Professional digital SLRs have rugged bodies, extremely fast focusing and shooting, and ultra-high resolution.

Checking for Key Camera Features

Check out Book II, Chapter 1 for a close look at all the features to consider for your digital camera. In this overview chapter, I provide a list of the key features that you should think about. I discussed resolution earlier because resolution is one of the key ways of categorizing cameras, but I've only touched briefly on other features. Here's a summary of what to look for:

✦ **Resolution:** Again, resolution determines how sharp your image will be, how much you can enlarge a photo before the pixels start to become distracting, and how much you can crop a photo and still be left with a decent image that you can enlarge and manipulate.

✦ **Lens:** The lens is the eye of your digital camera. Look for the following in your lens:

- You'll want good-quality optics that focus a sharp image on your camera's solid-state sensor. The best way to gauge the quality of the lens is to take a test photo or two. A vendor's reputation or lab tests in magazines are other ways to evaluate a lens.

- The lens also needs enough light-gathering power to let you shoot in reduced light levels. A camera's light-gathering capabilities are measured in something called *f-stops*, and I explain this in more detail in Book II, Chapter 1.

- The magnification power of the lens (how large or small an image appears to be from a particular shooting position) is another factor. A digital camera's lens magnification can usually be varied by *zooming* in and out to make the image larger or smaller.

- A related factor, the zoom range, is another key characteristic to look at. Where magnification tells you only how large or small the image can be made to appear, the zoom range tells you the difference between the two. As I mention under the discussion of general camera categories, some lenses have only a small zoom range, say 2:1, whereas others have a longer range, up to 12:1 or more (which means the image size can be varied up to 12X).

What's the difference between magnification and zoom range? Magnification deals purely with how large or small an image appears to be. For example, one lens may extend from a 28mm (35mm equivalent) to 85mm (35mm equivalent) magnifications, a 3:1 zoom range. Another lens might go from 35mm to 105mm (both 35mm equivalents) and also qualify as a 3:1 zoom range optic. However, the second lens would provide more relative magnification.

✦ **Storage:** The kind and amount of removable storage is another key feature. The more storage space you have for photos, the more pictures you can take before "reloading" your digital camera. Most cameras use CompactFlash, Secure Digital, or other electronic "film" media. You can find more on this topic in Book II, Chapter 1.

◆ **Exposure controls:** Except for the least expensive models, all digital cameras include automatic exposure controls that adjust the amount of light reaching the sensor based on the lighting conditions of your subject. If the illumination is low, an autoexposure system uses a wider lens f-stop or exposes the sensor for a longer period of time. If there is a lot of light, the exposure system reduces the amount of light reaching the sensor. Cameras with more versatile automatic exposure controls let you specify what type of exposure to use.

For example, when shooting action, it's often preferable to use the shortest shutter speed possible to freeze the motion and to adjust the size of the lens opening instead. Conversely, if you want a lot of your image to be in sharp focus (say, objects very close to the camera and very far are both important), you may be able to choose an exposure mode that favors maximum depth of field. You probably want a digital camera that can handle several different exposure modes and lets you set exposure yourself. I explain more about these modes in Book II, Chapter 1.

◆ **Focus controls:** Most digital cameras also have an automated system for sharply focusing your images. Some are more versatile than others, and many cameras also let you focus manually to ensure that the subject matter you want to emphasize is the sharpest.

◆ **Viewfinders:** Digital cameras generally have four ways to let you preview and compose your images prior to exposure. The color LCD panel on the back of the camera shows you the same image that the sensor is capturing. The LCD is often hard to view in bright light, so digital cameras also may have optical viewfinders that let you see a nonelectronic version of the frame. More-advanced cameras might include a second LCD (EVF) in the camera, where it is shielded from the glare of the surrounding light. Single lens reflexes (SLRs) let you see an optical version of the picture through the same lens used to take the photo. I explain more about your viewfinder options in Book II, Chapter 1.

◆ **Other equipment, other features:** Finally, as you choose your digital photography gear, think about accessories, such as tripods, filters, add-on lenses, external electronic flash units, scanners, printers, and additional stuff. Even the storage media you use to archive your photos, such as CDs or DVDs, can all be important.

I reveal the mysteries of these extra pieces of equipment in various parts of Book II. This overview has given you enough to think about.

Chapter 3: Acquiring Your Digital Pictures

In This Chapter

↳ **Transferring from your camera to your computer**

↳ **Scanning images**

↳ **Getting photos online or on Photo CD from a photo lab**

*H*ow do you acquire digital photos? The quick answer is, "With a digital camera!" However, the digital photography process involves more than simply snapping a picture. Indeed, you can use other ways of acquiring a digital picture that don't even involve a digital camera. Scanners, for example, can convert any printed image into a digital image. Some scanners, such as those with slide scanning attachments or dedicated slide scanners, can even capture color transparencies or negatives.

This chapter provides an overview of all the ways you can acquire digital pictures and points you to chapters that explore these topics in more detail.

Transferring Images from Your Camera to Your PC

The first challenge you have to face is getting your digital images from your camera into your computer so that you can edit them (if necessary), store them on some archival medium (such as CD or DVD), and make prints.

Today, transferring images to your computer is a fairly painless process. It wasn't always so. My first digital camera back in the last millennium had no removable storage. It was bad enough that when the camera's internal storage was full, I had to stop taking photos. But what was even worse was that it often took 10 to 20 minutes to move those photos from the camera to my computer. The only option was an old-fashioned serial cable that moved an image one bit at a time, like a line of soldiers, from the camera to the serial port on my computer at about 64 kilobits per second.

Even at a prehistoric resolution of 640 x 480 pixels, I had roughly 2.5 million bits (307 kilobytes) to move *per picture*. So at best, I spent a minimum of 40 seconds transferring *one* photo. It seemed longer.

To make things worse, this was back in the days when PCs didn't share peripheral ports very well, so my computer really had only two functional serial ports. I used one for my mouse, and the other for both a modem and my camera's serial cord. I had to unplug one to use the other. This may seem bizarre in these days of USB (Universal Serial Bus) ports, which enable you to connect a mouse and dozens of other peripherals at once, and FireWire connections, which speed files between computers.

Today, you have multiple options for transferring your images. I can plug a USB cable directly into my favorite camera and transfer multi-megapixel images in a few seconds. I also have a card reader that accepts memory cards and lets me move images between the card and my hard drive as if the memory card were another disk drive.

Card readers are so inexpensive these days that they are often built right into computers or printers, as you can see in Figure 3-1, which shows the slots of a reader included below the DVD drive in a Windows PC. Usually, such a reader will be your best choice for transferring photos. Compared to transferring using a cable connection, the reader is faster and uses less juice from your digital camera's battery.

Figure 3-1: Card readers built into computers allow transferring photos quickly without the need for a cable.

I outline all the options and explain the pros and cons of each storage medium in Book VIII. You can find everything you need to know about transferring images from camera to PC or Mac there.

Grabbing Digital Images of Prints and Slides

Another way to create a digital image is to capture an existing print or slide with a scanner. As far as your image editor or printer is concerned, these kinds of digital images are just as digital as those that began their lives in the sensor of a digital camera.

Indeed, before digital photography became common, the only way most of us who worked with images could acquire a digital picture was with a scanner. Scanners remain a valuable tool for anyone who needs digitized graphics from hard copy originals. The good news is that the price of scanners has come down since the late 1980s, while the features have improved. Whereas my first "real" scanner (forgetting about toys such as the ThunderScan, available for the Macintosh in the mid-1980s) captured a whopping 16 levels of gray at 300 samples per inch, my latest has a true resolution of 2,400 samples per inch and can grab a few billion different colors. It's about 10 times faster and includes a capable transparency scanner. My first scanner cost me about $2,500; the list price of my latest is about $200. A typical scanner is shown in Figure 3-2.

Figure 3-2: Scanners have become less expensive, thinner, faster, and capable of better resolution.

You can find a lot of information about scanners in Book II, Chapter 4, but I can summarize a lot of what you need to know here in this overview.

Kinds of scanners

A variety of nonprofessional scanners has drifted off into the fog of history. My first scanner was a ThunderScan unit that (I am not making this up) replaced the ink ribbon in an Apple ImageWriter printer with an optical imager that captured a scan of a photo as it fed through the roller. Other scanners have included the hand scanner of the early 1990s, which looked like an overgrown mouse.

Yesterday's sheet-fed scanners became obsolete but lived on for awhile in the form of dedicated fax machines that sucked your documents past a stationary sensor. The flatbed scanner, which looks and works a little like a photocopier, has become today's standard.

Today, unlike times past, you don't have to agonize over what category of scanner to buy. That should be obvious from the kind of scanning you want to do:

✦ **Flatbed scanners** are used for scanning reflective copy, such as documents, photographs, articles torn from magazines, and other similar material. You simply place the original face-down on the scanner's glass *platen,* and a moving bar with a light source and a sensor (or a mirror that reflects the light to a sensor located elsewhere in the scanner) captures the image a line at a time when you close the lid and activate the scanning software.

Figure 3-3: A light source built into the lid allows a flatbed scanner to capture slides.

Some flatbed scanners have a light source built into the lid (or another component), as shown in Figure 3-3. This light source can transilluminate a negative, slide, or transparency so that you can use the flatbed to grab images from transparent originals. These scanners can do a good job in non-critical applications.

✦ **Slide scanners** are specialized scanners designed to scan slides and transparencies. They often have the higher resolution needed for scanning the 24mm x 36mm area of 35mm slides and often cost quite a bit more than flatbed scanners. There are also dedicated transparency scanners for larger size film, too, such as 120/220 roll film and sheet film, including 4-x-5-inch, 5-x-7-inch, and larger sizes. They're largely used by professional graphics workers.

✦ **Photo scanners** are simplified scanners that convert snapshots to digital format. Deposit your standard-sized photo in the scanner, and it grabs an image for you to edit. Photo scanners are sometimes mated with color printers so that you can make copies of prints as quickly as you can feed them into the scanner. Although popular at one time, this type of scanner is no longer widely available.

What to look for in a scanner

When shopping for a scanner, you'll want to look for a few important things. Here's a quick summary (see Book II, Chapter 4 for more details):

✦ **Resolution:** Scanners generally have a lot more resolution than you need, measured in samples per inch (spi). You'll also see the terms *dots per inch* and *pixels per inch* applied to scanners, even though scanners don't have dots (printers do) or pixels (monitors do). Scanner resolution varies from 600 x 600 spi to 2400 x 2400 spi or higher. Unless you're scanning tiny, very high-resolution originals (such as postage stamps), anything more than 300 or 600 spi is overkill. I explain why in Book II, Chapter 4. The difference between 300 spi and 2400 spi resolution is shown in Figure 3-4.

Figure 3-4: A 300 spi scan of a small, detailed object (left) isn't sharp enough. The 2400 spi scan (right) looks much better.

✦ **Color depth:** This is the number of colors a scanner can capture. The color depth is measured using something called *bit depth.* For example, a 24-bit scanner can capture 16.8 million different colors; a 30-bit scanner can grab a billion colors; and a 36-bit or 48-bit scanner can differentiate between . . . zillions of colors. You'll never have an original with that many different hues, however. In practice, the extra colors simply provide the scanner with an extended range (called *dynamic range*) so that the scanner can capture detail in very dark areas of the image as well as in very light areas.

✦ **Speed:** Some scanners are faster than others. If you're scanning a lot of photos, you'll want one that works quickly.

✦ **Convenience:** So-called "one-touch" scanners have buttons mounted on the front panel so that you can trigger the scanner to make a copy (that's sent to your printer), scan to a file, route a scan to e-mail, capture text with optical character recognition (OCR), or perform other functions.

✦ **Bundled software:** The best scanners are furnished with an easy standalone software interface plus a more professional scanning program that gives you total control over every scanning function. You also get drivers that let you access these interfaces from within programs, such as Photoshop. You may even get Photoshop Elements bundled with the scanner, plus software to create panoramas, build Web pages, manage documents, and do other fun stuff.

✦ **Accessories:** Some scanners include sheet feeders (for scanning a stack of documents) or can be fitted with them as an option. Others have slide-scanning attachments or built-in slide-scanning tools. Depending on the kind of work you do, these accessories can be a perk or a necessity.

Letting a Professional Do It

Sometimes you don't need to convert an image to digital format yourself. Professional services can do that for you. These range from stand-alone kiosks at your local department store (with a built-in scanner and printer) to services that your local photofinisher offers. When you take in your film for processing, your local lab can give you the same set of prints or slides that you have always received or return your images already scanned onto a Kodak Photo CD or Picture CD. Some mail-order firms offer the same service.

As long as your images are being scanned anyway, your professional service may post them on the Internet for you — as Web pages or as files that you can download directly to your computer. You can find more about these options in Book VIII.

Chapter 4: Editing or Restoring a Photo Electronically

In This Chapter

↳ **Deciding what can be done to restore and improve digital photos**

↳ **Choosing which repairs to make first**

↳ **Picking the right software for your image editing needs**

↳ **Solving common photo problems quickly and easily**

*R*emember when getting free double prints of your photos was a big deal? It was so convenient to have a spare copy of every photo on the roll. With the advent of digital cameras and scanners, however, the excitement of double prints has worn off. Today, it's routine for your local digital print lab to offer double prints of every shot you took with your digital camera, along with an index print or CD with all your images on it. In addition, you can make as many prints as you want at home with your own printer.

Today, the most exciting part of photography is that you no longer need to put up with images that don't look exactly like you want them to. While a retail digital print lab can make many fixes to your images, you can apply these adjustments in your own computer with an image editor. Why put up with damaged images or photos that are too dark or too light if you can fix them electronically?

With digital photography and a good image editor, you have the power to reproduce and repair your own photos or the photos others have taken, whether they originated digitally or were scanned from prints or slides. This chapter is an overview of what's possible with photo-editing software, which applications do the best job for the money, and how to make some quick corrections of common photographic problems, such as fixing red-eye and removing dust spots.

In this chapter, I also explain how you can improve the image quality and content of your photos by removing the tell-tale signs of age, poor photography, or bad lighting. (I even show you how to remove unwanted people or things — ex-boyfriends/girlfriends and the like — from the picture.) If the last remaining photo of a long-departed relative is looking shabby or has faded with time, there's no need for alarm or regret. Just open your favorite image-editing application (some programs to consider are discussed later in this chapter) and add color, remove spots, improve contrast, and in general make the image look like new. For example, Figure 4-1 shows before and after versions that illustrate how you can spruce up an old photo.

You can also remove unwanted content — that dumpster that nobody noticed when the picture was taken or the brother-in-law you really don't miss — and replace it with more desirable stuff, such as a hedge, a pet, or an extension of the background. You can make the photo look as though the item was never there in the first place.

Figure 4-1: Here's an old photo that's faded and scratched (left) and spruced up in an image editor (right).

Choosing an Image-Editing Program

In a digital photograph, you can fix just about anything — as long as your image-editing program has the tools you need. You don't want a program to limit what you can do, but you don't want to spend $600 when you could pay just $100. This section helps you figure out what type of editor meets your needs, and I offer you a guide to some of the different programs on the market.

Determining your needs

If you're using a powerful application, such as Photoshop Elements, the repairs and improvements you can make are almost unlimited:

✦ You can use a flexible and powerful set of selection tools to control where the edits and repairs take place, preventing changes to areas of the photo that are just fine as they are.

✦ You have access to a nearly unlimited set of brush tools for painting, drawing, and erasing anything you want.

✦ You can use filters to blur and sharpen images.

✦ You can work with a vast assortment of color, brightness, and contrast-adjustment tools (see Figure 4-2) to fix the results of an overachieving flash, a cloudy day, or old photo paper that allowed images to fade and colors to change with time.

Figure 4-2: Tinker with color, brightness, and contrast to bring images back to life.

If you're using Photoshop Elements, the tools at your disposal are virtually the same set of tools found in the full version of Photoshop. Some of the features that only hardcore professional photographers use have been weeded out in Elements, but the basic set of tools and features is still there.

Checking out different applications

So how do you know which application to use? Your needs are your most effective guide, but of course, your budget will have some impact as well. After you start pricing these applications, you'll notice that the prices vary from more than $500 to less than $50. How can that be? Is the least expensive software terrible? Is the priciest application great? No, and yes. It all depends on what you want to be able to do, how intuitive you are with software, and how much photo editing you'll be doing.

You can find a more detailed comparison of the various software packages in Book V, Chapter 3, but Table 4-1 gives you at least an overview of what various applications have to offer. We discuss these and other applications in more detail in the following sections.

Table 4-1	Overview of Image Editing Applications			
Product Name	*Expensive?*	*Mac or PC*	*Easy to Use*	*Editing Capabilities/ Interface*
Adobe Photoshop	Yes, over $600	Both	Yes	Professionals hands-down prefer this program. You can do quick fixes, restoration, or just about anything.
Photoshop Elements	No ($99 retail)	Both	Yes	Great for the home user. Also good for quick fixes and more substantial editing.
Corel Paint Shop Pro	No (about $99)	PC	Yes	Similar to Photoshop Elements.
Microsoft Digital Imaging Suite	No (about $99)	PC	Yes	Available in three versions, with additional clip art and templates the main difference between them. Excellent for those who need design help.
Ulead Photo Impact	No (around $99)	PC	Yes	Good, basic tools for photo retouching.
Corel Photo Paint	Yes (part of the CorelDraw suite, over $500)	PC	No	A fairly comprehensive set of retouching tools, but not quite as rich as Photoshop or Elements.
Corel Painter	Yes (costs $499, $199 for upgrades)	PC	Yes	Consider as a companion to whatever other retouching software you buy; it has painting features that are not available elsewhere.

Adobe Photoshop CS2 and Photoshop Elements

Photoshop CS2 is the photo-editing software for professional photographers, graphic artists, Web designers, and the like. Photoshop Elements was designed to put a good number of Photoshop's tools in the home and small business user's price range. The interface for these two products was similar until the most recent versions of Elements arrived dressed in a spiffy new interface. They're not "sit down and use it" applications. You'll want to read the guide that comes with either editor or buy a book about the software (or use Book VI of this title).

The top-of-the-line software (Photoshop) costs as much as $649 for a full version, but it offers the most powerful set of image creation, editing, and retouching tools you can lay your hands on. Photoshop Elements, which has functions similar to Photoshop for the average person's photo-editing needs, is only $99. Considering that, it's a steal at the price, and both Photoshop and Photoshop Elements are available for both the Mac and Windows PCs. You may even find Photoshop Elements bundled with your digital camera for free!

Corel Paint Shop Pro

Corel Paint Shop Pro is inexpensive (on par with Elements) and powerful. The interface is pretty intuitive, and it lets you do all the standard image editing stuff (resizing, cropping, rotating, color and contrast adjustments, and adding textures). It has some quick and useful tools for eliminating red-eye, scratches, tears, and so forth. If you feel intimidated by Photoshop or aren't big on using Help to figure stuff out, you'll like Paint Shop Pro. It was designed for regular folks, but it includes photographer-quality tools.

Corel PhotoPaint and Ulead PhotoImpact

Applications like Corel PhotoPaint and Ulead PhotoImpact are intended as true competitors to Photoshop, although neither does everything that Photoshop can do.

Corel Painter

Many serious digital photographers and artists own both Photoshop and Painter because Painter's natural media tools let you paint on image canvases in ways that are completely different from what you can do with Adobe's flag-ship image editor.

Lower-end products, shareware, and freeware

The lower-end products — such as Ulead Photo Express and others you can find by searching the Web — are great for quick adjustments to size, rotation, and even simple color and contrast changes. If all you want to do is capture images from your digital camera and make minor adjustments to their size and general quality before sending them to friends via e-mail, these packages may be just what you need. If you really want to restore and edit photographs for prints or Web pages, you'll probably be happier with one of the more powerful (and pricier) applications.

 Want to find freeware and shareware for photo editing? Search for **"Photo Editing"** at www.hotfiles.com or www.tucows.com. A search of either site's software libraries will yield a long list of downloadable freeware and shareware applications. Note that shareware is not free. If you keep and use the product, be sure to pay its author or manufacturer — it's the right (and legal) thing to do.

Performing Photographic Triage

How do you decide what needs to be done to a given image? Well, some problems are obvious. A torn photo (where the tear shows in the scanned version) is in definite need of plastic surgery. A photo with a row of red-eye-plagued children needn't look like a lineup of demons. You can remove the red-eye and return the little darlings to their normal states.

Some photos, however, have several problems, and you may not be sure which problems to tackle first. There may be fading from age, scratches and scuffs from improper storage, yellowing, stains, or maybe the picture was too dark or too light from the start. If your photo suffers from two or more problems, solving one might solve another if you attack them in the right order. Here's a series of tips to help you do a little image triage:

✦ Handle structural problems first. If there's a torn corner or a rip or hole in the photo, scan the image and repair the tear first in your image editor so that you're working with an intact "canvas" as you continue to fix other problems.

✦ Adjust light and dark problems before tinkering with color. Why? Because if you add color to an image and then adjust brightness and contrast, the color added with the software can become too bright or too dark or can change to a color you don't want.

✦ See if any of the content removal or replacing that you want to do will solve other problems, as shown earlier in Figure 4-1, in which the missing left edge of the photo was fixed by removing the person standing behind the boy on the bicycle. For example, if you need to get rid of a person's hand or shoulder, or some other content that was inadvertently included in a shot, maybe replacing that content with something else will also get rid of a big scratch that's occurred on that part of the photo as well.

Making Quick Fixes

For the purposes of this portion of the book, I use Photoshop Elements to demonstrate some *quick fixes*, or simple, fast techniques for solving the most common photographic problems. You can find similar techniques in other applications, assuming the applications can perform these tasks to begin with. If you're still up in the air about which photo-editing program to use, the inability to perform some of these quick fixes would be a good reason to take one or more of your alternatives out of the running!

Fixing red-eye

Red-eye results from the camera flash reflecting off a subject's retina. We've all had it happen, especially when taking pictures of children who get too close to the camera and of pets, whose pupils are quite large, letting in a lot more light. So what do you do when your niece's eyes look like two red marbles? You can use tools designed specifically to get rid of red-eye (see Figure 4-3), or you can use conventional editing tools to exorcise the demons that have possessed your image.

Red Eye tool

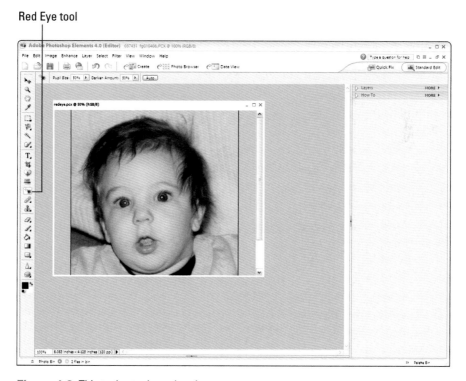

Figure 4-3: This tool gets the red out!

To use the Photoshop Elements new-and-improved red-eye tool, follow these steps:

1. **Click the Red Eye Removal tool; it's about halfway down the Tool Palette when it's docked (or press Y to select it).**

2. **Go to the Options bar that runs just above the document window and make sure the Pupil Size and Darken Amount are both set to 50%.**

3. **Drag a rectangle around one eye, as shown in Figure 4-4 (or just click in the area of the pupil and let Elements locate the red-eye unassisted).**

   You don't have to be too precise. When you release the mouse button, the Red Eye tool locates the red pupil, removes the red coloration, and darkens it. (It works only with red pupils; the yellow or green pupils found in animals are not affected.)

Figure 4-4: Drag a rectangle around the eye. You don't have to be precise.

4. **If the pupil is too dark, press Ctrl/⌘+Z to reverse the action and then change the Darken Amount to a lower value and try again.**

   Your results should look like Figure 4-5.

5. **Select the other eye, or try clicking inside the pupil. The Red Eye tool works either way.**

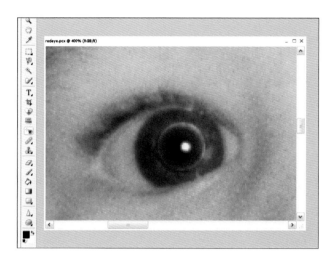

Figure 4-5: The Red Eye tool removes the red coloration from the pupil.

If your image editing software doesn't have a red-eye tool, you can still get rid of red eyes. Doing so just requires a few more steps and tools:

1. **Set your application's paintbrush tool to a size that matches the diameter of the red eye.**

2. **Manually choose a color to replace the red.**

   Choose a color that's darker than the person's real eye color so that the colorization looks natural.

3. **Zoom in tight on the eye so that you can apply the color to the right spot.**

4. **Click with the brush to fill the red area.**

   This step should require just one click if your brush is set to the right size.

Removing dust spots

Dust spots and scratches are common problems for old photos or photos that have been stored in desk drawers or shoeboxes or were tucked inside a book or a wallet. If the front of a photo has been rubbing up against other stuff — other photos, papers, pens and pencils — chances are that the photo has highly visible scratches. Dust can collect in these scratches, compounding the problem, or you may simply have scanned the photo without dusting it off first. Mold, things spilled on the photo, or just places where the emulsion has cracked and come off the photo can also create small, unpleasant blemishes.

Any image editing program provides the basic tools to clean up this sort of defect. Although the Clone or Rubber Stamp tool (discussed later in this chapter) is useful for touching up dust, if the background is a solid color, you can use your software's Paintbrush tool instead, along with color selection tools, to correct the problem by following these steps:

1. **Use your program's Eye Dropper tool to sample the color near the scratch, spot, or stain. If you're using Photoshop Elements, skip to Step 2.**

   Most applications have an Eye Dropper tool for selecting a color in the image and setting it as the paint color. You'll use the color you choose to paint over your blemish.

2. **Click the Paintbrush in the tool palette to activate it, and if possible, set the size of the brush so that you control how much color is applied. (If you're using Elements, hold down the Alt/Option key while clicking near the dust spot to sample the color; you don't need to access the Eye Dropper tool directly.)**

   Be sure to use a very small brush so you don't paint over nonblemished areas — to do so can leave obvious signs of the touch-up.

3. **Zoom in on the area you want to touch up and then click and drag in the image to paint that color over the blemish, as shown in Figure 4-6.**

Figure 4-6: The Paintbrush tool can touch up dust spots on a solid background.

If your image editing software has filters or other similar tools designed specifically for cleaning up an image, you can use them instead of repairing the spot or scratch manually. Photoshop Elements includes a Dust & Scratches filter, which allows you to select the portion of the photo to repair, and it provides settings so that you can control to what degree the photo is cleaned up. Figure 4-7 shows the Dust & Scratches filter dialog box, which you open by choosing Filter⇨Noise⇨Dust & Scratches.

To use the filter, follow these steps:

Figure 4-7: The Preview window shows how the settings affect the final results.

1. **Select the area to be repaired, using any of Photoshop Elements' selection tools.**

2. **Open the Dust & Scratches dialog box by choosing Filter⇨Noise⇨ Dust & Scratches.**

3. **Inside the dialog box, adjust the sliders by dragging both the Radius and Threshold sliders to the far left.**

4. **Ease back the Radius slider, dragging it slowly to the right until you see the scratches and spots in the preview area disappear.**

   You may have to tinker with the sliders to achieve a pleasing result.

5. **When you like how the preview looks, click OK to apply the repairs to the selected area in your photo.**

If the entire surface of your photo is damaged, you can select the whole thing or repeat the filter procedure on several different selected areas. The latter approach is probably best, unless the damage is absolutely uniform over the entire image. If it isn't, then you'll benefit from applying different levels of the Dust & Scratches filter to the different areas of the image.

Don't go too far when removing scratches and dust because you could end up with a blurry image or a portion thereof that looks obviously smoothed out. If the photo is old or is clearly an amateur photo, nobody expects absolute perfection, and going too far in removing every little tiny blemish can have an undesirable effect overall. However, Photoshop and Photoshop Elements share a handy feature under the Edit menu: You can choose to revert to a previous version of your image — and you can do this in steps if you go too far in the correction process.

Correcting color

Colors on printed photos can fade, and scanning a photo can magnify this problem. If you take a picture with a digital camera, you can lose color accuracy and depth, depending on the quality of the camera, the lighting at the time, and the file format and quality you choose when you save the captured image to your computer. No matter what the cause, though, your image-editing software should offer at least one or two options for fixing the color in a photo. These options are either automatic correction tools that do an all-over sweep for bad color or manually controlled tools that allow you to increase or decrease tones in your image.

In Photoshop Elements, the quickest fix is the Auto Levels command, which you can employ by using the following steps:

1. **Issue the Auto Levels command by choosing Enhance⇨Auto Levels.**

   After it's issued, the Auto Levels command goes over your entire image (or a portion thereof if you made a selection first) and adjusts the color levels.

2. **You can repeat the process for further adjustments or press Ctrl+Z (⌘+D on the Mac) to undo it if you don't like the results.**

   Figures 4-8 and 4-9 show before and after views of the same photo.

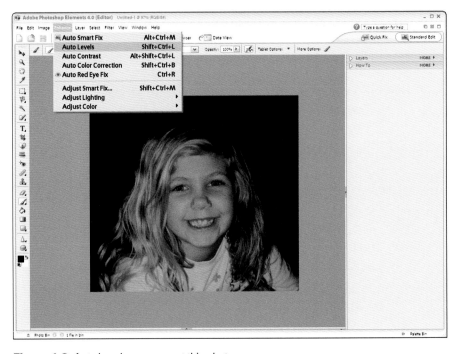

Figure 4-8: Auto Levels can correct this photo . . .

Figure 4-9: . . . producing results that look like this.

Typically, even the lower-end image editing applications offer a similar tool for correcting color quickly. If your application doesn't offer this tool or doesn't do what you want, you can switch to a more effective application.

Photoshop Elements offers a handful of commands (each with its own dialog box) that allow you to adjust brightness, contrast, tones, hues, and color casts. You can find these tools on the Enhance menu, under the Color and Brightness and Contrast submenus. Figure 4-10 shows the dialog box that appears if you choose Enhance⇨Adjust Color⇨ Hue/Saturation. The box's three sliders are for adjusting Hue (color),

Figure 4-10: Adjust multiple color attributes all in the same dialog box.

Saturation (amount of color), and Lightness (amount of white in the colors). To use this and similar dialog boxes, simply drag the sliders for whatever levels you are able to adjust (Hue, Saturation, and Lightness in this case) and watch the Preview. When you like what you see, click OK to apply the changes to your image. You can find out more about these specific tools in various chapters in Book VI, which focuses on Photoshop and Photoshop Elements.

Restoring, Replacing, and Removing Photographic Content

When my aunt was a child, she liked to draw on photos, especially those that included pictures of my mom. So we have a lot of old pictures with crayon and pencil strokes on them, and many of those strokes run through people's faces and parts of the picture that you couldn't crop away without losing the charm of the image. Other photos in our family's collection are torn or ripped, bear deep scratches, and generally look tattered. I've salvaged many battered photos by using Photoshop and Photoshop Elements to replace the missing content. Various tools in these applications enable you to take content from another spot in the photo and use that content to rebuild what's missing. For example, in the photo shown in Figure 4-11, rough handling resulted in a tear, and an unfortunate fold cost this photo its corner. Figure 4-12 shows the image after I repaired it.

Figure 4-11: A photo with tears and lost content.

Another problem you might encounter is unwanted content. Perhaps a truck is parked in front of the house you're trying to sell, and you can't take the picture without including the truck. Never fear — if you have the right software, you can easily get rid of the truck and replace it with a curb, grass, and even a few shrubs that may not really exist. You can do the same thing to get rid of people in a picture or to add people (or pets!) to a photo when they weren't there the day the picture was taken. How do you think the tabloids make it look like two people who haven't really even met went to a party together? Is that really Elvis in the background of Lisa Marie's wedding? It's all a matter of taking existing content, placing it in the image, and leaving unwanted or unimportant content in its wake.

Figure 4-12: I restored the missing parts by using other content in the image.

Replacing missing or unwanted content

So you want to replace a missing corner, which was lost to a big rip or deep scratch, or you want to cover up something that's undesirable in the photo. You can use a variety of tools, and most of the more powerful image editing applications let you take content from one spot in the image and repeat it in another spot. To finish the job, you may need tools to make the pasted content blend in, and those tools are normally available even in midrange image editing applications.

The tools you use to replace the missing content or cover up the unwanted content depend on the size of the area being filled. To cover a thin seam (such as a deep scratch) or fix a tiny corner, you can use the Clone Stamp in Photoshop or Photoshop Elements (other higher-end applications have their own versions). If the missing or unwanted content represents a large area of the image, it's better to copy and paste content from one part of the photo to another. I explain both techniques in this section.

Figure 4-13 shows a shot of two gargoyles perched on the Cathedral of Notre Dame in Paris. Unfortunately, a guard-rail protrudes on the image. The Clone Stamp is the best bet for getting rid of that rail.

Figure 4-13: Cloning can remove the guard-rail.

If you use the Clone Stamp, you can paint other content into the area that's lacking, filling as much or as little as you want. If you use the copy-and-paste technique, you may have to paste repeatedly to fill in the missing content.

Fixing small areas

To replace content in a small area with the Clone Stamp, follow these steps:

1. **Click the Clone Stamp in the tool palette to activate it.**

2. **Choose an appropriately sized brush.**

3. **Find the spot that contains the content you want to use to cover something else.**

   Zoom in if necessary to zero in on the spot.

4. **Press and hold the Alt key (or the Option key if you're on a Mac) and click to *sample* that spot.**

   Now, the software knows this is the area you want to clone and use elsewhere. The size of your brush dictates the size of the sampled area. You can set the brush size on the Options bar while the Clone Stamp is active.

5. **Now, click the spot that you want to cover to deposit the cloned content, as shown in Figure 4-14.**

   You can click over and over, and the cloned content appears wherever you click.

Figure 4-14: Your copied content is painted over the guardrail.

Be sure to turn off the Aligned option on the Clone Stamp Options bar so that the original sampled spot is used as the source each time you click to deposit the cloned content. If Aligned is on, the Clone Stamp continuously resamples content, and you can end up with undesirable results.

Fixing larger areas

To replace larger areas with the Edit, Copy, and Paste commands, follow these steps:

1. **Using the Marquee or Lasso tool, select the area you want to use to cover up something else in the image, as shown in Figure 4-15.**

   You can find more information about these selection tools in Book VI, Chapter 1.

2. **Choose Edit⇨Copy from the main menu.**

   You can also press Ctrl+C on a Windows computer or ⌘+C on a Mac to do the same thing.

   This places a duplicate of the selected area in your computer's memory, and it waits there until you tell your software where to place the copied content.

3. **Paste the content by choosing Edit⇨Paste from the main menu.**

   The keyboard shortcut for this is Ctrl+V for Windows and ⌘+V for Macs.

4. **Click the Move tool in the Tool palette to activate it and then drag the pasted content into the desired position.**

5. **Blur the edges of the added content so that it blends with the rest of the photo.**

   If you're not sure how, read on.

Figure 4-15: Select the area you want to use to cover up something else.

Adding the finishing touches

After you've positioned your cloned or pasted content, you can use the Blur tool to blend any obvious sharp edges. To do so, follow these steps:

1. **Click the Blur tool to select it.**

2. **Using a small brush size, scrub (brush) over the edges of the pasted content to make the edges disappear.**

   The content should look as if it were always there, as shown in Figure 4-16.

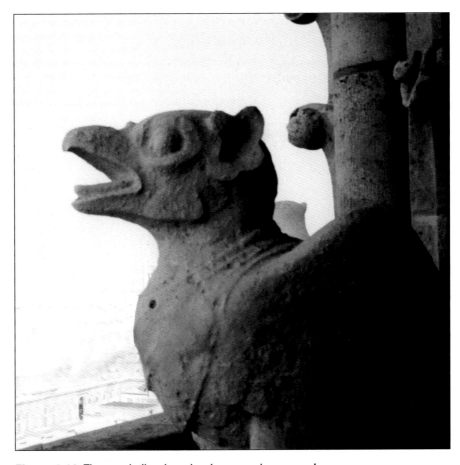

Figure 4-16: The guardrail and overlapping gargoyle are gone!

If you merge the layers of your image (Layer⇨Merge Visible), the photo becomes one layer again, and you can blur both the pasted content and the surrounding content, all with one stroke.

Rearranging parts of the picture

Moving part of your image requires selecting it with the Marquee or Lasso tools (or the equivalent tools in the software you've chosen to use). After you select the content, you activate the Move tool and then drag the selection to a new spot.

One thing to remember when moving content is that it leaves a hole where the content originally was. The hole is filled with the current background color, which is normally white. If you want to move content and also leave it in place, press and hold the Alt key (or Option key if you're using a Mac) as you drag. A duplicate of the content is moved, instead of the original content, as shown in Figure 4-17.

If you're wondering whether you can move content between images, the answer is yes — if you're using the higher-end image editing applications. Some of the lower-end applications don't allow more than one image to be open at a time, making it impossible to drag content from one image onto another or to easily use the Edit⇨Copy command in one image and then use the Edit⇨Paste command in another image.

Original   Duplicate

Figure 4-17: Holding down the Alt/Option key as you drag a selection creates a duplicate of the selection.

Getting rid of unwanted content

After you select an area of your image by using any of the selection tools, you can press the Delete key to get rid of it. Doing so leaves a hole, and the background color shows through. You can then use any tool you want — such as the Paintbrush or the Paint Bucket (which fills the area with a solid color or a pattern) — to occupy the hole where the content used to be. You can also use the Clone Stamp or the Edit⇨Copy and Edit⇨Paste commands to fill the hole with content from elsewhere in the image.

Another way to get rid of content in one place, but to not lose the content altogether, is to use the Edit⇨Cut command. This command removes content, but instead of simply deleting it forever, the content is placed in the computer's memory (in a space called the Clipboard), where it waits for you to paste it somewhere. This is similar to the copy-and-paste process, except for the fact that the Cut command deletes the selected content where it currently is. The Paste portion of the process is the same, whether you use Cut or Copy.

Chapter 5: Storing and Organizing Your Digital Photos

In This Chapter

✏ **Understanding your organizational options**

✏ **Choosing the right tools to organize and store your photos**

✏ **Keeping your treasured photos safe**

*W*e all have at least one box or drawer full of photos that we've never had the time to put in an album — vacation photos, pictures of the family at holiday dinners for the last 10 years, even collections of vintage photos, all waiting for someone to take them out of their envelopes and put them in a book so that people can actually look at them. What about your digital photos? They may not be languishing in a drawer, but if they're in different folders scattered all over your hard drive, they may as well be in a shoebox under the bed.

The most important things you can do with your digital images are first to organize them and then to store them in a way that keeps them safe from accidental erasure, unwanted changes, or loss due to fire, flood, or computer meltdown. You can easily achieve the proper organization and reliable storage of your digital images, and plenty of tools are at your disposal to make it all happen. The key, however, is to do it — so don't put it off any longer!

Organizing Your Photos

When it comes to taking control of your photo organization, you have a few different approaches to choose from. Your personality, your computer, and your access to the Web all dictate your choice. Here are some approaches to consider:

✦ Setting up a file structure on your computer

✦ Working with software that makes it easy to organize and store your images and view them through a special interface

✦ Organizing and storing your images in an online gallery

What do I mean about your personality influencing your choice of organizational tools? If you're a very organized person who enjoys straightening out closets and dresser drawers, always knows where the remotes are, and always puts things away after using them, then using the file management tools already on your computer might appeal to you.

If, on the other hand, you aren't too tidy and often forget where you left your glasses or your keys, you might prefer either using software that organizes things for you or posting your images to an online gallery. The tidy person might like these latter approaches as well.

Using your computer's file-management tools

You already have some great tools for organizing your images, and the tools have been on your computer all along. If you're running Windows, you have My Computer and Windows Explorer right there at your fingertips. If you're using a Mac, you can use the file-management tools that you've already been using to create folders on your desktop or hard drive.

Using these tools requires devising some sort of filing system — one or more folders that will help you categorize your images. You might start with one called Photos and create subfolders called, perhaps, Family Photos, Vacation Pictures, and Scanned Vintage Photos. You can create folders on your computer for whatever groupings fit the pool of images you have. After you create the folders, all you have to do is move your images into the appropriate folders and remember the folder names when you store new images in the future.

Using Windows Explorer to store and organize your photos

Working with folders under Windows is pretty basic but deserves a review in the context of organizing your digital image files. To create folders to store your images by using Windows Explorer, follow these simple steps:

1. **Choose Start⇨Programs⇨Windows Explorer.**

   You can also right-click the Start button and choose Explore from the context menu.

2. **When Windows Explorer opens, click the C: drive icon (see Figure 5-1).**

   If there's a plus sign next to the icon, click that plus sign to display the folders currently on the drive. If there's a minus sign next to the icon, that means you can already see all the folders.

 The Windows Explorer window is divided into two panes: the Folder pane on the left and the Content pane on the right. When you click a drive or folder in the Folder pane, that drive's or folder's contents are displayed in the Content pane. This two-sided display makes it possible to drag items from one folder to another simply by displaying the source (where the content is now) and target (where you want the content to be) folders in the separate panes.

If you don't see the Folder pane, you can open it either by choosing View⇨Explorer Bar⇨Folders or by clicking the Folders button on the toolbar.

Figure 5-1: Navigate your hard drive to locate the folder you want to use.

3. **If there's a My Pictures or other folder you want to use as the basis for your image organization, click it. If you want to start a new folder for your photos, choose File⇨New⇨Folder from the menu bar.**

   If you go the New Folder route, a New Folder appears in the Content pane, with its temporary name highlighted, waiting for you to type its real name (see Figure 5-2).

4. **If you go the New Folder route, give your new folder a name and press Enter to confirm it.**

With a folder created to house some or all of your photos, you can begin to place them in a single location. You can also make subfolders in that main folder to categorize your photos. For example, if you have a Photos folder, you can create a Vacation Photos subfolder and a Baby Pictures subfolder to keep those two, distinct photo subjects separate. Figure 5-3 shows just such a folder system.

Figure 5-2: Create a new folder if necessary.

To create subfolders of the main folder, simply click the main folder to select it (on the left side of the screen, in the Folders pane), and repeat Steps 3 and 4 from the preceding steps list. You're going to use the File⇨New⇨ Folder command to create a new folder, but because you're in an existing folder when you do it, the new folder appears inside the active folder.

The process is like taking one of those green hanging Pendaflex folders and putting one or more manila folders in it. The green folder represents the main Photos folder, and each of the manila folders is the same as the subfolders you create to categorize your photos. You can create as many subfolders as you want, and even create subfolders within subfolders. The folder hierarchy can become as complex as you want or need it to be, but be careful not to make managing files so cumbersome that the process becomes confusing when you need to place an image in the right folder.

If you don't need to categorize your photos by subject, consider creating folders that separate your photos by date. You can have a separate folder for individual years, months, or weeks, depending on how prolific a photographer you are.

Working with My Computer

You can also use the My Computer program on your Windows-based computer, and it works much like Windows Explorer. Instead of a two-paned window, however, you have separate windows for each drive and folder on your computer. The command for creating new folders is the same (File⇨New⇨Folder), but you have a visually different environment in which to work when creating and using your folders. Figure 5-4 shows the main My Computer window, displaying the C: drive, D: drive, E: drive, and other computer components.

Figure 5-3: Here's a typical folder system for organizing images.

Figure 5-4: You can also use My Computer to navigate your hard drive.

Organizing your photo images on a Mac

If you're using Mac OS, you can easily create folders to store your photos and other digital images. You can choose to store them on your hard drive or make them quickly accessible from your ever-visible desktop.

To create a new folder in OS X, follow these steps:

1. **Choose File⇨New Folder from the menu bar.**

   A folder called *Untitled Folder* appears on the desktop. You can also press Shift+⌘+N, or Control-click the desktop and choose New Folder from the context menu that appears.

2. **Give your folder a short yet relevant name that will make it easy to find the folder in the future.**

3. **You can leave the folder on the desktop or open your hard drive and drag the folder there.**

   If you store the folder on the desktop, it is quickly available at any time, but you also make it quickly available to anyone using your computer. If you don't want people poking around in your photos, store the new folder somewhere on your hard drive other than the desktop.

4. **If you want folders within the folder you just created, open the folder and then repeat Steps 1 through 3 to create the subfolders.**

You can duplicate an existing folder by choosing File⇨Duplicate. Alternatively, drag the existing folder to a new location on the same hard drive while holding down the Option button; this approach makes a copy of the original folder and leaves the original where it was.

Using photo album software

Setting up a series of folders to store and categorize your images is easy enough. To view them after they're stored, however, you either have to open them in the software you used to edit/retouch them or use the generic software that came with your computer to see the images. If you find that inconvenient (and you probably will, especially if you like to look at and work with your images frequently or to view them side by side), you'll probably be glad to know that several great photo-album applications are on the market. (I list a selection of them in Book V, Chapter 3.) These applications enable you to view one, two, or several of your images at the same time, all in one easily navigated workspace.

Figure 5-5 shows a group of photos viewed through Adobe Photoshop Album, which started out as a standalone application but is now part of Photoshop Elements. Similar programs are often furnished with cameras and software bundles from other vendors.

Figure 5-5: Album software makes it easy to organize, find, and retrieve your images.

Want more? Do a search at your favorite search site for **"Photo Album Software"** (use the quotation marks to make sure the search engine uses the full phrase). You can also check Web sites, such as www.buy.com and www.amazon.com, where you can do similar searches for the photo album software each site has to offer.

Your criteria for actually selecting photo album software is a personal thing. You may prefer ease of use and not care if you don't get a lot of fancy functionality. If you want a lot of bells and whistles, you may not mind it if the product is a little more complicated to use. Some photo album software serves as both an organizational tool and a vehicle for creative display of your photos, and some just do the latter job. If you already have a system for organizing your images, you may not need software that does double duty.

You can download and test many photo album products for free (with a time or number-of-uses limitation), making it possible to test-drive two or more products before plunking down any cash and making a commitment. It pays to shop around if you plan to use this software frequently. ThumbsPlus, available for evaluation at www.cerious.com/download.shtml, is shown in Figure 5-6. Other popular album applications include ACDSee, iPhoto, and Adobe Bridge, a standalone program included with many Adobe products, including Photoshop and Elements.

Figure 5-6: ThumbsPlus is a popular image management application.

Here are some features to look for when choosing photo album software:

+ Ability to categorize and classify each photo, using built-in or custom-designed categories

+ Provision for adding your own captions and other annotations

+ Search capabilities, so that you can locate all the images classified as Vacation pictures by using keywords such as *beach* and *2006*

+ Sorting abilities, so that you can permanently or temporarily arrange your photos by filename or other criteria (these features go hand-in-hand with search capabilities)

+ Features for uploading from your local album to your own Web space or picture sharing services, such as SmugMug (www.smugmug.com) or PBase (www.pbase.com)

+ Viewing capabilities that include looking at single photos and arranging them into slide shows

+ Simple image-editing features such as cropping, resizing, and rotating, so that you can make small changes to your pictures without firing up your image editor

Using online galleries

You probably already e-mail photos to friends, sending the images as message attachments that the recipients must open to view. Then, your recipients can save any images they want to keep on their hard drives. There may be a better way to share your images, assuming you don't mind having your images posted on the Internet, by using online galleries to display your photos. This section is an overview of using online galleries. You'll find a complete look at this valuable tool, including a discussion of some leading gallery providers in Book VIII.

The online approach to image distribution has some great advantages and some drawbacks. Check out the advantages first:

+ You can avoid the hassle of having to e-mail photos to lots of different individuals because you're placing all your photos on one Web site. All you have to do is let people know to check the site for your images. This makes it possible to share images that are larger than some e-mail services can handle (many services have a 2MB limit).

+ You can share more images with more people. Anyone with an Internet connection can view the images without owning any special software — other than a browser, which people need to surf the Web anyway.

+ You have yet another relatively protected repository for your images. If you lose the original files, you can download them from the online gallery.

Possible disadvantages — and only you can decide if they are real disadvantages — are as follows:

+ Your photos are on the Web, and, unless you use the provider's privacy provisions, anyone can view them. This can expose you and your family to people with whom you would not normally share your vacation, holiday, and otherwise personal photos. You have to be careful about posting photos that show your house number, last name, or any other identifying information.

+ Most online galleries charge a fee for providing space on their site for your photos. The fees are usually reasonable, but compared to e-mailing photos, which is free (you're already paying to have e-mail anyway), the cost may be more than you're willing to pay.

To find an online gallery to post your photos, you can search online for **"Online Galleries"**. You'll see quite a few that are devoted to actual artists (and this may be of interest if you are an artist), and some that are for the general public to use. If you add **"+free"** to the search criteria, you'll ferret out those sites that offer the space for free or that will let you test their services for free or for a limited time.

Archiving and Backing Up Photos

Not all your photos will require instant, easy access. Vacation photos from the past — especially if you visited a not-too-exciting place — may be a waste of valuable hard-drive real estate. But what if you don't want to delete those infrequently viewed images? There's no reason to make rash decisions; you can simply archive the ones you don't need to access quickly or frequently. If a photo is valuable to you on some level in the long run, but you don't imagine wanting to look at or print it within the foreseeable future, just save it to disc — a CD or DVD.

Backing up your best shots

First, because you've already organized your photos (assuming you've read the beginning of this chapter), you should already have your photos categorized and know which ones are especially dear to you. These cherished shots need to be backed up, stored in some way in order to protect them from anything that can happen to your computer or your photo albums (printed or electronic).

Your backup options are simple:

+ **Store the photos on a spare hard drive.** This isn't as freaky as it sounds. Plug-in external hard drives that connect to your USB or FireWire port may cost less than $100, and they can make a large-capacity, relatively inexpensive backup system. External hard drives in sizes of 160GB or less can cost less than $100 and will hold thousands of images. You can unhook the drive and store it in a safe place when you're not actually using the images you've backed up. Of course, hard drives are prone to failure (eventually), and even an extra external drive shouldn't be used as your only backup destination.

+ **Write them to a disc, using a CD or DVD burner.** This method enables you to store up to 800MB on a single CD, or almost 5GB on a DVD. If your computer already has a burner in it or attached to it, all you need is a package of writeable CDs or DVDs. The discs are so inexpensive that you can make two copies. To be 100-percent safe, you should plan on copying your important discs to fresh media every few years. Even good-quality CDs and DVDs can "fade" over time. Also plan to copy your media to whatever new kind of storage replaces CDs and DVDs five or ten years down the road. You don't want to end up with "antique" discs and no way to access them!

+ **Store them online.** Many Web sharing sites also can provide you with a sort of backup for your images. It's best to use these as a secondary backup (sort of as a backup to your backup) because there's no guarantee how long these services will be around!

Using CD-R and CD-RW

For a brief period, virtually every computer sold came with a built-in CD burner. These have largely been supplanted by combo drives that can burn both CDs *and* DVDs. So it's very likely that your computer has a burner of some sort that can make archival copies on CDs.

With the ability to write to a CD, you now can save up to 800MB of data on a very reliable medium. Unlike older magnetic media, such as floppy and Zip disks (remember them?) that could be ruined by exposure to magnets, heat, cold, sunlight, water, and rough handling, CDs are pretty stable. Other than breaking or scratching them, you can't really hurt them. They might eventually fade on their own, but it won't be your fault!

Although DVDs are the new (if temporary) standard, the old CD format still has a lot of life left in it. Here's a refresher course in CD media:

✦ Writeable CDs come in two types: CD-R and CD-RW. CD-Rs can be written to (the R stands for Recordable), but only once. CD-RWs can be written to and erased, and written to again.

✦ You can use a CD-R or a CD-RW like a floppy or Zip disk by using a mode called Packet Writing. In that mode, you can copy files or groups thereof to the CD. However, you can't interrupt the writing process as you can with a floppy or Zip disk, and the process takes a bit longer.

✦ Commercial CDs (like the discs that contain software or audio tracks) are pressed from a mold. CD-Rs and CD-RWs are marked with a laser, creating spots that represent data (in binary form). CDs are virtually indestructible (unless you crack, break, or severely scratch them) and can withstand a sunny day in the car or a night below freezing in that same glove box. Even so, CD-Rs and CD-RWs shouldn't be exposed to direct sunlight or extreme heat, although they are less vulnerable to such conditions than floppy or Zip disks.

DVD storage

DVD burners have largely replaced CD-only burners in most computers. Indeed, the older single-layer, 4.8GB DVD drives are themselves being phased out by double-layer drives that can record 8.5GB of data. In the home theater arena, there's even a bit of fierce competition going on between Blu-Ray style and HD-DVD formats, which can handle as much as 50GB of information!

For the digital photographer, plain old 4.8GB DVD drives make a lot of sense until the technology settles down more. For one thing, single-layer DVDs cost much less than half what dual-layer blank discs sell for. And you can be assured that your dual-layer drive will read your old single-layer discs when you do migrate. The only real problem with sticking with the older technology right now is that the 4.8GB drives are becoming harder to find.

Like CDs, DVDs also come in more than one variety:

+ DVDs (the prerecorded kind) come with stuff prewritten to them. You can view what's on them, but you can't erase and then rewrite to them.

+ DVD+R and DVD-R discs (note the use of the plus and minus signs) can be written to only once. The plus/minus varieties are separate formats, but most drives and burners can read both types. The -R version can be slightly more compatible with some television DVD players.

+ DVD+RW and DVD-RW discs can be written to, erased, and written to again.

+ DVD+/-RW burner/players can play DVD discs and play or write to DVD+/-R and DVD+/-RW discs.

   If your older computer has a DVD player in it, that doesn't mean you can write to DVDs; it simply means you can play them. To write to a DVD, you need the burner version.

+ DVD Dual Layer discs require a dual-layer compatible drive or player.

Offsite storage for maximum safety

If your photos are so precious that you'd be devastated if anything happened to them, or if they're important for legal, financial, or other compelling reasons, don't risk losing them to a fire or burglary. You can store your archives off-site in one of three ways:

+ Use a bank safe deposit box.

+ Use a safe located in a secure storage facility.

+ Arrange to keep one of two archive copies with a friend or family member.

If you save your precious images to a CD or DVD, you can make two sets and store one set offsite, selecting one of the aforementioned places based on the level of security you need. The bank could burn down, but the safe deposit boxes are usually in or near the vault and are protected from very high temperatures, even in the event of a fire. If you keep a safe in a paid offsite storage space, the place is likely to be fireproof or well-protected by sprinklers and video cameras, so it's probably more secure than your home. If neither of these is an option, find a friend or relative you trust and give the extra set to him or her.

Chapter 6: Printing and Sharing Your Pictures

In This Chapter

- ✓ Making prints while you wait
- ✓ Choosing among printer categories
- ✓ Recommended print sizes
- ✓ Sharing the wealth (of pictures you've taken)

*U*ntil the cost of those huge flat-panel digital displays that hang on the wall like a picture frame dip below their current stratospheric price levels, you'll probably want to use hard-copy prints of your best digital pictures to decorate your home or office. You'll also find that prints are more fun to pass around when you're sharing your vacation with coworkers. And have you ever tried to tuck an electronic image of a loved one in your wallet?

No, prints are here to stay. Digital technology is just making prints easier for anyone to produce. Instead of stacks of photos of every single picture you've ever taken (plus shoeboxes full of "lost" negatives), you can have great-looking enlargements of the photos you want to keep, perfectly cropped and carefully corrected in your image editing program. The ability to make prints is one of the best things about digital photography.

An alternative to sharing prints is sharing your pictures online through commercial sharing services or your own personal Web space. Such options let friends and colleagues view your photos even if they aren't close by.

This chapter provides a quick overview of printing and printers and picture sharing services. You can find a lot more detail in Book VIII.

Creating Prints on Demand

One of the reasons you'll want a printer for your digital camera is the sheer joy of being able to produce your own prints any time in only a few minutes. If you're used to dropping off negatives at a local photofinishing outlet and then waiting *hours* or even overnight to get sparkling 5-x-7-inch enlargements, you'll love your color printer.

For example, on the day I began this chapter, I was called over to my daughter's school to take a picture of her science class performing the infamous Egg Drop experiment. I snapped off a couple shots of carefully-cushioned eggs surviving (hopefully) a two-story plummet and then ran home and made two 5-x-7-inch enlargements (one for the class, and one for our local newspaper). It actually took longer to write the caption for the newspaper than it did to print the photos. Less than 30 minutes after the last egg fell to an untimely end, I returned to the school with prints in hand. Try *that* with a film camera!

Color printers have never been cheaper or more ubiquitous. Our local supermarket sells $50 inkjet printers in the school and office supplies aisle, just across from the microwave ovens. It's a 24/7 market, too, so if I'm ever stuck in the middle of a project at 3 a.m., I can dash out and pick up some ink or even a whole new printer before sunrise.

Here are your main options for making prints from digital cameras:

+ **Use your local MegaMart's print kiosk.** These typically accept a broad range of digital media, from CompactFlash and Secure Digital film cards to CDs or Picture CDs. They let you choose a photo, crop, rotate, and resize your pictures, maybe add some text, and perform other simple manipulations using a touch-screen video display. When you're happy with your picture, press a button and wait a few minutes until your photo emerges. If you don't make many prints, this can be a viable option. The quality will be equal to or better than the prints you can make at home.

+ **Try out your retailer's digital lab.** You didn't think that photofinishers would roll over and play dead after film was abandoned by a fickle public, did you? Although dropping off your film for overnight processing may be an activity that's riding off into the sunset, many finishers are building a thriving business from making prints, enlargements, and specialty items from your digital images. Many retailers now have in-store digital minilabs that can accept your digital film and produce prints while you wait. There are many advantages to this approach. For one thing, your retailer can probably make prints a *lot* more cheaply than you can, can do it faster, and can give you better quality.

+ **Do it yourself with an inkjet printer.** Inkjet printers can produce prints that look exactly like traditional silver-based photographs, on glossy or matte paper, at a cost of about $1.00 for large prints and about $0.25 per snapshot. Most digital photographers own an inkjet printer, and unless you are *very* fussy, they'll do the job for you.

✦ **Upgrade to alternative technologies.** Other types of printers, such as dye-sublimation printers, thermal wax printers, and solid wax printers, do a great job with color photos. Of these, only dye-sub printers are still easy to find, with Kodak and Olympus among the vendors offering high-quality dye-sublimation printers that are actually economical enough to compete with inkjets. You can find more information about all these printers in Book II, Chapter 4.

Getting the Most from Your Printer and Supplies

If you want to get the best from any of these printers, just follow a few simple tips:

✦ Calibrate your monitor so that what you see is what you get in your prints. Check the manual that came with your image editing software for instructions on calibrating your monitor to your application.

✦ Use the best-quality glossy photographic paper you can afford. You can't go wrong using the paper recommended by your printer manufacturer.

✦ Clean your inkjet's print heads from time to time and keep the paper path clean to avoid visible lines or blurry prints.

✦ Wait until your prints are completely dry before you touch them. Wet ink can smear easily, which spoils a $1 investment.

✦ Have fun with those special printing media offered to let you make transparencies or T-shirt transfers, print on fabrics, or create greeting cards.

✦ Don't ruin a perfectly good sheet of paper by making a print that's too large for your digital camera's resolution (and thus comes out a bit fuzzy-looking). Table 6-1 shows good sizes and maximum sizes for typical digital camera resolutions, past and present.

Table 6-1	Recommended Print Sizes	
Camera Resolution	*Good Size*	*Maximum Size*
640 x 480 pixels	2½ x 3½ in.	3½ x 5 in.
1024 x 768 pixels	3½ x 5 in.	5 x 7 in.
1280 x 960 pixels	4 x 6 in.	8 x 10 in.
1600 x 1200 pixels	5 x 7 in.	11 x 14 in.
3000 x 2000 pixels	8 x 10 in.	16 x 20 in.
3600 x 2400 pixels	8 x 10 in.	20 x 30 in.

Sharing Your Photos

You can always e-mail your photos to friends and colleagues, but there's a better way. You can post them to your own Web site or use one of the commercial photo sharing services. You can share your vacation photos, pictures from school, and brag shots of your new house or car, or you can create an online holiday newsletter.

Your ISP (Internet Service Provider) probably provides some free Web space you can use to create pages for your pictures. Check with your provider for instructions on how to use this space. Even easier is using the services provided by online companies like SmugMug, Yahoo!, and PBase. Their Web sites lead you hand-in-hand through the process.

If you use an online sharing system or online gallery to display your images, you'll find that many of them offer some space for free. In the case of an online community, such as America Online, your monthly fee to AOL includes access to the company's AOL Pictures (formerly You've Got Pictures) feature, which enables you and others to view your images online. You get free Web space, too, which you can use to store and display your photos.

Other commercial sharing services known as *online galleries* allow you to post your images for free in exchange for posting a few ads on your Web pages. Other sites make their money through software they sell, such as image editing or photo album applications.

Some sites, like Kodak's EasyShare Gallery, let you upload your photos for viewing but also offer the ability to send picture postcards and order prints, enlargements, mugs, T-shirts, and other related items.

Sound intriguing? Check out Book VIII for more on sharing your photographic treasures online.

Book II

Building Your Digital Photography Studio

The 5th Wave   By Rich Tennant

"My God! I've gained 9 pixels!"

*I*n this minibook, I show you how to assemble a suitable digital photography arsenal, with explanations of all the key features of the weapons at your disposal, including camera equipment, computer gear, printers, and cool accessories like tripods, electronic flashes, and (if you're going the digital SLR route) add-on lenses.

I also give you in-depth explanations of key features, including zooms, viewfinders, storage options, and whether you really do need a gazillion megapixels of resolution. You'll find out how to set up your computer, transfer pictures from your camera to your hard drive, and archive your photos effectively for posterity. I also explain some of the more puzzling aspects of printers and scanners and show you how a few accessories can make a dramatic difference in the quality of your photos.

Chapter 1: Choosing the Right Camera

In This Chapter

- ✓ Selecting a camera category
- ✓ Key components of digital cameras
- ✓ Evaluating lens requirements
- ✓ Understanding sensors and resolution
- ✓ Choosing exposure controls
- ✓ Selecting exposure options
- ✓ Exotic digital camera capabilities
- ✓ Finding a camera that's easy to use

*C*hoosing the right digital camera has gotten a lot more exciting recently! Digital single lens reflex (dSLR) cameras — the ones that have interchangeable lenses and show you an optical (not electronic) preview image through the same lens that takes the picture — have dipped under the $1,000 price point and are nosing around the $600 neighborhood, making them a reasonable choice for many more serious amateur photographers. Affordable 8-megapixel (and up) cameras provide sharper, better pictures without busting your wallet. Digital cameras are becoming smaller and easier to use and are packed with special features we never dreamed were possible as recently as a year ago. This is a great time to be choosing a digital camera, whether you're a snapshooter or a dedicated photo hobbyist.

Yet, selecting the right digital camera isn't as daunting a task as it might appear to be on the surface, even with the increased number of features and options to choose from. Most of the leading vendors of digital equipment produce fine products that take great pictures. It's really hard to go wrong. All you need to do is a little homework so that you're aware, when you make your purchase, of the features you need — and features you don't need. The vendors write their brochures and ad copy so that those who don't sort out features and benefits ahead of time might think that every feature is essential.

Trust me: They're not. The ability to shoot several pictures consecutively, each using different color settings to make sure that one picture is perfectly color-balanced, might sound cool, but it's not something many people need every day. But if you find yourself constantly taking pictures under varied lighting conditions, and color accuracy is very important to you, a feature like that might be a lifesaver. Only you can decide for sure.

The key is having the upfront information you need to wisely choose the camera that has the largest number of your must-have features — and a nice sprinkling of nice-to-have features — at a price you can afford. In Book I, Chapter 2, you can find an overview of the choices you need to make. There, you can find an introduction to the chief things to consider, which are

✦ Lens requirements

✦ Viewfinder options

✦ Sensor resolution

✦ Exposure controls

✦ Storage options

✦ Ease of use

This chapter looks at each of these considerations, plus others, in more detail, with a brief mention of the newest digital SLR cameras (which are covered more exhaustively in Book III). Although much of the information can help you select a camera, you can also find some basic explanations of digital camera nuts and bolts that will be helpful as you take pictures. If you ever wanted to know what shutter speeds and lens openings do, this is your chance.

Choosing a Camera Category

Digital cameras fall into several different categories, each aimed at a particular audience of buyers, as well as particular kinds of applications for them. You can find an extended discussion of camera categories in Book I, Chapter 2. However, as a recap, the major types include

✦ **Web cams:** Web cams are cheap TV cameras that also offer low-resolution full-motion and still images. They're fun to use and essential for things like videoconferencing. They aren't covered in this book because most don't have the kind of image quality and capabilities required for serious photography.

✦ **Camera phones:** Camera phones are those multipurpose cell phones that also have photographic capabilities built in. Some have 2-megapixel or better resolution that exceeds the picture quality available from some $500 digital cameras from only a few years ago. In Japan, cell phones with cameras built in have already cut heavily into the market for one-time-use film cameras. Folks who sometimes forget to take their digital cameras with them wouldn't be caught dead without their cell phones, so they're always ready for the kind of spur-of-the-moment photography that single-use cameras have traditionally served. I'm not covering these useful (but specialized) devices in this book (even though I own and use one myself), nor cameras built into other products, such as personal digital assistants (PDAs). None of them are intended for use as a primary camera.

✦ **Point-and-shoot models:** These entry-level digital cameras, priced at $100–$200, offer 4 to 5 megapixels of resolution (although it's becoming very difficult to find a 4-megapixel camera in stores), simple lenses (usually with zoom), and autoexposure. I recently tested a 6-megapixel camera with a 3X zoom lens and 32MB of built-in memory (a memory card was optional) that could be purchased for $169! Clearly, even the most basic point-and-shoot cameras are gaining resolution and features almost faster than we can keep track. This kind of camera is an excellent choice for someone looking for a basic camera with few manual adjustments, and for casual shots that will be enlarged no more than about 5 x 7 inches.

✦ **Intermediate models:** Priced in the $200–$400 slot, intermediate digital cameras have 5- to 8-megapixel resolution, a 3:1 or 5:1 or better zoom lens, and Secure Digital (SD), xD, or CompactFlash storage. Many have close-up focusing, burst modes that can snap off seven or more frames in a few seconds, and some manual controls. The average snapshooter would be very happy with a camera in this category and would be satisfied with the few tweaks that can be made to add a little creativity to selected photos.

✦ **Advanced consumer models:** In the $400–$800 range, you can find deluxe digital cameras with roughly 6 to 10 megapixels of resolution, decent 5:1 to 12:1 zoom lenses, lots of accessories, optional exposure modes, and a steep learning curve. These cameras are easy to operate so the average snapshooter can use them with a little training and practice. Yet, they are also versatile, with features like electronic viewfinders and manual settings, that serious photographers can invoke for those special picture-taking situations.

✦ **Prosumer non-SLR models:** Serious amateurs and some professional photographers use these. They cost $600—$800 and have all the features you could want, including 8 to 10 megapixels or more of resolution, the highest-quality lenses, an electronic viewfinder (EVF), and every accessory you can dream of. Expect automatic and manual focus, multiple automated exposure modes, and motor drive multishot capabilities. (Read more about motor drive capability in Book IV, Chapter 5.)

✦ **Prosumer SLR models:** The prosumer SLR is very nearly a whole new category of camera, created in 2003 when Canon introduced the Digital Rebel for $999 (with lens), and other vendors, including Nikon and

Pentax, followed. In price, there is some overlap with the prosumer non-SLR cameras. However, the true SLR type offers interchangeable lenses and other features found in the traditional advanced-amateur favorite.

✦ **Professional models:** Professional-quality digital SLR cameras used to cost $5,000 and up and had 6–14 million pixels of resolution. Today, you can still pay around $5,000 or more for a pro camera (without lens), and resolutions now go up to 22 megapixels, but some very fine professional-worthy models are available for a few thousand dollars less, too.

The manufacturers of the top-end cameras are feeling the pressure of competition from the sub-$1,000 digital SLRs, so you can expect prices to drop even further as features proliferate. However, professional photographers will continue to pay a premium for these cameras because they frequently operate more quickly, allowing the pro to grab shot after shot without pausing for breath. They're rugged, too, which means they can withstand the harsh treatment pros often subject their equipment to (not because they're mean, but because they're *working*).

You can find some general tips in Book I, Chapter 2 that can help you determine what category of camera you should look for. Read here, though, for the lowdown on everything you need to consider.

Examining the Parts of a Digital Camera

If you're very new to digital cameras, you might be wondering what all those buttons, LEDs, and windows are for. Here's a quick introduction to the key components of the average non-SLR digital camera. Not every camera will have all these features, and some will have additional features not shown in Figures 1-1 and 1-2.

✦ **Shutter release:** Pressing this button halfway locks exposure and focus; press all the way to take a picture.

✦ **Control buttons:** Miscellaneous control buttons might turn on/off close-up mode, automatic flash, or other features; set picture quality; or activate the self-timer.

✦ **Shooting mode dial:** Most cameras use this button or dial for changing among different scene modes (such as Night, Portrait, or Sports), adjusting automatic or manual exposure choices, selecting Movie mode, or switching into close-up mode.

✦ **Microphone:** This captures audio for movie clips and voice annotations; it can even activate a sound-triggered self-timer.

✦ **Focus-assist light:** This is an auxiliary illumination source that helps the camera focus in dim lighting conditions.

Figure 1-1: The front of a typical digital camera.

✦ **Electronic flash:** This provides light under dim conditions or helps fill in dark shadows.

✦ **Optical viewfinder:** This window, which doesn't show exactly the same view that the lens captures, is for framing and composing your picture.

✦ **Zoom lens:** This magnifies and reduces the size of the image, taking you closer or moving you farther away.

✦ **Lens cover:** This protects the lens when the digital camera is turned off.

✦ **Tripod socket:** This allows you to attach the camera to a firm support, such as a tripod or monopod, plus other accessories, such as an external flash bracket.

✦ **Docking port:** Some cameras have a special dock that can be used to transfer photos, recharge the batteries, make prints, or perform other functions.

✦ **Battery compartment:** This contains the cells that power the camera.

✦ **Power switch:** Here is where you turn the camera on or off.

Figure 1-2: The back of a typical digital camera.

+ **Indicator LEDs:** These indicators show status, such as focus and expo-sure, often with green and red go/no go LEDs (light-emitting diodes).

+ **LCD (liquid crystal display) panel:** This shows the sensor's view of an image before exposure, shows preview images after exposure, and displays status, photo information, and menus.

+ **Display control/Menu button:** This controls the amount of information shown in the LCD and produces menus. Some digital cameras have multi-ple buttons for recording menus, setup menus, and special functions.

+ **Picture review:** Press this button to review the pictures you've already taken.

+ **Print/e-mail/share photos:** Some digital cameras allow printing directly from the camera to compatible printers or marking pictures for printing or e-mailing later.

✦ **Cursor pad:** Use this to navigate menu choices. Many digital cameras use the cursor buttons to activate frequently accessed features, such as flash options, macro mode, exposure value adjustments, and a self-timer.

✦ **Set/Execute button:** Press this to activate a feature or set a menu choice to the current selection.

✦ **Memory card slot:** This accepts digital memory cards.

✦ **USB port:** Use this to connect your camera directly to your computer or to a printer via a USB cable.

✦ **File-save LED:** This light usually flashes or lights up to indicate that an image is currently being saved to the memory card.

✦ **Power zoom control:** Press this to zoom the lens in and out.

Evaluating Your Lens Requirements

The lens and the sensor (or film, in the case of a conventional camera) are the two most important parts of any photographic system. The lens gathers the light from your scene and focuses it onto the capture medium, digital or analog. The sensor or film transforms the light into something that can be stored permanently and viewed as a picture after digital or chemical processing.

Sharp lenses and high-quality sensors (or film) lead to technically good images; poor lenses and bad sensors lead to poor photos. Indeed, in one sense, most of the other components of a camera are for your convenience. Theoretically, you could mount a simple lens on one end of an oatmeal box, focus it on a piece of film or a sensor affixed to the inside of the other end of the box, and make an exposure by covering and uncovering the lens with a dark cloth. Of course, the digital version of this science fair project would require some additional electronics to handle the captured signal, but such a system could work.

When you're choosing a digital camera, the first thing to concentrate on is the lens furnished with it. You probably don't need to go into as much detail as I'm going to provide, but understanding the components of a camera lens does help you use your optics as much as it helps you choose them. The major things you need to know fall into four simple categories:

✦ **The optical quality of the lens itself:** Just how sharp is the piece of glass (or, these days, plastic)? The better the lens, the better it can capture — *resolve* — fine details. In most cases, the optical quality of digital camera lenses marches in lockstep with the price of the camera and the resolution of the sensor. Even at the low and medium ends of the price spectrum, digital cameras have good-quality lenses that usually can resolve a lot more detail than the 4- to 5-megapixel sensor can capture.

Camera vendors have been mass-producing lenses like these for film cameras for decades, and any film camera can capture a lot more detail than an inexpensive digital camera. At higher price levels, lenses have better-quality optics, which are necessary to keep up with the detail-capturing capabilities of 6- to 8-megapixel (and higher) sensors.

✦ **The amount of light the lens can transmit:** Some lenses can capture larger amounts of light than others, generally because they have a greater diameter that can transmit more light. This factor, called *lens speed,* is a bit more complicated than that. Think of a 1-inch-diameter pipe and a 2-inch-diameter pipe and visualize how much more water (or light) the wider pipe can conduct; now you're thinking in the right direction. Lens speed, in part, controls how low of a light level you can take pictures in. If you take many pictures in dim light, you'll want a *faster* lens. I look at this factor in greater detail later in this chapter.

✦ **The focusing range of the lens:** Some lenses can focus closer than others. The ability to get up-close and personal with your subject matter can be very important if your hobbies include things like stamp or coin collecting or if you want to take pictures of flowers or bugs. Indeed, close-focusing can open whole new worlds of photography for you, worlds you can explore in more detail in Book IV, Chapter 2.

✦ **The magnification range of the lens:** Virtually all digital cameras have a zoom lens, which allows you to vary the amount of magnification of the image. You might be able to take your basic image and double it in size (a 2:1 zoom ratio), triple it (a 3:1 zoom), or magnify it 12X or more (a 12:1 zoom). The zoom range determines how much or how little of a particular subject you can include in an image from a particular shooting distance. As you might expect, the ability to zoom enhances your creative options significantly. At the widest settings (wide-angle settings), you can take in broad sweeps of landscape, whereas in the narrowest view (telephoto), you can reach out and bring a distant object much closer.

Understanding How Lenses Work

You don't need to have a degree in optical science to use a digital camera, but understanding how lens openings (*f-stops*) and some other components work can help you use those components more effectively.

Lenses consist of several optical elements made of glass or plastic that focus light in precise ways, much like you focus light with a magnifying glass or with a telescope or binoculars. The very simplest lenses, like those used on the least expensive digital cameras, are *fixed focal length* lenses, usually comprising just three or four pieces of glass. That is, the elements can produce an image only at a single magnification. You find these in the simplest point-and-shoot cameras that have no zooming capabilities. There aren't many of these around, but I did run into a camera with no "real" zoom recently: an extra-compact model that used a 3:1 digital zoom as a substitute for optical zooming capabilities.

Most digital cameras have zoom lenses, which have very complex optical systems with 8, 10, 20, or more elements that move in precise ways to produce a continuous range of magnifications. Zoom lenses must be carefully designed to avoid bad things, such as stray beams of light that degrade the image bouncing around inside the lens. For that reason, when choosing a digital camera with a zoom lens, you need to pay attention to the quality of the image. All 4:1 zooms are not created equal; one vendor might produce an excellent lens with this range, whereas another might offer a lens that is less sharp. Among digital cameras with similar or identical sensors, lens quality can make the biggest difference in the final quality of an image. You'll discover how to select the best lens for your needs as we go along.

You can get a top-quality lens and still save some money if you know how to interpret digital camera specifications. Many vendors share lenses and sensors among similar models in their product lines. I tested two cameras from the same manufacturer that had identical resolution and lens specifications, but one model was more compact, was outfitted with a rechargeable battery, and included rubber gaskets that made it water resistant. (It also cost $100 more!) A penny-pinching photographer who doesn't mind a tiny bit more bulk, is willing to use AA batteries, and doesn't plan any photography in rain showers could buy the less expensive version and save enough money to buy some extra memory cards or other accessories.

Magnifications and focal lengths

Comparing zoom ranges of digital cameras can be confusing because the exact same lens can produce different magnifications on different cameras. That's why you usually see the zoom range of a digital camera presented either as absolute magnifications or in the equivalents of the 35mm camera lenses that the zoom settings correspond to.

Zoom range doesn't relate to lens quality. You'll find excellent 4:1 zooms and average 4:1 zooms. However, the longer the zoom range, the more difficult it is to produce a lens that makes good pictures at all zoom settings. You should be especially careful in choosing a lens with a longer zoom range (8:1 or above); test the camera and its lens before you buy. However, lenses from the major manufacturers (Canon, Sony, Nikon, Fuji, and so forth) are all generally quite good.

Until the advent of digital cameras, figuring the magnification of consumer camera lenses was relatively easy because, in recent years, most consumer (and the workhorse professional) film cameras used a standard film size — the 35mm film frame — which measures a nominal 24mm x 36mm. Some cameras also used Kodak's now-discontinued Advanced Photo System (APS) film format, which produced images in three different configurations.

Optical zoom versus digital zoom

Non-SLR digital cameras have two kinds of zooming capabilities: optical and digital. *Optical zoom* uses the arrangement of the lens elements to control the amount of magnification. Usually, optical zoom is the specification mentioned first in the camera's list of features. *Digital zoom* is a supplementary magnification system in which the center pixels of an image are enlarged using a mathematical algorithm to fill the entire image area with the information contained in those center pixels.

Digital zoom doesn't really provide much in the way of extra information; you could zoom in on an image in your image editor if you like. However, digital zoom is a way of turning a 4:1 zoom into an 8:1 (or better) zoom lens even if the results aren't as good as those you'd obtain with a true optical 8:1 zoom. I tend to discount digital zoom capabilities when buying a camera because I want the sharpest picture possible, and many of the digital zoom pictures I've taken have looked fuzzy and pixelated. The feature doesn't cost you anything, and you can usually switch it off so you won't accidentally grab a digital zoom picture by mistake.

The magnification of any particular lens with a standard film size is easily calculated by measuring the distance from the film the lens must be positioned to focus a sharp image on the film. (This is the focal length of the lens.)

By convention, in 35mm photography, a lens with a 45–50mm focal length is considered a *normal* lens. (The figure was arrived at by measuring the diagonal of the film frame; you can calculate the focal length of a normal lens for any size film or digital camera sensor by measuring that diagonal.)

Lenses with a shorter focal length, such as 35mm, 28mm, 20mm, or less, are described as *wide-angle* lenses. Those with longer focal lengths (such as 85mm, 105mm, or 200mm) are described as *telephoto* lenses. We've lived happily with that nomenclature for more than 75 years, since the first 35mm camera was introduced. Wide-angle and telephoto images are shown in Figure 1-3.

Then came the digital camera, and all the simple conventions about focal lengths and magnifications went out the window. For good and valid technical reasons, most digital camera sensors do not measure 24mm x 36mm. You wouldn't want a sensor that large (roughly 1" x 1.5") anyway in a compact digital camera because the camera would have to be large enough to accommodate it. In addition, as with all solid-state devices, the larger a device such as a sensor becomes, the more expensive it is to manufacture. Sensors that are as large as the full 35mm film frame are available for an increasing number of digital SLR cameras, which means the magnification effect I'm about to describe doesn't apply for those models.

Most sensors for non-SLR cameras are more likely to measure, say, 16mm x 24mm or less. Even the larger digital camera sensors might be no bigger than about 38mm x 38mm. So, a normal lens on one digital camera might be 8mm, whereas another normal lens on another camera might be 6mm. A 4:1 zoom lens can range from 8mm–32mm or 5.5mm–22mm. What a mess! How can you compare lenses and zoom ranges under those conditions?

Figure 1-3: Telephoto (top) and wide angle shots (bottom) provide different perspectives on a subject.

Camera vendors have solved the problem by quoting digital camera lens focal lengths according to their 35mm equivalents. If you're already familiar with 35mm camera lenses, that's great. If you're not, at least you have a standard measurement to compare with. That's why you often see digital camera zoom ranges expressed as "35mm–135mm equivalent (roughly 4:1)" or some similar expression. You can safely use these figures to compare lenses in your quest for the perfect digital camera.

Because digital camera lenses have such short focal lengths in the first place, most models tend to be deficient in the wide-angle department. Expect to see most digital cameras with no better than a 35mm–28mm wide-angle equivalent. That's barely acceptable because 35mm isn't very wide. If you really need a wide field of view, consider a wide-angle attachment that fits on the front of your lens.

What focal length (equivalents) do you look for? Your preferred range will depend on what kind of photos you want to take. If you shoot architecture or indoor photos, you'll want the shortest focal length possible. An alarming number of digital cameras seem to have settled on a 38–39mm (equivalent) focal length as their widest setting. There are several reasons for that. First, a lens with that meager wide-angle field of view is easier to design (and usually more compact) than one with a broader perspective.

In addition, a lens with a particular magnification will have a longer telephoto effect if you're starting from a base focal length that's narrower to begin with. Consumers tend to get more excited about long telephotos than they do about wider wide-angles, even though both perspectives have an important place. Table 1-1 shows how a 4:1 zoom lens gains a more impressive telephoto "look" when the vendor snips millimeters from the wide-angle portion of the range.

Table 1-1	4X Zoom Lenses (35mm Equivalents)
Minimum Focal Length	*Maximum Focal Length*
28mm	112mm
32mm	128mm
35mm	140mm
38mm	152mm

Hey, wouldn't you prefer a 152mm medium telephoto over a 112mm short telephoto? You would until you find yourself with your back up against the wall trying to take a picture of an entire (albeit moderately small) room and discover that your 4X zoom lens would give you no more than the field of view of a 38mm lens. You might be happier with a lens that has a wider minimum focal length but which accepts a telephoto attachment for those times when you really need to reach out and touch something.

Lens apertures

The *lens aperture* is an adjustable control that determines the width of the opening that admits light to the sensor. The wider the aperture, the more light that can reach the sensor, making it possible to take pictures in dimmer light. You can think of an aperture as the pupil of your eye. When it's bright outside, your pupils contract (and you squint), letting in less light. When it's dim, your pupils dilate.

A narrow aperture reduces the amount of light that can reach the sensor, letting you avoid overloading the imaging device in very bright light. These lens openings are used in tandem with *shutter speed* (the amount of time the sensor is exposed to the light) to control the exposure. (I explain more about exposure later in this chapter.) Your digital camera needs a selection of lens apertures (*f-stops*) so that you can take pictures in a broad range of lighting conditions.

**Book II
Chapter 1**

Choosing the Right Camera

F-stops aren't absolute values; they're calculated by measuring the actual size of the lens opening as it relates to the focal length of the lens, using a formula that I won't repeat here. The easiest way to visualize how f-stops work is to imagine them as the denominators of fractions. Just like ½ is larger than ¼ or ⅛, f/2 is larger than f/4 or f/8. The relationship is such that as the amount of light reaching the sensor is doubled, the f-stop increases using an odd-looking series of numbers: f/2 is twice as large as f/2.8, which is twice as large as f/4, and so on through f/5.6, f/8, f/11, f/16, and f/22 (which is just about the smallest f-stop you'll encounter in the digital realm). Figure 1-4 shows a lens opening that's partially closed down.

Figure 1-4: Lens opening, f-stop, aperture — all mean the doorway that light passes through to the sensor.

If you're taking photos in automatic mode, you don't need to know what f-stop you're using because the camera selects it for you automatically. Your digital camera probably displays the f-stop being used, however, either in the viewfinder or on an LCD panel, and the information can be helpful. Just remember these things (see Figure 1-5):

✦ The larger the f-stop (the smaller the number), the more light that is admitted (*faster*). An f/2 lens (small number, large f-stop) is a fast lens, whereas one with a maximum aperture of f/8 (larger number, smaller f-stop) is *slow*. If you need to take photos in dim light, you want to buy a camera with a fast lens.

✦ The smaller the f-stop (larger the number), the more of your image that is in sharp focus. (More on this later.)

✦ As the f-stops get smaller (larger number), exposure time must be increased to let in the same amount of light. For example, if you take a photo at f/2 for one-half second, you need to double the exposure time to one full second if you *stop down* (reduce the aperture) to f/4. I look at exposure a little later, too.

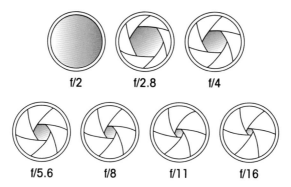

Figure 1-5: As the f-stop gets larger (the number gets smaller), more light is admitted.

Typically, you'll find that among non-SLR digital cameras, the *speed* or maximum aperture of camera lenses is smaller than is common among 35mm film cameras, and the range of available apertures is more limited, too. For example, even an inexpensive snapshooter 35mm film camera might have an f/1.9 lens (pretty fast), and serious photographers with 35mm SLRs probably own f/1.4 or faster normal and wide-angle lenses. Although zoom lenses usually have smaller maximum apertures, in the 35mm film world, f/2.8–f/3.5 are common numbers.

In the digital camera realm, things are a bit different primarily because the very short focal lengths of the lenses are more difficult to design with large lens openings. So don't be alarmed if your favorite digital camera has an f/4 or f/5.6 maximum aperture. You might even find that the lens is labeled f/4–f/5.6 because the effective widest opening can vary as a lens is zoomed in and out. A lens might have an f/4 opening when zoomed out to 38mm but only f/5.6 at its maximum telephoto setting of 152mm. (In most cases, as the focal length increases, the lens opening itself moves along with the optical glass, so the opening is farther away from the sensor and looks smaller.)

To make things really interesting, your digital camera lens might have only a limited number of different f-stops available, perhaps f/4, f/5.6, and f/8, or maybe none at all. You won't miss the lack of f-stops: Modern electronic shutters are fast enough to provide the proper exposure without smaller lens openings. Further, in 35mm photography, smaller lens openings have been used to increase the range of sharpness (called *depth of field*). As you can read in Book IV, Chapter 2, though, the short focal length of non-SLR digital camera lenses usually means that just about everything is sharp, anyway.

Focus range

The focus range of a digital camera is simply how close it can be from a subject and still create a sharp image. Digital cameras vary in their close-focusing (also called *macro*) capabilities. If you want to photograph flowers, hobby collections, items for sale on eBay, or anything else up-close, you want to make sure that your camera is up to it. Close focus can vary from model to model. Some vendors deem anything less than about a foot as macro capability. Other cameras take you down to 1/2 inch from your subject. Here are some things to consider when evaluating focus range:

✦ **There's such a thing as too close.** When you get to within a few inches of your subject, you'll find that the subject is difficult to light. The camera itself can cast shadows and keep sufficient light from reaching your subject. You'll find more about lighting close-ups in Book IV, Chapter 2.

✦ **Some lenses don't allow close focus at all zoom settings.** You might want to step back a foot and zoom in to get the best view of your subject. However, some lenses don't allow automatic (or even manual) focus at longer zoom settings. Some restrict macro capabilities to midrange or wide zoom settings.

✦ **Close focusing is tricky.** You want to make sure your digital camera includes automatic macro-focusing capabilities so that you don't have to focus manually when shooting up tight to the subject.

✦ **Keep attachment friendliness in mind.** If your favorite digital model doesn't have sufficient built-in macro options, see whether you can attach close-up lenses to the front of your lens. Not all digital cameras can accept screw-on attachments of this type.

Exposure controls

Because light levels vary, digital cameras must vary the amount of light reaching the sensor. One way to do that is to change the f-stop, as described earlier in this chapter. The second way is to alter the length of time that the sensor is exposed to the light. This is done either electronically or with an actual mechanical device — a shutter — that opens and closes quickly to expose the sensor for a set period — the *shutter speed*.

Like f-stops, shutter speeds are the denominators of fractions. The larger the number, the less light reaches the sensor. Typical shutter speeds include 1/60, 1/125, 1/250, 1/50, and 1/1000 of a second. Your digital camera readout might show them as 60, 125, 250, 500, or 1000 because the numerator is always 1. However, a recent trend has been to include the numerator anyway to avoid confusion with longer shutter speeds, which are whole numbers. Otherwise, you'd have no way of telling whether an 8 in the viewfinder means 1/8 second or 8 seconds.

Cameras (chiefly film models) that use mechanical shutters might have only exact intervals, although most film cameras have electronic shutters these days. Electronic shutters aren't limited to fixed incremental values and can provide you with any actual interval from a few seconds through 1/2000 (or sometimes even 1/4000) of a second. The traditional shutter speed values are useful only when calculating equivalent exposures.

For example, suppose a basic exposure were 1/250 of a second at f/16 (which is a typical exposure for a digital camera in bright daylight). If you wanted to stop some fast-moving action, you might want your camera to switch to 1/500 of a second to freeze the movement with the shorter exposure time. (You can find out more about stopping action in Book IV, Chapter 5.)

Because you've cut the amount of light in half by reducing the shutter speed from 1/250 to 1/500 of a second, your camera needs to compensate by doubling the amount of light admitted through the lens. In this example, the lens is opened up from f/16 to f/11, which lets in twice as much illumination.

Usually, all this happens automatically, thanks to your digital camera's handy autoexposure modes, but you can set these controls manually on some models if you want. It's probably a better idea to choose a different autoexposure mode (described later) that gives you the flexibility you need. Sometimes, you'll look at an image on your LCD review screen and decide that the picture is too dark or too light. A digital camera's autoexposure modes can take care of this, too. When shopping for a digital camera, you'll want to look for the following exposure options.

Plus/minus or over/under exposure

With these modes, you can specify a little more or a little less exposure than the ideal exposure that your camera's light-measuring system determines. These adjustments are called *exposure values* (EV for short), and most digital cameras let you fine tune exposure +/– about 2EV, using half- or third-stop increments. The most conveniently designed cameras have the EV adjustment available from one of the main buttons on the camera, such as the Up-cursor key. Beware of cameras that make you wend your way into the menu system to make an EV adjustment. Fortunately, after it's set, the EV setting "sticks" so that you can continue to take pictures in the same environment with the modified setting.

Full autoexposure

With this option, your digital camera selects the shutter speed and lens opening for you by using built-in algorithms, called *programs,* that allow it to make some intelligent guesses about the best combination of settings. For example, on bright days outdoors, the camera probably chooses a short shutter speed and small f-stop to give you the best sharpness. Outdoors in dimmer light, the camera might select a wider lens opening while keeping the shutter speed the same until it decides to drop down to a slower speed to keep more of your image in sharp focus.

Some digital cameras have several autoexposure program modes (sometimes called *scene settings*) to select from, so if you're taking action pictures and have chosen an action-stopping mode, the camera tries to use brief, action-stopping shutter speeds under as many conditions as possible. These program modes are different from the aperture/shutter-preferred modes described next because they frequently include other factors in their adjustments. They might have names like Sports, Night, Night Portrait, Landscape, Fireworks, or Portrait. I used a camera with a scene setting called Cuisine (I kid you not), which (after a little digging) I discovered also increased the sharpness and color richness of the picture to supposedly make food pictures look better. Some cameras have both an Auto (A) and Program (P) setting.

Aperture-preferred/shutter-preferred exposure

These options let you choose a lens opening (aperture-preferred) or shutter speed (shutter-preferred), and then the camera automatically sets the other control to match. These settings might be indicated by A or S markings — commonly, Av and Tv (Time value). For example, by choosing shutter-preferred, you can select a short shutter speed, such as 1/1000 of a second, and the camera locks that in, varying only the f-stop.

Unlike the programmed modes described in the preceding section, if your camera finds that the selected shutter speed, for example, can't be mated with an appropriate aperture (it's too dark or too light out), it might not take a photo at all. I've run into this at soccer games when I've set my camera to an action-stopping shutter speed, but clouds dim the field so much that even the largest lens opening isn't enough to take a picture. Figure 1-6 shows an action shot taken with the camera set on shutter priority.

Full manual control

With this option, you can set any shutter speed or aperture combination you like, giving you complete control over the exposure of your photo. That means you can also completely ruin the picture by making it way too dark or much too light. However, complete control is good for creative reasons because seriously underexposing (say, to produce a silhouette effect) might be exactly what you want.

Other factors to consider

In addition to exposure options themselves, you must consider other factors when evaluating the exposure controls of your dream digital camera. Here is a quick checklist of those you should look out for:

Figure 1-6: Choosing shutter priority lets you select an action-stopping shutter speed.

✦ **Sensor sensitivity:** Like film, sensors have varying degrees of sensitivity to light. (For film, this is its *speed.*) The more sensitive the sensor is, the better it can capture images in low light levels. Most digital cameras have a sensitivity that corresponds roughly to that of ISO 50 to ISO 100 film (so-called *slow* film), and the specs often use that terminology. Many cameras let you specify the sensitivity, increasing from the default value of, say, ISO 100 to ISO 400 or even ISO 800 (fast) to give you a "faster" camera.

Unfortunately, upping the ISO rating usually increases the amount of random fuzziness — *noise* — in the image. It's like turning your radio up really loud when you're driving a convertible with the top down. The wind flying past your ears tends to cancel out some of the audio information that your too-loud radio produces. Increasing the ISO boosts image information while increasing background noise in the image. If you plan to shoot many pictures in very dim light, any camera you buy should be tested first to see whether ISO settings can be set manually. Then check how noisy the pictures become when you increase the sensitivity.

✦ **Measurement mode:** Just how does your digital camera's exposure system measure the light? Sometimes it measures only the center of the picture (which is probably your subject anyway); sometimes, it might measure the entire frame and average out the light that the sensor sees. You don't always want the camera to measure the light the same way.

Measuring a center spot sometimes produces the most accurate reading. Other times, such as when the scene is evenly lit, an averaging system works best. On still other occasions, say, when there is a lot of sky in the photo, you might want the camera to measure only the light in the lower half of the picture. Many cameras have multiple exposure modes that allow you to choose what part of the image is measured. One clever exposure system I've used works in conjunction with the camera's automatic focus, selecting the part of the image that is in sharpest focus to calculate the exposure.

✦ **Compensation systems:** Many exposure systems can sense when a picture is *backlit* (most of the light is coming from behind the subject) and add exposure to make the subject brighter. Sophisticated cameras can analyze your scene and choose an exposure mode that best fits each individual picture, compensating for potential trouble spots in the photograph. Or the camera might have an override to the exposure system, allowing the sensor to receive more light from backlit subjects when you choose to activate it.

✦ **Manual exposure:** If you're seriously interested in photography, you'll want at least the option of setting exposure (both f-stop and shutter speed) manually so you can custom-tailor your exposure to the artistic effect you're trying to achieve.

Selecting Your Resolution

The best lens can't produce any more sharpness than the sensor used to capture its information. For that reason, the resolution of most digital cameras is the specification most people use to choose their equipment. They want a 4-megapixel camera or a 5-megapixel model or maybe a 6- to 8-megapixel camera. They figure (with some justification) that the more pixels they have, the more features the vendor packs into the camera. After all, you can expect a 6-megapixel camera to have a decent zoom lens, lots of exposure control choices, close focusing, and all the other goodies, right?

Most of the time, that's true. The sensor is usually the most expensive part of any digital camera, so if you're building a camera that's going to cost $600 anyway, you might as well load on the other goodies to justify the price. However, as sensors get less expensive, you'll see cameras with (supposedly) equivalent sharpness with widely varying feature sets. For example, I've used cameras in the 6-megapixel range that cost as little as $169 (and had sparse lists of features to match) and others with the same nominal resolution that cost $800 and were chock-full of advanced capabilities.

And even when dealing with sensors, all pixels are not created equal. For one thing, the *true* resolution of a sensor is likely to be somewhat less than you might think. Take a sensor measuring 3008 x 2000 pixels. You'd think that such a sensor could image about 6 million different details. Bzzzt. Wrong answer! That would be possible only if the camera were designed to capture an image only in black and white.

In practice, the sensor has to capture red, green, and blue pixels. With current sensors, each pixel can capture only one particular color, so those 6 million pixels are actually divided up into red-sensitive pixels, green-sensitive pixels, and blue-sensitive pixels. If the pixels were divided up evenly, you'd wind up with three 2-megapixel sensors — one each for red, green, and blue — rather than the 60-megapixel sensor you thought you had.

However, the pixels aren't divvied up in that way. Because our eyes are more sensitive to green light than to the other colors, sensors typically divide up their pixels unevenly: 50 percent are green, 25 percent are red, and 25 percent are blue. That's done by alternating red and green on one line, and green and blue on the next, as shown in Figure 1-7.

Figure 1-7: The typical sensor pixel is sensitive to red, green, or blue light.

Your camera's brain examines the picture and calculates (or *interpolates*) what the red and blue values probably are for each green-sensitive pixel position, what the green and blue values are for each red-sensitive pixel position, and the likely green and red values for each blue-sensitive pixel.

Other digital cameras use technologies that are a little different — or a lot different. For example, Sony offers a sensor that captures what it calls RGB+E (for emerald) light, producing what it describes as color fidelity that is closer to human color perception, with more life-like rendering of blue, blue-green, and red hues. Another vendor, Foveon, produces a sensor that has separate layers for red, green, and blue light, as shown in Figure 1-8, so that each pixel is capable of capturing any color light without interpolation. This sensor has been used only in a couple digital cameras from Polaroid and Sigma.

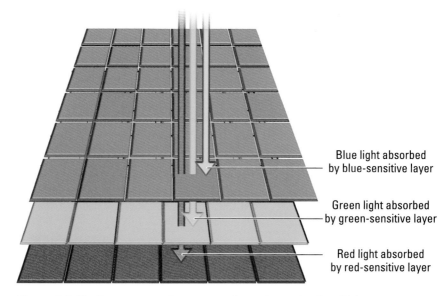

Blue light absorbed
by blue-sensitive layer

Green light absorbed
by green-sensitive layer

Red light absorbed
by red-sensitive layer

Figure 1-8: The Foveon sensor has separate layers for each color of light.

Beyond the capture scheme used, other factors affect sensors. Some sensors are more sensitive than others, and other factors make a particular sensor not perform as well as another one with the same number of pixels. For example, some sensors don't register some colors well or have pixels that bright light can easily overwhelm.

When choosing a digital camera, you want to choose one with the resolution you want. If possible, compare the pictures taken with each camera under consideration to see whether that resolution is being put to good use.

When it comes to megapixels, you can estimate the resolution you require with these guidelines:

✦ **Low *res* (short for *resolution*):** If you're shooting pictures intended for Web display, for online auctions, or for pictures that either won't be cropped or enlarged much, you can get by with a lower-resolution camera in the 4- to 5-megapixel range.

✦ **Medium res:** If you often need to crop your photos, want to make larger prints, or need lots of detail, you want at least a 6- to 8-megapixel camera.

✦ **High res:** If you want to extract small portions of an image, make 8-x-10-inch prints or larger, or do a lot of manipulation in an image editor, you want a 6- to 12-megapixel (or more) camera.

Keep in mind that most digital cameras allow shooting in a reduced mode, so if you own a high-resolution camera, you can still shoot in low resolution to pack more images on your digital film or to reduce file sizes on your hard drive. Resizing images is rarely a good idea, even with a good image editing program, so you usually want to shoot at the resolution you intend for your finished photo. Resize later, if you want, but keep your full-size version for printing, just in case.

The mode in which your camera stores the image on your digital film can affect the final resolution of your image, too. Digital cameras usually store photos in a compressed, space-saving format known as *JPEG* (Joint Photo-graphic Experts Group). The JPEG format offers reduced file sizes by discarding some information. In most cases, a JPEG file is still plenty good, but if you want to preserve all the quality of your original image, you might want to set your camera to store in a *lossless* image format (that is, one that doesn't discard any image information when compressing the file), such as TIFF, RAW, or EXIF. You might be able to choose from different JPEG quality levels, too.

Expect these alternate formats to eat up your exposures quickly. One of my digital cameras can store 200 images on a particular digital film card in JPEG format but only 150 in RAW and 40 in TIFF. TIFF and RAW also take more time to store on the film card, too, so they're not a good choice when you're shooting sports or other sequence-type photos.

Some cameras generally label their resolution choices with names such as Large, Medium, Small; Standard, Fine, Superfine, Ultrafine; and so forth. These terms can vary from vendor to vendor.

Choosing Your View

Generally, you want what you see to be what you get, but that's not always the case with digital cameras. That's because the viewfinders available are usually a compromise between what works best and what can economically be provided at a particular price level. In the digital photography realm, the solution has long been to provide you with two viewfinders per camera, each with its own advantages and disadvantages. In a non-SLR camera, you usually find

+ A **color LCD screen** on the back of the camera, which you can use to preview and review your electronic images.

+ An **optical viewfinder,** which you can peer through to frame and compose your image. Some digital cameras with large LCDs don't have optical viewfinders at all.

Some cameras have two LCDs: one on the back in the traditional location, and a second one inside the camera and visible through an optical system.

This variety is an *electronic viewfinder* or EVF. None of these are ideal for every type of picture-taking application.

LCD viewfinders

In a non-SLR, the liquid crystal display, usually measuring 1.5–2.5 inches diagonally, shows an electronic image of the scene as viewed by the sensor. (Digital SLRs can't preview images on their LCD because the mirror, shutter, and other components get in the way of the sensor until the moment of exposure.) On the one hand, that's good because you can view more or less the exact image that will be captured. It's also not so good because the LCD screen is likely to be difficult to view, washed out by surrounding light, and so small that it doesn't really show what you need to see. Moreover, the backlit LCD eats up battery power. I've used digital cameras that died after 20 minutes when the LCD had depleted their rechargeable batteries. Luckily, some digital cameras let you specify that the LCD is turned on only when composing a picture or only for a few seconds after a picture is taken (so that you can quickly review the shot).

Although often not usable in bright daylight, LCDs, such as the one shown in Figure 1-9, are better in more dimly lit conditions. Some third parties offer LCD hoods that fit over the back panel of the camera to shield the LCD from direct illumination. If you mount your camera on a tripod and make sure all the light is directed on your subject, an LCD is entirely practical for framing, focusing, and evaluating a digital image (even outdoors, if you use one of those protective hoods).

Figure 1-9: LCD screens work fine in dim light.

As you shop for a digital camera, check out the LCD under a variety of conditions to make sure it passes muster. Here are some things to look for:

+ **Brightness controls:** Many cameras include a brightness control that allows you to increase the brightness of the LCD to make it easier to view in full sunlight, or to decrease the brightness indoors to use less battery juice. A related factor is whether the LCD automatically "gains up" by amplifying a dim image to provide a usable view when it's very dark.

+ **Swivel mount:** The LCD doesn't have to remain fixed rigidly to the back of the camera. Some swivel and rotate, allowing you to point the camera in one direction and move the LCD so that you can easily view it at an angle. (Alternatively, the part of the camera with the lens can swivel while the part with the LCD remains in place.)

+ **Resolution and size:** Ultracompact digital cameras often have tiny LCD displays, on the order of 1½ inches (measured diagonally), and others have more generous 2.5-inch LCDs. The size of the LCD and the number of pixels it contains will partially determine how easy it is to preview your image. Some may have as few as 80,000 pixels; others may have 230,000 pixels or more. Guess which is easier to view!

+ **Display rate:** Some digital cameras update their LCD images more efficiently, so the view is smooth even when the camera or your subject is moving. Others offer up blurry images or ghost trails that make it difficult to view images in motion.

+ **Vanishing images:** What happens when you press the shutter release? Does the image instantly freeze as soon as you start to press the button but before you actually take the picture? If so, what you saw might not be what you get because your subject matter might have changed in the time between the initial press and the actual photo. Or, does the LCD go completely blank, leaving you with no clue about what you're shooting? Ideally, the LCD should display a real-time image right up until the instant before the picture is taken.

+ **Accurate viewpoint:** Believe it or not, even though an LCD viewfinder's display is derived from the same sensor used to make the exposure, the LCD might not display 100 percent of the sensor's view. Instead, it might trim a little off the sides, top, and bottom, and show you 80 to 90 percent of the actual picture. That's not good when you're carefully composing a photo to make the most of your pixels, particularly with lower-resolution cameras that don't have pixels to spare.

+ **Real-time corrections:** Some cameras have live *histograms* — graphs that show the distribution of the tones in the image — that can be viewed on the LCD and used to correct exposure manually while you shoot. These are all non-SLR types, of course. With a dSLR, a histogram is visible only after the exposure.

✦ **Accurate rendition:** I've found that some LCDs don't let you evaluate just how good (or bad) your picture is because they provide an image that's more contrasty, or brighter, or with more muted colors than the actual digital picture. You don't want to reshoot a picture because you *think* it looked bad on the LCD, or worse, make a manual exposure or other adjustment to correct a defect that appears only on the LCD and not in the finished photo.

Optical viewfinders

Most of the time, you use an optical viewfinder, which is bright and clear, uses no power, and lets you compose your image quickly. However, optical viewfinders have problems of their own, most notably *parallax*. Parallax is caused by the difference in viewpoint between your camera's lens and the optical viewfinder. They don't show the same thing.

If the optical viewfinder happens to be mounted directly above the camera lens, its view will be a little higher than that of the lens itself. This becomes a problem chiefly when shooting pictures from relatively close distances (3 feet or less). Such a viewfinder tends to chop off the top of any subject that is close to the camera. Optical viewfinders usually have a set of visible lines, called *parallax correction lines,* which you can use to frame the picture. If you keep the subject matter below the correction lines, you can avoid chopping off heads. Of course, you get *more* of the lower part of your subject than you can view.

Parallax becomes worse when the optical viewfinder is located above and to one side of the lens, as shown in Figure 1-10. In that case, a double set of parallax correction lines is needed to help you avoid chopping off both the top and the side of your subject. Yuck! Here are some things to look for in optical viewfinders:

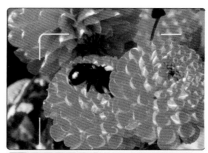

✦ **Magnification:** I get to use dozens of digital cameras in a year, and one of the first things I notice is the difference in magnification of the optical viewfinders. Put the camera up to your eye, and you might see a tiny image floating off in the distance, with the details of your scene barely discernible. Other cameras provide a big view that makes it easy to frame and compose your photo.

Figure 1-10: Parallax correction lines help you avoid chopping off heads or worse.

+ **Zoom:** Believe it or not, some digital cameras with zoom lenses have optical viewfinders that don't zoom! Ideally, the image should match the view of your LCD and lens, but some cameras keep a fixed view and use indicator marks to show the picture area.

+ **Parallax correction:** As I mention earlier, optical viewfinders might not accurately frame the image when you move in close to your subject. The position of the viewfinder window can have an effect: If the viewfinder is directly above the lens, the side-to-side view will be accurate, but you might cut off the top of your subject if the camera doesn't provide parallax correction. If the viewfinder is immediately to the side of the lens, your problems will involve accidentally cutting off the side of your subject. Some viewfinders are both above the lens and to one side, which can produce parallax problems in both directions.

+ **Accurate viewpoint:** As with LCD screens, the optical viewfinder might not show everything you're framing, with some image area clipped off the top, bottom, or sides.

+ **Diopter adjustment:** Eyeglass wearers might want an optical viewfinder that offers adjustment for common prescriptions so the camera can be used without wearing glasses.

+ **Extended eyepoint:** The *eyepoint* is the distance your eye can be from the viewfinder's window and still see the entire view. Some viewfinders mandate pressing your eye up tightly against the window. Others let you back off a few millimeters, which is handy when you want to be able to see *around* the camera to monitor the whole scene (and not just what appears in the viewfinder) or prefer to wear your glasses while using the camera (and are thus not able to get close to the window because the glasses get in the way).

+ **Readouts:** What information is available within and around the optical viewfinder? Some cameras show nothing but the unadorned image. Others have framing or parallax correction lines or perhaps a faint grid to help you line up the image. Perhaps some camera status indicators appear in the viewfinder, too, such as a flash-ready LED, within the field of view or located just outside the viewfinder window where it can be detected by the eye.

Electronic viewfinders (EVFs)

Some affordable cameras are available with hybrid viewfinders that work like optical viewfinders (that is, you put your eye up to a window to view your subject) but that use an electronic display to show you the image. These LCDs are much like the LCDs found on the backs of cameras, but because they are automatically shielded from extraneous light, they are much easier to view. Because they form an image by using the signal from the sensor, when compared with optical viewfinders, they offer a potentially more accurate and SLR-like picture-taking experience.

However, poorly designed EVFs can be a pain to use, so you'll want to examine the view through any camera so equipped before you sink your money into one. Here are some of the considerations to think about:

✦ **Magnification:** EVFs can suffer from the same viewfinder magnification issues as optical viewfinders. Because you'll be composing and (in some cases) focusing manually via the internal LCD, make sure your view is as large and sharp as possible.

✦ **Extended eyepoint:** Just as with optical viewfinders, you might not be able to (or want to) press your eyeball up to the viewfinder window, so an EVF with an extended eyepoint is a plus, particularly with eyeglass wearers.

✦ **Readouts:** Compared with optical viewfinders, EVFs usually contain a lot of information, including status readouts, grids, focus and exposure area indicators, and so forth, as shown in Figure 1-11. Make sure you can turn off these distracting elements when you don't want to see them.

Figure 1-11: Electronic viewfinders can contain a lot of distracting information.

✦ **Swivel mount:** Some eyepieces for EVFs can swivel 90 degrees to allow taking pictures from especially low or high angles. I find this capability handy when I have the camera mounted on a tripod at about waist level and I don't want to crouch down to look through the viewfinder.

✦ **Resolution and size:** The LCDs in EVFs typically have more detail than their camera-back counterparts. Vendors have raised the bar on EVF resolution, with at least one offering a full megapixel display on its top-of-the-line camera. These high-resolution electronic viewfinders are easier to see to discern detail and more reliable when used for focusing.

✦ **Display rate:** EVFs can have ghost images, too. A brand-new feature on some models is so-called *smooth mode,* which refreshes the EVF image 60 times a second (about twice as fast as normal), providing an especially good preview of your photo.

✦ **Vanishing images:** Obviously, the EVF can't provide a continuous image because the sensor's view must be collected and captured at the instant the photo is taken. During that interval, the image might freeze onscreen or vanish entirely. Some cameras switch into *high-gain mode* under dim lighting conditions, in which the image signal is amplified to provide better viewing, sometimes offering only a fuzzy or black-and-white view in that mode. Better cameras give you an accurate, full-color preview up until the exact moment the photograph is taken.

✦ **Accurate viewpoint:** EVFs don't always display 100 percent of the sensor's view, either. The best show at least 92–99 percent of the actual picture area in the viewfinder.

✦ **Accurate rendition:** As with any LCD, the image you see might not be exactly like your final photograph, but the results should be close.

SLR viewfinders

And there's always the single-lens reflex (SLR) camera, which shows you (more or less) the exact image the sensor sees through the lens via an optical system. It's done with mirrors (really). In the most common configuration, you view the subject through the lens by using an image bounced off mirrors and (sometimes) a glass prism. When you take the picture, the mirror moves out of the way to expose the sensor. You lose sight of the image for a fraction of a second, but film SLR users have been tolerating that inconvenience for decades.

Both general types of SLR viewfinders use a mirror to bounce light upward, where it then reflects off a series of surfaces until the final image (erect and nonreversed from left-to-right) is viewed through an optical window. Less-expensive cameras use a series of mirrors (often called a *pentamirror* because of the five total surfaces in the structure), and more costly models use a solid glass prism, called a *pentaprism.* The latter provides a brighter, higher-contrast image that looks better and is easier to use for viewing and focusing. However, pentamirror viewfinders can also be very good, particularly if you don't compare them directly with models using a pentaprism. The light path for an image viewed by a pentamirror/pentaprism viewing system is shown in Book III, Chapter 1.

Regardless of what optical or SLR viewing system you use, if you wear glasses and want to shoot without them, you want to make sure your camera either has built-in eyesight (diopter) correction to adjust for your near/far-sightedness or can be fitted with corrective lenses matched to your prescription. This vision correction enables you to get your eye close enough to the viewfinder to see the whole image. Some viewfinders make it difficult for those wearing glasses to see through the optical system because a bezel or other part of the viewfinder prevents the glasses from getting close enough.

Considering Your Storage Options

The kind of storage your digital dream camera uses will never be a factor in making your selection (unless it's a truly odious choice, and that's a matter of personal taste). The days of the digital cameras that used floppy disks and other oddball media are long gone. Today, all digital cameras use one (or more) of the following options:

+ **Secure Digital (SD):** Among non-SLR cameras, the SD format is by far the most popular memory card format. These postage-stamp-size cards, which allow manufacturers to design smaller cameras, are available in roughly the same capacities as CompactFlash, and cost about the same. The chief drawback (to date) is that there are no mini hard drives in the SD format. If you want to use a mini hard drive, you need a camera with a CompactFlash slot. Some digital cameras can also use the similar (but slower) MultiMediaCard (MMC).

+ **CompactFlash (CF):** CompactFlash is the second-most-favored format in the United States. Although physically larger than SD, CompactFlash cards are still very small and convenient to carry and use. As larger capacities are introduced, they usually appear in CF format first. As a bonus, the CompactFlash slot can also be used for mini hard drives, such as those from IBM, with capacities of a gigabyte or more. They are the most popular memory card format for digital SLRs.

+ **xD and mini-xD:** The xD and mini-xD formats are new, smaller than Secure Digital, and supported by fewer vendors (currently only Olympus and Fuji). Although it's wise to avoid getting stuck using a Betamax format when everyone else has converted to VHS, you're safe in choosing a camera using an xD variant. The vendors are important enough that even if the format eventually fails, you should be able to purchase memory cards for as long as your camera works. Indeed, because memory cards are typically used over and over forever, the cards you purchase with your camera or shortly thereafter are likely to serve you throughout your camera's useful life.

+ **Sony Memory Stick:** About the size of a stick of gum, Sony's Memory Sticks are useful because you can also use them with other devices, such as MP3 players. They're not going to replace CompactFlash, though. Sony has had an unfortunate tendency to flip around among memory choices for its digital camera, and didn't stop when the Memory Stick was introduced. It's now available in Memory Stick (up to 128MB sizes), Memory Stick Pro (larger capacities), Memory Stick Duo (a smaller version that needs an adapter to fit memory card readers outfitted for Memory Sticks), and, most recently, Memory Stick Pro Duo (in capacities up to 4GB). Whew!

✦ **Mini hard drives:** For a long time, mini hard drives were your only option when you needed more than a gigabyte of storage. If you're using a 6-megapixel or better camera and like to save your images as TIFF files or in another lossless format, you need more than a gigabyte of storage. However, with CompactFlash cards now available in 4–8GB sizes, the mini hard drive is losing its capacity edge, and it has always cost more than the equivalent silicon memory card. Although not excessively prone to failure, mini hard drives do have moving parts and must be handled with more care than memory cards.

✦ **CD-R/RW:** Sony, in its never-ending quest to change its digital camera media options annually, actually tried out both floppy disks and mini CD-R and CD-RW discs for its digital cameras. Although not really a bad idea, because the media is relatively inexpensive (a 240MB mini CD-R is a lot cheaper than a 256MB CompactFlash card), this option never caught on because digital camera memory requirements eventually exceeded the capacity of mini CDs. Sony seems to have settled into an ever-changing Memory Stick groove now.

Digital memory cards might be offered in various speeds, such as *standard, high-speed, 40X, Ultra,* and *Extreme,* depending on the nomenclature used by the vendor. The faster, more expensive media are able to store images more quickly. Unless you're shooting sequences and don't want to wait even a short time between pictures, standard media will probably do the job for you. Some newer digital cameras that provide a high-speed burst-photo mode require these higher-performance digital cards to function as advertised, however. With memory cards now being offered in 133X and 150X speeds, there's no telling where the speed race will end.

No Flash in the Pan: Determining Your Lighting Needs

Your digital dream camera's electronic flash capabilities (or lack of them) should be on your list of things to evaluate before you make a purchase decision. Not every photo is possible using existing light. Even if there is plenty of light, you might still want to fill in those inky shadows with an electronic flash. Your camera's built-in flash features are definitely something to consider.

Most digital cameras have a built-in flash unit that can be turned on or flipped up or swung out or otherwise activated when you want to use a flash — or when the camera decides for you that the flash is required. (Usually, a tip-off is a flashing red light in your viewfinder or next to it. Time to flip up that flash!)

You should be aware that most flash units are good only over a particular range. If you've ever seen a fan stand up in the balcony at a Bruce Springsteen concert and take a flash picture of the Boss from 100 feet away, you'll understand just how limited flash is at long distances. Some units are so feeble that they can only illuminate subjects 2 to 12 feet away. Others have special settings to spread the flash illumination for wide-angle shots or tighten it up for telephoto pictures.

Here are some features to look for in an electronic flash:

✦ **Auto-on:** It's useful to have a flash that can be set to flash only when it's needed. Some cameras require you to flip up the flash to use it. Others build the flash into the body of the camera in such a way that the flash can be used anytime.

✦ **Autoexposure:** An electronic flash can sense the amount of light reflected back from the subject and turn itself off when the exposure is sufficient.

✦ **Red-eye prevention:** Some flashes can be set to produce a short preflash just before the picture is taken. That causes the subjects' irises to contract, reducing the possibility of the dreaded red-eye effect. Alternatively, the preflash can fool your subjects into thinking that their ordeal is over and produce some priceless weird expressions.

✦ **External flash capabilities:** At times, you want to use an external flash, either in concert with or instead of your camera's built-in flash. See whether your camera has either a built-in flash-sync socket or a *hot shoe* that you can use to mount an external flash and connect the camera to the flash. Keep in mind that many digital cameras require that you use only a particular brand of flash to retain the automated exposure features or (in some cases) to avoid frying your camera's flash triggering circuit with too much voltage. If you're thinking of using a slave sensor to trigger the flash, make sure that it can be used with your camera. The preflash of some cameras will set off the slave unit. Figure 1-12 shows an external flash unit fitted with a diffusing dome to soften the illumination.

Figure 1-12: External flash units add power and flexibility to your lighting repertoire.

A Dozen Exotic Digital Camera Features

After automobile manufacturers introduced heated seats and the Global Positioning System (GPS) for their luxury cars, everyone wanted them, so the designers had to come up with other high-end features, like holographic rearview mirrors and rocket-powered ejection seats. Digital camera vendors are in a similar race to develop features that are similarly too-cool-for-school. (Believe it or not, some high-end cameras can use GPS to record the camera's current geographical location when each picture is taken!) Here are some of my favorite features that are exotic now but probably won't be exotic by the time you purchase your next camera:

+ **Sound-activated self-timers:** I had a ball playing with a new camera that could be triggered by sound. Just set the audio sensitivity, go get in the picture yourself, and shout, "Cheese!" No more racing to beat the self timer or ending up with a photo showing you holding your camera's infrared (IR) remote control.

+ **Ultra-fast shutter speeds:** At least one camera has a shutter speed of 1/16,000 of a second. You might need a supernova as your illumination source, but you can stop the fastest action with this baby.

+ **Image stabilizers:** Several cameras offer internal stabilization that cancels the effects of shaky hands or the blur induced by the high magnification of a telephoto lens. My favorite is the camera that automatically moves the sensor in time with your camera jiggles.

+ **Night shot capabilities:** Digital camera sensors are inherently sensitive to IR illumination, so vendors like Sony provide enhanced night photography capabilities by taking advantage of this sensitivity.

+ **Infrared photography:** Many cameras have a device called a *hot mirror* to filter out infrared light but allow flipping this filter out of the way or leaving enough remaining IR sensitivity to allow you to take interesting weird-tonal infrared pictures.

+ **Predictive focus:** Slow autofocus is the bane of digital cameras, which is why I was glad to see the introduction of high-end models smart enough to figure out where focus *should* be set ahead of time when you're photographing subjects for which the focus changes rapidly.

+ **Enhanced movies:** Traditionally, digital cameras have been able to shoot only short video clips (perhaps 15–30 seconds) at abysmal resolutions (some no better than 320 x 240 pixels) and not necessarily with sound. That's changing with the latest crop. Some recent digital cameras are virtual camcorders, letting you grab VHS-quality clips for as long as your digital memory card holds out. Make sure your card is a capacious one because digital video can eat up a megabyte a second!

✦ **Unlimited burst mode:** I loved using an advanced digital camera that uses a technique called *pipelining* to keep the images flowing onto the memory card at high speed (when used with a high-speed card). I managed to take more than 150 3.3-megapixel resolution photos in a row at around 4 frames per second (fps) before my 256MB memory card filled up. Set to a lower resolution, I took 1,500 shots in a little more than five minutes. My finger got tired before this ultra-fast camera started slowing down. Think how well you can analyze your golf swing with a camera like this!

✦ **Panorama photography:** A growing number of digital cameras have cool panorama capabilities that make it easy to shoot a series of pictures that can be automatically stitched together in your computer. You find out more about panorama photography in Book IV, Chapter 6.

✦ **Two-in-one shot:** Don't have a tripod but want to get in the photo yourself? Some cameras let you take a picture of the background, have someone else take a picture of you, and then merge the two shots automatically.

✦ **Underwater photography:** I once purchased a Nikonos underwater film camera specifically so I could take surfing photos at Huntington Beach, California. (I wasn't surfing; I was *photographing* surfers.) Now, anyone with a digital camera and an inexpensive underwater housing offered for Canon and other models can take pictures in, around, and under the sea. Digital cameras are much better than my old Nikonos: You get to see exactly what you shot right away, so you can jump back in and do it over until you get it right.

✦ **Time-lapse photography:** Thirty or forty years ago, the big thing was time-lapse photos of flowers opening and paint drying. Today, every television show includes a sunset-to-sunrise time-lapse sequence to demonstrate that time marches on. Whether you have some flowers you want to watch opening or you need to document a construction project, digital cameras with time-lapse capabilities can snap off a picture every few seconds or every few hours, depending on how you set them. This is a great feature that's fun to play with.

Checking Out Ease of Use

I've saved the most important topic for last because I want it to sink firmly into your mind as you put this book down and continue to think about what you're looking for in a digital camera. *Usability* is one of the most important factors to keep in mind when choosing a camera. The sharpest lens, the most sophisticated sensor, and the most advanced features are all useless if you can't figure out how to operate the stupid camera! I've owned digital cameras that absolutely could not be used without having the manual at hand. Even common features were so hard to access that I sometimes avoided taking certain kinds of pictures because activating the feature took too long.

Ease of use is not limited to digital cameras, of course. Difficult-to-operate cameras have been creeping up for 15 or 20 years. This was not always so. When I began my photographic career as a newspaper photographer, film cameras had a limited number of controls. There was a shutter speed dial, f-stops to set on the lens, focusing, and maybe a rewind knob to move the film back into the cassette when the roll was finished. Over the years, electronic exposure controls were joined by exposure modes and a ton of other features as film cameras became more and more computer-like.

Today, even digital cameras that most resemble their film counterparts bristle with buttons, command dials, mode controls, menus, and icons. That's not necessarily a bad thing. What is evil is an interface that's so convoluted that even advanced users might have problems. You might have to wade through nested menus to change the autofocus or exposure control mode. Switching from aperture-priority to shutter-priority can be a pain. Something as simple as changing from automatic focus to manual focus can be difficult, particularly if you don't make the switch very often and forget which combination of buttons to press.

Ease of use varies greatly, depending on which sets of features are most important to you. A camera that one person might find a breeze to use might be impossible for another person to manage simply because a particular must-have feature is hard to access.

I urge you to try out any digital camera that you're seriously considering buying before you plunk down your money. A camera's feature set, the vendor's reputation, or recommendations of a friend won't tell you how the camera will work for you. Hold the camera in your hand. Make sure it feels right — that its weight and heft are comfortable to you. Be certain your fingers aren't too large or too small to handle the controls. Can you see through the viewfinder?

If possible, take the camera for a test drive, borrow a similar camera from a friend or colleague, or at least shoot some photos in the store. Can you find the features you use most? Can you figure out the menus and buttons? Is the camera rugged enough to hold up under the kind of treatment you'll subject it to?

As much as I like buying by mail order or over the Internet, a digital camera is too personal a tool to buy from specifications lists and photos. If you're reading this book, you're probably serious enough about digital photography that you'll be spending a lot of time with your camera — and probably will spend more than you expected to get the camera you really want. Make sure it really is the one you want by giving it a thorough workout.

Chapter 2: Setting Up a Computer for Digital Photography

In This Chapter

✐ **Choosing between a Mac and a PC**

✐ **Understanding your memory and storage needs**

✐ **Selecting a microprocessor**

✐ **Doubling your display pleasure**

✐ **Pointing with a pen**

*Y*ou might be ready for digital photography, but is your computer up to the task? The good news is that virtually any computer of recent vintage probably has the horsepower and features you need to work with the digital images that you capture with a camera or scanner.

Even so, the differences between a computer that's good and one that's good enough can be significant. Your system might be exceptional, or it might be the exception. You probably don't want to work with the minimal system possible even if you'd rather invest your money in a better digital camera. (I know, if faced with the choice of a new, superfast computer and a digital single lens reflex, I'd choose the camera every time.)

This chapter helps you develop your own checklist of recommended hardware, shows you how to upgrade to make your work even easier, and offers tips on setting up your computer to make working with digital images a breeze.

In this chapter, I cover only the main equipment options for setting up a computer for digital photography editing and storage. You can find information on equipment used to transfer images between your camera and computer in Book I, Chapter 3.

Hardware Wars Revisited

Macs versus PCs. Why are we even having this conversation?

Well, it wasn't my idea. Then Steve Jobs and his crew decided to abandon the IBM microprocessors that have been inside every recent Macintosh and replace them with something called a "dual core" chip from Intel. The new Intel-based Macs are faster, still sexy, and have aroused the interest of even dedicated Windows PC operators. Anyone weary of the weekly "critical security flaw updates" that plague Windows computers or who covets the stylish and common-sense design of the Mac is now taking a serious look at the computer arena's "other" platform. That's become especially true with the introduction of the Macintosh Boot Camp software, which lets you install Microsoft Windows XP on the new Intel-based Macs and boot either operating system.

Of course, digital photography, graphics work in general, and multimedia production were the key arenas in which the Macintosh versus PC battle never died out. In most other areas, Windows-based systems have taken over the desktop, with Macs relegated to specialized or oddball applications. Apple keeps coming up with compelling hardware, interesting computer designs, and lots of quirky but cool applications (Garage Band, anyone?), but those computer troops solidly camped in the Windows realm usually take notice of what's going on only when those cute Macintosh commercials interrupt prime-time TV.

Not so in the digital photography world. Visit any newspaper or magazine that relies on digital cameras, and you'll find Macs. Drop in to any professional digital photographer's studio, and you'll see a brawny Macintosh perched on the desktop. Talk to the top Photoshop users in the country. Most of them are using Macintoshes, too, either exclusively or in tandem with a Windows box.

Indeed, for a long time the only logical choice for most photographers has been the Macintosh. The decision was along the lines of selecting a 35mm Nikon or Canon SLR for photojournalism or a Sinar view camera for studio work: a no-brainer. Although I don't have hard figures, my gut feeling is that Macs outnumber PCs in many imaging production environments by at least 8 to 1. In the rest of the business world, the figures are reversed, except on television, where anyone shown with a laptop computer is always using an Apple PowerBook.

By and large, the latest Macintoshes provide enough muscle for virtually any still-image work, particularly when equipped with dual processor chips (which provide extra speed with applications designed to work with multiple CPUs) and gigabytes of memory. No photographer need be ashamed of driving a properly equipped Mac.

In the digital photography world, Macs are not only viable but are often the system of choice. However, in some cases, you might not have a choice — maybe you already own a computer or need to use a particular system to remain compatible with friends and colleagues.

Yet, if you aren't locked into a particular platform and operating system, should you be using a Macintosh or a Windows computer? If you want a definitive answer, I'd say, "It depends." (Which isn't very definitive, is it?) Each platform has its pros and cons. Here is a summary of some of the things you should consider:

✦ **The bandwagon effect:** If you plan to make your living (at least in part) from digital photography, you need to learn two things: how to use a Mac and how to perform image magic with Photoshop. Both skills are expected to be part of your résumé. Jump on the bandwagon while you can. On the other hand, Windows proficiency is expected for most jobs outside imaging. Unless you're a full-time graphics professional, you might have to learn to wear two hats.

✦ **Ease of use:** The Macintosh is generally acknowledged to be a bit easier to learn and somewhat easier to use for many tasks. Of course, the Macintosh system's vaunted ease of use has been subverted over the years as Apple has tried to catch up with Windows systems. (For example, if you want to stick with the Mac's sublimely simple single-button mouse, you must augment it by holding down the Control key while clicking to reproduce the Windows two-button mouse's right-click option. You can also reprogram certain Macintosh mice to provide the same results.) If you're just starting out in computing and don't want to climb a steep learning curve, the Mac is your computer.

✦ **Software compatibility:** Not all applications are available for both Mac and PC. Most key applications are offered for both, including the Photoshop CS2 image editor, shown in Figure 2-1 in both Mac and Windows incarnations; the StuffIt archiving tool; browsers such as Netscape and Internet Explorer; and word processing applications such as Microsoft Word. Plus, Microsoft is now offering Virtual PC for the Macintosh, making it possible to run Windows XP and Windows applications under Mac OS X on many different Macs. Boot Camp does the same thing for the latest Intel-based Macintosh models. But if you must be totally compatible with Windows, you still need Windows.

✦ **The cost factor:** Macs have generally been more expensive than PCs, although the cost difference has decreased over the years. Even so, with powerful Pentium systems available in barebones configurations for $500 or so, even the least expensive Mac capable of image editing still costs a bit more. In the Mac's favor, however, most peripherals and add-ons, such as memory, hard drives, DVD devices, monitors, and so forth, cost the same whether you're purchasing them for a Mac or a PC.

**Book II
Chapter 2**

**Setting Up a
Computer for Digital
Photography**

Figure 2-1: Photoshop looks the same on PCs and Macs.

✦ **Hardware reliability:** Reliability is a double-edged sword. Macs are wonderfully crafted machines, a beauty to behold when you dismantle one, and filled with high-quality components. The insides of some of the assembly-line-built PCs have a decidedly industrial look, and if you examine the parts, you might find a mixture of known brand-name pieces and *what's this?* components. On the other hand, if something does break on your PC, you can run down to the local MegaMart and buy a new floppy drive, a CD burner, and maybe some memory off the shelf next to the cell phone batteries. My local *grocery store* carries these items. Macs also use many off-the-shelf components, but some specialized parts for your Mac might be harder to come by, and it's unlikely you'll know how to replace them anyway. So, even assuming the Mac is more reliable than the average PC, is that always an advantage?

✦ **Operating system reliability:** Trust me, Macs do crash, especially when Apple is making a transition, as it did from Mac OS 9.x to OS X or from the current version of OS X to the next one. Early versions of a Mac OS can crash and burn as spectacularly as any Windows release. On the other hand, Mac users don't add hardware or new applications at the same clip as Windows users, who seem to be constantly trying this new utility or that, applying the monthly patches Microsoft issues for its software and OS, and doing other fiddling that can lead directly to the Blue Screen of Death (BSOD).

Anyone who swears his or her Windows installation never crashes is probably using Windows XP, never runs more than two or three applications at once, and avoids installing new software more often than once every six months. I'm an exception to that rule: I haven't had a crash in more than a year. That's when I uninstalled XP Service Pack 2 and stopped applying Microsoft's monthly patches. The secret is that none of the updates in the past year fixed any *operating* flaws in Windows XP; they were all repairs for security defects. As long as I hide behind my firewall, don't use Internet Explorer, and am careful about what Web sites I visit, I'm able to run my antique installation of Windows with no crashes. Still, if avoiding crashes is on your holiday gift list, the Mac still has the edge. This may eventually change as Apple completes the transition to Intel processors, and virus-happy hackers turn their attention to producing viruses and ill-behaved applications that exploit the weaknesses that exist in Mac OS.

✦ **Technological superiority and coolness:** If owning a computer that looks like a Tensor lamp or is built into an LCD screen is your cup of tea, and you like the idea of having cool stuff before anyone else, you really, really need a Macintosh. The most exotic hard drive interfaces (from SCSI in the '80s to FireWire in the '90s) came to the Mac first, along with flat-panel displays, DVD burners, and other radical innovations that turned out to be a little (or a lot) before their time.

Book II
Chapter 2

Setting Up a Computer for Digital Photography

Hardware differences aside, the most visible differences between Macs and PCs (after you get past transparent, multicolored cases and eye-catching design tricks) stem from the two competing operating systems. A few years ago, a dual-barbed joke was circulating, implying that the current version of Windows was almost identical to the Macintosh operating system of 1984. But of course, the same observer noted, the *current* Mac OS was also almost identical to the Macintosh operating system of 1984. The more things change, the more they stay the same.

The gibe is no longer true. Windows has been transformed into Windows XP, which is the most stable, easiest-to-use operating system Microsoft has ever offered, even if it does still resemble some of the older versions of Mac OS. At the same time, Mac OS is completely different, too. Mac OS X is now a thinly disguised version of Unix, which is both good news and bad news. Unix is more stable than the OS 9.x and earlier versions that preceded it, but Mac-Unix has some underlying complexities (including — horror of horrors — a command line interface if you want it) that didn't intrude themselves on Macintosh users in the past.

Windows has its advantages and disadvantages. One advantage is that it's almost universally available and has the broadest range of widely used applications written for it. One disadvantage is that Windows still forces you to do things the Microsoft way when you'd really rather do them your own way. For example, Windows XP is fond of setting up your network the way it likes, bludgeons you into using Internet Explorer even if you prefer Firefox, Opera, or Netscape, and has a tendency to coerce you into using the Windows Media Player for everything and anything.

Mac OS, on the other hand, lets you do things your own way quite easily. Would you prefer that your digital camera application be installed on your secondary hard drive rather than the one you first installed it on? Just drag it to the new hard drive; there's no need to uninstall it and reinstall it as you must do with Windows.

Although you probably won't choose a computer based on the operating system, these things are nice to know.

What Equipment Do You Need?

Digital cameras themselves make few demands on a computer system, of course. The real drain on your system is running your image editing program and storing your images for editing or archival purposes. Make no mistake, image editing is among the most demanding types of work you can lay on a computer, so before you start down this road, you'll want to know about the minefields that lie along the way. If you want the flying short-course, the ten most important things you'll need to consider are

+ Memory

+ More memory

+ Even more memory

+ Adequate local storage (a fast, big hard drive. Or two.)

+ A fast microprocessor

+ Archival storage

+ Advanced video display capabilities (maybe two monitors)

+ Other peripherals, such as digitizing tablet and pen devices

+ A little more memory

+ More RAM than you thought you'd ever need

The rest of this chapter examines each of these needs thoroughly.

Determining How Much Memory You Need

If you noticed that I listed memory five times in the preceding top ten list, there's a reason for that. Memory makes everything else possible. A fast, big hard drive is also important because it gives you room to work with your current project's files and can substitute for RAM (memory) when you finally do run out. But nothing can replace memory when decent performance is your goal.

You can finish reading the rest of this section if you want to know the hows, whys, and how muches of memory, but I can give you a two-word recommendation that will let you skip ahead, if you want:

Two gigabytes!

That much RAM will cost you very little, perhaps a couple hundred dollars; it's the most RAM the current version of Photoshop can use; and it will solve most of your problems. We now continue with the technical portion of our program (for those of you who aren't skipping ahead).

I can't emphasize this point enough: When you're working with images, you must have, as a bare minimum, at least six to ten times as much RAM as the largest image file you plan to work with on a regular basis. With inexpensive 8-megapixel cameras now available for a few hundred dollars, many digital photos in their native RAW format can be huge, requiring 180–600MB of RAM for each image you want open at once. If you're working with more reasonably sized 4MB images but need to have ten of them open at one time, you still need tons of memory to do the job.

Without sufficient RAM, all the bucks you spend on a super-speedy micro-processor are totally wasted. Your other heavy-duty hardware is going to come to a screeching halt every time you scroll, apply a filter, or perform any of a number of simple functions. That's because without enough RAM to keep the entire image in memory at once — plus your image editor's Undo files (basically copies of the image in its most recent states) — your computer is forced to write some or all of the image to your hard drive to make room for the next portion it needs to work with.

Digital photography can produce some large images, too, especially if you're working with a serious camera in the 8- to 12-megapixel range and choose to save your files in the highest-quality mode. An 18MB image is fairly common these days, so you should be prepared with as much RAM as you can cram into your computer.

Most systems have two to four memory slots, which can each hold a 256–1024MB memory stick. Loading your computer with 2GB of memory is not at all outlandish and is relatively inexpensive. You can purchase that much memory for a few hundred dollars. Any Mac or PC with 512MB or less of RAM is hopelessly under-equipped for digital photography. Beefing up your memory can be the least expensive and most dramatic speed enhance-ment you can make.

Indeed, a few years ago, when I upgraded from my ancient 800 MHz Windows computer to a spiffy new 2.8 GHz Pentium 4 model, I was annoyed to find that my new computer seemed to be significantly slower than my old one. It didn't take long to discover the reason. My older computer had 2GB of RAM, but my new "faster" one was initially equipped with a mere 512MB of memory. When I worked with large digital photos, Photoshop didn't have enough RAM to keep more than one or two images in memory at one time. It was forced to continually swap image information out to the hard drive to make room for the changes I made. Having a processor that was more than three times faster made no difference: Lack of memory was slowing everything down through a poky hard-drive bottleneck.

Within a week, I upgraded the Pentium system to 2GB of RAM, and guess what? It really flew! If you feel your current computer is slow, try adding memory before upgrading to a faster processor. You might be surprised. With any luck, an upcoming version of Photoshop will be able to use more than 2GB of RAM, and we'll get even better performance. (With *real* luck, that version will be available when you're reading this!)

Choosing Local Storage

Your graphics powerhouse is only as fast as its narrowest bottleneck, so you should pay special attention to that looming potential roadblock I just mentioned: your mass storage subsystems. You need one or more big hard drives for several reasons:

◆ **To keep as many images as possible available for near-instant access:** A large hard drive enables you to store all your current projects — plus many from recent months — all in one place for quick reference or reuse. With a large hard drive, you can store a vast library of your own photographic clip art, too, and avoid having to sort through stacks of archive CDs.

◆ **To provide working space for your current projects:** You'll want *scratch* space — space on your hard drive — to store images that you probably won't need but want to have on hand just in case. Alternate versions of images eat up more space as you refine your project. Image editors such as Photoshop also need spare hard drive space to keep multiple copies of each image you're editing.

◆ **To let you store additional applications:** Good bets here would be panorama-generating programs, a second or third image editor for specialized needs, utility programs, extra plug-in programs, and so forth.

In the recent past, your hard drive storage options were limited to internal hard drives in one of two categories: fast, expensive hard drives using a Small Computer System Interface (SCSI; *SKUZ-zee*); or inexpensive, slow hard drives using the Enhanced Integrated Drive Electronics (EIDE) interface or ATA (Advanced Technology Attachment). Today, the technologies have converged. SCSI drives no longer cost that much more than ATA disks, but they are now used only for specialized applications, such as file servers, where the SCSI interface's ability to address many drives simultaneously comes in handy. Fortunately, ATA drives have gotten much, much faster. Moreover, new options have appeared, chiefly in the form of external hard drives that link to your computer via FireWire or Universal Serial Bus (USB) and a new kind of internal drive called Serial ATA (or SATA.)

SCSI and EIDE hard drives

You don't see SCSI disks used much outside server environments these days. Their chief advantage is that your computer can transfer information to and from several SCSI disks simultaneously. That's because SCSI is a system-level interface that conveys information in logical terms: Multiple devices can use the same connection in parallel fashion, although more intelligence is required to decode requests from the computer. Other kinds of hard drives, particularly EIDE/ATA drives, might have to take turns talking to your computer, which can reduce performance. Peripherals are so fast these days that the difference in performance between SCSI and other systems is seldom important outside the server farm.

The chief advantage of drives in the EIDE/SuperATA and the very latest serial ATA (SATA) categories is that they are almost free. As I was writing this book, even mammoth 500GB hard drives could be purchased for a lot less than 50 cents per gigabyte, and I expect the cost per byte will drop even more dramatically during the life of this book as the latest 750GB and larger disks become standard. However, even at 50 cents per gigabyte, hard drives aren't that much more expensive than CD-R media.

External hard drives

With external hard drives, you're no longer limited to the number of disk drives you can cram into your computer's housing. These disks link to your computer using an IEEE 1394 (FireWire) or USB 2.0 interface, such as the one shown in Figure 2-2.

Figure 2-2: This drive uses slide-out trays to allow hot-swapping one disk drive for another.

The advantage of external storage is that you can install and remove FireWire and USB 2.0 drives without opening your computer's tower, and you don't need to worry about how to fit them in the case. You can also easily move such an external drive from computer to computer.

Archiving and Backing Up

Digital photos can fill even the largest hard drive faster than Yankee Stadium on Bat Day. Your graphics powerhouse needs open-ended storage that is relatively cheap and reliable and that provides near-online (permanent storage) access speeds.

Zip disks (R.I.P.)

I mention Zip disks because they eventually became a part of popular culture, almost turned into a generic term, and threatened to replace the floppy disk before $40 CD and DVD burners killed them off. Today, you see Zip disks only in old spy movies in which a secret agent copies crucial data while a bar graph on the computer display shows the progress. Today, solid state "thumb" or "jump" drives do the same thing more cheaply and plug right into your USB port. (The latest spy movies show the agents using a thumb drive, but the bar graph remains maddeningly slow because the need for suspense hasn't been eliminated by the pace of technology.)

CD-Rs and CD-RWs

CD-R and CD-RW discs have a bit more credibility in this arena because you can cram a healthy 700MB on a CD that can cost as little as a nickel. You still wouldn't want to back up your 160GB drive to 200 CD-RW discs (even though the media itself might cost you only $20), but it's entirely practical to archive your digital photos on this media if you are using a camera with no more than 5 or 6 megapixels of resolution. For cameras that produce larger files, even CDs don't have much capacity.

DVDs

DVDs have become a more viable long-term storage medium, even though the basic one-layer DVD barely holds the contents of a 4GB memory card. (And those of us with higher-resolution cameras can fill up a 4GB card *very* quickly; on a recent trip I snapped roughly 4GB of photos every day for ten days running.) Depending on how many layers are used, DVDs can store up to 8GB or more each. The cost of DVD burners is coming down, and this medium should become more popular when the industry settles on a single, standard format. In a world with DVD-ROM, DVD-RAM, DVD+RW, and DVD-RW, the best plan is to buy a DVD burner that supports them all. Things might become more complicated in the future when the newer, extra-high capacity DVDs (including the blue-laser Blu-ray discs) become available.

Avoiding Microprocessor No-brainers

The fastest microprocessor might not be absolutely essential for image editing if you're using a digital camera with about 5 megapixels of resolution. Higher resolutions call for more horsepower, however, and if you're buying a new machine, there's no reason not to buy one with the fastest microprocessor available, within reason. The microprocessor is what processes many of your program instructions — everything that isn't handled by a separate digital signal processing chip. So the faster the microprocessor runs, the faster your image editing software will work, generally speaking.

Each individual element of an image involves from 1 to 4 or more bytes of information. An RGB (red/green/blue) image requires 3 bytes per pixel, a CMYK (cyan/magenta/yellow/black) image needs 4, and additional alpha (selection) channels take up 1 byte each. Even a relatively minuscule 640 x 480, 24-bit image can involve nearly 1MB of data.

If you ask your image editor to apply an image-processing filter to an entire image, your microprocessor must calculate the effects of that filter on each and every one of those million bytes. That can take a second or two with a very fast system or as long as a minute or much more with very slow computers.

And although there are other constraints (such as memory or hard drive speed), the speed of the microprocessor affects nearly everything you do on your system. As you might guess, a fast CPU should be a major consideration when assembling a graphics workstation from scratch. You might not need the fastest microprocessor available, but then again, you never hear anyone complaining that a computer is just too darn fast.

Determining What's Most Important

Even though I went three years between new computers, I generally buy a new system more often than that, and upgrade most other components more frequently than that. However, I keep three pieces of equipment for years and years. I lavish all available funds on the original purchases and hang onto them as long as possible. Those three items are my display screen, my keyboard, and my mouse.

This trio involves the components you interface directly with all day, every day, usually for long periods of time. For efficiency and sanity's sake, you should insist that these pieces of equipment be only the very best available, and don't change them capriciously. I liked the IBM keyboard that came with my IBM PS/2 in 1987 so much that I am still using it about two decades later (even on my Macintosh, thanks to a keyboard/video/monitor switch). My ball-less, cordless, infrared wireless mouse has been serving me well for several years, and I only recently replaced my beloved 19-inch CRT monitor with an almost-identical model. I look at or touch these components all day, every day, and they're worth every penny I spent.

For digital photographers, your display and video card are two of the most important components in your system. You need a video card with 64–128MB of fast memory (or more) so that you can view 24-bit images with 16.8 million colors at resolutions of up to 2048 x 1536 (or more) on a 19- to 24-inch monitor.

A combination like that enables you to examine your photos closely, array several large images side-by-side, and view pictures at a size very close to their printed size. Here are some specific recommendations:

✦ Unless you also play computer games, you don't need to spend hundreds of dollars on video cards with video accelerators so powerful that they require their own fans. Instead, sink your funds into a video card with enough RAM to display images at high resolution. Think 2-D instead of 3-D.

✦ Consider buying a dual-head video card capable of displaying separate images on two different monitors. You'll find that most serious Photoshop users and digital photographers work with two monitors (at least). One monitor can contain your image editor, and another can display a Web browser or another application. Or, you can move Photoshop's palettes to the second monitor to make more room for your images.

Book II
Chapter 2

Setting Up a Computer for Digital Photography

Another trick is to use different resolutions for each monitor, say 1920 x 1440 on one for a high-res display, and 1024 x 768 for a larger view on the second monitor. If a Web page is hard to read on my main display, I often just slide it over to the second monitor at 1024 x 768 for a closer view. Figure 2-3 shows a dual monitor setup in the Display control panel.

Figure 2-3: Dual monitors can be set up in your Control Panel.

✦ Two video cards can also give you dual monitor capabilities. When I upgraded, I purchased an "obsolete" 64MB PCI video card for about $40 and installed it in tandem with my system's original AGP card. I then purchased a 17-inch monitor with multiple rebates for a net cost of $49. For less than a C-note, I was in dual monitor heaven.

✦ Check out the monitor you buy in the store before you purchase it. You'll be staring at it all day, so you want a sharp image that you can live with.

✦ If you've been using CRT monitors for awhile, expect a surprise when you go to replace your display, as I was when I got my latest 19-inch tube-based monitor. These displays are starting to become hard to find and are being replaced wholesale with LCD monitors. That's not good news for the budget-minded because LCD displays are still a bit more expensive than the CRT type, and the cheapest models are *not* suitable for image editing. The cheap-o models have colors that aren't accurate, they don't offer an easy way to calibrate them, and their fixed resolution may not be fine enough for image editing.

Of course, on the plus side for LCDs, you can tuck one of these flat beauties into the most confined desktop or even hang one on the wall. And they don't require geometry (shape), convergence (alignment of the electron guns), or focus adjustments. They're easier on the eye, emit no radiation, use as little as ten percent of the power of a tube-based display, and are not affected by electromagnetic fields.

However, LCDs might not be as bright as your trusty CRT monitor, and most have a rather limited viewing angle, making it difficult for more than one person to see the screen clearly. Most LCDs also have a narrower color gamut than a CRT and are more difficult to calibrate. But if you are able to do so, they rarely need to be recalibrated.

Look for an LCD with a high contrast ratio (700:1 to 1000:1 is good), and with the resolution you need. A 20–21 inch LCD should offer 1920 x 1200-pixel resolution. You don't want to edit images on a 1280 x 960-pixel display. Also find one with a DVI interface so you can connect to your video card's digital connector rather than analog link.

If you insist on a CRT monitor, you must consider a few monitor specifications and controls. For example, sharpness is often measured in terms of *dot pitch,* which is supposed to be the distance, measured diagonally, between the centers of two RGB phosphor dot triads (found on a CRT). Some vendors, however, measure horizontally, yielding a smaller dot pitch figure that doesn't reflect the true sharpness of the image (anything between .22mm and .27mm is acceptable).

Other specs, such as color *convergence* (how accurately the electron guns are aimed); video bandwidth (measured in megahertz; determines how well an analog signal is displayed onscreen without ghosting or the loss of brightness in thin lines); or refresh rate (the number of times per second an image is renewed) affect your viewing experience. Of these three, the refresh rate is the most important. Most people perceive a 75 Hz refresh rate at most resolutions as flicker-free, compared with, say, a 60–68 Hz refresh rate. The less flicker, the longer you can stare at your monitor without going blind (or at least getting a whopping headache). When buying a monitor, your best bet is to try one out in the store and purchase the one that looks good to you.

Choosing Pointing Devices

Can you sign your name with a bar of soap? No? Can you sign your name with a pen? If so, you probably would be more comfortable doing graphics work with a pen-based graphics tablet rather than a clunky old mouse. Pressure-sensitive tablets with cordless pens are especially cool. Used with applications that support pressure-sensitive pads, such as Photoshop, they enable you to draw thicker lines just by pressing harder. Tablets and pens are a very natural way of working with graphics; if you can draw, you can use one faster and more accurately than you can sketch with a mouse. Trackballs and alternate mice are also choices if you prefer them. A typical pressure-sensitive pad and stylus are shown in Figure 2-4.

Figure 2-4: Digital photos can be edited more precisely with a pressure-sensitive tablet and stylus.

Chapter 3: Getting Your Pictures from the Camera to the Digital Darkroom

In This Chapter

- Connecting the camera to the computer
- Using various connections and memory cards or disks
- Moving your images from camera to digital darkroom

When you take pictures with a conventional film camera, you end up with a roll of exposed film that must go to a photo lab (or the minilab at your local drug store) for processing and printing using special chemicals and darkroom equipment. When you get the prints back a few hours or days later, you get to see how your pictures turned out. Often, a fair number of pictures end up in the trash, and you keep the rest. If you want extra prints or enlargements of the good shots, it's back to the lab to order reprints.

One of the great things about digital photography is that you don't have to process and print every single image you shoot. Most digital cameras let you preview your images right in the camera, so you know immediately how you did. And you can discard the obvious blunders and bloopers before anyone else sees them. What remains are the pictures you want to print.

With digital photography, there's no need to go to a photo lab to get prints from your pictures. The darkroom and lab are as close and convenient as your own computer. But unlike conventional photography, there's no roll of exposed film to send off for processing. Instead, you move your digital pictures from your camera to your computer by copying the image files from one device to the other.

How you do that depends on the features of your camera (and to a lesser extent, your computer). This chapter first addresses the various camera-to-computer connections you're likely to encounter and then describes the process of transferring images from camera to computer.

Making the Connection between Camera and Computer

Before you can use your computer as a digital darkroom to process and print pictures from your digital camera, you must get your picture files out of the camera and into the computer. After you save the images as files on your computer's hard drive, you can manipulate them with the image editing software of your choice and print them on your printer. Books V and VI describe the basics of editing images and working with Photoshop products to do so.

Some printers are capable of accepting images directly from a digital camera and printing them without going through an image editing program or other software on your computer. These use the PictBridge standard, which was created for printing from digital cameras to printers by using a direct connection, without the need of a PC. The camera and printer can be made by different vendors; all devices that support the new PictBridge specification (and the number is growing all the time; check your camera manual) should work fine with any other device that conforms to the standard.

Several technologies for transferring pictures from your camera to your computer are available. The range of options might seem confusing, but you don't need to worry about most of them because a given camera rarely supports more than one or two options.

In general, the image-transfer technologies fall into three broad categories:

✦ **Wired connections:** A cable, wire, or other connection enables you to transfer picture information from the camera to the computer. Some vendors offer docks with a niche for certain model cameras, like the one shown in Figure 3-1, allowing direct transfer between the camera and the printer and/or your computer. The communication between your computer and your camera is similar to that between your computer and other peripheral devices, such as printers, scanners, or external modems. I discuss wired connections in the following section.

✦ **Wireless connections:** In the future, more digital cameras will use wireless transfer to beam pictures directly to a computer or printer. Today, you'll find such connections chiefly on high-end digital SLRs and a few consumer cameras, including new Kodak EasyShare models, and cameras that use Bluetooth technology.

✦ **Removable media:** The camera stores picture data on a memory card that you can remove from the camera and then insert into a drive, slot, or reader on your computer. This process is much like saving files to a floppy disk and then moving the disk to another computer and accessing the files there. For information about different types of removable media, see the later section, "Memory cards."

Figure 3-1: Docks allow slipping your digital camera into a connector that's already wired to your printer or computer.

Book II
Chapter 3

Getting Your
Pictures from the
Camera to the
Digital Darkroom

Getting Wired

When you look at the back (or, often, front) of a typical computer, you see a variety of sockets and ports in different shapes and sizes. Some of them probably have cables attached that lead to assorted peripheral devices, such as your mouse and your printer. Camera manufacturers can choose from several of these ports in order to connect the camera to the computer. However, you rarely find any one camera with more than one type of wired connection.

Serial cable

The serial port was the old standby for connecting miscellaneous peripheral devices to a computer. It was used for everything from external modems to pointing devices, and, of course, it was used in the past for many digital cameras. Nowadays, most digital camera manufacturers use a USB connection instead of the older serial connection, and USB connections are also used for modems, mice, and keyboards. There is very little application for the original serial connection these days, and I mention it just for completeness. Enough said.

USB

The USB (Universal Serial Bus) port is the all-purpose connection that has largely replaced the older serial, parallel, and PS/2 (mouse/keyboard) ports. The older alternatives haven't gone away completely yet, but USB is increasingly becoming the connection of choice for many computer devices, including digital cameras. The original USB 1.1 port has already been supplanted by the faster USB 2.0 version now found on new computers. Cameras and other peripherals will work with either type, although at a slower speed when connected to a USB 1.1 port.

USB connections are capable of moving data faster than the older serial and parallel connections. Because USB connections are also hot swappable, you can safely plug in and unplug USB cables without shutting down your computer. You can also expand the number of USB ports available by adding a *hub* (a small box containing multiple USB ports) or a device, such as a keyboard or monitor, that has extra USB ports built in. Then, you can plug your camera or other USB device into the added ports, just as you can the USB ports on the back of your computer. Your USB hub may need a power adapter to run some equipment. Some gear works from the unadorned port, drawing power from your computer, but others require more juice.

Some older computers might not have USB ports built in. You can upgrade most of those computers with a relatively inexpensive add-in card to provide the needed USB ports.

Figure 3-2: A powered USB hub allows connecting many different peripherals at once.

The USB port is a small, flat, rectangular socket approximately $\frac{3}{16}$ x $\frac{1}{2}$ inch. You usually find at least two of them on the back of your computer, clearly marked with the special symbol shown in the margin. USB ports might also be available on the front of the computer, on a USB hub (like the one shown in Figure 3-2), or on a keyboard or other device that has a built-in hub.

You can use any of these ports to connect your camera to the computer. Just follow these steps (with your computer turned on):

1. Plug one end of the cable into the USB port on your camera.

The USB connector is often hidden behind a small door on your camera. It's sometimes a squared-off, D-shaped socket, approximately $\frac{1}{4}$ x $\frac{5}{16}$ inch. If your camera includes a standard USB port, you can use a standard USB cable, which has a rectangular plug on one end and a square plug on the other. However, most digital cameras now use a smaller mini-USB connection to save space. In that case, you may need to use the special cable supplied with your camera if it's not a standard mini-USB connector.

2. **Plug the other end of the cable into the USB port on your computer or USB hub.**

3. **Insert the camera manufacturer's driver disc into your computer if prompted to do so.**

   Windows automatically recognizes when a new device is added to a USB port. The first time you connect your camera to the computer, Windows versions prior to Windows XP might need to load drivers supplied by the camera manufacturer in order to access the camera. Mac OS also recognizes new peripherals when plugged in.

4. **Use the camera manufacturer's software (or other file-management software) to transfer image files from the camera to the computer.**

Book II
Chapter 3

**Getting Your
Pictures from the
Camera to the
Digital Darkroom**

FireWire

FireWire connections (formally known as IEEE 1394) are an alternative to USB connections. Like USB, FireWire transfers data faster than serial and parallel ports and is hot-swappable. You can also connect multiple FireWire-equipped devices to the computer. FireWire connections are a standard feature on all Macintosh computers built in the last few years. FireWire is also available for PCs, but built-in FireWire on a PC is only now becoming common because USB does most of what Windows users need to do. You might need to purchase and install an add-in card for your PC if your camera needs a FireWire connection.

FireWire isn't common on digital still cameras; you encounter it more frequently on digital video cameras. But because some digital video cameras can capture still images as well as digital video, I guess that qualifies them as digital photography devices.

The FireWire port (shown in Figure 3-3) is a small, rectangular socket that looks similar to a USB port. The FireWire port is a little fatter than a USB port, however, so there's no chance of mistakenly plugging a FireWire cable into a USB port or vice versa.

Figure 3-3: The two business ends of a FireWire connection look like this.

Follow these steps to connect your camera to your computer via a FireWire port:

1. Plug one end of the cable into the FireWire port on your camera.

The FireWire connector is often hidden behind a small door on your camera and is identified with the symbol shown in the margin. If your camera includes a standard FireWire port like the one on your computer, you can use a standard FireWire cable, which has identical plugs on each end. However, if your camera uses a special cable configuration to save space, you need to use the special cable that came with your camera.

2. Plug the other end of the cable into the FireWire port on your computer.

3. Insert the camera manufacturer's disc into your computer if prompted to do so.

Like USB, Windows and the Mac automatically recognize when a new device is added to a FireWire port and will prompt you for a disc if it needs to load drivers supplied by the camera manufacturer in order to access the camera.

4. Use the camera manufacturer's software (or other file management software) to transfer image files from the camera to the computer.

Riding the (infrared) light wave

An IrDA (Infrared Data Association) port enables you to transfer computer data from one device to another by using pulses of infrared light instead of a physical wire. The process is similar to how most TV remote controls send channel and volume adjustment instructions to the TV. Infrared connections are slow and not very reliable, but those drawbacks are countered by the convenience of not having to poke around the back of your computer every time you want to make a connection or deal with wires that get tangled and lost.

An IrDA port looks like a small, dark red (nearly black) lens or window. You find them on some digital camera models from Kodak and Hewlett-Packard, and on a few printers and laptop computers, but rarely as standard equipment on a desktop computer. If your computer doesn't have an IrDA port, you can purchase an adapter that will probably connect to your computer via a cable to one of the standard serial or USB ports.

To use an IrDA port to transfer pictures to your computer, follow these steps (with your computer turned on):

1. Turn on your camera and set it for infrared data transfer.

Use the camera's controls to select the infrared data transfer mode. Each camera model is different, so refer to your camera's instructions for details.

2. **Position the camera's infrared port so that it points toward the infrared port on your computer.**

   Although it's possible to make an infrared connection from several feet away, you generally get better results when the two infrared ports are close together (just a few inches apart). Ensure that no obstructions are between the two IrDA ports and that no bright lights (such as sunlight from a nearby window) are shining on the infrared sensors.

3. **Use the camera manufacturer's software on your computer to start transferring picture data.**

Transfers with teeth (blue)

Some computers and printers have Bluetooth adapters that can be used to accept images from Bluetooth-enabled devices (which these days are mostly cell phones). To transfer images from your device, you must first "pair" your two Bluetooth components so they recognize each other. Then follow the instructions that came with your camera and computer or printer to make the exchange.

**Book II
Chapter 3**

**Getting Your
Pictures from the
Camera to the
Digital Darkroom**

Memory Cards

All digital cameras have some form of built-in memory to store the pictures you shoot. In many cases, the memory medium that the camera uses is a card that you can remove from the camera. Using removable media to store image data has a couple of advantages over fixed, built-in memory.

First, you can swap out a full memory card (sometimes referred to as a digital film card) and insert another to increase the number of digital photos you can take without erasing some from memory. It's like putting a fresh roll of film in a conventional camera.

Second, you can use the removable memory media to transfer images to your computer for processing and printing. All you need is a suitable card reader on your computer, and you can read the image files directly from the memory card without attaching the camera to the computer.

The following points give you some insight on inserting, removing, and accessing files on cards (which can be a trickier endeavor than you might think):

✦ To remove a memory card of any type from your digital camera (or computer), just press the eject button next to the card slot (for some kinds of cards) to pop the card loose from its connection. Then you can grab the end of the card and pull it out of its slot. Other kinds of cards pop out automatically when you press them.

✦ To insert a memory card into a laptop computer, card reader, or digital camera, insert the card connector-edge first into the slot. Slide the card all the way in and press it firmly but gently to seat the connectors along the edge of the card. If the card won't go all the way into the slot, it's probably upside down. Flip it over and try again.

✦ After you insert the memory card into your computer, you should be able to access it as a virtual disk drive. You can use your normal file-management techniques to copy and move image files from the memory card to your computer's hard drive. See Book I, Chapter 5 for more on managing your digital photo files.

Windows XP and Mac OS X will usually recognize your digital memory card in a card reader or when you connect your camera and will pop up a dialog box like the one shown in Figure 3-4. You can choose one of the actions available, including copying the files to your computer and erasing them from the memory card when finished. Some applications, such as Photoshop Elements, come with a utility that recognizes a memory card and performs the transfer under your direction.

Figure 3-4: Your computer may recognize when a memory card is inserted and offer to make the transfer for you.

CompactFlash cards

CompactFlash cards, like the one shown at right in Figure 3-5, are used as removable memory in a few other devices, but their primary application is for image storage in digital cameras. They provide a much smaller and more efficient form of removable memory than PC cards (which I discuss a bit later).

Book II
Chapter 3

Getting Your
Pictures from the
Camera to the
Digital Darkroom

Figure 3-5: Secure Digital (left) and CompactFlash (right) are the most popular digital memory card formats.

At about 1½ inches square, a CompactFlash card isn't much larger than a postage stamp, and it's just a little thicker than a credit card. Still, there's room for two rows of holes for connector pins along one edge. All CompactFlash cards are physically about the same size (there are Type I and a thicker Type II variety), but they can have various memory capacities ranging from 4MB (generally no longer available) to 8GB or more. A higher-capacity version seems to come out every few months.

Card-reader adapters are available for your computer, or may be built into the computer itself. These adapters enable you to read and manipulate the contents of a CompactFlash card. The card reader is usually a small, external device, like the one shown in Figure 3-6, that attaches to your computer via a FireWire, USB, or serial cable. Sometimes, a card reader for your computer comes with the camera. If not, you can purchase one from most computer supply stores for less than $30. PC card adapters are also available. The adapters enable you to access your CompactFlash cards via a PC card slot in a laptop computer.

Figure 3-6: Card readers generally have multiple slots that accept every kind of memory media used in digital cameras.

For tips on removing, inserting, and accessing files on CompactFlash cards, see the bulleted list in the preceding section.

Secure Digital/MMC cards

Secure Digital (SD) cards and the identically sized but less flexible MultiMediaCard (MMC) are still other memory card formats similar to CompactFlash. Secure Digital cards are a newer format that has swept the industry in a relatively short period of time because the smaller size (roughly ⅞ x 1¼ inches) of the SD card allows designing smaller cameras. One key difference between MMC and SD cards is that the Secure Digital version allows encryption of the files to prevent tampering. SD cards also offer higher performance and thus are preferred over MMC cards for digital cameras.

Using a Secure Digital card for image storage is essentially the same as using a CompactFlash card except that the card itself is slightly smaller, which means that the sockets in the camera and the card reader must be made to fit the Secure Digital card. The Secure Digital format is not interchangeable with the other formats.

Memory Stick

The Sony Memory Stick is one more form of memory card, functionally similar to the CompactFlash and Secure Digital cards. Sony uses the Memory Stick in several of its high-end digital cameras and also in digital video cameras, music players, and so on, which means that you can move your Memory Sticks between devices and use them for storing pictures, music, and other files.

The Memory Stick is about the size of a stick of chewing gum and comes in capacities of 32 to 128MB. The newer Memory Stick Pro offers higher capacity but is not backward-compatible with earlier devices that used the original Memory Stick. There is also the half-sized Memory Stick Pro Duo. The latest versions can be purchased in sizes up to 4GB.

Several models of Sony laptop computers include a built-in Memory Stick slot so that you can use the laptop computer to access the contents of your Memory Sticks. You can also use a card reader similar to the card readers for CompactFlash and SmartMedia cards to access Memory Sticks from your desktop computer. The card reader is usually supplied with your camera and attaches to your computer via USB cable.

Here are some pointers for removing, inserting, and accessing files on a Memory Stick:

✦ To remove a Memory Stick from your digital camera (or card reader), press the eject button next to the slot to pop the stick loose, grasp the exposed end of the stick, and slide it out of its slot.

✦ To insert a Memory Stick into the camera (or card reader), insert the stick into the slot in the direction of the arrow marked on the surface of the stick. The arrow and a clipped corner help you orient the stick properly. The stick goes into its slot in only one way. Push the stick in firmly but gently to seat it properly.

✦ Like the other memory cards, after you insert a Memory Stick into the card reader attached to your computer, you can access and manipulate the files on the stick as if they were located on a virtual disk drive. Copy, move, and erase the files using your normal file management tools.

The Memory Stick includes an Erasure Prevention Switch that lets you protect the contents from accidental erasure. Make sure the switch is in the Off position when you want to record images onto the stick in your camera or erase files in the card reader.

CompactFlash cards, Secure Digital cards, Memory Sticks, and the like are often called *digital film* because inserting a memory card into a digital camera is analogous to loading a conventional camera with a fresh roll of film.

Book II
Chapter 3

Getting Your
Pictures from the
Camera to the
Digital Darkroom

SmartMedia cards

SmartMedia cards have faded almost completely from the scene and exist today only as memory options for older digital cameras. They are similar to CompactFlash cards but in an even smaller package, and they are limited to only 128MB capacity.

PC Cards

The oldest format for a memory card still in use is the PC Card, also known as ATA Type II PC Cards or PCMCIA cards. PC Cards come in many different forms and are not limited to memory configurations. They are typically used to provide plug-in components, such as modems or network interface cards, for laptop computers equipped with a PC Card slot. Memory cards and miniature hard drives have in the past also been furnished in the PC Card form. Today, PC card slots are used primarily for plugging in devices like wireless network cards. My own Toshiba laptop has a memory card slot for SD cards, but accepts Compact Flash cards only through an adapter plugged into its PC Card socket.

Mini-CD

To combat the problem of the limited capacity of floppy disk drives (used in some very early Sony digital cameras), Sony built some digital cameras with a mini-CD drive in place of the floppy disk drive. The camera actually includes a CD burner to record picture data onto mini-CDs, which are smaller-diameter versions of standard CDs. A standard CD-ROM drive can read the mini-CDs, and because CD drives are standard equipment on almost all computers, the mini-CD enjoys the same universal accessibility as floppy disks. The downside is that the mini-CDs aren't readily available for purchase like floppy disks or even memory cards are.

Microdrive

The Hitachi (formerly IBM) Microdrive is a tiny hard drive that's a little thicker than the standard CompactFlash card but otherwise the same. Such drives are also available from other sources, including Seagate. If your camera is equipped with a CompactFlash Type II slot, you can use the Microdrive. The Microdrive has recently been less expensive than solid-state CompactFlash cards of the same capacity. It's available in sizes up to 8G or more. Using the Microdrive is just like using a standard CompactFlash card except that because it is actually a miniature hard drive, it must be handled with more TLC than a CompactFlash card.

Transferring Images from Camera to Computer

As the previous section shows, different digital cameras offer different tools for connecting the camera to your computer. It might be a direct connection, such as a cable from the camera to a port on your computer, or it might be an indirect connection, such as a memory card that you can remove from the camera and then insert into a reader or drive attached to your computer.

After you make the connection between your camera and your computer, you might have a few more options available regarding what software you use to transfer pictures from the camera connection to your computer. Most digital camera manufacturers supply a program with the camera that is designed to handle the task, but you might also have the option of transferring pictures to your computer via image editing software or your computer's normal file management utilities.

Book II
Chapter 3

Getting Your
Pictures from the
Camera to the
Digital Darkroom

Transferring pictures using camera utility software

Windows XP and Mac OS X can recognize memory cards or cameras and offer to transfer your photos for you. However, you'll often prefer to use the utility software provided with your digital camera because such software frequently has additional features, such as the ability to edit your photos after you transfer them.

Just about every digital camera on the market today ships with a disc containing software designed specifically to transfer pictures from the camera to your computer. Often, the software has a number of other features as well, but its main purpose is to allow you to use your computer to access the pictures you shot with your camera.

The details of the installation and use of the software accompanying the various digital cameras vary as much as the cameras themselves. Covering all the different programs in detail in this book is not possible, but the general process goes something like this:

1. **Make sure the camera (or card reader) is connected to the computer and is turned on.**

   This ensures that the software can find the camera/card reader connection if the installation searches for it.

2. **Insert the disc that came with your camera into your computer's disc drive and launch the installation utility (if it doesn't start automatically).**

The software disc is usually a CD, and the installation routine usually starts automatically a few seconds after you insert the disc into your computer. However, if the installation doesn't start automatically, you can usually get things going by using Windows Explorer to double-click a file icon labeled Setup or Install. You can probably find the file in the root folder of the drive where you inserted the disc. With Macs, click the program's icon on the Desktop.

3. **Follow the onscreen instructions to install the software.**

   A couple of mouse clicks to accept defaults are all it usually takes.

4. **Start the camera utility software.**

   Sometimes the utility software sits in the background and waits for your camera to be connected. Then it pops up automatically and goes to work. If not, double-click the Desktop icon that the installation program added or look for the new addition to your Windows Start menu. If the camera or card reader is connected and turned on when you start the program, it will usually find your camera automatically. In some cases, you might need to help the program locate the camera by choosing a command such as File⇨Connect and selecting the appropriate location in a dialog box.

   Figure 3-7 shows the Photoshop Elements transfer utility.

5. **Click an icon or menu command to view the image files on the camera or removable media.**

   Here's where the different software programs really go their own way. There is usually an icon or menu command that you can use to display a list of picture files on your computer. You might even be able to preview the pictures as *thumbnail* (small) images.

6. **Select the picture files you want to transfer and click an icon or menu command to begin moving the files to your computer.**

   Again, the details vary greatly in the different programs, but there is usually a prominent icon that you can click to start the transfer process. If you don't see an obvious icon, check the File menu for a command such as Import.

The same utility program that enables you to transfer pictures from your camera to your computer often includes features that enable you to edit or manage your image files. You can also erase pictures from your camera's memory after transferring them to your computer so that you have room to shoot more pictures with the camera.

After you transfer the images to your computer, you can view, edit, and print them using any appropriate program on your computer. Windows' and Mac OS X's built-in utilities are sufficient for basic viewing and printing, but you'll undoubtedly want to use more capable programs for most image editing tasks.

Book II
Chapter 3

Getting Your
Pictures from the
Camera to the
Digital Darkroom

Figure 3-7: In Photoshop Elements, select the images you want to download in the Photo Downloader window.

Copying files to your hard drive

Perhaps the simplest and most straightforward way to move pictures from your camera to your computer is to treat them like any other computer file. In other words, you simply use your standard file-handling utilities to copy, move, and delete the image files. This is the technique you use with most forms of removable media, and you can often use it with direct camera connections via USB or FireWire as well.

The biggest advantage of this approach is that you don't need to deal with a specialized program in order to access your pictures. Instead, you use familiar tools, such as Windows Explorer and the Open dialog boxes, in your favorite programs.

In order for this technique to work, your computer operating system (Windows or Mac) must be able to access your camera or card reader adapter as part of the computer's file system. Fortunately, that's exactly how most memory card readers and many cameras (most cameras that connect via USB or FireWire) work. They appear to your computer as virtual disk drives, and you can read, write, and erase the files on those devices just like you can files on your hard drive or floppy disk (if your computer has one).

To transfer pictures from your camera to your computer, you can use any of the same techniques you would use to move files from one disk drive to another. The only exception is the extra steps needed to connect a virtual drive (your camera or card reader) to the computer. The following steps summarize the process for the Windows environment (similar techniques work for Mac OS):

1. **Connect the camera or card reader to your computer and turn it on.**

   After a moment or so, Windows displays a message box saying that it has found new hardware and is installing the necessary software drivers. An icon appears in the system tray portion of the taskbar next to the clock.

2. **If prompted to do so, insert the manufacturer's disc containing drivers for your camera or memory card reader.**

   You only need to do this the first time you attach your camera or card reader to the computer.

3. **Open Windows Explorer and navigate to the virtual disk drive representing your camera or card reader.**

   You can double-click the My Computer icon on your desktop to open an Explorer window and then double-click the appropriate drive icon to display the contents of the camera memory or the memory card in your card reader, as shown in Figure 3-8. Look for a new drive letter that doesn't correspond to one of the standard disk drives installed in your system.

Figure 3-8: In Windows Explorer, double-click the appropriate drive icon to display the contents of your memory card.

The name of the drive might be the brand name of your computer or card reader.

4. **Open another Windows Explorer window and navigate to the folder where you want to store the picture files from your camera.**

Be sure to position the two Explorer windows on your desktop so that you can drag and drop between them.

5. **Drag and drop one or more files from the first Explorer window onto the second window.**

That's all it takes to copy pictures from your camera to your computer. If you copy them in this way, you'll need to delete them from the memory card if you no longer want them there.

Book II
Chapter 3

Getting Your
Pictures from the
Camera to the
Digital Darkroom

Of course, after you connect your camera (or the memory card from your camera) to your computer as a virtual disk drive, you can use all the standard Windows tools and techniques to manage your picture files. The default action for a drag and drop is to copy the files to their new location. However, if you click and drag with the right mouse button instead of the normal left button, Windows displays a contextual menu that gives you the option to move the files instead of copying them. The Move command copies the files to their new location and then erases them from the old location in one step. You can also return to the first Explorer window and erase the picture files from your camera memory in a separate operation.

After you finish transferring pictures from the camera to your computer, don't forget to disconnect the camera properly. To do so, you need to right-click the Safely Remove Hardware icon in the system tray, and in the dialog box that appears, choose to unplug, eject, or stop the device. Then, select the camera from the list in the dialog box that appears next and click the Stop button to tell Windows that you want to disconnect the device. Windows displays a confirmation message, after which you can physically disconnect the camera and its cable from the computer. With a Mac, you should drag the camera's icon to the Trash before disconnecting your camera.

Importing images into image editing software

The normal sequence of events is to use your camera's utility software to transfer one or more picture files from your camera to your computer. Next, you launch your favorite image editing software and open the image file to make some adjustments before finally saving or printing the picture. However, several image editing programs can do the transferring for you, which shortens the whole process.

If Windows recognizes your camera or card reader as a mass storage device (and most such devices that connect to the computer via USB and FireWire are), the device and all the files on it appear to Windows just like any other disk drive. Consequently, you can open a picture for editing in your image editing program by simply selecting it in the program's Open dialog box. The only thing you have to do is make sure the camera is connected and turned on (and recognized by Windows) before you attempt to open files in the photo editor.

Macs operate in the same way, recognizing your camera or card reader and offering to open the photos in iPhoto.

To transfer images from your camera directly to your image editing software, you first need to tell the program what camera you use and where to find it. Make sure that the camera manufacturer's software has been installed and is operating properly on your computer and then configure your image editing software to access images from the camera. The setup process varies in the different programs, but the following steps are typical:

1. **Connect your camera to the computer and turn it on.**

2. **Choose File⇨Import⇨Digital Camera⇨Configure (or an equivalent command) in your image editing program.**

   The program usually opens a dialog box, but it might present a submenu instead.

3. **Select your camera and (if necessary) the port where it's connected; then click OK to close the dialog box.**

After you configure your image editing software, you can use it to access images from your camera. Here's how:

1. **Connect your computer to the camera and turn it on.**

2. **Choose File⇨Import⇨Digital Camera⇨Access (or an equivalent command) in your image editing program.**

   A dialog box appears, giving you access to the images stored on your camera. This is usually a subset of the camera manufacturer's access software.

3. **Select the image or images you want to open in the image editing program and then click the button or choose the command to begin the transfer.**

   The software transfers the selected pictures from your camera to the image editing software.

4. **If the image editing software doesn't return to the foreground automatically, click its taskbar button.**

   The selected images appear in the image editing program window, ready for you to begin working with them.

Chapter 4: Adding a Printer and Scanner

Nothing reveals more dramatically how digital technology has changed the face of photography as the ways in which we use prints. We've gone from the days of the daguerreotype (in which every photographic image was a unique and original hard copy) to the digital age in which (if we wish) a photograph can exist entirely and solely in electronic form and never be transferred to a piece of paper or film. The photo-graphic print has gone from being the normal and expected result of taking a picture to nothing more than an option.

In the digital age, prints have taken on an additional role as a source for digital images. If you have a scanner, the photographic fodder for your image editing software can come as easily from a hard-copy photograph that you've scanned as from your digital camera. Indeed, some of the happiest marriages of imagery come from mixing and matching photos that originate in digital form with pictures that have been created on film, printed on paper, and then scanned.

Even when you have the choice of viewing your finished photographs on a computer screen, there are so many good reasons for making prints. A better color printer is probably the first accessory that a digital photographer purchases after upgrading to a digital camera. And a scanner used to convert existing prints and slides into pixels is probably the second accessory considered.

This chapter looks into the factors that you need to take into account when choosing a printer and a scanner for your digital photography outfit.

Why You Want Prints

Digital pictures are great when you want to show them on your computer screen, project them on a screen during a presentation, or incorporate them into your Web page. Even old-fashioned color slides have their uses. Professional photographers like transparencies for their unsurpassed reproduction capabilities. Amateurs have long used slides as a tool for lulling neighbors to sleep during discussions of their vacations.

Yet, when it comes time to share your photographic efforts seriously, nothing beats a print. You can hang a print in a frame over your fireplace. You can pass around a stack of photos of your kids without worrying whether your captive audience has the right viewing hardware or software. Photo prints are used as proofs submitted for approval or as samples in a portfolio. When you open an old shoebox of memories tucked away in your closet, you hope to find a slew of old prints inside, not a stack of CDs or DVDs.

Indeed, students of photography have already noticed a dramatic change in how the work of the very best photographers can be studied and evaluated since digital photography became common. The photographic masters of illustration and photojournalism of the past worked with prints and often made proof copies, called *contact sheets,* that contained a rough, uncropped, and uncorrected version of every picture they took. We can look at those old prints and see how photographic ideas evolved into the famous photos we know today.

With digital photography, though, test shots, alternative angles that didn't work out, and other material can be erased and forgotten. A digital camera's Quick Erase feature can obliterate unwanted photos before they ever reach a computer. Only the best images survive, and only the best of the best make it to print form (at least, theoretically.)

That doesn't mean that prints are an endangered species. The same digital technology that has eliminated some of the need for prints has given us whole new capabilities that make them more useful than ever. For example, when shooting pictures on film, you probably let your photofinisher make a print of every single shot on the roll so that you can see which ones are the good ones. (In these days of double prints, you probably get at least two copies of every shot, including the blurry ones and the pictures of your shoes.)

With digital photography and inexpensive color printers, you don't need to accumulate stacks of prints that you don't want. Not only can you print (or have your retailer print) just the pictures you like, but you can also easily crop them the way you want to see them, fix the color, sharpen the blurry parts, and print them as glorious 5 x 7s or 8 x 10s. Digital photographers might not end up with more prints, but they do have better prints, and they like them better, too.

Choosing a Printer for Digital Photography

The good news is that printers capable of producing photo-quality images are inexpensive, and printers from all the vendors are comparable in quality, ruggedness, and image quality. If all you want are a few photos now and then, it's hard to go wrong. All the well-known printer manufacturers and many of the companies that sell cameras are hard at work building faster, better, and less expensive printers for you to choose from.

The bad news is that the vendors have a nefarious purpose behind their industrious efforts. Those who sell printers these days want to make their devices so easy to use and to produce hard copies that are so pleasing to the eye that you'll be tempted to make more and more prints. And that's where the money is: The cost alone of special photo papers and inks used during the first few months can easily exceed the price you paid for a color printer. As you read the descriptions of the printing options that follow, you need to keep foremost in your mind not how much the equipment costs to buy, but how much it costs to use. I provide some guidelines and tips as you go along.

Here are your primary options:

✦ **Let somebody else do it.** If you don't need many prints, you can probably get by quite well without owning any color printer at all. Color ink cartridges tend to dry out and clog up if allowed to sit for a week or two without being used, so if you really aren't making many prints, you should consider just stopping by your local discount or drug store with your images on a disk/disc/media card and using a desktop Kodak Picture Kiosk, or a stand-alone kiosk such as the Kodak Picture Maker, shown in Figure 4-1. You pay $5 or so for a sheet of photos, but think of the

Figure 4-1: A stand-alone kiosk might be your best source for quick, high-quality prints.

money you'll save on equipment and dried-out ink cartridges! Many photo-finishers have digital minilabs that use conventional paper and chemicals to produce high-quality photographic prints; they can accept your digital film and deliver a stack of 4 x 6 prints. You can even send your images to labs on the Internet for delivery to you by mail.

+ **Use a laser printer.** If you have a black-and-white laser printer, you can make quick-and-dirty monochrome prints of your digital images that might be good enough for many applications, such as pasting up in publishing layouts or creating simple posters to promote your rock band's upcoming club date. Color laser printers, at less than $500 (and up), can create fairly decent full-color pictures, although these pictures don't have the glossy sheen and true photographic appearance of some of the other options. Color laser printers can be fairly economical, too, if used in moderation because their color toners can be applied to inexpensive ordinary paper stocks rather than more expensive photo paper. If you have some other use for a color laser printer (say, printing documents, newsletters, or other work that uses spot color), these devices can fill in for you as an output option for the occasional digital photograph.

+ **Use an inkjet printer.** These are the most popular color-output option for digital photography right now because they cost very little (decent inkjets can be purchased for $50–$100) and supplies for them can be purchased everywhere, including at your average, all-night grocery store. Their output looks almost exactly like a color photograph when printed on special glossy photo papers.

Unfortunately, for each photo you print, you can pay as much as $0.50 to $2 for the materials (ink and paper) alone. After paying $35 for an ink cartridge that was good for only 20–30 8 x 10 prints and then repeating the process once a week for a month, I junked a perfectly good inkjet printer and replaced it with a model that uses separate ink tanks for each color. Now, when I run out of yellow ink, I drop in a new $8 yellow ink cartridge instead of replacing the whole thing. I tried several of the inkjet refilling kits, but the ink seemed more easily applied to my hands and clothing than to the cartridge being refilled. So I like using separate, replaceable tanks, like those shown in Figure 4-2.

Figure 4-2: Using replaceable separate ink tanks is more economical.

✦ **Use a dye-sublimation printer.** Dye-sublimation (dye-sub) technology, although gradually being replaced by inkjet printers for most applications, is still used at the consumer level in small photo printers that are limited to, say, 4 x 6 prints. In those sizes, a dye-sub printer can be fairly economical even though it uses a fairly complex printing system that involves a roll with a continuous ribbon of color.

A dye-sub ribbon cartridge is shown in Figure 4-3. Each section of the color ribbon is used only once, so you always know exactly how many prints you're going to get before it's time to refill. The quality of these printers is unsurpassed, but unlike inkjet and laser printers, you can't use them for printing documents. Photos are all they can print. These printers cost $149 and up.

Figure 4-3: Individual color panels apply one hue at a time to your print.

✦ **Use a different type of printer.** You can also find various alternate printing technologies, such as thermal wax printers, solid-ink printers, and a few other offbeat types, each with its own advantages. Some of them, called *phase-change* printers, for example, can print photo-quality images on ordinary paper, partially offsetting the cost of their solid wax or resin inks. These are generally expensive printers, often costing $600 to $3,000 or more.

Choosing a Scanner

In many ways, digital cameras and scanners are two sides of the same coin, each with their own advantages and limitations. Both use solid-state sensors to capture a digital image of an object, providing you with fodder for your image editor's magic. Cameras are portable and can grab images of three-dimensional objects of virtually any size, at any distance (up to the moon and beyond!). Scanners pretty much reside on your desktop next to your computer, are limited (for the most part) to two-dimensional originals such as photographs, and can work only with objects that are 8.5 x 11 inches or smaller.

Digital cameras capture an image in an instant; a scanner takes a minimum of 20–30 seconds to produce a scan. High-resolution digital cameras are expensive; if you want 12 megapixels of information, you can pay $3,000 or more. A scanner fully capable of grabbing 135 megapixels of image information (1200 samples per inch over an 8.5 x 11 photo) can cost less than $100.

Whereas digital photographers carefully select what goes into a digital camera image through use of composition and lighting, scanners pretty much capture whatever is already on the original you slap down on the glass. The purposes and capabilities of digital cameras and scanners are so very different that if you're serious about digital imaging, you'll want both a digital camera and a scanner.

What you can do with a scanner

One of the best things about scanners is that you can do a lot of other things with them in addition to scanning photographs. Here are some highlights:

+ **Turn printed text into editable text.** If you create newsletters and want to convert hard-copy text documents (such as newspaper clippings) into editable text, a scanner can use optical character recognition (OCR) to capture the text. Using software usually bundled with the scanner, the scanner translates the image of the text into text files (often with formatting and photos preserved). You can also use OCR with faxes that are clear and perfectly legible to convert those faxes back into editable documents.

+ **Photocopy documents.** Most scanners have a Copy button on their front panels. Slap an original down on the glass, press the button, and the scanner captures the image and directs it to your printer. It's almost as good as having a dedicated copy machine.

+ **Send faxes.** If a scanner can serve as a copier, it also works admirably as half a fax machine. Whether or not your work environment has a dedicated fax machine, there's nothing quicker (or more confidential) than using your scanner with your computer's fax modem.

+ **Manage documents more easily than you can with microfilm.** Some types of records must be retained in some semblance of their original appearance, such as documents with signatures, checks, illustrated reports, and so forth. Offices used microfilm for this sort of document in the past. Today, you can manage documents by using a scanner as an input source and using a specialized document-management application to file and retrieve the images.

+ **Capture non-photographic images.** Perhaps you have line art, charts, logos, cartoons, or other artwork you'd like in digital form. A scanner works as well with non-photographic images as it does with photos.

Types of scanners

You can find a pretty good overview of the various types of scanners in Book I, Chapter 3. For digital photography, your choices really boil down to one of three kinds of technology as well as several categories based on price and features. I can dispose of the scanner technologies quickly:

+ **Photo scanners:** These are small scanners designed specifically for scanning snapshots and are often used in tandem with equally compact photo printers. You feed in a snapshot and get a digital image for editing, or you might skip the editing step and direct your scanned output to a photo printer. You can use such a setup as a sort of photocopier for prints, which is great when your scanning needs are limited to snapshots. These scanners can cost less than a few hundred dollars and are slowly being phased out as the use of film declines.

+ **Flatbed scanners:** These are the most widely used type of scanner. They look and operate something like a small photocopier. You open the lid, place your original face-down on the glass, and scan. Flatbeds are usually limited to scanning 8.5 x 11 (or sometimes 8.5 x 14) material, but the movable cover makes it simple to grab images of thick originals, such as books or even some 3-D objects. Larger originals can be scanned in sections and stitched together in your image editing software. Some flatbeds have an alternate light source built into the lid or available as an add-on that can illuminate transparencies, giving you slide-scanning capabilities. Flatbed scanners can run anywhere from $50 to $500 or more.

+ **Slide/transparency scanners:** These are high-resolution scanners used for scanning color slides (in 2 x 2 mounts), strips of film in sizes from 35mm to 6cm in width, or sheet film up to 4 x 5 inches (or sometimes larger). Photographers who use transparency (positive) or negative film — or who have archives of these kinds of film — prize the specialized capabilities of slide scanners. These scanners cannot scan reflective copy, such as photographic prints. A new crop of film scanners priced at $300 or less has opened up this option to just about any interested consumer who has slides or negatives to scan. However, at the high end, this type of scanner can easily cost $1,500 or more.

All three types of scanners use similar components. All have a place to position the original to be scanned. A light source either reflects off the surface of the original or *transilluminates* it (shines light through it, in the case of transparencies or negatives). A high-resolution sensor captures the original one line at a time, either by moving past the surface of the original or by capturing light reflected from a moving mirror. Electronics inside the scanner convert the analog information that the sensor captures into digital form. You can find out more about using scanners in Book VII.

Scanner Prices and Features

Like digital cameras, flatbed scanners fall into several fairly well-defined price and feature categories. You'll find point-and-shoot scanners just like you'll find point-and-shoot digital cameras. There are also general purpose and advanced (*prosumer* — advanced models that can be used both by advanced amateurs and professionals) scanners as well as true professional scanners.

Unlike digital cameras, the primary criteria used to choose a scanner is not the resolution of the scanner. Virtually all scanners on the market claim roughly the same resolution, even though, in practice, the image quality of these devices can vary widely, even among those with similar specifications. The primary things you should look at when choosing a scanner are the image quality, speed, and convenience. I address these separately later in the chapter, concentrating on general specifications and features for the main flatbed scanner categories first.

Entry-level scanners

Entry-level scanners are the $50–$100 scanners you see on special at your local electronics superstore. They are designed for the casual scanner user — someone who needs to grab an occasional photo or who doesn't have particularly high quality standards.

All you get with one of these are simple scanning capabilities. They're often quite slow and use inexpensive sensors that often can't capture the kind of sharp image that a digital photographer expects. They're easy to use, which makes them ideal for scanning neophytes, but they usually aren't expandable with accessories, such as transparency adapters. Don't expect Photoshop Elements to be bundled with a scanner like this; many are furnished only with the most basic image capturing/editing software or a driver that works with your own image editing program as a plug-in.

Entry-level scanners are a good introduction to scanning for people who don't know whether they want to get heavily involved with image editing. These scanners are also good for noncritical applications, such as photocopying, faxing, or grabbing images for Web pages.

Intermediate scanners

Spend $100–$200 and you can purchase an intermediate scanner with better quality and speed, more features, and a great deal more versatility. These scanners have enough quality to please all but the pickiest digital photographers and are fast enough that you won't fall asleep between scans when you're capturing a stack of photos on a lazy afternoon.

Intermediate scanners usually have all the convenience features you'd want. These include front-panel buttons that let you scan, make a photocopy, send a fax, or attach a scan to an e-mail. Some can be augmented with simple attachments for scanning slides and usually include a useful selection of software, such as OCR programs, stitching programs that let you stitch together multiple scans into a single image, and image management programs.

Book II
Chapter 4

**Adding a Printer
and Scanner**

Advanced (or business) scanners

Serious digital photographers will probably be happiest with a scanner in this category. Priced at $200 to $400 and up, these include everything you need to scan and manipulate photos and other originals, produce better quality, and are faster to boot.

You can find lots of flatbed scanners with slide-scanning capabilities in this group, as well as a few models with automatic document feeders so that you can scan whole stacks of originals one after another. The image quality is better, especially when you need to pull detail out of inky shadows or bright highlights. Improved speed can be very important because owners of these scanners can spend a lot of time during the day using them.

Expect a rich treasure trove of software with a scanner in this class, including a capable image editor (probably along the lines of Adobe Photoshop Elements), OCR, document-management software, fax software, and specialized image manipulation applications, such as applications that let you create panoramas from multiple photos (also called *stitching applications*).

Professional (or prosumer) scanners

I'm not sure there's really a prosumer category in scanners anymore. The advanced, or business, scanners described in the preceding category can handle most of the needs of digital photographers and others who aren't using their scanner professionally. True graphics professionals are really the only ones who need to spend $400–$2,000 or more for a flatbed scanner — and then only if they need some of the special capabilities these scanners provide.

Scanners in this category have all the features found in the advanced category but augment those features with the very best optics, sensors, and electronics available. You truly get the very best scans with these models, particularly if you know how to use the features.

These scanners are also very rugged, having what the automakers used to call (euphemistically) road-hugging weight. You can bang one of these scanners around without throwing anything out of alignment, and you can expect them to scan hour after hour, day after day, without protest.

These are the scanners to consider if you are scanning larger originals. An 8.5 x 14-inch scanning bed is a must, and some models have 11 x 17-inch or larger scanning beds.

Don't expect to get a copy of Photoshop bundled with one of these models, either. Anyone who can afford one undoubtedly already has a copy (or two) of Photoshop on hand. You can expect to receive a high-end scanning program, though, with dozens of controls and adjustments so that scans can be both automated and fine-tuned to the *n*th degree.

What Scanner Features Do You Need?

There's a lot of overlap in features within and between the various flatbed scanner categories. Some features are more useful than others for the digital photography–inclined. Other features can be deceptive. Later in this chapter, I spend a little time on the two most misunderstood features — resolution and the number of colors captured — and I describe the other features briefly in this section.

Scan quality

Scan quality is different from resolution, as I describe in the later section, "Resolution mythconceptions." Resolution of the sensor is only one of the factors that affect scan quality. The others include the number of colors (dynamic range) of the scanner, the quality of the optics, and the electronics used to translate the scanned image for your computer. The most important thing you want to think about is how good the final scan looks. Often, you need to rely on reviews in magazines or Web sites or your own testing to determine this.

Scanner speed

Some scanners operate much faster than others. One scanner might capture an 8 x 10 image at 300 samples per inch (spi) in 20 seconds, whereas another might require a minute and a half. You might not care about the speed if you make one scan a day. Conversely, if you're making 100 scans a day, speed matters. Reviews can tell you how fast a scanner is, relatively speaking, but you still might want to test a scanner before you buy it, using your own documents and a computer similar to your own.

Scanning size

Flatbed scanners have a fixed-size scanning bed, usually 8.5 x 11.7 to 8.5 x 14. Even though you might rarely scan a 14-inch-long original, the larger size is handy to have. I often slap down a bunch of 4 x 6 prints and scan them all at once, cropping and sizing within Photoshop. It's nice to have a larger scanning bed to accommodate more and larger originals when you need to.

Film scanning

If you have many color slides or negatives you'd like to scan and don't want a dedicated film scanner, a flatbed that can accommodate these originals is a plus. A light source built into the lid of the scanner can transilluminate the film so the sensor can capture your slides, negatives, or transparencies, using the scanner's highest optical resolution. Figure 4-4 shows such a scanner.

**Book II
Chapter 4**

**Adding a Printer
and Scanner**

Figure 4-4: A flatbed scanner with a light source in its lid can scan film.

Physical size

If your desktop space is limited, you might want a tiny scanner. I favor larger scanners because they tend to stay put without sliding and can better ignore vibrations when heavy-footed colleagues or family members stride past. In any case, even the largest flatbed scanners today are likely to be half to two-thirds the size of the behemoths of ten years ago, so you won't have to worry about giving over half your desktop to your image grabber.

Configuration

Along with physical size, other scanner configuration features can be important when desktop space is limited. For example, a few scanners can be set up vertically so they occupy a minimum amount of space. At least one new scanner comes apart, so you can place the scanning element directly on a large original that wouldn't fit in an ordinary scanner's scanning bed. The scanner in Figure 4-5 lets you see the original being scanned through a transparent lid.

Figure 4-5: Some scanners let you see the subject you are scanning through a glass sheet.

Bundled software

If you're already well equipped with software, you probably don't need to worry about the bundle furnished with your scanner. I have several copies of Adobe Photoshop Elements that came with scanners, but rarely use any of them. Of more interest to me are the advanced scanning programs, such as the versatile Silver Fast application that came with my high-end Epson scanner. You can always upgrade to better software if you're dissatisfied with the applications furnished with your scanner.

You might be more interested in OCR software (to convert documents to editable text), copy utilities (to let you use your scanner as a photocopier), document management programs (to let you file document images and retrieve them by keywords), and other software, such as applications that let you stitch images together to create panoramas.

Type of sensor

The kind of sensor used in a scanner can affect how you use it. In the past, *charge coupled device* (CCD) sensors were the most common sensors in consumer scanners. These solid-state devices capture an image that is conveyed by a sophisticated optical system, often a path measuring a foot or more in length, as mirrors and optics convey the light reflected from the original to the sensor itself.

More recently, a less expensive, solid-state sensor called a *contact image sensor* (CIS) has been used, especially for lower-priced scanners. A CIS sensor moves beneath the glass a few scant millimeters from the original in a much-simplified system that requires no optical path at all. CIS scanners can be very thin and compact (because there is no need to leave room for an optical path) and use inexpensive red, green, and blue (RGB) light-emitting diodes (LEDs) instead of the fluorescent light tube found in CCD scanners. This makes for a cheaper scanner, in more ways than one:

+ CIS scanners often produce poorer quality than the more sophisticated CCD sensor produces. Although quality is improving (some $150–$200 CIS scanners produce great quality), this technology has not been associated with the best overall quality.

+ CIS scanners typically have very little depth of field, which means they can scan only flat originals held in tight contact with the scanning glass. Even a wrinkle in a paper original can affect the sharpness of some CIS scanners. You can also forget about scanning 3-D objects.

Until CIS sensors catch up with their CCD counterparts, you probably want to stick with a CCD-based scanner when making your decision. Check the box or specs to find out which you have or visit the vendor's Web site if the information isn't easy to find.

Scanner interface

The kind of interface used to connect your scanner to your computer was once an important consideration. You had to choose between SCSI or parallel port scanners or even slow serial connections. Some scanners required a proprietary interface card.

Today, all scanners come with Universal Serial Bus (USB) or IEEE 1394 (FireWire) connections or both. Either of these interfaces is fast enough for

They help you shoot better pictures, too. This chapter highlights some of the most common and most needed accessories for digital photography.

Getting Support from Tripods

A *tripod* is a three-legged stand, like the one shown in Figure 5-1, designed to hold your camera steady while a picture is composed and taken. Although a tripod might be a little cumbersome to carry along, at times, you'll find one indispensable. Here are some of the things a tripod can do for you:

✦ **Hold the camera steady for longer exposures.** You need a longer shutter speed to capture an image in dim light.

✦ **Hold the camera steady for photos taken at telephoto zoom settings.** Telephoto settings do a great job of magnifying the image, but they also magnify the amount of vibration or camera shake. Even tiny wobbles can lead to photos that look like they're out of focus when they're actually just blurry from too much camera movement. A tripod can help eliminate this sort of blur.

If pictures keep ending up fuzzy when the camera's set for its maximum telephoto zoom setting, it's more likely that the problem is camera shake than a poor autofocus mechanism. At long zoom settings, most digital cameras often switch to a slower shutter speed. The slower shutter speed coupled with the telephoto's magnification of the tiniest bit of camera shake leads to a photo that appears out of focus. It's not that the picture is out of focus at all; it's just that the camera has been vibrating too much. Mounting the camera on a good, sturdy tripod is the best cure for this problem.

Figure 5-1: Get the support you need from a tripod.

✦ **Hold the camera in place so you can get in the picture, too, by using your digital camera's self-timer feature.** This way, you only have to worry about how you look as you make a mad dash into the picture.

✦ **Allow for precise positioning and composition so that you can get exactly the image you want.** This is especially important if you want to take multiple shots from the same spot, and is also useful if you're experimenting with filters or trying different lighting ideas.

✦ **Hold the camera for multipicture panoramic shots that you stitch together into one photo in your image editor, or hold the camera for close-up photography.** I discuss close-ups in Book IV, Chapter 2, and panoramas in greater detail in Book IV, Chapter 6.

Because most modern digital cameras are fairly lightweight, you won't have to carry a massive tripod like many pros do; just be sure the tripod is strong enough to keep the camera steady. Beware of the models that claim to go from tabletop to full height (roughly eye-level at five feet or more); odds are that they sway like a reed when fully extended. If you have one of the new, low-cost digital SLR cameras like those available from Canon, Nikon, Sony, and Pentax, you might discover that you need a slightly heftier tripod because these models are a bit heavier than the run-of-the-mill digital camera.

Getting multiple shots with a tripod

Here's a trick that shows you just how useful a tripod can be. Multiple shots can be merged to solve difficult lighting situations because using a tripod also allows multiple images from exactly the same camera position. This is important because it can help the photographer correct problems with lighting that's too contrasty.

Many times, a scene is lit in such a way that the difference between the brightest white and the darkest black is greater than the sensor can handle. When this happens, pictures end up with areas that are solid white or solid black and have no detail in them.

When circumstances permit, pros correct this by taking two or more images of exactly the same scene with the camera mounted on the tripod. The first image is exposed so that the highlights are properly exposed; the second image is exposed so that the shadows have detail. *Hint:* When in doubt, take one picture that's a little

overexposed and one picture that's a little underexposed. (One setting above what the camera recommends and one setting below what the camera recommends would be a good rough estimate.) Some cameras have this capability built-in, usually called *auto exposure bracketing.*

Back at the computer, the two images are merged in an image editing program such as Photoshop so that the combined image carries detail throughout the picture. Using this technique might stretch your comfort zone with both your computer and your camera, but it can also help you improve many photos, such as scenics, that can be taken with the camera mounted on a tripod. You can always take an extra shot at the setting the camera recommends so that you still have the shot you'd have gotten anyway. That's one of the nice things about digital cameras; you don't have to worry about wasting shots!

Types of tripods

Tripods come in several types of materials, styles, and sizes. Pro units are capable of handling heavy cameras and extending 5 to 6 feet high. These tripods are made of wood, aluminum, or carbon fiber and can cost anywhere from a couple hundred dollars to a thousand dollars or more. You probably don't want one of these. Your ideal tripod is probably a compact model made of aluminum. Here are the common types of tripods:

✦ **Less expensive units:** May range in size from 1 to 5 feet tall and cost just a few dollars to a hundred dollars or more.

✦ **Full-size models:** These range from 4 to 6 feet tall (or even larger) when fully extended and might have from two to four collapsing sections to reduce size for carrying. The more sections, the smaller the tripod collapses. The downside is that the extra sections reduce stability and provide more points for problems to develop.

✦ **Tabletop or mini-tripods:** These are promoted as lightweight, expandable, and easy to carry, which they are. They can be small enough to carry around comfortably. They're also promoted to be sturdy enough for a 35mm camera, which they probably aren't unless they're set to their lowest height. Most can easily handle a digital camera, however. If used on a tabletop or braced against a wall with a small digital camera, these units can do a decent job. They can come in handy in places where there's not enough room to use a full-size tripod.

To use a mini-tripod against a wall, brace it against the wall with your left hand while pressing your left elbow into the wall. Use your right hand to help stabilize the camera while tripping the shutter. Keep your right elbow tight against your body for added stability.

✦ **Monopods:** While not exactly a tripod (monopods have only one leg), a monopod does help reduce camera shake. These single-leg, multi-segment poles, like the one shown in Figure 5-2, can just about double the steadiness of the camera.

However, don't try to use a monopod around some protected buildings, such as museums and government facilities, because monopods resemble guns from a distance.

✦ **Hiking stick monopods:** Another option is a combination hiking stick/monopod. If you do a lot of hiking, these can be very worthwhile. Although not as sturdy or stable as a high-quality monopod, these hybrids can work quite well with the typical small digital camera. Most of them have a wooden knob on top that unscrews, leaving a quarter-inch screw that mates with the camera's tripod socket. (Check to make sure your digital camera has one; not all models do.) Mount the camera on the hiking stick, brace the bottom of it against your left foot, pull it into your body with your left hand, and gently squeeze the shutter release button.

Figure 5-2: Monopods provide a more compact means of support for heavier cameras, like this digital SLR.

You can find excellent tripods and monopods from Bilora, Bogen, Benbo, Gitzo, Lenmar, Slik, Sunpak, and Smith Victor at your photo retailer.

Scrutinizing tripod features

Not all tripods are made alike, so I encourage you to take a close look at how the tripod you're thinking of purchasing is put together. The following subsections are a rundown of what to look for.

Locking legs

All collapsible tripods offer some way of locking the legs in position. Most common are rings that are twisted to loosen or tighten the legs in place.

Some manufacturers use levers instead. When buying a tripod, check this part closely. Remember, every time you want to fully extend or collapse the tripod, you're going to have six or more of these locks to manipulate. A good tripod lets you open or close all the locks for one leg simultaneously when the legs are collapsed, as shown in Figure 5-3. (Cover all three rings or levers at the same time with your hand and twist; they're all released, and then with one simple movement, they're all extended. This also works in reverse.)

Range of movement

Some tripod legs can be set to a right angle from the camera mount. This feature can be handy if you're working on uneven ground, such as a hiking trail.

Extra mounting screws

Figure 5-3: Grip all three locks to open or close them simultaneously.

Some tripods offer an extra mounting screw on one of the legs. Hypothetically, this is useful, but its use is rare enough that I wouldn't choose one tripod over another just for this. A more useful extra is a reversing center column post, available on better tripods, that can accept a camera on its low end (for ground-level shots) or that has a hook that holds a weight or camera bag. Placing extra weight on a tripod makes it steadier for longer exposures, so this capability is actually very useful.

Heads

A *tripod head* is the device that connects the camera to the tripod legs. On inexpensive models, these are frequently permanently attached. On better quality models (although not necessarily expensive ones), they are removable and can be replaced with a different type. There are quite a few different styles of tripod heads. Many tripod heads that offer a *panning* capability (the ability to spin or rotate the camera on its horizontal axis) also offer a series of 360 markings to help orient the camera for panoramas. Here are some of the types of tripod heads to consider:

✦ **Pan/tilt heads:** These allow you to spin the camera on one axis and tilt it on another. These are generally the cheapest and most labor intensive because you have to make adjustments to multiple levers to reposition the camera.

✦ **Fluid, or video, heads:** These usually have a longer handle that extends from the head. Twist the grip to loosen it, and you can pivot and tilt the camera simultaneously.

✦ **Joystick heads:** Similar to the fluid or video head, this type has a locking lever built into a tall head. By gripping the lever and head and squeezing, you can pan and tilt the camera quickly and easily. These were designed and marketed for 35mm cameras, but they don't work particularly well for these cameras because they're subject to creep. Basically, creep occurs when you reposition your camera on a tripod head, lock it, and then notice the camera move a little as it settles into the locked position. Creep can be a very annoying problem with any tripod head, but the joystick models seem to have more trouble with it. *Note:* For a smaller digital camera, these heads might be a better choice simply because these cameras weigh so much less.

✦ **Ball heads:** These are probably the most popular style with pro photographers because they provide a full range of movement for the camera with a minimal number of controls to bother with. This type of tripod head, shown in Figure 5-4, uses a ball mounted in a cylinder. The ball has a stem with a camera mount on one end, and when the control knob is released, you can move your camera freely until reaching the top of the cylinder. A cutout on one side of the cylinder allows the stem to drop down low enough for the camera to be positioned vertically. Ball heads range in price from just a few dollars to $500 or more. The best ones don't creep at all, which is why photographers pay so much for them.

Figure 5-4: A ball head is the most popular style of tripod head.

Checking out tripod alternatives

Several other items on the market are also worth considering for those who need to travel light. A tried and true classic for supporting bigger camera/lens combinations is the beanbag. Whether you use the basic beanbag that you tossed around as a kid or the one specially designed for photography, by putting the bag on a wall or car roof and then balancing the lens on the bag, you can maneuver your equipment easily while letting the wall or car take the weight of the lens.

You can also find a number of clamp-like devices coupled with the quarter-inch screw necessary to attach them to your camera's tripod socket. You then clamp the camera to a tree limb or fence post or any other solid object, and *voilà!* Instant tripod (don't add water).

These camera-holding clamps range from a modest C-clamp device for just a few bucks up to the Bogen Super Clamp system (www.bogenphoto.com). The basic Super Clamp costs around $30. The basic C-clamp style should do the job for travelers using a shirt-pocket-size digital camera. Those working with one of the larger, digital SLR cameras might want to consider a Super Clamp. A local camera store can probably help you out.

Making Good Use of an Electronic Flash

Because available light (more commonly known as *available darkness*) is undependable, digital photographers should consider carrying an accessory flash unit. Although most digital cameras have some sort of built-in flash capability, these don't produce a very powerful light. The built-in flash unit is usually good only for a range of up to about 8 feet or so, which isn't always enough.

Accessory flash units do more than just provide extra light when it's too dark to shoot without it. Although I cover accessory lighting more thoroughly in Book IV, Chapter 3, here are some situations in which an accessory flash is useful:

✦ **Fill flash:** Is your subject standing in the shadows while another part of the scene is brightly lit? If you rely on your camera's light meter, you'll either get a properly exposed subject and overexposed area where the light was too bright or an unrecognizably dark subject and an okay scene. Using an accessory flash lets you balance the light throughout the scene by exposing for the bright area and using the flash to light up the shadows.

✦ **Painting with light:** Suppose you want to take a picture of a building or other large structure, and it's pitch dark out. One technique for handling this situation is known as *painting with light*. Set your camera on a tripod or something equally solid and then pull out your accessory flash unit. Set your digital camera to its bulb (B) or time (T) exposure setting if it has one — or if not, then use the longest exposure possible. While the shutter is open, use your flash to light up sections of the building one section at a time. Here's where the true wonder of the digital camera comes in: You can check your photo as soon as you're done taking it. Although film photographers have been using this technique for years, they've always had to wonder whether they got it right until they got their prints back or saw their negatives in the darkroom.

✦ **Macro, or close-up, photography:** Getting in close requires lots of light simply because as the camera gets closer to its subject, the area of sharp focus — *depth of field* — diminishes. Using your external flash helps provide enough light to allow an aperture setting for greater depth of field. The external flash also provides more-even illumination for your subject. It's best if you use a setup that allows your flash unit to operate while off the camera because lighting your subject from the side brings out more detail than lighting from straight ahead. Some flash units, such as ring lights, are specifically designed for macro photography. (I take a look at ring lights a little later in this chapter.)

✦ **Bounce flash:** Many accessory flash units include a tilt/swivel head that lets you point the unit toward a reflective surface instead of right at your subject. By bouncing the flash off the surface and toward your subject, you create softer light and shadows than you would if the flash was directed straight at your subject. Some include a built-in card or deflector that can help you direct the bounce light, as shown in Figure 5-5.

Bouncing a flash unit this way weakens its effective output because the light has to travel a greater distance to reach the subject. This isn't a problem if the surface is reasonably close, but distance matters. Beware of cathedral ceilings!

✦ **Multi-flash:** It's possible to use multiple flash units to create a lighting setup that comes reasonably close to studio lighting. By positioning these flashes properly, you can either create a nicer portrait lighting setup or distribute the lights well enough to evenly illuminate an entire room.

Built-in flash units can also speed the camera's battery drain tremendously. Because they're positioned right above the lens, the built-in strobes are also a prime cause of *red-eye*. This is a reddish tinge in human pupils (greenish or yellowish in many animals). Red-eye is particularly difficult to prevent when photographing (with flash) young children. An accessory flash can help reduce this effect because you can position it farther from the lens than a built-in unit.

Many higher-end digital cameras offer some method of triggering an accessory flash unit, either by a cable connection or via a *hot shoe* — the device on a camera that holds an external flash and provides an electronic connection to the camera. Many amateur and prosumer digital cameras, however, offer no such provision. The answer in this case is a "slaved" flash specifically designed for digital cameras (which I discuss in more detail in the next section).

**Book II
Chapter 5**

**Picking Up Some
Accessories**

Figure 5-5: An external flash unit can be bounced off any available surface.

Types of electronic flash units

There are as many different electronic flash units available as there are digital cameras. The following subsections provide a quick rundown of the kinds you'll want to consider.

Before buying flash equipment of any kind, be sure it works with your camera. Flash units can be triggered via the camera's hot shoe, by electronic slaves, by wireless radio triggers, and via several different types of cables. Some cameras can use a generic, old-fashioned connection called a *PC cable* (not named for a personal computer but for the Prontor-Compur shutters of the early film cameras that used this connection). These cables are inexpensive and work with any camera that has a PC connection, but all they do is trigger the flash unit.

A camera's manufacturer makes another type of cable, known by several different designations (TTL and E-TTL, for example); this proprietary type is designed specifically for the manufacturer's cameras (sometimes for just one segment of its camera line) and no other, although these cables do work with third-party flashes. The advantage to these types of flash cords (which are much more expensive than PC cords) are that they allow the camera and flash unit to communicate with each other so that the camera can turn the flash's output off when it determines proper exposure is reached.

Small, light minislaves

These units are electronic flash devices with built-in remote triggering and are designed to help augment the camera's built-in flash unit. They're generally useful for adding a little extra dimension to your lighting and as a way of filling in background areas. These units are slaved to fire when another flash unit goes off. Such photographic slaves are photoelectric sensors designed to trigger a flash unit when another flash is fired within the sensor's field of view (in the case of a digital camera, when the camera's built-in flash fires). These slave-triggering circuits are sold as independent units that you can attach to existing flash units, or the circuitry can be built right into a flash.

Hot shoe mount flashes

These are more powerful than both the minislaves and the camera's built-in flash units. They might or might not offer a tilt or swivel capability. Some camera systems (usually higher-end digital cameras) offer a cable that hooks up to the camera's hot shoe (shown in Figure 5-6) and allows the flash to communicate with the camera's electronics while being positioned in ways the hot shoe mount won't permit. The advantage to these cables over slaves is that they usually permit the camera/flash combo's full range of capabilities. (Some cameras are set to turn off the flash as soon as the correct exposure is reached, whereas a slaved flash will continue pumping out light as set.)

Professional models

These units tend to be the manufacturer's most powerful and most advanced flash units. They have lots of features, including built-in slave capabilities and the ability to work with wireless remote systems. In many cases, they're also capable of taking advantage of the digital camera's lack of a true mechanical shutter at higher shutter speeds. This means the flash can be used with faster shutter speeds than those used with film cameras. In addition to the manufacturer's flash models, dedicated flashes offered by third-party manufacturers also work with many existing camera systems.

Many third-party flash units and lenses are reverse-engineered to work on major brand-name cameras. Sometimes, this equipment might not work with later equipment made by your camera's manufacturer. If a third-party flash causes damage to your camera (and today's highly electronic cameras can be susceptible to damage from improper voltage discharge), the camera manufacturer might not repair the damage under warranty.

Figure 5-6: Dedicated electronic flash units use hot shoe connections.

Portable studio lighting

Portable studio lighting kits are available that enable a photographer to carry a complete set of lights with lighting stands and reflectors or umbrellas. These kits usually offer two to three lights or more and might also include a backdrop setup. Although these sets are fine for local or cross-country trips, it might be easier to rent such a kit while traveling overseas than it is to pack one along with all your camera equipment while flying. The flash units in these kits often have built-in slaves as well, which are triggered either via a connection to the camera or via a flash unit on or in the camera.

What to look for in a photographic slave flash

A basic slave unit is a small device designed to mate with the flash unit's hot shoe or other connection. The slave (good ones have on/off switches) triggers the flash when another flash unit is fired. These slaves have their own hot shoe foot (to mate with stands designed for such things or the L-bracket described in a few paragraphs) and also have quarter-inch tripod sockets in their base so that you can screw them onto an extra tripod.

Wireless or radio slaves also exist. These are significantly more expensive (although I paid just $75 for my radio unit), but worth it when other photographers and their accompanying flashes are in the vicinity. A regular photo-electric slave doesn't care that it's been triggered by the wrong photographer's flash unit; it simply does its job. Wireless triggers work via radio signals, not light. These devices generally offer multiple frequencies to minimize the likelihood of another photographer triggering them.

A standard photographic slave won't work properly with a digital camera because most prosumer and amateur digital cameras emit a preflash (to help the camera make some internal settings), which triggers earlier slave designs prematurely. If you're interested in a slaved flash unit, make sure it's designed to work with a digital camera. Nissin, an electronics firm, makes a flash unit known as the Digi-Slave Flash. You can find about a half-dozen different units, ranging all the way up to a pro unit. Check out SR, Inc., for pictures and descriptions of the models available (www.srelectronics.com).

Although the slaved flash doesn't help reduce the drain on the camera's battery, the more powerful light still helps improve photos. The photographer also gains the ability to position the light higher up from the lens (usually slightly to the right or left as well) to reduce the likelihood of red-eye and to provide a more pleasing effect. Generally speaking, setting the camera's exposure system to automatic can handle the increased flash okay; if you're not satisfied with the result, switch to aperture priority and experiment! The exception is with close-up photos, where overexposure is likely. Dialing in a correction (usually a reduction of about two f-stops) through the camera's exposure compensation system solves this problem.

Book II
Chapter 5

Picking Up Some Accessories

An electronic flash unit without power is an expensive paperweight. With the exception of the portable studio lighting kits, which require electrical outlets, electronic flashes usually require AA batteries, although the smallest might take AAAs instead. Rechargeable batteries generally provide an inexpensive option, although they tend to recycle (recharge the flash unit) more slowly than alkaline batteries do. PC cables and manufacturer flash cords malfunction (take care not to crimp them), so for important trips, carry extras (especially if you're going overseas, where it might be hard to find a replacement). Some rechargeable batteries also tend to lose their charge faster than alkaline batteries when stored.

Lighting/flash accessories

Depending on your shooting requirements and how much weight you can afford to carry, some accessories out there can help improve your photography. Here's my list of possibilities:

✦ **Brackets:** A nice complement to the accessory flash route is an L-bracket flash holder. This device mounts to the camera via the tripod socket and has a flash shoe at the top of the L, where you position the flash. In addition to providing a secure hold for the flash unit, the L-bracket tends to provide a steadier grip for the camera. You can even find models designed for the shorter, thinner digital cameras, such as the earlier Nikon Coolpix series (www.nikon.com).

✦ **Background cloths/reflectors:** Garden enthusiasts interested in photographing flowers can bring swatches of colored cloth large enough to serve as a background for a shot of a plant or bloom. Black is a good all-purpose color, whereas red, green, and blue complement common flower colors. Another helpful item is a collapsible reflector; camera stores sell small ones, or you can pick up ones designed as sun blockers for car windows. These reflectors can kick some sunlight back into the shadow areas to help create a more pleasing image. For the most serious flower photographers, a *ring light* or circular flash unit that mounts in front of the camera lens provides an even, balanced light for flower close-ups. A Digi-Slave flash ring light unit can be configured for many amateur and prosumer digital cameras.

Choosing a Camera Bag

Depending on the size of a digital camera and the accessories accompanying it, a camera bag or pouch could be a necessity. For just the basics — a small camera, extra batteries, extra memory cards, and a lens cleaning cloth — a simple fanny pack does the job and leaves room for hotel keys, money, and identification.

A more serious photographer who's carrying a larger digital camera needs more space. A larger camera bag might be the answer, but for the active traveler, there are some interesting options. Because camera bags are especially useful for traveling photographers, I've included a longer description of the options and features in Book IV, Chapter 6, which deals with travel photography.

Acquiring Other Useful Devices

Gizmos. Gadgets. Thing-a-ma-jigs. Many of these items don't fall into any particular type of category, except that they do something useful. Some are quirky but cool, such as little shades that fasten onto the back of your camera and shield your LCD readout screen from the bright sun. Others are serious working tools, like the add-on battery packs described in an upcoming section. Photographers love gadgets, and you'll find lots of them for digital cameras. Here are a few of the most practical.

A filter holder

A helpful device I especially like is a filter holder engineered by the Cokin company (`www.cokin.fr/`) and sold by most camera outlets. One Cokin holder, designed for cameras that can't accept filters, mounts to the base of the camera via the tripod socket. This adapter allows the use of Cokin's square filters, which slide right into the adapter to provide a variety of effects and corrections. Note, however, that you could achieve many of the same results in an image editing program. To those who are more comfortable tweaking things on the computer, filters aren't important. On the other hand, if you're new to computer photo editing, relying on traditional filters might be easier. You can always take one shot with a filter and one without and then try to tweak the filter-less shot to look like the filtered one. This process can help you figure out how to get the most from your image editing software.

A second camera

Sooner or later, you'll think about buying a second camera — say, when you're ready to leave on that vacation of a lifetime. A small, inexpensive digital camera doesn't cost much, and if the primary camera fails, it might prove worth its weight in gold, photographically speaking. Shop for one — or borrow one — that uses the same type of batteries and storage medium as your primary camera, if possible. The extra camera can also entice a spouse or child into sharing your love of photography.

Second cameras are easy to come by. Every time I upgrade to a new digital camera, the old one gets passed down to a family member or kept in reserve as a spare camera. My old 3.3-megapixel Nikon Coolpix 995 was great in its day, but it became a backup when I upgraded to an EVF model with a super-sharp 8:1 zoom lens. Then digital SLRs came along and I bought a Nikon D70, with my EVF camera relegated to back-up duty.

Cleaning kits

You'll also frequently need a good cleaning kit (see Figure 5-7). An inexpensive microfiber cleaning cloth is great for cleaning optics, but first use a blower to blow any dust particles from the lens. You can then hold the lens near your head, fog the lens with your breath, and gently (very gently) wipe the lens with the cloth. Canned (pressurized) air also does a good job of blowing dust and dirt off the camera, but make sure the can is held level, or solvents from the aerosol might contaminate the lens.

Damp or dusty conditions call for more serious efforts. Protect your camera inside heavy-duty plastic freezer or sandwich bags while inside the camera bag, thus reducing exposure to dust and moisture. Keep the little packets of silica that come with electronic equipment and place one or two of these in the camera bag to eat up moisture, too. The following section provides more detailed information about dealing with extreme weather conditions and bags and containers for protecting gear. (Call it the difference between shooting at a dusty ball field on a windy day versus shooting in a windstorm in the desert.)

Figure 5-7: Keep your camera clean with gear like this air blower, cleaning swab, and cleaning liquid.

If you have a digital SLR, you might need a special cleaning kit for removing dust from your sensor. Something as simple as a bulb air blower may work, or you might need to buy a kit containing a brush and swabs for liquid cleaning.

Waterproof casings and housings

Extreme conditions call for better protection for your camera. Better yet, photography in wet weather, or even underwater, can be fun, too. Waterproof casings that still allow for photography are available from several companies, including ewa-marine (www.ewa-marine.de). These are useful for both underwater photography (careful on the depth, though) and above-the-water shots when you're sailing or boating. Keep in mind that salt spray is very possibly the single worst threat to camera electronics. Make sure your camera casing provides good protection against wind and salt spray.

Another option for those who want to shoot in wet conditions often is a new underwater digital camera. The SeaLife ReefMaster underwater digital camera series (www.sealife-cameras.com) comes in a waterproof housing and works both on land and underwater. The cameras, which can be purchased for as little as $400, produce 3.3 to 5 megapixel images, and save you the trouble of trying to find a housing to fit an existing digital camera. The cameras also have an LCD that works underwater and a fast delete function to make it easier to operate underwater.

For serious underwater enthusiasts, heavy-duty Plexiglas housings now exist for small digital cameras. These housings are available for a wide range of digital cameras and may be found for as little as a couple hundred dollars.

Filters

Filters, those glass disks that can be screwed onto your camera's lens, are a popular accessory. Here are some of the different kinds of filters you can buy and play with:

✦ **Warming:** Some filters produce what photographers refer to as a *warming effect.* This filter can help make up for the lack of color in midday light and tries to add some reddish-orange color to the scene. Usually, these are coded in the 81 series as in 81A, 81B, 81C. Just ask for a warming filter.

✦ **Cooling:** These do just the opposite of the previous type. They add blue to the scene to reduce the reddish-orange color. These fall into the 82 series for daylight conditions.

✦ **Neutral density:** Another type of filter reduces the amount of light available. These neutral density (ND) filters (*neutral* because they have no color, and *density* because they block light) come in handy for things such as achieving the spun-glass effect from moving water. The filter blocks an f-stop's worth of light or more, making a slower shutter speed possible and increasing the blur of the moving water. You can use ND filters to operate at a wider aperture to blur the background in portraits, too.

✦ **Neutral density, take two:** Sometimes a photographer wants to photograph a street scene without cars driving through the photo. By stacking neutral density filters, it's possible to create such a long exposure that no cars are in the scene long enough to register in the image. Obviously, a camera support of some sort is required. (**Hint:** The ground's pretty stable, too, unless you're visiting California.) Having a camera capable of extremely slow shutter speeds is also necessary. A neutral density filter is shown in Figure 5-8.

✦ **Split neutral density:** Another version of the neutral density filter is a split neutral density design. This filter provides half neutral density and half clear filtration, preferably with a graduated transition from the light-blocking half to the clear half.

The main use for a split ND filter is for occasions when half the scene is brighter than the other. The most common example of this is a bright sky against a significantly darker foreground. This condition is typical of midday lighting conditions.

✦ **Polarizers:** Polarizing filters can reduce the glare bouncing off shiny surfaces in your photos. Simply attach the filter and view the image through your LCD. Rotate the polarizer until the glare disappears. Polarizers can also help deepen the contrast of the sky from certain angles.

Figure 5-8: A neutral density filter cuts down the amount of light reaching the sensor.

Battery packs

One of my digital cameras uses a lithium-ion (Li-Ion) rechargeable battery that's good for a couple hundred shots. Unless you're involved in a serious photographic project or leave home on vacation, a single battery (plus one spare) might be all you need. However, that same camera can be fitted with an add-on battery pack that fits under the camera body and holds two more of the same model Li-Ion batteries (increasing the shooting capacity to nearly 600 shots). More importantly, the accessory battery pack accepts standard AA batteries, which the camera itself does not.

You'll find an add-on battery pack like this extremely useful for those shooting sessions that involve treks into back country far from AC power. Or if you're on vacation, you might be unable to recharge your digital camera's batteries until you check into your next hotel, so the additional juice might be handy. If you need an accessory battery pack, you probably also need a charger that works on multiple voltage settings (so it can be used overseas) or with an automobile connector so that you can recharge your batteries on the road.

Book III
Using Digital SLRs

The 5th Wave   By Rich Tennant

"Try putting a person in the photo with the product you're trying to sell. We generated a lot of interest in our eBay Listing once Leo started modeling my hats and scarves."

$\mathcal{B}$e honest: If you're really serious about digital photography as a hobby, you probably turned to this book first because digital single-lens reflexes (dSLRs) have, in a few short years, become the dream camera of almost every photo enthusiast. Those point-and-shoot cameras are great to slip into a pocket or purse for spur-of-the-moment pictures, but dSLRs are really where the action is among photo hobbyists.

So, if you're the type who loves to be on the bleeding edge of technology, this minibook's three chapters will help slake your dSLR-knowledge thirst. I show you exactly why these cameras can do things that other types of picture-shooters (both film and digital) cannot. I'm even up-front with explanations of a few things that dSLRs can't do (and why you shouldn't care). I help you figure out how to manage a dSLR's controls to select the right focus mode, as well as choose between aperture-priority, shutter-priority, programmed exposure, or one of those intriguing Scene modes. I explain the differences between prime lenses and zooms and how to select an add-on lens that gives you the most flexibility without sacrificing image quality. This book is a concise introduction to an exciting camera technology.

Chapter 1: The Digital SLR Advantage

In This Chapter

- ✔ **A half-dozen advantages of digital SLRs**
- ✔ **Six downsides that aren't really downers**
- ✔ **How dSLRs really work**
- ✔ **Dealing with quirks**

*S*ome folks will tell you that digital single-lens reflex (or dSLR) cameras are destined to become the Next Big Thing. They're wrong. Digital single lens reflex cameras are *already* a Big Thing, and they're destined to get even bigger. Practically anything you can do with a traditional digital camera, you can do with a dSLR — and do it faster, with more creative options, and usually with a better picture. (I explain some of the things a dSLR *can't* do later in this chapter.)

Working with what most amateur photographers consider the "high end" of the digital photography equipment realm won't make you a better photographer. But upgrading to a dSLR will probably make you a *happier* photographer, particularly after you've mastered all the new controls and features these cameras offer.

As you may (or may not) know, single-lens reflex cameras are film or digital picture-takers that use mirrors and/or prisms to give you a bright, clear optical view (not a TV-like LCD view) of the picture you're going to take, using the same lens that is used to take the picture. Best of all, that lens can be *taken off* (it's *interchangeable*) so you can substitute another lens that brings you closer to your subject, offers a wider view, or maybe focuses down close enough to see the hungry look in the eye of a praying mantis. Is that cool, or what?

Whether you already own a dSLR or you're thinking of buying one, this chapter and the two that follow are your introduction to the exciting features of these top-of-the-digital-food-chain cameras. If you want to find out more, check out my book *Digital SLR Cameras & Photography For Dummies,* but everything you really *must* know right off the bat is in this book.

Six Great dSLR Features

All digital SLRs have six killer features that make your job as a photographer much easier, more pleasant, and more creative.

A bigger, brighter view

The perspective through a dSLR's viewfinder is larger and easier to view than what you get with any non-SLR's optical window, back-panel LCD, or internal electronic viewfinder (EVF). With a dSLR, what you see is almost exactly what you get (or at least 95 percent of it), although you might need to press a button called a *depth-of-field preview* if you want to know more precisely what parts of your image are in focus. The dSLR's viewfinder shows you a large image of what the lens sees, not a TV-screen-like LCD view. (See Figure 1-1.) If you have your heart set on using an LCD, you can still review the picture you've taken on your dSLR's LCD after it has been captured.

Figure 1-1: A dSLR viewfinder gives you a big, bright view of your scene for easy composition and focus.

Faster operation

Any non-SLR digital camera suffers from something called *shutter lag*, which is a delay of 0.5 to 1.5 seconds (or more) after you press the shutter release all the way but before the picture is actually taken. Lag is a drag when you're shooting sports action or trying to capture a fleeting expression on the faces of your kids. A dSLR responds to your command to shoot virtually instantly and can continue to take pictures at a 3 to 5 frames-per-second clip (or even faster). Try *that* with a non-SLR camera! All functions of a dSLR camera, from near-instant power-up to autofocus to storing an image on your memory card are likely to operate faster and more smoothly with a dSLR than with other types of digital cameras.

Lenses, lenses, and more lenses

Certainly, many non-SLR cameras are outfitted with humongous zoom lenses with 12X or more zoom ratios. A typical "superzoom" range is the equivalent of 35mm to 420mm on a full-frame digital or film camera. Yet, these "do-everything" lenses don't do everything. Only a digital SLR, which lets you pop off the lens currently mounted on your camera and mount another one with different features, has that capability. Non-SLR digital cameras rarely offer wide angle views as broad as 24mm to 28mm. Digital SLR lenses commonly offer views as wide as 10mm. You'll also want a dSLR if you need to focus extra-close or want a *really* long telephoto. The lenses offered for dSLR cameras are often sharper, too. For many photographers, the ability to change lenses is the number-one advantage of the digital SLR.

Better image quality

You'll find non-SLR digital cameras today with 8 to 10 megapixels of resolution. (There are even *camera phones* with resolution in that range.) But a good-quality dSLR will almost always provide better image equality than a traditional digital camera of the same or *better* resolution. Why? Because the dSLR's sensor has larger pixels (at least 4 to 5 times larger), which makes them more sensitive to light and less prone to those grainy artifacts we call *noise*. An 8-megapixel dSLR usually provides better images with less noise at a sensitivity setting of ISO 800 than an 8-megapixel non-SLR camera at ISO 400 — and the snapshooting camera probably doesn't even *have* an ISO setting of 800 or more.

Camera-like operation

The workings of a non-SLR digital camera have more in common with a cell phone than with a traditional film camera. If you don't like zooming by pressing a button, visiting a menu every time you want to change a setting, or fine-tuning focus with a pair of keys, you should be using a digital SLR.

More control over depth of field

Depth of field (DOF) is the distance range in which things in your photos are in sharp focus. DOF can be shallow, which is a good thing when you want to make everything in your image other than your subject blurry, so that your subject is isolated or highlighted. Depth-of-field can also be generous, which is great when you want everything in the picture to look sharp.

Digital SLR cameras allow you to choose between shallow DOF, extensive DOF, and everything in between. Non-SLR cameras usually give you two choices when you're not shooting close-up pictures: having everything in sharp focus, and having *virtually* everything in sharp focus. You can find out more about the technical reason for this (the extra depth of field provided by the shorter focal length lenses used in non-SLR cameras) in Book IV, Chapter 2. If you want to use focus creatively, a dSLR is your best choice.

Six dSLR Drawbacks You Can Live With

Although dSLRs can do many things that non-dSLRs can't, they do have some limitations. However, I think you'll find that those limitations make a worthwhile trade-off, considering all the additional capabilities you gain with a digital SLR.

No LCD preview

"Where's my preview?" That's the number-one question asked by new dSLR owners who started out using conventional digital cameras. Except for one scientific model offered by Canon and a line of cameras from Olympus, no digital SLR offers a live preview of the image you're about to take on the back-panel LCD. That's because the mirror and shutter of a dSLR block the sensor from receiving light until the moment the picture is actually taken. So, you generally must be satisfied with viewing your image on the LCD only *after* it has been taken, as shown in Figure 1-2.

A dSLR can't provide the real-time exposure "chart," called a *live histogram,* that many non-SLR cameras display on the rear LCD, either, although you can view this chart after the photo is taken and make corrections then. You can live with this drawback because the LCD preview isn't all that great or accurate, anyway.

Figure 1-2: A dSLR shows an image only after the picture has been taken.

Limited viewing angles

Cameras that offer an LCD preview, particularly those with a swiveling LCD, let you hold the camera at arms length, overhead, or down low to compose your pictures. With a dSLR, you must have your eye right up to the viewfinder to line up your shot. You can buy add-on viewing attachments (including right-angle adapters) that can give dSLR owners a little more flexibility, but this is one limitation you'll probably have to learn to live with.

Lack/expense of super-wide lenses

If your dSLR has a sensor that is smaller than 24mm x 36mm (a 35mm film camera's "full frame"), the perspective of each lens is cropped by this smaller sensor size, "increasing" the focal length's effective field of view by 1.3X to 2X, depending on the dSLR you're using. (The focal length isn't really multiplied, however.) This factor is good news for those who want to reach out with a longer telephoto lens, but bad news for those who find their 20mm super-wide-angle lens has become an ordinary 26mm to 40mm moderately wide or normal lens. This drawback is easier to live with if you have the funds to buy the special, often expensive, ultra-wide lenses made especially for dSLRs.

Other factors cause noise, too. If an exposure is very long, some spurious pixels can be produced, often because the sensor heats up after being sensitized for a long period (about a second or more). Some kinds of electrical interference can also produce noise in your images.

Non-SLR cameras are the worst in the noise department, which is why most snapshooting cameras top out at ISO 400, although a few cameras from Fujifilm, Sony, and others now go all the way up to ISO 1600 (with mixed results). Your dSLR has a distinct advantage. It has larger pixels, which are more sensitive to light because they have more area to capture photons. So, virtually all digital SLRs can be used at ISO 800 with little noise, and many go up to ISO 3200. The very best performers tend to be the full-frame dSLRs, such as the Canon EOS 5D, which has the largest pixels of all.

If you're new to dSLRs, you may be unfamiliar with the possibilities of high ISO shooting and, in particular, the relative image quality your own camera produces at various ISO settings. You'll want to take the time to capture a few shots at each available setting to find out what your dSLR can and can't do.

You'll also want to figure out how to use your camera's noise reduction (NR) features to reduce problems like those shown in Figure 1-4. Depending on the model you own, NR may be applied automatically to high ISO settings but be optional for longer exposures. Or your camera may have separate user-defined settings for each type of noise.

Excessive noise reduction can reduce the amount of detail in your image, so you should find out exactly how to use your camera's NR features. You'll also want to find out how to apply noise reduction after the picture was taken by using software like Adobe Camera Raw, Noise Ninja, or the filter built into Photoshop itself.

The real dirt on sensors

It might take awhile, but eventually you'll get some dust on your dSLR sensor and will need to clean it. Don't panic! The process isn't difficult or dangerous, but you can take some steps to minimize the number of times you'll have to clean your sensor:

+ **Minimize dust entry.** If you point your camera downward when changing lenses, dust particles are less likely to settle into the mirror compartment.

+ **Don't provide dust with a safe haven.** Make sure the mounts of your lenses and the rear lens elements are clean and dust-free when you attach a lens to your camera.

Figure 1-4: Without noise reduction, a long exposure at a high ISO (left) can be contaminated by the multicolored specks we call noise (right.)

✦ **Think clean.** Try to change lenses in relatively clean environments. Avoid dusty rooms or gusty outdoor locations.

✦ **Minimize the time your camera is lenseless.** Have your new lens ready to mount, with the rear cap off but placed loosely on the back of the lens. Then, remove the lens already on your camera, set it down, and immediately take the rear lens cap off the new lens (set it on the back of the old lens if you can do it quickly). Then pick up the lens to be mounted and fasten it as quickly as you can. It's okay to leave the old lens "naked" for a few seconds if you're careful — you can always clean dust that settles on it later. The goal is to get the old lens off and the new one attached as quickly as possible.

Do a Google search for "sensor cleaning" to find extensive discussions on the various ways of cleaning digital SLR sensors. You can use specially designed bulb blowers to waft the dust off, certain types of soft brushes to remove more firmly attached particles, and moist swabs to get the really stubborn artifacts off. Don't use general-purpose products intended for cleaning lenses or your vehicle's dashboard. Your Google quest will provide all the information you need to do the job right. (I also include a long discussion of the process in *Digital SLR Cameras & Photography For Dummies*.)

Going in crop factor circles

As I note earlier in this chapter, many digital SLR cameras use a sensor that is smaller than the 35mm film frame. Even so, most vendors (Olympus is a notable exception) rely heavily on lenses that were originally designed for these full-frame film cameras. Although many digital-only lenses are being introduced, there is still a momentum of thinking of optics in terms of the 24mm x 36mm format.

That means that if you cut your teeth on 35mm cameras, the apparent focal lengths of your dSLR camera's lenses are likely to seem "wrong" to you. The smaller sensors cause the image to be cropped, so a 50mm "normal" lens becomes a mild telephoto. A 105mm "portrait" lens that you used to take head-and-shoulder shots with a film camera might not be such a good choice for portraits anymore. (For one thing, you'll have to take a few steps backward to keep your subject within the frame.)

And, of course, your wide-angle lenses might not be so wide when cropped by your sensor. This effect is sometimes called, inaccurately, a *multiplication factor* or lens *multiplier* because the easiest way of representing the effect on the camera's field of view is by multiplying the focal length of the lens by the factor. A 100mm lens "becomes" a 150mm lens with a camera that has a 1.5X crop factor.

Of course, in truth, no multiplication is involved. That 100mm lens is still a 100mm lens and has the same depth-of-field. Your 180mm f/2.8 optic isn't magically transformed into an amazing 360mm f/2.8 super-telephoto. You could get the same effect and look by shooting a picture on a full frame camera and then cropping it down. That's why the correct terminology for this effect is *crop factor*. Common crop factors with today's dSLRs are 1.3X, 1.5X, 1.6X, and 2X, as shown in Figure 1-5.

As a dSLR user, you need to become accustomed to thinking about this factor as it really is — as a crop rather than multiplication factor. That will help you better understand what is going on in your camera, although it won't eliminate all the confusion that results from trying to equate your 70mm to 200mm (actual focal length) lens with what it "really" is in dSLR terms. The good news is that you'll eventually get used to the crop factor and begin thinking of 30mm as a "normal lens" focal range and a 50mm lens as a "portrait" lens before you know it.

Figure 1-5: Crop factors change the effective view of your dSLR's lens.

Book III
Chapter 1

The Digital SLR
Advantage

Chapter 2: Mastering Digital SLR Controls

In This Chapter

- ✔ **Exposure follies**
- ✔ **Focus features**
- ✔ **Other controls**

*D*igital SLR cameras have many more controls, buttons, dials, and options than their non-SLR counterparts. If you bought a dSLR because you wanted to take control of your photography and gain access to customization features that let you produce photos with the exact color rendition, sharpness, and focus you want, the additional layers of settings are a great thing. No other type of digital camera gives you access to so many different shooting parameters that you can use to optimize image quality or to manipulate your photos in creative ways.

Of course, if you bought your dSLR because you wanted a big, impressive-looking camera to overwhelm your friends with your photography prowess, you have some studying ahead of you. If they laugh when you sit down at the piano, they'll *really* be amused if you don't know how to tickle the keys and buttons of your shiny new dSLR!

One great thing about dSLRs is that you probably won't have to wade through menus to adjust many settings. These cameras frequently have dedicated (or multifunction) buttons for given types of settings, so all you need to do is press the button and twist a dial or thumb a cursor control. That's much faster!

In this chapter, I explain some of the key controls you use with your dSLR, and I revisit some of the exposure and focus topics covered in Book II, Chapter 2, with an expanded emphasis on the more advanced things you can do with a dSLR.

Exposure Controls

Point-and-shoot cameras don't give you much input into adjusting exposure. You point, you shoot. If you're feeling daring, you look at the results on your LCD and, if dissatisfied, rinse, lather, and repeat (or the photographic equivalent). You have a dozen or two Scene modes that can adjust exposure and some other settings based on the kind of picture you're taking (for example, Beach, Night Scene, or Portrait). You probably also have exposure value (EV) settings that can increase or decrease the exposure a bit, and, if you own a higher-end model, you might have aperture priority, shutter priority, and manual exposure modes (which are all introduced in Book II, Chapter 1).

Now it's time, as they say, for the *rest* of the story. As you'd expect, digital SLRs have the same roster of exposure controls found in even the most advanced non-SLR digital cameras (although a few dSLRs eschew the only semi-useful Scene modes or trim their roster drastically). But dSLRs give you a lot more to work with, too, because, while getting a good exposure is relatively easy, getting the *best* exposure can be tricky. For dSLR owners who are serious about photography, good is rarely good enough.

No digital camera (or film camera, for that matter) can capture every tone available in a scene. Some detail in dark areas is lost because not enough photons are captured by the sensor, and details in light areas vanish when pixels in a sensor are flooded with more light than they can handle. The range from the darkest detailed picture elements to the brightest is called the *dynamic range,* and the goal of proper exposure is to make sure that the most important tones in an image fall into that range.

Metering modes

All digital cameras have built-in number-crunching routines that let the camera read the lightness and darkness values from a range of locations (or *matrix*) in the scene and calculate the best compromise in terms of exposure. The most advanced cameras, including dSLRs, let you choose how the information is gathered and interpreted. So, your camera will offer a choice of metering modes:

✦ **Matrix metering:** This is usually the default mode. The camera collects information from multiple locations in the scene, which can range from a dozen or so to more than 1,000 locations, as shown in Figure 2-1. The camera's programming can use this information to make some good guesses about what kind of picture you're shooting and set exposure accordingly. For example, if the matrix system determines that the upper half of your image is light and the bottom half is dark, it may decide that you're shooting a landscape and will optimize exposure so there will be detail in the foreground, allowing the sky to be a little too light, if necessary.

Figure 2-1: Exposure info may be gathered from a few locations, or, as in this figure, from more than 1,000 invisible points arranged in a matrix.

✦ **Center-weighted metering:** In this mode, the camera puts the most emphasis on the information in the center of the scene, but takes into account the illumination in the rest of the frame. This mode is a good choice if you know your main subject will be in the middle of the frame, but the other areas of the picture have some importance, too.

✦ **Spot metering:** In spot mode, the camera derives its exposure setting exclusively from an area in the center of the frame. This setting is a good choice at, say, a concert, where you want to expose for the spot-lit performer and don't want the inky dark surroundings to affect the settings.

Correcting exposure

Digital SLRs have an adjustment system called EV (exposure value) compensation. (Other kinds of digital cameras often have EV settings, too, but they are sometimes buried down in the menu system.) With dSLRs, this adjustment is easy to apply: You simply press the EV button on your camera (usually it's on the top panel) and use a command dial or left/right cursor key to add more exposure (+EV) or reduce exposure (–EV) using 1/2 or 1/3-value increments. (+0.5 EV would give 150 percent of the metered exposure, +1.0 EV would provide 200 percent, and so forth.)

You can determine whether to add or subtract EV by reviewing an image you've just taken on the LCD or by reviewing a picture's histogram, which can be displayed on the LCD along with the image itself (you usually must activate this option in a menu setting).

A *histogram* is a bar chart with 256 vertical bars spaced very closely together, usually forming a curve that looks like a mountain, with a high peak in the middle, trailing off to foothills at the left and right. All you really need to know to use a histogram is that the left side of the chart represents the darkest tones in your image, the right side represents the lightest tones, and the middle hump represents the tones in between.

Your goal is to produce a histogram in which the entire "mountain" is solidly in the center of the chart, with none of the dark tones lost at the left side or light tones at the right. If you look at a histogram of your most recent shot carefully, you can learn to add a little exposure (+EV) when the dark tones are cut off at the left side, or subtract a little (–EV) when the light tones are cut off on the right side. (See Figure 2-2.)

Other exposure adjustments

You have several other options for changing your camera's exposure setting:

✦ **Scene modes:** Scene modes are the modes offered on many digital SLRs that are similar to the scene options found in other digital cameras. They set up your camera to use specific exposure options (for example, long exposures for Night Scene or Night Portrait mode), set shutter speed/aperture preferences for action in Sports mode, as well as adjust parameters like color richness and sharpness.

✦ **Exposure Lock:** The exposure settings are fixed when you press a special exposure lock button or simply press the shutter release down halfway. Such a lock gives you the freedom to set exposure and then reframe the photo any way you like without worrying that the settings will change. Using a separate button has an advantage because you don't have to keep your finger on the release button.

✦ **Bracketing:** Bracketed pictures are a series of photos taken at a particular setting and then taken at a "plus" and "minus" setting. The plus/minus can be more or less exposure or other factors, such as color saturation, color balance, and flash exposure. Your camera might allow you to bracket more than one of these settings and in the order you choose.

✦ **Shifting equivalent exposures:** Most dSLRs allow you to choose equivalent exposures without changing the actual amount of light that reaches the sensor. For example, if the meter chooses 1/500 of a second at f/11, you might be able to flip to 1/1000 of a second at f/8 (which is the same effective exposure with a faster shutter speed for stopping action) or 1/250 of a second at f/16 (which is also equivalent, but would provide more depth of field).

Figure 2-2: An underexposed image (top), correctly exposed image (middle), and overexposed image (bottom).

Shooting modes

Metering modes, which I describe earlier in this chapter, are the options for collecting exposure information and calculating an exposure. Shooting modes tell your camera how to apply that information. I introduce the various shooting modes in Book II, Chapter 2. Here's a longer discussion of these modes, which are, after all, the exposure options most used by dSLR owners:

✦ **Auto:** Full auto mode handles all the settings for you, with (often) no options for adjustment. This is the mode you use when you hand your camera to a passerby and ask to have your picture taken. No fuss, no muss, no options.

✦ **Programmed:** Your dSLR uses its built-in smarts to analyze your scene and come up with a recommended exposure. However, you can override the camera's selections with EV settings, equivalent exposure shifts, or other tweaks.

✦ **Shutter priority:** You choose the shutter speed, and the camera locks it in, which makes this a good choice for sports shots like the one shown in Figure 2-3. The autoexposure system keeps the shutter speed you've chosen and varies *only* the aperture to achieve correct exposure. You also see the selected aperture in the viewfinder so that you can decide when, say, the f-stop is getting a little too large for comfort and you want to accept a slower shutter speed to gain a smaller aperture. Should light conditions change enough that your selected shutter speed won't produce a correct exposure with the available f-stops, you're alerted with a LO or HI indicator in the viewfinder or, perhaps, a flashing LED.

✦ **Aperture priority:** This mode lets you choose the f-stop, letting the camera select the shutter speed needed for correct exposure. Perhaps you want a small aperture to maximize depth of field or a large f-stop to minimize it. If you notice that the shutter speed is too slow or high, you can adjust the f-stop you've dialed in to one that's larger or smaller.

✦ **Manual exposure:** Use manual exposure when you want to set both the shutter speed and aperture yourself. Don't worry! You're not on your own and forced to guesstimate exposure. You can still use your dSLR's metering system to determine the "correct" exposure and then set it yourself — or set some other exposure entirely for a special effect. Manual exposure is also a good choice if you're using a non-automatic flash unit or an older lens that doesn't allow automatic exposure with your camera.

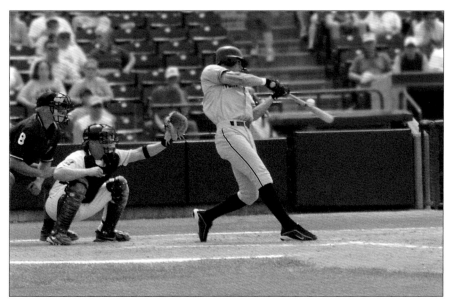

Figure 2-3: Shutter priority lets you lock in a high shutter speed to freeze action.

Focus Controls

Correct focus is important because, although you can often at least partially correct for bad exposure after a shot is taken, there isn't a lot you can do when your picture is blurred beyond recognition. Point-and-shooters actually have *less* of a problem with correct focus (in one way) than dSLR users do because the short focal length lenses on cheaper cameras render almost everything in sharp focus. Of course, that makes using selective focus (creatively placing parts of an image out of focus to emphasize other portions) more difficult, but you win some and lose some.

Digital SLRs give you back selective focus, while making it more critical to focus correctly. Fortunately, you have two ways to focus — manual focus and autofocus. Manual focus is accomplished by twisting a focus ring on the lens until the image looks sharp in your viewfinder. (Some cameras provide a viewfinder signal when you have focused correctly manually.) Automatic focus achieves the same results but with the camera deciding when the image is sharply focused. In both cases, the apparent contrast between your subject and its (relatively) blurry surroundings is used to determine that focus point.

Chapter 3: Working with Lenses

In This Chapter

✏ **The myth of the do-it-all lens**

✏ **Choosing prime lenses or zoom lenses**

✏ **Special features you might like**

All digital cameras have lenses, of course. Digital SLR owners just have more of them to choose from. The ability to change lenses is one of the top advantages of the digital single-lens reflex camera, especially for those who want to go longer, wider, deeper, or closer or want to shoot in less light. If the lens currently mounted on your camera doesn't do what you want, just remove it and replace it with one that does (assuming you have the funds to *afford* your dream optics).

You can find a basic discussion of lenses as they apply to all digital cameras in Book II, Chapter 1. This chapter concentrates on the special things you can do with the interchangeable lenses available for dSLRs.

Optical Allusions

You'll find references to a disease called "lens lust" all over the Internet. It's that strange malady that strikes dSLR owners when they discover just how much more they could do if they just had this or that particular lens.

Unfortunately, no single lens can do every job, although a few come close. Several vendors offer an 18mm to 200mm zoom lens (one of them, shown in Figure 3-1, with camera-shake-nullifying vibration reduction built in) that covers most of the focal lengths you need for everyday shooting. But even that lens won't give you ultra-wide-angle shots or superzoom perspectives, and it won't operate well at light levels that call for a large maximum aperture (say, f/2 or f/1.4).

So choosing the right lens is important when you want the best lens for a particular job. Here are some of the things that the "right" lens can do for you:

Figure 3-1: An 18–200mm lens with built-in vibration reduction (left) and a less expensive 18–70mm lens furnished with several digital SLRs as basic equipment.

✦ **Shoot in low light.** The basic zooms furnished with most digital SLRs have maximum apertures of f/3.5 to f/4.5, which is much too "slow" to be useful in low light levels. You can choose other zooms with f/2.8 maximum apertures (although they tend to be expensive) or select a fixed focal length lens with an f/1.4 to f/2.0. Some of these, such as the 50mm f/1.8 lenses offered for most cameras, can be very cheap — $100 or less. But if you're able to spend a little more, you can buy 28mm, 30mm, 35mm, 50mm, or 85mm f/1.4 lenses that can shoot under very dark conditions. They'll be optimized to produce pretty good results wide open, too.

✦ **Shoot sharper.** You can often get better results with a special lens that was designed to produce sharper images rather than to do everything passably well. That 50mm f/1.8 lens you pick up for less than $100 just might be the sharpest lens you own. Or, you might buy a close-up lens that's optimized for macro photography and produces especially sharp images at distances of a few inches or so.

✦ **Shoot wider.** Wide-angle lenses let you take in a broader field of view, which can be useful when there isn't room to move farther away from your subject. The lens that came with your camera probably has a field of view no wider than that of a 28mm lens on a full-frame film SLR. You can get a wider look from lenses designed to provide that extra-broad perspective with a dSLR.

✦ **Shoot farther.** Telephoto lenses let you bring distant objects that much closer to your camera, as you can see in Figure 3-2. The lens that came with your camera probably provides only a moderate telephoto effect, perhaps around 70mm, which, with a 1.5 crop factor, is the equivalent of a 105mm short telephoto on a full-frame 35mm film camera. Longer lenses are easy to find, are fairly affordable, and are fun to use when you want to reach out and almost touch something.

Figure 3-2: A wide-angle lens provides a broader view (top), while a telephoto lens takes you up close to your subject (bottom).

✦ **Shoot closer.** An interchangeable lens you buy may be able to focus on subjects a lot closer to the lens, giving you valuable close-up or *macro* capabilities. Macro photography is literally a whole new world, encompassing subjects that you couldn't capture before (such as small animals or insects), as well as new ultra-close looks at familiar objects.

Primes or Zooms

Digital SLRs can use one of two basic kinds of lenses: prime lenses and zooms. *Prime lenses* are fixed focal length lenses, the kind that were the mainstay of photographers 20 or 30 years ago, before *zooms* (variable focal length lenses) became as sophisticated as they are today. Because prime lenses were the best, sharpest, and fastest optics available, it was even common for photographers to carry around two or three camera bodies, each with a different lens, to avoid having to swap lenses.

Today, zoom lenses are sharper, faster, and more practical for all-around use, but they still lag a bit behind their prime lens cousins. Your own lens kit will probably end up containing a few of each type, each suitable for a different kind of photography.

Pros for primes

Primes have their advantages. For example, if you shoot architecture, you might want a fast wide-angle lens to let you shoot interiors without a tripod or capture images from unusual angles with less lens distortion, as shown in Figure 3-3. Sports photographers might want a similar wide-angle lens, for indoor sports like basketball, mated with a fast telephoto prime lens for night football or baseball under the lights. If you plan on shooting portraits destined for display on the wall, you'll want a sharp, short telephoto lens. Prime lenses with close-focusing capabilities are great for macro work. Wide-angle prime lenses produce results that are sharp enough to enlarge to 20 x 30 inches for display as home décor.

The main drawbacks of using prime lenses is that you must buy a bunch of different lenses to cover a range of focal lengths — plus you must be willing to swap lenses whenever you need to shoot something that doesn't suit the lens currently mounted on the camera. Digital SLR owners can be leery of changing lenses often, especially when working in dusty environments, because of the danger of getting dust on the sensor.

Prose for zooms

There's a lot to like about zoom lenses, too. They are convenient and flexible, allowing you to shoot several different magnifications without moving, so you can frame your photo carefully and precisely right in the camera.

That's important when you don't want to waste valuable pixels by cropping later in an image editor.

Zooms come in several types. There are wide-angle zooms with focal lengths like 10–20mm or 12–24mm. Depending on the crop factor of your camera, these offer the equivalent of 15–30mm to 18–36mm lenses on a full-frame film or digital camera. Because of the distorted looks that these super-wides can sometimes provide, they are often relegated to special situations that truly require an ultra-wide perspective.

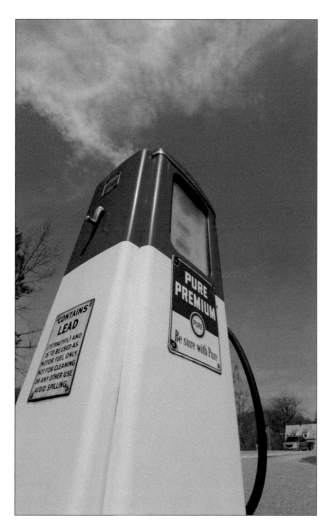

Figure 3-3: Wide-angle prime lenses let you capture photos from unusual angles.

Mid-range zooms are more general-purpose. These have ranges that start at 17 to 18mm and extend out to 55 to 70mm at the telephoto end. They're usually much less expensive than other types of zooms and may be furnished with your camera at an incremental cost of only $100 or so above the cost of the camera body alone. Expect the maximum aperture to shift as you zoom out; such a zoom may offer an f/3.5 opening at the wide-angle end, but only f/4.5 in the telephoto range.

Short telephoto to telephoto zooms sacrifice the wide-angle end of the range to give you a telephoto reach that may extend to 200mm or 300mm. Several popular lenses go from 28mm to 200 or 300mm. The affordable models suffer from the same limited maximum aperture as the mid-range zooms.

Telephoto zoom lenses cover only a telephoto range and tend to extend to much longer focal lengths. One of my favorite lenses is a 170 to 500mm zoom (although the same vendor also offers a very good 50 to 500mm version that is highly prized but much more expensive). Other popular telephoto zooms have ranges like 200–400mm. As with all very long lenses, you'd be crazy to use one of these without a tripod or other sturdy support.

Macro zooms are a specialized kind of zoom lens, usually in the medium telephoto range (from about 100mm to 200mm), that can focus especially close. You'll find these lenses useful outdoors for shooting small animals and insects that must be photographed from a few feet away but that require extra-close focusing. As your critter flits or hops around, you can follow him with your macro zoom while still remaining far enough away to keep him from becoming skittish. The same lens will work with non-moving objects like flowers, too.

Special Features

Some lenses have special features that let them do things that other types of lenses cannot do. Here's a summary of some of those capabilities that are common (or uncommon) among add-on lenses:

✦ **Image stabilization:** Referred to variously as *image stabilization* (by Canon and some other vendors . . . and me), *vibration reduction* (by Nikon and allied companies), *anti-shake, optical image stabilization,* and other names, this feature operates by shifting lens elements around to nullify the shakiness that can result when the camera or photographer wobbles during exposure. Image stabilization can give you the equivalent of two to three shutter-speed increments more steadiness, so you can shoot at 1/30 of a second instead of 1/250 of a second, or, with a long telephoto, 1/250 of a second instead of 1/2000 of a second. Image stabilization does *not* counteract a moving subject and may actually slow down your camera a little when shooting sports. You'll still need a fast shutter speed for that kind of work.

✦ **Perspective control:** These highly specialized and expensive lenses shift the lens elements from side to side and up and down to improve the perspective when photographing buildings or other subjects that converge in the distance, reducing that "falling backward" look, as shown in Figure 3-4.

Figure 3-4: Perspective control lenses compensate for distortion from tilting the camera up to take in the top of a building.

**Book III
Chapter 3**

**Working with
Lenses**

✦ **Close focus:** I've already described the close focusing capabilities of macro lenses. These lenses also offer improved sharpness and may include extra-small apertures (such as f/32 or f/45) to give you extra depth-of-field.

✦ **Focus control:** Some very specialized lenses lend themselves to portrait work by letting you adjust how the out-of-focus background appears in photographs in which single subjects are centered in the frame, such as portraits. The effects you get with focus control lenses are unlike those available with any other type of lens.

Book IV
Taking Great Pictures

The 5th Wave   By Rich Tennant

"Ooo-wait! That's perfect for the clinic's home page. Just stretch it out a little further... little more..."

This minibook is the main course in your digital photography banquet, a sumptuous repast for both veteran and aspiring photographers looking to improve their photographic skills. Each of the six chapters is devoted to a different aspect of digital photography. First, I reveal the basic rules for composing great photos. Then I give you advice on when you should ignore these rules to create even more powerful images. I also provide some tips on dramatic close-up photography and the best ways to produce pleasing portraits of individuals and groups.

If shooting for publication is on your to-do list, you'll want to read the chapter on taking print-worthy photos, accompanied by tips on how to market your pictures. I also provide meaty chapters on sports and action photography and tips on getting good travel photos as you trot the globe.

Chapter 1: Tools and Techniques of Composition

In This Chapter

- Developing a picture concept
- Centering on your main subject
- Selecting vertical or horizontal orientations
- Mastering the Rule of Thirds
- Using lines to draw interest
- Balancing and framing your image
- Avoiding unintentional mergers

*R*andom snapshooting can sometimes yield lucky shots — happy accidents that look good and prompt you to say, "Actually, I *meant* to do that" (even if it wasn't the case). Some Pulitzer Prize–winning photos have resulted from a photographer instinctively squeezing off a shot at what turned out to be a decisive moment in some fast-breaking news event. However, lacking a Pulitzer-winner's intuition, most photographers end up with a larger percentage of pleasing photos when they stop to think about and plan their pictures before putting the viewfinder up to their eyes.

In this chapter, I tell you about the essentials of photo composition that set you on the road to taking great pictures. I introduce all the basic elements of good composition, such as selecting what to include in and what to leave out of a well-designed photograph. You find out some basic rules, such as the Rule of Thirds, and most importantly, when you should ignore these rules in order to get a dramatic effect.

Some of the best photographs use composition to take a stand or say something beyond the photo itself. Figure 1-1 is an example of a photo that makes a subtle statement, juxtaposing the idyllic academic setting of Kent State University in Ohio today with a stark memorial that shows where the body of a slain student fell. In one sense, it's a less graphic version of those chalk outlines you see on police shows, but it's just as effective as a reminder of a place where a human died.

Figure 1-1: A memorial to a slain student stands out against the peaceful, tree-lined campus in the background.

Where will the image be used?

How the photo will be used can affect composition. If you plan to print the picture in a publication or enlarge it for display in a frame, you want a tight composition to maximize sharpness. If you want to use the shot on a Web page, you might want to step back to take in a little extra and crop later with your image editor because the resolution lost from cropping pixels isn't as critical for Web graphics.

Whom are you creating the image for?

You compose a photo for your family differently from a photo that your colleagues or strangers will view. Your family might like a picture better if the composition revolves around that cute new baby. Create a photo that says, "I've been to Paris," and you'll want to include the Eiffel Tower somewhere in the picture so your family and friends will know where you've been. Colleagues might want to see a product highlighted or the CEO shown in a decisive pose. Subject matter that's extraneous for one audience could be important for another.

Selecting a Subject and a Center of Interest

Photographs shouldn't send the person looking at them on a hunting expedition. As interesting as your subject is to you, you don't want viewers puzzling over what's the most important part of the image or perhaps conducting a vote by secret ballot to see who has successfully guessed your intent. Every picture should have a single, strong center of interest. You want to narrow down your subject matter: Rather than include everything of interest in a photo, choose one main subject. Then find secondary objects in the picture that are also interesting (giving the photo depth and richness) but that are still clearly subordinate to the main subject.

Narrowing down your subject matter

Narrowing your subject matter means eliminating everything from your photo that doesn't belong there and concentrating on fewer objects that can form an interesting composition.

Find something in the photograph that the viewer's eye should focus on, thus forming a center of interest. Your center of interest is usually a person, a group, or the object you're seeking to highlight. You don't want eyes roaming around your photo searching for something to look at. Some aspect should jump out and grab your viewers' attention. If other portions of the photo compete for attention, look for ways to eliminate or minimize them.

For example, you can crop more tightly, move to one side or change your angle, ask the extraneous person to leave (your brother-in-law is a good guy; he'll understand), or physically move something to omit it from your composition. Figure 1-2 shows photos of the same goose taken from the same distance, but with a clear center of interest in the second shot.

One good technique when shooting groups is to plan several photographs, each using a different part of the subject matter in view. That way, each person or object can take a turn at being the center of interest, and you won't be looking for ways to reduce the competition among them.

Figure 1-2: To avoid spoiling a shot with secondary geese in the background (left), wait until they move on (right) for a better composition.

Choosing one main subject

You can use several compositional techniques to ensure that the main subject you've selected is, in fact, the center of interest. Here's a quick checklist to follow:

✦ **Make sure that your center of interest is the most prominent object in the picture.** You might think of Aunt Mary as a worthy photo subject, but if she's standing next to a '60s-era minibus with a psychedelic paint job, she might not even be noticed. Large, distinctive, highly unusual, or controversial objects are likely to take on a life of their own and seize the focus of attention in your photograph.

✦ **See that the center of interest is either the brightest object in the photo or at least is not overpowered by a brighter object.** Gaudy colors or bright shapes in the background distract viewers from your main subject. Some elements — such as spotlights at a rock concert or a reflection of the sun on water — become part of the environment and aren't necessarily distracting. Other parts of a photo — such as a bright sail on a boat or a white automobile located behind your subject — can interfere with your carefully planned composition. Eliminate such objects, move them behind something, or otherwise minimize their impact.

✦ **Make sure that your composition has only one center of interest.**
Other things in a photo can be interesting, but they must clearly be
subsidiary to the main center of interest. A child seated on the floor
playing with a puppy would be interesting. However, other puppies in
the photo should be watching or vying for the child's interest, not off
somewhere else in the photo engaged in some distracting activity.
Figure 1-3 shows a photo of some flowers that is colorful, but there's no
real center of interest anywhere in the photo, although the clump of
blossoms at right do attract the eye in its frantic search for something
to focus on.

✦ **Avoid always placing the center of interest in the exact center of the
photograph.** There are many occasions when it's okay to center your
subject, such as for close-ups or portraits. But most of the time, you
want to move the important subject to either side and a little toward
the top or bottom of the frame. Don't take "center" literally in all
cases. Refer to Figure 1-2, shown previously, for an example of a center
of interest moved to one side but still somewhat centrally located.
I explain how to locate your center in interesting spots later in this
chapter.

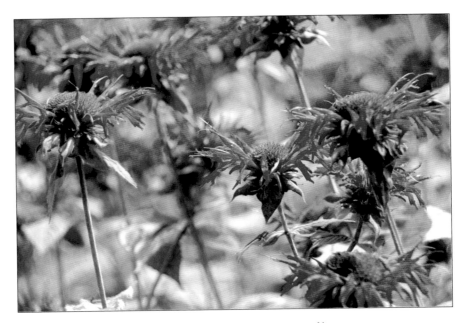

Figure 1-3: This is a bad photo because it has no true center of interest.

full-length or portrait photos), and similar compositions all call for a vertical orientation, as shown in Figure 1-5, which shows a massive blown glass sculpture.

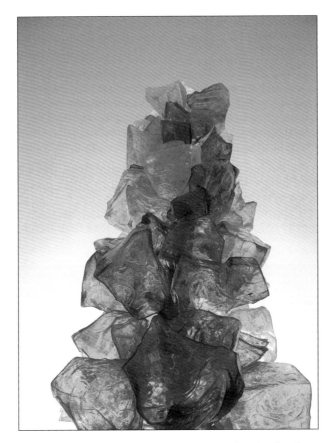

Figure 1-5: Vertical pictures are also appropriate for showing height or vertical movement.

+ **Use a square composition if vertical and horizontal objects in your picture are equally important and you don't want to emphasize one over the other.** A building that is wide but that has a tall tower at one end might look good in a square composition. The important vertical element at one end would keep the image from being too static. Circular images lend themselves to square compositions because the round form fits comfortably inside a square "frame," as shown in Figure 1-6.

Figure 1-6: Some compositions look best when presented within a square.

Arranging Your Subjects

A basic skill in composing great images is finding interesting arrangements within the frame for your subject matter. You need to position your subjects, make sure they're facing an appropriate way, and ensure that they are well-placed in relation to the horizon and other elements of your image. Your first consideration when arranging your subject is to choose the subject's distance from the camera.

Choosing subject distance

Choosing your distance from the subject to provide the desired point of view is one of the first things to do, but it's not something you do once and then forget about. While you take pictures, constantly examine your distance from the subject and move closer or farther away if adjusting your position will improve the composition. Here's how to choose a subject distance:

✦ **To convey a feeling of space and depth, use a wide-angle lens, or, if your back is not already up against a wall, move back.** Standing back from your subject does several things. The foreground area becomes more prominent, adding to the feeling of space. You also take in more of the sky and other surrounding area, giving additional depth.

✦ **Make sure that your subjects don't appear too small when you're moving back; they should still be large enough to be interesting.** Moving too far back is the most common mistake amateur photographers make, as shown in Figure 1-7. If you're showing wide-open spaces in your picture, be certain that it's because you *want* to.

✦ **For photos that emphasize a person, group of people, or a particular object, move in as close as you can.** A close-up viewpoint adds intimacy and shows details and textures of a subject that can't be seen at greater distances, as shown in Figure 1-8. A short telephoto setting is often the best route to getting closer; with a normal or wide-angle lens, you can get some apparent distortion of objects that are very close. With kids or animals, you should not only get close, but also get down to their level and shoot eye-to-eye.

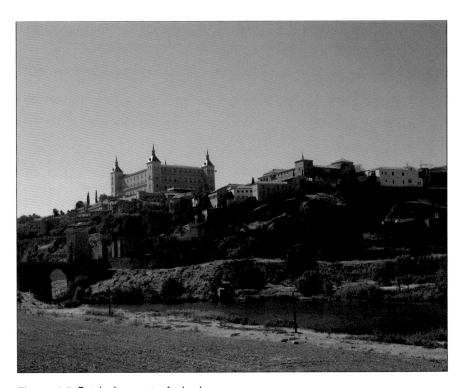

Figure 1-7: But don't move *too* far back.

Figure 1-8: Some kinds of backgrounds can be found in nature, but avoid the cluttered background in this shot.

✦ **Move so you fill the frame completely with interesting things.** Whether you're shooting close up to your subject or at a distance, your composition should not include anything that isn't needed to make the picture. Full frames mean less enlargement and sharper pictures, too!

Optimizing backgrounds

Unless you're taking a picture in the dead of night or on a featureless sand dune or snow field, you'll have some sort of background to contend with. A background can be a plus or a minus depending on how you use it in your composition. Here are some tips for making the most of your background:

✦ **Check your background to make sure that it's not gaudy, brightly colored, or busy.** The background should not be more interesting than the subject, nor should it be a distraction.

✦ **For portraits, a plain background (such as a seamless backdrop) can be effective.** A plain, featureless background can work for portraits as long is it isn't totally bland. Notice how professional photographers who pose subjects against a seamless background still use lights to create an interesting gradient or series of shadows in the background.

✦ **Outdoors, trees, grass, cloud-studded skies, plain walls, and other textured surfaces can make good backgrounds.** Such backgrounds are interesting without overpowering your subject (refer to Figure 1-8).

✦ **Watch for strong lines or shapes in the background that don't lead the eye to your subject.** Straight or curved lines are good for compositions but not if they distract the viewer from your subject. Also watch out for things in the background that seem to grow out of your subjects or the borders of the image. (These are called *mergers*, discussed later in this chapter.)

✦ **Consider using *depth of field* (the amount of the image that's in sharp focus) to make your background blurry.** Figure 1-8 uses this technique to make the foliage background less distracting.

Because of how their lenses are designed, consumer digital cameras often show *everything* in sharp focus. Workarounds include using longer lens zoom settings and wider lens openings. You find out exactly what these are and more in Book IV, Chapter 2.

The Rule of Thirds

The position of your subject matter within a picture is one of the most important decisions you make. Whether you can move the subject or objects around, change your position, or wait until everything moves to the right spot, you should constantly be aware of how your subject matter is arranged. Photographers often consciously or unconsciously follow a guideline called the *Rule of Thirds*. It's simply a way of dividing your picture horizontally and vertically into thirds (see Figure 1-9). The best place to position important subject matter is often at one of the points located one-third of the way from the top or bottom and sides of the frame.

Placing important objects at imaginary junction points

Follow these steps to compose your pictures effectively using the Rule of Thirds:

1. **Divide the frame into thirds horizontally and vertically.**

   Above all, you want to avoid having your subject matter centered. By imagining the frame in thirds, you automatically begin thinking of those ideal, off-center positions.

2. **Try to have important objects, particularly your center of interest, at one of the four intersections of the imaginary lines that divide the picture (refer to Figure 1-9).**

3. **Avoid having objects at the edge of a picture unless the part that isn't shown isn't important.**

Figure 1-9: To divide your image into thirds, picture the imaginary lines shown on this image.

If you're taking a picture of a group of people, cropping out part of the building they're standing next to or trimming off half a tree that's not an important part of the composition is okay. But don't cut off heads!

When to break the Rule of Thirds

Sometimes, you want to break the Rule of Thirds. There are almost as many exceptions to the rule as there are good reasons to apply it, which is why the rule should be considered only a guideline. Think of the Rule of Thirds as a lane marker on a highway. Sometimes you want to stay within the markers; other times, like when you see an obstruction in the road, you want to wander outside the lines. (If you happen to move from the United States to the United Kingdom, you'll find that it's wise to swap sides and use the lane markers on the opposite side of the road.)

You might want to ignore this handy rule when

+ **Your main subject matter is too large to fit comfortably at one of the imaginary intersection points.** You might find that positioning an object at the "correct" location crops it at the top, bottom, or side. Move it a bit to another point in your composition if you need to see the whole thing.

✦ **Centering the image would help illustrate a concept.** Perhaps you want to show your subject surrounded on all sides by adversity or by a threatening environment. Placing the subject at one of the intersection points implies motion or direction, as if the subject were about to flee the picture entirely. However, putting the center of interest in the very center of the picture gives the subject nowhere to hide.

✦ **You want to show symmetry.** Centering a symmetrically oriented subject that's located in a symmetrically oriented background can produce a harmonious, geometric pattern that is pleasing, even if it is a bit static. If the subject itself makes you think of motion, a square image can even boast a bit of "movement," as shown in Figure 1-10.

Figure 1-10: Sometimes a square picture can have an interesting geometrical arrangement.

Incorporating Direction and Movement

A photo composition creates an entire world for the viewer to explore. You don't want to destroy the illusion by calling attention to the rest of the universe outside the frame. Here's how to orient people and other objects in a picture:

✦ **If your subjects are people, animals, statues, or anything that you think of as having a front end and back end, make sure they are either facing the camera or facing into the frame rather than out of it.**

If a person seems to be looking out of a picture, rather than somewhere within it, viewers will spend more time wondering what the person is looking at than examining the actual person. The human doesn't actually have to be looking at any object in particular as long as they are looking somewhere within the picture.

✦ **If objects in the frame are moving or pointed in a particular direction, make sure they are heading into the frame rather than out of it.**

A stationary automobile, a windmill, a palm-tree bent over by a strong wind, anything with a sense of direction to it should be facing into the frame for the same reason that a person should be looking into it, as shown in Figure 1-11.

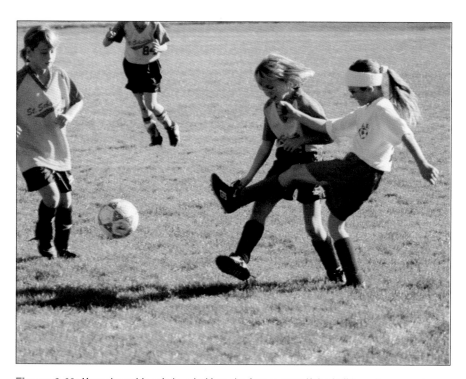

Figure 1-11: Here the subject is headed into the frame, even if the ball is on its way out.

✦ **Add extra space in front of any fast-moving object (such as a race car) so that the object has somewhere to go while remaining in the frame.**

If an object is moving, having a little more space in the frame in front of it is best so that the viewer doesn't get the impression that it's on its way out of view. In Figure 1-11, for example, you wouldn't want to crop the image any more tightly on the left because you'd need to leave room for the speeding ball.

Using Straight Lines and Curves

After you have the basics out of the way, progressing to the next level and creating even better compositions is easy. All you need to know is when to apply or break some simple rules. Just remember that one of the key elements of good composition is a bit of surprise. Viewers like to see subjects arranged in interesting ways rather than lined up in a row.

Lines within your image can help your compositions by directing the eye toward the center of interest. The lines don't have to be explicit; subtle shapes can work just as well. Try these techniques:

✦ **Look for straight lines in your image and try to use them to lead the eye to the main subject area.**

Some lines are obvious, such as fences or a seashore leading off into the distance. These kinds of lines are good when you want a dramatic composition, like the one in Figure 1-12, which includes multiple sets of horizontal and vertical lines.

✦ **Find diagonal lines to direct the attention to the center of interest.**

Diagonal lines are better than straight lines, which are static and not particularly interesting.

✦ **Use repetitive lines to create an interesting pattern.**

Repetitive lines could be multiple lines within a single object, such as the grout lines in a brick wall. Repetitive lines could also be several different parallel or converging objects, such as a road's edges, the centerline of the road, and the fence that runs along the road. Strong repetitive lines can become a pleasing composition in themselves, like the ones in Figure 1-12.

✦ **Curved lines, which are more graceful than straight lines, can lead the viewer gently from one portion of the composition to another.**

Curving roads are a good example of arcs and bends that can contribute to a composition. Other graceful curves include body parts of living things, such as the necks of flamingos, as shown in Figure 1-13.

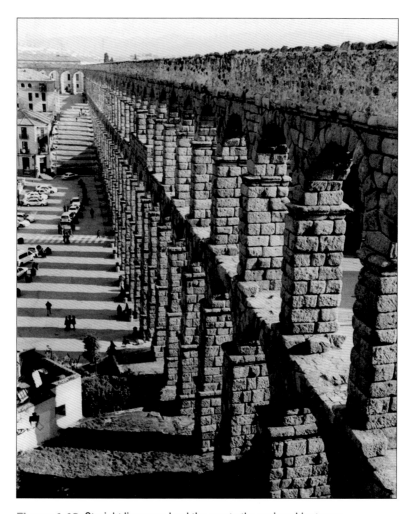

Figure 1-12: Straight lines can lead the eye to the main subject area.

✦ **Look for shapes within your composition to add interest.**

Three objects arranged in a triangle make a picture inherently more interesting than if the objects form a square shape. Your eye naturally follows the lines of the triangle toward each of the three points, or apexes, whereas squares or rectangles don't point anywhere. Instead of posing groups of people in rows and columns, stack them in interesting arrangements that make shapes the viewer's eye can explore. Figure 1-13 uses two flamingos to create an interesting set of repeating curved shapes that almost form a heart.

Figure 1-13: Curved lines form graceful, more harmonious pointers for the eyes.

Balancing an Image

If you place every element of interest in a photograph on one side or another, leaving little or nothing to look at on the opposite side, the picture is unbalanced, like a seesaw with a child at one end and no one on the other. The best pictures have an inherent balance that makes them look graceful.

To balance your image, arrange objects so that anything large on one side is balanced by something of importance on the other side. This is not the same as having multiple centers of interest. A group of people arrayed on one side need only be balanced out by having a tree or building on the other. Or a chess piece Queen can be balanced by other pieces on the opposite side of the image, as shown in Figure 1-14.

You can balance objects in two ways:

✦ **Symmetrical balance:** Have the objects on either side of the frame be of roughly similar size or weight.

✦ **Asymmetrical balance:** Have the objects on opposing sides be of different size or weight.

Figure 1-14: Other elements of the photo can balance the composition.

Framing an Image

Photos are frequently put in frames for a good reason: A border around a picture defines the picture's shape and concentrates attention on the image within the frame. You can use framing to provide an attractive border around your own pictures by using these tips:

✦ **In the foreground, look for obvious framing shapes in which you can place your composition.**

You won't easily miss the most readily apparent frames: doorways, windows, arches, and space between buildings. These have the advantage of being a natural part of the scene, like the cliffs in Figure 1-15, and not something you contrived in order to create a frame. In this illustration, the cliffs at the left side of the image partially frame the ocean inlet at right.

✦ **Make your own frames by changing position until foreground objects create a border around your image.**

Find a curving tree branch and back up until the scenic view you want to capture is wrapped in its leafy embrace. Climb inside something and use an opening as a frame.

✦ **Place your frame in the foreground.**

Shapes in the background that delineate your image don't make an effective frame. You want something that appears to be in front of your subject matter, just like a real frame would be.

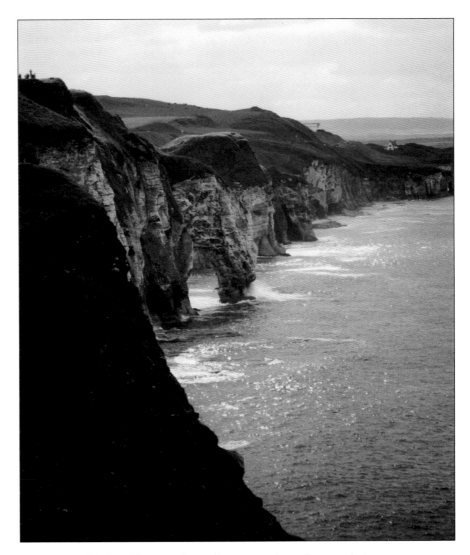

Figure 1-15: Existing objects can be used to create a frame for your photo.

✦ **Use a frame to create a feeling of depth.**

A flat-looking image can jump to 3-D life when it's placed in a frame. Usually, you want to have the frame and your main subject in focus, but you can sometimes use an out-of-focus frame to good effect.

✦ **Use a telephoto lens setting to compress your frame and your subject; use a wide-angle lens setting to add distance between the frame and your main subject.**

With a telephoto lens, however, you have to be especially careful to keep the frame in focus.

What's That Tree Doing Growing Out of My Head?

Mergers are the unintentional combining of portions of an image. With our stereoscopic vision, our eyes and brain distinctly separate objects that are farther apart. Other visual clues let us keep objects separate, such as the relative size of the objects compared with our knowledge of their actual size.

For example, we know that a tiny human is located in the distance whereas another human in the same field of view who appears to be four times as large is simply closer. However, viewed through the one-dimensional perspective of a camera lens, it's easy for objects that we know to be distinct to merge into one.

We've all seen photographs of hapless photographic subjects posed with what looks like a telephone pole growing out of their heads. Sometimes, the merger is with a border of the image or a simple joining of two objects, as in Figure 1-16, in which the penguin(s) at right appear to share a body. This mistake is easier to make than you might think — and easier to avoid than you realize. Follow these steps:

1. **When composing an image, look behind the subject at the objects in the background. Then, examine the borders of the image to look for things "attached" to the edges.**

   By concentrating, you can see how the background and foreground will appear when merged in your final photograph.

   Sometimes it helps to close one eye while viewing the scene.

2. **If an unwanted merger seems likely, move the subject to either side or change your position slightly to eliminate the juxtaposition.**

Like all the other rules discussed in this chapter, you can ignore the anti-merger guideline (even if you aren't a captain of industry looking to build a giant conglomerate). Keep in mind that you can creatively use mergers to make photographs that are humorous. You just might want that forest ranger to appear to have a tree growing out of his or her head.

Figure 1-16: A two-headed penguin at right? No, just an unwanted merger.

Chapter 2: Close-Up Photography

In This Chapter

- Mastering the jargon
- Previewing the fun of macro photography
- Choosing your location
- Assembling the necessary equipment
- Taking that photo
- Digital single lens reflexes and close-ups

One area that has really benefited from the digital single lens reflex (dSLR) revolution has been close-up, or *macro,* photography. Although digital cameras of any sort make close-up pictures fairly easy, you always have the pesky problem of trying to figure out whether you framed your picture properly — and whether it's in sharp focus. Tiny LCD (liquid crystal display) screens on the back of a camera should do the job — theoretically — but they're often difficult to view, especially under bright light. Fortunately, a growing number of digital cameras have back-panel LCDs that measure 2.5 inches or more, so even if you don't have a digital SLR, you can easily take good close-up photos.

With a digital SLR, though, you're *always* looking through the same lens used to take the picture (unless you choose to view the LCD on the back of the camera after the picture is taken). Digital SLRs are designed for bright, easy viewing and focusing of your image. Unless the light is very dim indeed, you can usually see almost exactly what you're going to get as well as whether your camera's autofocus mechanism (or your own trusty fingers) have zeroed in on the exact point of focus you want. Digital SLRs can turn a fun activity into an uproariously good time.

However, you don't need a dSLR or camera with an electronic viewfinder (EVF) to enjoy close-up photography. Macro photography can be one of the most satisfying forms of digital photography. Any intermediate digital camera has all the features that you need to take great close-ups that will astound your family, friends, and colleagues. And although a beautiful scenic photo or an attractive portrait will elicit praise and appreciation, a well-crafted close-up photo is guaranteed to generate *oohs* and *aahs* and "How did you ever take that picture?" comments. Close-up photography takes us into fascinating new worlds without the time or expense of an exotic trip.

For example, if you collect coins or stamps, miniature teddy bears, porcelain figurines, model trains, or nearly anything smaller than a breadbox (or bread-boxes themselves), you'll love the ability to document your collection. Have a garden full of prize roses? Display them even in the dead of winter through digital photos. Have a thing for insects? Grab a picture of the little beasts in their natural habitat. Some of the best applications of close-up photography involve crafts and hobbies.

You don't have to be a forensic expert specializing in crime scene investigations to find interesting photos in the macro world. Just about any household object, if photographed from an inch or two away, is transformed into an abstract scene worthy of the most artsy photographic expression.

If you haven't tried close-up photography, I hope this chapter encourages you to do so. I show you here how to set up a close-up "studio" and take macro photos the painless way.

Defining Macro Photography

The first thing to do as you begin your exploration of close-up photography is to get some jargon out of the way. There's nothing wrong with calling up-close-and-personal pictures *close-ups*, but within the photography realm, you commonly find some other terms in frequent use (and misuse). Here are some of them:

✦ **Close-up photography:** This term has been co-opted by the movie industry (as in "All right, Mr. DeMille, I'm ready for my close-up," from the film classic, *Sunset Boulevard*). A *close-up* is generally considered to be a tight shot of a single person (say, only the face and shoulders) or of another object of similar size. It's okay to refer to close-up photography for what you do with your digital camera, as I've done in the chapter title. That's a term that most people, even photographic neophytes, understand.

✦ **Microphotography:** *Microphotography* results in microphotographs — that is, microfilm images. You wouldn't apply this term to pictures taken through a microscope, although it is sometimes (incorrectly) used that way.

✦ **Photomicrography:** This is the correct term for taking pictures through a microscope. Although photomicrography is chiefly within the purview of scientists and researchers, it can also be a fun activity for digital photographers who have the special equipment needed to hook a digital camera up to a microscope. Everything from microscopic animals to human hairs can make fascinating photographs, but you generally need a higher-end digital camera and some specialized gear to capture the images. Photomicrography is beyond the scope of this book.

✦ **Macro photography:** This is the brand of close-up that is the focus of this chapter. Generally, *macro photography* is considered any picture taken from about 12 inches or less from the subject, down to half an inch or even closer. *Macro* is derived from the Greek word *makro*, meaning "long," but it has come to mean "large" and the exact opposite of *micro*. However, that's not exactly the case in photography. A macro photograph is not a huge picture (the opposite of a microphotograph), but rather a normal-sized photo of a tiny object that has been made to appear large, as shown in Figure 2-1. You might not even be able to recognize common objects when enlarged in a macro photograph.

Figure 2-1: Small objects becoming large are the result of macro photographic techniques.

Why Digital Macro Photography Is Cool

Digital cameras and macro photography were made for each other. In many ways, digital cameras can be far superior to an ordinary film camera when it comes to taking close-up pictures. Consider these advantages:

+ **Close-focusing lenses:** Digital camera lenses are ideal for focusing up close. Without getting too technical, macro photos are made with any camera by moving the lens farther and farther away from the film (or sensor, in the case of a digital camera). Film cameras require moving the lens quite a ways out to get a decent macro effect. For example, a 50mm lens on a 35mm single lens reflex camera (or a digital SLR with a full-size sensor) must be moved 4 inches out from the film or sensor to get a life-size (1:1) image. In contrast, an 8mm lens on a digital camera with a small sensor, roughly the equivalent of the 50mm lens on an SLR, needs to move only a total of about ⅝ of an inch to provide the same magnification. Clearly, close focusing is much easier to incorporate into a digital camera.

In the macro photography arena, you'll see close-focusing capabilities described in terms of magnification rather than the distance from the subject. As a beginning macro photographer, you might be more interested in how close you can get: 6 inches, 3 inches, or whatever. However, realize that the size of the final image at any given distance varies depending on the zoom setting of your lens. That is, an image taken from 6 inches away at the wide-angle setting might be one-fourth the size of one taken from the same distance at the longest zoom setting. Comparing the amount of magnification is more useful. For example, a 1:1 image is exactly the same size in your camera whether taken from 1 inch away with the wide-angle setting or 6 inches away with the zoom setting. (Although the size is the same, the way the image looks is quite different, and I discuss that later in this chapter.)

+ **Easy framing of your image:** Virtually every digital camera features an LCD screen, like the one shown in Figure 2-2, that shows almost exactly what you'll get in your finished photograph. (The LCD might trim a bit of the edges from the image, but getting more than you expected is far superior to getting less.) Inexpensive point-and-shoot film cameras, if they have macro capabilities at all, don't show you exactly what your image will look like. Cameras with an electronic viewfinder (EVF) are also easy to use for framing close-ups.

+ **Immediate results:** Close-up photography can be tricky, and the last thing you want to do is wait for your film to come back from the photo-finisher to find out whether your pictures came out. With a digital camera, you can review your results on the LCD immediately, delete bad shots, and keep taking pictures until you get exactly what you want.

Figure 2-2: LCD viewfinders make it easy to frame your close-ups.

Picking a Place to Shoot

Where you shoot your macro photos can be as significant as what you're shooting. You might want to take your photographs in the tightly controlled environment of your kitchen, using a tabletop as your platform for your model trains or other objects. Maybe you want to venture out into the field to stalk the creatures of nature.

Sometimes you have a choice of where you shoot, and sometimes you don't. For example, if you want to photograph sea life at the beach, you pretty much have to take your pictures there. Comparatively, you can photograph a tree frog on a tree or pop him in a mayonnaise jar along with a leaf and stick to re-create, as the late, great, comedian Mitch Hedberg said, his natural environment.

Table 2-1 shows some of the advantages and disadvantages of location and studio shooting.

Table 2-1	Location Shooting versus Studio Shooting	
Factor	**Location**	**Studio**
Setting	Natural environment.	Studio environment.
Transport	Equipment such as tripods and reflectors must be carried. Some items might not be available.	All equipment is right at hand.
Background	Little control over background, unless you bring some props.	Background can be chosen to complement subject.
Lighting	Realistic natural lighting, but you have less control.	Lighting might look artificial, but you have perfect control.
Environment	Bad weather can be a problem.	Weather is not a factor.
Setup	Setting up picture can be tedious; settings might be transitory and impermanent.	Setups can be left in place as long as desired.
Consistency	Taking groups of pictures with similar look is difficult.	Control over lighting and backgrounds means a consistent look that's useful for photographs of collections and so on.

Setting Up Your Macro Studio

You don't need a real studio for macro photography, of course. That's one of the cool parts of taking close-ups. Any nook or cranny that you can spare in your home or work environment can be designated as a studio area. All you need to do is keep the area reasonably neat and free of clutter so that you can set up and take macro photos on a few minutes' notice. You can also keep a semipermanent close-up studio, like I do, for stuff that my wife sells on eBay. I have a seamless backdrop up in a little-used corner so that an item that's destined for sale can be set up and photographed anytime. A macro studio, such as the one shown in Figure 2-3, requires so little space that you won't hesitate to dedicate a small portion of your living space in exchange for the convenience of having a special area you can use anytime.

Of course, you're free to create little macro studios on an *ad hoc* basis, using your kitchen table, hearth, or any convenient location as you need.

Many of the close-up photos in this book, such as Figure 2-1, were taken on impulse right here at the desk where I work. I just grab a piece of white paper from my inkjet printer, lean it against any convenient support, and drop the object I want to photograph on my miniature, seamless backdrop.

I often use the built-in flash of my digital camera with one or two other pieces of printer paper strategically located to reflect the light onto my subject. Less than a minute after I started, I plug my camera into the USB cable that rests by my keyboard and watch my photos appear on the screen.

Figure 2-3: Any small corner can become a macro studio.

Of course, you can get better results than I get with my quickie photos if you collect the right equipment and gear for your ministudio. This next section explains exactly what you need.

Background check

In many cases, you want close-up backgrounds that are plain and unobtrusive because they allow your subject matter to stand out without any distracting extraneous material. That generally means a light background for darker objects and a dark background for light objects. You don't need to stick with stark white or inky black backgrounds unless your plan is to drop out the background in Photoshop or another image editor so that you can combine the subject with some other photograph. A light pastel background often works well for dark objects, and a medium-dark shade looks good with very light objects.

TIP

The amount of light that falls on the background helps determine its lightness or darkness. A soft gray background can appear to be almost white or fairly dark depending on the amount of illumination that reaches it. Don't be afraid to experiment.

So-called *seamless* backdrops are very popular. They provide a continuous (seamless) surface on which the subject can rest while blending smoothly into a vertical background. Depending on how you light the seamless backdrop, it can appear to be a single shade or can provide varying amounts of separation between the foreground and background, as shown in Figure 2-4.

Figure 2-4: Seamless backgrounds make an attractive setting for close-up photos.

Here are the main types of backgrounds that you'll probably use for your macro photography:

✦ **A few yards of cloth:** I really like plain, solid-colored cloth as a backdrop because it's rugged and versatile. If it gets dirty, you can usually just throw it in the wash. I buy pieces about 45–54 inches wide and 8 or 9 feet long in several different colors, including pure black and pure white as well as soft pastels and bright colors. The longer lengths let me use the cloth as a portrait background if I need to.

Artificial velour is extremely useful. One side has a soft surface that really soaks up light. A black velour cloth can make a perfectly black background almost guaranteed not to show shadows. The other side of velour has a shinier texture that you can use for some types of photos. Leave the cloth smooth. Avoid fabrics with a pronounced reflective sheen, such as satin/sateen and vinyl. The simplest fabrics won't cost you more than a few dollars a yard.

✦ **A roll of seamless paper:** Rolls of true photographic seamless paper can be expensive (around $40 for a 9-x-36-foot roll) and hard to find — you need to seek out a camera store that sells to professional photographers. If you can't find such a store locally, online sources sell paper in 53-inch-wide by 12-yard rolls for about $20, although shipping can add a considerable amount to the cost. If seamless paper is what you want, however, you can take a hacksaw and cut the roll in half to make the size a little more manageable for ministudio work. Because seamless paper eventually gets torn and dirty, it's nice to be able to unroll a little more so that you always have a fresh background.

Check out craft and packaging stores for large rolls of sturdy wrapping paper as an alternate source for seamless backgrounds. Avoid the paper with mistletoe and bunnies and stick to plain colors. However, don't be afraid to experiment. A smooth section of Kraft paper (like that found on rolls of brown shipping paper) might make a handsome backdrop for some subjects.

✦ **Posterboard:** I've used a lot of posterboard as seamless backgrounds for close-up photos of smaller objects. *Hint:* Use duct tape to curve it into place. At a few cents a sheet, you can afford many different colors. However, watch for posterboard that has a slightly shiny surface. If you use it with soft and diffuse lighting, however, that shouldn't be a problem.

Visible means of support

You have to provide support for your background material, your lighting equipment (if you use some), and your camera. Fortunately, the same supports that work for close-ups serve admirably for other types of photography. (See Book IV, Chapter 3 for a discussion of gear for people pictures.) If you plan to take a lot of studio-type photos, buying some good-quality equipment of this type can be a shrewd move. I'm still using the same tripod and light stands that I purchased while in college. A few hundred dollars for that stuff seemed like a lot of money at the time, but I haven't had to spend a penny since then even though I've gone from large professional cameras to teensy digital cameras in the interim.

You can buy tripods, light stands, and other equipment relatively inexpensively. However, I can tell you from personal experience that a $100 tripod is a lot more than twice as sturdy and twice as useful as a $50 model. If you're going to spend the money replacing a flimsy tripod or two anyway, start out with a good one.

Here are some of the supports you can find:

✦ **Background supports:** You'll find that cloth backgrounds are so light-weight that you can support them with almost anything. Duct tape can suspend a piece of cloth from any piece of furniture that happens to be around. I tend to use 7-foot *light stands,* which are aluminum supports that telescope down to a compact size and have tripod legs at the bottom to keep them upright. Set up a pair of light stands, suspend a wooden dowel between them as a horizontal support for your cloth, and you're all set.

Light stands can also support some rolls of paper if you substitute a wood closet pole or metal pipe for the wooden dowel. You can also build a simple background stand out of lumber. Or, if you do a lot of shooting in a basement area (as I do), use metal supports fastened directly to the ceiling joists, as shown in Figure 2-5.

Figure 2-5: Seamless paper can be supported in a variety of ways.

✦ **Lighting supports:** Light stands are good but might be a little too large to position effectively for close-up photography. In many cases, you can skip light stands or special lights altogether and use household desk lamps that rest right on your background setup.

✦ **Camera supports:** A tripod is essential for macro photography. You need to be able to fix your camera in one position and lock it down while you take your photos. That's particularly true if you use your digital camera's

LCD screen to compose or focus your image. It doesn't matter whether you're relying on your camera's automatic focus or focusing manually: A tripod can give you the fixed position that you need. A tripod also allows you to photograph several subjects from the same distance and angle, thus adding an important measure of consistency.

You can find more information on choosing a good tripod in Book II, Chapter 5.

Lighting equipment

Unless your subject is a candle or a glow-in-the-dark Halloween skeleton, you need some sort of lighting to illuminate the scene. Your choices include the existing light in the room, electronic flash, and incandescent illumination, such as desk lamps or photoflood lights. The following sections explain what you need to know about each option.

Existing light

Photographers used to refer to existing light by the term *available light* until someone pointed out that a 400-pound Klieg light is technically *available* if you happen to have one left over from the last motion picture you shot. Today, we call it *existing light* on the presumption that lighting doesn't exist if it isn't already available on-site. Here are some tips for using existing light:

+ **Use with modulation:** You can *modulate* (modify) existing light, of course, if you have reflectors or other gadgets about. If existing light is too harsh, you can soften it by using a piece of white cardboard as a reflector. Foam board also works and is stiffer and easier to position than cardboard.

  Avoid colors other than white unless you really, really want a color cast in your photo.

+ **Foiled again:** A piece of aluminum foil can make a brighter, more contrasty reflector. Crinkle it up so that the light it reflects is more diffuse. Otherwise, foil behaves a lot like a mirror, which is something you don't want. Mylar space blankets also make a lightweight, portable metallic reflector.

+ **For all in tents:** Pros often use miniature white tents when photographing a shiny object. You can make a simple one out of a translucent milk jug. Place your subject inside the tent, apply plenty of light from the outside of the tent, and then shoot through a hole in the top or side. You'll end up with beautiful soft lighting and no reflections of the surrounding room on the shiny subject matter.

  Make sure that the camera lens itself doesn't reflect on the object!

✦ **Block that light:** Sometimes you want to subtract light rather than add it to your subject. Put black cloth or cardboard outside the subject area to absorb light and darken shadows for a dramatic effect.

When using incandescent lights, make sure that your camera's white balance control has been set for interior illumination. Many digital cameras can be set to automatically recognize and adjust the white balance for various lighting conditions. Fluorescent lighting often requires a different setting, and some cameras will have adjustments for both warm and cool fluorescent bulbs. You can find out more about correcting colors in Book V, Chapter 1.

Electronic flash

Electronic flash is often useful for quickie shots like those I take right at my desk, but flash is often not the best choice for close-ups. Here are some reasons why not:

✦ **Too much light:** Flash is often too powerful for close-up pictures taken inches away from the camera. Flash is intended for shooting from several feet or more.

✦ **Can't project the outcome:** The effect of the lighting isn't easy to visualize with electronic flash because the subject is illuminated for only a fraction of a second. After you take your photo and review it on the LCD screen, you might find that the light is too harsh, is placed incorrectly, or illuminates the wrong part of your image.

✦ **Don't need it for stop-action:** One of the major advantages of electronic flash, stopping the action of moving subjects, doesn't really apply to close-up pictures, which are usually taken of stationary subjects at a fixed distance.

You can use four kinds of electronic flash when taking close-up photos. You can find a more thorough discussion of these flash options in Book IV, Chapter 3 (where I discuss photographing people). However, here's a quick summary of your choices.

✦ **Your camera's built-in flash:** This is usually your worst choice for illuminating your subject. For one thing, the flash is likely to be aimed quite a distance past your area of interest — or, in many cases, blocked by parts of the camera or lens. When I use my camera's built-in flash for close-ups, I always include several pieces of white reflective material outside the field of view to bounce the light back onto the subject. Your flash is likely to be too harsh, thus washing out the details of your subject.

Light placed at an angle, rather than straight on, can often produce better close-up illumination.

✦ **External flash:** You can find a connector on many digital cameras for linking to an external flash unit, which you can buy for $50 to $400 or more (for the dedicated units built specifically for the more advanced amateur cameras). Sometimes these are located on top of the camera in the form of a shoe (a hot shoe) that can be used to mount the flash and provide an electrical connection at the same time. Or, your camera might have a special connector — a PC/X connector, as shown in Figure 2-6.

Figure 2-6: Your camera may have a connection for plugging in an external flash unit.

PC doesn't stand for *personal computer,* but rather *Prontor-Compur,* which is the German mechanical shutter–building company that invented the connection.

Optional flash units range from more powerful versions of your camera's built-in flash to expensive studio flash units. Check out Book IV, Chapter 3, for tips on how to use external flash units of this type.

✦ **Slave flash:** These are a kind of external electronic flash that includes a photocell that triggers the unit automatically when another flash unit is fired. Slaves let you use several flashes at once, if you can match the slave's operation to your camera's flash functions. (Some cameras use a pre-flash that can trigger some slaves prematurely.)

✦ **Ring lights:** These are circular flash units that can be fitted around the circumference of your camera's lens. They provide even lighting that is designed especially for close-ups. Usually, only professionals who do a great deal of macro photography can justify the price of a ring light.

Incandescent lights

Incandescent lights — including gooseneck desk lamps (which I use), high-intensity lamps, or photographic floodlights — are great for lighting close-ups. Their advantages include

✦ **Easy preview:** You can see exactly what your lighting effect will be.

✦ **Flexibility:** Your options are wide-open. Use one, two, three, or as many lamps as you need. Arrange them as you like. Create backlit effects or soft lighting. Use a high-intensity lamp when you want a very contrasty quality to your illumination. Turn to a soft-white desk lamp when you need diffused light.

✦ **Inexpensive:** I buy desk lamps for less than $10 and use them in various combinations to get well-lit close-ups. What other photographic equipment can you buy that cheap?

Their disadvantages include

✦ **Heat:** Don't let your high-intensity lamps burn your subject. And forget about using them to photograph ice cream sundaes.

✦ **Power:** You need lots of power and thick cords if you're using multiple incandescent lights.

✦ **Color of their light:** You need to make sure that your camera's white balance is set correctly for the reddish hue of incandescent lights.

✦ **Burnout:** Have some extra bulbs available in case one of your lamps burns out during a shooting session.

Other equipment

You might find some other equipment handy when shooting macro photos. For example, slide-copying attachments are available for some digital cameras. These attachments let you make high-resolution digital grabs of 35mm color slides without the need for an expensive slide scanner. (For more information on scanning slides, see Book VII, Chapter 2.) Even if your digital camera focuses closely, special close-up lenses let you get even closer.

Here's a rundown of some of the most popular add-ons for close-up photography:

✦ **Slide copiers:** Slide copiers are great for converting your existing collection of color transparencies to digital form. All you need is a close-focusing digital camera and a copier attachment, which mainly consists of a holder for the slide and a diffusing panel that sits behind the slide to soften the light you use to illuminate it. You might be able to get good quality with such a device, and the quality is certainly better than what you get with most flatbed scanners jury-rigged to scan slides.

✦ **Single-lens reflex add-ons:** If you happen to own a digital camera with removable lenses (with basic SLR digital cameras finally dipping below the $1,000 price point, that's not altogether unlikely), you can use similar accessories offered for film-oriented SLRs, such as bellows, extension tubes, and reversing rings.

- **A bellows,** such as the one shown in Figure 2-7, moves your camera's lens farther from the sensor, enlarging the image over a continuous range. The downside is that the farther the bellows is extended, the less light reaches the sensor, producing long exposures. Bellows attachments are also expensive.

- **Extension tubes** do much the same as a bellows but over fixed distances.

- **Reversing rings** let you mount your camera's lens on a bellows so that the front of the lens faces the sensor. With removable lenses that weren't designed for macro photography, reversing the lens can produce sharper results *and* increase the magnification.

Figure 2-7: This bellows is expensive but versatile if you have a digital SLR camera.

✦ **Close-up lenses:** Even if your digital camera focuses very close, you might want to get even closer. That's where close-up lenses come in. Although they're called lenses (because they function as one), close-up lenses look like clear glass filters with a curved surface. These lenses fasten to the front of your digital camera's lens using a screw mount or other arrangement. Labeled with designations such as #1, #2, and #3 (referring to a measurement of magnification called *diopter strength*), you can use only one or use them in combination to produce varying amounts of magnification. For example, you can combine a #1 and a #3 for a plus-4 magnification. The amount of magnification that a particular close-up lens or combination provides depends on the zoom setting of the lens and its normal close-focusing ability.

For example, if you have a lens that focuses as close as one meter, a +1 close-up lens enables you to focus down to half a meter, a +2 diopter to one-third of meter, and a +3 diopter to one-fourth of a meter (a little less than ten inches for the non–metrically inclined). As you can see, these close-up lenses can bring macro capability to optics that aren't able to focus very close (one meter is the pits, close-up-wise) and can bring super macro capability to lenses that already can focus very close to your subject.

Serious macro photographers purchase a set of several close-up lenses and use them in combination to get the magnification they want.

Shooting Tips for Macro Photography

The first part of this chapter helps outfit you for macro photography. Most of the equipment and gear discussed can be used for location shooting or in your home or office studio, although outdoor close-ups can make some of the tools, such as cardboard reflectors, tricky to use.

This next section provides you with tips for shooting good close-up photographs, using common techniques the pros take advantage of all the time, plus a few things I learned the hard way myself.

Positioning your subject and background

You've chosen your subject to photograph, whether it's a pewter soldier from your collection or a terrified tree frog. You've selected a background to isolate and/or flatter your subject. What's next?

Set up your subject on its background so that it won't move. Although that can be tricky with the tree frog, it's less of a challenge with an inanimate object, such as the pewter soldier. I often use bits of modeling clay that can be hidden underneath an object to hold it at the correct angle. I also use pieces of wood, bent paper clips, and inexpensive clamps. One of the advantages of digital photography is that you can easily remove any supporting device in an image editor.

In the studio, positioning your subject might be all you have to do. On location, you'll likely have to remove unsightly leaves, ugly rocks, maybe some bugs that are wandering through your frame. Clean up any dirt, dying stems, or other objects that you don't want to photograph.

Setting up your camera

In the studio, it's fairly easy to set up your camera on a tripod or other support and not have to worry about it shifting. On location, you might need to make sure that the ground underneath your tripod is firm and solid. Put a rock under one or more legs, if necessary. If you're shooting on a slope, you might want to lengthen one or more legs of the tripod and shorten others.

Set the tripod a little shorter than the height you actually want to use. You can use the center pole to raise or lower the camera a bit. Don't make the common mistake of setting the tripod too low because if you really crank up the center column, the tripod will become top-heavy and unstable. It sometimes helps to tie a weight onto the center pole to give the tripod a bit of ground-hugging heft. I use mesh bags, like what oranges or onions are sold in, as a receptacle for rocks. Mesh bags tend to be strong but lightweight, which makes them ideal for this particular task. (Plus, if you happen to encounter an orange grove during your shooting session, you're all set to bring home some dessert.)

You can reverse the center pole of many tripods so that it extends down between the legs of the tripod, thus letting you shoot at an angle down on your subject. Often that's the only way to get the viewpoint you want without having the tripod's legs interfere.

Lights, please

Use your lighting equipment or the existing light to illuminate your subject. In the studio, position two or more lights so that they light up the subject evenly. In the studio or on location, work with reflectors to fill in dark shadows, darken spots that are too bright, and even out your illumination.

The light that falls on the background can be just as important as the light that you use to illuminate your subject. The background light can separate your subject from the surroundings and provide a more attractive photo. See Book IV, Chapter 3, for more information on lighting backgrounds.

Remember that the more light you are able to use, the smaller the lens opening needs to be and better the *depth of field* (how much of your image is in focus) you'll achieve. If you want a really sharp picture with lots in focus, pump up the light as much as possible — although if you're using electronic flash, not having enough light is rarely a problem. I explain more about depth of field later in this chapter.

The quality of the light is as important as the quantity. If you're using electronic flash, you want to avoid the harsh illumination that flash typically provides. I often drape a handkerchief over my camera's flash. This reduces the flash illumination to a more reasonable level while softening the light.

If the electronic flash is still too strong, move back a step or two and zoom in closer. Bear in mind, though, that not all digital camera lenses can focus closely at all zoom settings. Because of the perverse square law (er, I mean *inverse square* law), a light that is 12 inches from a subject generates only one-quarter as much illumination as it does from 6 inches.

Ready . . . aim . . .

You're all set to frame your photo and press the shutter release. But first, a few words from our sponsor. Keep these final advisories in mind as you take your best shot when shooting up close:

✦ **Watch proportions.** For any particular magnification, the closer you get, the more emphasis is placed on objects very close to the lens. Photograph a figure of a clown's head from 2 inches away, and his nose will be very large in proportion to the rest of his face, as shown at left in Figure 2-8. Move back a few inches and zoom in to produce the same size image, and the proportions are much more realistic, as shown at right in Figure 2-8.

✦ **Don't forget focus and depth-of-field considerations.** When shooting up close, only a small portion of your image might be in focus. Make sure that's the most important part of your subject! If your camera lets you lock in a focus setting by pressing the shutter release button part way, make sure you've focused on the right area before locking. Depth of field is a range, extending one-third in front of the plane of sharpest focus and two-thirds behind it, as you can see in Figure 2-9. In this figure, very little in front of the cat is in focus, but the cat's face itself is fairly sharp. The background, of course, is too far away to be in focus at all, which is how the picture was conceived.

Figure 2-8: The clown's nose (left) appears proportionately larger than when photographed from a distance (right).

Figure 2-9: Depth of field extends one-third in front of and two-thirds behind the plane of sharpest focus (the cat's face).

✦ **Crop and center.** Crop (trim) extraneous material and center your subject in the frame (most of the time). Good composition, as I describe in Book IV, Chapter 1, usually calls for an off-center subject, but that rule might not apply when shooting close-ups. It might be best to feature your main point of interest right in the center of the frame.

✦ **Use your camera's close-up features effectively.** That includes double-checking to make sure the camera is in macro mode and keeping close tabs on the in-focus indicator (usually an LED) that might appear in your viewfinder.

✦ **Aim and frame.** Make sure that you've framed the subject correctly, without accidentally chopping anything off. You often have to use the camera's LCD screen to examine your composition because the built-in optical viewfinder doesn't show the image 100 percent accurately. (Read Book II, Chapter 1, for a basic discussion of viewfinder *parallax* error.) You don't want to chop off the top or sides of your image by mistake. Of course, if you're using a digital SLR, you won't need to worry about this at all.

**Book IV
Chapter 2**

**Close-Up
Photography**

Depth of field and digital cameras

Throughout this book, I mention the copious amounts of depth of field that digital cameras offer. This is a good place to mention it again. Because of the relatively short focal length of their lenses, digital cameras help ensure that just about anything you shoot at normal distances is sharp. Even at close-focus distances, you have to work a little to throw even part of your image out of focus.

If you *want* to reduce depth-of-field a little, say to blur a background for creative purposes, you can do several things:

✏ Try using the telephoto zoom position of your camera. One of my favorite digital cameras works fine in macro mode at its 200mm (equivalent) zoom setting, which has an actual focal length of about 50mm, and can cut down the depth-of-field a bit.

✏ Use your camera's aperture priority mode (if it has one) and set the camera for the largest lens opening available.

✏ If you want to throw the background out of focus, try focusing a teensy bit *in front* of your main subject, which will probably remain acceptably sharp as the background grows blurrier. Or, focus *behind* the main subject (but only a little) if you need to throw the foreground out of focus.

If your digital camera has a connector for linking the camera to a monitor or TV, you can often use that capability to frame your indoor close-up photos.

Fire!

When you press the shutter release button, a lot of things happen. One quite likely (and none-too-happy) event is that you press the shutter release button too hard, jar the camera during exposure, and produce a blurry picture. Another possibility is that you see something wrong with your composition in the last ohnosecond. (An *ohnosecond* is that interval between the time when you press the shutter release and the instant when you realize that you've made some sort of serious error. An ohnosecond also occurs when you're slamming your locked car door closed and notice your keys in the ignition.) It's not too late!

Avoiding blur

First, avoid human-caused blur by using your camera's self-timer to trip the shutter after a few seconds rather than using your big fat finger. In self-timer mode, you set up your composition, make sure everything is okay, press the shutter button, and then step back and take a few deep breaths until the camera actually takes the photo (blur-free).

An alternative is to use an electronic or mechanical remote shutter-release control to trip your camera's shutter without touching it. A remote release can be a cable that attaches to your camera or an infrared remote control like the one that operates your television, VCR, and virtually everything else in your household. Unlike a self-timer, a remote release lets you take the photo at the exact instant you want — say, when the tree frog has a cute expression on his face.

Some cameras and lenses have anti-shake features that can help you avoid blur, too.

Making sure the camera is done

For heavens sake, don't do anything after you press the shutter button until you're 100-percent positive that the camera has finished taking the picture. If your camera has an optional shutter release sound, turn it on so that you know when the picture is being taken. Learn to differentiate between the sound the camera makes when the shutter opens and the sound made when it closes again.

If your camera has a flashing LED that indicates that a photo is being saved to your digital film, look for it to begin flashing as an indication that the photo has been taken. The automatic exposure mechanism of your camera just might need to use a long exposure (several seconds or more) to take the picture, and you certainly don't want any sudden movements or grabs at the camera to ruin your shot. Wait a few seconds after you hear the camera's shutter click before doing anything until you're sure that your camera isn't making a lengthy exposure or time exposure. That click might have been the shutter opening (or the digital camera's simulation of a shutter sound), and the camera might still be capturing the picture.

Reviewing your shot

After the photo has been taken, do take the time to review your picture on the LCD for defects. Look for these common problems:

+ **Poor focus:** Correct and reshoot.

+ **Bad exposure:** Make adjustments by using your camera's available exposure compensation modes. (Check your camera manual.)

+ **Bad reflections you didn't notice before:** Move your lights or move your camera until the reflections go away.

+ **Missing tree frog that has departed the scene:** You know, they do make quite realistic-looking plastic tree frogs these days.

Digital SLRs and Close-Up Photography

As I mention at the beginning of this chapter, digital SLRs are the almost perfect choice for close-up photography because of the increased accuracy you can get with framing and focusing, as well as the greater control that most dSLRs provide over your picture-taking. Here are a few things to consider when using a digital SLR for macro photography. Some of these also apply to cameras with electronic viewfinders.

✦ **Don't forget to use depth of field preview.** The digital SLR typically shows you a bright, clear image with the lens wide open and then closes down the aperture at the moment of exposure. As you know, the depth of field at that smaller aperture is likely to be much greater than what you saw with the lens wide open, so if selective focus is important to you, you'll want to use your camera's depth of field preview button to glimpse the true focus just before you shoot. An object that appears soft and out of focus through the viewfinder can be objectionably sharp in the final image, as you can see in Figure 2-10.

✦ **Investigate add-on focus aids.** An SLR image is usually viewed as projected onto a focusing screen underneath the pentaprism/pentamirror. High-end digital SLRs can offer removable focusing screens that can be easier to focus in dim light or in close-up mode. If you have a dSLR with that capability, investigate the focus aids available to you.

✦ **Not all digital SLRs show the full frame.** When I began my photographic career, the Nikon film camera was highly prized because it was said to display a full 100 percent of the film image through the SLR viewfinder. Other cameras might not. Today, many digital camera viewfinders trim off some of the image, providing only 92–98 percent of the full image. You actually get *more* than what you saw through the viewfinder, but if absolute framing is important to you, be aware that what you see is only *most* of what you get.

✦ **Avail yourself of the mirror lock-up feature, if provided.** Close-up pictures can be especially sensitive to vibration, such as that caused by a pivoting mirror. (The mirror reflects the lens view upward to the viewfinder, then flips up out of the way during exposure to let the light pass unimpeded to the sensor. This quick up/down flip inevitably provides a tiny amount of vibration, no matter how carefully the camera was designed.) If you're shooting very close or if your exposure is long, see whether your digital SLR has a *mirror lock-up* feature, which will let you flip the mirror up prior to the exposure. Then, when vibration has been damped, take your picture with the self-timer or remote release.

✦ **Check out bellows, extension tubes, reversing rings, and special macro lenses.** These specialized devices can let you get closer, take sharper pictures, and improve your results, especially if you have a digital SLR with a full-frame sensor.

Figure 2-10: A background that appears to be out of focus (top) might be objectionably sharp at the taking aperture (bottom).

Chapter 3: Photographing People

*A*lthough the first successful photograph, a scene taken from a Paris rooftop by Nicéphore Niépce in 1827, was a scenic photo unpopulated by humans (largely because the exposure took eight full hours!), the most memorable pictures since then have included people. Indeed, the desire to photograph family, friends, and colleagues is why many people own a camera.

When you think of the daguerreotype, Civil War–era portraits probably come to mind. When you imagine a prize-winning photograph, images such as Dorothea Lange's *Migrant Mother* leap into your thoughts more quickly than, say, Ansel Adams's "portraits" of the U.S. National Parks. And when you photographed an architectural treasure such as the Eiffel Tower, didn't you include a family member in the picture?

We're fascinated by photographs of people, so we take lots of them. However, people are the most difficult of all subjects to photograph because of the complexity of human ego, awareness, and opinion. When was the last time the Eiffel Tower complained that your picture made it look fat? Has anyone ever told you that your photo of the Grand Canyon "didn't really look like the Grand Canyon"? Has anyone worried that the presidents on Mount Rushmore would blink during an exposure?

Satisfying people photography is within the capabilities of every digital camera owner. You don't need an expensive camera to take portraits (although digital SLRs can have some advantages when it comes to using certain accessories, such as multiple light sources.) Your basic 5- or 6- megapixel camera will do just fine. Available light or your camera's built-in flash might work for some kinds of portraits, but I show you the advantages of using off-camera flash in this chapter. The best part about taking digital pictures of people is that you can review the photos instantly, with your subjects, and retake them if the results are less than satisfactory.

This chapter is an introduction to the many facets of people photography. You find out how to take great portraits, capture vivid candid photos, and manage unruly group pictures. If you can handle those, all other forms of digital photography are a snap.

Capturing Satisfying Portraits

The two basic categories of people photography are portraits and candids. *Portraits* are posed photos taken in a controlled environment; *candids* are unplanned pictures taken of people in the act of being themselves. In general, portraits show people as they'd like to be seen, and candids portray them as they really are.

Each category can produce images ranging from the mundane to the sublime. To make the step up from mundane isn't hard. In fact, the average novice can achieve significant improvement through better composition and lighting alone.

You don't need a lot of training to shoot candid photos after you master the features of your digital camera and the rules of composition. You just go out and take pictures. Portraits, on the other hand, demand some special skills if you want the images to look like portraits. The good news is that these capabilities are within the range of the average photographer; you just need someone to fill you in on the tools and techniques that work. That's what this chapter is for.

But first, a few ground rules. Take care of these simple aspects and you can't go wrong:

+ **Make it possible for your subjects to look their best.** Suggest that they wear suitable clothes and also invite them to have a change of outfits so they can have pictures with different looks. Encourage them to use a friend or family member to help them prepare. Provide access to a good-sized mirror so that they can check their appearance. A portrait subject who feels confident about his or her appearance will photograph well!

✦ **Get to know your subject's personality.** Be careful about trying to make a somber, serious individual look cheerful and gay; the picture can look forced and fake. It's easier to get a happy type to look serious. Unless it's an executive portrait (where serious is good), go for the smile. Use what you know about the subject to create a portrait that reflects his or her personality.

✦ **Provide comfortable surroundings to help people stay relaxed.** A clean, organized shooting area puts your subjects at ease, as can some soft mood music. If your subject doesn't feel like he or she is standing in front of a firing squad, your photos turn out much better.

Successful portraiture begins with getting your subjects into the right frame of mind. Relaxed, confident people pose better than nervous, tense ones, so make every effort to start things off right if you want to get a portrait like the one shown in Figure 3-1.

Figure 3-1: A relaxed portrait is the best kind.

Shooting in the Studio or on Location

Because portrait sittings are generally carefully arranged, these kinds of shoots offer the photographer the advantage of being able to exercise a great deal of control over creation of the image, both in location and lighting. You can choose to shoot in a studio (which can be any indoor room, including your living room or garage) or on location (which can range from your backyard to a park or other site).

You don't need to have a real studio to shoot studio portraits. You might have a place that serves double-duty as a studio as well as some other function. For example, I took some of my favorite portraits in an attic studio that was little more than a large space hung with multiple rolls of seamless backdrop paper, a few painted backgrounds, and lots of room to arrange lights. When I moved to a newer home without an attic, my studio moved, too, to a 16-x-20-foot basement area with 10-foot ceilings directly under my home office. The background paper was easy to hang from the ceiling joists.

For one book I wrote that called for lots of head-and-shoulders portraits, I pinned a long length of fabric to cover the drapery in front of my patio door, set up a couple of lights, and was able to snap a quick portrait on a moment's notice without the need to run down to the basement where the roomier, full home studio was set up.

You can even take portraits in your own living room, which was the case for the mother-daughter picture shown in Figure 3-2. I've left the couch in the photo (at left) but probably would have cropped or retouched it out when making a print.

And even if you don't have room to set aside for a home studio, you probably have an area that can be temporarily reconfigured to serve as a photographic environment. For example,

Figure 3-2: Your own living room can be the scene for your portrait photography.

back the car out of the garage and hang a backdrop — and you have an instant studio.

When I refer to a *studio,* I mean any indoor location that can be used to take posed photographs. I don't mean to imply that you have to build a home studio to use any of the techniques described here.

Deciding whether to shoot in your studio or on location must be based on the kind of photos you want to take. Shooting in a studio offers the utmost in control for a photographer, particularly when you're working in a studio you've set up and become comfortable in. Your studio can become a warm, comfortable cocoon that lets your creativity and talent grow.

Of course, sometimes, we all have to leave our comfortable surroundings and brave the outside world. Location photography may pull us out of our comfort zone, but it also gives us something hard to find in the studio — scenery.

Think of location shooting as your outdoor studio. Most of the techniques described later in this chapter apply to location photography, although you might have to use reflectors instead of external flash units, and you have less control over your backgrounds. The chief differences between location and studio shooting are as follows:

✦ **Portability:** If you plan to shoot on location regularly, you need to assemble a versatile kit of equipment that you can set up and break down quickly. Find yourself a duffle bag or two you can pack your location equipment into quickly so that you can be ready to go at a moment's notice.

✦ **Flexibility:** Because no two location shoots are identical, try for a portable location kit that provides the greatest flexibility for lighting both your subject and, if need be, elements of the location appearing in the shot.

✦ **Creativity:** Put together a portable studio system that lets you create different shots and moods. Consider props that are portable and versatile. Make sure that your kit includes a good set of posing blocks (structures, often of wood or plastic, that can be sat upon or stood on) so that you can adjust the height of various posers. You won't always find a rock or fence post exactly where you need it out in the field!

Book IV
Chapter 3

Location shoots give you the chance to provide your subjects with something different from the typical portrait sitting. Every area has a special site of some sort that can serve as a backdrop for memorable images, such as a gorgeous hotel lobby, public park, forest, or lake. One photographer I know lives on some wooded acreage complete with meadows, stands of trees, and a pond. You can bet that he uses these environmental settings as often as possible for his people pictures.

Photographing People

Setting Up an Informal Portrait Studio

Many photographers who pursue their art as a hobby or sideline prefer a simple, informal home studio that can be set up easily and broken down when the shoot's done. Such a studio fills their needs without taking over part of their house.

Others want to have the option of taking their show on the road. A simple portrait studio can also be a transportable portrait studio. Even if you're working on a tight budget, you can come up with a lighting system that improves your photography.

Depending on your needs, a pair of accessory flash units helps give you the balanced lighting that you need if you want to capture that natural-lighting look. If your budget permits a better system, you can build up to a more powerful semiprofessional system. You'll find that an investment in slightly better equipment can be worth it. Portrait lights that I purchased for use with film cameras a few decades ago work just fine with my latest digital cameras, and their initial cost averages out to just a few dollars a year.

Choosing backgrounds

Sometimes you want to pose people in their natural environments, even for formal portraits. A family can be posed in their living room seated on a couch. An attorney can be pictured in front of a wall of law books. (This is almost a tradition. Don't forget to include a flag!) If you apply the same rules of posing and lighting to such a portrait as for more traditional studio portraits, the results will be quite good.

However, most formal portraits call for a real portrait background. For an indoor studio, you'll want something more attractive than just a bare wall for a background; fortunately a wide variety of choices is available for every budget.

✦ **Go disposable with paper.** The simplest choice is a roll of seamless background paper, like that used in the photo shown in Figure 3-3. These rolls are available in a wide variety of colors and are easy to use. Usually, you just suspend a roll on some kind of hanging support and then unroll as much as you need for a shoot. (**_Hint:_** Bring enough down to cover a couple of feet of floor and have your subject stand on it.)

When a section of the backdrop paper becomes dirty or wrinkled, you just roll down some clean paper, cut off the damaged part, and throw it away. You can keep a selection of three to five different rolls and switch them as needed.

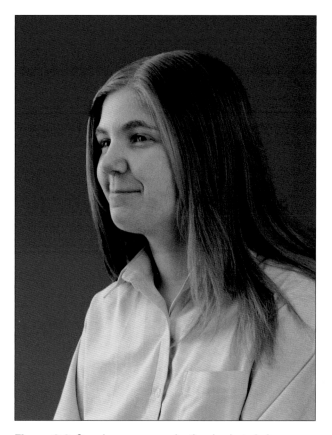

Figure 3-3: Seamless paper can be the simplest choice.

✦ **Upgrade to fabric.** Other background choices include painted linen backdrops that provide a more interesting texture and color gradient. Because these backgrounds are more expensive and weigh more than the seamless paper, they might not be a great choice for a portable setup or for the home enthusiast (who might need to use the studio for normal family things when not doing photography).

✦ **Use more than one backdrop:** A higher-end system for those making their living doing portraits offers a multiple-background setup that can be used for either a permanent studio or a traveling one. Such a rig has multiple rollers with different backdrops on it. The portrait photographer creates one set of portraits with one background and then another set with a second or even third background. Often, the backgrounds and poses complement each other — say, an athletic field for a sports-type portrait, with props such as a football in the child's arm. This way, you can create a combination of both formal and informal images.

**Book IV
Chapter 3**

**Photographing
People**

Nothing is more distracting than using a cluttered wall as a background. Even a simple roll of seamless paper as a backdrop can do a lot to make your portraits look more professional.

Selecting supports for lights, camera, and subjects

Good portraits really require lighting beyond the flash built into your digital camera. In most cases, you need two or more external lights. And because lights, cameras, and subjects all need to be moved from time to time, how you support them is important. Supports need to be light enough to move around easily, collapse small enough to be portable, and yet be sturdy and solid enough to safely hold your gear.

You need different supports for lights, backgrounds, camera, and people. As usual, the choices span all budgets and setups. Try to build a system that will allow for future upgrades or studio expansions.

When planning your support system, aim for versatility and portability. Here are some things to consider:

◆ **Lighting supports:** Your lighting supports should be strong enough to support an external lighting unit, up to and including a relatively heavy flash with soft box or umbrella reflectors (more on these later, in the upcoming section, "Lighting gadgets"). You want the supports to be capable of raising the lights high enough to be effective. Look for light stands capable of extending 6 to 7 feet high.

◆ **Camera support:** A good, solid tripod that's sturdy enough to support your camera represents the starting point. If your setup is likely to call for a lot of back-and-forth movement as you shift from individual to group portraits, you might want to consider a camera *dolly* device — a kind of wagon — that lets you roll your camera/tripod rig back and forth as needed.

◆ **Subject support:** Posing your subjects is easier if you can have them sitting rather than standing (which is why portrait sessions are usually known as *sittings*). The tool of choice for this sort of thing is the pneumatic posing stool. These stools are much easier to operate than corkscrew-type chairs, which have to be spun to raise or lower them to the right height for portraiture. With a pneumatic stool, you simply press a lever to control an air-driven piston that raises or lowers the chair. At less than $100 each, they are reasonably affordable. A posing table is also a useful option, particularly if you need to do a shot of a baby in his or her carrier. You don't need to spring for these devices, however: Stools and tables around the home can serve the same purpose.

If you do want to go with photo gear, you can find lots of different options at most camera stores or advertised in many camera magazines. A good basic setup includes at least one posing chair (preferably two), three light stands (two capable of reaching 6 to 7 feet high and a third, shorter one), a mobile tripod, a posing table, and posing blocks. *Posing blocks* are nesting wooden blocks made in varying heights that are big enough for people to stand on. Using these blocks helps you make people taller as needed to get the proper posing relationships.

Figure 3-4 shows a bird's-eye view of a full-blown portrait setup, including a tripod-mounted digital camera, seamless backdrop paper, a light to provide the main illumination, another light to fill in the shadows, and optional lights to brighten the hair and background. In the center of it all is our victim, seated on a folding chair (although a stool is often a much better choice).

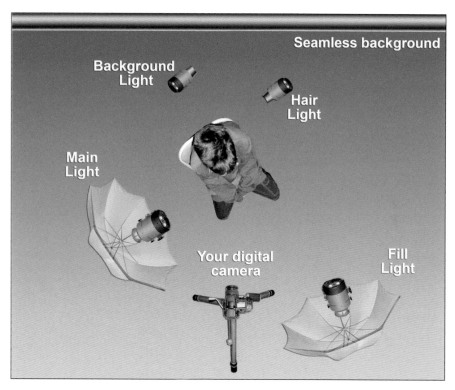

Figure 3-4: Lighting, camera, and subject supports are all important parts of a studio setup.

Basic lighting equipment

Lighting your subject properly is one of the most challenging aspects of portrait photography. At your disposal are many different approaches to lighting and also many different types of lighting resources.

A beginning photographer can definitely create a basic, inexpensive lighting system capable of delivering high-quality results. Putting together a lighting kit depends on your budget, what kinds of portraiture you hope to do, and how big a percentage of your photography this kind of shooting is. Obviously, the photographer who needs to shoot only the occasional portrait can get by with a less-sophisticated setup than someone who wishes to focus mainly on portraiture. Lighting choices fall into several different categories, as the following sections make clear.

Existing light

Existing light is the light that's already there in your environment — that is, before you add flash or other extra light sources. It's also called *available light* — or, by wags, *available darkness* — but all three terms are misnomers. After all, *all* light that you can use exists (unless you're into quantum mechanics, in which case, it only potentially exists until it's observed). *Available light* is equally murky: If you have an electronic flash or a flashlight in working order, both of those are technically available. However, I'll apply those terms to the light that's already on a site, and not the kind of illumination you'd use to photograph Shrödinger's cat.

To make the most of existing light, consider these points:

✦ **Reflectors:** *Reflectors* enable you to bounce light into areas of the scene that need it. Any material that can bounce light into areas of heavy shadow can help make existing light work in your favor. Whether your reflector is an assistant holding a piece of foam board or a reflective disk held in place by clamp and stand, this kind of illumination can be an inexpensive and portable way of making your lighting better. Although some pretty fancy (read *expensive*) reflectors are on the market, spending a lot isn't necessary. A simple piece of white foam board does the job beautifully.

Use your main light source (daytime outdoors, that will be the sun) to light a three-quarter section of your subject and then position the reflector to bounce sunlight onto the remaining quarter. This will lighten the shadows and give a greater sense of dimension to your photo. If you want a little less softness in the shadows, use a metallic reflector. You can even press a metal serving tray into use, like the one shown in Figure 3-5, if you can convince a friendly observer to hold it up for you.

Figure 3-5: A metal serving tray can function as a reflector in a pinch.

✦ **Room lights:** Sometimes your goal is the most natural possible setting and feel to an image. If this means working without accessory lights, managing the room's lights properly can be a big help. If you can position a lamp to throw a little more light to a shadow area, you can clean up a heavy shadow. Or depending on the mood you're aiming for, you can bring your lights all to one side and have your subject emerging from the shadows.

Working with available darkness is one of photography's greatest challenges. However, if you can use it successfully, you can produce exceptionally natural-looking images. Look for ways to control the impact of the building's lights; remember, you don't have to accept what's there. Shift a lamp closer or farther from your subject. Unscrew some light bulbs while leaving others on or mask lighting fixtures with cardboard or *gaffer's tape* (a special kind of tape that won't leave a residue when pulled off the lights when you're done). The difference is worth it.

Figure 3-6 shows an outdoor snapshot taken in bright sunlight (at left). In the version at right, the subject has been moved so that the sun isn't glaring in her face, and a reflector provides soft illumination and better skin tones.

**Book IV
Chapter 3**

**Photographing
People**

Figure 3-6: At left, glaring sunlight. At right, a softer snapshot using reflector illumination.

Electronic flash

Accessory flash units are your first tool in the battle to correct undesirable lighting conditions. These small, portable light sources provide you with a lot of options and can be used to produce some amazing results. Photographers using a multiple flash setup can produce lighting results similar to those found in the studio. You can put together a small, three-flash lighting kit that can fit in a small suitcase or carrying case. If you're planning to put together such a flash kit, here are some things to consider:

+ **Supports (again):** You definitely need some sort of system for holding your flash units in position. Lightweight minitripods that can be set on tabletops or other elevated surfaces and positioned as needed work well. The marketplace has also produced a wide variety of clamps with standard ⅜-inch tripod threads that can also hold a flash and be used to position it high enough to work effectively. Some tripods also come with feet or stands they can be mounted on so that they can be set erect on a flat surface.

+ **Light modifiers:** After you position your flash units, make the quality of your light as pleasing as possible. When used head-on, direct flash is harsh, showing every flaw and imperfection. Experienced photographers solve this problem in a number of different ways. One solution is *bounce flash.* Here, the flash units are pointed toward the ceiling, and the light is reflected back down to the subject, thus spreading and softening the light and making it more pleasing. Other tools for improving the quality of light are devices that attach to the flash head and reflect light (such as white cards) or ones that cover the flash head and soften the light as it comes through the device (such as the Sto-Fen Omni Bounce [www.stofen.com, about $20] or a small soft box, which is basically nothing more than a piece of white cloth or other material stretched over a frame).

✦ **Power:** Keeping your flashes firing during a long shoot can be a daunting task if you're relying solely on AA batteries. Devices such as Quantum rechargeable batteries (www.qtm.com, prices vary widely depending on your model) can provide enough juice for your flash units to keep pace even with your most frenetic shoots. Many of these units can provide power to a pair of flashes simultaneously.

Two or three good flash units with some form of supporting gear and the appropriate light modifiers can give you a very effective portable lighting setup. Such a kit can give significantly better results than just a single flash unit and is versatile enough to be useful in a variety of situations.

Photographic *slaves* — electronic units that trigger multiple flashes not connected physically to the camera — are needed to fire the flashes with either a photoelectric trigger or wireless radio transmitter.

Incandescent lights

Incandescent lighting is the same lighting most of us use to light our homes. Enterprising manufacturers have created inexpensive photo lighting kits that use regular light bulbs instead of more expensive tungsten-halogen lighting setups.

Professional studio lighting

If you're serious about portraiture, you might want to consider professional studio lighting, which isn't really all that expensive for the photo hobbyist who spends a thousand dollars or so on a camera alone. Many digital cameras are capable of firing expensive and high-quality studio lighting kits. These kits, which use very powerful flash heads, provide a predictable, steady light source.

There are several differences between these flash heads and the more common accessory flash units that I discuss earlier. For a start, their power output is measured in watt seconds (ws) versus the guide numbers (gn) that on-camera flashes are usually measured in.

Another difference is that these units draw too much power to get by on either batteries or portable power packs. Instead, an electric outlet feeds them either directly or via a separate power supply (which can usually feed two or more lights at a time).

Using such a high-power system has several advantages:

✦ **More output:** The nearly unlimited power supply means that you can get greater light output. This enables the photographer to shoot at smaller apertures (larger-numbered f-stops). The resulting greater depth-of-field provided by smaller apertures means that you can shoot larger groups of people and have them all in focus. Plus, you get sharper overall images.

✦ **No recycle lags:** You don't have to wait for your lights to recycle. You can blaze away taking shot after shot.

✦ **Flash previewing:** You can take advantage of *modeling lights,* which are incandescent lamps built into the studio flash that show exactly how the light from the flash will look. Many of the higher-quality studio lights have built-in modeling lights that stay on the whole time you're working. These lights aren't as powerful as the main flash heads, but they do show you where shadows will fall on your subject.

Use modeling lights to check for *hot spots* (bright specular reflections) on eyeglasses.

✦ **More control:** You have more control over lighting. You can set one light for full power and another for a lower percentage of power output — the full-power light acts as a main light while the second, less powerful light simply fills in the shadows.

Studio lighting kits can range in price from a few hundred dollars for a set of lights, stands, and reflectors to thousands for a high-end lighting system complete with all the necessary accessories. The good news is that you don't need the top-of-the-line system to produce top-of-the-line results.

Lighting gadgets

A huge assortment of lighting gadgets are on the market, all promising to be easy to use and to produce a higher quality of light. For the most part, these claims are reasonably true. Here's a quick summary of what's available, ranging from useful and just about free all the way up to high-tech and pricey.

Inexpensive (or free!) gadgets

No such thing as a free lunch? Guess again! Check out these great ideas that won't blow your budget:

✦ **The White Card Trick:** This is the all-time classic. Set your flash to bounce mode (point it at the ceiling) and take a 3-x-5-inch index card or other card and attach it to the flash with a rubber band. Have the card extend 3 or more inches beyond the flash head. When you fire the flash, some of the light bounces off the ceiling while more light kicks off the white card to throw some light into your subject's face.

Figure 3-7 shows an electronic flash that includes a built-in "white card" and also a wide angle diffusing lens to spread the light even more.

Figure 3-7: The White Card Trick provides fill lighting.

✦ **The Spoon Trick:** If your supply of index cards has been depleted, you can always give The Spoon Trick a try. Similar to the preceding method, use a cheap, white plastic spoon in much the same way as you would use an index card. Some photographers maintain that the curvature of a spoon throws the light out in a curve to provide a more pleasing effect. I've used both methods, and they both work pretty well. It's also pretty easy to carry some rubber bands, plastic spoons, and index cards in your camera bag or find the stuff at most shooting locations.

✦ **The Aluminum Trick:** A third version for those with just a hint of mechanical ability is to take a piece of aircraft aluminum (white or copper colored) and cut it in a roughly squarish or 3 x 5 shape. Use hook-and-loop tape on the square and the back of your flash head. Store the card by attaching it upside-down when not in use and then just pull it off, flip it, and reattach for use. Although white is pretty standard, using a copper-colored piece can warm the color of your light a little, which can be flattering for portraits.

✦ **The Alcohol Bottle Trick:** Just so it doesn't look like all I know is different versions of the White Card Trick, here's one that's a little different. Get one of those white frosted plastic bottles of rubbing alcohol (one whose waist is about the same diameter as your flash head). Remove the alcohol (this is important), and then cut the bottom of the bottle about 2 inches down the waist. Then snug the waist (the end with the bottom) over the flash head. You can now shoot with the flash head angled almost vertically with a much softer light. (The Alcohol Bottle Trick creates an inexpensive alternative to a product known as the Sto-Fen Omni-Bounce, described in the next group.)

✦ **The Clear 35mm Film Canister Trick:** If you have only a small, fixed flash — *fixed* as in it won't pivot or tilt, not fixed as in *repaired* (but this won't work if the flash is broken either) — here's another way to soften and spread the light from it. Take a clear 35mm film canister (see whether one of your less technologically advanced friends has one you can get from them or try a camera store) and tape it over the flash head. Variations of this trick involve placing a sheet of facial tissue inside the film canister to diffuse (soften) the light a bit or using colored tissue papers to change the color of the light the flash produces. This isn't as big a deal these days, when you can produce all sorts of similar effects in an image-editing program. Still, if you're not real comfortable trying effects in the computer, this method lets you experiment while taking the shot.

✦ **Flash brackets:** Many department stores carry cheap, L-shaped flash brackets. Your camera mounts onto the flash bracket, while your flash fits into a flash mount at the top of the L. To use a setup like this, you have to have some way of triggering your flash when it is not attached to the camera. There are several ways to do this. If your camera has a PC/X connection (and I don't mean the way to connect it to your computer or *politically correct;* I'm talking about a small circular electrical linkage, as shown in the previous chapter), you connect your flash via a PC cable. A second method is to use a photoelectric slave to trigger your accessory flash unit. To do this, you use your camera's built-in flash unit, perhaps blocking most of its light output with gaffer's tape or masking tape.

As you can see, you have many inexpensive ways of improving the quality of your artificial light. Even the simple White Card Trick combined with bounced flash gives you much better results than bombing away with direct flash. Keep this method in mind even when your available light is enough for a good exposure because the light kicked forward from the white card is a great way to fill in shadows from ball caps and other similarly billed haberdashery items.

Moderately priced gadgets

For just a few pennies (well, maybe dollars) more, you can add the following items to your lighting toolbox:

✦ **Omni-Bounce:** Sto-Fen (www.stofen.com) makes several inexpensive light modifier devices. Best known is the Omni-Bounce, which is a frosted plastic attachment that fits over the flash head and softens the light considerably. The device is used by setting the flash head to a 45-degree angle — unless your subject is more than 15 feet away, and then you set the flash to fire straight-on. It costs about $20. The company also makes colored versions of the Omni-Bounce, which cost a few dollars more.

✦ **Two-Way:** Also made by Sto-Fen, the Two-Way bounce is a sturdier approach to the White Card Trick and works in a similar manner. It also costs about $20.

✦ **Barn doors:** LumiQuest's barn doors attachment fits several of its bounce flash attachments. Barn doors are flat panels, like those shown in Figure 3-8, that can be swung open and closed to more finely tune light output.

✦ **LumiQuest attachments:** LumiQuest (www.lumiquest.com) makes a whole range of flash attachments offering a bunch of different capabilities. These range from simple bounce hoods that kick the flash's output forward and spread it out to ones that perform very specialized functions. Variations of the basic bouncer include attachments to allow some light to bounce off the ceiling while the rest is kicked forward. Another version sends the light through a frosted panel to soften it even more, and a third variation permits insertion of colored panels to change the color of the light that the flash produces while bouncing it.

**Book IV
Chapter 3**

**Photographing
People**

Figure 3-8: Snoots (at left) and barn doors (at right) let you direct your lighting with more precision.

+ **Soft boxes:** A *soft box* is an attachment that mounts on the head of the flash and extends out about 6 to 8 inches, with a frosted white panel at the end. This attachment lets the light from the flash spread out a little bit inside the soft box, softening it as it passes through the frosted end. (Pro portrait studios often sport a similar but much larger version on their studio flashes.) Lumiquest, as well as several other companies, also make soft box attachments for portable flash units.

+ **Snoots:** LumiQuest also makes a snoot. (No, the company is not snooty, it makes a snoot.) A *snoot* is a tube-like device (see Figure 3-8) that focuses the flash's light to a very small area. Photographers often use a snoot to create a highlight on someone's hair.

+ **Flash brackets:** Moderately priced flash brackets tend to be sturdier than their inexpensive counterparts. Plus, they usually tend to lift the flash higher up above the camera. Otherwise, things work pretty much the same way.

A decent light modifier can be a pleasure to work with, can significantly improve your photos, and needn't cost you an arm and a leg. You'll find that many can be had for less than $50. A wide variety of choices are available, depending on your needs. For photographers who work mainly out of a camera bag, a small, collapsible light modifier is a better choice than one of the bigger, more cumbersome units. Those who work from a home studio are better off with one of the bigger soft boxes that give a nice-quality light.

Higher-priced gadgets

I'm not talking thousands of dollars here, but costs for the following items can still add up a bit. (***Note:*** Quality rises with the price.)

+ **Soft boxes:** Some companies make a fancier soft box attachment that mounts on the flash head via spring-loaded clips. These devices are bigger and feature a deeper well for the light to spread out in before hitting the frosted panel. They also tend to be sturdier than the less expensive versions.

+ **Umbrella units:** Another option is to mount your flash on a combination flash stand with photographic umbrella, like the one shown in Figure 3-9. This kind of rig lets you set up a multiple-flash lighting system that produces very pleasing lighting without the expense of buying portrait studio flash heads. Usually, these devices need to be triggered via some form of slave. The price is about $100.

You can also get by with *real* umbrellas as long as they're plain white with no pattern. Fold-up umbrellas are inexpensive and easy to carry. I pay less than $5 for mine, not including clamps to fix them to light stands or other supports. If one gets dirty, just throw it away and use a new one. The chief disadvantage is that these translucent rain-stoppers let as much light through as they reflect. In fact, you might have better luck using them to illuminate your subject by the light that leaks *through* the umbrella rather than bounces off.

Figure 3-9: Umbrellas make good reflectors.

✦ **Flash brackets:** Examples in this category tend to be very sturdy and can extend the flash as much as one foot or more higher than the camera. Some offer expanded capabilities, such as the ability to accept a flash umbrella, making for a heavy but versatile rig. Many of the more expensive units, such as several made by Stroboframe, offer the ability to rotate the camera and/or flash for vertical orientation. Go to the following Web site for more information about Stroboframe products:

    www.tiffen.com/products.html?tablename=stroboframe

If you're serious about using your digital camera for portrait photography, the equipment mentioned here adds a lot of bang for your buck. The umbrella rigs tend to be better for studio setups, whereas the soft boxes and heavy-duty flash brackets stay manageable for photographers who do most of their work on the road.

Choosing power sources

Keeping your portrait flash units supplied with power is a key to effective flash photography. You have several ways of getting juice to your flash heads, and they vary in both price and effectiveness. Don't skimp here if you expect to rely on your flashes. The wrong choice will cost you images and make you miserable. Choose from these power sources:

✦ **AA batteries:** These are the standard power source for your average accessory flash unit. The advantages are that they're inexpensive and can be found almost anywhere. You can choose from alkaline, lithium, and standard types. Alkaline and lithium are better choices because they recycle faster than the standard type. Rechargeable versions are available in several different versions, including nickel-cadmium (NiCads), alkalines, and nickel metal-hydride (NiMH). The big disadvantage to all of these is that they drain fairly quickly, leaving you to frantically change batteries while hoping you don't miss a shot.

✦ **Portable battery packs:** Several different manufacturers make high-capacity portable battery packs that can provide power for a wide variety of flash units. The best-known manufacturer is Quantum, which makes several different styles along with adapters for most current flash units. Although these rigs are much more expensive than AAs (figure between $150 and $200 for a new battery pack and flash module), they can power tons of flash cycles before running out of juice. They also keep your flash firing longer during motor drive bursts (although not indefinitely).

A good, portable power pack can provide enough juice to power a couple of flash units through a wedding, prom, or public affairs event. Having one available can really make your life easier.

Lighting Basics

The idea behind using artificial light is to provide enough illumination to adequately light your subject in a pleasing manner. The simplest, most basic method is to use a single flash — preferably with some form of light modification or bouncing — with the flash unit raised higher than the camera.

There are several ways to maximize the effectiveness of a one-light photographic system. First and foremost is to get the flash higher than the camera. The closer the flash is to the lens, the greater the likelihood of *red-eye* (that nasty red glare that appears in the eyes when light bounces off the subject's retina), so extending your flash unit's height helps your photography quite a bit. Ways to do this include

✦ **The ol' Statue of Liberty play:** Use an *off-camera shoe cord* (an intelligent cord that communicates between the camera and dedicated flash unit to retain the camera's ability to meter light through the lens) or a PC cord to lift the flash high above the camera. Then either point the light directly at your subject or bounce it off the ceiling.

✦ **L-brackets:** Use an L-bracket — or something based on an L-bracket design, such as a Stroboframe grip — to raise the flash up above the camera.

✦ **Use a flash stand with an umbrella reflector:** This requires either a long PC cord or a wireless transmitter to trigger the flash unit.

One advantage of getting the flash higher than the camera is that it re-creates the single high light source that you're used to seeing naturally — the sun. A second advantage is that by getting the flash higher than the camera and at a higher angle, you reduce the likelihood of red-eye. That's because red-eye is caused by a flash reflecting straight back off the retina of the eye into the camera lens. When the light strikes the back of the eye at a higher angle, it's reflected downward and away from the lens.

Using multiple light sources

A more advanced but still basic lighting system calls for multiple lights arranged in one of several possible ways. Although a multiple-light system doesn't re-create the natural light of the sun, you can create a very pleasing and effective lighting package.

Advantages of a multiple-light system include

✦ **Precise control over how much illumination you provide for a scene:** Even if your lights are more powerful than you want, you can add screens to reduce output or shift your lights farther back.

✦ **More control over the mood of the image:** You can control the location and intensity of shadows and highlights, which can affect the overall mood of the image, whether it's stark and full of contrast or soft and moody.

✦ **An adaptable lighting kit:** You can adapt your lighting kit to a wide variety of shoots and to any number of subjects. Some lighting kits are even versatile enough to be brought on location.

Multiple lighting setups can mean the difference between an adequate portrait photo and a good one. Although a multilight setup doesn't guarantee better quality, getting the hang of such an arrangement will do a lot to improve your portrait photography.

Arranging a multiple-light setup

After you decide you want to use a multiple-light setup, you need to know where to put it. Setting up a multiple-light system isn't very hard; it's just a question of positioning your lights to illuminate your subject attractively.

With a multiple-light setup, each light has a different role to play. Understanding the basic arrangement helps you get started down the road to good portrait photography.

Main light

Surprise, surprise. This is your primary light source. The main light provides most of the illumination for your subject. An effective two-light studio system can even be set up with a big main light firing straight on your subject through a big soft box (not the kind that mounts on an accessory flash, but a big studio model about 18 inches tall and 36 inches wide) with a second back light to separate your subject from the background (more on back lights in minute).

This principle also works with a smaller shoe-mount flash and soft box, but the quality of the light won't compare with that of the studio system. Generally, the difference is noticeable when you're trying to shoot larger groups or doing a lot of sittings. For an occasional small group and a limited number of exposures, the small portable system does the job pretty well.

The following list fills you in on some ways to maximize the effectiveness of your main light:

✦ **Get it up high.** Your main light should be higher than your subject. You don't have to be ridiculous here; keeping the light about a foot or so higher than your tallest subject will do the trick.

✦ **Make an effort to improve the quality of your light.** You can do this either via a soft box or by using an umbrella system.

✦ **Provide enough power to shoot at a small aperture, thus giving you greater depth of field.** Because shooting through a soft box or off an umbrella costs you some light, you need a lot of power to shoot a big group at f/11 or f/16.

✦ **Recycle quickly.** How quickly your main light recycles (recharges so that it can be ready to fire again) is very important. You want your lights to keep pace with your workflow, not the other way around. During a sitting, it's important to develop a rhythm with your clients while posing and photographing them. A break in that rhythm, particularly one caused by your lights not being ready, can make your life difficult.

You want your main light to provide a soft, even illumination with enough power to keep your subject in focus from front to back. Most often, the main light is set up a couple of feet to the right or left of your subject's center line and angled toward that center. Figure 3-10 shows a portrait subject illuminated by a main light off to the right of the subject.

Fill light

The fill light is the light that fills in the shadow areas created by the main light, as you can see in Figure 3-10. For the most versatile system, plan on using the same model flash for your fill light as you do for your main light. This gives you the option of setting the same power ratios — the settings on your flash that reduce or increase the amount of light emitted — for each light. Such a lighting system with two comparable lights about 6 feet apart angled toward the center point of your sitting enables you to build up your group size without having to reconfigure your lighting — which is a huge advantage if you're doing a large number of portraits during the course of a day.

Just because you can bomb both flash heads away at their highest power settings and create an even light doesn't mean that you have to. You can always dial down the power setting on your second flash head and create a more interesting lighting effect for your subject. Experiment with 2:1 and 3:1 power ratios to see which you prefer.

If you have a fill light that doesn't let you reduce or increase the power, try moving the flash back a bit or perhaps placing a diffuser (such as a handkerchief) over the flash. Thanks to your digital camera's review feature, you can quickly see whether you've reduced the amount of light enough.

Here are some tips for setting up your fill light:

✦ Your fill light should be roughly the same height as your main light, although slightly lower is okay.

✦ The fill light should also receive some kind of modification, via an umbrella, a soft box, or a *diffusion screen* (a thin screen-like material that diffuses or softens the light).

The fill light helps balance your portrait lighting and creates a sense of depth to your image. Used properly, it can also create a moody or romantic image through the carefully controlled play of shadows.

Hair light

A *hair light* is a small, carefully controlled light that puts a highlight on the subject's hair. This type of lighting can also be referred to as a kind of *rim lighting* (described later in this chapter.)

Figure 3-10: A fill light brightens the shadows.

Most often, hair light is controlled via either a snoot or through a barn doors attachment on a flash head. (See the earlier section, "Moderately priced gadgets," for more on snoots and barn doors.) The light itself doesn't need to be particularly powerful because it's responsible for lighting only a small area. Most often, a hair light is positioned closely to the subject (just out of the camera's view) via a *boom* (raised arm attached to a lighting stand) that allows it to reach into the portrait area from up high.

To use a hair light, position it so that the light is directed almost straight back into the camera, raking across the top of the subject's head, as shown in Figure 3-11. The hair light is emphasized in this example for clarity, but would be more subtle in your final portrait.

Figure 3-11: A hair light emphasizes the edge of the head.

Background light

A background light, as its name suggests, lights up the background and creates some separation between the subject and background by making the background lighter than the main subject.

This light is generally mounted on a small lighting stand and is pointed upward at the background; a small screen is usually mounted on the light to help spread the light over the backdrop. Be careful to position it so that the lighting stand stays hidden behind your subject.

When using the background light, keep the following tips in mind:

✦ Set the background light about 2 feet from the backdrop and about 2 to 3 feet off the ground.

✦ Try to keep your background light on a separate power circuit than your main and fill lights. Because the main, fill, and background lights are usually the most powerful lights in your setup, having them on the same power supply or circuit will probably stress your power source more than it can handle.

✦ Angle the background light upward about 45 degrees so that the light spreads upward and outward from below your subject(s).

✦ Mount a diffusion screen (which can be as simple as a handkerchief or any other diffusing material) on the light head to soften it as it spreads up the backdrop. Using the screen helps prevent the light from creating a *hot spot* (those annoying bright areas that can crop up in a background if the light isn't spread evenly).

Adding a background light to your portrait setup makes for a cleaner, more pleasing portrait — like the one shown in Figure 3-12 — because it helps separate your subjects from the background. Although hardly the most important light in your setup, your subjects can get lost in a dark background without a background light.

Additional light sources

Using the four lights discussed in the preceding sections will take care of the majority of lighting situations, but they're certainly not the only tools to create interesting lighting. For some neat alternatives, try one (or more) of the following:

✦ **Reflectors:** Rather than using a fill light, a photographer sometimes bounces light from an angled main light into a reflector positioned near the model but still outside the picture area. This can be a good solution if you don't own a second electronic flash.

✦ **Window lighting:** Another charming source of light can be the nearest window. Window-lit portraits require a bright, sunny day with sunlight pouring through the window. Position your subject on a chair near the window. Make sure that your digital camera takes its exposure reading from the portion of his or her cheek that's illuminated by the sunlight. If done properly, your subject appears to emerge from the shadows bathed in a golden glow. A variation of this lighting technique is to use a reflector to kick some light back into the shadow area so that some detail is returned to the side that doesn't receive sunlight.

Figure 3-12: A background light separates the subject(s) from the background (natch!).

✦ **Sun and fill:** A typical example of this form of lighting is the swimsuit model at the beach. The model is positioned so the early morning sunlight acts as the main light, and a reflector is positioned to direct some light into the shadow areas. This is a very nice style of lighting; unfortunately, it requires you to get up early!

REMEMBER

The latter two methods can produce some beautiful lighting but are hard to use for groups or a large number of sittings. It can be hard to schedule a sitting for this kind of lighting technique, too.

Here are some ways of using this lighting style:

✦ **Full backlighting:** In this technique, the main light is positioned directly behind the subject, about even with the subject's head. Check your composition carefully to make sure that the light is hidden from the camera's view.

✦ **Side rim lighting:** Here you're trying for just a hint of backlighting to add some glow to one side of the head. This is similar to hair lighting. In this case, though, use a small light rather than your main light. Set up a small light with a snoot (a conical light modifier discussed earlier in this chapter; refer to Figure 3-8) on a boom pointed at the side of the head, away from the camera. If you don't have a boom arm, try using a light stand as close to your model as possible while keeping it out of the shot.

Practice this technique and get the hang of it. Rim lighting and backlighting are valuable lighting techniques for certain types of portraiture, such as a bride's portrait. Just be careful not to overdo it.

Preparing to Take Your First Portraits

Studio portraiture is about making your subjects look as they would like to appear — not necessarily as they really are. When you're setting up your poses, reflect upon how to make people look their best.

A good portrait photographer inspires confidence not only in himself but also in the client. The better you can make a person who's posing for you feel about how they look, the better her pose — and the better her feeling about the whole portrait experience. This works in your favor because your subject will likely be interested in buying your photographs. This section provides the basic information you need to get started.

Working on a tight schedule

People pose for portraits for different reasons and in different situations. If you're working on a tight schedule with a lot of sittings in a relatively brief period of time (say a wedding or church directory shoot), you don't have a lot of time to get to know your subjects or establish a rapport, especially for a family. Instead, consider a routine that works something like this:

1. **Pose the family.**

   Have Mom seated and Dad as one of the side elements in the diamond pose. (See the sidebar, "The diamond pose," elsewhere in this chapter.) Then build the rest of the pose with the other family member(s).

2. **Shoot the family portrait.**

3. **Pull the kids from the family pose.**

4. **Keep Mom and Dad in place and photograph their portrait.**

5. **Pull Mom and Dad from the sitting and set the kids up into a new diamond pose (depending on how many kids you need to photograph).**

   Usually, it's best to pose a group of male children in a line from tallest to shortest. If there's a sister or two, seat the eldest boy and pose the eldest girl as the next diamond element with her hands on his shoulder.

6. **Ask the parents for any special poses they would like.**

   Don't be afraid to take special requests; they're usually very likely to be appreciated.

When you're doing large numbers of portraits (after word gets out about how good you are, you're bound to be the hit of the next family reunion!), strive for the most efficient posing setup and flow possible. People who are sitting around in their finery waiting to be photographed can get pretty grumpy, particularly if there's more than one group waiting. A typical pose, using the diamond configuration, is shown in Figure 3-17.

Book IV Chapter 3

Photographing People

Figure 3-17: You end up with an attractive pose like this one when using the diamond arrangement.

With most families, Mom is usually the decision maker when it comes to family portraits. Make sure you keep her happy. Have brushes, combs, and lint brushes on hand so that everyone can make sure they look their best.

Try to be flexible enough for a special request because sometimes these can be very profitable. I was once part of a team shooting portraits for a church directory when a husband mentioned that he and his new wife never had a wedding portrait done. We suggested that they come back after our shooting schedule was done in their best suit and wedding gown, and we'd do a series of portraits for them. The couple loved the idea, and we spent an hour creating different poses and portraits and ended up with a huge order! Most importantly, we accomplished this without inconveniencing other members of the church and gained a reputation for enthusiasm and service amongst that particular church's members.

When you have more time

If you're working under a more generous time schedule and aiming for a higher-end product, take the time to make your subjects comfortable and see what they're looking for in a portrait sitting.

Although you might still be looking at the basic family portrait package (family, couple, children), it's also very possible that each family member might need individual portraits as well. This could be the time to bring out more specialized types of lighting, such as the broad lighting and short lighting discussed earlier in this chapter.

Be sure to offer your clients some extra poses for each family member, particularly for those kids who go for a variety of sports in a big way. Have props such as soccer balls, baseball gear, footballs and helmets, and other such items on hand.

Here are some of the kinds of groups to expect:

✦ **Husbands and wives:** Offer husbands and wives the basic couples pose, but also suggest a second pose that illustrates their love and commitment to each other (standing close, gazing into each other's eyes). Depending on their age and demeanor, a more whimsical pose, like the one shown in Figure 3-18, might also be in order. If you want a whimsical pose, having the husband get down on one knee to re-create his marriage proposal while the wife "thinks" about it can be cute.

✦ **Kids:** A brother and sister can be posed in a diagonal with the boy seated and the girl angled behind him with her hands folded on his shoulder. This is a basic couples pose, but the relationship issue isn't important. If you have two posing stools, you can seat both diagonally one behind the other. A pose that works with two boys is to have them sit back to back with their heads turned toward the camera.

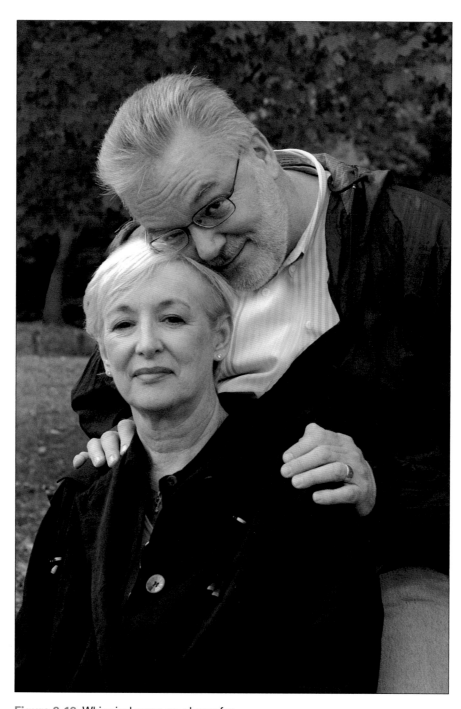

Figure 3-18: Whimsical poses are always fun.

✦ **Mothers and daughters:** Seat Mom and have her daughters arranged in the appropriate number of elements for a diamond pose. Another option — if you have the posing boxes to do so — is to seat Mom on a posing stool and have a daughter or two seated at her knee. A third daughter (the eldest) would be diagonally behind Mom with her hands on Mom's shoulder. If I had them, I'd load the scene with flowers.

✦ **Fathers and sons:** A simple pose would be to seat Dad and build a diamond around him. A more adventurous pose would be to have Dad standing slightly sideways with his off-camera hand in his pocket looking at his son(s) posed about a foot away (one diagonally behind the other) while one tosses a ball in the air (the sons watch the ball; Dad watches the sons). A simpler variation would be to have the sons remove their suit jackets (if this is a dressy portrait) and sling them over their shoulders (off-camera side) while Dad regards them with arms folded across his chest (still properly attired).

✦ **Infants:** For a fancy pose, look for an old-fashioned baby buggy or other such prop. A lot of choices are available, including simulated giant seashells for the baby to sit in or bearskin rugs to lie on. Generally, how you pose an infant depends on his or her age and physical abilities, such as whether or not the infant can sit up unsupported. Babies younger than six weeks old usually can't focus their eyes on any specific point, so they present a special challenge. Usually, it's best to leave them in their carrier and go for a reasonably tight shot.

The diamond pose

Diamonds are a photographer's best friend. Professional portrait photographers use a diamond formation as their basic foundation for a group photo. Establish your anchor person (usually the mother in a family portrait) and seat him or her. Place the father (or second individual) behind the anchor and halfway to the side. Elevate the seated person so the top of his/her head is level with the nose of the standing person. Have the standing person place his or her hands one on top of the other, slightly angled on the seated person's shoulder. (This is the basic pose for a couple, by the way.) Then do the same with the third person to balance the trio. (This gives you a basic pose for three people.) Place the fourth person directly behind the first person and positioned so that the heads of Subjects 2 and 3 come up to the nose of the fourth person. (Have sturdy wooden boxes or blocks of varying sizes for people to stand on.) Have Subjects 2–4 lean slightly forward from the waist so that their faces are as close as possible to being on the same plane as the first person. Avoid gaps between bodies, and make sure that people are close to each other. This basic posing system is expandable to fit 20 people or more.

As a general rule, pose multiple people closer together than they would normally stand if left to personal space comfort levels. Your goal is to maximize the use of space by filling the frame as effectively as possible with people, not backdrop or props. This doesn't mean that you're doing nothing but headshots, though. If you're doing a wedding or prom shoot, people will be in their finest clothes, and showing that clothing is appropriate. Certainly, the bride in her wedding gown deserves at least one photo that shows her entire dress, including the train.

Shooting the Portrait

Now that the previous section has made you more comfortable shooting portraits, you're ready to begin. Your first family enters your studio ready to have a portrait taken. After you exchange pleasantries, be sure to point them in the direction of the mirrors and check their appearance for any last-second adjustments.

Seating your subjects

When everyone's ready, begin arranging the sitting. Start by seating the mother and build your diamond around her. Make sure each person is sitting or standing up straight. (Place your hand on the front of a shoulder and two fingers at the base of the spine and apply gentle pressure to straighten them up.)

Have your subjects focus their eyes slightly to one side of the lens. Have them bring their chins up slightly so they're looking slightly up and away from the camera.

While seating your subjects, remember the following:

✦ **Make sure that your subjects are sitting up straight.** Slouching just doesn't look flattering to anyone.

✦ **Check to make sure clothing is as wrinkle-free as possible.** Tug suit jackets to straighten out wrinkles if need be.

✦ **Use your modeling lights (if you have them) to make sure you minimize the glare from eyeglasses as much as possible.** No one wants to look like Little Orphan Annie with no eyes.

✦ **Provide a mirror, as shown in Figure 3-19, so your subjects can check themselves over just before you take the picture.** Knowing they look good helps people relax.

**Book IV
Chapter 3**

Photographing People

Figure 3-19: Putting every hair in place.

Use this time to get your subjects in position and into the right mood for the portrait. Remember to stay positive and encouraging. Be sure to tell them they look good. Crack a few jokes while positioning people to keep them relaxed, too.

Posing your subjects

In order to properly pose your subjects, keep in mind that you are dealing with two separate tasks: positioning them in such a way to make them look their best and creating a pose that's not too unbearable to maintain for several minutes.

Start out by posing the lowest seated person, as follows:

1. **Pose the bottom person in the diamond so that he or she is comfortably seated on a posing stool; elevate the person's legs so they are at a right angle to his or her body.**

2. **Place a small posing box for the subject to place his feet on for best comfort while he is holding the pose.**

3. **Angle the subject so that he is at about a 45-degree angle to the camera lens.**

Make sure this subject is comfortable in the basic pose because he has to hold the pose longer than anyone else. I usually put the mother in this position for these reasons:

✦ She looks natural as the base of the diamond.

✦ She's usually trying to set a good example for the rest of her family.

✦ If she's already in the pose, she can't meddle with your work with the rest of her family. (Don't underestimate this reason, whatever you do.)

With your first person in place, it's time to move on to Subject 2:

1. **Set the second person on a posing stool angled behind the first person.**

   Normally, this would be the father, but there are no hard and fast rules here. Position him so that his head is properly oriented in relation to the mother within the diamond pose.

2. **Have your subject place his on-camera hand (the hand facing the camera) on his hip.**

   Be forewarned: Couples are always trying to put their arms around each other's waists. Don't let them; it's touching, but it doesn't photograph well. If dealing with spouses or a couple in a relationship, let them put their off-camera hand on their partner's hip out of sight of the camera.

3. **Have the second subject lean slightly into the first person so that you don't have any gaps between their bodies.**

   Make sure both are still sitting up straight. If a gap exists, you can turn the stools slightly to bring the shoulders a little more square to the camera and close the gap. You can also slide the chairs a little closer together.

Keep in mind that the pose you're setting up with the husband and wife (or whatever significant pair you're posing) also makes an excellent pose for when you do the couple's portrait. Don't let them get up when the family/group shot is done, or you'll just have to re-create this pose all over again.

After you have Mom and Dad posed, add the kids. Start with Kid 1:

1. **Place the smallest child on the bottom person's other side, using a posing box to raise her up to an appropriate height.**

2. **Turn the third subject toward the bottom person (roughly at the same angle as the second subject).**

3. **Move the third subject so that he or she is about halfway behind the bottom sitter.**

   The second and third subjects should be close together, but it isn't mandatory that their shoulders touch. Just avoid a gap between those two posers and the bottom subject.

You've set the base for a diamond pose and created a good three-person sitting. Remember to keep the relationship between the three heads consistent so that a line drawn across Subject 2 and Subject 3's faces travels over their eyes. Their mouths should be even with the first poser's eyes.

Now add Subject 4:

1. **Place your fourth person behind Subjects 2 and 3 and raise him or her up (if necessary) by using a posing box.**

   Subject 4 fills any gap between Subjects 2 and 3, which is why it wasn't that important to squeeze them in tight.

2. **Square Subject 4's shoulders toward the camera.**

3. **Adjust the height of Subject 4 so that his or her mouth is on a line with the eyes of Subjects 2 and 3. Have Subject 4 lean slightly into the others.**

That last little part about leaning is important. Ideally, you want all the faces in the same plane for the best possible focus. Even when shooting at f/11 or f/16, it's still better to have all faces on a line for best appearance. After you get everyone lined up properly, check your modeling lights to make sure that no one is casting shadows somewhere they shouldn't be.

If you need to pose more than four individuals, take the following guidelines to heart:

✦ **Use the topmost person in your original diamond as the base person for another diamond group.**

   This lets you add three more people the same way you added Subjects 2 through 4.

✦ **If you have more than seven sitters, start building diamonds outward by using the left- or right-most person in the lower diamond as the side anchor of a new diamond.**

✦ **As you build your additional diamonds, take care to make sure that everyone's faces line up properly in the same focal plane.**

✦ **Make sure that everyone is on steady ground.**

As more and more people stand on posing blocks, your group's inherent stability suffers. You don't want to see them collapse into your backdrop and lights.

Working with a large group is a difficult challenge because the number of variables increases to almost unmanageable numbers. Take a moment before setting up the pose to do a little planning.

Visualize the group pose before you start assembling it to avoid wasted time and effort after you get started. Take a moment to explain to the whole group that you're going to take a lot of shots of the group pose to maximize your chances of getting an exposure with as many good expressions as possible.

Arranging your lighting

Create a triangle with your base posing stool as its apex. Set up your main light and fill light about 6 feet apart and 6 feet from the posing stool.

Position your background light about 2 feet behind the posing stool and then position the background approximately 1 to 2 feet from the background light.

If you're using a hair light, position the light angled about 45 degrees behind the subject's head pointed toward the camera. Take a moment to check your viewfinder to make sure that no part of the hair light protrudes into the photograph. (Read about positioning a hair light in the earlier section, "Hair light.")

Taking the picture

After setting up the lights and arranging your subjects, start thinking about taking the picture.

I recommend triggering the camera via a remote so that you can maintain eye contact with your subjects. Many digital cameras (both professional and point-and-shoot types) offer some method of triggering the shutter without tripping the shutter button. If yours doesn't, you can still fire the camera via the shutter button while looking over the camera at your subjects.

Before tripping the shutter, go through this very quick checklist:

1. Is everyone standing up straight?

2. Are their heads properly arranged so that their faces are directed toward the camera?

3. Is everyone looking either directly toward the camera lens or in the direction you've designated? (Some poses may look better if you have your subjects looking slightly past the lens.)

4. Is everyone smiling?

Be ready to work fast. Holding a pose is a tiring chore. People lose their patience if you take too long to trip the shutter, so be ready to run through the checklist quickly.

Don't be afraid to stop and correct someone who's relaxed his or her pose. It doesn't do you any good to trip the shutter if someone doesn't look good.

I usually hold the remote behind my back when tripping the shutter during a portrait session in order to keep people from realizing I'm about to take the picture. This is important for two reasons:

✦ I don't want to give people a reason to shift their eyes in the direction of my hand when I'm taking the shot.

✦ Many people anticipate the flash firing and blink their eyes when the lights fire.

Remember to keep watching your subjects as you trip the shutter. You can usually catch any blinkers and know that you need to take another shot.

Advantages of Digital Cameras

Digital cameras offer you many advantages in portrait photography. Most important of all is the chance for the photographer to review the pose before the subjects leave. Because you can spot problems before your victims skedaddle, you have a chance to correct them while everyone's still there.

Another huge advantage of the digital camera is that it gives you a chance to make sales while your customers are still excited from their sitting and still in high spirits after all that positive feedback you've been giving them. (You have been giving them positive feedback, haven't you?)

Film photographers have to factor the cost of film, processing, and making proofs into their costs of doing business, thus driving up their margins. As a digital photographer, you can afford to take all the shots you want without damaging your bottom line (provided you have enough media to get you through a long shooting session, of course).

Learn to use your digital camera's review feature to its best effect. Here's a list of some of the things you should analyze as you play back your shot:

✦ **Make sure that the photo is properly focused.** Although you can't be dead sure while reading your camera's LCD screen, you can at least eliminate really poor shots. If you have a digital camera that can be hooked up to a television to play back images, by all means do so! This will help you get a better look at your images. You can also show the images to your clients while at the same time taking their orders. (If they're not satisfied, you can also offer to reshoot the sitting while they're still dressed for it.)

✦ **Check for any obvious errors.** Such errors could be gaps between people, bad expressions, or wrinkled clothes. Straighten out the clothing, as shown in Figure 3-20. Also make sure the subject's hair looks good and that the image is properly exposed.

Figure 3-20: Make sure the subject's clothing isn't in disarray.

✦ **Check for any lighting errors.** These include lights that shine where you don't want them to, bad shadows, and so forth.

✦ **If your subjects are wearing glasses, check for any hot spots that might be too difficult to clean up in an image editing program.** Repositioning someone's glasses is easier than heavy computer retouching, so make your job easier when you can.

✦ **Check for any blinkers.** This can be pretty tough with small LCD screens; a TV monitor makes this easier.

I once worked for a portrait firm (before the digital revolution hit its stride) that spent quite a bit of money developing a portrait system that simultaneously exposed a piece of film plus captured a low-resolution digital image. The photographer would hand the salesperson a floppy disk with the images, who would then show the images to clients while giving the sales pitch. Such a system made portrait sales much more effective because people were seeing the results of their sitting while they were still excited and upbeat about the process — and thus more likely to buy prints.

Most of today's digital cameras offer a similar capability via an RCA or video-out jack that allows you to hook up a TV monitor, as shown in Figure 3-21. You (and your subjects) can view images on a larger screen.

Figure 3-21: Connect your digital camera to a TV and preview your portraits as you take them.

Chapter 4: Shooting for Publication

In This Chapter

- Finding outlets for print publication
- Shooting for local newspapers
- Publishing in magazines and similar markets
- Photographing for company newsletters
- Effective public relations photography
- Taking photos of products

For some readers of this book, becoming a published photographer might be a lifelong goal. Many avid photographers hone their skills, trying to reach professional levels in a quest for a published credit line.

However, the average digital camera buff more often ends up shooting for publication for more practical reasons. Perhaps your parent-teacher association drafted you to publicize school events. Or maybe your small company doesn't have a full-time photographer, so you — with your digital camera wizardry — seem perfect to snap a portrait of the founder for the organization's newsletter. Perhaps you're a recognized expert in your hobby, customizing vintage Atari game consoles perhaps, and would like to have a few photographs published in one of the technical magazines devoted to '80s-era games.

Digital photography lends itself to all these situations because you can take a picture on a moment's notice, review your results on your camera's LCD, take *another* picture if you need to, and then produce a digital file or print that's ready for publication in a few minutes. Most professional photographers shooting for newspapers, magazines, catalogs, and other publications now use digital cameras — and you can, too.

In all these cases, your digital pictures are going to end up in print, and you need to know some things in order to shine when shooting for publication. This chapter explains the differences between taking pictures for print and for Web sites, desktop presentations, or a personal photo album. You can also find some tips on how to get published and advice on preparing your work for publication.

Finding Outlets for Print Publication

Whether you want to get published simply to satisfy yourself or you need to have your photos published to satisfy the expectations of your friends, boss, or colleagues, you can find lots of outlets for your digital work. Here are a few of the most common:

+ **Local newspapers:** Although larger newspapers rarely publish photos from readers, smaller local papers usually welcome submissions of photos on behalf of your school, club, or even business. Or, you can make a habit of showing up at public meetings or fast-breaking news events. Supply enough good shots in a variety of situations, and the paper might take you on as a part-time *stringer* (a freelancer with an ongoing affiliation with a publication). Because digital pictures can be snapped and transmitted to a newspaper over phone lines just minutes after an event takes place, electronic photos are especially apt.

+ **Trade magazines:** These are the unseen publications that nobody knows about, except for the millions of people within a particular industry. You might never have heard of *Repro Report* magazine unless you're a member of the International Reprographics Association. I had never heard of it, either, when I started taking pictures for the magazine (way back when it was still called *Plan and Print.*) However, that publication (and many like it) are constantly looking for photos taken at member businesses, conventions, and other venues. These trade publications are good outlets for digital photography, and I've managed to have my own photographs published in hundreds of them. You can do it, too.

+ **Company publications:** Companies of any size can never have enough photographers. If your organization is small, management might be delighted to find a photographer who's outfitted with fast and flexible digital gear and who's also ready, willing, and able to snap photos for company newsletters, annual reports, and other official publications. Even larger organizations with a full-time photography staff might be receptive to photos that you take at events that their pros are unable to cover.

+ **Special interest publications:** Every hobby or special interest, from collecting Seat Occupied signs from defunct airlines to protecting your right to arm bears, probably has a publication of some sort. If you share that interest, you can easily get your digital photos published.

✦ **External PR and advertising:** Most organizations can use photos for public relations or advertising purposes. If you're good, your work can accompany news releases or be incorporated into less formal advertising layouts. Digital cameras are good for these applications because you can create a photo in a few minutes, ready for review and approval by the high mucky-mucks in an organization.

✦ **Self-publication:** The fastest route to getting your digital photos printed is to publish them yourself. Whether your interests stem from a favorite hobby or from the most arcane conspiracy theories, if you have a computer, you can create a newsletter, fanzine, or other publication and spice it up with your own photos.

The best part about self-publication is that you have absolute control over which images are used, how they are sized and cropped, and who gets to see them. And who knows? If your work is good, you might get paying subscribers to cover part of your costs. In my case, I knew that no publisher would possibly want to print my illustrated guidebook to repairing vintage video games, so I took the photos, laid out the manual, and published it myself, as you can see in Figure 4-1. I've sold thousands of copies on eBay of something that I put together just for fun.

Figure 4-1: Publish your own fan magazine or other publication and put your photos to work.

✦ **Product photographs:** Your company probably needs photos of its products for use in advertising, PR, and so forth. You can take them with your digital camera.

Shooting for publication isn't as hard as many people think provided you remember that you don't start out shooting for slick, nationally distributed magazines any more than aspiring ball players begin by playing shortstop for the New York Yankees. If *National Grocer* is your target, rather than *National Geographic,* you have a shot.

Breaking into Newspaper Photography

Your local paper is probably willing to consider your digital photos of a local event, particularly if it's a small paper. Larger newspapers prefer to use their own photographers — not because they don't think your photos are good enough but because of journalistic ethics reasons. Big papers frequently face charges of journalistic bias and must be able to vouch that a given photograph hasn't been manipulated in ways that would make it misleading. Photographs supplied by businesses can't be used unless they are clearly labeled as a photograph originating with that organization. However, bear in mind that even big cities have small, special-interest papers that can be a market for your pictures.

Newspaper photography is fun and challenging. This type of shooting isn't especially rewarding financially, but it does provide valuable experience because you learn to adapt your photographic ability to the environment. No other type of photography offers the shooter as little control over the shooting conditions as photojournalism. For some of us, that's the best thing about it.

Submitting photos to your local newspaper

The key to getting published in your local paper is understanding what it does and doesn't need from you. Newspapers have small photo staffs and can't be everywhere at once. They'll send a photographer (*shooter* in the lingo of photo editors) to a major event or fire or accident, but if several events happen at the same time, shooters probably will have to cover one or two events and let the others slide. For example, I regularly cover events at my kids' school and submit them to the newspaper. Our paper even prints the articles that accompany the photos, as you can see in Figure 4-2.

Here are some of the kinds of photos that smaller newspapers would love to receive:

✦ **Events:** Your club or fraternity is having its annual barbecue or banquet or get-together of whatever form. It's not a big enough deal for the local paper to send someone to cover. If you can produce some usable images along with enough information to caption them properly, you can probably get at least one of them published. Newspapers are willing to run photos like these because people like to see their pictures in the paper — and that helps sell newspapers.

✦ **Sports:** The paper's shooters cover the big events, such as football, basketball, baseball, and so on. Your opportunity comes with the sports that don't quite get their due. For example, shoot track and field events (not necessarily the big weekend meets with 50 schools and a thousand athletes, but the local dual meet). Sports like tennis, field hockey, and lacrosse seldom get as much coverage as the big three (football, basketball, and baseball). Study your local paper to see what sports it seems to favor and then try submitting shots for the sports it doesn't seem to cover. Good action photos are particularly important. If you can regularly capture peak action well, your photos will be used. See Book IV, Chapter 5, for more information on how to take good sports photos with a digital camera.

Figure 4-2: Local newspapers are welcome territory for freelancers.

✦ **Spot news:** Spot news includes things such as traffic accidents, fires, and robberies. It can be tough to succeed at selling this kind of photo unless it's your main focus. If so, a police/fire scanner is a must. Remember, though, that it doesn't do you any good if you're covering the same news as the paper's staffer. Small-town papers tend to need this kind of material most and are sure to send out their own staffers at the first hint of a big story, but you might have a shot at publication if you're in the right place at the right time to take a photo of something that no one else managed to grab. (Some spot news opportunities don't last very long, which is why they're called *spot news*.) And because your digital camera film doesn't need processing, your photos are timely.

Although dramatic photos of spot news events can produce eye-catching portfolio shots, don't forget that human emotion creates the most memorable images. This is perhaps the most difficult part of photojournalism — intruding upon the tragedy of others and recording it for the world to see. Pros don't really have a choice in this matter — it's part of the job. Freelancers, however, can choose either side of the deal.

You might run across groups claiming that, as part of their membership fee, you'll receive a press pass that will get you across police lines or into events. *Be very skeptical of such claims.* Usually, an organization, such as the state police (in some states at least) or event organizers, issues a press pass. There is no universal press pass that gets you into any event. In fact, even working news photographers with state-issued press passes won't get into many events (pro sports and rock concerts for instance) unless they're specifically cleared for that event by the event organizer as well.

✦ **Hard news:** These are major news events, such as a speech by the mayor, a visit by the governor, certain press conferences, demonstrations, and political rallies. They're frequently open to the general public, although official photographers might be given a special area to shoot from.

✦ **News feature photography:** Feature photos and *news* feature photos are different. A news feature image accompanies a legitimate story with a feature edge — say an article on family TV-watching habits or a story on an upcoming play that will be performed this weekend (as shown in Figure 4-3).

✦ **Feature photography:** This part of the paper deals with the lighter side of life. You might shoot a feature package on Elvis impersonators or pictures of a local restaurant for a review. This is the one section of the paper where you'll frequently see *created images,* or what are sometimes called *photo illustrations.*

You can often tie some local happening in to a historical event to give your feature photo an interesting angle. For example, on May 4 of every year, I always find a ready market for photos of the 1970 shootings of four students on the Kent State University campus.

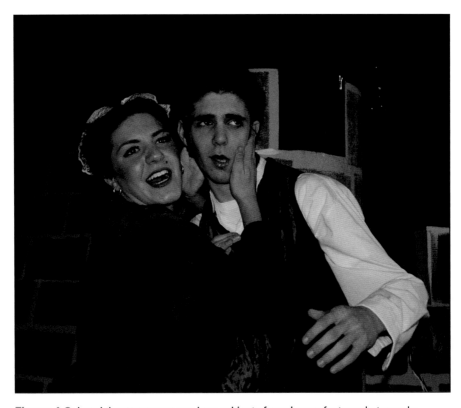

Figure 4-3: Local theater groups can be a subject of good news feature photographs.

You don't have to limit yourself to just one community newspaper. More often than not, neighboring newspapers have circulation areas that overlap. If you know your neighboring communities well, you can also market your talents to their newspapers.

Working as a professional newspaper photographer

Whether you submit photographs to newspapers as a representative of your organization, as a freelancer for pay, or as an official stringer for the newspaper, you want to conduct your business professionally. There are lots of points to consider. For example, do you want to be a freelancer or a stringer?

Being a stringer versus freelancing

Nonstaffers come in two types of affiliations: being a stringer and being a freelancer. The difference is in just how attached you and the newspaper are to each other.

Here's what being a stringer involves:

+ **Regular assignments:** Stringers receive assignments from the paper they're affiliated with, frequently with a guarantee of pay, even if a shot isn't used.

+ **Pseudostaffer:** Still considered an independent contractor, stringers are generally issued a newspaper press pass, like the one shown in Figure 4-4, or the paper gets a state credential for them (if it's in a state that issues them).

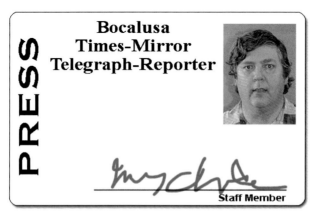

PRESS

Bocalusa Times-Mirror Telegraph-Reporter

Staff Member

Figure 4-4: If your work is good, a small-town newspaper might issue you a press pass.

+ **Free supplies:** Stringers frequently receive supplies, such as film (in the old days), notebooks, pens, and pencils. You might be able to get your newspaper to chip in for some extra digital film, which could be handy if you're rushed to get a shot published and need to simply hand over your memory card.

+ **Loyalty:** Both the stringer and the newspaper are expected to show some level of loyalty to each other, although it might not be a lot. Generally, a paper has a specific number of stringers and a rotation policy to have some fair manner of distributing assignments. By the same token, a stringer doesn't shoot for the paper's competition. (Usually the expectation is that you won't shoot for a newspaper that is sold in your paper's distribution area.)

Additionally, stringers are generally considered independent contractors for tax purposes. This is occasionally a point of contention between newspapers and state employment officials who scrutinize such arrangements carefully

Avoiding the Grip 'n' Grin cliché

Grip 'n' Grin — it's the standard shot of any event. You know, one person is giving an award, and one person is receiving it. They stand there gripping the award, each looking right at the camera and grinning. Photo editors hate these pictures. They all look alike, and the only people who are interested in looking at them are the ones receiving the award and maybe the ones giving it. Take the shot, give the awardee a print, and then get a shot that has a chance of being used.

Rather than take a Grip 'n' Grin shot, provide a sense of what the event is about. If it's a barbecue, get behind the grills and take a shot of somebody getting a hot dog through a haze of smoke with a big smile on his or her face (hopefully wearing a cap or T-shirt with the name of the organization on it). You can mention the award presented at the event in the *cutline* (caption), but there's really no need to show it. More information on preparing images for publication appears later in this chapter.

to see whether such relationships should be considered employer/employee instead of contractor/client. You should be aware of tax responsibilities in this situation, too.

Working as a freelancer also has some advantages and disadvantages:

✦ **Freedom:** Freelancers have no affiliation to any particular newspaper, so they receive no support from any paper. However, they are free to work for any newspaper and to sell pictures to the highest bidder if they stumble on a potential Pulitzer Prize winner.

✦ **More freedom:** Because freelancers are unaffiliated, they either don't get assignments or are at the very bottom of the list of those who do. That simply means that freelancers have to develop their own opportunities, which can help sharpen their news sense.

Freelancers don't have to worry about employee/employer relationships because they're total free agents as independent contractors, but the same tax responsibilities apply. As a stringer or a freelancer, you can likely deduct the cost of your equipment and expenses involved in doing business. You might also have to make quarterly tax payments if this is your primary source of income. (I'm not an accountant, however, so I can't give you tax advice; I urge you to consult a professional for the details.)

Newspaper Web sites have created a new concern for freelance photographers. Many papers now require freelancers to sign over more rights or all rights to any images used in the paper as a result of some recent court decisions. These rulings have said that freelancers still retain the other rights to their images even if a photo appeared in the paper. Because many newspapers were making their entire issue available online, the decisions

Book IV
Chapter 4

**Shooting for
Publication**

meant that the papers were violating the freelancer's copyrights. Most of the time, the loss of the additional copyright doesn't receive any additional compensation. Only you can decide whether giving up all rights to a particular image is worth the chance to get your work published.

Special considerations for news photography

Here are some things to think about when photo—graphing news events:

- **Be aware of emotions.** Tempers can run high at both spot and hard news events. Sometimes, law enforcement personnel can overreact when things go wrong. Cameras can be broken, film can get confiscated, and photographers can be threatened. More and more often these days, police (although to be fair, still not that often) try to stop press photographers from working, First Amendment considerations be damned. In such situations, newspaper photographers tend to have their newspaper's resources behind them, whereas a freelancer probably doesn't. It's best to accept that you're not on a level playing field in such circumstances. There are stories of photographers who've played sleight of hand with their film and turned over an unexposed roll of film when someone demanded their images. I've been ready to do so myself once or twice, but it's a judgment call for each photographer to decide what risk he or she is willing to take. In small towns, you can avoid problems by getting the police and firefighters on your side. Give them prints and work hard at getting favorable photos in the newspaper.

- **Be different.** Your best bet as a freelancer is to deliver something different from what everyone else is doing. One of the best news shots I've ever seen came from a presidential campaign several decades ago. The photo is of a president answering questions with a mountain of photographers pressed together shooting away. One enterprising shooter had enough of a sense of the moment to take a few steps back and record the insanity of the situation. In the process, he got a timeless photo that far exceeded the images his counterparts created.

- **Look for unusual angles.** Shoot from up high and down low. Try and get the shot with several different focal lengths, too.

- **Be careful not to get locked in on the main event.** Sometimes, the best shot comes because you look beyond the setting and uncover human nature at work. Young children can offer interesting opportunities because they don't hide their reactions or feelings as much as adults do. A sleeping child at a political event or wedding can show humor and make a comment about how sometimes adults take themselves too seriously.

- **Look at the participants who aren't center stage.** Is there a clandestine conversation going on? Do they look bored? Are they looking in the opposite direction of everyone else?

News photography strives for impact. Eye contact and emotions are key ingredients. Don't be afraid to compose your shot tightly. The image should have a single focal point, not multiple ones. Whether you're shooting for a newspaper or the World Wide Web, space is valuable, and images should be tightly cropped and easily understood.

Getting your foot in the door

How do you become a stringer or freelancer? I recommend making initial contact by mail. A simple introductory letter identifying yourself as a photographer interested in working as a stringer or freelancer, plus some samples of your work, should be enough. Don't overdo it on the number of samples you send. Two or three shots that demonstrate your ability are enough.

Then, follow up. In your letter, say you're going to call in a day or two to discuss how you might be able to help the paper. All you're aiming for at this point is a chance to meet the editor, show him or her your portfolio, and sell the idea of your contributing. The smaller the newspaper, the better your chances (although the smaller the pay, too).

Be thorough in your examination of the potential marketplace. Many areas have more than one newspaper and thus more than one opportunity for freelancing.

Magazines and Magazine-Like Markets

Breaking into magazine, book, or stock photography presents a different set of challenges and opportunities. Magazines offer the most opportunities.

Making the leap to published photographer is within the reach of many talented amateurs. It's just a question of understanding what markets are out there, how to make contact, and what the markets need.

Exploring magazine photography

You can find many different types of magazines that aim toward a variety of audiences. These magazines include

✦ **Trade journals:** Although perhaps not glamorous, these specialized publications are good potential sources of sales for enterprising digital photographers. A *trade journal* is a magazine that covers a specific industry or profession. These magazines are seldom found on newsstands but are instead distributed mainly via subscriptions. Although they might not pay very well (if at all), they tend to be the easiest magazine market for novices to break into.

If there's a trade journal for your particular profession or trade, you probably have a good place to start because you already have knowledge and experience in the industry. Your chances of acceptance improve even more if you can package a story with your photos. This is also a good market for event photos within your industry, particularly if you can produce interesting images. You can also cover local stores and companies in your area with the idea of doing a feature about their operations for the trade publication.

✦ **Special interest magazines:** These are mass-market publications geared toward a specific interest — think magazines like *Tennis, Popular Photography, Cat Fancy*, and so on. This market is harder to break into than the trade journal market because these magazines tend to pay better than trade journals and also because more writers and photographers want to be published in them. Read the guidelines, study the magazine thoroughly, and query the editor before submitting anything. In many cases, these magazines are more receptive to photo-only queries. Regional travel magazines can be a good bet. If you get a good photo of an unusual or out-of-the-way travel destination, like the one shown in Figure 4-5, you could have a sure sale.

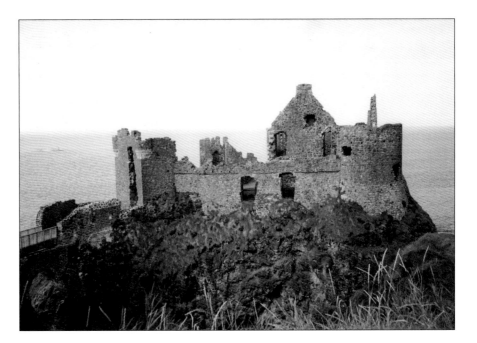

Figure 4-5: Photos of hard-to-get-to locations are easy to sell.

✦ **Major mass-market magazines:** *Time, People, Cosmopolitan* . . . these are the heavy hitters of the magazine world. They're also incredibly difficult publications for beginners to sell to. Many times, these magazines won't even consider unsolicited submissions and probably won't take your query letter seriously, either, unless you have some kind of established track record as a professional photographer. An amateur photographer generally needs a remarkably newsworthy image to have a chance to sell to one of these magazines.

Getting into book publishing and stock photography

Other markets include

✦ **Books, textbooks, and photo books:** The good news is that this market can be a reasonably easy one to break into. The bad news is that book editors are notoriously cheap, grumpy, and hard to deal with. (Just kidding! They're actually kind, supportive, and generous; plus they edit books such as this one.) Unfortunately, the book publishing industry is extremely competitive, and the sad truth is that many books don't turn a profit. (Please buy an extra copy of this one! It will make a great gift.) So although there is a need for good photography, there's seldom a lot of money in it. Find a publisher whose line of books appeals to you and query about its photographic needs and policies or check the appropriate market guide book. A coffee table or photo book is a tough sell even for established pros and requires the highest quality photographic images to support the higher resolution these books demand.

✦ **Stock photography:** The concept sounds great: Sell the same image over and over and make lots of money. No, it's not a telemarketing scam or multilevel marketing scheme; it's the world of stock photography. You deal with stock photo agencies, which keep carefully categorized images in a database that they can access to provide virtually any sort of picture (including yours) at the request of a client. To break into this business, you'll need lots and lots of photos (thousands) to make taking you on worth the agency's time. Figure 4-6 shows an example of a generic photo that *might* be useful as a stock picture.

✦ **Web stock agencies:** A number of growing stock agencies (often called microstock organizations) have sprung up on the Internet thanks to its worldwide reach, easy accessibility, and relatively low cost compared with the prime real estate used to house the big agencies. The advantage to them is that they can provide a starting point for photographers whose portfolios are too small to interest the big agencies. Of course, if your stock of images is that small, the odds are against your having much success. Still, most offer the photographer 20 percent or more of the revenue received, which can be as little as $1.00 per download, so it's an opportunity for you to get a lot of images online without having to have a Web site or server of your own.

Shooting stock pictures is one area in which having a spouse and kids might actually pay off. Photos of family interaction, pensive teens, and children at play are all marketable stock images. How about a boy and his dog? A girl and her cat? Study advertisements and brochures. Although teams of professional artists, designers, and photographers sometimes create images specifically for an ad or brochure, more often than not, they've been put together from stock images. Advertisers sell products by showing normal everyday people whose lives are enriched by their products. Theoretically, your family qualifies as normal. (Heaven knows I wish mine did!)

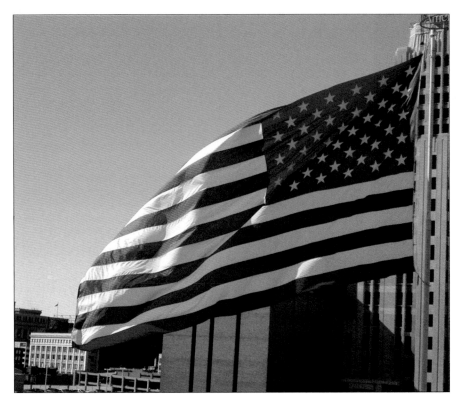

Figure 4-6: For stock photography, you don't want just one flag picture; you need dozens for clients to choose from.

Gathering publishable photographs

Never forget this omnipresent law of the photograph seller-to-be: *In focus and properly exposed.* It's amazing how often these basics aren't met when people submit photos to their local newspaper. I know from personal experience: At one newspaper I worked for, I was the one who had to weed through all those pictures trying to find something we could actually use.

So start by sending your best work. Publishable photographs are different from fine art. Their purpose is to communicate as simply and effectively as possible. Because you can do that, here's how to take the next step toward seeing your work in print:

✦ **Be organized.** Have a filing system that enables you to identify and locate a particular image.

✦ **Be ready to do some research.** Your local library is sure to carry references, such as the publication you're interested in selling to as well as *Photographer's Market.* Consider investing in your own copy because *Photographer's Market* provides information on a wide range of possible markets.

✦ **Consider ordering your own business cards and stationery in order to look professional.** If your budget allows, consider a promotional piece, such as a four-color postcard or print showing some samples of your best work.

Making contact with a publication

The magazine industry does not respond well to unsolicited photographs and manuscripts. Although you have a better chance of getting published with a trade journal than with most other types of publications, you improve your chances by sending the publication's editor a carefully worded missive indicating what he or she can expect.

Sometimes, a publication accepts unsolicited photos or manuscripts. You can usually find this information noted in the magazine's *masthead,* located inside the first few pages of the magazine and listing the publisher, staff, and contact information. If a publication does accept unsolicited submissions, be selective. Don't bombard an editor with a submission per week or more. (Editors can get restraining orders, too.) Instead, send your best. Either include an SASE (self-addressed, stamped envelope) with enough postage for the editor to return the photos to you or attach a note saying they don't have to come back. (Back in the days of typewritten manuscripts and hand-printed photos, this whole issue used to be a much bigger deal than it is now.)

Introduce yourself in a query letter. Talk about your experience in the industry, plus your experience as a writer and photographer if it might help. Let the editors know what your photo or story idea is and how you plan on approaching it. Also indicate that you're familiar with the publication's guidelines for writers.

Writer's and photographer's guidelines are frequently available on the Web or by mail and are sometimes even noted in the publication itself. Books such as the *Writer's Market* and *Photographer's Market* appear yearly, providing useful information about many publications. Generally, this information tells you how publications want materials submitted. (Do they accept digital photos? Should you submit prints with them? How should prints be packaged? Do the publications even accept work from freelancers?) Publications such as trade journals are more forgiving if you violate their writer's guides than other magazines are, but it's still best not to do so. (Remember, you're trying to convince them that you're a professional.)

Whatever individual guidelines a publication has, you'd be wise to keep the following in mind:

✦ **Be enthusiastic!** You can't expect editors to get fired up about your idea if it sounds like you find it dull. Tell them why you think their readers will want to read your story.

✦ **Submit on spec.** If the editor is interested in your work, mention that you'd be willing to submit it on speculation *(spec)*, which means that you prepare the work at your own risk, with no guarantee that the publication will use it. This kind of thing lets the editor know that he can encourage your submission without having to worry about what will happen if you're rejected. (Editors have nightmares about beginning contributors threatening lawsuits because they expected to be published even though all the editor did was agree to look at a submission.)

✦ **Send in your tear sheets.** If you have samples of published work (usually referred to as *tear sheets*), go ahead and submit the best one or two (three at the most) pieces you've done, like those shown in Figure 4-7. Quality is tremendously more important than quantity here. If you don't have something good to submit, don't submit anything at all unless the editors or guidelines ask for it. Frequently, editors take on mediocre writing with good photography simply because they can improve poor writing but might have trouble finding good photography.

Figure 4-7: Send in some clippings or tear sheets of your published work.

Trade journals are the best place to start if you're interested in expanding beyond newspaper work. They tend to be receptive to freelancers and provide the opportunity to contribute both photos and text. If writing isn't your thing, see whether you can team up with a newspaper staffer or stringer who's also looking to expand his or her reach.

Editors hate submissions and query letters that make it obvious the people contacting them haven't even looked at their magazine. Most publications offer copies at a reasonable rate for would-be contributors, or your local library may have back issues available. Get to know the magazine before you propose a story idea. Studying back issues tells you whether you've been beaten to the punch by another contributor, or you might find out that a publication is the wrong market for your submission.

Submitting your photos

Quite a few publications remain cautious about digital submissions for final publication (perhaps accepting CD submissions for portfolio samples) and might not even be willing to consider them. If the fact that your images are digital is the only thing preventing them from acceptance, consider converting them to analog artwork. A few publications accept prints, but these are in the minority. Generally, the hands-on favorite for submission even now is transparencies, or *slides*. The good news is that you have a couple of ways to get 35mm slides made from digital files:

✦ Online photo labs frequently offer this service. One such lab is www. slides.com, which charges about $2.50 per slide.

✦ Get a 5 x 7 or 8 x 10 print made from your digital file and load your film camera up with a good quality slide film. Then, either set up a *copy stand* (camera is placed perfectly parallel to print with two lights placed at 45 degree angles to the print) or your tripod and photograph the print.

As time goes by, more and more publications are accepting digital images. Odds are high that your local newspaper will. It's a nice feeling to discuss an image with an editor, e-mail him or her the image, and find out that it has been accepted, all in a single afternoon (particularly when you're selling a shot for the second or third or fourth time).

Getting model releases

A *model release* is written permission to use a person's likeness. These documents, available from any photo store, are popular with publishers because they help protect the publisher from nuisance lawsuits. The need for model releases depends upon how the images are to be used. Newspaper photographers, for instance, seldom bother. Editorial use is generally recognized by the courts to support the public good and provides some protections to such publications expected to meet that need. Usually newspapers, news magazines, and books are considered to meet the editorial-use standard, although most book publishers desire model releases anyway. Advertising photography, on the other hand, receives no such help. If your photo is going to help sell a product, have a model release for every *recognizable* individual in the shot.

Even as a newspaper photographer, I still try to be careful when it comes to photographing children. Usually, I look for the adult caretakers first, introduce myself to them, explain my purpose in taking pictures of the kids, and give them one of my business cards before asking their permission to shoot. Perhaps this was more than I needed to do, but parents rarely object after they know who I am and why I am taking pictures of their kids. Skip this approach, and you might end up explaining yourself to a state trooper instead. Also, a parent or guardian must sign model releases for minors if you want those releases to count.

A model release doesn't give you *carte blanche* to play with a person's image, which is something that's very easy to do with a digital photograph. Taking someone's image under innocuous circumstances and then placing it into what could be considered an embarrassing photo composite could leave you open to a lawsuit. When in doubt, be careful and consult with a lawyer or discuss the potential use with your subject (making sure your model release reflects the potential use and the subject's awareness of it). Model releases are particularly important for stock photography, where the image could end up being used for just about anything.

In some cases, public figures receive less privacy protection than private citizens when it comes to editorial photography. (Think of how the paparazzi chase celebrities. If you followed your private citizen neighbor around that way, no doubt your future cellmate would probably be amused to learn how you ended up in jail.) No such leeway exists to advertising-related uses, particularly because celebrities can argue that their likeness does have a monetary value and that your image is lowering its value.

Shooting Groups for Publication

This section details the special needs of each of the most common types of group photography for publication, such as groups and PR photos. In each section, you can find suggestions for taking great photos in a variety of situations. You'll find that these photos fit in with many different types of publications, from newspapers to trade magazines to company in-house newsletters to popular magazines. The tips in this section can be applied to many different types of print destinations.

Understanding group photography basics

Photographing groups can be an interesting challenge, one that calls for greater skill as the number of people in the shot grows. As you add more and more people to the frame, it becomes more difficult to catch a moment when everyone has a pleasant expression. As the numbers increase, faces get smaller, making it increasingly difficult just to make sure everyone is visible in the shot.

Group shots are popular — and for the photographer who can do a good job, rewarding. As souvenirs of large events, they're a well-accepted and comparatively easy way to commemorate a gathering. People have also become so trained to expect a group shot that trying to get through an event without taking one is almost a sacrilege. Thankfully, good group photos aren't impossible; they just need some planning and the right tools. They're perfect for trade publications looking to publicize member groups, or for your local newspaper.

Pose your group to conform to your camera's image area. For virtually all digital cameras, this means a horizontal rectangle that conforms to a roughly 2:3 aspect ratio.

Posing a group depends upon how many people you're working with. Book IV, Chapter 3 covers this topic in more detail, but the following sections dish out some helpful information.

Photographing groups of two to two dozen

Although 20 people might not seem like a small group, the techniques that you use to photograph collections of two dozen people or fewer are similar. Diamonds are a photographer's best friend. Professional portrait photographers use a diamond formation as their basic foundation for a group photo. You can find more about the diamond formation for groups in Book IV, Chapter 3.

The way it works is to establish your anchor person (usually the mother in a family portrait) and seat that person. Place the father (or second individual) behind the anchor person and halfway to the side. Elevate the anchor person so that the top of his or her head is level with the nose of the standing person. Have the standing person place his or her hands, one on top of the other and slightly angled, on the anchor person's shoulder. (This is the basic pose for a couple, too.) Now, on the opposite side of the anchor person, pose the third person the same way you posed the second person to balance the trio. (This gives you a basic pose for three people.)

Book IV
Chapter 4

Now place the fourth person directly behind the anchor person and positioned so that the heads of subjects two and three come up to the nose of the fourth person. (Have sturdy wooden boxes or blocks of varying sizes for people to stand on.) Have subjects two through four lean slightly forward from the waist so that their faces are as close to being on the same plane as the first person as possible. You do this so that everyone is on the same plane of focus. Make sure that people are close to each other so there aren't any gaps between bodies. Now you have a basic posing system that's expandable to fit 20 or more people.

Shooting for
Publication

Lighting groups

See Book II, Chapter 5, and Book IV, Chapter 3, for more information on lighting. Here are some general tips that you can use when lighting group photos that you hope will be publishable:

- **The pro way:** To light this setup, use a pair of studio lights firing into umbrellas or soft boxes about 6 feet apart and angled toward the center of the group. A third light is positioned behind the group and pointed at the backdrop to provide some separation from the backdrop. Set your light's power output to maximize your depth of field. *Safety tip:* If you're doing multiple sittings, use masking tape or gaffer's tape to tape your cables down so that people don't trip over them.

- **The serious amateur way:** A less professional setup that can still deliver good results is to use multiple slaved portable flashes (see Book II, Chapter 5 for an explanation of photographic slaves) without the backdrop. This approach has three problems: The flashes don't recycle as quickly as the studio lighting setup, the flashes don't put out as much light (meaning you have to go with shallower depth of field), and the lack of a backdrop means the photo's background will probably detract from the overall image quality. Few publications will use a photo that has a distracting background.

- **The not-so-serious amateur way:** One flash, straight ahead. It's not elegant, the light's kind of harsh, and you run the risk of red-eye, especially with kids. Getting your flash up higher helps prevent red-eye and gives you a nicer light, but even one flash can do you some good because it helps clean up shadows on your subjects' faces.

- **The "Oh My God, What Were You Thinking?" way:** The camera's built-in flash. You've got to be kidding. Most built-in flash units have a range of about 8 feet. It might do some good with a small group, but it's useless with a big one. Publications will reject large group photos poorly lit with a puny flash unit.

If you can't use a diamond-shaped pose, switch to a row arrangement, with a mix of sitting, kneeling, and standing subjects. Generally, four people or fewer make your first row. If you have five people, you can shift to a two-person front row and three-person back row.

Composing effective group shots

The general rule is that people don't buy portraits because their knees look good. Compose the shot from roughly above the waist to a little bit above the tallest person's head. Of course, this rule has a couple of exceptions. Wedding portraits should include all the finery, and so should formal events in which people are wearing gowns and tuxedos. When in doubt, take two shots — one long and one tight — and let your subjects pick the ones they prefer. Most professional portrait photographers offer at least two different poses to pick from. Here are some tips for arranging groups:

✦ **5 to 7 people:** Start with your basic four-person diamond pose (see the preceding section) and then start building a second diamond on top of the fourth person of the first diamond. Use that person as the anchor person for the second diamond.

✦ **8 to 20 or more people:** As you add more and more people, keep joining new diamonds with existing diamonds until this system starts becoming unwieldy. Generally, this happens somewhere between 10 and 20 people although experienced portrait pros can manage bigger groups. As the numbers grow, pay careful attention to whether your lights and backdrop are up to the challenge. (As your diamond stack grows taller, the height of the backdrop might not reach as high as the top of the uppermost diamond.)

✦ **More than 20:** At whatever point you feel uncomfortable with fitting a larger number of people into diamonds, switch to rows. Once again, remember the dimensions of your viewfinder. Keep the number of rows and columns proportioned so that you fill the frame effectively. With the rows and columns approach, divide each row in half and angle the halves into each other so that you can bring people closer together. Have your tallest rank kneel, position your shortest rank behind them, and then work your way back (tweaking if the tallest and shortest are so extreme that this alignment doesn't work). As you position each row, make sure that you can see each person's face from your camera position. When you use this technique for a large group, your first and most important goal is to make sure nobody's face is blocked.

Managing the group

People tend to get impatient in such situations, especially if they're among the first to get posed. Staying enthusiastic and cheerful buys you time and patience from your subjects. Here are some ideas that have proven to work in the past:

✦ **Don't worry, Mon.** Explain to your subjects not to worry about posing until everyone is in place. Keep them relaxed as long as you can because posing is tiring and stressful for most people.

✦ **Please, stay put.** I usually stress to people that I'm going to take more than one photo and ask them not to flee like startled deer the first time my flash goes off. (Every time they laugh at one of your jokes, you've gained a couple of more minutes of patience from them.)

✦ **Avoid flashers.** If your digital camera uses a preflash or red-eye reduction of any sort, either turn it off (if possible) or alert your subjects to ignore the preflash. Otherwise, they'll release their poses just as the main flash fires. When you're ready to shoot, tell everyone to look directly into the camera lens. Look carefully through your viewfinder and quickly check each person to make sure you can see everyone's face. If you can't, stop and correct poses. If you can, start shooting.

Keep your sense of humor no matter how challenging the group shot gets. If you can keep everyone smiling and relaxed, you'll get a good shot sooner or later.

Try to have people say something that will make them smile. *Vacation!* is usually successful, as is *Hawaii. Stock options* used to work well with business types, but with the current market conditions, you might get tears these days. (Remember, you're going for smiles, not hysterical laughter here.) Having people say, "Cheese" is a no-no. Every portrait photographer has a bag of phrases to get his or her subjects to smile.

Back in my days shooting portraits, I had different phrases for families, parents, boys, and girls. *Vacation* and *Hawaii* work for just about anyone. *Yes, dear* and *honeymoon* work nicely with couples, as does *10 more kids!* (Some moms get a look of terror when they hear this one, though.) Young children generally smile for *Cowabunga, Dude* (even if it is getting kind of dated), but any cartoon hero catchphrase will probably work. For teenage boys, a sequence beginning with *girls* for shot one, *lotsa girls* for shot two, and *lotsa girls in skimpy bikinis* for shot three is just about guaranteed to work. These days, a similar male-oriented sequence for teenage girls also works.

PR Photography

Public relations (PR) photography frequently looks like photojournalism, but note an important difference: Newspaper photography tries very hard to be balanced, objective, and unbiased, but PR photography doesn't.

The goal in this kind of shooting is to present your client in the best possible light. This kind of photography calls for a good sense of diplomacy and the ability to work as a member of the team with the company's public relations personnel. Generally, the PR department has some specific ideas of what message it would like the image to convey.

PR photography can take many forms, ranging from creating executive portraits for senior company personnel to special event photography to taking photos for the company newsletter or a sales brochure. PR doesn't apply only to businesses, either. Your social organization or church might need some useful PR. Perhaps a new church has been opened, and the parish could use an attractive photo, like the one shown in Figure 4-8, for publicity or for the bulletin. Anything newsworthy is ripe for PR photography. The next sections cover the particular varieties of PR photography in greater detail.

Executive portraits

If you have a staff position with a company or operate your own photography business, you may be called upon to shoot pictures of the top brass of a company or organization. Executive portraits can vary and include basic head-and-shoulders portraits, commanding-executive-in-charge-at-the-helm/ desk photos, and leader-with-his-or-her-troops pictures. You can find more on shooting portraits in Book IV, Chapter 3, but for now, check out the basic kinds of executive portraits you might be asked to shoot.

✦ **Head-and-shoulders shot:** This is a basic portrait. Use a portable studio lighting setup and take a variety of shots and poses, including smiling, visionary, and serious. Don't be surprised if an executive has some very clear ideas about how he or she wants to look. You and the PR staffer should look the execs over carefully to make sure they look their best. If they don't, offer them a mirror and a comb (if their hair is out of place) or a lint brush if their clothes need it. Also use an appropriate backdrop. The PR types in your organization might be able to suggest the best backdrop for a particular executive.

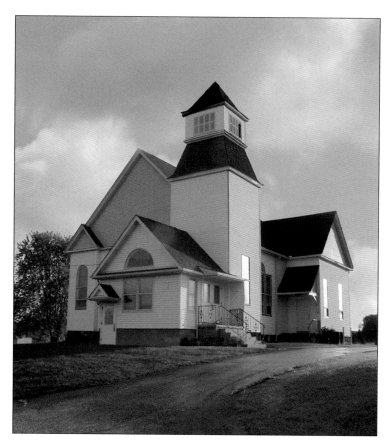

Figure 4-8: You might be the only one qualified to take an attractive shot to publicize the opening of a new building in your area.

+ **The desk shot:** This portrait shows the captain of industry hard at work at his or her desk. Skip the backdrop, but check the background thoroughly through your viewfinder. Some honors and photographs are fine, but if it's too cluttered, consider changing camera angles a little to clean things up. Because you're shooting the exec at his or her desk, indications that it's a working space are important. A neatly arranged pen set and a single document on the gleaming mahogany desk is plenty. Whatever you do, don't show a messy, cluttered desk.

+ **The confab:** This shot's a bit trickier. The idea is to show the exec as an in-charge leader. Usually, it's done with the standing exec giving instructions to a pair of underlings. The exec is turned toward the camera (slightly angled) with the underlings posed mostly away from the camera. Underlings should be carefully selected (this is the PR department's job) because it's an opportunity for the company to show it's an equal opportunity employer, or minority employer, or whatever.

+ **Setting:** The setting is usually in the nicer section of the company headquarters, but it could also be in a location shoot that showcases something about the firm. The location could be anywhere business-appropriate, such as a shipyard, an oil field, a factory assembly line, or a restaurant.

+ **One of the gang:** This shot is for the charismatic executive whose rapport with the troops is legendary. Forget the suits, mahogany desk, and rich carpeting. Instead, he or she is dressed casually. In fact, it should be hard to tell the executive from the employees, except for the fact that everyone in the photo is hanging on his or her words.

+ ***Really* one of the gang:** From time to time, you'll need to take a head-and-shoulders shot of someone who really is one of the gang: a non-executive, non-manager, ordinary star-of-the-warehouse type. Maybe she had a great bowling score on behalf of the company team. Or he had perfect attendance for 10 years. In such cases, a formal portrait would be inappropriate. You need to be prepared to grab a simple, flattering, head-and-shoulders shot, like the one shown in Figure 4-9.

Figure 4-9: Sometimes you'll photograph non-executives for the company newsletter, too.

Being able to produce a wide range of executive photos is a good skill for a PR photographer because there's always a place for these images, whether it be the company newsletter or the latest annual report.

Company events

Shooting company events usually revolves around documenting activity for outside company publications and also for distribution among employees. Usually, this means that the photographer is expected to take a lot of pictures — and the biggest challenge is being thorough enough.

Here are the main types of company events you'll be called on to capture:

✦ **Company dinners:** A company holds a dinner for a lot of reasons. Plan on getting photos of the speakers, award recipients (if any), company executives, and as many attendees as possible. Special-event dinners (fund drive events, seasonal parties, recognition of company accomplishments) should also include photos that show why the event is being held. For tips on how not to shoot presentations, see the "Avoiding the Grip 'n' Grin cliché" sidebar, earlier in this chapter.

✦ **Company outings:** Sometimes, an organization holds a retreat or conference. These gatherings feature a variety of events — some meant for fun and others for training. Plan on lots of shots of individuals participating in these events. Start by making sure you get the bigwigs. While you're looking for good photographs, make sure that your shots are positive and also present the employees in a good light.

✦ **Company-sponsored sporting events:** The information in Book IV, Chapter 5 applies here, with the added reminder that you're still shooting a corporate event first and an athletics meet second. Document elements that show the company relationship to the sports event (banner, logo, or whatever) and get good souvenir photos for the amateur athletes (particularly if they are company employees). Posed shots and camaraderie photos are good, too.

✦ **Family events:** Sometimes a company holds an open house for employee families to come see what their family members do and where they work. Get plenty of shots of employees demonstrating their jobs for their families.

✦ **Community relations events:** Many companies work hard to be good corporate neighbors. Employees are encouraged to volunteer as mentors or to give time to public service efforts, such as Habitat for Humanity. If you're asked to shoot a community relations event, plan on getting newspaper-type photos for use in the company newspaper or newsletter (and remember, positive images here). You should also take pictures for the company to hand out to its workers as well. (Companies motivate and reward employees for doing things like this. T-shirts, coffee mugs, and souvenir photos are the top three incentives.)

Arranging a PR event worth photographing

If you're shooting for your own company and your company is a small one, you might find yourself dubbed the in-house PR "expert" and be asked to help put together events covered by other photographers. You really need to understand the needs of other photographers, too! Putting together a photo-worthy event calls for an understanding of the needs of the photographers you're inviting and for optimizing your own chances to get good photos along-side them. Press photographers are paid to create strong, exciting visuals.

Here are some things you can do to make an event more likely to be a success:

✦ **Pick a location that provides a strong backdrop for the speaker or ceremony.**

✦ **Include elements that reinforce the purpose of the event.** For example, at a groundbreaking or building dedication, try to get some construction equipment in place to frame the podium or platform. Hang banners from the buckets of front-end loaders that identify your company and project.

✦ **Give the other photographers handouts that will make it easier to identify each person participating in the event.** This should include a photo of each person, with his or her name and title securely attached to the picture. (It can be a printed sheet with bio. It doesn't have to be an actual print.)

✦ **If holding an outdoor event, be prepared for bad weather by having an awning available on-site.** Try to set up things so that photographers can still get a good backdrop for their photos.

On the day of the event, check on all the small details that can come back to haunt you, such as confirming the presence of equipment, banners, handouts, and so on. Next, check the weather forecast. Have some people available to help answer questions from the photographers or provide extra handouts.

Refreshments for the press and guests are a good idea, but you don't need to go to extremes. Actually, you should probably worry more about having the appropriate refreshments for the company bigwigs than for the media.

Other photo-worthy events

Sometimes, your company welcomes members of the community inside its doors. This can be a welcome opportunity for creating images that you can place in your local papers.

✦ **School tours:** Does your company do something that might make a good tour for the local school? If so, bringing a group of school kids in will provide tons of photo ops (opportunities). Some typical images include an employee demonstrating a piece of equipment to the kids or one of the kids learning to use a piece of gear (keeping safety in mind at all times). Be sure to have your company's name or logo on equipment so that it shows up in the photo.

✦ **Mentors:** Does your company have a mentors program? If so, the interaction between your employees and their protégés can also make a good image. In this case, you're shooting at the school instead of your facility, so you won't have as many ops to get your company's name in the shot, but at least make sure it's in the caption.

Producing placeable PR photos

Successfully placing images taken specifically for PR purposes for your local media is both an art and a science. Remember that you're trying to meet your needs (placing your company's photos) as well as the newspaper's (strong images).

Newspapers know what you're trying to do — namely, get your company some free publicity and credibility. They also know that they have an advertising department that exists to help pay the bills. They're not giving away free space, but if you supply a good image, it has a chance at being used.

Also, understand your markets. Many local newspapers are willing to consider photo submissions, but each paper has its own criteria for acceptance. Newspapers use PR photos for a variety of reasons, including these:

✦ The images are of high quality and show members of the community doing something newsworthy (building homes for Habitat for Humanity, running a dunk tank to raise money for charity, and so on).

✦ The images fill a need that the newspaper couldn't fill on its own because it was understaffed or it was a weekend and too many events were going on to cover them all.

✦ The newspaper is willing to "sacrifice" a couple of pages to run photos from groups and organizations that want publicity. It's easy to tell whether your newspaper does this; look for the section near the back that has a couple of solid pages of Grip 'n' Grins (those trite photos of two people shaking hands and grinning at the camera).

Many newspapers also run a Neighborhood or Region section. (There are lots of names for this part of the paper.) Such a section is geared toward the local community. In fact, when a newspaper hits a certain size, it will probably print a different section for local communities as a special insert, which gives you even more opportunities to place photos. Even if your company isn't located in a community that the paper has a section for, some employees who work for your company probably live there.

Printing your PR photos

After you create your publishable PR images, give yourself the best chance that you can to get them used. Read Book VII, Chapter 1 to find out about printing digital images in detail, but here are some general observations.

As a bureau chief for one publication I worked for, I was frequently amazed at the number of low-resolution inkjet prints that I received from PR and marketing people. To make matters worse, they were frequently printed on cheap typing paper. Needless to say, they weren't used. (I'm not referring to proof images accompanying a digital file here either; those are okay.)

Instead, you should use one of the newer, high-resolution ink-jet printers (1400 dpi or higher) capable of producing photos that are as good as those you get from conventional film and photofinishers. If you don't have such a printer, your local drugstore or department store might have a stand-alone kiosk or an in-house digital mini-lab that can produce high-quality photos from your digital files.

Writing cutlines

Cutlines, or captions if you prefer, are vital to getting your photos used. Newspapers know nothing infuriates a reader more than seeing his or her name misspelled or being misidentified in a newspaper photo. As a result, most papers set very strict policies for their own staff on this kind of thing (usually three strikes and you're out of a job).

Good cutlines provide the basic information and get it right. Here's the kind of information to include:

✦ **Identify subjects.** Make sure that each name is identified with the proper person. Usually, it's done from left to right (or *l to r*).

Make sure that you have the correct spelling for the names of everyone appearing in the picture and triple check to make sure that no typos sneak through.

✦ **Summarize the event.** Describe what they're doing and why it's important. Make sure to also identify your company or client.

✦ **Identify yourself.** Provide your photo credit (*Photo by*). Include contact information in case the publication needs more information about the people in the picture or the event.

Cutlines need to be accurate, concise, and informative. Plus, the cutline is your chance to mention your organization's name in the publication. Although short cutlines will do the job in most cases, longer versions can serve as a mini news release. Here's a (slightly modified) example of a longer cutline, from a photo actually published in my local paper:

When faced with a barnyard full of animals who didn't want to help, "Do It Yourself" was the solution for the Little Red Hen in a production of the children's play, performed by the kindergarten class at Immaculate Conception School in Newtown. The young thespians who demonstrated the importance of cooperation included, from left, Johnny Smith, Janie Doe, William Roe, and Samantha Brown. For more information on the kindergarten or preschool classes, call the school office at (331) 555-1212.

Preparing the cutline for submission

After you write your cutline, affix it to the print — and do it in such a way that the print and cutline won't be separated by accident, as shown in Figure 4-10. The standard method is as follows:

1. **Set your margins for the cutline so they're narrower than the print's horizontal dimension and give your cutline a top margin of about one and a half inches.**

2. **Print out the caption and trim the sides and bottom to about a quarter-inch from the text while leaving the top margin alone.**

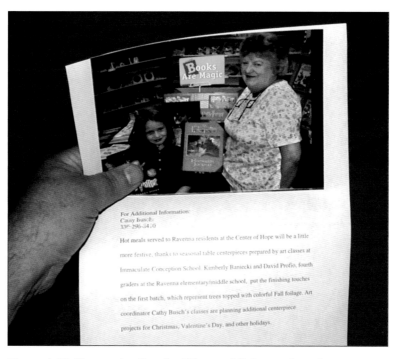

Figure 4-10: Photo and cutline should be carefully fastened together.

3. **Turn the print face-down and position the face-down cutline on top of it. Line the cutline up so that the top line of text is slightly below the bottom of the print and use a small piece of tape to affix the cutline to the back of the print.**

4. **Turn the print and cutline back face-up and fold the cutline sheet up and over so that it covers the photograph.**

   Now your picture and cutline, as shown in Figure 4-10, will fit neatly into an envelope, and with the cutline sheet offering some protection for the face of your print.

5. **Before sticking your print in the envelope, though, sandwich it between two pieces of corrugated cardboard and rubber band the sandwich together to keep it from being damaged in transit.**

Professional packaging and presentation will help you put your best foot forward and will improve your chances of getting your photos accepted.

Submitting the photo

After you assemble a nice professional package, prepare a cover letter telling the editor why you're sending these photos.

✦ **Be brief.** You need only a few paragraphs to explain what the event was about, when it was held, and where.

✦ **Include contact info.** Make sure that the appropriate contact information is also provided in your letter.

✦ **Send to the photo editor.** Check the newspaper's masthead and address the envelope to the photo editor (if the paper is big enough to have one), to the Neighborhood section editor if the paper has a Neighborhood section, or just to the editor if it's a really small paper.

✦ **Keep a log.** Identify the image (something like 20070821.03 for "2007, August 21.third photo release of the month"), the newspaper(s) you've sent the photo to, and the date you mailed it. Make sure your cutline includes this release number. Also identify whether the photo is for immediate release or for use on a particular date.

Following up

A few days after mailing your photo submission, call the newspaper and ask to speak with the appropriate editor. Tell whomever answers the phone that you're calling to follow up on a photo submission. When you're connected, identify yourself and say you're checking to see whether the editor needed any additional information.

Also be sure to check the appropriate papers to see whether they've already run your image. If so, buy a couple of copies for tear sheets for your files. Note the log number on your file copy so that you can match it with the appropriate photo. Get in the habit of comparing your successful and unsuccessful images so that you can see what kinds of images your local paper favors.

Product Photography

Product photography is certainly a specialized type of photography, but one that offers good opportunities for the enterprising photographer. *Product photography* is all about making your clients' products look as good as possible, such as in Figure 4-11. You can do this in several ways, and you can find more information on photographing objects close-up in Book IV, Chapter 2.

Although you could think of this type of photography as the exclusive domain of the big-name advertising photographers, agencies, and art departments, the reality is far different. Opportunities for this type of work are very open to talented freelance photographers.

**Book IV
Chapter 4**

**Shooting for
Publication**

Figure 4-11: Close-ups are the meat and potatoes of product photography.

Product shot opportunities

Lots of manufacturers sell their product lines through catalogs. There is a constant need for fresh images because some these catalogs come out as frequently as once a month. Success in this type of photography calls for several skills:

✦ **Speed:** Be prepared to work quickly and efficiently. Set up a standard lighting package that provides clean, even lighting. Generally, this means setting up a tabletop station with a pair of lights that rake across the product at 45-degree angles and that are positioned at a right angle to the camera.

✦ **Simplicity:** Your tabletop setup should be as simple as possible. Plan on using seamless paper that you can advance on a roller. Then, when one section gets dirty, you can just advance it to another stretch of clean paper. Your close-up photography skills should be well-honed, too, because many product shots are close-ups of components, like those shown in Figure 4-11. See Book IV, Chapter 2, to read more about snapping close-up photos.

✦ **Flexibility:** Your digital camera and tripod rig should be versatile enough for you to be able to change their position quickly and easily. Some tripod manufacturers offer *dollies* (small platforms with rollers) that the tripod can be mounted on so that you can reposition it easily.

✦ **Record keeping:** Be sure to have a workable record-keeping and -indexing system set up so that you can keep track of what you've shot and when; clients frequently need this info.

Product demo shots

Product demo photos are designed to show either what the product can do or how it is correctly used. The idea is to create an image that shows a typical user successfully using the product for its designed purpose. Some examples include

✦ **An attractive person reclining on a pool float, looking relaxed and happy.** (Selling the pool float.) Shoot this scene from a variety of angles, including getting up on a ladder to shoot down on her. Use an image editing program to tweak the pool water's color to be a nice rich blue. Be careful in your choice of lenses here, though: Longer focal lengths are more flattering. You probably need flash here to clean up any shadows, too.

✦ **Cyclists standing with their bikes happily discussing their planned ride.** (Selling the bicycle.) Use a long telephoto for this image. The cyclists and their bikes should be in focus, but the background shouldn't be. Use late-afternoon light to give a rich glow to the scene.

✦ **A woman stroking her pet cat while it laps up a saucer of milk — and not just any milk, but a specially formulated milk just for cats.** (Product box can also be in the photo or composited in later.) Use your portable studio lighting setup here and a short telephoto or modest wide-angle lens, depending on how much space you have to set up your photo.

✦ **A business person working on a portable computer.** (Selling the computer.) If the shot's outside, use fill flash and a medium telephoto. If it's inside, use your portable studio lighting kit and a medium telephoto lens. Set your aperture depending on your background.

For the outside shot, generally a wide-open lens that throws the background out of focus works fine. Inside, if you have a particularly good background (say, a nice study), take advantage of it and stop down to increase your depth of field.

✦ **The product posed as it is set up for use.** Figure 4-12 shows a shot arranged to show how a product is used. All the extraneous information has been excised, making the final photo abundantly clear.

Figure 4-12: This photo shows exactly how the product is hooked up.

The idea is to sell viewers on the idea that buying this particular product will enrich their lives in some way.

Of course, sometimes you don't want to show the product being used. When this happens, the photographer must invoke a mood the product manufacturer finds desirable. For instance, I'd never show a sample of kitty litter being used the way the manufacturer designed. Instead, I'd create an image of a cat bathing itself in the foreground with a dinner party in the background. The text for the ad could then read, *Brand X Kitty Litter — you'll never know it's being used.*

How the pros do it

When Philadelphia Mayor John Street wanted to announce his plans for an anti-blight initiative, his staff put together a carefully crafted day for the press. The day began with a morning briefing with coffee and pastries. More importantly, the media was given a full briefing manual describing the mayor's plan. During the briefing, Mayor Street and his team introduced his plan and the people whom he hoped would make it succeed. Although those of us who were working press photographers grabbed some photos at this point, we all knew these images weren't going to get much play.

After the briefing was over, we headed out to waiting city trolleys for a tour of the areas that the mayor hoped to turn around. At this point, we were informed that we'd be getting a three-hour tour of the city, which caused the press corps to begin singing the theme song from the old TV show, *Gilligan's Island*. (You know, "A *three-hour tooour!*") We were also given box lunches.

During the next few hours, we were presented with a number of carefully planned photo ops. Face it — a city like Philadelphia has a large number of abandoned buildings (several thousand according to the briefing we were given), and yet every time we stopped, it would be in front of a single derelict structure instead of a row of vacant houses.

When it came time for the mayor to climb into a front-end loader to knock down a derelict structure, there was just one small section of a building left for him. Every other building in that development had already been demolished.

The reason for these photo ops was obvious. The mayor's staff wanted to make sure the images in the media created the impression that the problem was manageable. The mayor facing a city block of vacant, ruined buildings would have looked too much like an underdog taking on an insurmountable challenge.

Chapter 5: Sports and Action Photography

In This Chapter

- ✔ Choosing your equipment
- ✔ Taking outstanding sports pictures
- ✔ Choosing your spot for your sport
- ✔ Capturing your first action photo
- ✔ Shooting sequences

*D*igital cameras offer at least one advantage and one disadvantage when used for sports and action photography. The big advantage lies in the ability to shoot an almost unlimited number of pictures in your quest to capture the peak moment of action but without burning up dozens of rolls of film. In times past, professional photographers had an edge in this department because they could justify using tons of film at a single event. Today, mistakes and bad shots can be erased from reusable digital film, so your errant photos aren't necessarily captured for eternity.

The chief disadvantage to digital cameras is that the models that are *not* digital single lens reflexes (dSLRs) don't respond as quickly as you like when the shutter release button is pressed. Even a pause of half a second is too long when the decisive moment in a contest is framed within your viewfinder or LCD for only an instant. If you are using a dSLR, you're in good shape: Most of these cameras will snap off a picture as quickly as you can press the shutter release. If you *don't* have a digital SLR, you can work around this potential problem by using some techniques I show you later in this chapter.

Choosing Your Weapons for Sports Photography

Sports photography calls for a range of tools that can help put you in the best possible position to get the shots you need. This doesn't mean that you need to break the bank to get good images, though. Many of the current crop of digital cameras — from digital single lens reflex cameras (dSLRs) to point-and-shoot versions — offer powerful capabilities of their own.

I cover the basics of choosing a camera, lenses, and accessories in more depth in Book I, Chapter 2. However, sports photography does have several particular needs. Here are some of the things that you should consider when assembling your sports photography arsenal. I explain these key needs in more detail later in this chapter, but this summary will get you in the proper equipment frame of mind:

✦ **Go long with telephotos.** To get the best sports photos, you want to get as close to the action as possible. That's enough of a challenge for pros equipped with press passes and access to areas set aside for their use. Imagine how tough it is for someone who has to get shots from the stands. If you can't get close, your digital camera's telephoto zoom setting or add-on telephoto attachment is your best friend. For sports photos, a camera with a 3:1 or 4:1 zoom lens is almost essential. You can find pro-sumer digital cameras that take you even closer with 10:1 to 12:1 zoom ratios. These long lenses provide the equivalent of a telephoto lens in the 200mm to 400mm range on a traditional full-frame (film or digital) camera. Of course, if you're using a dSLR, you can swap the lens you have on your camera right now for one that is longer, up to preposterous focal lengths. (There are lenses with 1000mm and longer focal lengths.)

✦ **Go wide.** Wide-angle capability also comes in handy for sports photography. Certain sports, such as skateboarding and roller blading, photograph quite well from a low position using an extreme wide-angle view. A wide-angle capability is also great for getting an overall view of a sports venue or crowd, as you can see in Figure 5-1.

✦ **Light up your sports life.** If you want to shoot sports at night, an accessory flash unit can greatly improve the quality of your photography because that brief flash of light can freeze action. External flash units can even be a big advantage during the day if you're photographing outdoor sports such as baseball because the flash lights up those inky shadows under the caps many athletes wear to shield their eyes. Of course, you have to be close enough for the flash to be useful.

✦ **Take along lots of digital film.** Sports photography can fill your digital storage media faster than most other photographic enterprises. At an exciting game or match, you might find yourself shooting more photos in two hours than you took during your entire vacation. Yet, other than timeouts or halftime, you have very little time to review your photos and erase the duds to free up storage space. The solution is to take a lot of digital film with you and use it freely.

Figure 5-1: A wide-angle lens attachment for your digital camera can provide ultra-wide views of the crowd.

Digital Camera Features and Action Photography

You can find information on specific digital camera types and their features in Book I, Chapter 2. The following sections review how some of those features can best be applied to action photography.

Viewfinder

Most non-SLR digital cameras have an optical viewfinder and a color LCD panel or, perhaps, an LCD alone. Others have an electronic viewfinder (EVF) and a color LCD panel on the back of the camera. And, of course, dSLRs have optical viewfinders that see the same lens used to take the picture. You need to determine when to use each of them when taking sports photos. Some general rules to keep in mind are

+ **Non-dSLR owners should use the optical viewfinder to follow action prior to squeezing off a shot.** You can view the subjects continually through the viewfinder under just about any lighting conditions. Although optical viewfinders can be difficult to use under very low light levels (when you need to use a flash instead of existing light to take the picture, anyway), optical viewfinders are still a better choice than the LCD panel for following fast-moving events.

✦ **Try keeping your other eye open while looking through the optical viewfinder.** This trick gives you some peripheral vision that will alert you when the action is about to enter the frame.

✦ **If your camera has an EVF, you might find it convenient for viewing fast action prior to snapping the shutter.** Note, though, that some EVFs produce a smeared image when you move the camera to follow action and may blank out a split second before the photo is taken, so you'll be shooting blind.

✦ **Digital SLRs are even better for sports photography.** They provide a bright, clear view (like an optical viewfinder), but you can see through the taking lens except for a tiny fraction of a second when the picture is actually being taken. You'll be "blind" for a much shorter period than with an EVF; you might barely notice the interval.

✦ **The LCD screen is invaluable for reviewing your images immediately after creating them.** Most cameras can be set to display an image on the LCD for a few seconds while it's being saved to your digital film. Take the opportunity to review the image. Even if it's great, you might learn something that will enable you to do better on the next shot!

Using your camera's LCD review feature

Here are some things to look for when reviewing your action shots:

✔ **Composition:** One of the most valuable things that your LCD screen can do for you is confirm that your composition is what you want it to be. With sports photography, you're dealing with athletes moving quickly and sometimes (seemingly) at random. Being sure they're where you want them to be in the frame is a good thing.

✔ **Sharpness:** LCD screens aren't necessarily an accurate way to judge image sharpness. However, some cameras offer the ability to magnify a portion of your image, which can help you see whether your camera's autofocus or your manual focusing is close. If not, you can switch autofocus modes (some cameras let you choose which area of the frame to focus on, or whether the camera locks the focus when you press lightly on the shutter release) or switch to manual focus.

✔ **Exposure:** Your camera's LCD screen can help you determine whether your exposure is on target. Some cameras let you call up a *histogram*, which is a kind of scale that shows the distribution of brightness values throughout the image. The histogram can help you judge your exposure. If your exposure isn't spot on, you can make changes immediately so that subsequent action shots are better.

Shooting outside in bright sun makes it hard to use your LCD screen effectively. The Hoodman company (www.hoodmanusa.com) makes a variety of hoods that offer some shade for the LCD screen and make it easier to read in the sun.

Electronic flash

An electronic flash unit can be a big help to your action photography whether it's day or night. You can use flash for good photos in a number of ways. Here are a few:

✦ **Let there be light.** An accessory flash unit can provide enough light for you to shoot by when it gets too dark for even your highest ISO (film speed) setting to be usable. (For more on ISO ratings, see the upcoming section, "Setting your ISO speed.")

✦ **Freeze your frame.** Accessory flash units produce an incredibly brief burst of light (somewhere on the order of up to 1/10,000 of a second). Also, because the flash unit, if it has enough power, provides the main source of light, it has the ability to stop action. You should be careful, however: When using flash at a slow shutter speed setting, the *ambient* light (the available light other than the flash itself) can register a ghost image trailing the image captured by the flash. This can sometimes be a cool effect — but only if it's intentional.

✦ **Cleaning up the shadows.** Even when you have more than enough light for good sports photography, many times even the brightest conditions can't change the fact that athletes wear ball caps or that tree limbs cast shadows. An accessory flash unit can help get rid of those shadows if you are close enough.

Tripods

Sports photography usually calls for such high shutter speeds to stop action that no photographer would use a tripod to prevent blurry photos from camera shake, unless working with a high-end digital camera with a huge telephoto lens (which isn't something the average digital photographer needs to worry about). Instead, sports photographers use a tripod to simply help support the camera. Here are some considerations specific to sports photography that you should consider. (Read Book II, Chapter 5 for more detail on tripods.)

✦ **Great support:** A good sturdy tripod can be invaluable for holding and steadying your camera, particularly at telephoto lens settings. Some sports, such as football, call for too much movement on the photographer's part for tripods to be useful. (You'll constantly be running up and down the sidelines.) When photographing track and field, baseball, and softball, however, you benefit greatly from having a tripod to support your camera.

✦ **A second camera rig:** When shooting baseball and softball games, I frequently prefocus a second, tripod-mounted camera on a key spot, such as first base, second base, or home plate. A tripod enables you to switch back and forth between two cameras easily and quickly.

✦ **Panning:** This technique involves following the action as it moves across your image frame. Panning is discussed in greater detail in the "Panning" section a bit later, but a tripod with a panning head can greatly improve your efforts at this technique because it allows free horizontal movement while keeping the camera steady vertically. Figure 5-2 shows some action stopped by panning in the direction the base runner was moving.

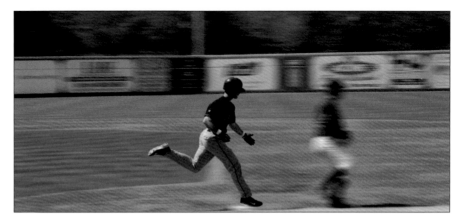

Figure 5-2: Pan the camera in the direction of movement to stop action at slow shutter speeds.

✦ **Monopods:** For sports that call for photographers to be active, a monopod frequently works better than a tripod because it's easier to pick up and carry around. A good monopod is fairly thick and heavy, both to be strong enough to support the weight of a big telephoto lens and also so that you can brace against it. A lot of inexpensive units promise all sorts of capabilities; make sure you hold out for a good solid monopod and not one of the flimsy ones.

✦ **Shoulder stocks:** These devices are modeled after rifle stocks and work on the principle that by bracing the lens into your shoulder, you can hold it steady.

Lenses and attachments

Because sports photography requires you to cover large swatches of field and fast-moving athletes, long lenses or attachments to extend the reach of your point-and-shoot camera's built-in zooms will really help improve your results. Your choice of lens or zoom settings is in part dependent on what sports you plan on shooting.

Because the effective focal length of a digital camera lens depends on the size of the sensor, when I give focal lengths in this chapter, I use the traditional "equivalent" figure; that is, the magnification you'd get if using the lens on a 35mm film camera or a full-frame digital camera.

✦ **Wide-angle settings:** Wide-angle settings will be a big part of your sports photography if you're shooting up close. For example, wide-angle lenses are currently in vogue for skateboarding photography. These lenses can give your sports shots a very different look, if you can get close enough to your subject to fill the frame.

✦ **Short telephoto settings:** Telephoto settings equivalent to a 35mm camera's 85mm–135mm lengths (which is how digital camera manufacturers measure their optics' magnifications) have a lot of uses in sports photography. These are great for indoor sports, such as basketball and volleyball, and can also be handy for nighttime sports under the lights. If your digital camera has a maximum aperture of f/2.8 or larger, you can take photos in lower light levels. Make sure that your camera doesn't use a smaller lens opening, which would defeat your ability to take indoor shots.

✦ **Medium telephoto settings:** These are usually in the 180mm–200mm range. This is a very versatile setting that can come in handy when shooting almost any type of sport.

✦ **Long telephoto settings:** Some digital cameras have long telephoto settings that are the equivalent of 300mm–400mm on a 35mm film camera. These are the lenses of choice for both football and baseball photography because they allow great reach and the ability to keep shooting even when outdoors under lights. Be careful that your long lens doesn't reduce your shutter speed beyond the ability to capture the action.

✦ **Super telephotos:** You probably won't have access to super telephotos unless your digital camera is a dSLR with interchangeable lenses. I'm talking about the really big guns here — the 500mm and 600mm telephotos. These lenses are almost too big for many kinds of sports photography and are almost the exclusive reserve of nature and bird photographers. They can be useful when you just can't get very close to the action and have a pretty small subject. (Gymnastics events and skiing come to mind.)

✦ **Add-on lenses for point-and-shoot digital cameras:** Many point-and-shoot digital cameras can accept lens converters that attach to the front of the camera's built-in zoom lens. These converters can screw into the lens filter mount, clip onto the lens barrel, or attach via an ingenious adapter barrel and are frequently available in both wide-angle and telephoto flavors. I recommend going with the manufacturer's version, which is specifically designed for your camera, but if your camera's manufacturer doesn't offer the accessory lens you need, look at third-party options.

Book IV
Chapter 5

Sports and Action Photography

Be very careful if someone tries to sell you an add-on lens for a video camera. Video cameras get by with much lower resolution than digital still cameras. A lens designed for a video camera probably won't produce very good results on a digital still camera.

Latency and Shutter Lag

Before you move on to tips for taking great digital sports photos, you probably should spend a few minutes considering the deep, dark secret that digital camera manufacturers don't want you to think about: When you press that shutter release button, many cameras have a noticeable time lag before the picture is actually taken. Although this lag is but a minor inconvenience if you're taking a photo of the Eiffel Tower, that delay can be fatal (to the shot, not to you) when photographing sports. Fortunately, there are some things you can do about the phenomena known as *latency* and *shutter lag*.

Once upon a time, you pushed the shutter release button and the camera took the picture. As cameras have gotten more and more sophisticated, more and more things have to happen before an image is created.

Dealing with latency of your camera

Latency is the time required to write the image you've just taken to your storage media. When you take a picture with a film camera, the shutter releases, and the image is immediately registered on the film at the speed of light, so to speak. When you take a picture with a digital camera, the image has to be captured and then recorded onto your memory card. The image capture and storage process can take a second or two — or even longer. How long the process takes and whether your camera will continue taking additional photos while writing to the card are important questions.

Digital cameras use *buffers* (built-in memory) to temporarily let you keep shooting while the buffer contents write to removable memory. If you keep shooting, eventually the buffer fills, and you have to stop until it has made enough room for you to resume shooting. Other cameras might not be able to use their buffers quickly enough for their highest resolution files but will let you keep shooting if you choose a lower-resolution setting. It's a tough choice, but sometimes the ability to keep shooting overrides the desire for the highest possible resolution. Things that affect latency (that you can control) are

✦ **Media:** Some forms of media accept data faster than others. CompactFlash cards tend to write information faster than *microdrives* (tiny hard disk drives). Some CompactFlash cards write data faster than others. Look for ones rated for faster write times (frequently marked 8X, 50X, 80X, or 133X). Several photo-oriented Web sites have conducted their own tests of CompactFlash cards. Check out `www.robgalbraith.com` for the most highly-respected card test results.

✦ **Resolution:** The more data the camera has to write to the card, the greater the latency period. Non-compressed formats like RAW and TIFF can take the longest to write. If you know that you can get by with a lower-resolution setting, you can speed up things considerably by going with the lower resolution. This can be a tough decision because after you give up quality, you can't get it back. On the other hand, missing a shot because you're waiting for your last few images to write to your memory card is one of the more frustrating experiences that a photographer can endure. Film photographers miss shots while changing rolls of film, but digital photographers miss them because of latency. It's not a perfect world, but it is a great reason to get a second camera.

Understanding your equipment and its capabilities and limitations is important for the digital photographer interested in making winning sports photographs. If sports photography is your overriding concern, several cameras on the market are geared toward the sports shooter. Both Canon and Nikon's top-of-the-line digital SLRs are highly capable photographic tools well designed for this kind of work (but they're not cheap!). For those of us on a tighter budget, Olympus makes a lower-resolution digital camera capable of 15 fps (frames per second) bursts (for a max of 10 frames). It may be worth considering.

Coping with shutter lag

Latency isn't the only thing that can slow down your picture taking. Many things happen when you press the shutter, including activating light-sensing features and bringing autofocus up to speed. If you have a microdrive hard disk storage device, the time needed for its drive platters to start spinning is a factor as well. The result is *shutter lag,* which is the delay between the moment when you squeeze the shutter and when the camera actually fires. In practice, most of the delay is caused by the autofocus system. Thus, you have to anticipate the decisive moment and trigger the shutter early enough to cause the image to be created at the best possible moment.

Timing your shot properly

Here are some ways to time your shot so that you can take a great picture even when shutter lag delays capture of that decisive moment:

✦ **Anticipate the action.** Many sports and non-sports action activities have a particular rhythm. If you can become sensitive to that rhythm, you can anticipate that peak moment of action and learn how far in advance to trigger the shutter. If you're shooting a baseball or softball game, you can position yourself down the third base line and wait for a play at first. It takes a certain amount of time for a throw to make it across the field to the first baseman, so you can trip the shutter in time for the ball to reach the mitt. When shooting a basketball game, you can usually tell when someone is about to drive to the basket. Anticipation can work for you in non-sports action photography, too. You can wait until just before the real action starts, as shown in Figure 5-3, which was taken just as the flume ride started down the incline.

Figure 5-3: Pressing the shutter button just before the flume ride started down helped freeze the action.

✦ **Go with the flow.** Follow the action with your camera and gently squeeze the shutter as you keep your eye on the ball (or athlete). In sports like basketball or soccer, you can track the person bringing the ball down the field.

✦ **Pick your spot.** Many sports direct action to a particular location. For instance, long jumpers are headed toward the landing pit, so you can know within a couple of feet where the athlete will land. Be prepared to trigger the shutter as the athletes launch themselves and stay with them until landing. Some sports have goals, some bases, and some baskets; sooner or later, every sport has a spot that you just know will see action.

✦ **Use manual focus.** Some digital cameras allow more control over their capabilities than others. If your camera lets you deactivate autofocus, for instance, you can prefocus on the expected action spot and reduce your camera's shutter lag time. A similar technique works for cameras that let you lock focus. Lock focus on the spot you're keying on just before the play starts, and you give yourself a head start on the action.

✦ **Lock in your focus.** If your digital camera requires you to press the shutter halfway to activate autofocus and autoexposure (and with cameras using mini-hard disks, to start your microdrive spinning), you can do this in advance and have everything operating at just the right time. The problem with this technique is that it can drain your camera's batteries in a hurry, so plan on having lots of extra juice if you want to do this.

✦ **Choose your autofocus mode.** Most digital cameras, dSLR and non-dSLR alike, have two autofocus modes: AF-S (autofocus single) and AF-C (autofocus continuous.) AF-S locks in focus when you press the shutter release halfway and keeps focus at that point until you release the button or take the picture. AF-C also sets focus when you press the shutter release part way, but then continues to refocus if your subject moves or you reframe the shot. Usually, AF-C is best for sports (if you're using autofocus at all), but it does run down your battery more quickly and can be fooled if something moves between you and your primary subject, even momentarily.

✦ **Use autofocus selectively.** Does your digital camera let you pick a different button to activate autofocus instead of the shutter button? If it does, you can combine this feature with the previous technique to decrease battery drain. (Autofocus uses lots of power.) Keep the shutter pressed halfway while awaiting the next event. Then, as soon as you need to, press the second button to activate autofocus. (This takes a little practice, but it does work.) It also works well for the prefocusing suggestion made a couple of paragraphs earlier. Some cameras have a continuous or single autofocus setting. Switching to the single setting can save power because your camera doesn't constantly refocus each time you move the camera a little.

Choosing Your Sport and Your Spot

This section deals with tips for taking great digital action photos in a variety of sports situations. That's the great part about sports photography: There are so many different sports. Just when you think you've explored everything that can be done for soccer, soccer season is over, and it's time to grab some basketball shots!

Elementary, middle, and high school sports are great training grounds for people who want to become good sports photographers, for several reasons:

✦ **Speed:** Because the players aren't as fast and as skilled as those at the college level (and up), the excitement generally unfolds at slower speeds, making life easier for the novice sports photographer who's trying to follow the action.

✦ **Access:** School athletic events are much more accessible than college or the pros. Return the favor by offering the coach or the boosters a copy of your shots for their awards dinner.

Don't be afraid to experiment, either. There are always elements of an event that provide dramatic imagery, even if it's not the typical sports action shot. Think about close-ups of equipment, low-angle shots of the playing field, and portraits or studies of spent, exhausted athletes at the end of the game. Look for shots that show the emotion and intensity that the athletes bring to the sport.

Knowing where to position yourself can be a real challenge for novice sports photographers. It's also vital to give yourself the best possible opportunities to get great shots. Your goal is to be in position to capture peak action in the right direction (getting that great catch with the athlete's back to you doesn't do you much good). Generally, this means you want to be far enough in front of the action to be effective, yet close enough to fill the frame.

Determining the right spot is largely dependent on the sport you're shooting. Your choice of available zoom settings can also play a role.

Football

If you're photographing high school or peewee football, you can often get right down on the sidelines to take photos like the one shown in Figure 5-4. At the lowest levels of the sport, you can pretty much get whatever access you want. Even at the high school level, you can probably get on the sidelines if you explain that you're trying to build a sports portfolio. For most college and professional games, you need some form of accreditation from the team itself. Still, sometimes even a small, local newspaper can secure such access for its photographers, so working for such a publication could get you in.

Here are some tips for photographing football:

✦ **Keep your distance.** Photographers generally stand about 8–15 yards up field from the line of scrimmage. Don't get much closer than this, or the line officials block your view. This puts you in place for a shot of a running play or quarterback sack in the backfield while still giving you a chance to turn and lock on to a receiver in case of a pass play to your side of the field.

✦ **Use a second camera.** A second digital camera set to its wide-angle setting can also be a good idea. This camera can be quickly grabbed and brought up to shooting position if a play comes right at you. (Be careful to avoid being run over.)

✦ **Keep other spots in mind.** As teams approach the goal line, you can move to the area behind the end zone and shoot straight at the quarterback or running back attempting to leap over the defensive line. Because the team's players sit near the midfield, you can't shoot around this area. Also, plan on getting some shots of the coach yelling from the sidelines and players on the bench. Cheerleaders are good for a couple of shots. If it's a particularly cold day, some shots of the fans bundled up in the stands are worth taking.

✦ **Be patient.** Football demands patience and determination on the part of the sports photographer simply because so much of the sport takes place too far away from where you're standing for you to be able to shoot it effectively. Just stay with the game and be prepared for the action when it finally does head toward you.

Football is one sport for which the more you know about the game and the particular teams that are playing, the more effective you can be. Understanding that one team favors short, quick passes while another favors a more conservative ground game helps you predict where the next bit of action will take place.

**Book IV
Chapter 5**

**Sports and Action
Photography**

Figure 5-4: Most football action can be captured from the sidelines.

Baseball and softball

For these sports, there are several likely places for a photographer to work from. One of my favorites is directly behind the backstop, shooting through the links to get a shot of the pitcher just as he or she releases the ball (ideally framed between the batter and umpire). I also like shooting from just behind the dugout, which is where I took the picture shown in Figure 5-5.

Figure 5-5: Shooting from behind or next to the dugout can give you a great perspective at baseball or softball games.

Here are some other tips for shooting ballgames:

✦ **Get behind the plate.** Many times, I start behind the plate to make sure I get a usable image as quickly as possible before moving on down either the first or third baselines. Usually, I head down until I'm about 5 or 10 feet below the base. From this spot, I can get good shots of the batter, a side view of the pitcher, and a good angle for plays at second base.

✦ **Move down the baseline.** After that, I continue on down the line until I'm as much as 15 or 30 feet past the base. This position gives me a shot at the runner racing to first or third.

✦ **Watch that runner on first.** If there's a runner on first, sometimes I pre-focus my tripod-mounted camera on second base in case there's a close play there. Here's where knowledge of the sport and the teams involved can give you a big advantage. The stolen base is one of the more exciting plays in baseball or softball. If you're ready before the play begins, you have a much better chance of getting a good shot of the action.

Much like football, baseball's lowest levels of skill are wide open to any photographer who cares to shoot them. College and the pros are much harder to gain access to — although once again, a newspaper job might give you a chance. Softball tends to be easier to gain access to. Sometimes, a one-sided game is easier to shoot than a close one. There tends to be lots of scoring, including plenty of people stealing home.

Basketball

Hanging out behind the backboard is a great place for getting good shots. I probably spend 80 percent of the game here. Rebounds, scoring, fights over the ball — it all happens under the boards. Here are some other good locations for shooting hoops:

✦ **Take to the bleachers.** I take some shots from up in the bleachers with a telephoto prefocused on the rim. This is a good location for getting the rebounder pulling the ball off the rim and a good look at the player's face. Try to find a spot a little higher than the rim. This generally calls for a longer zoom lens setting, about 100mm–135mm for a digital camera.

✦ **Head for the sidelines.** I also shoot along the sideline with a longer zoom setting to get a shot of a ball handler bringing the ball up court. From this position, I can also look for a shot of the coach yelling instructions to the players and pivot to grab some crowd intensity shots. Sometimes you can catch a tense moment as the ball is thrown back into play, as shown in Figure 5-6.

Figure 5-6: Sometimes the tension of putting the ball into play can make a good photo.

✦ **Don't forget half-time.** Half-time is the time to look for shots of the coach and players talking strategy. A wide-angle gets you in close when possible (easy for high school ball and younger, but you probably won't be able to get that close for college and the pros).

Basketball is a great sport for a novice photographer who's looking to build a sports portfolio. It's possible to get good photos without having to break the bank on a camera with an ultralong telephoto lens zoom setting.

Soccer

Soccer is a little like football in terms of the field and sidelines action, but this sport has lots of unique aspects, as well. Here are some tips:

✦ **Get behind the net.** Behind the net and to one side of it are good locations to catch scoring attacks, but you spend long periods of time counting blades of grass when the action moves to the other side of the field.

✦ **Take to the sidelines.** Positioning yourself on the sidelines puts you in place for good ball-handling shots. If you move down the sidelines closer to the net, you'll be in position to get the goalie in action.

✦ **Reach out and grab someone.** If you have a digital camera with a long zoom lens, you can try to reach from one end of the field to the other to get the goalie straight-on. Or, you can even grab a shot from way up in the stands, as in Figure 5-7.

✦ **Going for the wide look.** For variety's sake, try a shorter focal length while lying on the ground. This will give you a second shot, but not a main photo.

Soccer can be a difficult sport for the point-and-shoot digital camera simply because of the size of the field. The best place to work from is the spot behind the net and to one side. An occasional shot through the net works, too, but becomes a cliché if this is the only image you ever capture.

Other sports

Other sports all have their own special challenges and opportunities. Here's a brief rundown on some other popular action opportunities:

✦ **Hockey:** Stand behind the goalie or on the sidelines just above the goal. Players tend to make a lot of contact behind the net trying to control the puck, so there's some good action there. Another place where big hits happen is the area between the blue lines — the neutral zone. If your lens is long enough, get some shots of the face-offs. Don't forget about reaction shots either. Hockey is tough simply because your movement can be so restricted.

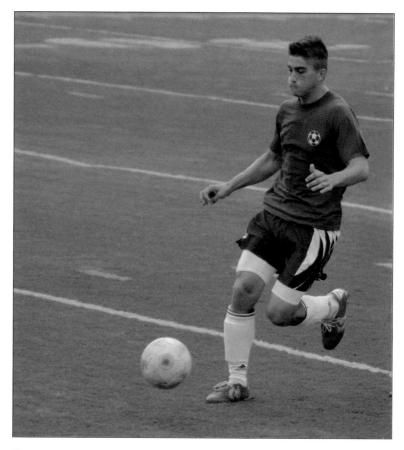

Figure 5-7: This action photo was taken from the stands with the longest zoom setting I had available.

✦ **Tennis:** You can stand behind the court shooting the player on the far side of the net straight-on. Don't worry about the fence; if you're using a telephoto setting, you can shoot through the links. On the sidelines, I favor shooting when the player is running from side to side after a ball, but only when the player is moving toward me. Either a monopod or tripod will work for tennis.

✦ **Golf:** Shoot from the side when the player is teeing up (but not during their swing) or straight-on if the course conditions permit. You can also shoot straight-on from a safe distance when a player is putting.

✦ **Track:** So many events, so little time. Whenever possible, I try to shoot track events from as close to straight-on as possible, generally as runners are coming around the turn or at the start of a race when the line of runners is beginning its break.

✦ **Field events:** So many events, so many different ways to shoot them. Unlike track, which tends to use the same quarter-mile track surface for its events, the field competition presents more challenges. Fortunately, shot put, javelin, and discus can all use the same basic philosophy: Namely, get in front of the athlete with a little offset to the side (and far enough away to be out of range) so that you can shoot straight-on as the athlete releases whatever it is he or she is throwing. Setting yourself up behind the landing area is a good strategy for both the long jump and pole vault, while positioning yourself to the side and slightly behind the bar works well for high jumping. (The hard part is racing from side to side because jumpers will come from both the left and right.)

✦ **Gymnastics:** Any position that lets you shoot the athletes coming directly toward you is a good location. If circumstances allow you to get close to the action, wide-angle lenses can give your images a different look.

✦ **Adventure water sports:** I'm talking white-water rafting, kayaking, and canoeing here. Generally, you have a choice of two good locations. The first is downstream, just below a rapid, so that you can get the boaters in action. The second is from a bridge, looking down on the river, which gives you a nice alternate shot. Don't be afraid to get in tight and compose from the top of the boater's head down to his or her paddle in the water. It's not necessary to show the entire boat.

✦ **Rock, alpine, and speed climbing:** If possible, either get on top of the rock and shoot down on the climbers, or get on a ledge that's level with a point the climbers will reach during their ascent. If you're on the ground when they begin the climb, a wide-angle shot from the side and below gives a usable image, and you can play with silhouettes if you want to try something different. Also from ground level, you can try a telephoto shot of the climber against the wall. For a speed climbing competition, a longer telephoto setting gets you in tight and compresses the competitors more closely together. I prefer to shoot speed climbing from the side because it emphasizes the extreme body contortions the climbers go through.

✦ **Extreme sports:** Both straight-on and profile shots provide good images for many of these sports. For skateboarding, inline skating, and BMX bike events, shorter focal lengths work well, depending on how close to the event you can get. Wakeboarding calls for very long lenses, a monopod, and a position on the riverbank that gives a good view of as many jump points as possible.

✦ **Motor sports:** These sports are among the fastest growing events from a fan standpoint. Auto racing is one of the toughest photographic challenges, even for modern professional camera equipment. Those cars are fast! Try to catch them on the curve when they're moving a little bit slower. This can also give you a three-quarter view of the car. Or, pick a spot where you can get the cars coming at you. This type of action is easier to capture. Fast moving racing cars can also present a good opportunity for creative blur shots (more on this topic later). Use a modest shutter speed (say 1/125 of a second) to keep the starter sharp as he waves the flag to begin the race. If you do it right, the starter stays sharp while the cars and flags are blurred. Other good opportunities include shots at the starting line or in the pits. For motor-cross events, where the motorcyclists are catching big air, you want to be some distance away from their take-off point. Side shots of the athlete and bike as they come even with your position are also good.

✦ **Horse racing/dressage:** For horse racing, station yourself where the track curves so that you can shoot the animals coming straight toward you; then get three-quarter and profile shots as they round the curve. For the specialized horse maneuvers called dressage, study a book on the desired movements and looks each animal should present. Be ready to shoot them head on and in profile and three-quarter pose.

✦ **Swimming:** Shots from head-on and from the side are pretty much your only choices here. Start by shooting head-on and time your shot to catch the swimmer rising up from the water. You might need an accessory flash unit and a butane-powered hair dryer for battling lens fogging. Don't underestimate just how difficult it is to keep your equipment in working condition because of all the moisture and humidity in the air. Keep extra packets of *desiccant* (a powdered moisture-grabbing agent) in your camera bag and a microfiber cloth within easy reach. Try to get to the swim meet site at least a half hour early so that your equipment has a chance to come up to room temperature and humidity. Package your camera and lenses in sealable plastic bags during this warm-up period so that condensation forms on the bag, not the lenses.

Increasing dynamic range

High-contrast situations, such as ski slopes, present a special challenge for digital cameras. Because sports photography frequently revolves around frame-filling action with just one or two athletes, the easiest way to deal with high-contrast lighting is to use flash to balance the light between your subject and the background.

✐ **Metering:** Take a meter reading off a *mid-tone* (something equivalent to medium gray, such as the palm of your hand) and find the correct exposure for the overall scene. Then set your flash to output enough light so that your subjects' illumination matches

the background. (This tip probably applies only to those with higher-end cameras and very powerful flash units.)

✐ **Filtration:** Special low-contrast filters have appeared on the market in the past few years. Although sticking another piece of glass in front of your high-quality lens risks degrading image quality, a well-made filter can be worth the investment. Photographs made with low-contrast filters generally require a little extra tweaking in an image editing program (nothing extreme), but the results can be well worth it.

Winter sports: A special case

The 2006 Winter Olympics renewed interest in shooting sports like skiing and snowboarding. These sports present a special challenge for the digital photographer because of the amount of contrast inherent in snowy conditions. Such lighting conditions often fool your camera's exposure system. If your digital camera lets you shoot in RAW mode (a relatively unprocessed mode that captures the image information before the camera's settings are applied — check your camera's instruction manual to see how), use that option. It gives you the maximum amount of information when you're editing the image later. You'll be glad you did.

Generally, a good image occurs when the skier or snowboarder turns about 15 or 20 feet from your position. (Try to avoid the snow spray.) Another good shot is when the athlete becomes airborne. Be careful that you aren't so busy looking through the viewfinder that you lose track of the skier or boarder coming right at you. (Don't laugh; it happens.)

Accessibility

Most events are accessible at all but the highest levels of play. Even high school and junior college sports cut serious amateurs some slack if they want to get closer to the action (on the sidelines or behind the baseline).

When you get to the point at which the athletes are making their living playing the sport — or for the highest levels of NCAA play — that starts to change. Even minor league ball has restrictions on what you can do and what kind equipment you can use. Pro-level events are even more restrictive. Plus, most professional organizations grant access based on your agreement to use your images only for editorial purposes. High-profile sports organizations like Major League Baseball, the National Football League, and the National Basketball Association guard the marketing potential of their sport and athletes very closely.

At least one type of competition, extreme (or *action*) sports, provides unparalleled access for the average enthusiast. Many times, while shooting events at the X-Games, I've been on one side of a fence chatting with spectators a foot or two away on the other side, and we're all close enough to the action to get the exact same shot.

Extreme sports tend to be very photogenic, too. Plus, the athletes tend to be fan-oriented, which can lead to good fan-athlete interaction shots. Because the financial rewards for many of these sports come more from endorsements than from prize money, the athletes actually try to cultivate their fans — a lesson that some professional sports seem to have forgotten. Extreme sports fans tend to be almost as flamboyant and colorful as the athletes, too. Look for mohawks, spiked hair, body piercings, and tattoos. Most fans don't mind if you want to get a shot of their particular fashion statement; they're usually pretty proud of it. Just ask whether it's okay first.

I usually rely on medium to longer zoom lenses plus an accessory flash. Because these sports are done on snow-covered mountains, I try to travel light and with my equipment balanced in waist pouches or equipment belts rather than a camera bag. A camera backpack works well, too, but makes it harder to get at your equipment in a hurry. Having a flash available is very important because, otherwise, you have to choose between overexposed snow and an underexposed subject.

Exploring Action Photo Techniques

As a would-be sports photographer, one of the most important things you can do is become knowledgeable about the sports you want to shoot. The most successful sports photographers are the ones who can anticipate the next play or event and put themselves in position to trip the shutter in time to record the moment.

Many times, you have decisions to make long before the action starts. Is this a situation in which you'll use the zoom on the camera and try to react to what happens? Or are you picking a spot, prefocusing, and waiting for action to reach that location? Both are valid methods, and most photographers alternate between them as the game goes on.

Whenever possible, sports shooters try to analyze the situation to see whether they can understand what will happen next. Third and long yardage or first and 10 in football are good examples. In the former, a pass is likely; in the latter, a running play. You can follow the receiver on your side of the field if you think a pass play is likely or key in on the quarterback to get a shot of the pass or the pass rush. For the running play, you can key in on the backfield and be ready to catch the hand-off and ensuing running play.

Setting your ISO speed

Being able to change the film speed or ISO (International Standards Organization) rating of your camera on the fly is one of the great benefits of owning a digital camera. Be sure to check your camera's instructions to see how to change the ISO setting.

When conditions permit, I always try to work at 100 or 200 ISO to get the highest quality images. Most digital cameras are optimized to provide their best quality at those settings. If I'm shooting outdoors under most daylight conditions, an ISO setting at 100 to 200 usually allows me an action-stopping shutter speed of 1/2000 of a second or higher, which is good for the majority of sports. (For more on choosing shutter speeds, see Book I, Chapter 2.) If I have to move indoors or if the sun is getting lower in the sky, I ratchet the speed up to 400 ISO and use a flash unit if circumstances permit. In uneven lighting situations, being able to change ISOs whenever you want is a great help.

sports participants are stopped dead in their tracks. Here are some tips for stopping action at slower shutter speeds:

✦ **Look for momentary pauses.** Many times, a sport has a moment of peak action where the action hesitates before movement returns. Think of a jumper on the ascent. At the top of the leap is a moment of stasis — hanging in space before dropping back down, as shown in the bicycle shot in Figure 5-9. If you're forced to shoot at too low of a shutter speed, try to time your shot for that moment. Another example is a tennis player, just after tossing the ball to serve. If the server uses a high toss, he or she has to wait for the ball to drop before hitting it. The tennis player up at the net is another example. Although the racket and ball might be moving very quickly, the athlete's body usually isn't traveling very far or fast.

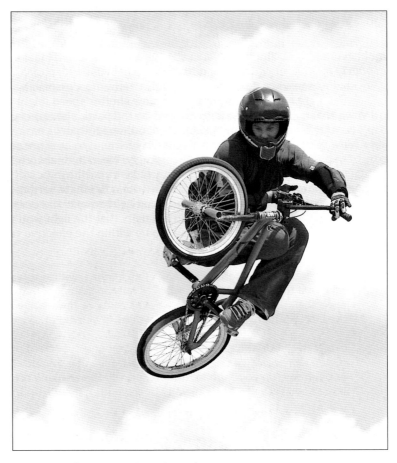

Figure 5-9: Catch the action at its peak.

✦ **Try to shoot the action moving directly toward the camera.** Athletes and machines moving toward the camera require a slower shutter speed and faster autofocus to freeze motion than those moving laterally across the camera's field of view.

✦ **Concentrate.** The most dramatic image can be the concentration of the athlete the moment before he or she begins play. Think of the pitcher looking to the catcher for a sign, or a tennis player just before serving the ball. Another example is the linebacker poised for the snap of the ball before rushing the quarterback. There's also the free-throw shooter pausing a moment before shooting.

✦ **Find action in nonaction moments.** Another shot to look for is one that shows the price the athlete pays for his or her sport. This can be football players on the bench with steam rising off their heads or a spent distance runner leaning on a teammate at the end of a race. A shot of a distraught athlete being consoled by a fellow athlete is a classic sports photograph. Also watch for the emotions of the fans or cheerleaders.

Panning

Panning (moving the camera horizontally in the same direction of motion as your subject) is a valuable technique that should be part of every serious sports photographer's repertoire. This procedure gives you the best of both worlds: freezing the important part of the scene while blurring the background to show the furious motion of the moment.

The idea behind the technique is to use a slower shutter speed while following an athlete or an object laterally with the camera. The result is a subject that's in relatively sharp focus while the background is blurred.

Here's how to put panning to use:

1. **Select a moderately slow shutter speed to give yourself a long enough stretch of time for the lateral movement of the camera to register — but not so long as to create overall blurriness from camera shake.**

   Don't you just love precise directions like this? But seriously, if I could give you exact numbers, your camera would already be programmed to do it for you. There's no exact recommendation; you have to experiment to see what works best for you. The speed will vary from sport to sport as well. Start out by trying something in the 1/45–1/60 of a second range for running humans. Work your way to around 1/350 of a second for motor sports and see how this works for you.

2. **Begin following your subject with the camera before tripping the shutter.**

   You want a smooth lateral motion here, so beginning the move first and then shooting helps you do that. Your panning movement is steadier if you limit your movement to your waist and hips while keeping your feet planted and your knees together. This will also help reduce camera shake.

Also make sure to keep your elbows braced against your body to help turn yourself into a human monopod. Most people find that using an actual monopod generally doesn't work very well, but for a few, it works. If circumstances permit, a tripod with a tripod *panning head* (one that allows the tilt and yaw controls to be locked while the panning direction swings free) can make for a smoother pan. Certainly, a photographer who's just starting to experiment with the panning technique might find that a tripod makes things easier.

3. **Trip the shutter as gently as possible.**

   You're trying to avoid a downward snap in your movement. The old cliché is to squeeze the shutter — not press it.

4. **Continue your lateral panning movement for a second or so after the shutter has closed.**

   This is a case where proper follow-through is just as important for the photographer as it is for the athlete.

5. **Repeat this process at least a half dozen times or more.**

   It seldom works perfectly the first time. (It's okay; you're not paying for film here.) Good panning is something you have to work at. Don't give up on the technique if your first few attempts (or more) don't *pan out*. (Sorry, just couldn't resist the pun!)

This technique gives you dramatic images that accurately convey the sense of motion the sport involves. Sometimes, the photograph of the athlete flying through the air or running down the baseline with the background blurred (see Figure 5-10) does a better job of conveying the speed of the event than a moment of frozen action.

Capturing action approaching the camera

Action approaching the camera is also more dramatic because the camera can maintain eye contact with the athlete or create a sense of power from the approaching machine coming right at the viewer.

Because these images produce such drama, work on capturing them well. Mastering this aspect of sports shooting will do much to improve your sports photography. Help your camera's autofocus system work its best by prefocusing on a spot a few feet ahead of where you hope to take the picture. Lock on to the approaching athlete and give your camera a chance to acquire the athlete and bring its autofocus up to speed. If you're working with a digital SLR with a zoom lens, you can give yourself more time and distance for the shot by acquiring your subject at the extreme telephoto end of its range and continuing to shoot while racking the zoom through its full range to its widest setting.

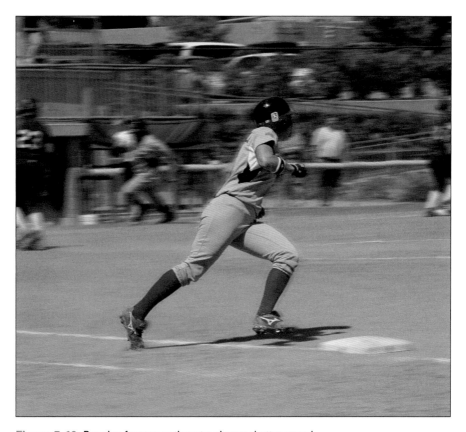

Figure 5-10: Panning freezes action at a slower shutter speed.

Circumstances don't always permit you to get this shot. Still, photography is about putting yourself in a position to give yourself the best possible chance to catch the action. If you couple that with shooting a large number of images, you can increase the likelihood of success.

Using blur creatively

In some circumstances, you just don't have enough light or a fast enough lens to set the shutter speed as high as you would like. Stopping action can be a good photographic technique when you're covering sports, but it's certainly not the only one. When circumstances don't allow you to freeze motion or when you want to create something that looks different from what everyone else is doing, deliberately trying to blur your image can create something special. Blur works for non-sports action, too. Figure 5-11 shows a picture in which the blurring creates a photo that says "action!" more clearly than any frozen-in-time photo.

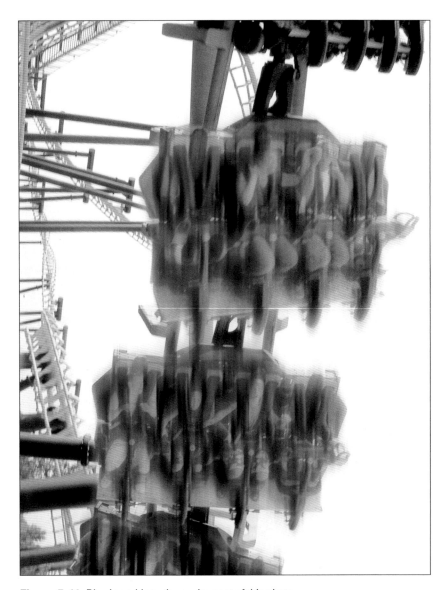

Figure 5-11: Blurring adds to the excitement of this photo.

To create a successful photograph, the key elements of the image — not necessarily every single part of it — need to be in focus. Your subject's eyes and face need to be in focus. If his or her body, hands, or feet are blurred, that shows just how fast they're actually moving. Some sports, such as tennis, are easy. There's a pretty forgiving difference between the shutter speed you need to freeze the athlete's body and the speed necessary to freeze the moving tennis racket or ball. The same goes for hockey because the player's stick and the puck blur quite easily at shutter speeds that comfortably freeze the player.

When successful, this kind of image can actually be more dramatic than freezing action. Here's how to try this technique:

1. **Figure out what shutter speed is slow enough to blur the faster moving parts of the body while being fast enough to freeze the face.**

   This varies from sport to sport, so be prepared to experiment.

2. **Time your shot to coincide with a moment of peak action, such as the athlete at the top of his or her leap.**

   Many sports call for the athlete's head to stay still while the rest of the body explodes in action. (Think of a golf swing where the player's head stays down through the entire stroke.) Other sports require the head to travel through a range of movement as they stroke through the ball. (You know, *keep your eye on the ball.*) For these sports, the head eventually stops as the athlete follows through to complete the stroke. The end of this follow-through determines where the athlete's body movement is frozen, although the ball or puck and stick or racket might still be moving.

After you get the hang of using blur creatively, you've added a powerful tool to your photographic arsenal. The essence of many sports is the athlete's ability to move as fast as possible. Blurred hands, feet, limbs, and wheels convey the speed of modern athletes and machines in a way that frozen figures can't. Try to experiment with creative uses of blur each time you're on a shoot. Just manage it the way most of photographers do: We start out working for an image that we know gets the job done. After we get our "money" shot, we can start looking for something a little more creative. This is the time to try the panning or creative blur photos.

Taking the Picture

After you choose your shutter speed, take a strategic position, and know what kinds of opportunities might be coming your way (literally!), take the picture. Watch the action closely, frame the image in your viewfinder, and snap away.

Capturing great sports moments

As you shoot, keep some simple concepts in mind. For example, here are some things to look for in a great sports image:

✦ **Full extension:** The athlete at the top of a leap or in full stride represents one example of the decisive moment in sports photography.

✦ **The coiled spring:** The moment before release when muscles are tense and the body is coiled represents another key moment in sports. This image shows the athlete just before he or she explodes into action. Think of the shot put thrower just before release, the shot still pressed into the chin; or the baseball pitcher, arm reared back ready to reverse direction and fire the ball at the batter.

✦ **Emotion:** A great sports image doesn't even need to be a good action shot. Catch the athlete or fan in a moment of extreme emotion, and you've gotten a memorable image. Watch the fans, watch the coaches, and watch the athletes watching the other athletes.

Most sporting events are carnivals of colors, patterns, and personalities. They provide a wealth of photographic opportunities not limited to just the playing field. Enthusiastic photographers, curious about the world around them and with an eye to more than just the game, can produce great sports photos no matter what camera they're using.

Setting up for predictable action

Having an understanding of the sport you're photographing can put you in a position to take advantage of your ability to predict impending action. Here are a couple of ways to use that ability.

✦ **Prefocusing:** Sometimes an athlete needs to reach a specific location as part of a play. If I'm photographing a baseball or softball game and a runner makes it to third, I swing my tripod-mounted camera to cover home and prefocus on home plate. I still follow the action with my hand-held camera, but I also position myself so that I can quickly fire the second camera for a shot of a runner sliding home. Prefocusing on the forward end of the basketball rim is another example. You're now ready to get a shot of the center leaping for a rebound.

✦ **Zone focusing:** This technique takes advantage of the depth of field that comes with using a smaller lens opening. (Depth of field is covered in greater depth in Book IV, Chapter 2. In simple terms, the smaller the lens opening, the greater the range of sharp focus from one point to another on a line from the lens.) The idea here is to choose a lens opening that's small enough to create a zone of sharp focus. The zone should be deep enough to give you about a 5-foot range in which everything is in focus.

Zone focusing works well for a sport like basketball, where you know you can expect action to take place in a location about 5 to 10 feet from the basket. Using an external flash unit (which many point-and-shoot digital cameras can do) should enable you to shoot at f/5.6 or f/8, which gives you that 5-foot range or greater. In Figure 5-12, the focus was set ahead of time for the ramp, so when the athlete spun around, the camera was already set for the picture.

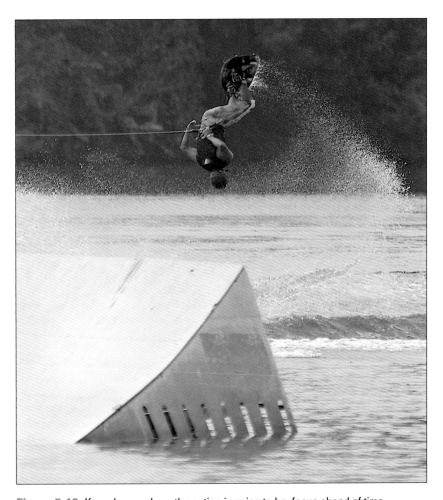

Figure 5-12: If you know where the action is going to be, focus ahead of time.

Photographing action sequences

Sometimes, you need to do more than just capture one good shot of sports action. You need to get the sequence of movements that make up an entire run or the execution of a particular move or trick.

Pros get these sequences by using cameras that can capture as many as eight pictures per second (usually expressed in fps — frames per second). Although one or two non-dSLR digital cameras are capable of high-speed, motor-driven photography, most are good for only about 2 or 3 fps at best. Usually, you must work with a digital SLR to get 3 to 5 fps and have one of the high-end pro models to get as many as 8 fps.

Even with a limited burst mode capability, a photographer can still create effective photo sequences. Once again, a little planning and foresight can help you get the best possible results. If you can predict the path the athlete is going to take, you can better follow that path with your camera. Another thing that you can do is back out your composition a little to give you some margin for error. You don't want to have a great sequence of shots with your subject ruining it by drifting in and out of the frame.

Here are some tips for getting good action sequences:

✦ Visualize the path that you expect your subject to travel.

✦ Prefocus on the point where you expect to start shooting.

✦ Set the fastest shutter speed you can to give your motor drive the best possible chance of advancing at its best speed.

✦ Compose your shot to give your subject some room to move within the frame.

✦ Shoot several sequences to make sure you get at least one usable sequence. Remember that you're trying to get four or five good shots in a row, not just one, so it becomes that much harder to be sure that they're all in focus and well composed. Take lots of shots.

Don't expect to get a good sequence on your first attempt. This is another one of those techniques that you need to practice beforehand. You're trying to understand how your camera works in this kind of situation and determine whether you can tweak your gear to perform better. Some cameras require you to drop down to a lower resolution in order to shoot fast enough to get a good sequence of images. Because you're trying to get multiple images, the loss of resolution might not be as bad as you think. After all, you'll have the group of images to take the place of one shot.

Some digital cameras don't offer a continuous shooting capability. Others offer it only at a lower resolution setting than you're really comfortable using. Just because you can't blaze away like the pros doesn't mean you can't tell a multiple-picture story of a sports event.

A good sequence of photographs tells a story. If you're shooting an event in which an athlete makes more than one run or attempt (long jumpers get six tries, for instance), work on getting the sequence you want by shooting a different aspect of each attempt. Be careful how you identify the finished result, though. There's nothing wrong with showing how each element of the jump works through a sequence of images, but representing it as the individual elements of one jump is the kind of thing that gets photographers in trouble.

Chapter 6: Travel Photography

In This Chapter

▶ **Choosing the right equipment**

▶ **Getting ready to go on the road**

▶ **Mastering the best travel photography techniques**

*T*aking pictures while traveling can be the most rewarding long-term benefit of a trip. Although memories of a particular location fade as the years go by, the images that you create will still be there to remind you of a special time in your life. Plus, face it: Photography is fun! Knowing that you've taken a good picture of that special location gives you a particularly satisfying feeling. Lasting friendships can be made during a trip, and being able to send your new friends pictures of the time you shared together can help cement your friendship.

If you've traveled with a film camera in the past, you'll find that vacationing with a digital camera offers some terrific advantages over traditional picture-taking tools. Digital cameras can be smaller and lighter than their film counterparts, so they take up a lot less space in your luggage. They have no film that airport security X-ray cameras can damage. And as you take photos, you can check them using your digital camera's built-in LCD screen.

This chapter offers advice for aspiring photographers who are intimidated by the idea of trying to take good pictures in unfamiliar surroundings. If you want to know more, I recommend *Digital Travel Photography Digital Field Guide*, also from Wiley Publishing and written by yours truly.

Getting the Right Gear

A photographer on the road needs a selection of gear that's versatile enough to handle the unexpected without burdening the photographer like a Sherpa on a Mount Everest expedition. Carefully considering which key pieces of equipment to take — and which to leave behind — can make the trip less stressful and more productive.

Selecting a camera for your needs

Choosing a camera to use while traveling is an important decision, one that you might have already made long before your trip. After all, most of us are unable to buy a camera specifically for a vacation. You'll want to keep a camera's travel photography capabilities in mind whenever you purchase a digital model. Key decisions revolve around lens versatility (for more options while taking pictures), file size (more megapixels equal bigger pictures), and how much control the camera gives you over shooting decisions.

When purchasing a camera, most of your decisions revolve around what kind of photographer you are and what kind of travel pictures you expect to take, as the following sections make clear. No matter which category you fall into, your digital camera should have the basic features that you need to make a broad range of travel photography easy and carefree.

Professional photographers

Pros like to be ready for anything, even when they're not on the clock. You never know when a quick shot taken while on vacation can turn into a salable image. If you're a professional photographer, look for

+ Compatibility of a digital system with your current film camera's interchangeable lens system, if at all possible. Right now this means Canon, Nikon, Fuji in Nikon mount, Sigma, Sony (which took over Konica Minolta), Pentax, and a few other vendors.

+ A choice of camera bodies offering 6–16-megapixel sensors, rapid sequence shooting ability, and other features, depending on your shooting needs. Travel photography can sometimes be as fast-paced as sports shooting and can require high-resolution images for reproduction.

+ A choice of flash units and accessories. A professional system needs to be flexible enough to accommodate all the gadgets needed for top-of-the-line travel photography.

Serious amateurs

The best serious amateur photographers are often professionals in every aspect except monetary reward. They frequently spend a lot on their hobby and might even be looking at the same systems desired by pros. Their needs will certainly include

✦ A high-resolution (6–10-megapixel) camera with large capacity memory (with the ability to accept interchangeable memory cards). These features enable you to grab travel photos suitable for printing at large sizes, which you can then display on the wall.

✦ Extreme zoom lens capabilities, preferably with a 10X range or the equivalent of 300mm to 400mm on a full-frame camera. This range is ideal for reaching out and grabbing a small detail from a panoramic scene.

✦ Add-on accessory lenses (called *teleconverters*) to extend a zoom's capability even farther.

✦ Rapid-shooting capability to allow taking pictures quickly at festivals or other fast-moving travel experiences. (The running of the bulls at Pamplona comes to mind!)

Enthusiastic amateurs

Amateur photo enthusiasts love photography but have other interests — such as travel! With more limitations on their budgets, they need top-quality *prosumer* cameras. These cameras are aimed at consumers but have features that will please advanced photographers. These include

✦ Medium- to high-resolution (6–10-megapixel) camera with decent capacity memory (with the ability to accept interchangeable memory cards). These cameras enable you to print vacation snapshots in sizes as large as 5 x 7 to 11 x 14 inches.

✦ Versatile zoom lens (between 3X and 10X — up to the equivalent of a 300mm to 400mm lens on a full-frame camera) for taking close-up shots of distant scenic features or for capturing locals being themselves. Figure 6-1 shows the "reach" of various typical zoom ratios.

✦ Add-on accessory lenses to extend range even farther or to widen the view to take in monuments, castles, or cathedrals penned in by their surroundings.

Vacationers who simply want to take good photos

You know who you are: You want pictures that are sharp and clear, colorful, and good enough to make a batch of 4-x-6-inch snaps of your best shots. You like digital photography and want to capture some travel memories, but can't spend a huge amount for your equipment. These photographers need

✦ Low- to medium-resolution (5–7-megapixel) cameras (especially pocketable compact models) with the ability to accept interchangeable memory cards.

✦ A versatile zoom lens, at least a 3X zoom, preferably a 5X or longer zoom.

3X

5X

10X

Figure 6-1: Zoom lenses let you reach out and capture distant details.

Choosing key features for travel photography

Here are some key features to look for in a camera, no matter what kind of travel photographer you are. You can find more information on these features in Book I, Chapter 2.

✦ **Optical zoom range:** A powerful zoom enables you to compose your image carefully and cover a lot of photographic territory on your travel treks. With a good zoom, you can also take advantage of lens effects, such as selective focus.

✦ **Interchangeable memory cards:** Some camera vendors try to get by supplying just a small amount of built-in memory, which may be a skimpy 32MB, and expect you to buy memory cards if you need more. When the memory is full, you either stop shooting or delete images, neither of which is a happy option during a once-in-a-lifetime vacation. The ability to change cards enables you to just keep shooting. Fortunately, all digital cameras that do have non-removable, built-in memory also include a slot for a flash memory card. It's just something you have to pay for.

✦ **Sufficient megapixels:** The more megapixels, the better. This is true for several reasons. First, higher resolution (more megapixels) allows for larger prints of your prized vacation shots. Second, higher resolution lets you crop down to a smaller view of that monument you just couldn't get close enough to and still get a good-quality print.

✦ **Interchangeable lenses:** These days, an increasing number of affordable digital cameras use interchangeable lenses. These give a photographer a wide range of choices for high-quality travel photography. Being able to select from a range of different focal lengths — plus being able to control depth of field (the range of image sharpness as it appears throughout the photograph) — gives the photographer tremendous power over the photographic image. Sometimes manufacturers offer add-on lenses for non-interchangeable-lens cameras, too.

Think about taking a second camera along, too, particularly if this is more than just a run-of-the-mill vacation. A small digital camera might not cost much. If your primary camera fails, your backup camera could be worth its weight in gold photographically. Shop for or borrow one that uses the same type of batteries and storage media as your primary camera, if possible. The extra camera can also entice a spouse or child into sharing your love of photography. Encourage them to shoot their own photos on the trip.

Selecting lenses for travel

Look at your camera's built-in capabilities, including the range of magnifications available from your zoom, as well as the ability to add supplementary telephoto, wide-angle, or close-up lenses. You can find more about lenses in Book I, Chapter 2. Travel photographers need three basic capabilities:

✦ **Wide-angle:** Being able to fit more into a picture comes in handy when you're shooting scenics and architecture, like the image shown in Figure 6-2.

Figure 6-2: Wide-angle lenses, like the one used to take this shot, can be useful in tight quarters.

✦ **Telephoto:** Capturing native wildlife or sports shots without getting dangerously close is an invaluable capability.

✦ **Macro:** These lenses are essential for getting close-ups of native insects, signs, or documents.

With at least some capabilities in each of these ranges, you can shoot a broad selection of travel photos without necessarily having to physically move closer or farther away from your subject.

Considering a tripod

A *tripod* is a three-legged stand designed to hold your camera steady. You can find more detailed coverage of tripods in Book I, Chapter 2.

Although a tripod can be a little cumbersome to carry along on a trip, this camera support can do several things for you. A tripod is great for holding the camera steady if you are using longer shutter speeds in dim light or using a telephoto lens. If your camera has a timer feature, you can use a tripod to get yourself in the picture.

A tripod definitely leads to better pictures, but only if you use it. If you find the idea of lugging one around too much of a bother during your vacation, plan on a different tool, such as a monopod, beanbag, or one of the other options discussed later in this chapter. It's okay — you're on vacation!

Investing in an accessory flash

Although most digital cameras have some sort of built-in flash capability, these are usually only good for a range of about 8 feet or so, which isn't always enough. Because available light (more commonly known as *available darkness*) is undependable, the traveling photographer should consider carrying an accessory flash unit.

Accessory flash units do more than just provide extra light when it's too dark to shoot without it. The reasons why an extra flash can be particularly helpful for travel photography include the following:

✦ **Using fill flash:** If you're planning to shoot a companion who is in partial shade or is wearing a ball cap, an accessory flash can help you clean up the shadows. Because the supplemental light isn't trying to light the whole scene, filling can be accomplished by smaller, less powerful flash units (such as the camera's built-in flash) or even by a reflective surface.

A 3-x-3-foot piece of folding Mylar or a silver-coated auto sunshield held by a helper to reflect the sunlight into the area where the sunlight can't reach provides a nicely lit photo, as shown in Figure 6-3.

✦ **Painting with light:** If part of your trip takes you into a dark place, such as a thirteenth-century church that doesn't have any spotlights shining on it, an accessory flash might help. You can use the *painting with light* photo technique, covered later in this chapter, with a tripod or firm support.

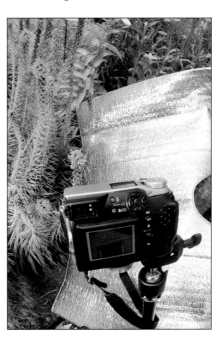

Figure 6-3: Keep a compact reflector in your travel bag to fill in shadows.

✦ **Macro/close-up photography:** If you want to take close-up shots of typical local jewelry, markers, or insects, you need to provide a lot of light in order to get enough image sharpness to create a good-looking image.

Many higher-end digital cameras offer some method of triggering an accessory flash unit, either by a cable connection or via *hot shoe* (the connection found on the top of many digital cameras that holds the flash and provides electrical contact with the camera). Figure 6-4 shows the hot shoe found on one Olympus digital camera model. Many consumer-priced digital cameras, however, offer no such provision. If your camera doesn't have the means for adding an additional flash, a slaved flash specifically designed for digital cameras might be your answer. (A *slaved* flash has a built-in light sensor that triggers the slaved flash when your camera's flash fires.)

Figure 6-4: A hot shoe lets you attach an external flash.

Accessory lighting is covered more thoroughly in Book II, Chapter 5.

Selecting a camera bag

Depending on the size of a digital camera and the accessories accompanying it, a camera bag or pouch could be a necessity. For just the basics — a small camera, extra batteries and memory cards, and a lens cleaning cloth — a simple fanny pack will do the job and leave room for hotel keys, money, and identification.

If you're a more serious photographer who's carrying a larger digital camera or an interchangeable-lens digital SLR, you need more space. Although a larger camera bag could be the answer, the active traveler should consider these factors:

✦ **Size:** Your camera bag should be roomy enough to hold your basic camera setup and also leave some room for an extra piece of gear or two, such as filters or extra batteries that you'll be glad you have when you're hundreds or thousands of miles from home.

✦ **Flexibility:** An ideal bag includes multiple compartments that can be reconfigured (with hook-and-loop tape) so that you can adapt the bag to the different configurations of camera outfit that you might need. You'll often find that your equipment needs vary from place to place on vacation. At one destination, you might need easy access to your extra flash unit. At another, you'll want to grab your add-on wide-angle lens quickly.

✦ **Sturdy strap:** Much travel is done on the run. A travel-friendly bag has a main strap that runs around the sides and bottom of bag and that's securely stitched, not grommetted into the fabric. (Don't underestimate the importance of this one, folks!)

✦ **Toughness:** To stand up to the rigors of travel, a bag should be made of rip-stop nylon or canvas. If you're really into leather, though, you don't have to rule this material out, either — if the bag is well constructed.

✦ **Security and convenience:** The bag should offer multiple methods of closing. Usually a good bag offers a fast method of closing (frequently with hook-and-loop tape or clasps) and a more secure method of closure (zippers or clips) that takes more effort to open and close but makes accidental opening less likely. Figure 6-5 shows such a bag.

Figure 6-5: A sturdy bag with multiple ways of closure offers the most flexibility.

✦ **Protection from the elements:** The bag needs a top flap that closes over the main compartment in such a way that if it's hit by rain, the water is channeled down the bag sides. Water shouldn't be able to seep through a zipper channel or closure point. Although the zippered closure on this bag looks secure, it does little to protect the sensitive digital camera equipment inside from rain.

At some point, you can cross over the line that divides vacation photographer from pack mule. Do a dry run with all your gear before leaving. Now ask yourself whether you're comfortable with the idea of lugging that stuff around with you on your vacation. The only right answer to the question is the one that satisfies you.

Keeping your camera powered

Modern cameras use batteries like there's no tomorrow, particularly digital cameras with their power-draining LCD screens and built-in flashes. That's not much of a burden when you're shooting close to home. But if you're traveling — far from AC power or a ready source for batteries — power is a prime consideration. If you plan to shoot pictures for more than a couple of hours, take along spare batteries to use until you get back to civilization.

Camera bag alternatives

If a traditional camera bag doesn't do everything you need, consider some alternatives. Here are some of the most popular:

- ✔ **Backpacks:** An alternative to the camera bag is the camera backpack. These range in size from small — big enough for just the camera, a couple of lenses, and some accessories — to massive carry-alls. One drawback is that you have to take the pack off and put it down every time you need to retrieve something.

- ✔ **Modular belt systems:** I use one of these myself, and it's great if you don't plan on sitting down very often. It puts the weight on your hips and leaves multiple lenses and accessories within easy reach even when wearing a backpack. The modularity of the system means that it can be configured for almost any sort of shoot.

Several manufacturers make modular belt systems, including Tamrac (www.tamrac.com), Lowepro (www.lowepro.com), and Kinesis (www.kinesisgear.com). These belts are festooned with loops, and separate pouches are mated to the belt with hook-and-loop tape. The advantage to this system is that the belt can be configured for different needs and matched to each day's shoot. Pouches are also available to hold cell phones, water bottles, and other non-photographic items.

- ✔ **Chest bags:** A chest bag enables you to carry your camera harnessed to your chest, where you can get to it quickly and easily. Most of these style of bags can also be switched to a belt and positioned to ride on the hip as well.

Predicting battery life is a bigger challenge than taking good pictures simply because the figure varies depending upon your particular camera, how much you review your shots on the LCD finder, how many pictures you take, what kind of media you're using, how often you use your internal flash, what type of batteries you're using, and what the temperature is. (Batteries drain faster in the cold.) If you're careful with the LCD screen and flash and keep the camera warm, four AA batteries could last for several hundred to 1,000 or more shots, depending on the camera.

Here's how to maximize your battery life when on vacation:

- ✦ **Short reviews:** Most digital cameras let you set how long the LCD stays on for review after a shot is taken. Choose the briefest setting. You can always review an individual shot for a longer period if need be.

- ✦ **Flash with care:** Built-in flash units reduce battery life by half. Use an accessory flash if possible.

✦ **Battery choices:** AA lithium batteries tend to last longer than other battery types, so if you use these, you can extend the active life of your shooting session before replacements are necessary. They also handle cold weather better. You should always carry at least one set of extra AA batteries (more if you shoot a lot).

If you're traveling in your home country, chances are you already know how easy or difficult it is to feed your camera, but even here in the United States, not every type of battery can be found in the "boonies." If your camera requires one of the less common types, your digital camera can become a paperweight before your trip is half over.

If your camera uses AA or AAA batteries, rechargeable batteries are the best answer (with an extra set of backups, or two or three sets) for each device you bring that needs them. Choose nickel metal-hydride (NiMH) rechargeable batteries if you can because they have more power, are safer for the environment, and have several technical advantages over other types. If your camera doesn't use a common battery type, bring lots more than you think you'll need. Remember, if you have to buy batteries at a popular tourist destination, you'll probably pay a lot more than you normally would at home.

If you're lucky, you'll have a camera that can accept a rechargeable battery pack and use regular AA batteries as well. Some packs, like the one shown in Figure 6-6, are the same form factor as a pair of AA cells.

Figure 6-6: Some rechargeable packs can be replaced with conventional AA cells.

Of course rechargeable batteries need to be recharged. If you're going overseas, make sure that you have the proper adaptors for whichever country you're visiting. Don't automatically assume there will be plenty of outlets, either. I recently went on a Bahamas cruise and found that our stateroom had only one outlet. Because I'd come prepared with a power strip, we could still plug in my laptop, battery chargers, fan, and my wife's hair dryer and curling iron. Without such foresight . . . well, my wife and I would surely have ended up fighting over a single outlet.

Another option, especially for those headed for a week or two in the backcountry, is a solar-powered battery charger from ICP Global Technologies (www.icpglobal.com/html/pp.htm). This unit can charge four AA batteries in four hours or so, depending on how bright a day it is. (Good luck if you're hiking in the Pacific Northwest.) The hard part might be finding a way to keep the device pointed toward the sun while you're backpacking through the forest. You may also want to consider whether carrying the unit's weight (1.3 pounds) in extra batteries would be more efficient.

By the way, many of today's camera makers have resorted to marking the battery compartment orientation markings through indentations (+ or –) in the molds used to make the compartments, rather than painting the markings on with white paint. If your camera is one of those, consider finding a way to mark it yourself with something more visible, such as nail polish.

Picking up other useful devices

Gizmos. Gadgets. Thingamajigs. Many of these items don't fall into any particular category except that they do something useful. Here are some of the most popular photo widgets:

+ **Cleaning kit:** A cleaning kit includes these items:

  • *Microfiber cleaning cloth:* These are useful for keeping lenses and bodies clean.

  • *Blower brush:* Use this first and blow off any dust or small particles.

  • *Silica packets:* These absorb any moisture that gets in your camera bag. Keep in a plastic freezer bag that can double as a camera raincoat in bad weather.

+ **Rain poncho:** I always keep a cheap plastic rain poncho in my camera bag, along with a better rain poncho in my car. Add to that a supply of plastic bags of various sizes and some artist's tape that's easy to apply and remove from the camera.

Make a raincoat for your camera from a plastic freezer bag. Draw the end of the bag over the camera's lens barrel and cut a hole large enough for it to shoot through. Wrap the artist's tape around the end of the barrel and bag to hold the bag in place, and you've got a low-cost rain poncho for the camera. Thread the camera strap through the end of the bag that opens and press as much of the seal together as possible. If it's hard to see through the viewfinder, turn the LCD display on and use that to compose the photo. Figure 6-7 shows you what this camera raincoat looks like. Put a clear or ultraviolet filter over the front of your lens to provide even more protection from the moisture.

Figure 6-7: A zip-closure bag and tape can make a raincoat for your camera.

✦ **Towel:** Carry some paper towels so that you can towel off any moisture that gets inside the freezer bag. Toss a silica packet or two in with the camera before closing the bag to help keep the inside dry. It's also a good idea to have something to dry your hands with so you're not touching the camera with wet hands. A good choice for this kind of thing is a Pack Towel, which is a lightweight towel that dries quickly and is sold in many department stores' camping sections.

✦ **A pencil eraser:** Sometimes a thin film of corrosion builds up on the battery and terminal contacts. The cure for this one is to gently rub both the battery and terminal contacts with a pencil eraser and reinsert the batteries, making sure that they're right-side-up.

✦ **Polypro gloves:** Several outdoor clothing companies make lightweight gloves out of polypropylene or some brand-name version, such as Capilene or Thermax. Outdoor enthusiasts prize these synthetic materials because they *wick* (transfer) moisture away from the skin to the outside of the material, making them seem warmer because the skin stays dry. Wearing a pair of these in damp conditions will help keep your hands dry. When you need to touch the camera, pull a glove off, and you have a dry hand to work with.

✦ **Artist's or masking tape:** If the conditions are both dusty and windy, protecting the camera can be vital and difficult. Fine-grit sand or dust can blow inside the camera's seals and mess up internal mechanisms.

The same plastic bag technique described in a preceding bullet is good, but consider taping as much of the bag end shut as possible to get the best possible seal.

 If you're traveling abroad and want to be sure you won't be hassled on your return, visit a U.S. Customs and Border Protection Office and ask for a Certificate of Registration (form CF4457). You have to bring your gear to the customs office where they will confirm your gear and stamp the form. This will guarantee you won't be asked to pay a duty on your gear. Find the location of the nearest customs office at `www.customs.ustreas.gov`. Most travelers skip this step and do just fine, but if you have new gear and are going somewhere known for electronics, filling out the form can be a good idea.

Getting Ready to Go on the Road

You won't like surprises after you leave home and begin taking pictures. One key to successful travel photography is making as many preparations as you can ahead of time so you'll be organized and confident when you begin capturing memories. Here is a checklist of things to do before you leave:

✦ **Create a packing list:** As you prepare for the trip, put together a packing list for the photographic gear. Plan a dry run to make sure everything fits in whatever camera bag or case you're using.

✦ **Carry it on:** All but the cheapest camera equipment should be included with carry-on luggage. If you're taking more than just a basic digital camera and memory cards, make sure that the camera bag is small enough to meet carry-on space limits. Record serial numbers for pieces of equipment that have them and have a packing list in a separate bag in case the camera bag gets lost or stolen. Check with your insurance company to see whether camera equipment is covered under your policy. If it isn't, see whether you can add a *rider* (a special add-on to your policy) for the trip.

✦ **Have some in-flight reading:** How familiar are you with your camera and accessories? Maybe it would be a good idea to dig out the instruction manuals and pack them in your carry-on so that you can reacquaint yourself with some of the camera's more esoteric features. The book you're reading right now also makes for some good travel reading. I also recommend *Digital Travel Photography Field Guide,* also from Wiley and yours truly.

Meeting Your Storage Requirements

Just like going on vacation with a film camera, the digital camera needs a steady supply of (digital) film. Because of the newness of the technology (particularly overseas and in Third World countries), photographers need to ensure that they have enough memory capacity for the trip.

Here are some considerations when bulking up your storage for a trip:

✦ **Have enough memory.** Will you be able to get an entire vacation's worth of pictures with your current supply of memory? Remember that you tend to shoot a lot more while traveling. If you don't think you're going to have enough capacity, consider buying more. Alternatively, you can carry a laptop computer (if you have one) so that you can transfer images and free up memory each night. (Test this process before you go to make sure you have what you need to transfer images.)

✦ **Try a portable hard drive or CD/DVD burner.** In between a pocketful of memory cards and a notebook computer are portable hard drives and CD/DVD burners. These drives can accept CompactFlash cards and other types of removable storage with the proper adaptor (floppy users are out of luck). For about $200–$300, far less than a laptop, you can get a portable hard drive (like the one shown in Figure 6-8) with 40–60GB of storage space for fewer dollars per byte than a CompactFlash card. The portable CD/DVD burners, although a bit larger, can copy your photos to durable CDs and DVDs, which can hold gigabytes of information at a very low cost. If you go this route, try to acquire the device a couple of weeks before the trip so you have time to make sure you can work it properly.

Figure 6-8: A portable hard drive will let you copy your photos and free up your memory cards.

Even with all the extra memory cards or a portable hard drive, you're still carrying less weight than the equivalent in number of shots worth of film.

Tried-and-True Travel Photography Techniques

If you've prepared well, you'll be ready to take great pictures when you reach your destination. This section tells you a little about some of the most popular types of travel photography and provides tips on getting the best shots.

In all cases, keep local, regional, and national sensitivities in mind when choosing your subjects. Some buildings, installations, and people shouldn't be photographed because of security, personal, or religious concerns. When in doubt, ask for permission.

Shooting scenics

Scenic photos are high on the list of pictures people try to bring back from their travels. After all, you have to prove you went someplace nice, don't you? Here are some tips for shooting great scenics:

+ **Don't hurry.** The effort to record a site's beauty all too often results in quick snapshots hurriedly snatched while with a tour group or during a sightseeing drive. Some places are spectacular enough that this approach actually works; most of the time, it's hit or miss.

+ **Not all light is created equal.** The best light of the day occurs when the sun is low in the sky. Early morning and late evening sunlight produce dramatic shadows and rich, warm colors, when the sun's light is more red/orange than any other time during the day. If a site on your trip is particularly important, plan on being there during the *golden hours* (early morning and late evening). Try to do a reconnaissance of the location a day or two beforehand so that you can see whether the sun rises or sets behind what you're shooting.

When the sun is rising or setting behind the scene, it creates the opportunity for a dramatic backlight silhouette. This is a difficult exposure situation because the camera is pointing directly into the sun. Don't underestimate the additional risk for the photographer, who must be careful not to stare directly into the sun.

+ **Create silhouettes.** For a good, solid black silhouette of a building, structure, landscape feature, or person, the camera should be set about two full f-stops smaller than what the light meter indicates for the main scene. Your goal here is a bright, orange-red sun (the most dramatic kind). Depending on your camera, you can either change aperture settings directly, or use the exposure compensation dial to get the exposure you need. Take several shots at one f-stop increment to make sure there's a good exposure, like the one shown in Figure 6-9.

+ **Keep it steady.** Have your camera mounted on a tripod while doing scenics. The added stability reduces the effects of camera shake and allows for a slower shutter speed. Reducing the shutter speed enables you to use a smaller aperture (larger f-stop number), which creates greater overall depth of field for the sharpest possible picture.

If a tripod isn't available, try to find something sturdy to brace the camera on or against. Walls, car roofs, wooden chairs, and countertops can all make excellent emergency tripods. Bracing the camera vertically against a post or column will also help keep it steady enough to help compensate for too slow a shutter speed for hand holding.

Figure 6-9: A sunset offers the opportunity to create dramatic silhouette photos.

✦ **That cloud looks like a. . . .** Take advantage of cloudy skies, which provide more visual interest than a plain, washed-out blue sky, as you can see in Figure 6-10. When the clouds are in hiding, compose the image so that it has minimal empty sky at the top of the frame.

Capturing monuments and architecture

The Arc de Triomphe, the Empire State Building, the Golden Gate Bridge. Monuments, architecture, and engineering marvels can provide stunning images and a record of your journey. You can take your photography to a whole new level by following some simple techniques.

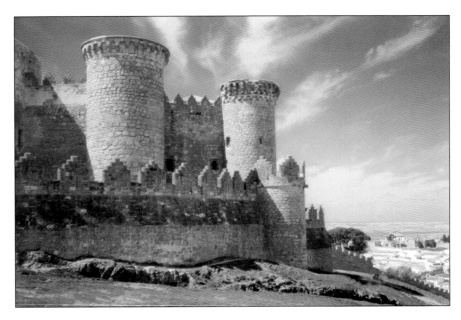

Figure 6-10: Clouds can add a dramatic element to travel photos.

Many of the techniques described earlier for scenics also apply to photographing these man-made wonders. Some special techniques, however, apply only to man-made objects.

Taking a shot in the dark

Don't put your camera away when the sun sets. Buildings, monuments, and bridges take on an entirely different look at night when they're all lit up. Here are some of the things to keep in mind when taking pictures of monuments after dusk:

✦ **Support your camera.** Once again, use your tripod or some other camera support. Many cameras suggest using flash at this point; don't. Some cameras automatically set the flash under such conditions; override it if you can. You don't want to overpower the existing illumination with flat, bright, electronic flash. Most of the time, flash used in night-time scenes spoils any existing mood or ambience.

✦ **Go long.** The idea here is to get a long enough exposure to turn the headlights from cars and trucks into long ribbons of color wrapping around the base of the structure, while its own lights help give a sense of its form.

✦ **Shoot by the sea, by the sea, by the beautiful sea.** Finally, if you're photographing in a river or ocean town, a boat can make a fine shooting platform. Just keep in mind that motor vessels' powerful engines cause the decks to vibrate, and a tripod isn't much help in such circumstances.

When the sun goes down, check out the nearest amusement park. Set your camera on a tripod or something solid and do a long exposure of the Ferris wheel or roller coaster or any of the other rides with bright lights and fast motion.

Painting with light

Sometimes, a building is too big and too dark for normal photographic measures to do the trick. For these situations, the pros paint with light. This technique calls for using a long exposure and firing off multiple flash bursts to illuminate the object in sections. Here's how to do it:

1. **Set your camera on a steady surface.**

   A tripod is good, but so is a short wall or the ground. Keep your camera steady because if the camera moves, the illuminated areas move, too, putting them out of alignment.

2. **Adjust the camera for a time exposure.**

   Check your camera manual to learn how to set your camera for a time exposure.

3. **Decide what areas of your subjects need painting.**

Keystoning

Keystoning, also known as *perspective distortion,* happens when the photographer tries to fit an entire building in a photo by tilting the camera up. The problem with this approach is that when the camera is no longer perfectly parallel with the building, any straight lines on the long axis of the image converge until they meet at the top. The photographer ends up with a photo of a building with a wide base and a pinpoint top that appears to be falling away.

How to avoid it? Because the problem comes from the lens and the building not being perfectly parallel, the easiest way to correct that problem is to bring them into line. You might be able to do this by finding a way to gain some elevation. Sometimes, a nearby hill can provide a distant vantage point. Sometimes, another building with an accessible roof is available. Unfortunately, all too often, neither solution is available, and the only option is to point the camera up and take the picture.

Book IV Chapter 6

Travel Photography

4. **Trigger a time exposure (or have helper do it) using your digital camera's particular time exposure controls.**

   Experiment with different times, from ten seconds to a minute or longer.

5. **Paint by triggering your external flash multiple times.**

   Move the flash around to illuminate the subject in sections. As you move, keep your body between your light source and camera if you don't want the light source to appear in the photo.

Photographers use another technique called *writing with light,* which can be lots of fun. It's an especially apt technique for travel photography, because it can be used to photograph buildings, monuments, and other scenes that would otherwise be difficult to capture at night. This is another trick that takes advantage of a long exposure and a solid shooting platform, such as a tripod, a wall, or the ground. The idea is to take a pencil torch (penlight) and point it toward the camera lens while the shutter is open. You can either swirl it around, or try to write a specific message. Here's how to do it:

1. **Plan what you want to do. It's good to rehearse a couple of times with someone watching through the viewfinder.**

   This way, you know if the camera's positioned properly to get everything. Besides, you have to write backward — don't you think that takes some practice?

2. **Set the camera to shutter priority and give it a long time (long enough for you to do what you want, probably several seconds or more).**

3. **Write with light by pointing the light at the camera lens from your subject position.**

4. **Review the image with the camera's LCD screen.**

5. **If necessary, make some adjustments to your shutter speed based on what you see in the LCD, using a longer or shorter speed as required.**

6. **If you want to get really fancy, have a friend or spouse fire off a small flash after you're done writing but before the shutter closes.**

   This helps illuminate you while still allowing your writing to show.

Don't forget that fireworks, like those shown in Figure 6-11, are a kind of "writing with light." You can use the same techniques that I just described except that you let the aerial display create your image for you. Use a tripod and set your camera for exposures of a second or two. Set the camera for about ISO 100 and start your exposure just before the fireworks reach the top of their arc. Try leaving your shutter open for several sets of displays, covering the lens with your hand between displays to capture several in one exposure. Take along a penlight so you can adjust your camera's settings in the dark! Time exposures of moving lights and traffic (think the Strip in Las Vegas) are also great ways to paint with light.

Figure 6-11: Fireworks are a kind of writing with light.

Shooting panoramas

One of the most frustrating moments of travel photography comes when you find yourself literally surrounded by the beauty of nature and have no way to capture all that surrounds you in a single photo. A digital camera, tripod, and the right image-editing software, however, make capturing a 360-degree panorama possible. Basically, you take a series of shots for your panorama and then stitch the shots together (line up the images into one image) on your computer. Although you can stitch images together in any image editor, specialized stitching applications are easy to use. Follow these steps to shoot a panoramic shot:

1. **Mount your camera on a tripod and set the camera's appropriate zoom setting.**

   You don't have to set the zoom lens to its widest setting. Zooming in a little closer means that you'll capture more detail per photo. If your main subject is distant, zooming in lets you capture more of the important part of the scene without wasting space on unnecessary foreground details.

The more shots you take, the more you'll have to stitch together, and the greater the chance the software might have trouble creating a seamless panorama. Generally speaking, three to six images are most manageable.

2. **Level the camera.**

   The closer you can come to a perfectly level camera, the better job your software can do with the final image. Buying an inexpensive level (as small a unit as possible) at the local hardware store is highly recommended. Set the level on top of the camera and adjust the tripod until the camera is level.

3. **When you take the first picture, waste a shot by photographing your fingers in front of the lens. Don't worry about focusing or exposure.**

   This makes it easy to see where you began the sequence. Do the same when you've completed each sequence.

4. **Make your first shot of the scene at either the left or right end of the panoramic swing that you intend to make.**

   If your camera is capable of manual exposure, take several readings throughout the scene and try to come up with an average setting for the entire range.

5. **Take subsequent pictures.**

   Make sure each shot overlaps the previous one by 20–30 percent.

6. **If possible, do a second sequence of images, particularly if lighting was erratic.**

7. **Stitch them all together back home, using an image editor or stitching software.**

   Packages such as PhotoStitch (furnished free with Canon cameras for Windows and the Macintosh) or Photoshop and Photoshop Elements' built-in PhotoMerge panorama capabilities (see Figure 6-12) are easy to use and a lot of fun. Your digital camera may come with similar applications.

Photographers who are really serious about getting good 360-degree panoramas can try a special tripod head made by Kaidan (www.kaidan.com). The Kaidan head enables you to mount the optical center (or *nodal point*) of the camera lens directly over the tripod's pivot point for the most accurate positioning possible. These heads range from a little over $140 to several hundred dollars or more. Unless you're a perfectionist, though, you can get satisfactory results without one.

Figure 6-12: Stitch images together in Photoshop or Photoshop Elements.

Shooting adventure sports

Adventure sports, such as white-water rafting, rock climbing, scuba diving, and similar activities, entail different risks and require different precautions and tools to protect your precious equipment:

✦ **Dry boxes:** Climbers and hikers need to keep their gear dry by using waterproof camera bags or other equipment. Sports like white-water rafting and kayaking call for even greater protection. Usually, these boaters protect their gear in a dry box setup. The best known manufacturer of these is Pelican (www.casesbypelican.com), which makes cases with foam insides that can be cut to fit specific camera gear. If using one of these, take very good care of the O-rings that provide the watertight seal for the box.

Veteran river runners sometimes rely on Army surplus ammo or rocket boxes, which also provide a watertight container for gear, but without the form-fitting foam. If you use one of these, make sure that the camera is properly cushioned from the bumps and jolts that white-water rafting entails. If you protect your camera from water, you can easily take photos like the one shown in Figure 6-13.

**Book IV
Chapter 6**

Travel Photography

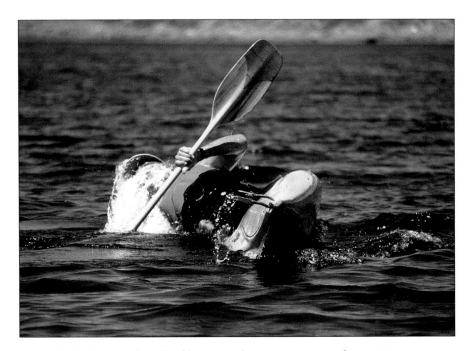

Figure 6-13: To take a photo like this, you need to protect your gear from water.

✦ **Carabineers:** These are the oval clips that climbers use to secure themselves to safety ropes; you can use them to clip the dry box to your off-
road vehicle. If you're immersed in a water activity, the clips can also
secure your dry box to the raft or inside the kayak. The boaters will run
the rapid, catch an eddy at the end of it, unpack the camera, and start
shooting. Once again, placing a silica packet or two in one of these cases
will help keep dampness from damaging equipment.

✦ **Underwater digital cameras:** Another option for those who want to
shoot a lot in wet conditions is a new underwater digital camera. I've
used underwater cameras even when I wasn't *planning* to go in the
water. (You never can tell where a hike will end up.) The SeaLife
ReefMaster underwater digital camera comes in a waterproof housing
and works both on land and underwater. The camera, which retails for
under $400, produces only a 3.3-to 5.0 megapixel image but saves you
the trouble of trying to find a housing to fit an existing digital camera.
The camera also has an LCD screen that works underwater and a fast
delete function, both of which make it easier to operate underwater.
Check out the manufacturer's Web site at www.sealife-cameras.com
for more information.

✦ **Waterproof casings:** More extreme conditions call for better protection. Waterproof casings that still allow photography are available from several companies, including ewa-marine (`www.ewa-marine.de`). These are useful for both underwater photography (careful on the depth, though) and above the water if sailing or boating.

Keep in mind that salt spray is very possibly the worst threat to camera electronics there is. A camera housing provides good protection against wind and salt spray.

✦ **Deep-diving housings:** For serious underwater enthusiasts, heavy-duty Plexiglas camera housings now exist for small digital cameras. These housings are available for a wide range of digital cameras and can be found for as little as $200.

Photographing people

There are lots of reasons to photograph people while traveling, and also some reasons not to. Photographing law enforcement or military personnel without getting their permission first can be a bad idea.

With the heightened concern about terrorism these days, many security forces, including our own, have become much more sensitive about people photographing and videotaping government facilities and employees. While traveling in Israel and South America, it wasn't unusual to see armed military personnel walking the streets. Even a decade ago, it wasn't a good idea to grab a snapshot of them, and I wouldn't even consider it these days unless I'd gotten their permission first.

When photographing people in other areas of the country or in foreign lands, remember that effective travel photography needs to create a sense of place. Any time the photographer can use lifestyle, surroundings, work, or clothing to show the region or culture involved, he or she has achieved at least one measure of success. Certain elements can help your photos convey your location:

✦ **Clothing:** Different cultures have different tastes in clothing and jewelry.

✦ **Design:** Advertisements, homes, and buildings will look different whether you're overseas or in the United States.

✦ **Products:** Soda cans, candy bars, and other packaging is different in other countries, and sometimes even in the United States.

✦ **The natural world:** Plants and wildlife might be noticeably different in other locations.

In addition to creating a sense of place, these tips can help you effectively photograph people while traveling:

+ **Be aware of cultural sensitivities.** Some cultures frown upon photographic images of other human beings (that includes cultures in the United States, as well). In many Middle Eastern and Third World countries, women wear clothing designed to hide their appearance. In some of these countries, photographing them can be a serious taboo (as can a man speaking to one of them to even ask permission to take their photo).

+ **Check out the local customs.** Although taboos that have their origins in religious beliefs can stay constant for millennia, official taboos can shift frequently. Check with the U.S. consular office for the country that you're visiting to learn what's okay and what isn't. The Web site `http://travel.state.gov/travel/warnings.html` also has information on individual countries and policies.

+ **Ask first.** As a newspaper reporter and photographer, my philosophy was to shoot first and ask questions later. (You can always talk to people after an event's over, but you can't re-create photos.) Photojournalists working in a newsgathering capacity are afforded some liberties that are considered out of line for tourists, though. (And that's in this country; the rules vary from country to country.) In the case of a traveler photographing others without their permission, it's a behavior that many would at least consider rude.

+ **Pretend I'm not here.** One of the reasons why pros prefer to shoot first and then ask is because people appear more natural when they don't know that they're being photographed. A common way of dealing with this problem is to ask permission and then explain you'd like the picture to look "natural" and could they please go back to what they were doing and forget you're there.

+ **Be forgettable.** Although your subjects likely start out self-conscious, after a few minutes, they tend to become involved in their activity and forget you're there.

+ **Give them feedback.** Be aware of human psychology. People who are posing tend to wait for some feedback at first — namely the click of the camera that tells them you're satisfied. If they don't hear it because you're waiting for them to forget you're there, they tend to become concerned that you're not happy with what they're doing. Use your digital advantage (being able to delete bad shots) and take a photo or two at the start. Your subject will relax a little and begin to forget you're there.

Another technique works well if you have a camera with a fairly wide-angle lens. Set the zoom to the widest possible focal length and hold the at camera waist level and as perpendicular to the ground as you can. I usually try to do this one-handed with the camera strap helping me keep the camera under control. Most people relax even more at this point because they don't expect you to shoot now. At this point, when I see the shot I want, I trip the shutter. This technique works better if you're familiar enough with your camera to have a good idea of what its wide angle covers from a certain distance.

This "shooting from the hip" can be a tricky proposition ethically. At least one journalism professor I know feels that it's a violation of trust between a photographer and the subject.

As a photographer, I believe it's important to be sensitive to your subject's feelings on the matter. Because I'm shooting digitally, I take the shot and then explain that I've taken a shot and show it to the person I've photographed. I then let him or her decide whether or not the photo should be deleted. Most people don't mind at all, but I've slept better at night by immediately deleting the shot if the person is unhappy with it. This all gets a lot harder if you and your subject don't speak the same language. Sometimes, the combination of pantomime and the preview capability of the digital camera can be enough for you to get by.

Capturing people and their environments

After the issue of getting permission from your subjects is out of the way, consider how to photograph them. Being able to capture people in their own environment is where you can really feel the advantages of your digital camera. It's lightweight and versatile and can take plenty of photos. Here are some ways to make the most of its advantages:

✦ **Shoot as much as it takes.** If what you want can be achieved in just one shot, so much the better. Still, there's nothing wrong with multiple shots to achieve the same thing, provided the images build upon one another.

✦ **Capture the environment.** At least one shot should show the individual within his or her cultural environment. After that image is out of the way, focus on smaller details. Look for things that would be unusual back in your own home.

✦ **Move in close.** Medium shots and close-ups provide greater intimacy than full-body or head-and-shoulder shots. A well-focused, tight composition of a person's face (cropped in to just eyes, nose, mouth, and not much more), packs a lot of intimacy. Whatever you do, don't make the mistake shown in Figure 6-14, in which the subject is so far away that you can barely tell who he is.

✦ **Hands can speak volumes.** Sometimes a person's hands can reveal his or her work history. Work roughened, they can speak of years of manual labor and toil. Or a close-up of hands holding small tools or repairing a watch, for instance, can show great dexterity.

✦ **Capture the essentials.** Who is this person? What shows your subject's identity? A new mom cradling her baby, a farmer on his tractor, and a cyclist on her bike are just a few possibilities.

✦ **Use lighting.** Don't forget to consider lighting. Unless your subject's in direct sunlight, some sort of fill flash is necessary. (The term *fill* flash comes from its use not as a main light source, but as an additional light to fill in areas that are hidden from the main light.)

✦ **Go for variety.** Make sure to take a mix of horizontal and vertical photos. For people shots, take lots of verticals because the human body breaks down to a series of elements that are taller than they are wide.

✦ **Show people working, playing, and relaxing.** Even on a mountain climb, like the one shown in Figure 6-15, quiet moments reveal another side of your subjects. Social gatherings and religious meetings are also prime opportunities for good photographs. Look for community festivals, too, where you can get lots of people, costumes, and events going on. In such freewheeling settings, people are less concerned about being photographed, and you can probably get away with taking wider shots without having to check with every individual for their permission. Performers, in particular, are quite used to being photographed.

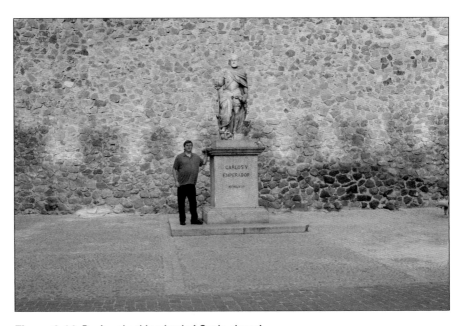

Figure 6-14: Don't make this mistake! Get in closer!

Figure 6-15: Even on a mountain slope, you can capture a quiet moment.

Documenting Your Trip

Pull together everything from the earlier sections in this chapter to create memorable photos of your trip. Documenting a vacation is more than grabbing some pretty pictures of your travels; it's creating a visual narrative that re-creates the magic of your trip all over again. This section wraps up travel photography with some final tips for getting great vacation pictures.

Varying your shots

Try for a mix of shots and camera angles. Shoot some close-ups, and shoot from far away. You can do a lot of things to avoid having all your photos look alike:

✦ **Put the camera on the ground for a worm's-eye view.** Makes that church look even more imposing.

✦ **Get a bird's-eye view.** Renting helicopters gets expensive, but there are other ways of getting up high and shooting down. You were going to climb that monument anyway, right? Take advantage of the elevation. Even simpler, climb a staircase and shoot straight down. Take advantage of cable cars. Take advantage of a hot air balloon ride for some once-in-a-lifetime scenic photos, like the one shown in Figure 6-16.

Figure 6-16: A bird's-eye view can provide an unusual vantage point for travel photos.

✦ **Turn the camera vertically when appropriate.** Many scenes lend themselves to vertical images, yet most people still grip the camera horizontally. Monuments, people, and buildings are all taller than they are wide. Turn the camera on its side.

✦ **Shoot from more than one vantage point.** Do like the pros do. Shoot it high, shoot it low, shoot it horizontally, vertically, get closer, move back, walk around it. While doing this, remember to consider what's in the background.

Composing your shots

How you arrange the elements within your photo has a lot to do with how much impact they convey. I talk about composition in more detail in Book III, Chapter 1, but here are some things that can help improve your photographic composition:

✦ **Leading lines:** Strong linear elements can pull the eye into an image. Straight lines, diagonal lines, and S-curves all show movement and can depict strength, direction, or grace. For example, a U.S. flag rippling in the wind combines an S-curve with the strong lines of the stripes.

✦ **Framing:** Use natural elements, such as window frames or tree branches, to form a natural border along a corner or around the image. Figure 6-17 is an example of this concept.

✦ **Rule of Thirds:** Divide the frame in thirds horizontally and vertically. Where the thirds intersect is a good place to position your subject. You can also use this to show a course of movement. For example, putting an airplane coming into the frame into the top-right third conveys a sense of moving downward through the frame.

✦ **Balance:** Ever see a picture of someone sitting on a park bench with one end of the bench missing? Without the missing support, it seems like the person is going to drop like a rock off the unbalanced bench. You can find examples of photos using balance and these other prime rules of composition in Book III, Chapter 1.

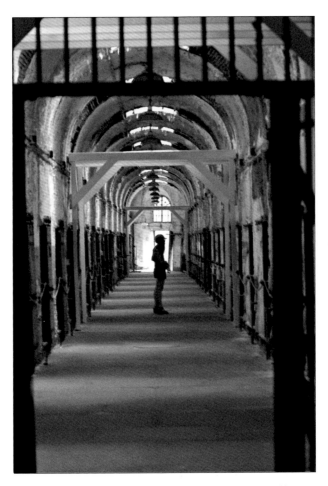

Figure 6-17: Lines and framing are used effectively in this interior photo.

Getting organized

Close focusing (or macro capability) is another one of the digital camera's best features. By introducing details of the location you're visiting, you can trigger memories of your experience years after the trip has ended.

On that cruise I mention earlier in this chapter (in which the stateroom had only one electrical outlet), my wife and I were fortunate to stay in an owner's suite, one of the nicest cabins on the ship. Each afternoon, we received a treat of some sort from one of the ship's staff along with a card announcing whom it was from. Before enjoying our delicacies, we made sure to photograph the dish and card together, as shown in Figure 6-18, and kept the card for a scrapbook as well. The photo album from this trip includes many such details and provides a much fuller and richer representation of our trip.

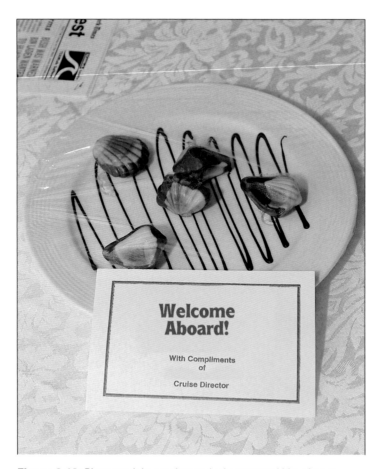

Figure 6-18: Photograph keepsakes and other unusual bits of your environment as you travel.

Now take it a step further. Think of your photographic coverage as a series of still images that tell a story rather than a group of individual pictures that stand on their own (even though they should).

✦ **Signs, signs, everywhere there's signs:** Use street and highway signs, or even the one and only South Pole (shown in Figure 6-19), to show where you are or where you're going. Photograph maps and brochures, too. Don't just settle for snapshots of these images; try to use lighting and depth of field to turn them into interesting images in their own right.

✦ **Cultural and language differences:** Signs differ from country to country. In the United States, signs read *End of construction.* Years ago, on a trip through New Zealand, I photographed a sign, shown in Figure 6-20, that proclaimed, *Works End,* with a cemetery in the background.

✦ **More signs:** Street and road crew signs are only one type of photographic target, though. Distinctive shop, restaurant, and tavern signs also provide reminders of where you've been.

✦ **Newspapers/newsstands:** Check the local newsstands. In at least some countries, newsstands say something about where you're visiting. For that matter, a close-up of the day's headline during your visit can make a good introductory graphic if you're giving a presentation.

**Book IV
Chapter 6**

Travel Photography

Figure 6-19: The South Pole is one sign that you've traveled far and wide.

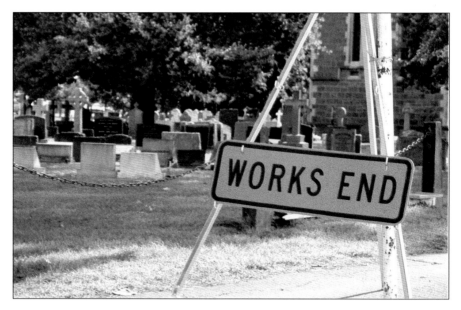

Figure 6-20: A sure sign that your travel work is never really at an end.

✦ **Trailheads:** On a wilderness trip, most trailheads are well marked. Photograph the signs. Shoot the trail maps, too. Your packs, supplies, and other gear should also be documented. Follow the same approach if you're on a white-water, skydiving, or ski trip.

✦ **White water:** For white water, shoot as many rapids as possible. (Only my fellow paddlers will get that pun.) Photograph the rapids from the side because that field of view gives a better sense of scale than a head-on shot. If you can, get a raft or kayak in the photo because that will help show the rapid's size.

✦ **River scenes:** Wilderness rafting trips include many other photo opportunities as well. Photos of *swimmers* (the white-water euphemism for someone who's inadvertently become one with the river) and their rescue provide dramatic images. The lunch buffet (if on a commercial trip) provides an opportunity for humor if you get shots of some of the sandwiches the guides make. (Guides traditionally eat after the paying guests have gone through the buffet. As a result, some of the sandwich ingredients get pretty creative. Mine usually included cold cuts, veggies, chunky peanut butter, and thick slices of onion.)

✦ **River scenes (part 2):** Don't forget that white-water rivers generally offer spectacular scenery, too. Plus, you can take shots of all the preliminaries — inflating the rafts, getting gear together, putting on wet suits and life jackets.

✦ **Rock climbing:** Scenery, gear, climbers. Oh yeah, don't forget the rocks. Seriously, mix close-ups, wide-angle shots, and action images of the climbers. Take advantage of the bright colors and patterns of the clothing that rock climbers wear, and the chocks, friends, and *nuts* (protective equipment climbers use to anchor into the rock, for all you nonclimbers) are great subjects for close-up shots. So are chalk-covered fingers. Also, get lots of angles: Shoot from below, above, and alongside the climbers.

✦ **Moods:** Everything doesn't have to be bright and sunny in your travel photos. Don't be afraid to shoot moody, misty, rainy days, like the one shown in Figure 6-21, to show yet another side of your journey.

✦ **Papers, please:** Don't forget close-ups of your travel documents. They're also part of the story you're telling.

Figure 6-21: Even moody scenes can tell part of your travel story.

You'll soon discover that good photography is all in the details. Visiting foreign cultures provides a wealth of these details that help show how different or similar we are. Close-ups of jewelry, magazines, and candy and food packaging help emphasize that you've gone somewhere different.

Book V
Basics of Image Editing

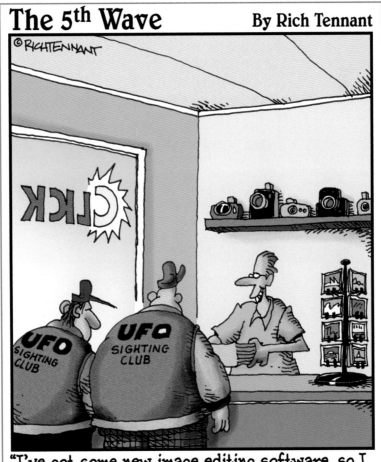

The 5th Wave   By Rich Tennant

"I've got some new image editing software, so I took the liberty of erasing some of the smudges that kept showing up around the clouds. No need to thank me."

*E*very journey begins with a first step, and if you still haven't taken the plunge into image editing, this minibook helps make that step a gentle immersion rather than a plummet from the high-dive platform. I show you exactly what you can and can't expect to do with image editors such as Corel Paint Shop Pro, Corel PhotoPaint, Ulead PhotoImpact, and Adobe Photoshop and Photoshop Elements. You'll see the capabilities of each of these applications and discover the full range of tools each puts at your disposal.

I close out this minibook with a chapter that compares and contrasts the most popular image editors so you can choose which one (or perhaps two!) of these image editing programs you really need to make your digital photos look their best.

Chapter 1: What You Can and Can't Do with Image Editing Tools

In This Chapter

- Fixing faded and distorted color photos
- Adjusting lights and darks
- Fine-tuning sharpness and contrast
- Eliminating dust, blemishes, and other artifacts
- Rearranging, removing, and adding content
- Merging images

*W*ith all the seemingly miraculous things that you *can* accomplish with image editing tools, it would be easy to assume that there's nothing you *can't* do. You'd think that you could take any image, in any condition, and make it beautiful — but is that really the case? Not always. Although you certainly can do a great deal to repair serious tears, rips, stains, and scratches, as well as the effects of aging and improper photographic technique, you can't solve every problem every time — at least not easily.

You can't, for example, take a photo in which everything is out of focus and make it as crisp and clear as the photographer probably intended. If, however, one part of the photo is in focus and the other parts are a blurry distraction, you can blur them out even further so that they're just a pleasant backdrop to the properly focused portion. Or, you can remove them altogether, eliminating the unpleasant aspects of the image. You'll find that in some extreme cases, your images might require some compromise when editing them, giving up one thing to gain another. Or success might require a willingness to work with only the parts of the photo that are salvageable, discarding the rest. This chapter provides a quick introduction to the kinds of fixes you can expect to make with image editing tools.

Correcting Colors

As you probably know, digital camera images are made up of the red, green, and blue primary colors of light. (You can find more about this in Book II, Chapter 1.) These three colors can be combined to produce the colors you see on a video monitor, within the limitations of the monitor's color reproduction capabilities. When your digital pictures are printed, these colors are expressed as combinations of their complementary colors, which are the primaries of pigments. The complement of red is cyan, and it is printed by combining yellow and magenta; the complement of blue is yellow, and it is printed by combining magenta and cyan; and the complement of green is magenta, and it is printed by combining yellow and cyan. Everyone has seen a color wheel, like the one shown in Figure 1-1, that shows these relationships.

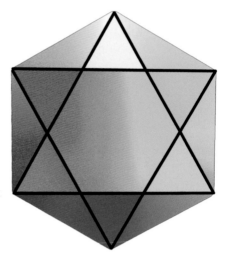

Figure 1-1: The relationships between the primary colors of light and their complements can be represented by a color wheel.

Knowing these relationships can be useful when it comes time to correct colors. For example, as you'll find out later in this chapter, you fix a photo that appears to be too red by removing some red or by "adding" its complement, cyan. (You'll see why "adding" is in quotes in the next subsection.) Similarly, you can remove green or "add" magenta; remove blue or "add" yellow.

We've all seen photos with a strange green, yellow, or red tinge, where skin looks weird, hair colors aren't anything close to what appears in nature, leaves are blue, grass is yellow, and basically everything looks alien. The color problem can happen either when the photo was taken or during development. Sometimes photos that looked okay in the beginning change color over time. Regardless of the cause, you can fix most color problems — with some exceptions, of course.

Most image editing applications provide tools for adjusting a photo's color levels. Depending on the features of your favorite application, you might or might not be able to add color or change color effectively, and this is perhaps one of the most important tests for evaluating multiple image editing applications. If you can't get rid of a ruddy, sunburned look in a photo or eliminate the nausea-green tinge in a picture, consider looking to another application for serious photo editing.

You can't add color that isn't there

Typically, adjusting image color involves changing existing color levels. If the photo is a color image, you can adjust the levels of whatever color is in unwanted abundance so that the tones are more natural. However, color correction can't add color that isn't there in the first place. For example, in an overpoweringly red image, removing the red cast might not leave enough green and blue colors to produce a realistic image. One of the things that you can't do with an image editor is fix the color of images that are too far off the deep end in terms of color balance.

Similarly, if the image is in black and white or has faded so much that it's hard to tell whether it was ever in color, adding that touch of color to a photo might not be so easy. You can't simply increase or decrease one or more colors if the colors aren't there in the first place.

You can, however, add layers to your image and color them in by using your editing software's fill color and painting tools. In doing so, you create a color wash on top of a faded or black-and-white photo. Think of it as the clear plastic overlays in the old anatomy books, in which each successive layer added some content (the respiratory system, the digestive system, and so on) until the body was complete. You can add layers of color on top of the faded image, achieving the look of rich color that's currently missing.

Do keep in mind, however, that when you add color layers to a very faded or black-and-white photo, the results often look fake, sort of like how colorized black-and-white movies look a little funky. To put it bluntly, people's teeth look blue instead of white, and natural things (grass, trees, flowers, and so on) never look quite natural. If you want to brighten a faded color, you can probably use an editing tool or two to bring back a bright blue dress or some lush green lawn, provided that there's enough color to work with in the original.

Fixing color casts

A *color cast* is a tinge — a shade of red or maybe yellow — that discolors your image in whole or in part. Casts occur for a variety of reasons, including the age of the photo, the quality of your scanner (if you scanned a printed original), the print from which you scanned the image, or the film used to take the picture. If a cast appears in an image captured with a digital camera, you might need to adjust the white balance of your camera to compensate for the different colors offered by various types of illumination. (See your camera's instructions to learn how.)

Most digital editing applications offer tools for getting rid of a cast, like the greenish tinge in Figure 1-2, usually with a name like Color Balance or Color Cast.

Figure 1-2: The greenish tinge makes this lemon resemble a jaundiced lime.

Here's a general description of the necessary steps for eliminating a color cast:

1. **Open the image with the unwanted color cast.**

2. **Choose your image editor's Color Balance, Color Cast, or similar command.**

   The dialog box opens with an array of tools, similar to what you see in Figure 1-3.

3. **Choose whether you want to apply the change to the Shadows, Midtones, or Highlights.**

4. **Move the Cyan/Red, Magenta/Green, or Yellow/Blue slider away from the color of the unwanted hue.**

   For example, if your picture is too blue, move the Yellow/Blue slider toward Yellow.

5. **Click OK to apply the change when you're satisfied.**

Applications such as Paint Shop Pro, Photoshop, and others have a Preview option. Make sure that you leave the Preview option selected in the dialog box. Leaving it checked means that you don't have to apply the changes just to see them in your image. If you do apply them and then decide you don't like the change, choose Edit➪Undo (or your image editor's equivalent) to go back.

If your application doesn't refer directly to a color cast, you can use any tool that adjusts tone, including dialog boxes and toolbar settings that allow you to adjust the levels of color in the image, one color at a time. This enables you to increase the level of blue, red, green, or yellow (or perhaps cyan or magenta), and you can tweak one or more of them until the photo looks more natural and normal.

Another tool in Photoshop and Photoshop Elements is the Variation tool, which gives you several different versions of an image to choose from, enabling you to add more red, green, or blue. You can adjust color intensity for any one of these colors in your image and view Before and After versions of the image. In Photoshop, choose Image➪Adjustments➪Variations. If you're using the lower-priced and nearly as powerful Photoshop Elements, choose Enhance➪Adjust Color➪Color Variations. Figure 1-4 shows the Elements Color Variations dialog box as well as our lemon portrayed in a variety of tones.

 What do you do if none of the color correction tools in your image editing software does the trick? You can try a different application, or you can appreciate the photo for what it is. If it's an old photo, the color problems can add charm. If it's a new image and there's no excuse other than film or technique, just chalk it up to experience. You can also try rescanning a print on a different scanner or after recalibrating your scanner (follow the manufacturer's instructions). You can find out more about scanners in Book VII, Chapter 1.

Figure 1-3: Use your image editor's Color Balance to help rebalance colors.

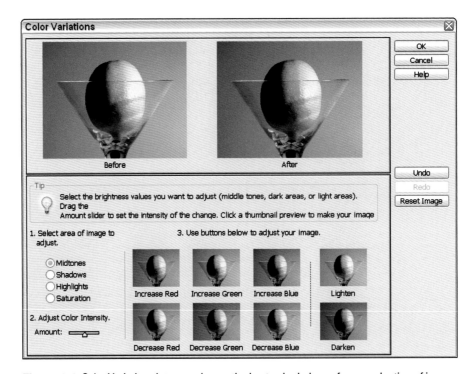

Figure 1-4: Color Variations lets you choose the best color balance from a selection of images.

Causes of color catastrophe

Where does bad color come from? Generally it comes from a digital camera that has been adjusted to the wrong *white balance* setting (say, set to indoor light when you're shooting outdoors), environmental color casts (such as sunsets or bright snowy conditions), or, in the case of film images, age of the film, bad film, bad development technique, poor print quality, or a bad or poorly adjusted scanner. These factors apply to most color problems in a poorly colored photo — unnatural tones, images that are too bright, too dark, faded, and so on.

Of course, if you have nondigital photography experience, none of this is news, and you probably know what to do to make sure that the images you take, develop, and print are not color-challenged. However, if you're a fledgling photographer or simply enjoy taking photos of family, friends, and vacation spots (and have no idea what you're doing beyond focusing and shooting), you might not know how to prevent problems in the future. Some things to consider include

✦ **Use appropriate film and/or white balance settings.** When shooting with a traditional (not a digital) camera, use film intended for the types of shots you'll be taking. Some films are balanced for indoor use; some are better for outdoor use. Digital cameras, too, need to be balanced for the light source, so you'll want to make sure that your camera is set for Automatic White Balance (AWB) or adjusted manually for the type of lighting you'll be shooting under.

✦ **Check printer settings.** If you're printing a digitally captured image, the color could go wrong entirely because of the printer's color settings, eliminating the need to edit the image. Use your image editor's calibration tools to correct for the vagaries of your particular printer. Try printing the image on someone else's printer to determine the common denominator.

✦ **Calibrate your monitor.** Use your software or monitor's instructions to calibrate your monitor to help insure that what you see is what you can expect to get.

✦ **Fix problems by using scanner software.** If you're scanning from a print, you get whatever sins were committed when that photo was taken, developed, and printed. Take note of any problems and be ready to accommodate them by using your scanner software — if color correction tools are included in its toolbox — or by using your image editing software. Better to have noticed the problem before you scan, print, and/or share the image online!

✦ **Store images properly.** Because aging causes many color problems when the dyes in the three color layers of prints fade at different rates, store your images in a cool, dark place and make sure that they contact only acid-free paper. Acids in some papers damage photos, and you can avoid it by using photo albums and storage boxes that were made in the last 10–20 years. Don't reuse the old photo albums that came over with your family on the Mayflower; the paper could contribute to the aging process.

If you have a precious image that you display in a frame, don't expose it to direct sunlight. Hang or stand any framed images in a place that gets only reduced ambient sunlight or low-level incandescent or fluorescent light from bulbs. Direct, bright sunlight fades images the worst. And because the colors in photos don't fade at the same rate, your previously natural-toned image can turn yellowish, reddish, greenish, or some combination thereof.

Adjusting Brightness and Contrast

Other components that you'll want to fix with your image editing software include brightness and contrast. Detail can be lost when an image is overexposed, faded, or just too bright. Detail can also be lost when an image is too dark because of a failed flash or simply a very dark subject. A day that looks perfect for picture taking to you can result in washed-out faces, shiny foreheads, light-eating shadows, and an overall lack of definition. You can eliminate many of these problems by adding and removing light in your image with the help of the brightness and contrast controls found in just about any worthy image editing package. Figure 1-5 shows a photo that has been improved simply by adjusting the brightness and contrast.

Figure 1-5: Sometimes photos need adjustments to brightness and contrast.

With most image editors, you have several choices for fixing these problems:

+ **Quick Fix:** Many image editors have a *quick fix* command with a variety of tools for tweaking just about any aspect of an image. You can adjust brightness, color, focus, contrast, flash, and backlighting. You can also rotate the image.

  Like with the Variations feature (which I discuss in the earlier "Fixing color casts" section), you can also preview a Before and an After version of your image, as shown in Figure 1-6. Previewing versions enables you to see whether the adjustments are having the desired effect before committing them to the image.

+ **Auto Contrast:** This is an easy one. Many image editors, including Paint Shop Pro and the Adobe products, have an Auto Contrast or Automatic Contrast Enhancement command. Choose this command, and voilà! Your image is adjusted, using existing color and brightness levels to determine a happy medium.

Figure 1-6: Photoshop Elements' Quick Fix feature helps tweak your images.

+ **Auto Levels:** This automatically adjusts the relationship of the tones for you.

+ **Adjust Lighting:** You can also find special commands to adjust for *backlighting* (images that are illuminated primarily from behind) or *fill flash* (to provide additional front illumination).

+ **Adjust Brightness and Contrast:** Use your image editor's manual Brightness/Contrast dialog box, like the one shown in Figure 1-7. You can enter values or move sliders or other controls to change these two integral levels in the image. Some image editors, such as Photoshop and Elements, show you the original image at all times so you can preview the effect.

Figure 1-7: Change values to modify the brightness and contrast of your image.

Other image editors might have a Preview option that you must use to see your changes before committing to them by clicking OK.

Original   Dodge   Burn

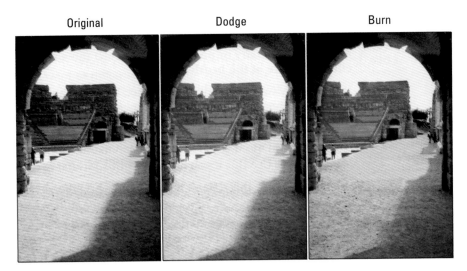

Figure 1-10: The original photo is dodged to lighten some shadow tones and then burned to darken some light tones.

When you're adjusting the lights and darks in your image, keep this delicate balance in mind. You don't want to make the lights and darks uniform over the whole image, yet you don't want to have very dark darks in one spot and very light lights in another. Artistic images that are meant to convey a message, and in which you want people to see that you've tinkered with reality, are another story — there are no limits or boundaries there. But for photos of people, places, and things that are meant to be realistic and clear, you want to keep the signs of your tinkering to a minimum, and you want to achieve the right levels of consistency.

How is that done? By using the right tools the right way. If you're dodging or burning an image, use brush sizes that allow gentle effects. Using very small brushes over a large area is bound to show the strokes or clicks. Using the tools too much causes some areas to be much lighter or darker than others, probably giving you unnatural results that look like you went overboard.

Of course, using the tools that apply to the entire image also gives you consistency. Any Auto command makes universal adjustments based on what's in the image to start with, and your results will be pretty tame and consistent. Using tools that allow you to drag sliders or enter new levels and have the settings affect a selected area only or the entire image if nothing is selected also creates consistency because your mouse skills and brush-based tool settings are not part of the equation. This gives you less control over the degree of lightening or darkening but can provide gentler, subtler results.

Reviving lost detail

Perhaps your photo has too much contrast, and the details of the items caught in the brightest spots are unrecognizable. Or maybe your photo has faded with time, and fine details are lost. Are the details lost forever? Probably not, assuming that you have time, patience, and the right tools to bring them back to life.

Choosing the revival method

The method used to bring back lost details varies by the situation and the situation's cause. For example, if the details were lost to too much brightness, using the Burn tool darkens the light areas and brings out the missing features, textures, or whatever has been blighted by the light. If the details are hidden in shadow, the Dodge tool can reveal these details once again. Adjusting contrast and brightness levels can revive details lost to too much or too little of those levels, and you can even use color to bring things out. How do you choose? The best strategy is to figure out what went wrong and reverse it, using a tool that applies the opposite attribute.

Re-creating lost detail

If you're skilled and patient and have good eyesight, you might be able to zoom in extremely close to your image and use painting and drawing tools to re-create details that are irretrievably lost. You have to be very careful, though, and avoid it in faces and natural things (such as flowers and plants) because pulling it off is nearly impossible. Things usually look drawn and end up drawing attention to the problem. You can, however, re-create textures (such as a brick wall or a stubbly patch of cement) and industrial or man-made items (such as the edge of a car bumper or the handle on an umbrella). The results can be surprisingly good, even for someone who might be a bit shaky with the mouse. You can use your image editor's Paint Brush and Pencil or similar tools to draw missing items.

Does what's missing appear elsewhere? If so, steal a copy and replace the missing detail. I've successfully replaced lost content with faces, furniture, grass, trees, walls, cars, and sleeping dogs. You can, too, by using the tools that I discuss in the section, "Removing Unwanted Image Content," later in this chapter.

Not to be negative (pardon the photographic pun), but sometimes lost detail is simply lost. If an overzealous flash completely washed out someone's face, short of drawing in his or her features by hand, you might not be able to bring back eyelids, a nose, cheekbones, the contour of lips, and so on. Not every photo can end up framed and admired or viewed by adoring millions online. If you've used every brightness, lighting, and contrast tool that your software has to offer, you can try a different or more powerful package, or you can do your best and hope nobody notices that Aunt Mary doesn't have a nose.

Using Blurring and Sharpening Tools

Another way to revive lost details is to apply a filter that sharpens the image by heightening the difference between adjacent pixels. This increased intensity of color and brightness makes everything stand out, as shown in Figure 1-11, where the top portion of the image has been sharpened, and the rest was left as it was. You can use the Sharpen filters that come with all image editing applications or use the Sharpen tool found in the toolbox of just about any image editing program. Using the filter requires selecting the area to be sharpened and then applying the filter, whereas the tool requires the standard brush-related adjustments (such as the size of the brush and the degree of sharpening it applies). You can find more information on the Blur and Sharpen tools in Book V, Chapter 2.

Figure 1-11: Sharpening enhances the contrast between adjacent pixels.

Sharpening here and there

If you want to sharpen the entire image, use a filter to do the sharpening. If your software doesn't have filters, check for a Sharpen command or reasonable facsimile thereof — any command that performs an automatic, all-over sharpening will do. The other benefit of this process is that it's a simple one in most image editors. Corel PhotoPaint, Paint Shop Pro, and Adobe's image editors, for example, all have a simple Sharpen command that you can apply directly, along with more sophisticated versions if you need more control.

If you want to sharpen an area, you can also use the filter or automatic sharpening command, but you have to make a selection first, directing the software to the spot you want to sharpen. You can repeat the process to sharpen two or more noncontiguous areas. Or if your software supports selections that are not touching, select all the areas that are to be sharpened and then apply the filter or related command.

When I need to sharpen a little here, a little there, a bit more here, and a whole lot there, I use the Sharpen tool that some image editors provide for "painting" sharpness. It works like a painting tool in that you click and/or drag your mouse over the image to apply the sharpening effect, and you can repeat your mouse movements in the same spot if you want more of a sharpening effect in one place than in another. You can dictate the size of the sharpened area by adjusting your brush size, and you can control the intensity of the sharpening by adjusting the strength setting.

To use a Sharpen tool, follow these steps:

1. **Turn on the Sharpen tool by selecting it from your image editor's toolbox or menu.**

2. **Set your brush size so that you can control how big an area is sharpened with each click or drag of the mouse.**

3. **Set the strength for your sharpening effect.**

   A good default value is 50%, but you can raise or lower that level as needed by dragging the slider or other control.

4. **Begin sharpening by clicking or dragging over the area to be sharpened.**

   Clicking sharpens an area the size of your brush tip, and dragging allows you to sharpen in a freeform area, following an edge or working within a desired region of the image.

Be careful not to sharpen too much. Too much sharpening results in bizarre-looking bright pixels that end up hiding details because the individual pixels stand out too much. Figure 1-12 shows an image in which the sharpening went a little overboard. Sharpening can also increase your file size.

Figure 1-12: Too much sharpening is not a good thing!

To keep the sharpening results as subtle as possible, avoid using a very small brush size (10 pixels or fewer) if you're sharpening an area that's more than 20 pixels wide and/or tall. Why? Because you'll be able to see your brush strokes as you apply the sharpening. An exception would be the sharpening of a very small spot, which would obviously call for a very small brush, and you can select the area first, which helps control your effects by restricting them to the selected area.

Blurring for effect

Sometimes the best way to draw attention to something is to draw attention away from something else. The bride doesn't *have* to wear the biggest, most ostentatious dress to stand out against her bridesmaids; she can instead dress them in colors that blend in with the flowers — and by contrast, she stands out. The same is true for photos, especially those with a lot of content that you need to keep but want to keep people from noticing too much.

Figure 1-13 shows a photo of a dandelion against a leafy background. The outdoorsy setting is important to give the image context, but the dandelion is the real focus. To make it stand out, the background has been blurred, and its details are diminished. Other than being able to tell that the background consists of foliage, there isn't much about it that you would notice or be drawn to visually.

Figure 1-13: Blurring everything else makes your main subject stand out.

Blurring is the exact opposite of sharpening in that instead of heightening the contrast between adjoining pixels, the color and brightness differences are reduced so that pixels are much closer to each other in terms of their color levels, brightness, and contrast. You can go too far with blurring and end up with something that isn't even recognizable; conversely, you can blur not enough, leaving the content as distracting as ever. The key is to find a happy medium where objects are still recognizable, but nobody will spend much time looking at them.

Like sharpening, you have choices as to how to apply blurring. You can use your image editor's Blur tool (which works just like the Sharpen tool, except for its results), or you can use the Blur filters. Many image editors offer specialized Blur filters that do cool things, such as making an image look like it's whipping past the camera (the Motion Blur) or like it's spinning in place

(Radial Blur). The plain old Blur filter simply blurs the entire image or a selection therein — it's as simple as that. In Figure 1-14, Motion Blur has been applied to the entire image.

Figure 1-14: Motion Blur adds the appearance of movement to an image.

To apply a blur to everything but the focus of the image, follow these steps:

1. **Select the object or area that should not be blurred.**

   This can be done on an image that's all on one layer. Or, if your software supports layers, you can select the object or area and then cut it to its own layer to keep it separate from the rest of the image during the blurring process.

2. **If you're working all on one layer, invert the selection so that everything but the selection can be blurred.**

   Most image editors, including Corel PhotoPaint, Paint Shop Pro, and the Adobe Photoshop products, let you invert a selection by pressing Ctrl+Shift+I (or ⌘+Shift+I if you're using a Mac).

   With the not-to-be-blurred section protected, you can begin blurring the rest of the picture.

3. **Click your image editor's Blur tool to activate it and then set the way the tool should work by choosing the brush size and strength, just as described for the Sharpen tool.**

4. **Begin dragging the mouse in the area to be blurred. You can go over some areas more than once, increasing the blurring effect in those spots.**

   Unlike many other types of retouching, blurring is very subtle and is hard to overdo.

5. **When you've finished blurring the area, turn off the selection and view your results.**

If you chose to use the Blur filter, after making the selection and inverting it so that everything but the selected area can be blurred, you can choose your image editor's Blur filter. The blurring effect is uniform throughout the selection, and you can intensify it only by repeating the command.

Unlike the regular Blur command, the special blur filters found in most image editors have dialog boxes that allow you to set how much blurring will occur and exactly what special effect will be achieved.

When blurring your photos, keep the following points in mind:

+ Try combining Blur effects. For example, blur by hand and then apply one of the special Blur filters, or combine more than one special blur filter for a completely unique effect. If your software doesn't offer special blurs, you might consider one that does, such as Photoshop Elements, which I used for all the figures in this chapter.

+ If your editing software supports layers, you can do a very cool thing with the Motion blur (or with a manually created motion effect, created by horizontal or vertical strokes with the Blur tool). Duplicate the object that should be in motion and put it on its own layer. Then blur that duplicate, and place it behind the static version on the original layer. Voilà! Your object is sitting still after rocketing into position via the Motion blur.

+ If you're a Photoshop or Photoshop Elements user, don't confuse the Smudge and Blur tools. The *Smudge tool* literally smears adjoining pixels, as though you've run a greasy paw across a chalk drawing. You can use the Smudge tool to blend two contiguous areas of color or texture, but the effect is much more dramatic than blurring.

Removing Artifacts (Tiny Blemishes)

Damage comes in all shapes and sizes — little specks of dust; scratches thin and wide, short and long; water marks or discoloration from tape; missing corners. In this section, I explain how to remove artifacts from your photos. No, I'm not talking about ancient clay pots unearthed by archaeologists. *Artifacts* are the little stray marks, blips, and other tiny blemishes that appear on images when they're captured and manipulated electronically — the kinds of blemishes you can see in Figure 1-15.

The term *artifact* is also sometimes applied to the dust and scratches that accumulate on printed photos and that end up in the digital version of the photo after it's scanned. Unlike an ancient clay pot that you'd probably want to keep, artifacts in your images are usually not desirable, and you'll want to get rid of them. Although few photos are as damaged as the example shown in Figure 1-15, most scanned images will have at least a few dings.

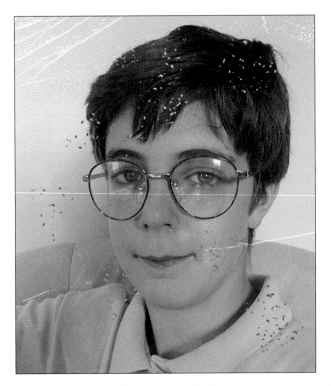

Figure 1-15: Dust and scratches inevitably show up on scanned photos.

Finding an artifact's source

When dealing with artifacts, it's useful to note how they got there. If the artifacts appeared after you resized an image or a portion thereof (stretching it with your mouse to increase its width, height, or both), the solution might be to undo the resizing and then save the file in a format that's more supportive of the resizing process. If the artifacts were there from the time the image was scanned, you can try brushing off the original to make sure none of the spots are from dust that can be removed (as opposed to the nastiest kind of dust, which becomes embedded in the photograph itself) and then rescanning it. In lieu of that, remove the marks with your software's various painting and cleaning tools.

So what file formats support the resizing process? JPG is a good choice as a final destination because it supports more colors than GIF (assuming that your image is bound for the Web or that you're trying to keep the file size small to facilitate sharing online). TIFF is another good choice if your image file size doesn't matter and you plan to print the image rather than display it on the Web.

Sweeping away dust

Dusting off your originals before scanning them is an obvious preventative measure, but it rarely removes the ground-in dust or the scratches and scuffs that appear over time, even on relatively new photos. If you store your pictures in a box or desk drawer and they rub up against each other, damage is bound to occur. For very old photos, the porous papers used back then absorb moisture and dirt, so stains and dust attack them much more easily than newer, coated photographic papers. Obviously, storing your images in a safe, protective environment (remember to use only acid-free paper!) is best, but if you haven't done that, all might not be lost.

You have several choices for removing dust and scratches, and in most cases, personal preference, skill, and the degree of damage will dictate which tool you choose. For example, you can use any of the following tools found in editors such as Photoshop, Photoshop Elements, and others to get rid of small spots, scratches, and other tiny blemishes:

✦ **The Brush tool:** The Brush tool can be used to paint out the spots.

✦ **The Pencil tool:** For tiny, tiny spots, you may like the precision of the Pencil tool, which works much the same as the Brush tool except that the dots or lines drawn are sharp-edged.

✦ **The Smudge tool:** The Smudge tool found in some image editors is a favorite of mine if I just need to smear a little of the surrounding color onto the spot, much as I'd do if I had a painting with an unwanted dot of color on a field of another color. You can find more information on the Smudge tool in Book IV, Chapter 2.

When you paint, pencil, or smudge out a dot or small scratch, you can't duplicate any pattern that's in place. For example, if the spot is on a piece of fabric, such as a coat or dress, the fabric's texture will be lost on that tiny spot even if the color is restored and the spot is no longer visible. For the kind of tiny spots and marks I'm talking about here, this is rarely a problem. For larger areas, however, the lack of texture stands out as clearly as the original mark did, so use the Clone tool (found in both Photoshop and Photoshop Elements, as well as other editing programs) to copy sections of the pristine textured area onto the damaged area. I discuss using this type of tool in the section, "Removing Unwanted Image Content," later in this chapter.

Painting over the dirt

Because your image contains only little marks on a plain background that you can easily remove with the Brush or Pencil, you decide that painting or drawing out the spot is the answer. You're ready to make the artifacts go away. With the photo in question opened and on-screen in your favorite editing program, follow these steps:

1. **Click the tool that you want to use.**

   - *Brush:* Use this tool if you're painting out a small dot or a tiny scratch.

   - *Pencil:* Choose this tool if you need a thin, precise line to get rid of the artifact in question.

2. **Set the size of the brush or pencil, choosing one that's roughly the same size as the dot or scratch that you want to eliminate.**

   If you're dealing with a scratch, draw or paint a line that's only a tiny bit wider than the scratch itself.

3. **Use the color-sampling tool — the Eyedropper — to sip up the color from the surrounding unmarred pixels.**

   With Photoshop or Photoshop Elements, hold down the Alt/Option key to convert the Pencil or Brush tools temporarily into an Eyedropper.

   This sets the painting/drawing color so that it matches when you brush or pencil the marks out. Figure 1-16 shows sampling in progress.

4. **With the proper color selected, go back to the desired tool (the Brush or Pencil) and paint or draw out the unwanted artifacts.**

You can click to get rid of a small dot or drag to get rid of a scratch.

Smudging or blurring out the paint lines

If you painted out a mark but feel that your retouching is too visible, you can use Undo (usually Ctrl+Z, or ⌘+Z if you're using a Mac) and start over, or you can use the Blur or Smudge tools (set to an extremely tiny brush size) to make the edges of the painted dot or line just a bit fuzzy. This action removes any visible edge to the color that you apply to the image. Figure 1-17 shows a painted-out scratch being repaired by blurring the edges of the scratch with the Blur tool.

Figure 1-16: The Eyedropper samples a selected color so you can paint with that color.

Figure 1-17: Blur a painted-out scratch.

To address any concerns about dust and scratches that can't be repaired, let me say this: Every image editing application that I know of offers the ability to select a color from within the image and then use that color for painting or drawing so that you can brush or pencil out tiny blemishes. The tools involved are simple to use, and this sort of repair is easily within the grasp of beginning users.

Spackling Over More Serious Damage

More extreme than scratches and scuffs, missing content is the kind of serious damage that might make you think a photo is unsalvageable. Not all image editing packages are capable of fixing dramatic problems, but many are. If your software has cloning, patching, or similar tools, you could be in luck. However, if all you have are paint brushes and the ability to copy and paste selections, you might not be so lucky. Figure 1-18 shows a seriously damaged photo with a corner missing. Painting, drawing, and pasting are clearly not going to work in a situation like this! But given the right tools, you can restore the missing corner by filling it with the remaining image content and thus creating a nearly seamless repair.

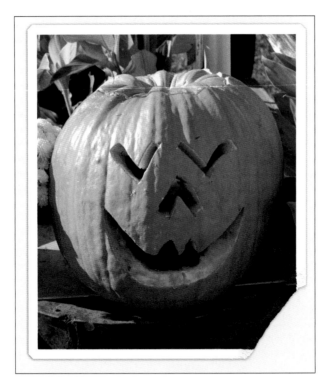

Figure 1-18: When you have an entire corner missing from your photo, serious repairs are needed.

Fixing more serious damage requires *digital spackle,* which works a lot like the gloppy white spackle that you apply to your walls to fill in holes from where pictures were hung or where someone gouged the plaster while moving furniture. Photos can also suffer from the same sort of dents and dings, and you need to fill in the holes and gashes with something, right? You can use content from within the image (or from another image), or you can create new content from scratch.

Preparing your digital spackle

Unfortunately, image editors don't come with a spackle tool, but you can create your own spackle by using the various tools at your disposal. The most common tool for this application is the Clone tool or Clone brush, depending on your image editor. The spackle that you create depends on what kind of damage you're repairing. You can fill in small areas with solid colors, applied with a Brush tool, or you can clone existing content from nearby and place it over the damage. Your choices are virtually unlimited, and the success that you see is based only on your mousing skills (for those tight corners and tiny repairs), patience, and how much time you can devote to the task.

Replacing content that's ripped or torn away

Although you might not be able to put the corner back exactly as it was, you can make it look as if there were never a missing corner. If that sounds like a contradiction, consider that what was in the corner might be unknown. What if the corner were missing before you even got the photo? If you don't know what used to be in that corner, you can't put it back. What you can do, however, is create a new corner from existing content and make it look like it has always been there. To get started, follow these steps:

1. **Think about what you could use to replace what's missing.**

   If you know what's missing, this isn't difficult, but if the missing or damaged portion doesn't tell you anything about its original state, you might have to decide what remaining content can be used to rebuild the corner.

2. **Click the Clone tool.**

3. **Choose a brush size and set the Opacity to 100%.**

4. **Zoom in to the area you want to work with.**

5. **Choose the source area for cloning, as shown in Figure 1-19.**

   Some image editors require right-clicking to select a source area. Others ask you to hold down the Alt key (if you're a Windows user) or the Option key (if you're on a Mac) as you click the area that you want to clone.

6. **Click and/or drag over the damage, watching as the sampled content covers it.**

   Figure 1-20 shows cloned content filling in the missing corner.

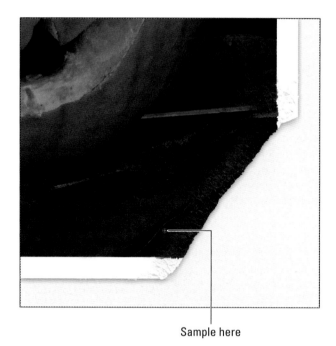

Sample here

Figure 1-19: Sample the area you want to clone.

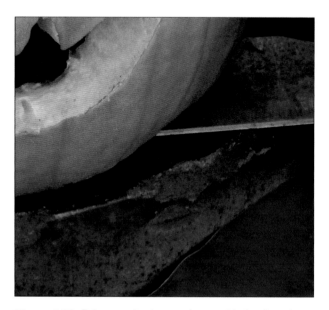

Figure 1-20: Paint over the damaged area with the cloned texture.

If you want to be able to apply the same exact cloned spot to the entire damaged area, be sure to select the Aligned option on the Options bar (or the Cumulative option with some image editors) before you start painting the cloned content onto the damage. With Aligned marked, the tool clones from a position relative to where you first started cloning. When unmarked, the Clone tool always starts cloning from the same point.

Your filling needn't come from the same image! You can use the Clone tool to sample content from another image and then apply it to the damaged photo. Just open up the new image, sample the content (press the Alt or Option key as you click the content to be cloned), and then switch back to the damaged photo. With the Clone tool still selected, click and/or drag to place the cloned content in the image.

Removing Unwanted Image Content

Signs of wear and other types of physical damage aren't the only things you might want to get rid of when editing your images. A person, car, garbage can, building, plant, tree, or just about anything can become objectionable if you didn't want it to be in the picture in the first place. Rather than tearing all your wedding photos in half, consider replacing the unwanted spouse with more of the background or a large potted plant. Someone forget to move the car before taking a picture of your house for the real estate brochures? Get rid of the car, replacing it with curb and grass as though the car had been in the garage all along.

It might seem like some sort of complicated sleight of hand, but replacing one piece of content with another is really rather simple. If you've already tried repairing scratches, stains, and tears, you're more than ready to tackle the process of removing unwanted people, places, and things. You need software that has Clone and/or Patch tools (or reasonable facsimiles), and you need to understand how the Clipboard works (so you can copy and paste content in big chunks). Sound like too big a job? Never fear — it becomes clear in the next few paragraphs!

For example, no matter how much we love them, we sometimes wish family members would make themselves scarce, if only for a little while. But what if your ex–family member — someone you thought you'd never have to see again — is still haunting your family photos? Starting with a group photo, follow these steps:

1. **Identify the unwanted person and use a selection tool — preferably a freeform or magnetic selection tool — to select him or her.**

   Book V, Chapter 2 has descriptions of the generic selection tools found in most image editors.

You don't have to worry about getting a little of the surrounding image as long as it doesn't remove someone else's arm or the side of a face.

2. Press Delete to get rid of the selected person.

The background layer or any other underlying layer's content now shows through the hole.

3. Fill the hole with other content — more of the photo's background content if you were all standing in front of one of those lovely painted backdrops, or use the sky or extend a nearby wall or stand of trees.

Whatever's behind the rest of the group can be extended to fill in where the now-missing person once stood. Your choices for filling in are as follows:

- Copy content from elsewhere and paste it onto the hole.

- Use the Clone tool to fill in the hole with sampled content from elsewhere in the image.

Which method you choose depends on three things:

- How big a hole the deleted person left behind

- Whether you have a lot of alternate content to use as fill

- Whether there are lighting issues

Perhaps everything but the deleted person is in shadow, and you can't seamlessly apply that dark content in his or her place. If lighting is the problem — and you have Photoshop — you'll want to use the *Patch tool* (a kind of super-Clone tool that adjusts for texture and lighting) so that the lighting of the destination is preserved when you patch the hole. If the hole is huge or there's no background to use, you might need to copy content and paste it into the hole, perhaps even going to another image to get the filler. Figure 1-21 shows a Before and an After of the same image. In the after version, the unwanted element (in this case, a goose in the background) has been replaced by more of the surrounding pond.

What if the unwanted person isn't against a background or is sitting in front of someone else and deleting him or her will leave you with half of a person? Consider bringing someone in from another picture and putting him or her in place of the person you're deleting. You can always resize a new person from a smaller or larger image, and you can use your image editor's Burn or Dodge tools to adjust lighting if the substitute person comes from a darker or lighter image. Use the Blur or Smudge tools to make the stand-in blend in so that none of the edges are obvious.

Figure 1-21: Hide the extra goose behind the water of the pond.

Combining Pictures

Throughout this chapter, most of what I discuss is repairing and improving individual photos by fixing spots, scratches, and tears, replacing missing content, and moving stuff around to make things better. This isn't the end of even a low-end image editing application's capabilities, however. You can do a lot with multiple images, combining them into a single image and using special effects for a really creative result.

When combining images, there really aren't any rules. You can combine black-and-white photos with color images, professional portraits or photographic artwork with amateur or family photos, pictures of people with pictures of places — anything that makes sense to you. You can create a collage, assembling parts of various photos into a *composite image* like the one shown in Figure 1-22, or you can mix content from two or more photos and retouch the combined result to make it look like the combined content had been together from the start.

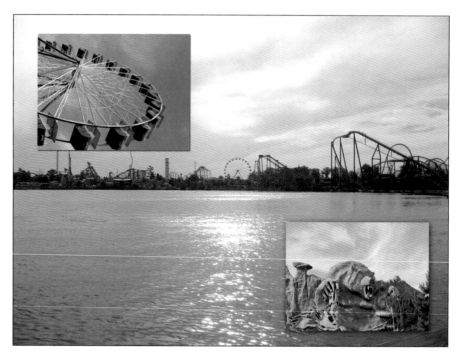

Figure 1-22: You can combine several photos into one.

Is there anything along these lines that image editing software *can't* do? With the midrange to top-level packages, the limitations are fairly . . . limited. You might run into limitations in terms of special effects and retouching capabilities, which can hamper the success of the creative side of your combinations, but those are software-specific limitations, such as not being able to adjust the opacity (see-through quality) of content within a photo, or not being able to place different parts of a composite image on separate layers.

Pasting content from other images

Whether you're using a Windows-based PC or a Mac, you have the ability to cut, copy, and paste content from one file to another or to share and duplicate content within the same file. These capabilities make it easy to take content from one photo and add it to another, either by removing content from its original location or by making a copy that appears in both photos.

To copy content from one photo and paste it into another, follow these steps, which work in virtually any image editing package:

1. **Open both the *source image* (the one where the content you want currently resides) and the *target image* (the one that will receive the copied content).**

2. **In the source image, use a selection tool to select the content that you want to copy.**

   You can use either a freeform or geometric-shaped selection tool. Your choice depends on the shape of the object that you want to copy.

3. **Choose Edit⇨Copy.**

   This places a duplicate of the selection in your computer's memory, where it will wait for you to paste it.

4. **Go to the target image and choose Edit⇨Paste.**

   In Figure 1-23, a moon that was cut from an image is now pasted into a different photo.

5. **When the pasted content appears in the target image, activate the Move tool and then drag the content into the desired position within the photo.**

Note that if you're using software that allows you to put different parts of an image on separate layers, the pasted content is probably on its own layer — a layer created automatically through the pasting process. You can leave the content on this separate layer or use your software's layer-handling commands to merge the paste layer with the rest of the photo (sometimes called *flattening*). Of course, you'd do this only after your pasted content was placed in the desired spot and you're sure you don't want to move it again.

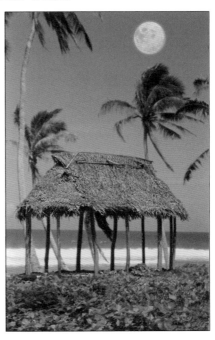

Figure 1-23: This moon has been copied from one photo and pasted here.

You can activate the Copy and Paste commands with your keyboard as well as through the Edit menu. To copy, press Ctrl+C, and to paste, press Ctrl+V. If you're on a Mac, the shortcuts are ⌘+C and ⌘+V, respectively.

Using layers to create overlapping images

Assuming that your software supports layers, your pasted content will be on separate layers — one new layer per paste. This is good in that it makes it easy to move things around, repositioning pasted stuff so that it's in just the right spot. Separate layers also enable you to hide pasted content if you're not sure you really want to use it. Rather than deleting the pasted content (which you might regret if you change your mind), you can simply hide the layer that it's on, and then you won't see it until and unless you choose to display that layer again.

Keeping things on separate layers has another benefit. By having different elements of your image on individual layers, you can overlap the layers and rearrange the layers to restack the overlapping content. As shown in Figure 1-24, the same image was copied, overlapped, and stacked in several layers. Images can be restacked in as many configurations as you can imagine but only because each individual part has its own layer.

Figure 1-24: You can stack layers to overlap content.

Hiding layers

After something is pasted into your image, the pasted content is on its own layer. If you no longer want to see that layer's content, just hide the layer by clicking the icon next to the layer number. The icon varies from image editor to image editor. In Paint Shop Pro, the icon is a pair of spectacles; in Photoshop Elements, it's an eyeball.

In any case, after the layer is hidden, its content doesn't display on-screen, nor will it print. If you want to bring it back, simply click the box where the icon was, and the icon reappears, as does the layer's content.

Rearranging layers to change object stacking order

If you want to change the stacking order of two or more overlapping elements in a photo, simply drag the layers up or down in the Layers palette. The top-most layers represent the content that's on the top of any overlapping stack, and the lower layers are underneath. Dragging a layer up moves it up in the stack, and dragging a layer down puts it beneath the other layers.

Deleting layers

If you just plain don't want a layer anymore and hiding it isn't the answer, delete the layer. To do this, just drag the unwanted layer to the trash can icon, located at the bottom of the palette in some image editors (Photoshop) or at the top in others (Photoshop Elements and Paint Shop Pro, for example).

Adjusting opacity for interesting effects

When layers overlap, you can achieve very cool results by making one or more of the layers less opaque (more see-through) so that underlying layers can be seen. Reducing the opacity of the elements on top of a background makes it possible to see that background image and recognize its content. Or, you can use transparency to de-emphasize some parts of an image and emphasize others. The elements on top of the background remain visible, but their slightly see-through nature integrates them more fully with the image as a whole. Figure 1-25 shows a picture used in an eBay auction: Only the widget in the center is for sale. The semi-transparent objects at the left and right are shown to illustrate how the widget works.

For applications that support layers, the opacity controls are found in the Layers palette, and you adjust the opacity of an entire layer, not just portions thereof, although some editing applications allow you to select content on a single layer and reduce or increase its opacity independently. Using the popular Photoshop Elements program as an example, follow these steps to adjust a layer's opacity, making the objects on underlying layers more visible:

Figure 1-25: You can make some layers semi-transparent.

1. **Open the image containing the layer that you want to adjust.**

2. **Access your image editor's Layers palette or dialog box.**

3. **Within the Layers palette, click the layer you want to make more or less opaque.**

4. **Choose your image editor's layer opacity control and use the slider to adjust the opacity level.**

   Opacity is set at 100% (not see-through at all) by default.

   As you adjust the opacity, the results appear immediately within your image. You can undo your result if you don't like it, or simply go back to the Layers palette and readjust.

An opacity of 0% renders the active layer completely invisible, and you can use this to your advantage, making a layer disappear and then slowly increasing its opacity until you achieve the very level of visibility you want. You can also back down from 100%, but starting at 0% can make it much easier to find the right setting for a layer that you want to be very, very faint.

Chapter 2: Common Editing Options

In This Chapter

✓ **Touring typical image editing tools**

✓ **Creating original content with painting tools**

✓ **Focusing your efforts with selection tools**

✓ **Smoothing the rough spots with blending tools**

✓ **Fixing photographic errors with correction tools**

The main editing tools found in virtually all image editing applications fall into four categories: painting, selecting, blending, and correction. There are no hard and fast rules, however, as to when to use these tools, and you'll find yourself using painting tools to make corrections, blending tools to create original painted effects, and any other variety of mixing and matching of tools and tasks that your editing jobs require.

This chapter provides an overview of the editing tools common to most image editing programs. I use Adobe Photoshop Elements and Corel Paint Shop Pro as the primary examples, but most of these tools are available in other image editors, such as Microsoft Digital Imaging Suite, Adobe Photoshop, Corel PhotoPaint, and others. Whatever application you're using now or will use in the future, the basic concepts are the same for these four tool categories and the tasks you perform with them. So don't worry about not being able to apply instructions or examples from one application to another!

This chapter is intended to be an introduction to the tools that you'll find in virtually all image editors. I show you how to use some of these functions in more detail using Photoshop and Photoshop Elements in Book VI.

Checking Out Your Editing Toolkit

As shown in Figures 2-1 and 2-2, your tools in both Photoshop Elements and Paint Shop Pro are very similar. You might even notice that some of the tools' buttons are nearly identical. These similarities exist for a very simple and logical reason: The things people need to do to photographs — reversing the signs of aging, wear and tear, and photographic errors or applying aesthetic preferences — are universal. Nobody has thought of something that the other guy hasn't added to his software. Other than some of the very low-end packages with extremely limited toolsets, a full set of tools for performing these tasks is found in pretty much the same arrangement, and the tools are used in pretty much the same way. So, the information you pick up in this chapter can be applied across the board. You can find a summary and comparison of the features in a broad selection of image editors in Book V, Chapter 3.

Figure 2-1: The tools in Photoshop Elements 4.0.

In both Elements and Paint Shop Pro, you can choose where toolbars are displayed. They can be docked along an edge of the main window or pulled loose as free-floating strips of tools, as in Figure 2-1. Paint Shop Pro lets you resize the floating toolbar into a rectangle with several columns, as you can see in Figure 2-2.

Figure 2-2: The tools in Paint Shop Pro.

If you don't see your application's tool kit, you can usually redisplay it by choosing it from the Window or View menu. The preferences settings that control features of the image editor are normally found in the Edit menu, as shown in Figure 2-3, which shows the Photoshop Elements Edit menu and Preferences submenu. As you can see from this list, you can control just about every aspect of the image editor's functions as well as some general settings for the application as a whole.

As you take the time to visually check out your tools, you can identify them quickly by placing your cursor over a tool to display a *ToolTip,* which shows the names and sometimes the purpose of the individual tools. As you mouse over a tool, its name appears in a small box.

Figure 2-3: You can set preferences for each tool.

 Just a key or click away if you're a Windows user, Help can be found by pressing the F1 key at any time. Most applications support *context-sensitive help*, which means that if you're using a particular tool or have a particular dialog box open and press the F1 key, information pertaining to that tool or dialog box appears when the Help window opens. The Mac OS also offers a Help menu, and the same Help articles appear when you search by topic.

Painting Tools

Spotting the painting and drawing tools in any image editing package isn't difficult. They look like paint brushes and pencils, and there are often air-brush and spray-can alternatives as well. When you use a painting tool, you can customize several options in just about any application. Although some applications definitely offer more options than others, any program worth its salt lets you set the following paint brush options:

+ Brush size and type

+ The shape of the brush bristles

+ The strength of the flow of paint coming out of the brush

+ The opacity of the paint applied by the brush

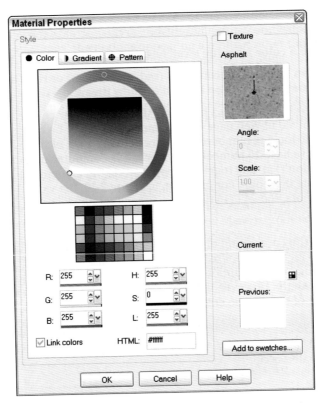

Figure 2-10: Paint Shop Pro puts the key color selection tools in this chooser palette.

After your color is set, you can use any painting, drawing, or filling tool available to you, and then that color is applied to the image.

Sampling colors from the image

If a color already appears in your image (or anywhere on the workspace or your Windows or Mac desktop), you can *sample* it, which means sipping up the color with a sampling tool, such as the Eyedropper tool or variation found in all image editors. When you sip up a sample of the color, the color information is stored, and the color that you sampled becomes the new foreground color. Figure 2-11 shows sampling in progress.

Sampling colors makes it easy to find compatible colors and to keep your colors consistent throughout a single image or in related images that need the look of a running theme. If, for example, you retouch a photo by adding brighter colors to clothes, cars, flowers, and other objects, you can sample those colors afterward, which will allow you to use those same shades in other places.

Figure 2-11: You can sample existing colors to duplicate any particular hue.

To sample a color, click the sampling tool, and your cursor changes to an eyedropper. Then click the image at the spot where the desired color is currently in use. The color you clicked then becomes the foreground color.

Remember that you can also click title bars, buttons, backgrounds, or images on your desktop — anything that's visible while the sampling tool is active can be sampled and turned into a paintable color in your editing software.

Applying the paint

After you customize your painting tool by choosing the size, style, opacity, strength, and color for the brush, pencil, or other painting device, you're ready to get painting! The technique for painting doesn't vary much from application to application. With your mouse or other pointing device in hand, you're ready to go. Just click and drag and watch the paint flow onto the image.

Painting and drawing freeform lines

When you're painting by hand and applying freeform lines, there are no real rules. You can set the line to just about any width, shape, style, and color you desire, which you see as you paint. If you set the line to a particular level of opacity, you see that, too. The only control that's not easily established is your mouse ability. If your hand is shaky, you're working too quickly, or you're not paying attention, you might not like your results.

 Take your time, go slowly, and don't do the entire job in one stroke. Why? If you make a mistake at the very end, using Undo from the Edit menu will undo the entire job. Instead, paint in shorter strokes. You can see from the Undo History palette found in Paint Shop Pro, Adobe Photoshop and Photoshop Elements, as well as other image editors (see Figure 2-12) that the Brush tool has been used several times in succession to form the apparently continuous line in the image. Every time you release the mouse button, you create an individual stroke, even if the pause doesn't show on the line itself.

Figure 2-12: Photoshop Elements' Undo History palette (left) and the Paint Shop Pro equivalent (right.)

Filling a shape with the Brush tool

Remember coloring books? You scrubbed away with your crayons, filling in shapes, trying to stay within the lines. Or, if you were like me, you went outside the lines and created new shapes altogether! In any case, you can use your editing software's painting tools to fill in shapes and areas simply by applying paint the same way you'd apply crayon to a shape on a coloring book page. Figure 2-13 shows a shape being filled in with the Brush tool, set to a large size and a soft style so that no obvious scribbles are visible.

If you want a nice, uniform fill for a shape or an area, consider using the Fill tool that comes with your software. The *Fill tool* applies a solid color with no visible brush strokes. On the other hand, if you want a brushed look or want to vary the intensity by painting over certain spots more than others, you can use the Brush tool. Don't use the Pencil tool, though, or the result will look too sketchy.

Figure 2-13: You can fill a shape with color as easily as with a coloring book.

Painting and drawing straight lines

With all image editing packages, holding down a key (the Shift key in Photoshop Elements and Paint Shop Pro) while you use the Brush and the Pencil tools constrains the drawing to a single direction. This trick is helpful when you need to draw straight lines.

To use this feature, follow these steps:

1. **Click the painting or drawing tool you'd like to use (Brush or Pencil) to activate it.**

2. **Click the image at the spot where the straight line should start.**

3. **Press and hold the Shift key.**

4. **Click where the line should end.**

A straight line connecting the beginning and ending points will be painted/drawn automatically, with the visual characteristics of the Brush or Pencil settings you established. Figure 2-14 shows a box that was painted with a textured Brush tool.

Figure 2-14: This border was painted with a textured brush.

Because the Pencil tool provides a sharp-edged, crisp line, it's a good tool to use if you need to create a very clean line or lines. It's also great if you need to draw very fine lines that measure as small as one pixel.

Using specialty painting tools

Specialty painting tools refer to any painting or drawing tools that aren't your basic Brush or Pencil. These tools often work like the basic ones, at least in terms of how you apply them. Just drag and/or click your mouse and the paint is applied. The look achieved is where these tools deviate from the basic painting and drawing tools.

With some image editors, the specialty tools are actually variations on the basic tools. For example, in the Adobe products, you can turn on the Airbrush option when you're setting up the Brush tool to give the lines and strokes an airbrushed look. In Paint Shop Pro, the airbrush is a separate tool; it has its own settings for size and intensity of the lines drawn, as shown in Figure 2-15. When you paint with this tool, your results really look like paint that was sprayed on.

Figure 2-15: Paint Shop Pro includes a separate Airbrush tool.

Paint Shop Pro also has a Picture Tube tool that, by default, applies color as if you were squeezing thick paint out of a tube. Its results are shown in Figure 2-16, where you can see the 3-D look of the lines drawn. Not all applications have a tool like this, but many do. In Photoshop or Photoshop Elements, you could apply drop shadow and beveling options to the lines after drawing them, ending up with a 3-D-looking result.

Figure 2-16: The Picture Tube lines look like you've squeezed thick paint out of a tube.

✦ **Paintbrush or Mask Select:** Some applications offer a paintbrush-like tool that allows you to make a selection by painting. Others allow you to enter a Mask mode, where your standard Brush tool acts as a selector to create a mask of what you want to include in the selection, and when you switch back to the normal mode, your mask has turned to a selection. Alternatively, you can specify that what you don't paint turns into a selection instead.

Making geometric selections

Geometric selections — rectangular and oval-shaped regions — are good if you're preparing to make an adjustment or to apply a fill to a large area and don't mind if the area doesn't follow the shapes within your image. As shown in Figure 2-19, you can select a square area and apply paint to it to create a frame around the central images in a figure.

Figure 2-19: Paint around the edges of a selection to create a natural-looking frame.

Before shape tools were added to most image editing applications, using the Marquee selection tools was the only way to map out an area and fill it with color — creating solid-filled squares, rectangles, circles, and ovals. Most applications come with shape-drawing tools now, enabling you to draw just about any geometric shape or symbol (hearts, arrows, and so on) and then fill it with color. This strips the Marquee tool of one of its original jobs, but it remains an important weapon in your image editing arsenal.

Using the Marquee selection tools

To use the Marquee or geometric selection tools, simply click the tool and drag from the upper or lower corner of the desired selected area and diagonally away from that starting point. The farther away you drag, the bigger the selection becomes, as shown in Figure 2-20. Here, a rectangular area is being selected, and the distance and angle from the starting point dictates the selection's size and proportions.

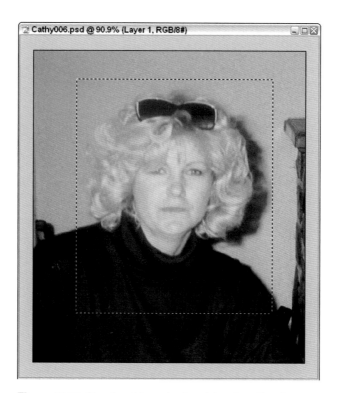

Figure 2-20: The size of the selection determines the shape of the frame.

Selecting perfect squares and circles

If you want to select a square or circle instead of a rectangle or oval (often called an *ellipse*), you can add keystrokes to the process. In most image editors, holding down the Shift key while you drag the Marquee or other geometric selection tool creates a perfect square — if you're using the Rectangular Marquee tool. If you're using the Elliptical Marquee, holding down the Shift key creates a perfect circle. Paint Shop Pro offers a set of selection options, as shown in Figure 2-21, in which the Freehand Selection tool is chosen. You can use the drop-down list within the Tool palette to select square or circle rather than rectangle or ellipse. You can also select rounded-corner rectangles in Photoshop, Elements, and Paint Shop Pro.

Figure 2-21: Paint Shop Pro includes a variety of selection tools.

Changing and resizing selections

If you've already selected a geometrically shaped area on your image and realize you want a different area or a larger or smaller area, you can always deselect and start over. If the area you've selected is fine but you want to add to or take away from it, however, you needn't restart from scratch. You can simply augment or reduce your selection by using keyboard shortcuts or tool options that are provided while the selection tool is active.

If you're using Paint Shop Pro or any of the other higher-end applications, you can use the Shift key to add to a selection or the Ctrl key (⌘ on a Mac) to reduce a selection. Make your selection first. Then hold down the Shift key or Ctrl/⌘ key and create an additional selection. The new selection will be added to or subtracted from the first selection you made. You see a plus or minus sign, respectively, appear with your selection cursor.

With most image editors, you can choose from four alternative selection modes on the Options bar. In Figures 2-22 through 2-25, I use the *Magic Wand tool,* which selects contiguous pixels based on their color, to add or subtract from the main selection. (I could have used one of the other selection tools instead, however.)

Here are the most common selection options:

✦ **Selection:** Figure 2-22 shows a rectangular selection made out of the overlapping rectangle and circle. The dotted lines represent the limits of the selection.

Figure 2-22: A standard selection created with the rectangular marquee.

✦ **Subtract from Selection:** In Figure 2-23, I held down the Alt key (Option key on the Mac) and used the Magic Wand to click in the circle area, subtracting the circle from the selection and leaving a corner cut out of the rectangular selection.

✦ **Add to Selection:** In Figure 2-24, I went back to the original rectangular selection and held down the Shift key while clicking in the circle with the Magic Wand. This added the circle's area to the selection.

Figure 2-23: The area of the circle has been subtracted from the selection.

Figure 2-24: The area of the circle has been added to the selection.

✦ **Intersect with Selection:** In Figure 2-25, I used the Intersect option, which produces a selection that results where two selections overlap — in this case, creating a quarter-circle.

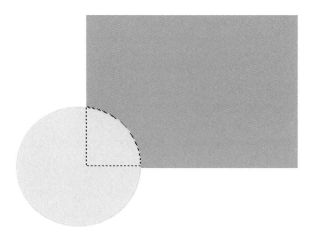

Figure 2-25: This selection results from the area in which separate circle and rectangle selections overlap, using the Intersect option.

Want to make a selection that looks like a frame? Use your application's tool for reducing a selection to select a rectangle or square within a larger rectangle or square selection. The smaller selection cuts the center out of the first selection, leaving a frame-like selection that you can fill with a solid color or pattern. This can also be done with concentric circular or elliptical selections.

You can move your selection without moving the selected content within the image if you point to the very edge of the selection (the dashed line) and drag *after* drawing the selection. This allows you to reposition the selection before you fill it with paint, delete its contents, or apply a filter or special effect to the selected area.

Drawing freeform selections

The ability to draw the borders of a freeform selection is what really enables you to do fine editing in a photo. Without the freeform selection tools in your application, you can't select a person's face, a scratched area, a shadowy area that needs to be lightened, or any other nongeometric region within an image. Most applications offer alternatives for the Lasso or Freeform selector tools — the ability to have the selection follow along like-colored pixels or to draw a polygon (an irregular, straight-sided shape) with the selection tool. With these alternatives, there isn't anything too large, small, or oddly shaped to be selected.

Using the Lasso or Freehand selection tool

Using the Lasso (in Photoshop and Elements) or the Freehand selection tool (in Paint Shop Pro) is really easy if you follow these steps:

1. **Click to activate the tool.**

2. **Move your mouse onto the image and find the spot where you'd like to begin your selection.**

3. **Click to begin the selection and then drag, drawing the shape selection you want.**

4. **Come back to the beginning of the selection.** When you've met or passed the starting point, release the mouse button to complete the selection. If you release the mouse button anywhere else, the program will draw a straight line from that point to the original starting point, closing the selection.

Selecting polygonal areas

When you click the Lasso or Freehand selection tools, options become available. In Photoshop and Elements, the Options bar displays different Lasso modes, as shown in Figure 2-26. Similar options are available for the Freehand tool in Paint Shop Pro through the Tool Options palette.

Figure 2-26: The Lasso tool's Options bar in Photoshop Elements.

With the Polygonal Lasso (Photoshop Elements) or the Point-to-Point Freehand tool (Paint Shop Pro), you can make your selection by following these steps:

1. **Click to activate the selection tool.**

2. **Use the tool's options to set it to Polygonal or Point-to-Point mode.**

3. **Click your starting point on the image.**

4. **Rather than dragging, move the mouse to the next point in your polygon — where you want to make a corner and start another side — and click.**

5. **Continue clicking and moving, each time drawing a new side for your selection, until you come back to your starting point.**

6. **When you're back to the beginning of the selection, click the starting point to close the shape.**

   If you can't find the exact pixel where your selection began, just double-click when you get close. The software closes the shape for you, forcing the endpoint to meet the starting point that you couldn't see or find manually.

> **TIP**
> Your freeform selections needn't be a single closed shape. You can draw figure eights or any kind of freeform looped shape, using either the freehand or polygonal modes. Go crazy!

Using magnetic selection tools

Magnetic selection tools create a selection that "clings" to the outline of an object as you drag, according to pixel colors that define the object's edge. These tools are very handy because they enable you to follow the edge of an object or objects, restricting your selection to very finite areas of the image. Nearly every editing package has a tool like this. In Photoshop and Elements, it's the Magnetic Lasso; in Paint Shop Pro, you select the Smart Edge option for the Freehand tool.

To use the magnetic selection tools, follow these steps:

1. **Click the Lasso or Freehand tool (or other similarly named tool in your application) to activate it.**

2. **From the tool's options, choose Magnetic (Photoshop or Elements) or Smart Edge (Paint Shop Pro).**

3. **Click the spot where you want to begin your selection.**

4. **Continue making the selection by dragging along the edge of the object or area you want to select.**

   The tool adheres to the edges of that object or area, following the like-colored pixels, as shown in Figure 2-27.

5. **If you see an area coming up where the tool might fail because the pixels aren't diverse, click again to reroute the selection process, and then continue dragging.**

   You can click as often as you like along the way, controlling the direction that the selection takes.

   The same process in Paint Shop Pro uses the Smart Edge tool, from which a rectangle follows you as you drag. While you click to continue in a new direction, the previously dragged selection adheres to the shape.

Figure 2-27: The Magnetic Lasso in Photoshop and Elements sticks to the edges of objects.

6. **Come back to your starting point and click (or double-click if you're not sure you're at the exact starting point) to end and close the selection.**

Selecting with the Quick Mask mode

Photoshop offers a Quick Mask mode, in which you can use the Brush and the Pencil tools (as well as the Fill tool) to paint a protective mask over parts of the image. This makes it as easy as painting to make a selection because when you return to standard working mode, the mask turns into a selection. Alternatively, everything *not* painted can become a selection.

To work in and make a selection with Quick Mask mode, follow these steps:

1. **Click the Quick Mask Mode button in the bottom section of the Photoshop toolbox.**

2. **Click the Brush or the Pencil tool, adjusting its settings just as you would if you were painting or drawing color onto an image.**

   You want to increase or decrease the size of the tool's tip to accommodate the level of detail that you want to achieve in your selection.

3. **Begin outlining the area you want to select, and note that a see-through red mask appears wherever you paint, as shown in Figure 2-28.**

Figure 2-28: The selection you're painting appears as a semi-transparent red mask.

4. **After you outline the shape or area, use the Fill tool to fill in the shape that you want to turn into a selection.**

   This makes a solid mask that will translate into a selection of the entire area.

5. **When you finish masking the area you want, switch back to Standard mode.**

   When you leave Quick Mask mode, your mask turns into a selection. You can now work with the selection as you would one that you created directly with any of the other selection tools or methods.

If you want to select everything but a particular object or area, first mask that area. Then, when you get back into Standard mode, choose Select⇨ Inverse from the main menu.

Selecting with the Paintbrush Selection tool

Photoshop Elements has a Paintbrush Selection tool that you can use to paint a selection. The tool gives you the flexibility and familiarity of a Paint Brush tool and also allows you to select snaking paths or to select a freeform shape by filling in an area with the Brush tool.

Selecting pixels by color with the Magic Wand

The selections that you can make with the Magic Wand (or like-named tool) often resemble those you'd make with the Lasso or Freehand selection tools. They're freeform shapes and — like selections made with the Add to Selection option turned on — they can encompass multiple noncontiguous areas.

The difference between those selection tools and the Magic Wand, however, is that the Magic Wand makes selections based on an initial pixel sample. For example, this enables you to select all the blue areas, all the white areas, or all the areas that are the same as or quite close to any color or shade within your image.

Abracadabra! Using the Magic Wand

The Magic Wand selects pixels within your image based on the color of a pixel you click. It's a simple process, but one that you can master and use to your advantage if you know exactly how it works.

To use the Magic Wand tool, follow these simple steps:

1. **Click the Magic Wand tool to activate it.**

2. **Click a pixel that's the color of the pixels that you want to select in your image.**

   Figure 2-29 shows the sampling in progress.

3. **If you don't get all the pixels you wanted, press and hold the Shift key while you continue to click pixels around in the image, adding to the Magic Wand selection.**

   Figure 2-30 shows a selection in progress.

Figure 2-29: Click a pixel that's the same color as the pixels you want to select.

Figure 2-30: Add pixels to your selection by holding the Shift key and clicking another area.

If you get more pixels in the selection than you want, reduce your selection by switching to Subtract from Selection mode (Photoshop or Elements) or by holding down the Ctrl key (⌘ for Mac) to take away from the existing selection. When you click an unwanted area within the selection, those pixels are no longer selected.

If you didn't get as much of the image as you wanted, tweak the tool's options settings, such as Tolerance, to include more pixels. You can tweak the number of selected pixels by expanding the tolerance, or press the Shift key and click in the additional area you hoped to select in order to add to the selection.

Controlling the wand's magic

Any wand settings that you could possibly tweak are located on the tool's Options bar in Photoshop and Elements or in the palette or Tool options bar of other image editors. The settings work differently, depending on the application you're using.

In any case, you will see a Tolerance setting, which is a threshold for the sensitivity of the wand. The higher the number you set for the Tolerance setting, the more pixels that the software sees as selectable — a risky approach if you're working with a black-and-white photo or a color photo without a lot of color diversity throughout. You can make other application-specific adjustments that, when used in conjunction with the Tolerance setting, can assure you of the exact selection you wanted. These adjustments include the following:

✦ **Match Mode** (Paint Shop Pro) allows you to choose what pixel attribute is compared to the surrounding pixels. You can choose from RGB Value, Hue, Brightness, All Opaque, or Opacity. If you choose RGB Value (the default), the surrounding pixels are compared in terms of their levels of red, green, and blue. And, if they're close enough to the sampled pixel (based on the Tolerance you set), they are selected.

✦ **Contiguous** (Photoshop/Elements) is a check box that allows you to choose whether the selection includes pixels that aren't touching the sampled pixel or any of the pixels that were selected on the first click with the wand. If you turn on the option (it's off by default), you get a smaller selection, which might be just what you want. If you turn it off, any pixels meeting your Tolerance setting are selected, no matter where in the image they're found.

✦ The **Use All Layers** option (Photoshop/Elements) allows you to select pixels on (who'd have guessed it) all the layers of the image. If you turn this on (it's off by default), you can select all the pixels that meet your tolerance requirements, no matter which layer they're on. If you want to restrict your edits to a particular layer, however, make sure this option is off.

You might find it easier to set your Tolerance setting low so that you don't get more of a selection than you wanted and then use the Add to Selection option or the Shift key to augment the selection by clicking again on a new spot, which resamples the image and compares surrounding pixels against a different sample pixel. Like most things in life, it's easier to start small and add what you need than to grab too much and then have to give some of it back or start all over again.

Blending Tools

Blending is another word for mixing — combining separate things to make a new thing. When it comes to photos that you're retouching or editing for content, use blending to make new content seem as though it has always been in what's really a new environment. Blending is for retouching — applying strokes of paint that cover a stain or pasted areas that fill in a hole and then disappear into the neighboring content.

Any good image editing application offers at least one or two blending tools, and again using Photoshop, Photoshop Elements, and Paint Shop Pro as examples, you'll find no lack of blending tools available, including

+ The Smudge tool (Photoshop/Elements)
+ The Blur tool (Photoshop/Elements and Paint Shop Pro)
+ The Scratch Remover tool (Paint Shop Pro)

You can use other tools to blend one thing into another, but they're not necessarily tools that are classified as blending tools per se. For example, you can use the Clone Stamp tool to eliminate the signs of an obvious patch job, to add consistency to an area with spotty colors or textures, or to heal a damaged area that stands out like a sore thumb. Sometimes, the Clone Stamp's results need a little blending of their own, though, and that's when the actual blending tools come into play.

Smudging and smearing your colors

The *Smudge tool* smears color from one area of the image onto another area, much like how you blend dry pastels with your fingertip or how children finger-paint. You can use this tool to blend hard edges, to soften blemishes (when actually patching them would rob the image of too much texture), and to smear away small spots or scratches. You can use the tool in black-and-white or color images.

Using and controlling the Smudge tool

To use the Smudge tool, just click it and start smudging. The default settings are appropriate for most uses, but you can adjust them. The most effective setting to adjust is Strength, which controls the degree of smearing that the Smudge tool achieves. A low strength creates very subtle results, and a high strength achieves dramatic results. A setting in the middle (50%) gives you an effective smudge without making a mess.

Other adjustments are available on the Mode drop-down menu, which allows you to control which aspect of the smudged pixels is affected by the smudging process. You can choose to Darken or Lighten the pixels or to affect their hue, saturation, color, or luminosity (brightness). Not sure which one to choose? Tinker a bit and undo your handiwork by pressing Ctrl+Z (⌘+Z) if you don't like the results.

Smearing with the Finger Painting option

The Finger Painting option — available with Photoshop and Photoshop Elements' Smudge tool — allows you to smear the current foreground color into the area you're smudging. You can use this option to incorporate new colors or brighter, more vibrant versions of existing colors by virtual finger-painting.

Don't forget the role that the brush size can play in the Smudge tool's effectiveness. Too big a brush can smear more of the image than you want it to, whereas too small of a brush can result in obvious, sketchy-looking smudges. It's a real Goldilocks situation: You want the one that's just right, and sometimes only experimentation helps you find the right size.

Blurring the edges

The Blur tool found in most image editors works by eliminating a little — or a lot — of the contrast between adjacent pixels, thereby making parts of your image blurred or out of focus. You control how much of an effect the tool has by adjusting its settings — Strength and Brush Size being the most dynamic. You also control where it works by where you place your mouse as you scrub over unwanted edges and distinctions. You can use it to draw attention to part of the photo by blurring nonessential content. Or, in the blending context, you can use it to make hard lines, the edges of pasted content, and other unwanted edges disappear into the surrounding image.

Figure 2-31 shows an image that's ripe for blurring; you can see the hard edges where the white flowers were pasted into the image. Figure 2-32 shows the blurred result. The hard edge is gone, and you can hardly tell that the new content was pasted into place.

These flowers were pasted into the photo.

Figure 2-31: The edges around the pasted-in flowers are too harsh.

How do you know when to blur and when to smudge, when to clone and when to paint? There are no hard and fast rules, although I wish there were. We all spend time trying one technique and then undoing it in favor of another. A good guideline to keep in mind, though, is the old adage that *Less is more*. A small problem (such as tiny scratches or minor stains or spots) should require a small solution, and that usually calls for a subtle tool. If you have a large-scale problem — such as major amounts of unwanted content, big tears, or missing portions of the photo — a larger-scale solution is probably required.

Figure 2-32: The hard edge is gone after blurring.

Using the Scratch Remover

Paint Shop Pro offers a very cool tool — the Scratch Remover. Unlike Photoshop's multistep Healing Brush and Patch tools, this tool works quickly and easily. (If you want to remove spots in an image in one step using Elements, try the Spot Healing Brush instead. You can find more on removing scratches with Adobe's healing tools in Book VI, Chapter 4.)

1. **Click the Scratch Remover (as shown in Figure 2-33) to activate it.**

   The Tool Options palette appears.

2. **Check the options palette for any adjustments you'd like to make to the size and shape of the Scratch Remover itself.**

3. **In the image, click and drag over the unwanted scratch.**

4. **When the Scratch Remover's shape encompasses the scratch, release the mouse.**

   The scratch is gone, a seamless duplication of surrounding content in its place.

Figure 2-33: Paint Shop Pro's Scratch Remover tool removes dust and scratches.

You can also use the tool to get rid of unwanted small content, such as an unruly cowlick sticking up on someone's head, a blemish on a face, a stain on a tablecloth, or whatever tiny imperfections you'd like to be rid of.

Finding it hard to decide which application is best? Don't make a decision — use two or more applications and work with them on a situational basis. I love Photoshop and Photoshop Elements and would consider either one a required program for anyone working with photos or just about any other types of images. However, I love Paint Shop Pro's Scratch Remover tool, and I use it instead of Photoshop's Healing Brush and Patch tools whenever I can. You might find yourself in the same boat — torn between two applications — but you needn't choose, especially if you're shopping in the under-$100 range!

Correction Tools

The word *correction* implies the presence of a mistake — something to be fixed. Photos, both those taken professionally and those captured by total amateurs, can be rife with color, lighting, and exposure problems. Whether your image was printed and then scanned or taken with a digital camera, it can suffer damage from poor storage, low-end equipment, or even inadequate previous attempts to clean up the image.

Whatever the source or cause of your photos' problems, you can find a comprehensive set of corrective tools in just about any image editing application. If you don't find them, move on and find an application that offers tools such as

✦ Color-correction tools that saturate and desaturate colors

✦ Brightness and contrast adjustment tools that add and remove light

✦ Red-eye removers

✦ General retouching tools that make quick, overall color, light, and exposure corrections in a single step

I admit that the number of corrective options can be confusing. However, like choosing the right blending or selection tool, choosing the right correction tool is done on a case-by-case basis. Don't underestimate the value of some reasoned trial-and-error editing!

Using the Sponge tool to add and remove color

Discussed briefly in Book V, Chapter 1, the Sponge tool, found in both Photoshop and Photoshop Elements, adds color (in Saturate mode) or removes color (in Desaturate mode), depending on how you set up the tool. There's a Sponge version of Paint Shop Pro's Retouch tool, too. Figure 2-34 shows how I used the Sponge tool to remove some — but not all — of a yellow cast in a bird's feathers.

To use the Sponge tool in Photoshop or Photoshop Elements, follow these steps:

1. Click the tool to activate it.

 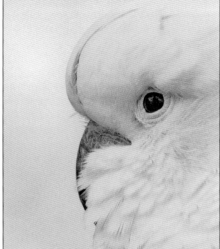

Figure 2-34: The Sponge tool removed most of the yellow cast seen at left, producing the image shown at right.

2. **On the tool's Options bar, choose Saturate or Desaturate mode.**

3. **Adjust the Flow, which controls how much saturation or desaturation occurs.**

4. **Choose the right brush size for the area to be sponged.**

A small brush might give you undesirable results when used in a large area, and a big brush can go too far. Choose a brush that allows you to fix the problem area with the fewest number of clicks or brush strokes.

5. **Apply the Sponge tool to the image, clicking and/or dragging to add or remove color where desired.**

Passing over the same spot more than once intensifies the sponge effect. You wash out or add more color on each successive pass.

Why would you want to take color away? Perhaps you added too much color in a previous editing session, and the edit can't be undone. Or maybe you simply want a subtler, more faded look to your image. New photos are often faded for a more vintage look or to prepare for the use of an artistic filter that makes the photo look like a drawing or painting.

Adjusting lights and darks

Although you can use dialog boxes galore to adjust the light levels in your photos, the tools on the toolbox/toolbar that allow you to paint light and shadows where they're needed are always a real timesaver. It's also much easier to control the amount of light or shadow you're applying and to control where you're applying it if you use a brush-based tool to apply it. You can set the brush to as large or small a size as you want, and you can zoom in and adjust single pixels or very small groups thereof as needed. You can also apply light and shadow to very large areas; by going over the same spot more than once, you can easily intensify the effect.

Dodging to add light

Photoshop and Photoshop Elements offer a Dodge tool, described briefly in Book V, Chapter 1, that allows you to add more light to any image simply by clicking and dragging the tool over the area needing more light, as shown in Figure 2-35. Many other image editing applications have the same tool. In the case of Paint Shop Pro, for example, the application offers a retouching tool that has dodging capability.

The term *dodge* is not specific to any software product; it's a photographic term for holding back the light that forms part of an image as a print is exposed onto photographic paper by an enlarger, lightening part of the image.

Figure 2-35: The Dodge tool lightens areas, such as the shadows under this scary ride.

To use the Dodge tool, follow these steps:

1. Click the tool to activate it.

2. Check the tool's Options bar and make any desired adjustments.

Your options are

- *Size:* The size of the brush that you use to dodge the image. Use a size that won't show the individual strokes but that isn't so large that it dodges an area larger than you intended.

- *Range:* Choose which tones the dodge will affect in the image — the Highlights, Midtones, or Shadows.

- *Exposure:* This percentage is set to 50% by default and allows you to control the intensity of the dodge effect. Lower numbers result in a subtler effect than higher numbers.

3. Click and drag over the area to be dodged.

If you feel that you need to confine the Dodge effect to a very specific area, you can select that area first, using a freeform selection tool, such as the Brush selector or the Lasso. That way, you don't end up with obvious blocks or circles of lightened image content.

You can go over areas more than once. Each pass heightens the dodge effect, so don't go overboard!

Burning to add depth and shadow

Burning is another photographic term, and its definition is the opposite of *dodging*. It involves adding extra exposure to part of an image while a print is exposed by an enlarger. That sounds contradictory, doesn't it? Adding more exposure time darkens the image? Note that image-forming light is held back — that's the key. The Burn tool reduces the amount of light, which deepens shadows and reduces the detail-killing light that can wash out parts of your image. Figure 2-36 shows an image in dire need of the Burn tool — if only to even out the very stark effects of the sun on specific parts of the road image.

Figure 2-36: The Burn tool darkened the road in this country scene.

Using the Burn tool in most image editors is very much like using the Dodge tool. Even though their effects are opposite, their functioning is nearly identical:

1. **Click the tool to activate it.**

2. **Adjust any desired settings on the tool's Options bar, including Size, Range, and Exposure.**

   These options have the same meanings as they do for the Dodge tool except that increasing exposure here increases the darkening effect. Your software might have different terms for these settings, but they do the same things.

3. **Click or drag over the area of the image to be darkened, being careful not to lose more detail by creating shadows that are too dark or too obvious.**

Living up to its name, overuse of the Burn tool can make your image look singed. If yours is a color photo or a black-and-white photo in RGB mode (which has more color information beyond simple shades of gray), the Burn tool can add a brownish tone, making the photo look as though it were exposed to high heat or flame. Unless you *want* your photo to look toasted, take it easy with the Burn tool.

Chapter 3: Choosing the Right Image Editor for You

In This Chapter

- Choosing an image editor that matches your needs and skills
- Comparing the capabilities of the popular image editors
- Using different image editors for different tasks

Choosing the right image editor is a lot like selecting the best digital camera for your needs. Like digital cameras, some editors have lots of bells and whistles that you really don't need and that can, in fact, get between you and easy access to the functions you really must use. Other image editors correspond to point-and-shoot digital cameras, with lots of automation that helps you avoid making decisions on your own. That's great when you're in a hurry, but not so helpful when you want to apply your creativity to an image.

In many ways, choosing your image editor corresponds to choosing a photographic lab to perform the physical and chemical processes required to generate prints from your exposed film. The lab technicians at your finisher routinely adjust exposure, color balance, and other details to improve the quality of your photographic prints. You place a lot of trust in their skills.

Today, you often end up making those adjustments yourself in an image editor, even if the final prints are still made at a digital lab at your retailer or via a walk-up printing kiosk instead of on your own printer. You want to have the same trust in your image editor and your capabilities that you had with a traditional photo lab, especially since you can't switch from one editor to another as easily as you can switch photo labs when you shoot film. When you choose an image editor, you're making a long-term commitment — unless you have the resources to buy and use multiple image editors.

In Book V, Chapter 1, I fill you in on the kinds of things that you can and can't do with image editing tools. In Book V, Chapter 2, I describe some of the basic features common to all image editors. In this chapter, I compare the features of some of the leading image editors and help you decide which is best for you.

 You can download free trial versions of most of these image editors from their corresponding Web sites. The trial versions are limited in some way — often the length of time you can use them, and sometimes they also have limits on their capabilities — but using them can help you choose the right image editor before you plunk down the big bucks for a full version.

Looking at Popular Image Editors: The Basics

No single image editor is right for every digital photographer. Different image editing programs offer different feature sets and take different approaches to manipulating digital images. The trick is to find the program (or programs) with the features and approach that most closely match your needs and working style. Image editing programs range in capabilities from extremely limited to impressively powerful. And you probably won't be surprised at the correspondingly wide range in price, from free or low-cost for programs with limited capabilities to several hundred dollars for high-end programs.

A simple image editor was probably included on the disc that came with your digital camera. Dozens of others are available on the shelves of local computer stores or as free downloads from the Internet. Like the one-hour photo lab, these programs are quick and easy to use for viewing your images and producing simple prints, but the capabilities are usually quite limited. Your search for an image editing program will undoubtedly extend beyond the simple view-and-print utilities and those already included with the Windows and Mac operating systems. However, wanting more capabilities than the low-end programs offer doesn't necessarily mean that you should go all the way to the other end of the spectrum. An assortment of midrange programs just might fit your needs very nicely.

The available image editing programs can be grouped into roughly four tiers:

✦ Adobe Photoshop stands alone at the top as the *de facto* standard for professional image editing. If you're working with images professionally, you need to own and use Photoshop. Although you might also find one of the other editors helpful for specialized tasks, Photoshop is your meal ticket.

✦ The second tier is composed of highly capable image editors. Although they might not match Photoshop's every feature, they have the power and versatility to meet the needs of many digital photographers. The image editors in this tier often include wizards and dialog boxes that automate common tasks, but the main focus is on direct access to the image with a variety of manual selection, retouching, and painting tools.

✦ The third tier of image editors sacrifices some of the raw power and versatility of the first- and second-tier programs in favor of dramatically improved ease of use. Most common image editing tasks are automated or made more accessible through the use of wizards and dialog boxes that walk you through the steps required to complete the task. The programs in this group might also have the ability to access your image for direct manipulation with retouching and painting tools, but the manual editing features are somewhat limited. The main emphasis is on the program's automated editing tasks.

✦ The fourth tier is composed primarily of the simple view-and-print utilities, although some of the programs also have some limited image editing capabilities. These programs often feature simple and attractive user interfaces with big graphical buttons for each task. They are very easy to use but offer only a very limited assortment of simple image editing options, such as cropping and overall color balance. Generally, these programs don't enable you to select and edit a portion of an image with manual retouching tools.

Because the purpose of this chapter is to give you a brief overview of some of the popular image editors and to assist you in identifying the program that might be right for you, I skip the bottom tier. These programs come and go and don't usually have the level of support needed for serious image editing. The focus in this chapter is on the other (top) three levels.

Adobe Photoshop — Alone at the Top

Adobe Photoshop, as shown in Figure 3-1, is the big kahuna of image editing programs. Available for both Windows and Mac OS, it is the industry standard by which all the other image editing programs are measured.

Over the years, Photoshop has earned a place in nearly every digital imaging professional's toolbox. The latest version only cemented that position. In fact, for many graphics professionals, Photoshop is the primary tool for everything from resampling image files and changing the file format to photographic retouching and image enhancement to creating original illustrations and artwork.

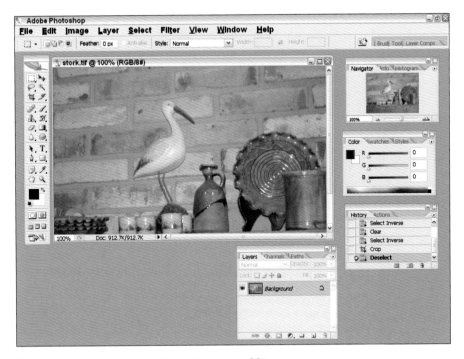

Figure 3-1: An image being edited in Photoshop CS2.

Photoshop is a professional-level tool, but you don't have to work at a major advertising agency, photography studio, or printing plant to use it. Even though buying a copy of Photoshop requires a significant investment of money and of time spent learning to use it, it's not beyond the reach of small businesses, serious digital photography hobbyists, artists, and others who need access to its powerful tools and advanced features. You'll need a computer powerful enough to run it, of course. You can find attractive upgrade offers from time to time that let you purchase a full copy of Photoshop for a fraction of its regular list price. When you own Photoshop, additional upgrades (as Adobe releases new versions) are relatively economical.

What's good about Photoshop

Photoshop didn't attain its stature as the leading high-end image editing program by accident. It has a well-deserved reputation for delivering a complete feature set. In short, this is one powerful program. No matter what you want to do with an image, odds are that Photoshop contains the tools to let you do it.

Photoshop can read, write, and manipulate all the industry-standard file formats, such as TIFF, JPEG, and, through its Adobe Camera RAW plug-in, the RAW formats that more advanced digital cameras produce. It also supports many not-so-standard formats as well. You can resample images to change the image size, resolution, and color depth. Photoshop excels at providing images that are optimized for specialized uses, such as commercial printing and Web graphics. Photoshop also enjoys close ties with several leading page-layout programs and Web-development programs (especially the other Adobe products, PageMaker and InDesign).

Photoshop provides a rich set of tools for everything from simple image manipulation (cropping and color balance adjustments, to name two) to selecting complex shapes from an image and applying sophisticated filters and effects to the selected area. Photoshop also includes a full set of painting tools that you can use to retouch your images or to create original artwork.

As if Photoshop's built-in features weren't complete enough, Adobe designed Photoshop to accept filters and other program extensions provided by third-party suppliers. As a result, a robust aftermarket has evolved to supply a wide assortment of plug-ins that make it quick and easy to apply all manner of textures, edge treatments, special effects, and other image manipulations to the images that you edit in Photoshop.

What's not so good about Photoshop

Photoshop is undeniably a powerful program, but you do pay a price for all that power: Photoshop is expensive. The price of admission for accessing Photoshop's power is a significant investment in money and learning time.

At a little over $600, Photoshop is expensive to purchase initially (later upgrades won't cost you as much). But the cost of the program doesn't stop there. If you're a serious Photoshop user, you probably want to add one or more plug-in packages, which each cost as much as a typical mid-level image editor. And then there are the inevitable upgrade costs when Adobe releases the next version of Photoshop with all its cool new features. The upgrade price for a new version of Photoshop is more than the full purchase price of most other image editors, but the cost is still reasonable when you consider what you're getting.

In addition to its monetary cost, Photoshop is also expensive in terms of the time that you need to invest in order to use it. The demands of learning to use this program are probably the most significant barrier for the casual user. Photoshop's power and versatility make it a complex program, and that complexity creates a steep learning curve. Getting started working with the program right out of the box can be challenging. Even after you learn the ropes, performing some simple tasks can sometimes be cumbersome in Photoshop. The program's breadth and depth make it difficult to master. Often, even the graphics pros who use Photoshop on a daily basis haven't explored all its many capabilities.

Photoshop is an ongoing commitment, too. It's not the sort of program that you can use once a month and pick up where you left off. It works best when used daily so that the commands and shortcuts become second nature. Attempt to use a special feature after not working with Photoshop for a month, and you'll probably find yourself diving into the (excellent) built-in Help system.

What you can do with Photoshop

What can you do with Photoshop? The short answer is, "Almost anything!"

In fact, it's difficult to come up with anything that you'd want to do to a digital image that can't be done in Photoshop unless it's outright impossible in the first place (such as transforming a total train wreck of a photo into a work of art). Oh sure, a few tasks are faster or easier to perform in some other programs. However, it's hard to find a visual effect that can't be duplicated in Photoshop if you're willing to invest the time and effort to get acquainted with the program's tools and to use those tools in innovative ways. Best of all, Photoshop has many features that are useful to those using digital cameras, including the ability to work with RAW camera files (the basic, unprocessed camera file with all the original information captured by the camera) for many popular models, facilities for matching colors between images taken under different lighting conditions, and a new feature for stitching panorama photos seamlessly. You'll find a description of Photoshop CS2 improvements in Book VI, Chapter 1.

Here's just one very simple example of an image enhancement that you can create with Photoshop. Suppose you don't like the flat, uninteresting sky in the picture shown in Figure 3-2. No problem — you can quickly add some better clouds by following these steps:

1. **Click the Magic Wand tool and then adjust its settings.**

   The Magic Wand tool is the second button down in the right column of the toolbox on the left side of the Photoshop window. You adjust the settings for the Magic Wand tool in the Options bar across the top of the Photoshop window. In this case, I used a tolerance setting of 50 and selected the Anti-Aliased and the Contiguous options. Those settings tell the Magic Wand to select only the pixels in the sky. (For more information on how the Magic Wand tool operates, see Book VI, Chapter 2.)

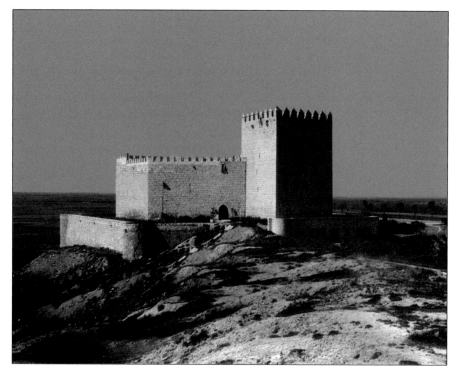

Figure 3-2: This image needs a more interesting sky.

2. **Click the sky with the Magic Wand tool.**

   Photoshop selects the sky for editing and marks the selection by surrounding it with a "marching ants" marquee.

3. **Open a file with better clouds and select the clouds by using the
   Marquee tool.**

4. **Copy the clouds by pressing Ctrl+C (or ⌘+C on the Mac) and then
   switch to the original castle image and press Shift+Ctrl/⌘+V to paste
   the image into the selection.**

   Figure 3-3 shows the finished image with clouds added to the sky.

Where to get Photoshop

Photoshop CS2 costs about $600 and is available from most computer stores,
catalogs, and online software outlets. For more details, or to purchase
directly from the manufacturer, go to www.adobe.com.

Figure 3-3: Clouds have been added to the image.

The Best of the Rest

Photoshop's chief competitors are a diverse lot. They all have the ability to edit and manipulate digital images, and they emphasize direct access to the image over wizards and other automation for editing tasks. They are all less expensive than Photoshop. However, that's where the uniformity ends.

Some of the programs in this group are niche products that excel at dealing with particular kinds of images, whereas others are general-purpose image editors with nearly as much versatility as Photoshop CS2. Each of the programs in this collection has its own set of strengths and weaknesses. Depending on your specific needs, the program that is a perfect fit for you might be unsuitable for another digital image maker.

Adobe Photoshop Elements

Photoshop Elements 4.0 is the little brother of the full Photoshop program and is available in similar, but not identical, versions for both Windows and Mac

OS. Adobe created Photoshop Elements (often shortened to just *Elements*) as a more accessible version of Photoshop for the numerous people who want to use Photoshop but don't need some of its more advanced features.

Photoshop Elements, as shown in Figure 3-4, shares much of the same user interface with its big brother, Photoshop, although in a revamped form because Elements 4.0 was introduced after Photoshop CS2. Compared with the full version of Photoshop, Elements has an abbreviated feature set, but it includes most of the basic image editing tools that the typical digital photographer needs on a regular basis. That includes image selection, retouching, and painting tools; a generous assortment of filters; and the ability to expand those filters by accepting the same Photoshop plug-ins as its sibling program.

Figure 3-4: Photoshop Elements 4.0 at work.

What's good about Elements

Photoshop Elements is competitively priced at about $100. Elements is considerably less powerful than its big brother, but by sacrificing some of the immense power of Photoshop, Adobe created a program that is significantly less complex and is therefore easier to use than Photoshop.

In general, Adobe did a pretty good job of selecting which Photoshop features to include in Elements. The program's feature set is a reasonably good match for the needs of the typical digital photographer. Most of Photoshop's standard selection, retouching, and painting tools are available in Elements. If your image editing needs revolve around retouching and manipulating individual pictures one at a time, you'll probably never notice the more advanced Photoshop features that are missing from Elements.

Rest assured, though, that Elements isn't just a slimmed-down version of Photoshop. The program includes a few interesting features that Photoshop lacks. For example, Elements features an un-Photoshop-like Palette bin (shown at the right in Figure 3-4) with quick access to features like How To, Styles and Effects, and Layers. You can also store palettes in more traditional Photoshop nested tab palettes, as you can see in the lower right in the figure.

The automated commands on the Enhance menu make quick work of common image editing tasks, such as adjusting backlighting or color cast. As a result, an occasional user working with Elements can complete those tasks faster and more accurately than a seasoned graphics pro working with Photoshop. You can find out more about color casts in Book IV, Chapter 1.

Elements also makes a good set of training wheels for Photoshop. After you master this program, you can use Photoshop much more easily than if you started with Photoshop from scratch.

What's not so good about Elements

The similarity of the Elements *user interface* (the arrangement of menus and floating palettes superimposed on the workspace containing multiple document windows) is a boon to Photoshop users and wannabes who might need to switch back and forth between the two programs. However, the Photoshop interface (and thus, to a large extent, the Elements interface) isn't known for its ease of use. Many newcomers to the program don't find the menu arrangements and other details to be very intuitive.

What you can do with Elements

One very nice feature of Elements is the broad array of automatic fixer commands, which can adjust color, contrast, lighting, or even all of these at once via the Smart Fix feature. (Elements also has an Auto Smart Fix command that does all these things automatically.) Follow these steps to apply the Auto Contrast command to an image you're editing in Photoshop Elements:

1. **Open the file containing the image you want to edit.**

   The image opens in the Elements workspace and is shown in the Photo Bin at the bottom of the window, as shown in Figure 3-5.

Figure 3-5: Changing the contrast of an image automatically.

2. Choose Enhance⇨Auto Contrast from the menu.

Elements examines your photo and applies the necessary contrast changes.

3. Save the enhanced file.

If your image looks muddy and unnatural after applying the Auto Contrast command, try applying the Enhance⇨Auto Levels command to restore a more natural tonal range.

Where to get Elements

Photoshop Elements 4.0 retails for about $100 and is available from most computer stores, software catalogs, and online software outlets. For more details or to purchase directly from the manufacturer, go to www.adobe.com.

Corel PhotoPaint

Corel PhotoPaint, one of three upscale image editing packages available from the graphics powerhouse Corel, is the image editing program that is included in the popular CorelDRAW Graphics suite. Various versions of this program are available for both Windows and Mac computers.

PhotoPaint, shown in Figure 3-6, is a full-featured photo retouching and image editing program. Although its feature set cannot match the full version of Photoshop, PhotoPaint stands solidly among the second group of products, delivering a large portion of Photoshop's functionality for a relatively small portion of that program's price. PhotoPaint is far more powerful and versatile than programs that stress ease of use.

Figure 3-6: Corel PhotoPaint comes with the CorelDRAW graphics suite.

PhotoPaint offers a full set of selection, retouching, and painting tools for manual image manipulations and also includes convenient automated commands for a few common tasks, such as red-eye removal. PhotoPaint also accepts Photoshop plug-ins to expand its assortment of filters and special effects.

New in Version X3 (13!) is the PhotoPaint Image Adjustment Lab, a one-click facility that lets you correct the color and tone of photos quickly and easily. By using the automatic correction control, you can fix most color and contrast problems. You can also manually remove color casts and adjust the brightness, contrast, highlights, shadows, and midtones of a photo. To help you choose the best photo-editing results, you can compare snapshots of a photo with different settings applied.

The "Cutout Lab" simplifies making selections, making it easier to isolate parts of your images. You can touch up your cutouts by adding and removing detail, and you can redo and undo actions if necessary. In addition, you can choose to keep both the cutout and the original image or to create a clip mask from the cutout.

What's good about PhotoPaint

Corel PhotoPaint is a respectable product as a stand-alone image editor. However, its greatest strength is its integration with CorelDRAW and the rest of the Corel graphics suite. If you use CorelDRAW to create and edit graphics, you probably have PhotoPaint installed on your computer, and you'll feel right at home using the product. All the menus, dialog boxes, and palettes behave just as you expect from your experience with DRAW.

What's not so good about PhotoPaint

Perhaps the worst thing about PhotoPaint is that it's available only as part of the CorelDRAW graphics suite. That's also one of the best things because the Corel Graphics applications are a powerful combination. At a $159 upgrade price for the downloadable version (it's a $179 upgrade if you want the retail package), the CorelDRAW graphics suite is a good value, provided that you need the main CorelDRAW program and any of the other components of the suite. However, that might be a lot to pay for PhotoPaint alone, especially because other image editors in this tier are available for around $100.

What you can do with PhotoPaint

You can do many of the things possible with Photoshop except for complex color separation tasks. It's an all-around good editor for the average user.

Where to get PhotoPaint

To get PhotoPaint, you need to purchase the CorelDRAW graphics suite for about $159 to $400, depending on whether you are upgrading or buying it as a stand-alone product. The suite includes the CorelDRAW graphics program, PhotoPaint, PowerTRACE (a bitmap-to-vector conversion utility), Corel CAPTURE (a screen capture utility), and an assortment of 1,000 fonts and 10,000 clip art images. The CorelDRAW graphics suite is available from the usual list of computer software suppliers. For more details, or to purchase directly from the manufacturer, go to www.corel.com.

Corel Paint Shop Pro

Corel Paint Shop Pro, shown in Figure 3-7, is one of the leading second-tier image editors. It's a general-purpose image editor for Windows only that has gained a reputation as the "poor man's Photoshop" for providing a substantial portion of Photoshop's capabilities at a fraction of the cost. The program lists for about $100, but you can often find it for sale at a substantial discount.

In recent years, however, Corel has stuffed in the features, going beyond achieving feature parity with Photoshop in many areas and exceeding Adobe's flagship product with specialized tools and effects. Indeed, the program has more than 500 special effects, counterparts to Photoshop's filters, that can add an amazing number of interesting looks to your photos, from the fading of an aged newspaper clipping to *faux* infrared transformations.

Figure 3-7: Paint Shop Pro has some features you won't find anywhere else, including more than 500 special effects filters.

Paint Shop Pro features a complete tool kit that includes selection, painting, and retouching tools for direct manipulation of your images. It also includes a sizable collection of wizard-like commands that automate common tasks, such as removing red-eye and scratches. Paint Shop Pro includes an incredible assortment of filters and effects, and you can expand that assortment by adding most any of the Photoshop plug-ins.

What's good about Paint Shop Pro

Paint Shop Pro has been around for a while, so the program has had time to evolve and mature. Over that time, it has developed a reasonably robust feature set and a refined user interface. Many people rate Paint Shop Pro as the easiest to use of the general-purpose image editors, and it's among the lowest priced programs in its class.

The latest version, Paint Shop Pro X, includes a friendly Learning Center that can show you how to edit your photos, remove objects from your photos, and assemble composite photos. If you just want your photo fixed, fast, Smart Photo Fix corrects color, exposure, and lighting problems. The new Makeover Tools remove blemishes, whiten teeth, lather on a suntan, remove wrinkles, and zap red eyes.

This version adds 16-bit editing — useful for those who have cameras that can produce files with expanded color palettes — advanced CMYK and color management, and screen calibrations options you might have needed Photoshop for in the past.

The program includes Corel's Photo Album 6 digital asset management program and Pixmantec RawShooter Essentials, a fully functional RAW converter that simplifies translating RAW files.

What's not so good about Paint Shop Pro

The breadth and depth of the Paint Shop Pro feature set is a little uneven. The program shows surprising depth in some areas (such as the availability of layers) and shallowness in others (such as the limited choice of selection and paint tools). Also, some tools (such as the Histogram Adjustment command) require more knowledge and experience to use effectively than do the corresponding tools in some of the other editors.

You need to evaluate the program carefully to determine whether its particular strengths and weaknesses are a good match for the mix of work you need to do.

What you can do with Paint Shop Pro

Paint Shop Pro includes a huge number of special effects filters. It also includes a useful little command that helps you select the filter you want to use. Here's how it works:

1. **Choose Effects⇨Effect Browser from the main menu.**

   The Effect Browser dialog box appears, as shown in Figure 3-7. The dialog box contains a list of effect filters on the left and thumbnail (small) previews on the right.

2. **Click an item in the Effects list to preview the effect.**

   When you click an item in the list, a short description of the effect appears, and a Sample Preview thumbnail for each effect shows an approximation of how the effect will look on your image. Continue trying different effects until you find one you like.

3. **Click Apply.**

   The Effect Browser dialog box disappears. This is the equivalent of choosing the corresponding effect from the Effects menu. If no settings are available for the selected effect, the effect is applied immediately, and you're done. Otherwise, the effect's dialog box appears.

4. **Adjust the settings in the effect-specific dialog box as needed.**

   Depending on the specific effect you selected, you might need to set options to control the intensity and other attributes of the effect.

5. **Click Apply.**

   The dialog box disappears, and Paint Shop Pro applies the effect to your image.

Where to get Paint Shop Pro

Paint Shop Pro started life as a shareware program but has since expanded its market presence and gone mainstream. As a result, now that Corel has taken it over from Jasc, it now sports the slick packaging and complete documentation that most people expect from a commercial software product. You can buy the boxed version of Paint Shop Pro at all the usual computer software outlets. You can also order the product from the Corel Web site at www.corel.com.

Corel Painter

If PhotoPaint and Paint Shop Pro don't suit you, Corel has a third image editing program for you to consider. Surprisingly, there is very little overlap among Corel's three image editing options. Painter, available for Windows and Mac computers, is a unique image-editing program. In fact, the term *image editor* is a bit of a misnomer for Painter. It's more of a program for creating original images than it is an editor for images from your digital camera.

Painter IX.5, shown in Figure 3-8, specializes in re-creating in digital form a wide range of traditional artist media, such as charcoal, pastels, and various kinds of paint. Painter includes a basic assortment of tools that you can use to edit existing images, but the program is really designed for artists to use to create original illustrations.

Figure 3-8: An image being edited in Painter, with only a few of the scores of different palettes visible.

What's good about Painter

Painter's natural media effects are really impressive. Although other programs allow you to select different paintbrush tools and adjust their color, size, edge softness, and a few other attributes, Painter takes the concept of brush effects to a whole new level.

In Painter, you can define not only the characteristics of the brush but also the texture of the paper or canvas; the thickness of the paint on the brush; and how the paint, brush, and paper interact. As a result, the program can realistically simulate the very different effects of a watercolor wash on hot-press paper, oil on canvas, pastels on a sanded board, or any of a huge assortment of other media/material combinations. Painter comes with a large inventory of predefined brushes and art materials that you can use or modify to suit your artistic impulse. With the right settings, you can even watch the digital paint drip and run.

Note: A pressure-sensitive graphics tablet and pen is an essential tool for using a program like Painter. The pen gives you much better control of the cursor than a mouse does, and the pressure-sensitive tip adds a new dimension to your digital brush strokes. A graphics tablet makes any image editor easier to use, and you can't use Painter effectively without one. Expect to pay $50 to $150 and up for one of these.

What's not so good about Painter

Painter can be confusing and difficult to work with at first. It has a bewildering array of different palettes filled with options that allow you to exercise precise control over each brush stroke. Just figuring out where everything is can be a challenge, and working your way through the various options each time you want to do something can be tedious. After you gain experience with the program, it becomes easier to use, but learning to use Painter effectively takes no small amount of time and commitment. This isn't a program that lends itself to occasional, casual use.

Painter's image editing capabilities are more attuned to the needs of an artist who wants to incorporate a portion of an existing image in a new composite composition — not so much for routine image enhancements and corrections. If you're looking for a digital darkroom where you can crop, color correct, and repair your digital photographs before printing, you need to look elsewhere.

Painter is second only to the full version of Photoshop as the most expensive product in this roundup of image editors. Its price tag (about $199 for an upgrade, $399 if you want a full boxed version) is not unreasonable if you really need its specialized natural media brush effects, but its high price puts Painter beyond the reach of most hobbyists equipping a typical digital darkroom. Few people can afford to buy Painter for casual experimentation.

What you can do with Painter

Painter is designed for digital artists to use when creating illustrations from scratch. However, you don't always have to start every image with a blank canvas. Painter can also apply its rich assortment of paper textures to an existing image. Here's how:

1. **Select the paper texture that you want to use by expanding the Papers menu in the Art Materials palette and then clicking a paper sample.**

2. **Choose Effects➪Surface Control➪Apply Surface Texture from the main menu.**

   The Apply Surface Texture dialog box appears, as shown in Figure 3-9.

3. **Adjust the settings in the dialog box as needed.**

   Drag the various sliders to change the settings. You can exercise precise control over the depth and character of the texture, how the light strikes and defines the texture, and how the texture is applied to the image. As you adjust the settings, the Preview box shows a sample of how the settings affect your image.

4. **Click OK.**

   The Apply Surface Texture dialog box disappears, and Painter displays a progress box as it applies the texture to your image. After a moment, your newly textured image appears.

Figure 3-9: You can apply surface textures to your electronic canvases with Painter.

Where to get Painter

Like most of the other programs in this roundup, Painter IX.5 is a commercial software product that is available through the normal purchasing channels. It's a bit of a specialized product, so you might need to go to a larger software dealer or one that specializes in graphics products. The suggested retail price is close to $400. A time-limited free trial version of the program is available for download. For more information on Painter, including how to get the free trial download, visit `www.corel.com`.

Macromedia Fireworks

It's hard to predict what will happen to Fireworks, the image editing program from Macromedia, which Adobe acquired along with the market-leading Web development software (Dreamweaver) and Web animation software (Flash). Fireworks has been available as either a separate, standalone program or bundled with Dreamweaver, Flash, and Freehand (a drawing program) in the Studio MX package, and it runs on both Windows and Mac machines. Now that Fireworks has joined the Adobe fold, its days as a separate program may be limited.

I hope it remains available, because Fireworks, shown in Figure 3-10, has all the features it needs to handle most any routine image editing chore and is especially adept at producing images for the Web. The basic selection, retouching, painting, text, and drawing tools are all present and accounted for, and the program supports layers and Photoshop plug-ins to expand its basic filters. However, Fireworks doesn't try to be the most versatile general-purpose image editor on the market. Instead, the program excels in the more specialized job of preparing images for use on the Web.

What's good about Fireworks

Fireworks really shines at two kinds of Web-related activities:

+ **Creating Web graphics, such as banners, image maps, and rollover buttons:** Fireworks provides an excellent set of tools for working with text and shapes, and the program can automatically generate the HTML and JavaScript code needed for rollover effects and image maps.

+ **Optimizing images for use on the Web:** The Preview tab of each document window in Fireworks allows you to instantly preview different image optimization settings while you edit your image. The Image Optimization dialog box pulls all the various file format, color depth, size, and resolution settings together into one place where you can experiment with various settings and observe their effect on file size and image quality.

Figure 3-10: An image being edited in Fireworks.

Fireworks is bound in a symbiotic relationship with Dreamweaver. Although each product works independently, using them together can dramatically streamline the usual process of optimizing images for a Web page under development. For example, if you're building a Web page in Dreamweaver and need to optimize an image on that page, all it takes is a couple of mouse clicks to open the image in Fireworks' Image Optimizer dialog box. With a few more mouse clicks, you can optimize and save the image and then return to Dreamweaver, where the newly optimized image appears automatically on the Web page being edited. You have to see this feature in operation to appreciate just how slick it is and how much time it saves.

What's not so good about Fireworks

Fireworks' concentration on creating and optimizing images for the Web leaves it a bit weak in some other areas. For example, although the basic image editing tools are present in Fireworks, the selection of retouching and painting tools isn't as comprehensive as you might find in some of the other image editing programs.

The list of file formats available for import and export is also somewhat restricted. All the major file formats (such as TIFF, JPG, and GIF) are represented, as well as Fireworks' native PNG format and a number of others, but the list of supported file formats is less than half as long as its counterparts in some other image editors.

What you can do with Fireworks

One of key features of Fireworks is its ability to optimize images for the Web. Here's an example of that feature at work:

1. **Choose File⇨Export Preview from the main menu.**

   The Export Preview dialog box appears. On the right side of the dialog box is the preview pane that shows how your image will look when saved with the current settings. If necessary, adjust the zoom setting (the drop-down box showing a percentage at the bottom of the screen) to adjust the size of the preview image. Drag on the preview image to bring different portions of the image into view.

2. **Adjust the settings in the Options tab.**

   Select the file format, quality, smoothing, and other settings as needed. Depending on the file format that you choose, the other setting boxes change to reflect the options that are available for that file format.

3. **Experiment with different settings as needed.**

   Adjust the settings and note the effect on the preview image and on the file size and download speed display above the preview box. If necessary, adjust the image size settings on the File tab as well. Keep trying different settings on the Options tab until you achieve the smallest file size that still retains acceptable image quality.

4. **Click the Export button.**

   The Export Preview dialog box disappears, and Fireworks exports your image to a file using the settings that you selected.

Where to get Fireworks

Fireworks has been available from all the normal suppliers for less than $300 and is still being sold by Adobe at that price as Fireworks 8. For details about Fireworks (under whatever name Adobe will be calling it by the time this book is published) and the other Macromedia programs, go to www.macromedia.com.

Ulead PhotoImpact

Ulead PhotoImpact, shown in Figure 3-11, is a general-purpose, Windows-only photo editing program with a particularly robust feature set. In fact, PhotoImpact is arguably second only to Photoshop in the overall scope of its features, although Paint Shop Pro is virtually neck-and-neck.

In addition to the usual selection, cropping, and fill tools, PhotoImpact features a rich assortment of brushes for painting, retouching, and cloning. You'll also find tools for text and vector shapes as well as tools for creating slices and image maps for use on the Web. PhotoImpact supports layers and includes a generous collection of effects filters, which you can expand with Photoshop plug-ins. Auto-process commands are available to automate many of the most common image correction and enhancement tasks.

Figure 3-11: PhotoImpact is almost as versatile as Photoshop, for a lot less money.

What's good about PhotoImpact

PhotoImpact is one of the most powerful and versatile of image editors, and yet it's modestly priced at less than $100. This combination of high capability and low price makes PhotoImpact an excellent value.

If you frequently find yourself performing the same image manipulations on a number of files, you'll appreciate PhotoImpact's batch operations. With this feature, you can select multiple image files and then apply any one of a long list of filters, enhancements, or auto-process commands to all the selected files. What a timesaver!

PhotoImpact also includes some specialized features for creating Web graphics. The program includes wizards to help you create Web backgrounds, banners, and buttons, and its image-optimization features are especially strong. Although PhotoImpact's Web graphics features aren't quite as slick as those in Fireworks, they're quite good.

What's not so good about PhotoImpact

PhotoImpact's user interface can be a bit quirky and inconsistent in places. Some of PhotoImpact's features, although effective and very useful, feel like they are the result of grafting separate modules onto the program instead of seamlessly integrating the features into the program. Overall, the PhotoImpact user interface is not as polished as Photoshop, Fireworks, or PhotoPaint. To be fair, however, after you get past the program's quirks and idiosyncrasies, you'll find that PhotoImpact is a very capable, Windows-only image editor.

What you can do with PhotoImpact

PhotoImpact is a versatile image editor, capable of most any image manipulation you might want to do. Picking just one example to show here is difficult.

PhotoImpact comes with a generous assortment of effect filters, and playing around with the filters is lots of fun. Here's an example of a filter that gives an image the look of an oil painting:

1. **Open an image that might make a good painting.**

2. **Choose Effect⇨Artistic⇨Oil Paint from the main menu.**

   The Oil Paint dialog box appears, as shown in Figure 3-12. The Dual View tab shows two thumbnails: your original image on the left and a preview of the effect on the right.

3. **Drag the sliders to adjust the Stroke Detail and Level.**

   Adjust the sliders as needed to achieve the desired effect. You can also use the spin boxes to the right of each slider if you want to make more precise adjustments.

4. **Click OK.**

   The Oil Paint dialog box disappears as PhotoImpact applies the effect to your image.

Figure 3-12: The Oil Paint dialog box.

Where to get PhotoImpact

PhotoImpact is available from many of the same software dealers that carry most of the other programs in this chapter. The suggested retail price is about $90. You can also order PhotoImpact directly from the Ulead Web site at www.ulead.com. The site also offers a time-limited free trial version that you can download.

Microsoft Digital Image

Microsoft's image editing software doesn't get the attention that the big-name Microsoft programs like Microsoft Office get. Despite the Microsoft name, these Windows-only programs aren't the dominant programs in their class. However, all are respected players in the field, and you might find that one of the company's three tiered offerings can work for you

The three programs are Microsoft Digital Image Standard, Digital Image Suite, and Digital Image Suite Plus, ranging in price from $34.99 to about $99 (see Figure 3-13). Each of the upscale editions piles on more goodies that can be useful for digital camera owners.

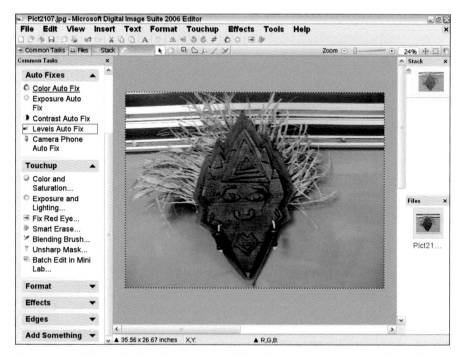

Figure 3-13: Microsoft offers three versions of its Digital Image program — all priced less than $100.

The entry-level version, which forms the basis for all three editions, is a simple program that makes accessing your images easy (whether they are in your camera or scanner or stored on your hard drive) and then lets you edit and print those images with a minimum of fuss. The image editing capabilities are limited when compared with some of the more advanced editors, but they cover the basics. You can perform tasks such as cropping, rotating, adjusting brightness or color balance, and fixing red-eye and scratches. It also includes a modest collection of effect filters and edge treatments that you can apply to your images. The program even includes some basic painting tools as well as tools for adding text and shapes to your images.

Microsoft's imaging software comes in several variations. The key difference among them is the number of artistic design templates and photos. Digital Image Standard comes with 1,500 designer templates and 2,400 photos, versus 3,000 templates and 5,000 photos in the Digital Image Suite and Digital Image Suite Plus. The two advanced editions add more filters (200-plus instead of 10 for the low-end version) and retouching tools, including flash and backlight corrections; dodge and burn tools; and the ability to adjust shadow, midtone, and highlight levels independently. Digital Image Suite/Plus also accepts Photoshop plug-ins for even more filter effects and has a total of 3,000 templates.

What's good about Microsoft image editors

Like most Microsoft products, the Digital Image Standard, Suite, and Suite Plus products have a slick-looking user interface that is well thought out and easy to use. Microsoft can afford to invest time and money in focus groups and usability testing — and it shows.

These editors also have the ability to select several image files and apply the same adjustment to all the selected files at once. This ability isn't unique to the Microsoft editors, but it's unusual in image editors at this level.

What's not so good about Microsoft Digital Image editors

The added features of the Digital Image Suite versions are an obvious attempt to give the program capabilities comparable to some of the more full-featured image editors. In my opinion, the attempt falls short. However, you might find that Digital Image Suite gives you just enough capability to handle your occasional image editing tasks without needing a more advanced editor.

What you can do with Microsoft Digital Image editors

Programs in this collection excel at quick fixes. Here's an example of making a couple of quick adjustments in Digital Image Suite to an image that needs color correction:

1. **Open a photo that you want to correct.**

2. **Click the Levels AutoFix button in the left toolbar (see Figure 3-13).**

   Digital Image Suite automatically adjusts brightness and contrast to achieve a full tonal range of blacks, whites, and all the tones in between.

3. **Click the Color Auto Fix button in the left toolbar.**

   The program displays the Color and Saturation panel on the left side of the program window.

4. **Click the Eyedropper icon and then click an area of the picture that should be gray.**

   Digital Image Suite automatically adjusts the color settings as needed to render the selected area as gray. If the image still doesn't look right, you can try clicking another gray spot or adjusting the Color Balance sliders manually.

5. Click the Done button at the bottom of the Color and Saturation panel.

The Adjust Tint panel disappears, and the program returns to the normal display with the changes applied to your image.

Where to get Microsoft image editors

All three Digital Image programs are available in many retail software stores and online outlets. You can also order the program direct from Microsoft. For more information, go to www.microsoft.com/products/imaging.

Roxio PhotoSuite

Roxio PhotoSuite, another Windows-only program, is perhaps the best known of the basic image editors. (***Note:*** Roxio PhotoSuite was formerly known as MGI PhotoSuite.) It's inexpensive (less than $50) and easy to use. At this writing, Roxio is selling PhotoSuite 7 for $29.95. I recommend spending a few dollars more for Easy Media Creator 8, which includes a later version of the program plus utilities for burning CDs and DVDs to boot.

PhotoSuite's opening screen is uncluttered and features big, graphical icons with lots of interactive feedback. This approach is in stark contrast to the multiple toolbars and floating panels that fight for the user's attention in most of the first-tier and second-tier image editors.

Despite PhotoSuite's apparent simplicity, it offers a reasonably good assortment of image editing tools for this level of image editor. You'll find basic versions of the standard selection, paint, clone, erase, and fill tools, plus an effect brush and tools for drawing simple shapes (but not text). And, of course, you can crop and rotate the image, remove scratches and red-eye, and touch up the brightness and color balance, among other things.

PhotoSuite, shown in Figure 3-14, also includes tools to help you organize and distribute your pictures. You can gather a set of pictures together into an album and then share an individual picture or an entire album on the Web, show them as a slide show, or send them via e-mail. You can even install your pictures as wallpaper on your Windows desktop or display an album of pictures as a screen saver.

What's good about PhotoSuite

PhotoSuite's strength is its ease of use. The uncluttered user interface keeps the screen simple and clean. A permanent panel on the left side of the screen contains either buttons that enable you to select a procedure or detailed instructions that walk you through the procedure step-by-step.

Figure 3-14: Roxio PhotoSuite is great for image editing neophytes.

The built-in projects make it easy to create greeting cards, calendars, report covers, and many other items that incorporate your pictures into the design. This is a nice bonus that enables you to use your pictures in fun and interesting ways without needing another program to do so.

What's not so good about PhotoSuite

The almost stark simplicity of the user interface means that most of the available tools and options are hidden from view at any given time. You often have to drill down through several layers of options to reach a specific tool or to apply an effect. The program's constant hand-holding is helpful for newcomers, but after you learn the ropes, you might find yourself getting impatient and wishing that you could jump straight to the desired effect with fewer intermediate prompts and clicks.

What you can do with PhotoSuite

Starting with one of PhotoSuite's project templates, you can create a pretend magazine cover containing a digital image from your collection. Just follow these steps:

1. **Open the image that you want to use for the cover and perform any needed enhancements and touch-ups.**

2. **Click the Compose button in the top toolbar.**

   A dialog box appears so you can select a new project.

3. **Click the Fun Stuff button in the Create New Project panel and then click the Magazine Covers button.**

4. **Select a category from the drop-down list, click the cover template of your choice, and then click Next.**

   PhotoSuite displays the magazine cover template, ready to receive your image.

5. **Drag the thumbnail for your image from the Library panel and drop it onto the template; then click Next.**

   PhotoSuite inserts the image into the template and automatically sizes it to fit. If your image wasn't already available in the Library panel on the right side of the PhotoSuite window, you could have used the buttons in the Magazine Covers panel on the left to open an image from your computer, camera, or scanner.

6. **Adjust the size and position of the image in the template (if needed) and then click Finish.**

   Your project is done and ready to print.

Where to get PhotoSuite

Roxio PhotoSuite is available from most software retailers. You can also order it from the Roxio Web site at www.roxio.com.

Apple iPhoto

Although it has very limited editing capabilities, Macintosh owners will want a copy of iPhoto, which started life free, migrated to become part of the iLife suite, and now works smoothly and intuitively (if you're running Mac OS X) and does a lot more than just edit pictures. In fact, iPhoto's strengths are in importing pictures from your digital cameras, organizing and albuming your photos into Photo Libraries, creating prints, and even sending pictures by e-mail.

You can touch up photos by rotating, cropping, removing red-eye, converting to black-and-white or sepia, and performing a few other fine-tuning steps. Apple finally added brightness and contrast controls, which had been lacking in earlier versions, to iPhoto. Figure 3-15 shows an iPhoto album open and ready for use.

Figure 3-15: Import, sort, and make minor edits to your photos with iPhoto for Mac OS X.

Deciding Whether You Need More Than One Image Editor

Sometimes one is just not enough.

Obviously, every image editing program doesn't have the same feature set as every other image editor. Some editing tasks, such as cropping a picture, are common to all the editors, but many other features are available in some editors and not in others. Not even Photoshop includes every available image editing feature.

If you evaluate your image editing needs thoroughly and inspect the features of the available editors carefully, you might be able to find one editor that has just the right mix of features to match your needs. If you're fortunate, you'll find an editor that has all the features you need, and whatever features are missing from that editor are in areas that you don't care about. It could happen (especially if your image editing needs are modest), but don't count on it.

A much more likely scenario is that you find one editor that fulfills most of your image editing needs. Then you need to find a second (or third) editor to handle the editing tasks that your main editor just can't manage.

You might also find that an image editor doesn't perform all editing tasks equally well. A specific editing task might be easier to perform in one editor but more cumbersome in another. If your main editor is a little awkward to use for some tasks that you do frequently, it might be worthwhile to keep another editor around that can handle those tasks with aplomb.

The following list summarizes some common situations in which multiple image editors are called for:

✦ **Artists:** Artists who use Corel Painter for its ability to create images with natural media effects often use another image editor (usually Photoshop) to further manipulate those images and prepare them for publication and other uses.

✦ **Web developers:** Fireworks is a favorite of Web developers who build pages in Macromedia Dreamweaver MX because of the close interaction between those programs. Although Fireworks MX is great for optimizing Web images and creating Web graphics, those users frequently turn to another image editor to retouch photographic images.

✦ **Photoshop users:** Serious Photoshop users often keep one or more other image editors around to take advantage of a particular feature that is available only in the other editor. Basically, the other editor serves as an auxiliary utility program.

✦ **Digital photographers:** Many digital photographers have Photoshop or one of the higher-end, second-tier image editors for serious work but find it easier to use one of the simpler programs to access images from their camera and make quick adjustments and prints.

Instead of investing the big bucks in Photoshop, some digital photographers find that they can get all the features and capabilities they need with a combination of two or three other less expensive image editors.

Book VI

Editing with Photoshop and Photoshop Elements

The 5th Wave   By Rich Tennant

SINCE INSTALLING PHOTOSHOP, THE 4th PRECINCT BECAME NOTED FOR ITS CREATIVE WANTED POSTERS

"Ooo-look! Sgt. Rodriguez has the felon's head floating in a teacup!"

*N*ow that you've gotten your image-editing feet wet, I show you more of what you need to know with two of the most popular image editing programs, Adobe Photoshop CS2 and Adobe Photoshop Elements. As I demonstrate, Photoshop isn't just for professionals anymore, and Elements now has enough tools to appeal to dedicated photography enthusiasts. In the six chapters of this minibook, I reveal the power of selections, the best ways to brush away problems, techniques for correcting faded or weird colors, and how to achieve special looks using the Adobe editors' built-in filters.

If you want to enhance your photos, I show you how to "heal" photographic wounds, replace unwanted content with other images, and adjust light and shadows to give your pictures extra snap.

Chapter 1: Latest Features of Photoshop CS2 and Photoshop Elements 4.0

In This Chapter

✓ **Photoshop and Photoshop Elements together**

✓ **New features in Photoshop CS2**

✓ **New features in Elements 4.0**

When I wrote the first edition of this book, the state of the art in high-end image editors was Adobe Photoshop 7. For powerful but easy-to-use entry-level image editors, Photoshop Elements 2.0 was the way to go. Within an impressively short period, however, both were replaced (twice) with newer, better, and more powerful editions with lots of extra features and improvements. For this book's third edition, the amazing advancements in digital cameras in the past few months were only half the battle. I also had to take into account the changes made for Photoshop CS2 and Photoshop Elements 4.0. (Alas, it's also likely that new versions of each program will be available during the life of this book.)

Some of the changes and improvements were small, but some were fairly Earth-shaking. If you were familiar with either of these image editors before (or are still using the older versions), you'll want to review this chapter to see what's new and different. You just might glean enough to prompt an upgrade to the latest release — or, if you're already working with Photoshop CS2 or Elements 4.0, you might discover some changes you didn't even know about.

The Relationship between Photoshop and Photoshop Elements

As most Photoshopoholics know, Photoshop and Elements share many of the same underpinnings and programming code. Indeed, in some respects,

Elements can be considered a version of Photoshop with some capabilities missing or disabled. Their interfaces, dialog boxes, and many features are virtually the same. They use the same filters and also have tool palettes that are quite similar.

However, the differences are not quite simple enough to allow Elements to qualify as a "watered down" version of Photoshop. Development on each of these applications is ongoing and staggered, with releases scheduled at roughly 18-month intervals.

The relationship between the two programs becomes even more complex when you consider that Photoshop includes some features that will *never* show up in Elements, and vice versa. Users of Elements probably don't need the ability to work with 16-bit channels or CMYK (cyan, magenta, yellow, black) files, and Photoshop workers wouldn't deign to use some of the quick fixes found in Elements. You can expect Photoshop and Elements to continue to converge and diverge, as appropriate, with features crossing from one application to the other during their overlapping development cycles.

What's New in Photoshop CS2

Photoshop CS2 has some new features that weren't available in its predecessors. Here's a quick listing of the most important changes for photographers:

+ **Bridge:** The old Adobe File Browser has been revamped into a new standalone product called Adobe Bridge, shown in Figure 1-1, which works with all Adobe applications, including Photoshop, Illustrator, InDesign, GoLive, and Acrobat.

+ **Vanishing Point:** This is a 3-D filter that lets you paint, add, or remove objects while retaining their perspective.

+ **Spot Healing Brush:** This tool popped up in Elements 3.0 first, and it was too good to withhold from Photoshop users. It speeds touching up photos by eliminating the need to sample pixels to use as a cover-up; it automatically samples the surrounding pixels as you click with it.

+ **Red Eye Tool:** The Red Eye Removal Tool from Elements was added to Photoshop and renamed the Red Eye Tool. Just click red eyes and watch the red vanish.

+ **New Layers palette:** The way the Layers Palette operates has been changed, most significantly in the use of Shift-click and Ctrl/⌘-click to choose multiple layers.

+ **Box, Shape, and Surface Blur filters** have been added.

Figure 1-1: Bridge is a new file browser shared among all Adobe applications.

✦ **Info palette:** This palette now includes additional information, new settings, and tips for using the current tool.

✦ **Lens Correction filter:** This new filter, shown in Figure 1-2, fixes barrel and pincushion distortion and corrects for other lens defects, such as fringing.

✦ **Reduce Noise filter:** Now you have a choice of reducing noise in your camera, zapping the noise when converting RAW files, or using this new filter in Photoshop.

✦ **Smart Sharpen filter:** More sophisticated than the Unsharp Mask filter, this new sharpening tool reduces the noise that inevitably results from sharpening up your image.

What's New in Elements 4.0

The biggest news about Photoshop Elements 4.0 is that it's finally available for the Macintosh. In a departure from its previous practice, Adobe upgraded Windows users from Version 3.0 to 4.0 without introducing a similar enhanced package for the Mac. Some months later, a version for the Macintosh became available.

Figure 1-2: The Lens Correction Filter fixes many kinds of lens distortion.

Mac owners shouldn't have worried because there aren't too many significant new features in the latest version of Elements. Here are the key upgrades:

✦ **Magic Selection Brush:** Just paint around the object you want to select, and Elements tries to isolate the object as a selection for you.

✦ **Magic Extractor:** This tool lets you paint around an object to select it and remove it from its background.

✦ **Skin Tone Adjustment:** Choose an area of skin in a photo, and Elements uses that area's characteristics to adjust the balance of the other colors in an image.

✦ **Straighten tool:** This tool is useful for aligning a crooked scan. Just draw a line across the image to indicate a horizontal or vertical line, and Elements will reorient the photo to match.

✦ **WYSIWYG (what you see is what you get) font menu:** Elements gets Photoshop's new font-display menu.

✦ **Red-Eye Removal on Import:** Elements 4.0 can automatically remove red-eye from your photos when you bring them into the program.

Chapter 2: Making Selections

In This Chapter

✓ **Making rectangular and elliptical selections**

✓ **Selecting single-pixel columns and rows**

✓ **Creating freeform selections**

✓ **Making polygonal selections**

✓ **Selecting image content based on colors in the image**

A wag once noted that "Time is what keeps everything from happening at once." In a similar vein, *selections* are what let you modify only part of an image without your changes slopping over into parts of a picture that you *don't* want to manipulate. Selections let you fine-tune your photos a little at a time, making it easier to get the effects that you want.

Creating selections of the parts of the image that you intend to modify is the key to successful image manipulation. Indeed, the first step in many editing procedures is to focus the software's attention on the stuff you want to edit — an area that needs to be lighter, darker, a different color, or removed altogether. For this purpose, Photoshop and Photoshop Elements both offer a series of specialized tools that let you select geometric shapes, rows and columns of pixels, freeform shapes, and polygons. You can also find tools for making selections based on colors and pixel comparisons. The selection tool that you choose is based on the kind of area you want to select and the nature of the image itself. There are no hard and fast rules for when to use a particular tool over another; experience and experimentation show you which ones work best for different situations.

Making Simple Selections with the Marquee Tools

Photoshop has four tools that all go by the moniker *Marquee:* the Rectangular Marquee tool (for rectangles and squares), the Elliptical

Marquee tool (for ovals and circles), the Single Row Marquee tool (to choose only one line of pixels), and the Single Column Marquee tool (to select a column that's one pixel wide).

The Marquee tools in Photoshop and Photoshop Elements are very simple to use. For example, you can drag the Rectangular or Elliptical Marquee tool to select a rectangle or oval. Hold down the Shift key to select perfect squares and circles. Photoshop's Marquee tools are shown in Figure 2-1. You can select the Marquee tools by clicking them in the Tool palette or by pressing Shift+M repeatedly until the Marquee tool that you want is highlighted in the Tool palette.

Photoshop Elements offers the same two basic shape selection tools as Photoshop — the Rectangular and Elliptical Marquees — but does not offer the Single Row or Single Column options. Figure 2-2 shows a rectangular selection in progress in Photoshop Elements.

Figure 2-1: Click the shape you want to select and then drag to make the selection.

Selecting geometric shapes

When you're ready to make your geometric selection, the procedure is quite simple. It requires only that you first select the layer that contains the area you want to edit. Then, you're ready to make the selection by following these steps:

1. **Click the Marquee selection tool in the Tool palette and choose the shape (Rectangular or Oval) that you want to use.**

2. **Move your mouse onto the image and click where you want the selection to begin.**

3. **Drag away from the starting point until the marquee outlines the selection you want to make.**

   If you want a perfect square or circle, press and hold the Shift key while you drag; release the mouse and then the Shift key when the selection is complete.

When you use the Shift key to make a perfectly square or circular selection (equal in width and height), be sure to release the mouse before releasing the Shift key when your selection is complete. If you release the key first, the selection will snap to the size and shape it would have been had you not used the Shift key at all.

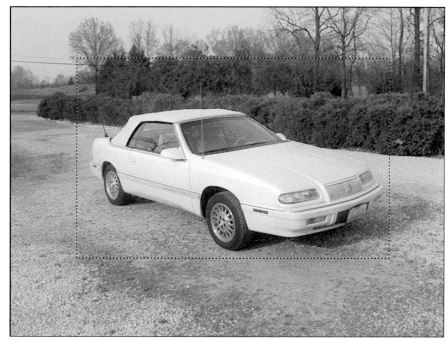

Figure 2-2: Click and drag diagonally to make the selection.

Both the Rectangular and Elliptical Marquee tools allow you to choose from different Style settings. Your choices are Normal, Fixed Aspect Ratio (Constrained Aspect Ratio on the Mac), and Fixed Size. If you choose either of the latter two, additional options appear on the tool's Options bar, through which you can enter the ratio or dimensions, respectively. If you use the Normal style, these options are dimmed.

Selecting single-pixel rows and columns

Photoshop's Single Row Marquee and Single Column Marquee tools allow you to select a row or column that's one pixel wide simply by clicking the image to make the selection.

After you make the selection, you can delete it, paint it, fill it, cut it, or copy it. You can use these Marquee tools to draw grids on the image, as shown in Figure 2-3, by filling selections with a solid color. These tools are also useful for creating a perfectly straight line anywhere on the image, going either up and down or left to right. If you want a soft edge to the selection, you can use the Options bar to set a Feather (fading) amount in excess of the default 0 pixels.

Figure 2-3: Use the single-pixel Marquees to draw grids on your image.

Adding to, reducing, and combining selections

The Marquee tools' Options bar (the Photoshop version is shown in Figure 2-4) offers four icons that you can click to customize your selections. You can find these same tools, with the same powers, in the Options bars for the Lasso and the Magic Wand tools, as well. The buttons are descriptively named, and it's quite clear what they do:

- ✦ **New Selection:** Creates an entirely new selection

- ✦ **Add to Selection:** Adds more area to an existing selection

- ✦ **Subtract from Selection:** Removes part of a selection

- ✦ **Intersect with Selection:** Creates a selection from only the overlapping area of two selections

Each button represents a selection mode and controls whether you can add to, take away from, or create a new selection based on the overlapping areas within two concurrent selections. If you're in New Selection mode, each time you click and drag the mouse, a new Marquee selection is created, replacing any other selections currently in place. If you switch to Add to Selection mode, you can select noncontiguous areas on the image, or you can make your current selection larger. Figure 2-5 shows both a set of noncontiguous selections (lower right), and a selection that was created by selecting three overlapping rectangles (upper left).

New selection

Subtract from selection

Intersect with selection

Add to selection

Figure 2-4: Choose one of the icons to create a new selection, or to add, subtract, or intersect with that selection.

Selection created
from overlapping selections

Two contiguous selections

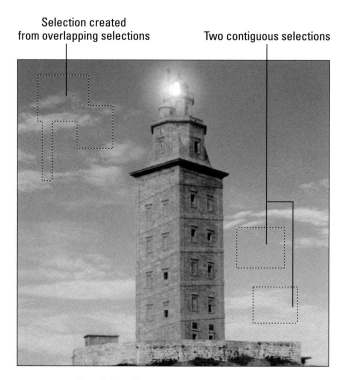

Figure 2-5: Use Add to Selection to create multiple selections or to extend a selection.

The Subtract from Selection mode lets you cut away from an existing selection or deselect noncontiguous parts of an initial selection. For Figure 2-6, I originally created a rectangular selection that went all around the tower; I tightened the selection by subtracting rectangular sections from the lower half of the original selection.

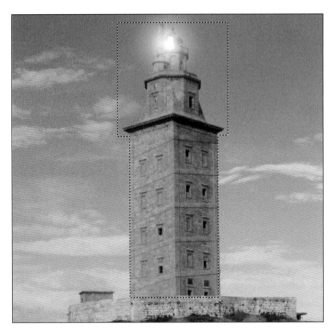

Figure 2-6: The original selection around the tower was trimmed by subtracting rectangular sections from it.

Using the Intersect with Selection mode allows you to create new selection shapes, such as the semicircular selection shown on the far right of Figure 2-7. This semicircle selection was formed from the overlapping areas of a circle and a rectangle. You can also move from one mode to another as you build or tear down selections.

Figure 2-7: The left and middle selections produce the selection shown on the right when intersected.

Snagging Irregular Shapes with the Lasso Tools

The Lasso tool, available in both Photoshop and Photoshop Elements, is a freehand selection tool. You can use the regular Lasso tool to draw freeform shapes that become selections, or use the Polygonal Lasso tool to select polygons by dragging around an object with straight lines.

You can also select by drawing with the Magnetic Lasso tool. In this case, you guide the cursor around an object, and the software selects pixels by comparing them with adjoining pixels and then chooses the ones that are different on the basis of color and light. In all its incarnations, the Lasso is a pretty powerful selection tool — probably the one I use most when retouching photos. A Lasso tool selection is shown in Figure 2-8.

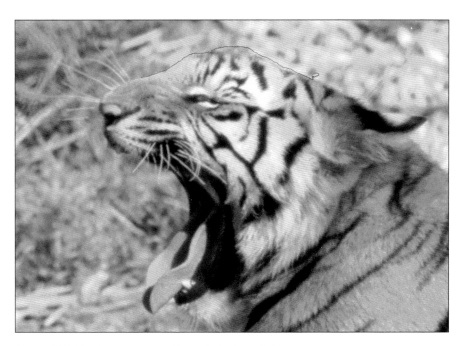

Figure 2-8: The Lasso can select irregularly shaped objects.

Selecting freeform shapes

The main Lasso tool is extremely easy to use. Just click and drag, drawing a loop around the section of your image you want to select.

The other important thing to remember is to *close* your selection by coming back to the starting point. This prevents the software from guessing how you'd like the shape to finish, which usually results in some of the intended selection (the tiger's head) being omitted, as shown in Figure 2-9. If you don't close the shape, Photoshop and Elements do it for you by connecting the start and end points with a straight line.

Figure 2-9: Don't let Photoshop or Elements close the selection for you.

The Lasso Options bar offers a Feather setting, which allows you to add a number of fuzzy pixels to the selection's edges. This gives any fills applied to the selection a softer edge. Obviously, the higher the Feather setting, the softer the edge. A higher Feather setting also extends your fill or other edits, such as filter effects, farther beyond the actual selection.

You might remember from geometry class that a *polygon* is any shape made up of three or more straight sides. Triangles are polygons, as are squares, rectangles, and octagons. The Marquee tool takes care of rectangles and squares, but what if you want to select a triangular shape, or a shape that looks like a big sunburst, or an irregular shape? You use the Polygonal Lasso tool, shown in Figure 2-10. From simple shapes to complex, many-sided stars, the Polygonal Lasso tool gives you freeform selections with the precision of straight sides and sharp corners.

Figure 2-10: Using the Polygonal Lasso tool.

The tool works easily enough, and you can make it select just about any size or shape on your image by following these steps:

1. **Make sure that the layer you want to edit is the active layer; use the Layers palette to choose the layer.**

2. **Click the Polygonal Lasso tool in the Tool palette to activate it.**

3. **Click the point in your image where you want to begin making the selection.**

4. **Click the point where you want to create the first corner.**

   This creates the first side, and you can now draw the next side.

   Don't drag the mouse; just click where you want the corners to appear.

5. **Continue clicking until you've drawn all the sides that your selection needs.**

6. **Come back to the starting point and click (double-click if you're using a Mac) to close the shape and create the selection.**

You can make your sides as small as you want (just a few pixels long) or as long as you want. You can select the edges of complex shapes by drawing many short sides. You might find this handy when there isn't enough color difference between pixels to use the Magnetic Lasso tool effectively.

Selecting magnetically

If you want to select a particular object, and that object is a different color or shade than the objects touching it, use the Magnetic Lasso tool to select it. The Magnetic Lasso tool works by following the edges of content in your image, comparing pixels while you drag your mouse, and automatically snapping to the edges where pixel values vary enough, based on your settings for the tool's options. Use the Magnetic Lasso's Options bar to control the Magnetic Lasso tool's sensitivity, detail, and the number of pixels it compares while you move along your desired path. Pen Pressure (or Stylus Pressure in some versions of Photoshop) might be dimmed unless you are using an accessory drawing device.

Before using the Magnetic Lasso tool, you can adjust the following settings in the Options bar:

✦ **Width:** Sets how far from the mouse path (as you drag) the pixel comparisons will be made.

✦ **Edge Contrast:** Set the sensitivity anywhere from 1% to 100%. The higher the percentage you set, the higher the contrast must be between compared pixels before the Magnetic Lasso tool snaps to pixels to build the selection.

✦ **Frequency:** Changes the number of fastening points (or nodes) that you see along the line, as shown in Figure 2-11.

Figure 2-11: The more fastening points you specify, the closer the selection will adhere to the object you're selecting.

To use the Magnetic Lasso tool, you follow a procedure that's similar to the one you use for the Lasso and the Polygonal Lasso tools, with minor variations:

1. **Make sure that the right layer is selected so that your selection applies to the right content.**

2. **Click the Magnetic Lasso tool in the Tool palette to select it.**

3. **Make any necessary changes to the tool's settings so that it will work to the best of its ability within the photo at hand.**

You can adjust the width of the Magnetic Lasso tool's attraction, how many points it lays down, and the amount of contrast that must be present for the attraction to take hold. The default values work best in most situations.

4. **Click the image to begin your selection.**

5. **Move the cursor and click along the edge of the desired object.**

A click redirects the line whenever it begins to veer off the path you'd like it to follow.

6. **When your moving and clicking takes you back to the starting point, click (or double-click) the starting point to finish the selection.**

Clicking to redirect the Magnetic Lasso's path is especially helpful if you get to a section of the photo where there isn't very much difference between the color and brightness of the pixels and the object you're trying to select. Sometimes, the Edge Contrast setting won't help you, and you have to redirect the selection yourself or use the other Lasso tools to augment or reduce the selection after using the Magnetic Lasso tool to make the main selection.

Has your Magnetic Lasso gone crazy, and you can't bring it back into line by clicking and moving? Press the Esc (Escape) key to abandon the current selection and start over.

The Magic Wand Tool's Digital Prestidigitation

The Magic Wand tool selects based on color. If you want to select all the flesh tones on a face or all the green leaves on a tree, you need only turn on this tool and click somewhere on the face or on a particular leaf, and the rest of the face or tree that matches the brightness level and color of that original pixel is selected. You can adjust how the tool works by increasing or decreasing the Tolerance level required for a match, which increases or decreases the number of pixels that are selected when you click the mouse in the image. The higher the Tolerance level you set, the wider the range of pixels included in the selection.

and the Art History Brush tool (which does the same thing but adds a brush stroke effect) are beyond the scope of this book. You can find an entire chapter on using these two tools and related implements in *Photoshop CS2 All-in-One Desk Reference For Dummies,* by Barbara Obermeier (Wiley). You can find more about the Impressionist Brush tool (which paints using artsy brush strokes) in *Photoshop Elements 4 For Dummies,* by Barbara Obermeier and Ted Padova (Wiley).

Table 3-1	Painting Tools by Application	
Tool	*Photoshop*	*Photoshop Elements*
Brush tool	✓	✓
Impressionist Brush tool		✓
History Brush tool	✓	
Art History Brush tool	✓	
Pencil tool	✓	✓
Airbrush tool	✓	✓

However, all the controls for setting the size, fuzziness, and other parameters of the Brush tool *do* apply to other brush-like tools, such as the Art History Brush tool, the Blur/Sharpen tools, the Toning tools (Dodge/Burn/Sponge), and the Clone Stamp. Thus, what you read in this chapter can be applied to those tools as well.

Some people consider the Smudge tool as a painting tool because it can be set to apply the foreground color if you put it in Finger Painting mode and also because it does manipulate colors in the same way a brush or your fingertip would if you were working with real paints or pastels. On the other hand, I think it's more of a retouching and special effects tool. I show you the basics of the Smudge tool in Book VI, Chapter 4.

Working with Brushes and Pencils

Photoshop's and Photoshop Elements' brushes and pencils are easy to use and customize and can apply a wide variety of colors, textures, and special effects. Painting and drawing with Photoshop or Elements mostly requires a steady hand and the proper view so that you're zoomed in close enough to see what you're doing. Figure 3-1 shows an extremely magnified view of a portion of an image, with the Brush tool at work filling in some rough spots in an old photo.

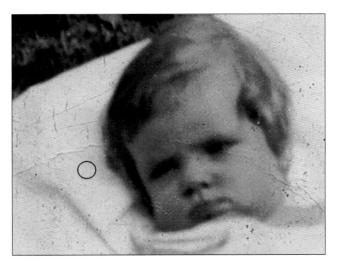

Figure 3-1: You can paint out scratches, stains, or dust spots if you zoom in tight enough.

You can also paint larger areas, filling in space lost to a tear or to add a colored frame around an image. You can even create new content: Just paint lines or shapes or simply apply a wash of color to a black-and-white or faded color photo for an interesting effect. Whatever your painting or drawing goal, these two applications offer the right tools for the job.

Painting with the Brush tool

The Brush tool, found in both Photoshop and Photoshop Elements, can paint tiny dots, short strokes, or longer lines as small as a single pixel in width or as large as several hundred pixels. Using the tool is easy. Just click it on the Tool palette (or press B on the keyboard) to activate it, and drag or click (or both) on the image. You want to make sure that you're painting on the appropriate layer first, of course.

If you want to control how the brush applies paint, you can change the following settings before you start painting:

✦ **Color:** The color or tone painted by the brush

✦ **Size:** The size of the brush. Note that in Elements 4.0, you can set the size directly from a slider in the Options bar.

✦ **Mode:** How the pixels painted by the brush blend with existing pixels

✦ **Opacity:** The transparency of the pixels

✦ **Flow:** How quickly the pixels are applied while you stroke

✦ **Airbrush:** Changes any brush tool to a fuzzy airbrush effect

With the exception of color, you can adjust all these settings from the tool's Options bar, shown in Figure 3-2. If you're using Photoshop, you can tinker with several more settings (and a few more for Elements users, too), but I get to those in the upcoming section, "Customizing Your Brushes and Pencils." The settings listed here are those that you'd want to adjust whenever you're painting. More elaborate changes would be needed in fewer, more specific cases.

Figure 3-2: The Brush Options bars for Elements 4.0 (top) and Photoshop CS2 (bottom).

One setting — Color — can't be set from the Options bar but can be set through the Color Picker. You open the Color Picker by clicking the toolbar's Set Foreground Color button, shown at left in Figure 3-3. From within the Color Picker (shown at right in Figure 3-3), you can choose a color in three ways:

✦ **By eye:** Click in an area that contains the color you want to choose.

✦ **By setting color levels:** Type values in the H, S, and B (hue, saturation, and brightness) or the R, G, and B (red, green, blue) boxes.

Figure 3-3: Click the Foreground Color button (bottom left) to access the Color Picker (right).

◆ **By using a hexadecimal number:** Enter this number in the # field to create colors in the language of your Web browser.

Select the Only Web Colors check box if you want the Color Picker to show only the 240 colors considered completely Web-safe. (With virtually all users having monitors that can show more than 256 colors, "Web-safe" colors are not the concern they once were.)

If you want to paint with a color currently in use elsewhere in the image or in another open image, click the toolbar's Eye Dropper tool and sample (click) the color that you want to use. This makes that color the new foreground color.

Working with the Pencil tool

The Pencil tool is also found in both applications and works much like the Brush tool. The only real difference is the nature of the line drawn. Just like you'd expect a paintbrush to apply a relatively soft line, you'd expect a pencil to draw a sharper line, depending on the hardness of the lead. The Pencil tool works just as you'd expect and also offers its own set of adjustments through the Options bar in Elements, as shown in Figure 3-4. (The Photoshop CS2 version is similar.) From the Options bar, you can control the Pencil's size and density so that you can make whatever large or small edits are required.

Figure 3-4: The Pencil Options bar in Elements 4.0.

Use the Pencil tool's settings to control the size, mode, and opacity of the line you draw. You can also choose from a smaller set of styles, most of which are solid, fine lines. The Options bar also has an Auto Erase option, which allows you to draw the background color over any pixels currently colored in the foreground color as well as apply the foreground color only where no color is currently applied. Auto Erase is sort of a confusing name because no real erasing occurs — but you get the idea.

Customizing Your Brushes and Pencils

Beyond the basic adjustments that you can make with the Brush and the Pencil tools' Options bars, you can work with an additional set of options in Photoshop Elements (see Figure 3-5) or with a set of Brush Presets (shown in the Photoshop interface in Figure 3-6).

The Photoshop CS2 Brushes palette consists of 11 different options, each of which has its own dialog box. To view each of the 11 sets of options, make sure Expanded View is selected in the Brush Palette's fly-out menu (that right-pointing triangle at the upper right of the palette). Then, selecting any of the 11 sets of options causes that option's dialog box to appear. Make the changes you want in each option's dialog box. You can activate or deactivate any particular option by marking the check box to the left of the option name. Figure 3-7 shows the settings for the Texture option.

Figure 3-5: Elements offers extensive brush controls.

Refer to the preview area at the foot of the Brushes palette to see how your new settings affect the brush size and shape that you select. The sample stroke provided shows you what effect the brush will have when you apply it to your photo.

If your Brushes palette is missing, simply choose Window⇨Brushes from the main menu to bring it back. You can also place it on the docking well (next to the File Browser) or drag it to the workspace to move it freely like the rest of the palettes.

Figure 3-6: Photoshop has an entire palette devoted solely to brushes.

Figure 3-7: Need to clean up a vintage photo's matte finish? Use a textured brush and customize the texture here.

Choosing the right size and shape

Whether you're working in Photoshop or Elements, the success of your brush with a given image depends on setting the right size and shape for it.

Photoshop Elements brush settings

Photoshop Elements offers a list of Brush Presets in the form of a drop-down list, as shown in Figure 3-8, accompanied by a separate Size setting and the More Options button.

Figure 3-8: Photoshop Elements' Brush presets provide an extensive set of styles and shapes.

To change the shape of your brush in Photoshop Elements, follow these steps:

1. **Click the Brush tool on the Tool palette to activate it.**

2. **From the Options bar, set the style and size of the brush by using the drop-down list and slider, respectively.**

3. **Click the brush next to More Options on the Options bar.**

4. **In the resulting dialog box, adjust the angle by entering a number for the angle you want to use or by dragging the arrow clockwise or counterclockwise, as shown in Figure 3-9.**

Figure 3-9: Drag the brush schematic's arrow to change the angle of the brush tip.

You might find that a specific angle is more desirable for painting the kind of strokes you want, and you can use this setting to set that angle.

5. **Adjust the Roundness setting the same way — by entering a number or by dragging the big black dots closer to or farther away from the center of the sample brush shape, as shown in Figure 3-10.**

Dragging inward makes for a horizontally flatter brush; dragging outward makes the brush vertically flatter.

6. **Tinker, as desired, with other sliders — Spacing, Hue Jitter, Hardness, and Scatter.**

7. **Click your image to begin painting or click somewhere on the workspace to close the More Options box.**

Figure 3-10: Make a soft, round, fat brush or a lean, mean, flat brush.

Photoshop brush settings

If you're using Photoshop, you can change your brush shape by using the Brush Tip Shape option of the Brushes palette, as shown in Figure 3-11. The resulting settings look very much like Elements' settings. You can drag a brush tip schematic to change the angle and roundness of the tip, and you can also adjust the size (diameter) of the tip itself.

Here's a quick summary of all the customization changes you can make to Photoshop's brushes:

+ **Brush tip shape:** Here, you can select the size and shape of the brush tip, including its diameter, angle, roundness, hardness, and spacing.

+ **Shape dynamics:** Make your brush strokes appear to be more natural and less machine-like

Figure 3-11: Control your Photoshop CS2 brush and its shape, size, and roundness setting.

(especially if you're using a digital tablet) with these adjustments. They modify the degree of randomness or variation produced when a stroke is drawn, including the amount of fade, size, jitter angle, roundness, and other options. The higher the value, the greater the amount of variance produced for each option. Note that some of these options apply only when you are using a pressure-sensitive digital tablet.

✦ **Scattering:** Use this control to vary the amount and position of individual brush marks in a stroke. The higher the value, the larger the number of brush marks and the farther apart they are. When Both Axes is selected, the brush marks are distributed radially, as if on a curve. The Count controls the number of brush marks at each spacing point. The higher the value, the greater the number of marks.

✦ **Texture:** The Texture control lets you add a preset or custom pattern to a brush stroke. It includes these options:

- *Invert:* Mark the Invert check box to reverse the light and dark pixels in the pattern.

- *Scale:* The Scale control adjusts the size of the pattern in each stroke.

- *Texture Each Tip:* Texture Each Tip applies each tip as it is stroked, giving a more saturated effect.

- *Depth:* The Depth control sets how prominently the pattern appears against the brush stroke.

- *Minimum Depth:* Minimum Depth specifies the minimum depth that the paint of each stroke shows through the pattern.

- *Mode:* Mode lets you choose one of Photoshop's blending modes.

✦ **Dual Brush:** Yes! You can have a brush with two tips. The second tip can have attributes of its own, which you can set here. You can also specify a blending mode between the two tips so that the strokes they draw merge together in a predetermined way.

✦ **Color Dynamics:** You can also create a multicolored brush with this control. It uses your foreground and background colors to generate variations that give the stroke a more natural, organic look. You can introduce jitter to the hue, saturation, brightness, and purity of the colors as well as some randomness between the foreground and background colors as a stroke is drawn.

✦ **Other Dynamics:** These controls add some natural-looking randomness to the opacity and flow factors of a brush, again making the brush stroke look more natural and less machine-like.

Here are some tip characteristics that you can modify:

✦ **Noise:** This adds random pixels to your brush tips, giving them texture, which works especially well with feathered brushes that fade out at the edges.

✦ **Wet Edges:** This option creates a stroke that looks like watercolor, with color that builds up along the edges.

✦ **Airbrush:** This option gives the brush tip a fuzzy, airbrushed look.

✦ **Smoothing:** Use this control to help smooth out curves when drawing arcs with the brush, which is especially helpful with a pressure-sensitive tablet.

✦ **Protect Texture:** If you want all your textured brush tips to use a uniform texture, apply this option.

Obtaining third-party brush sets

The brush sets that come with Photoshop and Photoshop Elements are fairly extensive (see Photoshop's in the Brush drop-down list options menu, shown in Figure 3-12), but you might pine for more of them.

A quick online search will net you several sites where third-party brush sets are available, usually for a small fee. Some sites probably offer brushes for free, but these are not in abundance. One site to check out is www.graphicxtras.com/products/psbrush.htm. This particular site is chock-full of interesting new brushes, which you can order for about $30 (U.S.). The site, which is based out of Great Britain, charges in pounds sterling, so the day's exchange rate dictates what you pay.

Figure 3-12: Lots of brushes come with Photoshop CS2, but you might want more, more, more!

Chapter 4: Restoring Images

In This Chapter

- ✏ **Shedding light and casting shadows**
- ✏ **Blending and bringing focus to your images**
- ✏ **Healing wounded photos**

*A*dobe's image editing applications do a great job of fixing problem images. Some of the most common problems that you'll encounter with your photos (both old and new) relate to lighting, clarity, detail, and damage caused by poor storage methods. Even a vintage black-and-white or sepia photo, if properly stored, won't show unacceptable signs of age. Any photo, however, that is tossed in a drawer or put in a frame and exposed to direct sunlight for years will start to look a bit shabby and will probably lose much of its detail and depth.

A color photo will lose some color due to fading. It might also have scratches and scuffs, as shown in Figure 4-1, which displays a photo with several problems that require Photoshop's or Elements' restorative tools. I show you how to repair this photo in this chapter.

Because digital images saved on a hard drive or removable media don't suffer from the same ailments as photographic prints, negatives, and slides, your restoration work will invariably involve scanned versions of these originals. This chapter focuses primarily on repairing scratches, stains, dust, and lightness/darkness problems in old monochrome images, but the techniques apply equally well to color photos with the same problems. It's just a little easier to concentrate on lightening, darkening, and repairing photos when color isn't a major concern. I show you how to work with color photo restorations in Book VI, Chapter 5.

Figure 4-1: You can paint out scratches, stains, or dust spots if you zoom in tight enough.

Adding Light and Shadows

Whether because of fading with time or from poor original photographic technique, many of your photos might need more light or more shadows — or more of both — in different areas of the same photo. What to do? Photoshop and Photoshop Elements' Dodge and Burn tools rush to the rescue!

Using the Dodge tool to lighten tones

The Dodge tool lightens portions of your image. The process is simple:

1. **Click the Dodge tool in the Tool palette to activate it.**

   You might need to switch to the Dodge tool if the Burn or Sponge tool is currently displayed on that button in the Tool palette. Hold down the Shift key and press O until the tool that you want is active.

   Multiple tools that are nested under a single icon are indicated by a triangle in the lower-right corner of the icon on the Tool palette.

2. **Check out the Options bar, shown in Figure 4-2, and decide whether you need to make changes to the range of tones that will be affected or to the exposure (degree of intensity) that the tool will apply.**

   The Range drop-down menu determines which tones the Dodge tool affects: Shadows (the dark areas), Highlights (the light areas), or Midtones (everything in between). Most of the time, you want to stick to Midtones, but if you want to open up some inky shadows or darken areas that are a little washed out, you can do that, too.

The Exposure menu determines how rapidly the lightening process occurs. Avoid lightening too much, too quickly. A value between 15 and 35 percent enables you to lighten slowly. You can always return to an area and lighten it some more if you haven't applied enough dodging.

Figure 4-2: The Dodge tool's Options bar in Elements; Photoshop's Options bar is similar.

3. **Using the Options bar, set the size of the brush that you'll use to apply the light.**

   You can choose the kind of brush you use just as you would the ordinary Brush tool. Both use the exact same Brush palette. You can find more on setting brush sizes in Book VI, Chapter 3.

4. **Drag over the area to be lightened or click a single spot, such as a face or some other distinct area that's suffering from too much shadow.**

Figure 4-3 shows the woman's face before and after dodging.

Figure 4-3: Use the Dodge tool to lighten shadows in faces.

If your image isn't very crisp or detailed and you have no desire to make it that way, use one of the textured brush settings for the Dodge tool. This can apply light in a dappled or mottled way, matching the image's overall look — perhaps a desirable one, in the case of vintage photos.

Burning your image to darken areas

The opposite of the Dodge tool, the Burn tool darkens areas. This can bring out facial features lost to a sunny day or faded details in clothing or a garden, or it can add depth lost to a photo that has faded with time or exposure to sunlight.

To use the Burn tool in either Photoshop or Elements, follow these simple steps:

1. **Click the Burn tool in the Tool palette to activate it.**

   The Burn tool might be hidden under the Sponge or Dodge tool; they all share the same position on the toolbox. Hold down the Shift key and press O until the Burn tool is active.

2. **Check the Options bar (as shown in Figure 4-4) for any adjustments you'd like to make.**

   You can adjust the range and exposure, which respectively control which elements of the image (Shadows, Midtones, or Highlights) are affected by the Burning process and how quickly the darkening process takes place.

Figure 4-4: The Burn tool's Options bar.

3. **Choose a Brush size in the Brush palette.**

4. **Begin darkening your image by dragging over the areas to be made more shadowy or by clicking a single spot.**

   Figure 4-5 shows a face being darkened by a single click with a brush that's set to the same diameter as the face.

Don't go too far with the Burn tool. If your image is in color, excessive use of the tool creates a brownish, singed look that makes the image appear literally burned. If your image is in black-and-white or grayscale, this won't happen; the worst that can occur is that your burned areas look so dark that details are obliterated.

Figure 4-5: Paint with the Burn tool to darken an area.

Using Smudging, Sharpening, and Blurring Tools

When it comes to retouching photos with Photoshop and Photoshop Elements, you'll probably use the Sharpen and Blur tools quite frequently. These tools are good for heightening or diffusing details in some of an image, an entire image, or along the edges of content that's been pasted into the picture from elsewhere. The Smudge tool is also a powerful ally, but you might find that good mouse skills are required before you can make really successful use of it. Figure 4-6 shows these three tools in Photoshop Elements. As in Photoshop, the tools share one button, and you must switch between them by holding down the Shift key and pressing R until the icon for the tool that you want appears. This isn't an operational hardship, but it makes identifying them in one image here rather difficult!

Figure 4-6: The Blur, Sharpen, and Smudge tools in Photoshop Elements.

Although the Sharpen tool's name clearly indicates what it does, the Blur and Smudge tool names might lead you to believe that the tools essentially do the same thing. In reality, however, the Blur tool is a more finely grained tool than the Smudge tool is in terms of its results. Whether applied to a small area or painted over a large field, the Blur tool's effects are uniform: It makes the affected area fuzzy and less distinct. (Technically speaking, the Blur tool reduces the contrast between the pixels, and our eyes see this reduced contrast as blur.) The Smudge tool smears the pixels into each other, and its effects are entirely dependent on the length and direction of your mouse or pen strokes.

What the three tools do have in common is how highly dependent they are upon their Options bar settings — or rather, how much *you* are dependent on the settings. Without controlling how drastic or subtle an effect these tools have, you might end up with very little blurring or too much sharpening — or perhaps some smudging that makes it look like you were drunk when you tried to retouch the photo. Figure 4-7 shows an image in which the Sharpen tool was taken a bit too far; instead of adding contrast between pixels (to make them all stand out just a bit), the result is a very unpleasant effect — definitely not what you want.

Figure 4-7: A little goes a long way with the Sharpen tool. Take care as you set up how the tool works.

Finger painting to blend colors and textures

You use the Smudge tool to drag tone from one spot to another spot right next to it. Think of it like blending pastels or chalk on paper with your finger. The smudging process can smooth an edge, blend two adjoining colors, or smoosh out a background, as shown in Figure 4-8. You can also turn on a Finger Painting option and bring the current foreground color into the mix, smearing it into the image at whatever point you're dragging the mouse.

Figure 4-8: Blend a background or soften sharp edges with the Smudge tool.

To use the Smudge tool, follow these steps:

1. **Click the Smudge tool in the Tool palette to activate it.**

   This displays the Options bar, shown in Figure 4-9.

Figure 4-9: Control the effects of the Smudge tool.

2. **Using the Options bar, change the setting in the Strength drop-down menu to make the smudging more dramatic (a high percentage) or subtle (a low percentage).**

3. **If you'd also like the Smudge tool to adjust the lights, darks, tones, and colors of the area that's smudged, choose an appropriate setting in the Mode drop-down menu.**

   The Mode setting controls how the original pixels and smudged pixels are blended together. Your options are as follows:

   - *Normal:* No change to the quality of the colors or tones where you smudge. They just get smudged.

   - *Darken:* In addition to smudging, a Burn tool effect is applied.

   - *Lighten:* In addition to smudging, a Dodge tool effect is applied.

   - *Hue:* Smudges only the hue or color of one area onto another, dragging the tone from your starting point onto another adjoining area of the image.

   - *Saturation:* By smudging with this setting in place, you're smudging the color intensity instead of the image content.

   - *Color:* Smudge color (both hue and saturation) from one area to another without distorting the physical content.

   - *Luminosity:* This mode smudges the brightness of your starting point onto the adjoining areas through which you drag the Smudge tool.

The last four mode options allow you to adjust the color and quality of the color as you smudge. I recommend that you tinker with the area using other color- and hue-adjustment tools first and then smudge in Normal mode.

4. **Set the Brush size by using the Brush palette, just like you set all other Photoshop brush-like tools.**

5. **Click and drag to smudge the image.**

   You pull color from the starting point onto the ending point.

Don't use the Smudge tool to smudge large areas of your image unless you're going for a really smudgy background, as in the case of Figure 4-8. In most other instances, although you can use a large brush size and make a big smudge, you'll regret it because you'll end up distorting the image instead of blending areas within it. For the best results with most images, use a small brush and use it in small areas.

Using the Sharpen tool to add detail

The Sharpen tool heightens the contrast between adjacent pixels so that each of the pixels stands out more. This can help you improve the apparent detail in a blurry or faded photo. Small features, textures, and the like can be brought out by making the pixels in and around them more diverse.

In versions 1.0 and 2.0 of Elements, the Sharpen tool lived all by itself on its own button on the Tool palette, but from Version 3.0 to the latest version 4.0, it shares a button with the Blur and Smudge tools just like in Photoshop. In either case, the tool has the same options (see Figure 4-10) and works the same way.

Figure 4-10: Using the Sharpen tool in Photoshop.

To sharpen some of or the entire image, follow these steps:

1. **To control the area in which the sharpening will take place, use a selection tool — Marquee, Lasso, or Magic Wand — from the Tool palette to select an area within the photo.**

2. **Click the Sharpen tool to activate it.**

3. **Use the Brush palette to adjust the brush size and whether you want a hard-edged or soft-edged brush.**

   A smaller brush enables you to sharpen a very specific area, whereas a larger brush heightens pixel diversity in a wider area, with more generalized results.

4. **Reduce or increase the intensity of the sharpening effect by adjusting the Strength setting from its default of 50%.**

   Be careful not to sharpen too much, or you'll end up with pixels that are so bright and diverse that detail can actually be lost.

5. **From the Mode drop-down menu, choose the mode setting that you want for the Sharpen tool.**

   The mode setting controls how the pixels are blended. The modes are the same as those for the Smudge tool — described in the preceding section's steps list — and include Color, Hue, Saturation, or Luminosity. Normal mode is good for most jobs.

6. **Click and/or drag over the area to be sharpened.**

   You can go over the same spot more than once, but again, don't go too far. Figure 4-11 shows both effective (left side of face) and ineffective sharpening (right side of face). Subtle effects are usually preferable.

Book VI
Chapter 4

Restoring Images

Figure 4-11: At left, the unsharpened version. At right, the left side of the face has been sharpened effectively, but the right side of the face has been sharpened too much.

Sharpen and Blur filters are available through the Filter menu in both Photoshop and Photoshop Elements, and you can achieve more uniform results with them than with the brush-applied Sharpen and Blur tools because the mouse is removed from the equation. The filter is applied evenly over the selected area or the entire active layer of the image. You can read more about filters in Book VI, Chapter 6.

Blurring some or all of your image

The Blur tool is the Sharpen tool's opposite. Instead of increasing the diversity between adjoining pixels, the pixels are made more similar (reducing the contrast), with their color and light levels adjusted so that no individual pixels stand out too much. Obviously, you can blur a lot or blur a little: The degree to which the tool is applied determines how much contrast is removed from the pixels that you brush over with the Blur tool.

Blurring can be used as a quick-and-dirty substitute for cloning over unwanted pixels. Figure 4-12 shows at left a scan of an old photograph that was folded and wrinkled along the bottom edges. I could have used the Clone Stamp to copy pixels over the wrinkles, but because this area of the subject would look better if de-emphasized anyway, blurring the lower-left and lower-right corners was faster.

Figure 4-12: Blurring the lower corners of this photo, as shown at right, de-emphasizes the wrinkles that are clearly visible at left.

To use the Blur tool, follow these steps:

1. **Check to see that the layer you want to work with is selected in the Layers palette.**

   If the Layers palette isn't visible, you can choose it from the Window menu.

2. **If you want to restrict the blurring to a particular area of the image, use the appropriate selection tool (Marquee, Lasso, Magic Wand) on the Tool palette to select that area.**

3. **Click the Blur tool to activate it.**

   The tool shares a spot with the Sharpen and Smudge tools.

   Check out the tool's options on the Options bar, shown in Figure 4-13.

Figure 4-13: The Blur tool's Options bar.

4. **Adjust the setting in the Strength drop-down menu (set to 50% by default) to increase or decrease the amount of blurring that each click or stroke applies to the image.**

   Obviously, a low setting results in very subtle effects.

5. **Set the brush size and type (such as hard- or soft-edged) for the area you'll be blurring by using the Brush palette.**

   Use the smallest brush you can if you need to blur a very small or detailed area. If you want to blur a large area, use a large brush so that you can avoid the obvious signs of retracing your steps with the tool.

6. **Click or drag over the area to be blurred.**

   Some scrubbing with the mouse might be required if you want to get rid of a very sharp edge between two parts of the image. Figure 4-14 shows the edge of content that was pasted into a photo, and the Blur tool is making the edge disappear so that the pasted content looks like it was always there.

Figure 4-14: For maximum control and subtle (yet effective) results, scrub along the unwanted hard edge with a low-strength Blur tool.

Sometimes you can use the Blur tool to make another part of the image seem sharper in comparison. For example, if the Sharpen tool is having undesirable effects on your image, use the Blur tool to soften or remove the details surrounding the parts of the image to which you want to draw attention.

Finding Relief with the Healing Tools

Both Photoshop and Photoshop Elements have tools that are considered purely restorative. They're intended for removing the signs of age, wear and tear, and outright damage in the form of tears, rips, scratches, and missing content.

In Photoshop CS2 and Elements 4.0, you can find two tools nested with the Red Eye tool designed specifically with healing in mind:

✦ The **Healing Brush,** which copies pixels from one place to another while modifying the copied pixels so that they take into account the texture and brightness of the underlying image.

✦ The **Spot Healing Brush,** which performs its healing magic only on specific areas you click, such as dust spots, taking its samples from the surrounding pixels automatically.

Photoshop CS2 has a third tool not found in Elements 4.0:

✦ The **Patch Tool,** which overlays a portion you want to repair with a patch taken from another area, but modified so that the patch takes into account the texture and brightness of the image underneath.

You can also find a Clone Stamp tool in both applications, which copies undamaged content and allows you to paint it over damaged areas. You can do this to replace missing content, cover up damaged content, or simply edit the content of the image by painting over things you don't want. Unlike the Healing Brush and the Patch tools, the Clone Stamp obscures any detail being copied over.

The Clone Stamp isn't purely a restorative tool. It has many uses in the creation of original artwork and in images that aren't photographic in nature. Its restorative uses are extensive, however, so I've grouped it here with the healing tools.

Using the Healing Brush

The Healing Brush is so named because it repairs or heals the current image being painted over — using it doesn't replace it completely. The Clone Stamp (to be discussed shortly) replaces content in one place with selected content from another spot in the image. The color and lighting in the source spot are cloned and placed in the target location as well, which might not be what you want if you'd like to preserve a realistic look.

The Healing Brush is a bit more intelligent and a bit less heavy-handed than the Clone Stamp. As shown in Figure 4-15, this view of a single image shows the Healing Brush effects. The tear on the right side of the photograph is partially healed, and the healed portion matches the surrounding content even though the healing content was derived from a spot on the other side of the image (marked by the cross hairs to the left of the woman's face).

**Book VI
Chapter 4**

Restoring Images

To use the Healing Brush, follow these steps:

Figure 4-15: Select the healing content (at the cross hairs) and then paint over the "wound" on the right side of the image.

1. **Identify the area to be healed and pick content from elsewhere in the image that you can use to heal the wound.**

2. **Click the Healing Brush in the Tool palette to activate it.**

   A set of options appears in the Options bar, as shown in Figure 4-16.

Figure 4-16: The Healing Brush's Options bar.

3. **Using the Options bar, establish the following settings. You can leave them at their default settings if you want, but you might want to make adjustments:**

   • *Brush:* The Brush setting allows you to choose the size of the brush you'll use and whether it is hard- or soft-edged. This is the same setting that you use to control the way any content is applied with a brush-based tool.

- *Mode:* Choose how the pixels will blend. Normal is the default setting and is probably your best choice because it lets the tool work as it's intended. With the Normal setting, the Healing Brush takes the healing content and applies it to the damage and then lets the "band-aid" content blend in with the surrounding area. You can also use the modes described in Book VI, Chapter 3.

- *Source:* If the *Sampled option* is selected, the Healing Brush copies pixels from a place that you select in the image. This is the default because it assumes you're going to choose a spot on the image — somewhere where there is no damage — and use that as the band-aid for the damaged area.

  If the *Pattern option* is selected, you can paint a pattern over the area to be healed instead of pixels from another part of the image. If you select this option, the pattern that you apply takes on the color and lighting of the surrounding pixels. This can be a useful option if you're replacing missing content and have to invent the fill entirely. Figure 4-17 shows a pattern applied to an area and the interesting effect that it creates to cover a stain on the carpet. The content within the circular cursor has not yet changed to match the surrounding pixels, but you can see the previous clicks that place a pattern in context.

- *Aligned:* When you select your source area (where the healing content is taken from), you can select this option so that the distance and direction between the source and target remains the same as you paint over larger damaged areas. This option is unchecked by default, which means that the tool copies from the original source spot each time you click the mouse to paint over the damaged area with the Healing Brush. If you enable this option, new source areas are selected each time that you apply the Healing Brush.

Figure 4-17: Applying a pattern.

4. **After you adjust all the settings you want or need to, begin using the Healing Brush. First, sample the spot that's used to heal the damage by Alt-clicking (Option-clicking on the Mac) the healing content that you want to use.**

5. **With your healing content chosen, go ahead and click or drag over the damaged area.**

   The content you sampled (with the Alt or Option key and your mouse) covers the damage.

You might have to wait a few moments for the healing effect to finish. A lot of calculating goes on as Photoshop matches the copied pixels to the new location's darkness and texture. At first, it might look like the exact color and lighting from the source area is being duplicated on the damaged (target) area. If you wait a second, however, you'll see the Healing effect occur — the content you applied with the Healing Brush automatically blends into its surroundings, like a chameleon blending into the leaf or twig on which it sits.

The Spot Healing Brush in both Photoshop and Photoshop Elements works the same as the Healing Brush, but doesn't require clicking within your image to select an area to be used as a sample. Just select the tool and click over the area you want to "heal." The pixels surrounding the "wound" will be examined and used to construct the new pixels painted over it during the healing process.

Working with the Patch tool

Unlike the Healing Brush and Spot Healing Brush, which allow you to paint content from one place to another, the Patch tool works by applying a selected shape from one spot on the image to a damaged spot somewhere else in the image. You can use this tool to cover damage (such as scratches, spots, and stains), or you can use it to replace unwanted content with something more visually appealing.

Photoshop Elements doesn't offer the Patch tool; only Photoshop does (starting with version 7.0). It's similar to copying and pasting content from one place to another, which is a procedure supported by both applications. The difference between using the Patch tool and doing a simple copy and paste to cover up unwanted content or damage is simple: The Patch tool is a little more intuitive and a little more chameleon-like in that when you place the patch over the unwanted content, the lighting and shading in the target area is applied to the patch.

To use this really helpful tool, follow these steps:

1. **Check the Layers palette to make sure the right layer is active.**

   If the Layers palette isn't visible, you can activate it from the Window menu. Using the correct layer prevents you from patching the wrong layer's content onto another part of your image.

2. **Decide which part of the image you want to use to cover the unwanted or damaged area.**

3. **Click the Patch Tool to activate it.**

   You might have to switch to it from the Healing Brush because these two tools share one spot on the toolbox.

4. **Using the Options bar (shown in Figure 4-18), choose either Source or Destination for the patch.**

   If you didn't select the patch area before turning on the tool (and I haven't had you do that in these steps), select Destination.

Figure 4-18: Source or Destination? Choose which direction your patch will follow.

5. **Using the mouse, drag a line around the area that you want to use as the patch.**

   It's a lot like using the Lasso tool, as shown in Figure 4-19.

Figure 4-19: Select the Destination patch to place on top of the damaged areas or unwanted content.

6. **Drag the selected patch area onto the damaged/unwanted spot.**

Wait a second and see the lighting and shading change to make the patch match the surrounding pixels so that the patched content blends in.

7. **If you have a large area to patch, you can do it in small pieces, repeating Steps 5 and 6 for each piece.**

Figure 4-20 shows an extra kitten's face added to a former pile of three kittens. The shading and lighting of the new face match its location among the existing kittens.

Figure 4-20: Patch a portion of the image over other content to make more of a good thing.

When your entire damaged or unwanted area is patched, you can use the Blur or Smudge tool as needed on any visible edges. If you placed one large patch over a large trouble spot, you might have to blend it with any drastically different adjacent pixels. Sometimes, if the damaged area is a very light color and a dark area is right next to it, the patch-matching won't be as smooth as you'd have hoped.

Cloning content to cover damage and unwanted content

The addition of the Patch tool, Healing Brush, and Spot Healing Brush to Photoshop might have eliminated more than half the uses for the Clone Stamp for many users, but you'll find the Clone Stamp to be a helpful tool in many applications.

The Clone Stamp duplicates content from one place and lets you click to place it one or more times in the image, covering existing content (thus the term *stamp* in the tool's name). Figure 4-21 shows a good candidate for Clone Stamp fixing. Unlike the Patch tool, there is no matching of the stamped content to the surrounding pixels in the target area. If you stamp green grass on a blue couch, you get green grass on a blue couch — you don't get a blue, grassy texture on a blue couch.

Figure 4-21: Can we create a portrait of the bugle boy alone? Unfortunately, his mom's hat and shoulder intrude into the picture.

To use the Clone Stamp, follow these steps, which are quite similar to the steps for the Healing Brush and Patch tool combined. I use Photoshop Elements here:

1. **Verify the layer you're in, making sure that the layer containing the content you want to clone is highlighted in the Layer palette.**

   You can switch to another layer later when you stamp the content onto the image.

2. **Click the Clone Stamp tool in the Tool palette to activate it.**

   The Options bar (shown in Figure 4-22) appears, offering several settings that you can tweak to control how the tool is applied, including

   • *Brush:* This pop-up palette on the left side of the Options bar contains the brush styles you set for painting, erasing, or using any brush-applied tool. Pick a brush from the palette based on your target area, going for a size that's just a bit smaller than the area you want to stamp over. You don't want to leave an obvious edge to a single stamping of content. With two or more stamps in the area, you can avoid a clumsily pasted look.

- *Mode:* You can choose a mode to control how the pixels will be merged when the cloned content is pasted. The Mode controls were discussed earlier, in the section, "Finger painting to blend colors and textures." Normal works for most jobs, but you might want to experiment.

- *Opacity:* If you want to see through your stamped content, reduce the opacity from the default 100%.

- *Aligned:* This keeps the same distance/offset between the sampled spot and the stamped area. If you deselect this option, the tool returns to the original sampled spot as its source each time you release the mouse button and continue stamping.

- *Use All Layers:* If you want your cloning and stamping to affect all the layers of your image, select this option. It's unchecked (off) by default, just so you don't make more of an impact on your entire image than you had intended.

Figure 4-22: The Clone Stamp's Options bar.

After you customize the tool as needed, you're ready to clone and stamp.

3. **To clone the spot that will be used to cover unwanted content, hold down Alt (Option key on a Mac) while you click the spot that you want to clone.**

   The mouse pointer changes when you're in clone mode, and a crosshair appears in the center of your brush point.

   In this example image, I Alt-clicked in the bugle boy's sleeve to cover his mother's arm at the lower right corner of the picture.

4. **Release the Alt or Option key and apply the cloned content by clicking to cover the unwanted content, as shown in Figure 4-23.**

   Here, multiple copies of the cloned content have been applied over a large area to cover the seated woman's shoulder and hat.

Note that I've also used the Clone Stamp to remove some dust spots and other artifacts from the background and uniform.

Figure 4-23: Remove the edge of the hat and shoulder with the Clone Stamp tool.

Chapter 5: Correcting Faded, Funny, and Funky Colors

In This Chapter

- ✏ **Mastering the color balancing act**
- ✏ **Controlling the intensity of color**
- ✏ **Improving color quality overall**
- ✏ **Eliminating red-eyed demons**

*P*hotos displayed on a sunny wall or desk can fade from the exposure to sunshine, even if you live in a rainy climate. You'd be surprised how just a small amount of sunlight or fluorescent light can fade a photo if it's exposed long enough. Time, too, can fade photos printed from old negatives on old photo paper. You might also have photos that looked a bit odd from the start — perhaps there was too much red or green, or the colors looked washed out from the minute you had the photo developed or captured it with your digital camera.

Regardless of the cause, color photos present a whole host of color-balance, level, and quality issues, and Photoshop and Photoshop Elements are well prepared to deal with them. This is where Photoshop's status as the standard for photo retouching software kicks in. You can find several ways to manually and automatically adjust color levels and quality. Photoshop Elements has many of the same tools that Photoshop does, as well as a few of its own.

In Book VI, Chapter 4, I show you how to adjust tonal values and eliminate artifacts while fixing old photos. This chapter focuses on the color adjustments you can make to bring your images up to snuff.

Using Automated Tools in Photoshop and Elements

Your first stop when attempting to correct your colors and tones is the automated tools built right into both Photoshop and Elements. These tools are a training wheels of a sort that work well for some basic image problems, but they don't allow the kind of fine-tuning that you want to apply to really optimize your photos. Try these automatic tools first and then turn to some of the more advanced options described in the rest of this chapter.

Auto Correction in Photoshop

Your automated toolkit in Photoshop is located in the Adjustments submenu of the Image menu and includes

✦ **Auto Levels:** This command automatically examines the tonal values in your image, including the lightest tones (highlights), the middle tones, and the darkest tones (the shadows). Then it attempts to provide a balance among all those tones so that the lightest tones aren't washed out, the darkest shadows still have some detail, and the middle tones are right in the middle.

✦ **Auto Contrast:** This command looks at how many different tones are in your image. If only a few are present, your image could have excessive contrast. If the image information is spread evenly among hundreds of different tones, your image might be low in contrast. Photoshop attempts to redistribute the tones to provide a more pleasing picture.

✦ **Auto Color:** This command attempts to determine whether the color in your image is heavily biased toward one color or another and then removes excessive color to provide some correction. (Remember, no image editor can *add* color that isn't there; colors can only be removed, leaving whatever other colors are present.)

None of these commands have any options. You just invoke them and evaluate your results.

Auto Correction in Photoshop Elements

Elements has the same three tools found in Photoshop, under the Enhance menu: Auto Levels, Auto Contrast, and Auto Color Correction. Elements also includes an Auto Smart Fix command that attempts to apply all three of these commands, as appropriate, simultaneously.

You can throttle back the amount of correction applied by Smart Fix by moving a slider in the Adjust Smart Fix dialog box. Choose Enhance⇨Adjust Smart Fix and move the Smart Fix slider from 0 percent (almost no correction)

up to 200 percent (a whole lot of correction) until you get the effect you like. The current effect can be viewed in the original image's window as you adjust the slider.

Photoshop Elements also has a Quick Fix mode (select it by clicking the Quick Fix tab on the right side of the main window), shown in Figure 5-1, with an assortment of correction tools for general fixes, lighting and contrast, color, and sharpening. Each of these has an Auto button that you can click to apply the automatic version of that correction, as well as sliders for applying the fixes manually. Read more about manual fixes in the next sections.

Adjusting Color Balance

Say a photo has too much red or yellow, or the whole picture is too dark or too light. These problems — problems you might think would require multiple tools and several steps to solve — could just be a couple of clicks away from their solutions. With automatic color and lighting adjustment tools, commands that address specific color levels, and Photoshop's Channels palette, you have the power to make sweeping changes to your photos or sections thereof, significantly shortening the amount of time that you spend editing and improving your photos.

Adjusting color levels

Both Photoshop and Photoshop Elements offer a Levels command. In Elements, it's squirreled away under the Enhance⇨Adjust Lighting submenu; in Photoshop, you can find it on the Image⇨Adjustments menu. Or, just press Ctrl/⌘+L to bring up the dialog box directly.

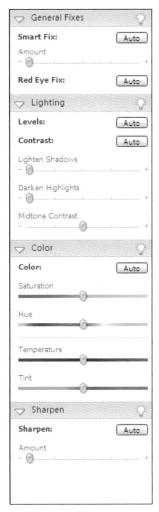

**Book VI
Chapter 5**

Correcting Faded,
Funny, and Funky
Colors

Figure 5-1: Elements' Quick Fix mode gives you fast access to automated and manual correction tools.

The Levels command in either application allows you to set the highlights and shadows in an image by dragging three Input Levels sliders (in this case, a set of three black, gray, and white triangles along the slider axis) to adjust the

Levels histogram. A *histogram* is a visual representation of quantities — in this case, levels of tones. The sliders, as shown in Figure 5-2, allow you to adjust levels of shadows, midtones, and highlights.

As you drag the Input Levels sliders, the levels of lights and darks change in the photo. You can control the effects by using the Set Black Point, Set Gray Point, and Set White Point eyedroppers. (The eyedroppers are located under the Options button in Figure 5-2.)

Figure 5-2: Adjust shadow, midtone, and highlight levels.

While in Levels, double-click each of the Eyedroppers in turn to open the Color Picker so that you can choose new colors for these three levels (Shadows, Midtones, and Highlights). Alternatively, you can choose new color levels by clicking existing shades within the image. As you make your selections (using the Color Picker or the image itself) and okay them, you see the results in your image.

You can find more about working with the Levels command in *Photoshop CS2 All-in-One Desk Reference For Dummies,* by Barbara Obermeier (Wiley).

Using the Variations dialog box

The Variations command (Color Variations in Elements 4.0) is a useful feature found on the Image⇨Adjustments submenu in Photoshop and on the Enhance⇨Adjust Color submenu in Photoshop Elements.

The Variations/Color Variations command enables you to view a series of thumbnails, each showing a different color or contrast effect. As you can see in Figure 5-3, clicking the Darker thumbnail shows you how adding more black to the image will affect it. If color adjustment is your goal, you can see what will happen if you bump up the Blue component just by clicking More Blue (in Photoshop) or Increase Blue (in Photoshop Elements).

While you're experimenting by clicking the Variations thumbnails, you can always click the Original thumbnail to return all the thumbnails to their default states. You can view the effects of multiple changes, such as making the image lighter, adding more of one or more colors, or switching between the Midtones, Shadows, Highlights, and Saturation radio buttons. No matter what variations you're considering, Photoshop lets you see your results in a Current Pick thumbnail, and Photoshop Elements shows an after version of the image, as shown in Figure 5-4.

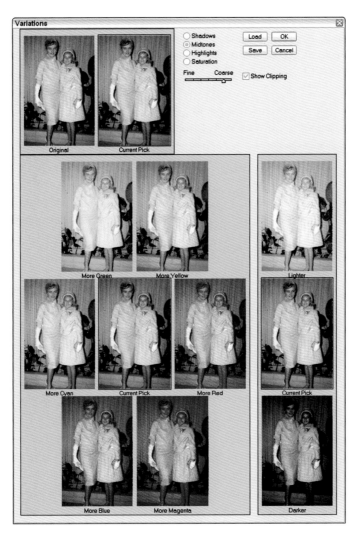

Figure 5-3: Photoshop's Variations dialog box lets you see your results in the Current Pick version of the image.

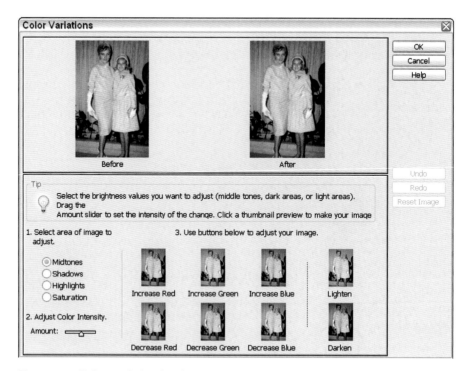

Figure 5-4: Before and after thumbnails in Photoshop Elements.

Equalizing colors

The Equalize command has been christened with a name that clearly tells you what it does. Choose Image⇨Adjustments in Photoshop or Filter⇨ Adjustments in Elements. The command evenly distributes color over the range of brightness levels throughout your image (or in a selected area) from 0 to 255. When the Equalize command is issued, Photoshop or Elements locates the brightest and darkest pixels, and the rest of the colors are adjusted, making white the brightest value and black the darkest. Then all the colored pixels that fall between these two extremes are *equalized,* or made to fall between the two extreme shades.

If you don't select part of your image before issuing the Equalize command, no dialog box appears; the changes just take place automatically over the entire image. If you do make a selection first, a dialog box appears, as shown in Figure 5-5.

Use this dialog box to indicate whether you want to equalize a selected area only or equalize the entire image based on the selected area. In Figure 5-6, only part of the image is equalized, and it's easy to spot it. Therefore, be careful that you don't make the rest of your image look shabby by improving just a small section so drastically.

The Equalize command affects each image differently. The effect depends on how damaged, faded, and light or dark the image was to begin with. Don't assume that if equalization was a big problem solver in one photo, it will be as successful with another.

Figure 5-5: Indicate how you want to use a selection to equalize colors.

Figure 5-6: Equalizing just part of your image might be too drastic, as it is in this case.

Fixing a color cast

A *color cast* is a tinge — a shade of red or maybe yellow — that discolors your image in whole or in part. Casts occur for a variety of reasons, including the age of the photo, the quality of your scanner (if you scanned a printed original), the print from which you scanned the image, or the film used to take the picture. If a cast appears in an image captured with a digital camera, you need to reset something on the camera (what you change and how you change it varies by the camera). A digital camera is rarely the culprit, however. Your cast probably came from a print, film, or age problem instead.

To get rid of a cast, use Photoshop Elements' Color Cast command (Photoshop doesn't have it) to rid an image of any unpleasant preponderance of a single color. Just follow these steps:

1. **Open the image with the unwanted color cast.**

2. **From the main menu, choose Enhance⇨Adjust Color⇨Remove Color Cast.**

   The Remove Color Cast dialog box opens, as shown in Figure 5-7, offering instructions.

Figure 5-7: Correct a color cast and get rid of any dominant shade.

3. **Use the dialog box's Eyedropper tool (already activated within the dialog box) to click the gray, and then white, and then black points in the image.**

   As you click in the image (about three times — one for gray, one for white, and one for black), the color cast in the photo changes.

   You can keep clicking different spots until you like the results or bail out entirely by clicking Cancel.

 Make sure that you leave the Preview option on in the Remove Color Cast dialog box. Most applications offer a Preview capability in dialog boxes that adjust visual elements. Leaving it on means that you don't have to apply the changes just to see them in your image. If you do apply them by clicking OK and then decide you don't like the change, choose Edit⇨Undo from the main menu.

Displaying and using channels

Channels are the different individual color layers that make up your image. Most photos are either in RGB (red/green/blue) or CMYK (cyan/magenta/yellow/black) modes, and photos in those modes have either three (in the case of RGB) or four (in the case of CMYK) channels.

Photoshop's Channels palette (not found in Elements) allows you to view the individual channels for your photo, as shown in Figure 5-8. If the Channels palette is not visible, you can display it by choosing Window➪Channels.

The channel that includes all the colors (the RGB or CMYK channel) is displayed when all the individual channels are showing in the photo, and it turns off (the eye disappears from that channel in the palette) if any one of the channels is hidden.

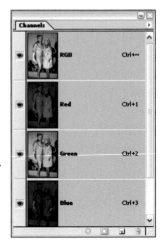

Use the Channels palette to focus your editing efforts on a single color channel's content or on a combination of two or more channels. For example, if you want to make changes only to the red portions of an image, you can edit the Red channel alone without disturbing the Green or Blue channels. You can edit any channel that's visible. When you hide all but one channel, your edits affect only the channel that's active. To edit a single channel, keep these rules in mind:

Figure 5-8: Photoshop's Channels palette lets you view an image's basic color components.

- ✦ White applies the selected channel color at 100 percent intensity.

- ✦ Black wipes out the channel's color wherever you paint or draw it.

- ✦ Use a shade of gray to apply the channel's color at a lower intensity.

To display a channel, make sure that the eye appears next to the channel in the Channels palette. If you want to hide a channel, click the eye to the left of the channel. You can't turn off the RGB or CMYK channel directly; it's visible only if all the other channels are visible, too. Using Channels is a complex topic, and I recommend checking out *Photoshop CS2 All-in-One Desk Reference For Dummies,* by Barbara Obermeier (Wiley), for more information.

Working with Color Intensity and Quality

Automatic tools that ask nothing — or ask just a few questions and then make global corrections to color and light — can fail you. In these situations, Photoshop and Photoshop Elements can help. These applications provide targeted tools that you can apply manually to adjust color, lighting, brightness, and contrast. Whatever your photo's color difficulty is, however, chances are that these tools offer a quick and easy solution:

+ The Sponge tool for saturating and desaturating color

+ The Brightness/Contrast dialog box

+ The Curve dialog box, for adjusting individual colors

Increasing and decreasing color intensity

Found in both Photoshop and Photoshop Elements, the Sponge tool adds color (in Saturate mode) or removes color (in Desaturate mode), depending on how you set up the tool.

The Sponge tool can come in handy if you added too much color in a previous editing session and the edit can't be undone. Or perhaps you simply want a subtler, more faded look to some or all of an image. New photos are often faded to look vintage or in preparation for the use of an artistic filter that will make the photo look like a drawing or painting.

Regardless of your motivation, the Sponge tool is very simple to use. To saturate or desaturate color in either Photoshop or Photoshop Elements, follow these steps:

1. **Click the tool in the Tool palette to activate it.**

   In Photoshop and Elements 3.0 and 4.0, the Sponge shares a space on the Tool palette with the Dodge and the Burn tools. Hold down the Shift key and press O to cycle through the three tools until the Sponge is active. Elements versions prior to 3.0 give the Sponge tool its own spot.

2. **Choose Saturate or Desaturate mode, using the tool's Options bar, as shown in Figure 5-9.**

Figure 5-9: The Sponge tool's Options bar.

3. **Adjust the *flow* — how much saturation or desaturation occurs — by using the Flow drop-down menu. In some Mac versions of Photoshop, Pressure does the same thing.**

4. **Use the Brush drop-down menu and choose the right brush size for the area to be sponged.**

   A small brush can give you undesirable results when used in a large area, and a big brush can go too far. Choose one that lets you fix the problem area with the least number of clicks or brush strokes.

5. Apply the Sponge to the image by clicking and/or dragging to add or remove color where desired.

Passing over the same spot more than once intensifies the sponge effect. You add or wash out more color on each successive pass, as shown in Figure 5-10, where too much color has been sponged away.

Figure 5-10: Too much Sponge in Desaturate mode can wash away all your colors.

Tinkering with brightness and contrast

Although automatic tools can correct brightness and contrast, you might want to control these levels manually. To do so, you can use the Brightness and Contrast command found in the Image⇨Adjustments submenu in Photoshop or the Enhance⇨Adjust Lighting ⇨Brightness/Contrast submenu in Photoshop Elements. In either application, the command opens a dialog box, shown in Figure 5-11, that offers two sliders. One adjusts the brightness, and the other adjusts the contrast.

Figure 5-11: Adjust brightness and/or contrast with this handy dialog box.

Although the Brightness/Contrast controls are tempting for the beginner, most of the time, they are the *worst* choice for making corrections to your photos. That's because they provide uniform changes in brightness or contrast to *all* the pixels in your image or selection. That might work out in some cases, but most of the time, the results will be terrible. If you bump up brightness to lighten shadows, you'll find that your highlights are now completely washed out. Darken highlights, and your shadows will turn black. And rarely will any photograph need adjustment in contrast over its entire image. I recommend using the Levels command (discussed earlier in this chapter) and Curves (discussed next) as your Photoshop or Elements proficiency increases. Each of these commands deserves most of a chapter of its own, and that's what you'll find in the companion books to this one, *Photoshop CS2 All-in-One Desk Reference For Dummies,* by Barbara Obermeier, or *Photoshop Elements 4 For Dummies,* by Barbara Obermeier and Ted Padova (both by Wiley).

Book VI
Chapter 5

Correcting Faded,
Funny, and Funky
Colors

Riding the curves

Another way to adjust the tones in your image is to work with the Curves dialog box, available in Photoshop (but not in Photoshop Elements) by choosing Image⇨Adjustments⇨Curves. You can use this box to adjust the entire range of colors in your image. To adjust the tones and color balance, drag the curved line up, down, left, or right, and watch the Preview to see how the adjustments affect your image. You'll also want to use the set of three eyedroppers to set the shadow, midtone, and highlight samples from within the image and then readjust the curve.

If you want to change only certain color levels in the image, choose which color channel you want to adjust by selecting that channel within the Channels palette. If you want to adjust multiple (but not all) channels, hold down the Shift key as you click to select more than one channel.

Removing Red-Eye

Another tool that originated with Photoshop Elements and migrated to Photoshop is the Red Eye Removal tool (called simply the Red Eye tool in Photoshop). This tool allows you to literally click or paint away those glowing pupils that affect children or anyone else wide-eyed and close enough to the camera and its overzealous flash. Figure 5-12 shows an image in dire need of red-eye treatment.

Using the Red Eye Removal tool requires using the Options bar; Photoshop's Red Eye tool has a similar Options bar, but without the Auto button. To use the Red Eye Removal tool, follow these steps to customize the tool's effects and apply them to the glowing eyes in question. In Elements, you can also click the Auto button and let the tool find and fix the red eyes without your help (it does a fairly good job.)

Figure 5-12: Have some demonic eyes to fix? Use the Red Eye Removal tool in Elements 4.0.

1. **Make sure that the layer with the demonic eyes is in fact the active layer in the Layers palette.**

2. **Click the Red Eye Removal tool in the Tool palette to activate it; then consider the following options:**

   - *Pupil Size:* The size of the brush you'll use to paint over the red-eye.

   - *Darken Amount:* The degree you want the red eyes darkened.

3. **Click in the area that includes the red-eye effect.**

   The tool automatically seeks out the red tone and darkens it, creating more natural-looking eyes.

4. **If both eyes are glowing (they usually are), you can repeat this process for the second eye.**

   Figure 5-13 shows both eyes exorcised, with no glow remaining.

Figure 5-13: The glowing-eyed demon has been exorcised.

The current version of the Red Eye Removal tool does not work with the similar yellow- or green-eye effect produced in animals. Try using the Color Replacement tool instead. For best results, be careful not to apply the same exact pupil color to both eyes.

Chapter 6: Enhancing Photos with Filters and Special Effects

In This Chapter

⊯ **Understanding how filters work and what they do**

⊯ **Using Photoshop Elements' special effects for images and text**

⊯ **Finding third-party filters and other plug-ins**

Filters allow you to apply groups of effects and formats to your images, whether to a specific selected area or to the entire image on one or more of its layers. You can use filters to add or change the color and texture of your images or to add patterns. Each of the filters in Photoshop and Photoshop Elements enables you to control how the filter affects your image, and most filters give you a preview so that you don't have to formally apply the filter to your image until you see how it will look.

Telling you everything you need to know about using filters is beyond the scope of this book. After all, Photoshop and Elements each include more than 100 different filters that span a broad range of special effects. But this chapter certainly gets you started using these fascinating tools. For more detailed information on using filters, check out the *Photoshop CS2 All-in-One Desk Reference For Dummies*, by Barbara Obermeier (Wiley).

The main thing to remember when using filters is to experiment and have fun with them. Several of the illustrations in this chapter are not simply digital photos with a filter applied to them. Some of them are digital creations in their own right, using a combination of digital photos cut and pasted together, special editing techniques, and a bit of filter special effects magic.

Working with Photoshop's and Photoshop Elements' Filters

Both applications provide the same filter categories, shown in the Photoshop Elements menu in Figure 6-1. Photoshop's Filter menu is similar, with Extract, Liquify, and Pattern Maker commands added for good measure. (Liquify has been moved to the regular Filter menu under the Distort submenu for Elements 4.0. It can also be found in the Styles and Effects Filter Gallery.)

Filters can be used for many different purposes, including creating original works of art from scratch. However, for the purposes of this discussion on editing digital photos, the filters I discuss fall into three categories: corrective, artistic, and special effects. These are the kinds of filters that you're likely to use to retouch photos for personal or professional use. As for those filters that fall out-

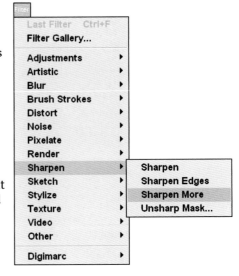

Figure 6-1: Choose a category in the Filter menu and then select a filter from the submenu.

side these categories, you can take your newly found knowledge of the filters that I actually cover and apply it when you experiment with other filters. And just think of the fun you'll have with the trial-and-error process!

Understanding how filters work

When you open the Filter menu, you see all the filter categories, each followed by a right-pointing triangle that spawns a submenu. Most of the categories have at least four filters in their submenus, and many of them have even more to choose from.

Just about all the Filter commands work through either a dialog box or the Filter Gallery found in both Photoshop and Elements. Either mode enables you to both preview and customize the filter's effect. Figure 6-2 shows a standalone filter dialog box for the Smart Blur effect.

You access other filters through the Filter Gallery, which presents you with a large number of filters, all of which can be quickly tried out from within the Gallery. You can even add several filters together, change their order, and preview the results of the combination before you apply the effects.

Figure 6-3 shows the Filter Gallery in Photoshop Elements 4.0. Elements also has other effects in the Styles and Effects palette.

Before I discuss individual filters, consider these important filtering tips:

+ Filters can be applied only to the active layer, and only if that layer is visible. If your photo has only one layer, this is a moot point.

+ You can limit the filter's effects to a selection by using the various selection tools before applying a filter.

+ If you don't make a selection before you apply a filter, the filter is applied to the entire active layer.

+ Certain filters work only with certain file types. If your file type doesn't support a certain filter, the filter command is dimmed in the submenu.

Smart Blur

| | OK |
| | Cancel |

14%

Radius   3.0

Threshold   25.0

Quality: Low

Mode: Normal

Figure 6-2: The standalone Smart Blur filter dialog box and preview pane.

Not all filters have a dialog box or appear in the Filter Gallery. Some of them, called *single step filters,* have no options to bother with and are applied the instant you click the command in the Filter menu within a particular category's submenu. The downside? You have no control over the effects, although you can select a section of your image beforehand. If you don't like the results, though, you can easily use the Undo command or the History palette to get rid of the effect.

Fixing flaws with corrective filters

Corrective filters are those that improve the quality of the image without distorting it, changing the content significantly, or applying any stylized effect. The three filters that are most appropriate for a discussion of digital photos fall into three Filter menu categories: Blur, Sharpen, and Noise.

These three categories contain several filters, each performing a relatively subtle effect, depending on the settings that you employ in the available dialog boxes.

Figure 6-3: Photoshop Elements' Filter Gallery is similar to the one found in Photoshop CS2.

Blur filters

Use the Blur filters (Blur, Blur More, Gaussian Blur, Motion Blur, Radial Blur, and Smart Blur) to soften the content of your image. The Motion and Radial blurs do a bit more than soften. They actually give the appearance of circular movement (Radial) or movement through space (Motion). The Blur and Blur More filters don't have dialog boxes; the commands automatically apply a modicum of blurring to your image in its entirety or to a selection made before issuing the command.

Use the Blur and Blur More filters instead of the Blur tool when you want uniform results. When you use the Blur tool, your mouse has the greatest effect on the results. You might be able to see the strokes that you used to apply the blur, or you might miss some spots or apply the effect unevenly. If you use the filter, the same amount of blurring is applied everywhere, with no strokes or places that are blurred more or less than somewhere else.

In Photoshop and Elements, the last filter you used is repeated at the top of the Filter menu so that you can access the filter quickly if you want to use it again in the current session. In both applications, the keyboard shortcut to reapply the most recently used filter is Ctrl+F (⌘+F on a Mac).

The specialized Blur filters — Gaussian, Motion, Radial, and Smart — have their own dialog boxes where you can choose the degree of blurring. You'll use the Gaussian Blur filter most often because it allows a high degree of control over the amount and type of blur applied. Figure 6-4 shows a Gaussian Blur applied to the background part of an image to make the foreground stand out.

Figure 6-4: Gaussian Blur lets you apply customized blurs to all or part of your image.

For the Motion blur, you can also choose the direction in which the object is supposed to be moving. Figure 6-5 shows the Motion Blur dialog box as well as a preview of its effect on an image created in Photoshop using actual photos blended together in a creative way.

The Radial blur completely distorts everything to which it's applied. If you want to create a background that appears to be spinning around or behind parts of the image, select the content that will remain static and copy it to a new layer. Then apply the Radial Blur to the original layer, which should be placed behind the static content layer. Voilà! Your objects are in the center of a hurricane, but they've not moved a bit. Figure 6-6 shows a fanciful image created in Photoshop from an actual vacation photo I took in London, with the addition of some type and special filter effects.

Figure 6-5: Zoom! The Motion Blur filter makes your image take off.

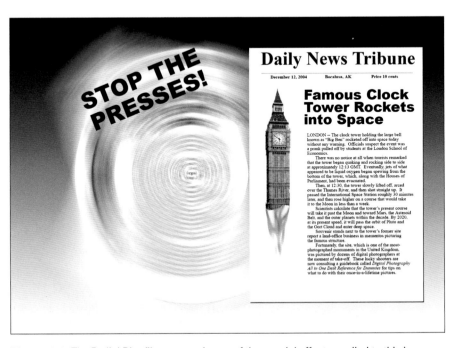

Figure 6-6: The Radial Blur filter was only one of the special effects applied to this image.

Sharpen filters

Just as the Blur and Sharpen tools are opposites, so are the Blur and Sharpen filters. They're the same in one respect, though — the filters apply the effect in a uniform way, whereas the tools are entirely dependent on your brush size, mouse movements, and selection to control them. These are the four main Sharpen filters (Photoshop CS2 has a fifth, called Smart Sharpen):

✦ **Sharpen:** This filter has no dialog box. Just choose the command, and a uniform, subtle sharpening effect is automatically applied. You might want to repeat it two or more times if you need more sharpening than it manages to apply in one pass.

✦ **Sharpen More:** This is Sharpen on steroids. The filter applies more sharpening in one fell swoop than the Sharpen filter.

✦ **Sharpen Edges:** This makes the edges, determined by a group of pixels varying in color and light levels from an adjoining group, stand out by sharpening the connecting pixels. If you have content in your image that just fades into its surroundings, this might be the filter for you.

✦ **Unsharp Mask:** Despite its confusing name, this filter *sharpens* images. Very similar to Sharpen Edges, this filter adjusts the contrast of edges. This filter is the only Sharpen filter with a dialog box, shown in Figure 6-7, which you use to control the effects.

Figure 6-7: The Unsharp Mask filter can refine the detail of any photo.

Noise filters

Among the Noise filters, the Despeckle and Dust & Scratches filters are the ones you use to retouch photos. You use them to deal with artifacts, such as dust spots or scratches that are distracting or that obscure parts of an image.

The Despeckle filter finds the edges in an image and blurs everything but those edges. Although this sounds overly destructive, it can create an interesting effect that blends together parts of an image despite differences in color and texture that existed in the original. It's also a good tool for minimizing the halftone screen effects of photos scanned from newspapers or magazines.

The Reduce Noise filter is a recent addition to the Photoshop and Elements repertoire, with helpful tools for removing multi-colored speckles from your images.

The Dust & Scratches filter eliminates much of the noise (dust, scratches, small spots) by making pixels that are very different from their surroundings more similar. You can use the Dust & Scratches dialog box (shown in Figure 6-8) to adjust the Radius and the Threshold settings, which determine the scope and degree of the effects, respectively. Figure 6-9 shows the result of adjusting these settings.

The steps for using this filter are pretty simple:

Figure 6-8: This photo needs the Dust & Scratches filter in a big way!

Figure 6-9: Although some details have been softened, the worst of the dust and scratches has been removed.

1. **Choose Filter⇨Noise⇨Dust & Scratches from the main menu to open the filter's dialog box.**

2. **Zoom in on the area with the greatest degree of dust and scratch damage by using the Hand tool and the + button.**

   The Hand tool appears when you mouse over the preview. Examining the image preview helps you determine whether your settings are doing the job.

3. **Adjust the Threshold setting by dragging the slider.**

   Watch the preview for the desired result to appear.

4. **Adjust the Radius, again by dragging the slider.**

   Don't go too far with your Radius adjustment. The image can become so blurry that any details in the photo are indistinguishable.

5. **Click OK to apply the filter.**

Turning photos into paintings with artistic filters

The filters found in three of the Filter menu's categories — Artistic, Sketch, and Brush Strokes — are not truly restorative or retouching filters, at least not traditionally. However, as more people are either capturing images digitally or scanning prints, their needs and desires with regard to those pictures have become more sophisticated and complex. It isn't good enough to just scan a wedding photo and enlarge it for a framed copy on the piano. You might want to make the photo look like a drawing done with pastels or a painting created with oils.

For gifts, cards, Web graphics, and interesting marketing materials, you can turn any photo into an apparent work of hand-done art, as shown in Figure 6-10. Here, a photo has been filtered to look like a painting, with soft shapes and a slight texture that mirrors the weave of watercolor paper. I used the Ink Outlines and the Accented Edges filters, followed by a heavy-duty application of the Unsharp Mask filter.

Using artistic filters also performs another important role. If your image is simply beyond repair or beyond your skills or interest level to repair, you can hide a multitude of sins with the right filter. If your image is scuffed and scratched and you don't feel like dealing with each individual injury, just clean up the most offensive or extreme of the marks and then apply a filter such as Colored Pencil or Dry Brush. This way, you create something entirely new while still preserving the content and history of the original image by hiding the damage that would have normally relegated the image to a drawer rather than a frame.

When you use these filters, you always get a dialog box, such as the one shown in Figure 6-11. Through the dialog boxes, you can customize how the artistic effect is applied — the thickness of the brush or pencil strokes, the frequency of them, how detailed the effect is, the intensity of the effect, and so on. You can select an area before using the filter to restrict the amount of the photo that's affected, or you can apply the filter to the whole image.

Going a little crazy with special effects filters

The Distort and the Stylize filters (found in both Photoshop and Photoshop Elements) and the Liquify command are the least conservative effects. These unusual effects change the appearance of some or all of your image by stretching, pulling, or pinching or by mimicking textures and overlays, such as rippled water, glass, or by appearing to be ripped apart by a strong wind.

Figure 6-10: Photos become paintings and drawings with the use of artistic filters.

Figure 6-11: Make sure you get the effect you're looking for by controlling the filter's attributes.

You might be wondering how on Earth you'd use these filters to restore or retouch a photo. Well, you wouldn't. However, you might use them to create an interesting piece of digital art, using one or more of your photos — or to achieve a symbolic look that's suggested, but not artistically realized, in a photograph you've restored traditionally. For example, if you have a photo of someone's boat, it might be interesting to apply the Ocean Ripple filter to the water in the image, and the Wind filter to the boat's sails. That's a bit literal, but you get the idea.

As you work with these filters, their dialog boxes help you control how the filters work their special effects magic. You can change the size of the tiles or cracks in an image, choose which texture to apply, and adjust the degree of pinching or twirling to use. Figure 6-12 shows the Emboss filter dialog box (one of the Stylize filters) and the settings you can adjust to create a very interesting relief map of your drawing. Check the preview window as you drag sliders and enter values. When you like the results, click OK, and they are applied to your image or to a selection within it.

For a brief description of the more creative filters, check out the following:

✦ **Texture filters:** These filters apply artificial textures to your image. Figure 6-13 shows Stained Glass (top), Craquelure (middle), and Grain (bottom) applied to different sections of a single image, purely for demonstrative purposes.

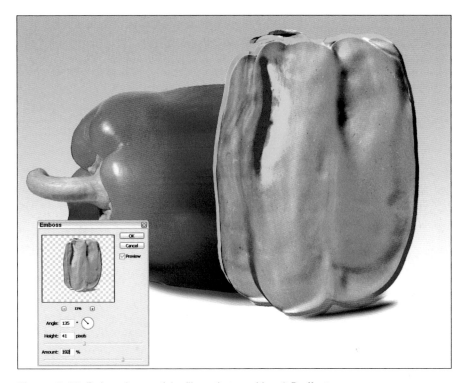

Figure 6-12: Emboss is one of the filters that provide a 3-D effect.

Use the Texturizer filter (found in the Texture category) to apply textures, such as Canvas, Sandstone, and Burlap to your photo. These textures make a photo look like it's printed on very textured paper or some sort of fabric.

✦ **Distorting filters:** These filters manipulate the apparent shape of your image content, as shown in Figures 6-14, 6-15, and 6-16, in which the Ocean Ripple, Pinch, and Glass filters have been applied to the same photo. By creating an apparent shape to the surface of the image, the content looks as though it's being viewed through some sort of distorting lens, or as though the photo exists within a substance and not simply on paper or a computer screen.

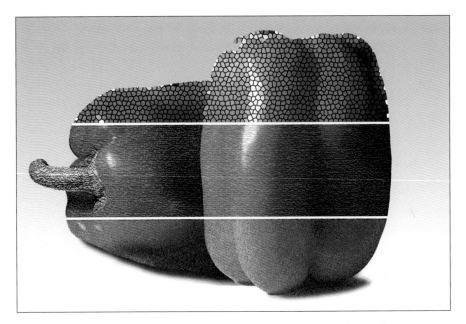

Figure 6-13: Stained Glass (top), Craquelure (middle), and Grain filters (bottom).

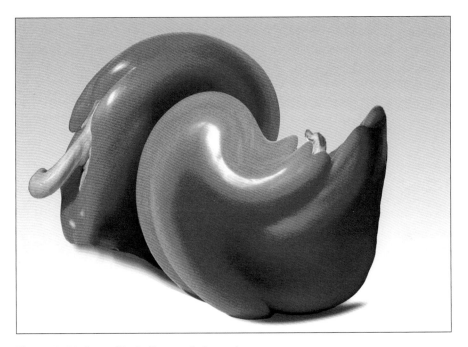

Figure 6-14: Ocean Ripple filter applied to an image.

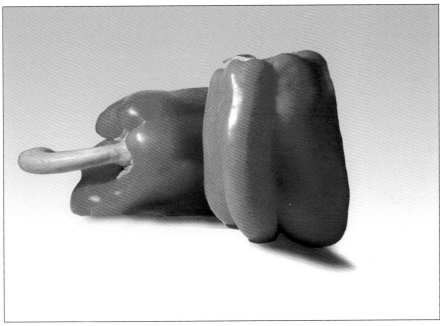

Figure 6-15: Pinch filter applied to the same image.

Figure 6-16: Yet another variation using the Canvas option of the Glass filter.

✦ **Stylize filters:** This category is sort of a hodgepodge of filters that don't really fit anywhere else. With names like Emboss, Glowing Edges, Solarize, and Wind, you'd be hard pressed to find a more descriptive yet nondescript name for them. In Figure 6-17, I applied the Wind filter to the pepper on the left and Glowing Edges to the pepper on the right. The results are extreme and might go beyond your intentions for dealing with digital photos. On the other hand, these examples might inspire you to create something unique.

Figure 6-17: Here are the Wind filter (left) and Glowing Edges filter (right).

✦ **Liquify:** This is a command on Photoshop's Filter menu and is found in the Distort menu in Elements (see Figure 6-18), but it isn't simply a filter. Instead, it's a miniprogram of its own that gives you a full set of distortion and manipulation tools for pinching, twisting, scrunching, pulling, bloating, shrinking, or doing just about anything that sounds like some form of torture to your image. Figure 6-18 shows the Liquify window and some distortion in progress.

Don't hesitate to mix and match with filters. Apply one, then another, then another after that. Stacking their effects can give you unexpected and often quite beautiful results. Don't be afraid to experiment with different combinations!

The Photoshop Elements Styles and Effects Tab Palette

Photoshop Elements has a list of effects that you can apply to a selection or to your entire image similar to the way you apply filters. The Effects are actually canned applications of Elements' filters using a predetermined series of steps, much like a macro. Watch the status bar at the bottom of the screen as an Effect is applied to see the names of the filters used as they are added in turn.

You can view Elements' effects as a list or as a series of thumbnails, as shown in Figure 6-19. The effects can either be applied to a selection within your image or to the entire active layer.

Figure 6-18: Turn your image to a liquid-like substance and then stir it up with the Liquify tools in this dialog box.

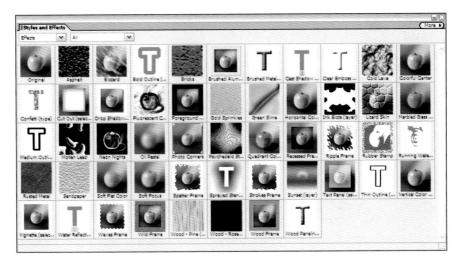

Figure 6-19: View the vast array of Photoshop Elements' Effects that you can apply to your image.

To switch between List and Thumbnail views of the Effects palette, click the More button in upper-right corner of the list and choose from the menu that appears.

If you choose to view the effects as a list, you see additional effects that apply only to text (the word *Type* appears next to them). These allow you to create type that looks like wood, chrome, glass, pipe, or just about anything you can imagine. Figure 6-20 shows the List view of the Effects palette, and a Type effect selected.

Displaying and moving the tab

The Effects palette is normally docked on the right side of the Photoshop Elements window when the Palette Bin is visible; if you click the tab, you can display the palette with its top still docked. If you want to move the palette around, you can simply drag it away from the Palette Bin by grabbing the tab with your mouse. You can move it anywhere on the workspace, and even minimize it in place by clicking the Minimize (–) button to shrink it to just a title bar. When you want to use it again, click the Maximize (X) button. You can also close the Palette by clicking the triangle on the left side of the tab.

Figure 6-20: View the effects as a list and access effects intended for use on text only.

Applying an effect

After you understand how to see either the thumbnails or list of effects, and you know how to manipulate the Effects palette (see the preceding sections), you can apply these cool effects to your photos and text. Just follow these steps:

1. Select the portion of your image to which you want the effect to apply.

If it's text, make sure that the Type layer in question is active and double-click the Type icon on the layer to select all the text on that layer.

2. **Display the Effects palette.**

3. **If you want to apply an effect to your image (not to text), drag the desired thumbnail onto your image.**

   After a delay — how long a delay depends on your available system resources — the effect is applied to the image. If you have part of your image selected, drag the thumbnail into that selected area. You'll get an effect like the one shown in Figure 6-21, in which I applied Psychedelic Strings to the background.

Figure 6-21: Photoshop Elements' Effects are an easy way to apply canned filter transformations.

If you want to apply a Type Effect, remember that you have to be in list view with the correct layer selected to see those effects. When you have the effect in view, either drag it from the list onto your Type layer or click the Apply button while your type is selected.

Click the drop-down list in the upper-left corner of the Effects palette to choose from different effect groups — Textures, Frames, Text Effects, Image Effects — to be displayed alone. The default setting for this drop-down list is All, which shows all the available effects. Choosing one of the groups in the drop-down list distills the displayed set down to just that group.

Getting Your Hands on Third-Party Filters

To find third-party filters for Photoshop (many of which work with Photoshop Elements as well), simply do a search online for *"filters for Photoshop."* Be sure to use the quotation marks to restrict your search to sites that contain that exact phrase. Otherwise, you'll find sites pertaining to filters (for coffee, oil, air) and sites pertaining to Photoshop but not to filters. Of course, the first few will pertain to both, but you'll have to wade through some losers, which is good to avoid.

 The Web is a great place to find other Photoshop products, such as *actions* (automated series of procedures that create special effects at the click of a button), brush sets, and pattern sets. Do a search for *"Photoshop add-ins"* or *"third-party Photoshop tools"* and you'll get an ever-growing list of sites where you can download all sorts of cool stuff — usually for a fee, but sometimes for no charge. Figure 6-22 shows the kind of looks you can get from non-Adobe filters.

Figure 6-22: Many amazing filter effects for Photoshop and Elements are available from non-Adobe sources.

In addition to searching the Web, you can find interesting filters and other stuff by poking around these sites:

✦ **Alien Skin Software** (www.alienskin.com) makes Eye Candy 4000, Xenofex, and Splat! plug-ins. Its three-pack (of all three programs) retails for $299. Eye Candy 4000 alone costs $169.

✦ **Auto FX's DreamSuite** (www.autofx.com) has two Series products. Series One provides special effects for graphics, text, and photos, and these effects are all easy to use. Series Two has features that allow you to turn your photos into puzzles (great gift idea for family photos or as a promotional item for clients) plus 11 other special effects. Series One retails for $199, and Series Two for $149.

✦ **Andromeda** (www.andromeda.com) offers several different filter sets, including light-scattering filters, lens filters, screen and mezzotint filters, outlining and woodcut filters, and special focus filters, ranging in price from $30 to $95. Andromeda also makes Velociraptor, a filter that puts trails on image contents, giving the objects the appearance of movement that's sort of a Photoshop fireworks display.

As you can tell, the variety of filters is quite wide, from conservative yet cool effects to real psychedelic experiences.

Check out www.photoshopuser.com, the official Web site of the National Association of Photoshop Professionals (NAPP). This site lists lots of *plug-ins* (software that adds to an application, expanding its capabilities), providing links to manufacturers and ratings of the various products so that you can avoid downloading any lemons. The association also offers other goodies, such as a great magazine. Your membership fee entitles you to subscribe to the magazine for just $10 a year and to attend seminars and training. You also get advance notice of Photoshop-related events.

Book VII
Restoring Old Photos

The 5th Wave   By Rich Tennant

RICHTENNANT

"Mary-Jo, come here quick! Look at this special effect I learned with the new graphics software!"

*P*erhaps you've mastered digital photography and now take only flawless pictures that need so little further improvement that most of your image-editing efforts are just minor tweaks. Fortunately, becoming a paragon of photographic prowess leaves you that much more time to tackle that wretched shoebox full of old photos you've inherited, each infected by tears, speckles, stains, faded spots, and, in a few cases, some vexing content (such as a tree) growing out of the top of some poor soul's cranium.

In this minibook, I show you how to use a scanner to capture those vintage prints, negatives, and transparencies, and then mend them using Photoshop and Elements. I explain how to brighten dark shadows, sharpen blurry images, correct and enrich faded colors, and replace torn or missing content. If you're waxing nostalgic, I even demonstrate some easy techniques for adding sepia tones to a photo. This book helps you restore vigor to even the most lifeless photos.

Chapter 1: Scanning Print Images

In This Chapter

⤶ **Preparing your originals**

⤶ **Selecting resolution**

⤶ **Choosing other scanner controls**

*Y*ou basically have three ways of scanning a color or black-and-white print into your computer: You can do it quickly, you can do it easily, or you can produce a high-quality digital image. If you're new to scanning, you can probably choose the fast route and do things the easy way or tediously create the best quality scan you can. If you want your scanning experience to be all three (fast, easy, and aesthetically satisfying), you need to read this chapter.

Modern scanning software helps you make the right decisions as you capture images from prints, but you still need to know what you're doing and what questions to ask yourself before you start. For example, what resolution should you use to scan a particular image? What other settings do you need to adjust? How can you scan problem prints with stains, scratches, bad color, or other defects?

How to get good scans is worthy of a book itself — indeed, I've written nine scanner books since 1990, including one just about scanning transparencies and negatives. But this chapter provides you with the basic information you need in order to grab good-looking images from prints, without hassles, 99 percent of the time. Whether you're restoring photos or planning to incorporate scanned prints into digital photo images, you can find what you need here.

In Book VI, Chapters 4 and 5, you can find more information on fixing old, blemished, or faded photos that you scan.

Prepping an Image for a Scan

The first thing to do before scanning is to prep your original. Although you might not have a lot of control over the artwork you need to scan, you can still prepare ahead of time to improve your chances of success. Here are a few tips:

✦ **Start with the best available original.** Don't use a copy print if you can avoid it. Use a print that was made recently from the original negative. Older prints are sure to have some scratches, or their colors might have aged over the years. You might even want to scan from the original negative or slide instead of from a print. (See Book VII, Chapter 2, for information on scanning transparent originals.) However, as long as you're scanning from a print, use the newest and best print you can find. If the print is housed in an album, frame, or cardboard display, carefully remove it before scanning unless removal will damage the picture.

✦ **Start with the largest print that fits on your scanner.** If you can choose between a 4 x 6 print and a 5 x 7 print, use the larger print. Because of the grain of the color emulsion in the print, a larger version is likely to be sharper and, more importantly, to have a larger *tonal range* — the range of colors from lightest to darkest. An 8 x 10 print might be even better, but there is a point of diminishing returns. An 8 x 10 might not be any sharper or better; it might simply show the grain of the film in a larger form, particularly if the print was made from a 35mm negative taken with an inexpensive camera. In addition, some scanners are known for having uneven illumination at the edges of the scanning area. A 5 x 7 print centered in the scanning glass won't suffer from this defect; an 8 x 10 print can't avoid it.

✦ **Clean the print and your scanner glass before you scan.** If you scan a dusty print, like the one shown in Figure 1-1, or if dust covers the glass platen or scanning bed of your scanner, you end up with an image that has dust spots that you must remove in your image editor. Dust the print carefully with a cloth and use Windex and compressed air on your scanner's bed.

✦ **Make sure the image is aligned properly on the scanner glass.** If you scan a print that's rotated slightly, you can always straighten it out in your image editor. Of course, you lose some quality, particularly when straightening horizontal and vertical lines that could have been scanned with proper alignment in the first place. Some scanner software actually can straighten skewed pictures for you, but you want to avoid that feature when possible. The straightening uses the edges of the photo for reference, and that might not coincide with the correct orientation of the image (if the picture itself was printed skewed, for example).

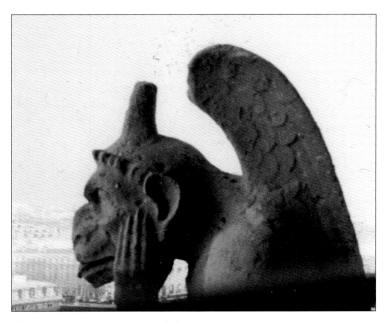

Figure 1-1: Dust off your prints before scanning!

Lining up images when they're face down on the scanner glass is tricky. Sometimes I hold the print up to the light and draw a straight line with a pencil on the back of the print. Then I can make sure the line is parallel to the top edge of the scanner glass so that the image in the photo is perpendicular to the direction of the scan. Hewlett-Packard has helped this problem by introducing a scanner with a transparent lid: You can see exactly how the print is aligned when you close the top. The latest versions of Photoshop Elements have a tool that can straighten up scanned images at the click of a mouse.

Working with Scanner Settings

When you're ready to scan an image, you'll find an array of settings, and this section is here to guide you through them. Setting the resolution probably gets the most attention, but your scanner likely has other settings — such as interpolation, sharpening, blurring/descreening, and halftone — that might also help you get the best possible scan. Read on to find out what these settings do, when they're useful, and how to set them.

Choosing a resolution

What's the best resolution to use for a particular scan? Note that this is very different from the question, "What's the top resolution I want for my scanner?" The thing is, the top resolution available in any scanner is unlikely to be of much use to you, and the figures the vendors provide don't really tell you much about the image quality you get at a given resolution, anyway. (For more on the sordid tale of how scanner manufacturers play with resolution numbers, see Book II, Chapter 4.)

Even so, particular tasks have recommended resolutions. Unless you're working with a special image, you probably want to keep within the guidelines that I lay out in the following sections.

Why not simply use the highest resolution of your scanner at all times and be done with it? Here are a few reasons why this is a dumb idea:

+ **Too much resolution wastes valuable hard drive space.** A 4 x 5 image scanned at 200 samples per inch (*spi* — the number of points in the image captured per linear inch) has 800,000 pixels and can be up to 6.4MB in size. (With the image compression provided by file formats such as TIFF and JPEG, the actual size on your hard drive is likely to be smaller.) Scan the same image at 2400 spi, and you can end up with a 76.8MB file! It wouldn't take long to fill up a hard drive with those babies; even if you archived them to a CD, you'd be able to fit only ten images on the CD and perhaps only 70 on a DVD. At 200 spi, you can pack 125 images on the same CD.

Printers measure resolution in dots per inch, and scanners measure it in samples per inch.

+ **High-resolution (hi-res) images take a long time to scan.** Depending on your scanner model, you might be able to scan that 200 spi image in ten seconds or so, but you're sure to wait for two or three minutes when scanning the same photo at 2400 spi.

+ **High-resolution scans of prints don't contain any more useful information.** This is the most important consideration, when you get right down to it. When you scan at a resolution higher than you need, all you're capturing is the grain of the paper (see Figure 1-2) or perhaps the film used to make the print. You're also getting beautiful close-up details of any scratches and dust on the original film plus any dust you forgot to remove before you scanned.

Also keep in mind that you actually need to consider three different resolutions:

✦ **The resolution of the scanner that captures the image:** I cover scanner resolution in this chapter.

✦ **The resolution of the display device that shows the image in your image editor:** Display resolution isn't something that you can do much about. You're probably working with a 17–19" color monitor and have the display resolution set to anywhere from 1024 x 768 pixels to (in my case) 1920 x 1440 or thereabouts.

✦ **The resolution of the output device, such as a printer that you'll use to reproduce the image:** The resolution of the output device, such as a 600 dpi laser printer, a 1440 dpi inkjet, or a high-resolution image setter, can affect the resolution you scan at. The higher the resolution of the output device, the more of your scanner's resolution that you can actually put to work.

Here are some guidelines for choosing a resolution for the two most common kinds of scanning tasks.

Figure 1-2: High resolution can just highlight the grain.

Line art

Line art includes black-and-white or color drawings comprising only solid lines, dots, or other strokes, with no shading. Artwork that has already been printed, such as photos clipped from publications, also qualifies as line art because although such images might look like photographs, they're actually composed of black and white halftone dots.

Line art can usually be scanned effectively at the same resolution that you'll use to print the image, or a fraction of it. If a 600 dpi laser printer outputs an image, use 600 spi. If you'll be using a 1440 dpi inkjet, consider using 720 spi (or something close). Doing this allows a 1:1 (or 4:1, if you halve the output device's resolution to make your scan) correlation between scanned pixels and printed dots. This reduces the chance of the stair-step effect known as *jaggies.* A 3200 spi scan is shown in Figure 1-3.

Figure 1-3: High-res scans of line art can provide sharp images.

Why not use 1440 spi when outputting to an inkjet printer? You'll find that the extra detail isn't needed, your image file is four times as large (compared with a lower resolution), and your file takes longer to print. However, if you're scanning something that really does have fine details and is so small that you can avoid mega-file sizes (postage stamps and other small engravings are the classic example), you can use the higher resolution.

Black-and-white and color photos

Black-and-white and color photos are known as *continuous tone* images because they contain a full range of tones from very light to very dark as well as all the shades in between. Photographs are a whole different ballgame than line art.

As you scan photos, choose a resolution based on two factors:

✦ What you plan to do with the photo and whether you'll be manipulating it in an image editor

✦ Whether you plan to enlarge it

For example, a print destined for a Web page might look just fine scanned at 75 spi because 75 spi is all you need for screen resolution. The same original scanned for reproduction using a printer should be scanned at around 150–200 spi. If you intend to manipulate the photo in your image editor or reproduce it at a size that's larger than the picture's original dimensions, use a higher resolution: perhaps 300 spi. Notice that none of these recommendations approaches the 1200–2400 spi top resolution of most scanners. High resolutions simply aren't required for photographs.

Most books about image editing, and even some scanning books, provide you with arcane formulas that you can use to calculate scanning resolutions for photos. These are usually based on the *halftone frequency* (the number of lines of halftone dots per inch in the "screen" used to create the halftoned version of your photograph). These formulas are needlessly complex. Who, other than professional photographers and other professional graphics workers, actually knows whether a photograph will be printed using an 85-line screen or a 133-line screen or some other frequency?

Today, digital photographers don't have to worry about these details. The halftoning is automatically handled by the printer driver that resides in your computer, and you don't need to know much about what's happening. If you scan a photo at 150–200 spi (or up to 300 spi if enlarging it), you'll get good results most of the time. The real pitfall is scanning at too high a resolution, which wastes your time and hard drive space. Your concern will probably focus more on how to remove moiré effects, discussed in the "Blurring/descreening" section, later in this chapter.

Many newer scanners can actually calculate an optimal resolution for you. You tell the scanner software what type of destination your image is intended for (Web page, laser printer, imagesetter, and so forth) and select a size for the image (50%, 100%, and so forth). Based on this information, the scanner then chooses the right resolution for you.

Book VII Chapter 1

Scanning Print Images

Interpolate, schmerpolate

I might as well tackle the topic of interpolation because you're going to e-mail me and ask about it anyway. Questions about scanner interpolation are the second-most-common queries (after resolution) that I have received in the last decade.

Interpolation isn't limited to scanners, of course. You would think so only because scanner vendors like to trumpet their products' interpolation prowess in their specifications lists. *Interpolation* is a process used to create new pixels any time an image is made larger or smaller or changed to a color depth other than the one at which it was captured.

Photoshop uses interpolation all the time. If you enlarge or reduce an image, Photoshop has to create more pixels (when you enlarge) or fewer pixels (when you reduce) to represent the same image. Photoshop also needs to come up with a new set of pixels when you change an image from, say, 24 bits at full color to 8 bits and 256 colors. Within Photoshop, interpolation is almost always a bad thing (even if it's a necessary thing) because you always lose some quality when your image editor obliterates real, actual pixels and replaces them with best-guess estimates. You should, therefore, try to retain your image at its original resolution (such as the resolution it was taken at with your digital camera) until you absolutely have to resize it. And always keep an unedited version of the file to fall back on, should you need to!

Sometimes, the term *interpolation* is reserved for making larger images from a given resolution. You'll see the term *downsampling* to describe the type of interpolation used to produce a smaller image. I'm not particularly fussy about terminology that's not often used correctly anyway, so I use *interpolation* to mean both enlarging and reducing images or scans.

When scanning, interpolation isn't quite as evil because the scanner is working with the original image and can avoid some of the quality loss that plagues your image editor.

Some sort of scanner interpolation takes place whenever you scan at anything other than the native resolution of the scanner. That means if you're using a 1200 spi scanner and scan at 2400 spi, the scanner actually captures 1200 samples per inch but creates 1200 new pixels to make the resolution seem higher. The same scanner at 300 spi must figure out which 300 pixels per inch best represent the full 1200 spi scan.

Actually, when scanning in even fractions or increments of the scanner's optical resolution, the results are usually quite good. The problems start when you try to scan at odd resolutions like 5000 spi or 332 spi.

As the scanner interpolates an image, it doesn't simply duplicate pixels (say, doubling all the pixels in a 1200 spi scan to produce a 2400 spi image) or throw away pixels (to create a 600 spi scan). Instead, the interpolation algorithm examines the pixels surrounding the new pixel and produces one with characteristics that closely match the transition between the pixels. That is, if one pixel is dark tone and the next pixel is light tone, a medium-tone pixel is created to insert between them, as shown in Figure 1-4.

Figure 1-4: Interpolation examines the pixels in the top line and creates the new pixels in the bottom line.

Interpolation is not all smoke and mirrors. A good interpolation algorithm can accurately calculate the pixels that would have been captured by the scanner if it had been able to scan at the interpolated resolution used. That is, you do get additional information through interpolation. However, there are diminishing returns. A 9600 x 9600 spi interpolated image is not eight times as sharp as one scanned at a true 1200 spi resolution.

Following are the most common interpolation algorithms, which have official names:

✦ **Nearest Neighbor:** With the Nearest Neighbor algorithm, the new pixels are created by examining the pixel nearest where the new pixel will go. This works fine with line art, in which the pixels change in predictable ways. However, the method doesn't allow for the fine and random gradations of tones found in photographs.

✦ **Bilinear:** This algorithm examines the pixels on either side of the target pixel and produces better quality images than the Nearest Neighbor method, although it is a little slower.

✦ **Bicubic:** The slowest commonly used method is also the best. Bicubic resampling uses sophisticated formulas to calculate the new pixel based on the pixels found above, below, and to either side of the new pixel.

Photoshop CS2 and the latest version of Elements have two new interpolation options: Bicubic Smoother and Bicubic Sharper. These can be used to fine-tune the most popular interpolation algorithm, making it (you guessed it) either smoother or sharper than the unadorned Bicubic version.

Sharpening

You might think of sharpening as a way to increase the resolution of an image without boosting its file size. That's not exactly true. All scanners include optional sharpening routines to enhance images as they are scanned. (In most cases, leaving this feature turned on is a good idea.) Sharpening actually only increases the apparent resolution of an image by increasing the contrast between pixels, but it works very well.

In use, a scanner's sharpening routines examine squares of pixels that are, say, 5 pixels on a side. Depending on the values of the other 24 pixels in the square, the scanner might (or might not) darken or lighten the center pixel to increase the contrast between that pixel and its neighbors. If the scanner determines that there is a significant difference in contrast between the center pixel and its neighbors, it can increase the contrast even further, making the pixel look sharper, at least in relation to its neighbors. The sharpening algorithms look at every pixel in an image as it relates to its neighboring pixels and increase the contrast as appropriate to enhance the sharpness. Pixels that are included in "edges" in your image are lightened or darkened to make them more distinct, as shown in Figure 1-5.

Figure 1-5: Higher contrast (right) can equal extra sharpness.

Because sharpening brings out details that are present in an image but that the scanner can't see otherwise, sharpening really can enhance the apparent resolution of the final image. That's why sharpening in the scanner is probably useful when making most scans. Don't overuse it with photographs, however, because the extra contrast can be objectionable.

Blurring/descreening

The opposite side of the sharpening coin is a common scanner feature called *descreening*. Descreening is used when you scan an image that has already been printed and that contains halftone dots, such as those found in newspapers, magazines, yearbooks, and other publications. The process blurs the image slightly by reducing the contrast between the edges (in this case, the dots) and tends to make the halftone dots merge together.

In practice, I've found that descreening settings in most scanners tend to overdo the blurring, and you can get much better scans of halftones by doing the blur yourself in Photoshop or another image editor, as shown in Figure 1-6. Descreening can also help you avoid the *moiré effect* (an objectionable pattern caused by interference between the arrangement of the original halftone screen and the pixels in the scanned image).

Figure 1-6: You can usually produce better descreened halftones, like the one at bottom, in your image editor.

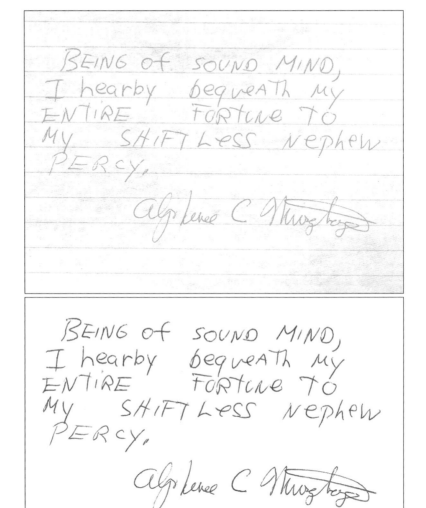

Figure 1-7: The blue lines are diminished while the reddish text is darkened in the bottom version.

Chapter 2: Restoring Images Captured from Slides, Negatives, and Other Formats

In This Chapter

- ✔ **Preparing your originals**
- ✔ **Selecting resolution**
- ✔ **Choosing other scanner controls**

*W*ith the introduction in the past few years of $200–$300 scanners designed especially for film, slide and negative scanning has finally come of age. If you have a collection of 35mm slides or discover a treasure trove of family negatives, you can now bring them into the digital realm easily and inexpensively. Although film's days as a primary snapshot medium are numbered, there's no reason why you can't enjoy working with your film-originated photos in your image editor.

Scanning old photos, slides, and negatives is a great way to preserve and share your family history, especially when you restore the images using the techniques described in the next chapter and elsewhere in this book. Your great-great-great-grandchildren will love you for it!

Of course, scanning prints and other opaque documents (or *reflective originals*) is far more common than scanning transparent originals, such as slides and negatives. In fact, most scanners can't handle anything but reflective originals. Sometimes, however, your only copy of an image is a transparency or negative. Other times, you might have both a hard copy reflective original and a transparency or negative film version, but the film is a better choice for scanning because film is usually in better condition and contains all the information originally captured. (You find out the difference between reflective and film originals in the "Examining Different Types of Film Originals" section, later in this chapter.)

Scanning film is not quite as intuitive a process as grabbing an image from a print. You can't slap the slide or negative down on the glass and press a button to begin scanning. Some of the same prep work I describe in Book VII, Chapter 1 is necessary, and you have additional considerations to think about as well. This chapter helps you put slide and negative scanning in perspective and offers some tips for getting the best results.

Film and Photography

Although film has long been a key part of the photographic process, the casual snapshooter has never given film itself much thought ever since the late 1960s. In the past three decades, "film" has come to mean those pesky strips, discs, slides, or canisters that you had to find when you wanted to have the best-quality print of pictures that had already been processed. Film became a necessary means to a desired end.

By the end of the film era, a sparkling color print for sharing or display became that desired end. As proof, consider your own pre-digital photographic work. You probably have prints filed away in albums and other prints in frames on your piano or over the fireplace. There are prints in your wallet and perhaps a few stuck to your kitchen appliances with magnets. The prints you aren't using right now are probably stacked in shoe boxes. But do you have any notion at all where the *negatives* used to make those prints are?

Of course you don't, despite the valiant efforts of film manufacturers and photofinishers to provide you with film storage envelopes or, in the case of the Advanced Photo System, permanent archiving in the same cassette used in your camera. Unless you're the fastidious type, when you want a reprint of a favorite picture, you probably take a print down to your finisher and have a copy made. Film is pretty useless, right?

Actually, film made photography as we know it possible. Until George Eastman introduced the first commercial transparent roll film in 1889, amateur photography was a daunting hobby indeed, pretty much limited to dry plates and other clumsy media that ordinarily only a professional photographer would be willing to mess with. For the hobbyist, photography was a daunting and potentially expensive hobby.

Black-and-white negative film made it possible to produce compact and more affordable cameras that anyone could use. By 1936, color photos (in the form of Kodachrome slides) became feasible, and in 1942, Kodacolor film for prints made the modern color snapshot possible. Is it a coincidence that the modern refrigerator, now universally used to display these prints, was invented at roughly the same time? I don't think so.

Amateur photographers used a mixture of color slides, black-and-white film/ prints, and color film/prints to capture their memories for several decades until automated, low-cost color printing in the '70s (and the ubiquitous mini-lab in the '80s) finally relegated both color slides and black-and-white prints to professional photographers and serious amateurs.

Today, if you take pictures, you either use a color print film (and end up with prints) or work with a digital camera (and end up with electronic images and prints). If you have slides or negatives to scan, you are probably a serious amateur or professional photographer or need to convert an older stash of film originals to digital form.

Why Scan Film?

One reason why you might scan film is that it's the only form of an image you have. You might not have a print at all, or the print you do have might be too small or might have suffered some damage. Scanning even a well-made 4 x 5 print won't yield the same detail you can get from a high-quality scan of an original negative or slide. The original always has more information than a second-generation copy, such as a print.

If you still shoot film regularly, you'll find lots of good reasons to shoot either slide film or print film and then scan the respective positives/negatives. Slide film — for the creative control it offers you — is the choice of professionals for a reason. What you shoot is what you get. When you shoot color negative film, the prints you get might vary significantly from what you saw through your viewfinder. For example, if you deliberately underexpose a shot to produce a silhouette effect, the automated printing system at your photofinisher will try to thwart your creative efforts by pumping extra light on your print. Instead of a silhouette, you get a washed-out image with highlights that are too bright. Figure 2-1 shows a typical image that has suffered these vagaries. Because the lab printed for the dark shadows, they are rendered lighter, while washing out the sunset. Scan the negative and make a print yourself, and you can optimize the image for the dramatic sunset, as shown in the right half of Figure 2-1.

Or maybe you took a picture at sunset and are surprised when the reddish colors you remember are printed a little bluer than you'd like by the automated machinery. And try as hard as you like, Kentucky bluegrass is going to come out green.

However, when you shoot slide film, what you see is what you get. If the film is processed well and if you were using the proper film for the lighting conditions, your image appears exactly as you composed and focused it. You can then scan your slide and get the exact picture you visualized.

Figure 2-1: Your photofinisher might give you a washed-out image (left), but you can scan and adjust your print to get the dramatic rendition you really want (right).

All this fuss probably makes you realize exactly how great digital photography is: You can take pictures the way you want them and never have to worry about your photofinisher messing with your vision. In one sense, slide film is the closest thing to digital imaging available. Transparencies can make a valuable complement to digital cameras for photographers who want the most versatility in their image-capturing options.

Scanning Options

If you want to scan transparencies or negatives, you have four primary options (ignoring the truly professional alternatives, such as drum scanners, which aren't available to the amateur digital photographer). I list them in order of descending quality.

Let the pros do it

Your photofinisher is equipped with high-resolution scanners that can convert your slides or negatives to a digital format. They can deliver the finished product to you on a high-resolution Photo CD (now available from a very limited number of labs, sometimes as a special-order item) or a lower-resolution Kodak Picture CD. Going this route is a good idea for several reasons:

✦ **No equipment to buy:** If you have an archive of film originals to convert and don't plan to scan slides or negatives on a regular basis, you'll find it economical to use your photofinisher's equipment and personnel instead.

✦ **Better quality:** The pros have better equipment than you're likely to purchase and can give you better overall quality.

✦ **Less time:** I scan slides and negatives all the time. It's time-consuming. After you've spent most of an afternoon scanning 30 or 40 slides, you'll wonder why you ever wanted to do the job yourself.

✦ **Lower cost:** Unless you have a ton of film originals to scan on a continuing basis, it will take you a very, very long time to amortize the cost of a good slide scanner compared with the small fee your finisher will charge for each scan.

Buy a slide scanner

Dedicated slide scanners are high-resolution devices designed specifically for scanning slides, transparencies, and negatives. With the new breed of inexpensive film scanners, just about anyone can justify one of these beasts. There are some advantages to choosing this method, too:

✦ **Customized quality:** Although your photofinisher will give you standardized results that look good, you might want to scan a particular original in a particular way to produce the exact image you want. Perhaps the information in the highlights is most important, and you don't care whether the shadows go black. Perhaps you want to scan only a particular portion of the original. If you have your own slide scanner, you can customize your scan to meet your own creative needs.

✦ **Quicker turnaround time:** I tell colleagues that I scan my own transparencies because of the turnaround time. My scanner sits on a table behind me, so all I have to do is turn around. I can have a scan on my screen in five minutes; if I used a photofinisher, I'd probably have to wait a week to get my results. If you're in a hurry, making your own scans is definitely faster.

✦ **Lower cost for higher volumes:** If you do your own scans, your biggest costs are the scanner and your own time. If you make many scans of slides and negatives over time, your in-house capability will eventually pay for itself if you factor in the time you expend running to the photofinisher. It takes a lot of scans to pay for a dedicated scanner, but serious amateurs and professionals can justify their expenditure more quickly than they realize. (Don't forget the fun factor, too.)

Use a transparency-capable flatbed

Many flatbed scanners come with a slide-scanning attachment (chiefly a light source to transilluminate [shine light through] the originals) and have sufficient resolution and dynamic range to do a decent job scanning slides. This option has a few advantages:

**Book VII
Chapter 2**

**Restoring Images
Captured from
Slides, Negatives,
and Other Formats**

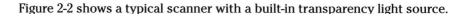

✦ **Lower cost:** There's no expensive dedicated slide scanner to buy. You can find flatbed scanners that can grab decent film images for $200 or even less.

✦ **Acceptable quality:** If "good enough" is good enough, you'll find that flatbeds do give you enough quality to work with. You can still do some of the same customization steps with your scanner that make the dedicated slide scanner attractive. Hey, it beats paying a gazillion dollars for a slide scanner, doesn't it?

✦ **Quicker turnaround:** Again, just turn around and scan your slide or negative. No running to the photofinisher.

Figure 2-2 shows a typical scanner with a built-in transparency light source.

Figure 2-2: Some scanners have transparency light sources built into the lid.

Try the Rube Goldberg approach

Before I ever had a slide scanner or flatbed with a transparency attachment, I was happily scanning my own slides by using my own cobbled-together apparatus. All you really need to scan film originals is a flatbed scanner with high-enough resolution to do a decent job with small pieces of film (probably a minimum of 1200 samples per inch [spi]); a carrier of some sort to hold the film or slide flat against the scanner glass while blocking off other stray rays of light; and a broad, even, diffuse white light source.

Do-it-yourself limitations

You'll probably run into some limitations when scanning film yourself using an inexpensive slide and negative scanner or when using your flatbed scanner. Here are a few things to keep in mind:

✓ **35mm only:** The least expensive dedicated film scanners handle only 35mm and smaller film formats. If you have 620/120 roll film or sheet film, like those used in old box-and-view cameras, twin-lens reflexes, or even "press cameras," you won't be able to scan it yourself. Dedicated film scanners that work with larger sizes typically cost $1,000 or more.

✓ **Size limitations:** Even flatbed scanners that can capture film can probably scan only limited sizes. Perhaps your unit can accommodate up to 2¼" wide film (6cm) but no larger. If you're lucky, you may have a flatbed that works with 4 x 5 or 5 x 7 sheet film.

✓ **Dust busting limitations:** More expensive scanners use a sophisticated feature called Digital ICE to remove dust from film. This hardware/software combination is actually able to discern dust spots on film and remove them without degrading the rest of the image. Lower-cost scanners might have some sort of software "dust brush" that actually blurs the image a bit.

I don't recommend such arrangements if you plan to do much film scanning, but if you're in a pinch, you might see what you can put together. Rube Goldberg would be proud.

I don't list bullet-point advantages of this approach because other than cost and the sheer joy of the do-it-yourself experience, there aren't any.

However, you can try to copy film by using your digital camera and a homemade rig if you're very daring. A few camera vendors offer slide copying attachments for their digital cameras, usually the digital single lens reflex (dSLR) versions. They can cost $100 or less and give decent results if your expectations aren't high. The more resolution your digital camera has, the better your results will be.

Book VII
Chapter 2

Restoring Images
Captured from
Slides, Negatives,
and Other Formats

Examining Different Types of Film Originals

To successfully scan film originals, you need to understand the differences between prints, negatives, slides, and transparencies. I summarize them in this section.

Prints

You already know about scanning prints if you used the tips in Book VII, Chapter 1. However, it's useful to go a little deeper into prints (so to speak) so that you can better understand the challenges that film originals present.

Like color slides and transparencies, negatives have the same long dynamic range. That makes them much better for making prints but increases the challenges your scanner faces in capturing all that extended information.

Exotica

As your reputation for old photo restoration magic grows, you'll be called upon to scan and fix up some really old, faded pictures of a rather exotic (for our 21st-century eyes) nature. These can include old daguerreotypes, silver prints, 19th-century glass plates, or even tintypes like the one shown in a wretched, unrestored version at top in Figure 2-4, and a wretched, partially restored version at bottom.

Figure 2-4: Family members who discovered this old damaged tintype (top) were pleased when even a small amount of the picture information was able to be restored.

Although these old photos were captured using different technologies, they all share some common attributes. First, they may be housed in folders, glued to cardboard, or tucked away in frames. You'll need to be very careful when removing them for scanning to avoid damaging the picture.

Second, it's very likely that the old pictures will be faded, dark, or low in contrast. You'll want to increase the contrast and sharpness in your scanner's controls, if possible, because the improvements you make can sometimes be even better than what you could achieve later in your image editor. That's because the scanner is working with the original material.

Finally, your old photos probably have dust spots, pits, mottling, and other defects that can't be removed by scanning alone. Your best bet is to try to correct these problems in your image editor. It's a good idea to scan the photo several times using different tonality settings. You'll end up with several versions, each with different details brought out. You can combine the best portions of each to create one finished photo.

Scanning Film

If I haven't scared you off scanning slides, transparencies, and negatives by now, it's time to get to work. You need to refer to the instruction manual for your scanner and the slide scanning software for the exact steps to follow, but here are some general tips.

Prepping the film

You absolutely must make sure the film is clean, particularly if you are scanning a 35mm slide or negative. Sometimes dust settles on the film when it's still wet and becomes embedded in the emulsion side; sometimes film just gets plain dusty. Because small film images are enlarged many times as you work with them, you magnify the size of the dust or other artifacts at the same time. For example, a 24mm x 36mm transparency enlarged to 5 x 7 inches is blown up to roughly five times its original size — and each tiny dust mote is visible when magnified that much.

Dust on either transparencies or negatives appears as dark black dots when scanned, of course, because the dots block the light from passing through to the sensor. However, when scanning a negative, you reverse the negative image to create a positive, turning the dust spot into a white speck. Tiny white specks can blend in with lighter areas of your image a little and are fairly easy to retouch out of the dark areas. (That's not to imply that you can go ahead and scan dusty negatives.) Dust on transparencies shows up as dark spots that are very visible and unsightly, so you should take extra care to make sure your transparencies are extremely clean when you scan them.

Clean dust from either a transparency or negative with a soft brush, an ear syringe, or a blast of canned air. Be careful not to allow the residual dust to scratch your soft film as you remove it. That's why soft brushes and air are your best tools. Figure 2-5 shows a typical slide scanner's film carriage. Dust off the film after you mount it in the carrier.

Figure 2-5: Dust off your film after inserting it in the scanner's carrier.

Film always has two sides: an emulsion side (where the image information is stored) and a base side. The emulsion side is usually dull looking when compared with the shiny base side. If you're somewhere that is fully lit, you can tell which is which by holding the film sideways and looking across the film. If you view a strip of negatives, you'll find that the film curls toward the emulsion side. If you plan to scan a Kodachrome slide, the emulsion side appears to be etched.

There is another way to tell which side is the emulsion side, and it works even in total darkness, but you're not going to like it. Back in my darkroom days, when I wanted to know which was the emulsion side of a piece of film or photographic paper, I'd put an edge between my lips. The emulsion side sticks to your lip. If you want to test this out, don't slobber all over the image area of an important image.

You can sometimes remove stubborn artifacts by soaking the film in distilled water. However, this works only if the dust hasn't replaced some of the image-forming part of the emulsion. In addition, the water removes the protective chemical applied to color film as a last step (black-and-white film is simply washed and allowed to dry after processing), so you need some of that solution if you want your film to last after cleaning. As you might guess, washing film should be done only as a last resort and only by those who know what they're doing. In the olden days, photographers used to do wild and crazy things with film to make it printable, including soaking it in oil to mask scratches and printing it "wet."

Performing the scan

When your film is clean and you're ready to start scanning, here are the steps to follow:

1. **Place the film on or in the scanner (depending on whether you're using a flatbed scanner or a dedicated film scanner) in a holder designed for it.**

   The holder masks off the areas outside the image portion of the film. This is an important step that reduces the possibility of stray light striking the sensor, thus reducing the amount of contrast in your image.

2. **Insert the film in the holder so that the emulsion side of the film is facing the sensor.**

   You want the light to pass through the film's base side and leave through the emulsion side. If you do the reverse, the light passes through the emulsion and is then diffused by the base side, giving you an image that is less sharp than it might be.

3. **Make sure you've done whatever is necessary to turn on your flatbed scanner's transparency light source.**

   Usually, this step is performed in the scanning software. If you're scanning a color negative, your scanning software has a dialog box, like the one shown in Figure 2-6, that lets you specify what brand and type of color film is being scanned. That ensures that the orange mask and other characteristics of that particular color negative film are dialed into the scanning software. You'll find the brand name of the film printed along the edge of the film itself.

4. **First do a *prescan,* which is the step that all scanner software provides to let you capture a preview image before doing the main scan.**

   While you're viewing the prescanned image, your scanning software might offer various controls that let you choose black points and white points (the darkest and lightest areas of the image that contain image information).

**Book VII
Chapter 2**

Restoring Images
Captured from
Slides, Negatives,
and Other Formats

Figure 2-6: Choose your film brand and type to optimize the scan.

5. Make any corrections that are appropriate by using the dust removal, sharpening, brightness, contrast, and tonal controls of your scanner software.

The options vary widely from program to program.

6. Set the black points and white points and then choose your resolution.

If you're making an important scan, you'll want to choose the highest optical resolution your flatbed scanner provides, typically 1200 to 2400 spi. A dedicated film scanner has resolution choices in the 2700 to 4000 spi range (and up). You can choose the setting recommended for the size of film you're scanning.

Be prepared for a long wait while the scanner painstakingly captures all that detail, and for the size of the file you end up with. A good scan of a transparency is a beautiful thing to behold, so I can assure you it's worth the wait!

Chapter 3: Some Common Fixes for Vintage Photos

In This Chapter

⮕ **Returning a faded picture to brighter days**

⮕ **Working with sepia-tone tools**

⮕ **Replacing what's been lost to rips, tears, and deep scratches**

This chapter concentrates on fixing up vintage photos. After all, vintage photos present a unique situation. They're often the most cherished yet the least cared-for photos we have. I don't know about you, but I have boxes of them in my house, and I'd despair for weeks if they were lost. But am I storing them properly and making sure they don't get damp, too dry, too hot, and so on? Nope. So they're precious to me, but I don't have the time to put them all into acid-free paper photo albums or frame them, and the boxes keep getting moved around, stored wherever there's room, with no regard for the temperature or humidity. Inside the boxes, the photos are scuffing each other every time the box is moved.

So what can I do? Of course, the first step is to properly store and archive them, but in addition to or in lieu of that, I can scan them, store the scanned files in my computer, use image editing software to clean them up, and then print them. The printed digital versions can be kept in frames, hung on the wall or stood up on the piano, with no fear of sun damage, because they can always be reprinted. I can give them as gifts and store the really precious ones in a safe place so that I always have a backup of the last known picture of my great-great-great-grandmother should anything happen to the original. Better yet, I can make copies on multiple CDs or DVDs and store them in several different locations (such as a safety deposit box) to guard against even the worst-case scenarios.

If this sounds like a good plan to you — and I assume it does or you wouldn't be reading about restoring old photos — then read on. In this chapter, I explain some common solutions to all-too-common problems — photos that show the signs of age, wear, and tear. If you need to get your old photos into digital form, check out the material on scanning in Book VII, Chapter 2.

Repairing Vintage Photos: The Basics

Vintage photographs present some very common problems, some of which are explored in earlier chapters. Over time, the image fades because of age, developing procedures, the paper it was printed on, or exposure to the sun, extreme heat, or dampness. Dampness can cause even more harm because it can cause mold to grow, which eats away the coating on the photos and can damage the paper as well. In many cases, multiple culprits have been and are at work, and you'll have multiple problems — faded image content along with scuffs, scratches, stains, mold, dust, and outright damage in the form of rips, tears, and missing corners. Some old images may be in the form of slides or negatives, which have their own deterioration problems.

Figure 3-1 shows a vintage photo that was originally glued to a piece of cardboard. Over time, the cardboard dried out, and one of the corners has cracked and fallen off. The image itself is quite faded; the original crisp blacks and whites are now very muted shades of gray.

When faced with an image like this, you need to perform a little triage. What do you do first? Improve the color? Replace the corner? Clean up the scratches and scuff marks? It really depends on the location and severity of the problems and which problems bother you the most.

Consider these ideas for how to approach an image with multiple problems:

Figure 3-1: Faded, worn, and torn old photos often present multiple problems.

✦ **If multiple problems appear in a single area, solving one might solve the other(s).** Consider a torn corner with a big stain along the tear. If you paste content from the opposite corner over it (rotating the pasted content, of course), you might get rid of the stain, too (assuming that the other corner isn't similarly stained). You find out how to replace torn or missing content later in this chapter.

✦ **If a portion of the edge or frame is missing, try to crop out the damaged part.** When you can crop around the image, you eliminate the need to replace the missing corner or side. Of course, you have to consider whether the missing portion includes part of the image that is important to its composition. Figure 3-2 shows an image that can be cropped to just the important parts, eliminating hours of restoration work that would have been spent rebuilding the damaged mat the image was glued to.

Figure 3-2: Crop away the damaged edges, leaving a cleaner, neater image.

If you can't crop, how bad is the damage? Does it lend an air of history to the picture? Part of the charm of vintage photos is that they look old. The places, people, clothes, scenery, and architecture all add to that charm. So if the photo itself looks like it was taken in 1897, what's the harm in that? If the damage is on someone's face or across the front of the family home, yes, try to fix it. If the damage is on the periphery or doesn't detract from the overall appeal of the image, consider leaving it alone.

+ **Tackle structural problems first.** First, replace that missing corner or fill in that the hole or deep crack in the photo. Then go about improving color quality, eliminating tiny scratches and spots, or bringing out detail lost to fading or bad lighting. You'll find more information on replacing missing or damaged content later in this chapter.

+ **Work slowly and deliberately.** Don't try to work fast or do too many things at once. Your results show your approach, and a slap-dash job leaves you with a slap-dash photo. If the picture is that precious or historically important, it's worth laboring over, zooming in to get things right, editing pixel by pixel.

When restoring photos, you probably want to go against my advice in Book VII, Chapters 1 and 2, in which I say that high resolutions aren't needed for scanning photographs. Scanning a photo for restoration is a special case. You may want to scan at a fairly high resolution of 600 samples per inch (spi) or more. You can always reduce file size later when optimizing a photo for use on the Web, or if you need to send the file via e-mail or store it on some low-density media.

By scanning it at a high resolution, you get all the color, light, and texture information possible, and all that information gives you more to work with. If you scan at a lower resolution, and a face's features have been lost to time, you won't have as many colors and details to work with as you rebuild that face. When the image looks right, you can reduce the resolution for a more reasonably sized file. You end up with a photo that's about the same resolution as an ordinary photo you've scanned, but you'll be glad you had some extra information to work with during the restoration.

Replacing Depth and Detail

One of the things that gets lost when a photo ages is the detail — the textures, the features, the small elements that gave the photo clarity and interest when it was new. The details can be scuffed off by constant abrasion of the photo's surface, or they can be bleached away by exposure to the sun. If your photo's details are lost to either or both of these causes, you can find tools in virtually any image editing application to solve the problem:

✦ **Burn and Dodge tools** deepen shadows and brighten highlights, respectively. You probably need to use these tools during restorations more than when working on ordinary photos because you encounter faded images and dark areas more often in old photos.

✦ **Sharpening filters and tools** bring image content into focus. Again, restorations need this kind of manipulation because, frankly, many old photos weren't that sharp to begin with.

Shedding light on the subject

I talk about the Dodge (lightening) tool found in Photoshop and Elements in Book VII, Chapter 4. However, most image editing applications have a Dodge or similarly named tool. *Dodge* is an old photography term, so it's not specific to any particular software manufacturer's lingo. You can use the Dodge tool to add light to images that you're restoring by clicking and/or painting over the image after customizing the tool as needed to make sure it creates the desired effect.

To use your image editor's Dodge tool, follow these simple steps:

1. **Click the Dodge tool to activate it.**

   You usually find the Dodge tool on your image editor's Tool palette. It might also be a special mode for the Brush tool.

2. **Check out the tool's options, whether they appear on a bar or in a dialog box or palette, and adjust the intensity or strength of the tool**

(how much light it will shed) and the size of the brush with which you're applying the light.

3. **After the settings you want are in place, click or drag over the area to be lightened.**

   If the results are too harsh or dramatic, undo them (press Ctrl+Z on a PC/⌘+Z on a Mac) and tweak the tool's settings. Then try again.

You might find that the Dodge tool actually removes detail if you use it too much. It's best used when shadows are so deep that detail is impossible to discern or when age has darkened (rather than lightened or washed out) image content.

Don't be afraid of dark shadows

In most image editing applications, you can find a Burn (darkening) tool, too. The Burn tool intensifies dark shadows to make a faded shadow in an old photograph dark again or to add darkness where there was none. In the process, using this tool can heighten the perceived level of detail in a photo. Adding detail to a faded photograph is difficult, but using the Burn tool can help. As shown in Figure 3-3, when a faded face in this old-time photo is slightly darkened with the Burn tool, the features become more distinct.

Figure 3-3: At left, the left half of the face is the original; the right half was burned to bring out details. At right, more shadows are applied.

The Burn tool works much like the Dodge tool, and here are the simple steps:

1. **Click the Burn tool to activate it.**

   You can find the Burn tool on the Tool palette of most image editors, or as a special mode of the Brush tool.

   This typically activates an Options bar or palette that gives you settings to control how the Burn tool works.

2. **Set the Burn tool's options to the levels needed.**

   These usually are settings to specify whether the burning is applied to highlights, midtones, or shadows, and how big a brush is used to apply the darkening effect.

3. **When your settings are in place, drag over the image to darken it.**

   You can also click one or more times on a spot that needs more darkness, as shown at right in Figure 3-3.

 Just like a big fire is much worse than a little one, a little burning is good, but too much is destructive. Don't go over and over a spot with the Burn tool because you'll end up scorching the image with so much darkness that you lose some or all of your image detail.

Creating focus by sharpening images

Many old photographs were taken with relatively long exposures by today's standards, resulting in blurs from the movement of fidgety subjects. In addition, many old-time cameras had what photographers would call *soft lenses* that produced a somewhat blurry rendition. You can sharpen such images with manual tools, such as brush-based tools that allow you to paint on a sharpening effect with your mouse, or you can use sharpening filters to do the job in a more uniform way. Either method has the same effect in terms of how the focus is achieved. When you *sharpen* an image, you increase the contrast between adjacent pixels. By making dark pixels darker and light pixels lighter, you make each pixel stand out — therefore, its neighbor stands out, too. The sharpen tools and filters can be taken too far, of course, but if used sensibly, they can bring out the details that you thought you'd lost forever.

Running with Sharp (en) tools

Using a Sharpen tool (you can find one in just about any image editing application) is pretty straightforward. Before using a Sharpen tool, however, make sure that you're on the right layer if your image has layers. Also, if you want to confine your sharpening to a specific area, make sure that area is selected. Now, go!

1. **Click the Sharpen tool to activate it.**

   You can usually find this tool in the Tool palette of your image editor. When you click the tool, an Options bar or palette appears.

2. **Use the tool's Options bar or palette to control the way the tool works.**

   You can usually adjust its intensity, and you can always choose a larger or smaller brush size to control how much of your image or selection is sharpened with each click or drag.

3. **Click and/or drag over the area to be sharpened.**

   You can go over the same spot more than once, but don't go too far. Figure 3-4 shows the results of sharpening that's been overdone, producing an exaggerated, pixelated effect.

Figure 3-4: Photos can be sharpened beyond recognition.

Focusing with filters

Sharpening with a filter requires, of course, that your software has filters — or at least special-effects tools that perform this particular kind of task. If you're using Paint Shop Pro, PhotoImpact, Corel PhotoPaint, or many other image editors, you have at your disposal various sharpening filters that you can use to apply generalized sharpening or edge-specific effects to your old photographs. Located on the Filter menu (or its equivalent) in most editors, you can apply an all-over sharpening or an *unsharp mask effect* — a mask that applies sharpening to the edges within a photo and blurs the rest. The results might be just what the doctor ordered!

To use the typical Sharpen filters, follow these steps:

1. **Locate the Filter menu, go to the Sharpen submenu, and choose the filter that you want to apply.**

   If you choose any of the Sharpen filters other than Unsharp Mask, the sharpening occurs without any intervention from you; there is no dialog box or anything to adjust.

2. Choose Unsharp Mask if it's available in your image editor.

Use the settings in this dialog box to control the intensity of the results. A preview window within the dialog box makes it easy to see how your adjustments to the filter's settings affect the outcome.

If you want all-over sharpening in your image or selection, you might prefer using the Sharpen filters because there's no chance of your mouse strokes being visible or of going too far in one spot and not far enough in another. You can focus the filter's effects by making a selection prior to invoking the filter command, which limits the filter's effect on the entire image but still gives you a uniform result within the selected area.

Correcting Faded Colors

Of course, not all old photos are black and white. Many treasured pictures date from the 1950s or later, when family photographers began the great changeover to color film. Unfortunately, films of that day weren't as stable as they are today, and the colors of many of these old pictures have faded drastically. When colors wash out over time, they take with them the information that was originally available in the image. Was it a sunny day with a blue sky? Was it summer? Winter? What color dress is your grandmother wearing? Was that a brown dog or a black dog? To get the answers to these questions, you go to your image editing software and ask whether the original colors can be restored. If you have the right software, the answer should be yes. You might have to make up some stuff, depending on how washed out and faded the photo has become, but some quick and easy tools can resurrect whatever color is still available.

Adjusting color levels

Most image editing applications have several automatic color-adjustment tools. Some of these tools work without requiring any information from you, and others present a dialog box that you can use to decide how much color and which colors to increase or balance. Using Photoshop and Paint Shop Pro as examples, you can use the following commands:

✦ Photoshop's Levels, Auto Levels, and Auto Color commands, located on the Image➪Adjustments submenu

✦ Paint Shop Pro's Color Balance, Hue/Saturation/Lightness, and Colorize commands, found on the Color➪Adjust submenu or on the Color menu itself

If you see an ellipsis (...) after a menu command, a dialog box appears when you choose the command. If there is no ellipsis, the command is one that just happens; you choose it, and it does its job, whatever that may be. The job it does is based on default settings that are part of the program, and you might or might not be able to edit these settings.

Increasing saturation

When it comes to controlling color, you don't have to rely purely on menu commands and dialog boxes to revive your image colors. If you'd prefer, you can use your mouse to manually adjust colors, clicking and dragging to add or take away color with the Sponge tool, found in both Photoshop and Photoshop Elements.

The Sponge tool adds color (in Saturate mode) or removes color (in Desaturate mode), and you can control how much color is added or taken away through the tool's Options bar.

To adjust your color intensity with the Sponge tool, follow these steps:

1. **Click the Sponge or Desaturate tool to activate it.**

   You can find this tool on the Tool palette of most image editors.

2. **Choose Saturate or Desaturate from the Mode drop-down list in the Options bar (or your image editor's equivalent).**

3. **Adjust the setting in the toolbar's Flow drop-down menu.**

   Some image editors use Pressure or Opacity to indicate this parameter.

   A greater number here could mean more saturation or more desaturation, depending on what mode you chose in Step 2.

4. **Use the image editor's Brush menu to set the brush size for the area to be edited.**

   You want to choose a brush that's big enough to do the job without a lot of repeated strokes. Each pass over the same spot increases the effects of the tool in that spot.

5. **Drag your mouse over the area to be sponged, being careful not to go over the same spot too many times.**

   Going over the same spot too many times or using a Flow setting that's too high makes your strokes seem too obvious.

Adding color adjustment layers

What if the color is really gone and you can't retrieve it or rejuvenate it? You're faced with the same decision that Ted Turner faced when his organization began colorizing old movies. What color was that dress, really? How about that hat? The sky is blue and the grass is green, but some of the other colors are pure guesswork.

Fortunately, however, guessing the color is the hardest part when making a photo restoration of a faded color picture. You can add any color you like via a new layer. Of course, this approach requires that your software supports the use of layers, and that you're familiar with the Layers palette in your application — how to select a layer, delete a layer, and so on. I use Paint Shop Pro for this demonstration.

So what does a new layer do for your color? Well, nothing if it's just a regular old blank layer. But if it's an *adjustment layer,* it can do a lot. Figure 3-5 shows Paint Shop Pro's Color Balance dialog box, which you access by choosing Layers⇨ New Adjustment Layer⇨Color Balance.

Figure 3-5: When you create a new Color Balance Adjustment Layer, this dialog box appears.

This same process is available in Photoshop — just choose Layer⇨New Adjustment Layer, and its submenu offers a similar set of choices for the role the new layer will play.

Adjustment layers

Adjustment layers are special layers that control a particular type of modification, such as brightness/contrast, color balance, hue/saturation, or even curves. Any changes that you make to a particular adjustment layer apply only to the layers stacked beneath the adjustment layer in your image editor's Layers palette. The advantage of adjustment layers is that you can change the adjustment at any time or even turn it off entirely to cancel the changes or to review what your image looks like without the adjustment. In contrast, if you apply a particular modification directly to a layer — say, to change color balance — there's no easy way to reverse that adjustment without reverting to an earlier state in your image editing process.

To create an adjustment layer, follow these steps:

1. **With your faded image open on-screen, choose Layer⬦New Adjustment Layer⬦Color Balance from the main menu bar.**

   The dialog box that appears lets you raise and lower the color components, one level at a time. If your image is in RGB mode, you can adjust the red, green, and blue levels. If your image is in CMYK mode, you can tweak the levels of cyan, magenta, yellow, and black in the picture.

   Each of the New Adjustment Layer submenu commands produces a different dialog box, and each dialog box offers sliders and text boxes into which you can enter levels for the image component being adjusted — brightness or contrast, hue, lightness, and so on. If it's not clear which of these components your image needs help with, be brave and do some experimenting. You can always undo an edit by pressing Ctrl+Z (⌘+Z on a Mac).

2. **Make your adjustments by dragging the sliders to the left or right or by entering new color levels.**

   You can also choose which elements of your image you're going to adjust: Shadows, Midtones, or Highlights.

3. **To see the results of your adjustments before you commit to them, click the Proof button (the big eye) to get a preview in the image window.**

   With some image editors, the results of your change appear in the main image window as you apply them.

4. **When you like the results, click OK to apply the changes to your image.**

   A new layer appears in the Layers menu, as shown in Figure 3-6.

Figure 3-6: Each adjustment layer you add appears on the Layers menu.

Of course, if you change your mind after adding an adjustment layer, you can use the Undo command or History palette (if you're using Photoshop or Elements) to go back in time before the adjustment layer was created. You can also delete the layer, and your image returns to its original state.

Eastman Kodak Company's Applied Science Fiction division (www.asf.com) offers a selection of Photoshop-compatible plug-ins that can streamline correcting colors and tweaking your images in other ways.

Getting Nostalgic with Sepia Tones

Don't you love those old brownish photos? They're so much warmer than black-and-white but not as garish as color. A sepia-tone photo just says *vintage photo*. Over time, sepia-tone photos can become less sepia. They can fade to a pale yellowish color or be mistaken for a dirty black-and-white photo if the fading is allowed to go too far.

If your sepia-tone photos aren't very sepia anymore, or if areas of them have been bleached by sun damage or abuse, you can restore the sepia-ness to the whole image or just to part of it. You can also make a black-and-white photo look like a sepia-tone image.

Evening out existing sepia tones

So your sepia-tone photo is blotchy; some of the photo still has those warm sepia tones, but other areas are faded and dull. What to do? Select the faded area and then, in Paint Shop Pro, choose Effects⇨Artistic Effects⇨Sepia. I use Paint Shop Pro here just as an example; most image editing applications have a similar feature. Even if your particular program doesn't offer it, you might be able to find a third-party effect that you can download off the Internet — a filter for Photoshop, for example.

To use Paint Shop Pro's Sepia Toning dialog box, follow these steps:

1. **Select the area to be adjusted.**

   I recommend using a freeform Lasso selection tool. Avoid the geometric shape selectors because they make the adjusted area stand out too much.

2. **Choose Effects⇨Photo Effects⇨Sepia Toning from the main menu.**

   The Sepia Toning dialog box opens, as shown in Figure 3-7.

3. **Use the Amount to Age slider to increase or decrease the amount of sepia added to the image.**

The Before version of the image appears on the left, and the After version on the right.

4. **When you like how the After version looks, click the Proof button (the big eye) to see the change previewed in your image window.**

5. **If you're happy with the preview, click OK to apply the changes to your image.**

Proof button

Figure 3-7: Sepia tones looking sapped? Restore their original glory with the Sepia Toning dialog box.

If you're tinkering with a very small area, use the Sepia Toning dialog box zoom tools (located between the Before and After images in the dialog box) to get close enough to judge the effectiveness of your adjustments.

Converting a black-and-white photo to sepia tone

The process of converting a black-and-white photo to sepia tone is virtually identical to the process of evening out the sepia tones in a photo that's already a sepia-tone image. The only difference is that you might have to change the color mode of your image beforehand. If your application (Paint Shop Pro, in this case) sees your image as a true black-and-white or grayscale image, the Sepia command is dimmed in the Effects submenu.

What to do if it's dimmed? Choose Image⇨Increase Color Depth. One or more of the submenu's commands (as shown in Figure 3-8) become available, depending on the photo's current color status. Choose the highest depth level possible (up to RGB - 8 bits per channel; more than that isn't necessary) because the more color information you add to your image the more color manipulation you can perform.

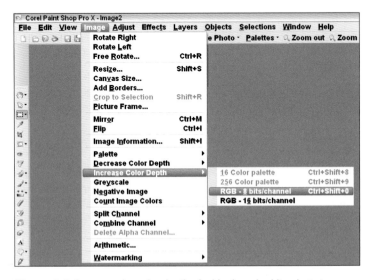

Figure 3-8: Increase the color depth of a black-and-white photo to access the Sepia command.

After you make this change, the Sepia command becomes available, and you can open the Sepia Toning dialog box and go to work making your black-and-white photo into a fake sepia tone.

Rip! Replacing Torn or Missing Content

Although you encounter physical defects in all kinds of photos, these defects seem more prevalent in old pictures that have been stored carelessly, maybe ripped out of an album a time or two or even pinned up on a bulletin board. Cracks and crevices are the sort of damage that you might think is beyond repair. How wrong you'd be if you thought that! Although not all image editing packages are capable of fixing these instances of very serious damage, most of them are. Certainly Photoshop, Photoshop Elements, and Paint Shop Pro — three of the most popular tools available — are capable of restoring even the most seemingly hopeless photo.

Sometimes the answer to your problem is much easier or straightforward than you thought it would be. In the case of photo editing, nothing is simpler than a paintbrush. You pick the color to paint with, set the size and style of the brush, adjust the shape of the brush, and paint over the scratch, scuff mark, or other type of small mark on your image. What could be easier? Most packages have more sophisticated tools, some that even let you borrow content from one spot in the image and use the content elsewhere. But if the scratch or spot is really tiny, do you need to go to any more trouble than you'd go to if you had to touch up a tiny chip in your car's paint? No. You probably wouldn't call the auto body shop and have the car sanded, primed, and painted; you'd whip out the touch-up paint, and good-bye chip.

When you're ready to take the easy way out, follow these steps with your application's Paint Brush or Brush tool. You can even use a Pencil tool if your scratch is very thin:

1. **Click either the Brush or Pencil tool.**

   Use the Brush for larger areas or with damage that has soft edges, such as scuff marks, abrasions, or tears. Use the Pencil tool if your scratches are very fine and sharp-edged.

2. **Set the options so that they fit with the task at hand.**

   When the tool becomes active, so do its options. As shown here for Photoshop Elements (Figure 3-9), you can adjust the size, shape, and style of the Brush tool, which controls how and how much color it applies.

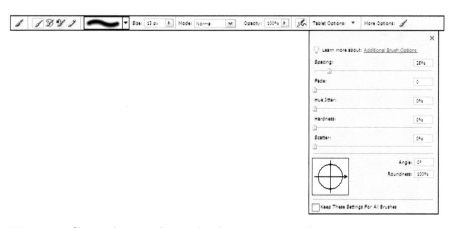

Figure 3-9: Change the specs for your brush to meet your needs.

3. **Select the color you want to apply in order to cover up the flaw in your image.**

   In Photoshop, you have the Color Picker, which you open by clicking the Foreground Color button on the toolbox. Other applications might have a color-sampling tool in the brush palette or along the side or bottom of the application window.

4. **With the proper color selected, go back to the desired tool (the Brush or Pencil) and then begin painting or drawing out the unwanted scratches, scuffs, and spots, as shown in Figure 3-10.**

   You can click to get rid of a small dot, or drag to get rid of a scratch.

Figure 3-10: Paint away the scratch, spot, scuff, or other small mark.

Got a long stretch of scratch to cover? Don't try to do it in one stroke. Instead, nibble at the problem with short strokes, one after the other. That way, if you mess up, you can undo the small changes with the Undo command or the History palette without undoing your entire painted line. Only the last short stroke where you went astray disappears.

Book VIII

Printing and Sharing Your Digital Images

The 5th Wave — By Rich Tennant

COSMETIC SURGERY

"This time, just for fun, let's see what you'd look like with bat ears and squash for a nose."

The best part about taking great digital photos is sharing them with your family and friends. In this minibook, I show you all the different ways you can make prints to pass around and techniques for sharing your best shots over the Internet.

After all, you can do a lot more with good photos than just admire them from afar. I explain how you can incorporate your top pictures into photo greeting cards, have them applied to T-shirts, and convert them into other gift items. I also provide tips for setting up online galleries so friends, family, and colleagues can enjoy the results of your photographic efforts from the comfort of their own computers.

Chapter 1: Printing Your Final Result

In This Chapter

✔ **Figuring out if and when you need to print your photos**

✔ **Choosing the right printer for the job**

✔ **Understanding the printing process**

✔ **Hiring a professional printing company or service bureau**

Digitally captured and retouched photos live on your computer. That's where they came to life, whether you captured them with a digital camera or scanned a printed original. It's also where they may have been doctored for any number of purposes — to make them smaller so that you can e-mail them to friends and family, to make them safe for use on a Web page, or to make them picture-perfect for printing.

However, unless you deal only in Web images or on-screen presentations, you probably need lots and lots of prints of your photos. In this chapter, you discover when and how to print your photos, which printers do what kind of job, and how to create the best-quality print of your digital images. You'll find more information about choosing printers in Book II, Chapter 4.

Why Do You Need Prints?

The reasons you might need to print your photos are as numerous as the photos themselves. Look for your own reasons among these:

✦ You need to create a suitable-for-framing version of a photo that was too small or too damaged to be framed before you edited it. You can transform that wallet-sized photo into a framed picture suitable for the top of your grand piano. Or, perhaps, a picture has wrinkles or tears you can fix with your image editor before making a pristine, new print. See Book VII for tips on restoring damaged photos.

✦ You want to create a backup print of a very precious photo in case something happens to the original. Better yet, display the duplicate and keep the precious original in a safer place, such as a safety-deposit box. Put a disc containing the digital version of the original in the box, too, so you won't have to duplicate your editing efforts.

✦ You're building a portfolio of your digital artwork, and you need a printed copy to show to prospective employers or clients. Make as many prints as you want economically, and distribute them far and wide.

✦ You need a *proof,* or printed evaluation image, that you can submit to someone who can't view the image online for his or her approval. You can fiddle with the proof print to make sure it's an accurate representation so the person passing judgment on it will have the best copy possible to approve.

✦ You require an evaluation proof for comparing the digital image with the hard copy original, and just viewing the file electronically won't provide the necessary information about print quality. The proof of the pudding, in this case, is in the viewing.

✦ Your photo is for printed marketing materials, such as ads, brochures, or flyers, and you need to create camera-ready art that a professional printer can use to create the finished materials. Although many professional printers today can work with digital files, some cannot. You need a print for the print shop's use.

✦ You'll often need prints for holiday greeting cards or birth announcements and other special events.

✦ When I prepare publicity pictures for my local newspaper, I always provide the original photo on CD. But I also include a print so the editor can decide whether the photo is worth using without having to pop the CD in a drive and go to the trouble of digging down into it to view the picture.

Although this chapter's title is "Printing Your Final Result," you may also want to print versions of your image as you go along in the editing process. Because computer monitors aren't capable of displaying colors exactly as they print, you may want to print at least one "in-progress" version of your image so that you can check for color, clarity, and other qualities before you commit the final version to that sheet of expensive photo paper. You can purchase lower-priced photo paper for your test prints (because printing on plain old inkjet paper may be misleading) and then use the good stuff for your final printout.

Why does the same photo look different if you print it on plain inkjet paper than it does on photographic paper? The porous nature of regular inkjet paper absorbs more of the ink, and this affects the reflective quality of the colors. Images look darker, contrast is lost, and overall quality is diminished if you print on porous paper. If you print on glossy or matte photographic paper, where a coating on the paper prevents absorption, your photo's color and content stand on their own, unaffected by the paper. No details, color, or contrast is lost.

Evaluating Your Printing Options

After you know that you need to print your photo, it's time to decide how to print it. If you have only one printer and no money for or access to another printer, then the decision is already made — you'll use your one and only printer. If you have the cash for the perfect printer for your particular photo, that's great. If you don't have the cash but have access to a variety of printers, that's great, too. With the assumption that you have some choices available to you, consider the list of printing possibilities found in Table 1-1. You'll find more information on choosing printers in Book II, Chapter 4.

Table 1-1		Printer Options
Type of Printer	*Price Range*	*Comments*
Inkjet	$75–$250	Great for color prints; good text quality, too
Laser	$400–$3,000	Fast, economical for text; not the best choice for images
Dye-sublimation	$150–$500 (and up)	Best color print quality, but can't handle text

Inkjet printers

The name *inkjet* gives you an idea of how the inkjet printer works — assuming that the word *jet* makes you think of the water jets on a whirlpool bath or spa. The way these printers work is rather simple. *Piezoelectric crystals* make the ink cartridges vibrate (the crystals are sandwiched between two electrodes, which make the crystals dance). Different levels of voltage cause the crystals to vibrate differently, which adjusts the colors and the amount of color sprayed through a nozzle onto the paper.

Color inkjet printers can create photo-quality images, assuming you use good-quality photo paper for the output. Price isn't necessarily an indication of print quality, and you should print a test page before making a purchase or go on the recommendation of someone who owns the same model.

Laser printers

Laser printers work very much like photocopiers. A laser beam is aimed at a photoelectric belt or drum, building up an electrical charge. This happens four times, once for each of the four colors used to make all the colors in your image — cyan, magenta, yellow, and black. The electric charge makes the colored toner stick to the belt, and then the belt transfers the toner to the drum. The paper rolls along the drum as it moves through the printer, which transfers the toner from the drum to the paper. Then, either pressure or heat (or both) makes the toner stick to the paper.

Color laser printers are more expensive than inkjets and black-and-white laser printers and are more expensive to operate. Indeed, now that the prices for color laser printers have dipped down to affordable levels, many users are complaining that they easily spend more on toner in the first few months they own these devices than they spent on the printers themselves! If you're creating camera-ready art for very important, detailed publications, you probably want a color laser printer (assuming the images are in color) rather than an inkjet, but the image quality is not as good as what you'd get with a dye-sublimation printer.

Dye-sublimation printers

Here, the name of the printer doesn't tell you much about the way the printer works. Despite their cryptic name, dye-sublimation printers work in a relatively straightforward way. A strip of plastic film, called a transfer ribbon, is coated with cyan, magenta, and yellow dye. When a print job is sent to the printer, a thermal print head heats up the paper-sized (4-x-6-inch or 8½-x-10-inch) panel of plastic transfer ribbon. Variations in temperature control what colors and the amount of color that are applied to the paper. Because the paper has a special coating on it, the dye sticks.

Dye-sublimation printers produce an excellent image, especially for color photos. The subtle results are great for professional designers, artists, and photographers. The expense for full-sized dye-sub printers may be prohibitive for small businesses and home users, but the lower-priced models that produce only snapshot-sized prints and cost less than $150 (plus about 30 cents per print for paper and ribbon) may be within reach.

Touring the Print Process

Regardless of the photo editing and retouching software that you're using to process your photographs, some aspects of the image-printing process are the same. With most image editors, the print process consists of the following options:

✦ You get to choose which printer to print to. If you have a black-and-white laser and a color inkjet, for example, you can choose to output to the color inkjet.

✦ You can choose how many copies to print.

✦ You can choose to print only part of the image by choosing the Selection option. This assumes you made a selection before issuing the Print command.

✦ You can adjust your printer's properties to print at different levels of quality, assuming the printout is the final version.

✦ You can choose to print crop marks, which can help you or a professional printer cut along the edges of the printout. If you want to frame a 5-x-7-inch photo, for example, and you're printing it on 8½ -x-11-inch paper (letter size), the crop marks can help you cut the paper down to fit inside the frame and within any mat you're using.

Preventing surprises with Print Preview

Before you actually commit your image to paper, you may want to see a smaller view of an image in the context of a sheet of the currently set paper size, just to make sure everything is okay. This prevents nasty surprises such as printing your favorite portrait in horizontal format and cutting your subject in half. In virtually all software programs, you choose File➪Print Preview (or just File➪Print, depending on which program you're using) to see how the printout will look. Figure 1-1 shows the Print Preview window in Photoshop Elements. If you're happy with what you see, you go ahead and issue the Print command (File➪Print or Ctrl+P) to open the Print dialog box.

Figure 1-1: A Print Preview window shows how your image will look on paper.

Higher-end photo editing packages (such as Photoshop) let you choose to print color separations, which means printing each of the image's colors on a separate sheet. This can be helpful to a professional printing firm that may be using your printout to create the films that will generate your prints.

Understanding your output options

In the Print Preview window, you can print the image by clicking the Print button, and you can also change the scale (size) and location of the image on the paper. With some image editors, a Show More Options check box opens an extension of the original dialog box. Options here may include applying a caption to your image or turning on crop marks. You may even be able to apply a background color and a border, which can be helpful if you're printing an image for framing and don't have a mat for the frame.

The Page Setup dialog box, which you open by clicking the Page Setup button in the Print Preview dialog box, allows you to change the printer you're sending the job to and to view your printer's properties (see Figure 1-2). It's also another place to choose the Background, Border, and Corner Crop Marks options. In many packages, the Page Setup dialog box also allows you to change the paper size and orientation.

Figure 1-2: You can specify paper orientation and size.

Printing your photos

When you're ready to print your work, choose File⇨Print (or choose Print from the Print Preview window) and use the Print dialog box to take advantage of your printing options — which printer to use, how many copies to print, and so forth.

If the software you're using offers a drastically different set of options through its Print dialog box, you can press the F1 key (in Windows) to open the software's help files. (Mac users can click the Help button in the dialog box.) If that doesn't work (though it should because most applications support this feature), use the Help menu and look for help articles that pertain to printing. The software may have also come with a *Read Me* file — a file that came with the software if you downloaded it from the Web — or a printed manual that you can refer to.

Of course, before you click the Print or OK button to begin the print job, you'll want to make sure the right paper is in the printer and be sure how your particular printer wants the paper fed — good-side down, the proper end in first, and so on. The printer should come with instructions, if not in a printed manual then right on the printer trays themselves, through little pictures of paper with arrows to show you how and where to insert the paper. Most photographic paper has a "good side," which has the image-enhancing coating on it, and a repeated brand name on the back, making it easier to tell which side you want to print on. If you're not sure, though, do a test print first. In the worst case, you'll print on the wrong side and have to do it again, wasting a single sheet of paper. If you're planning to print several copies of the image, it's better to waste a single sheet than to print all ten copies on the wrong side of the paper!

Using Professional Printing Services

Also known as a *service bureau,* a professional printing firm offers services to graphic artists, photographers, fine artists, businesses (for business cards, brochures, and so on), and the general public. Chains (such as FedEx Kinko's, AlphaGraphics, and Kwik Kopy stores) offer such services, and some office supply stores print your graphic files for a fee. You can also find small, privately owned printing services, which may charge more than the chains do, but you get very personalized service and may find the staff more willing to help you if you're not entirely sure what you need to provide in order for them to do a job for you.

I used service bureaus for many years, back in the days when laser printers could output text at no more than 300 dpi. Service bureaus were an economical way to produce black-and-white camera-ready pages (which can be photographed by the printer to make printing plates) without the need to purchase a high-resolution printer or imagesetter (a high-resolution printer especially suited for images). Those can be costly. Today, most laser printers have 600 dpi or better resolution, so the need for service bureaus for text output is reduced. They are still a good idea for making full-color prints from your digital photos if you don't own a color printer that provides sufficient quality.

Choosing a service bureau

Not sure who to call when you're ready to shop for a service bureau/printing service? You can always check the Yellow Pages online or in print, or you can ask friends and business associates for referrals. The best people to ask are graphic artists or people who work for an ad agency; they're likely to use service bureaus pretty extensively, and their recommendations would be valuable.

Before you hire a service bureau to print your photos, you want to ask the folks there a few questions:

✦ What do they charge, and how do they determine their prices? Do they have minimum fees?

✦ When can they finish the job? Note that most service bureaus will want to fit your job into their normal queue of projects. They may charge extra for "rush" jobs. Find out what constitutes a "rush" job — is that overnight service, or anything less than a week?

✦ What file formats do they support (so you know the format in which you should save your photo after editing it)? At one time, service bureaus could handle only Macintosh files and common Macintosh formats, such as TIFF or PICT. Today, most service bureaus support all platforms and all image file formats. It doesn't hurt to check, though.

✦ Can you view a sample of the printout before paying for the final copies? It can be helpful to view a proof or evaluation copy, even if you have to pay extra.

✦ Is the kind of output you're looking for something they've done before and done frequently?

With answers to these questions in hand, you can choose the right service bureau for your needs. If the person you're working with isn't open and cooperative with you, run, don't walk, to another company. I've worked with both kinds of service bureaus — the kind where the staff assumes you should know everything and doesn't want to be bothered explaining things, and the kind where folks are more than willing to help and answer any question, no matter how simple it is. Obviously, the former type of company doesn't deserve your business, and the latter type of company is best.

Tell them what you want, what you really, really want

After choosing a service bureau to work with, you need to discuss your exact printing needs. When you tell the person helping you how you plan to use the printout, he or she should

✦ Suggest the type of paper for the printout.

✦ Tell you what file format you need to use (a `.psd` file created in Photoshop, a `.tif` file, and so on) and whether you need to provide printed, camera-ready art.

If you do need to provide camera-ready art, ask whether you need to provide *color separations* (each color within your image printed on a separate sheet of paper) and what kind of paper the bureau prefers you print to. If you have only an inkjet printer, the serviceperson may balk at your using it to create the camera-ready art. In general, though, any good service bureau prefers to get the image as an electronic file so that the staff can work with the image as needed to give you the printout you require.

Knowing when you need a service bureau

In the end, the choice as to whether to work with a service bureau will come down to money. Time is money, and money buys quality if you shop carefully for printing services and/or your own printer. If you need a perfect, absolutely beautiful printout of the photo and can't afford a high-end printer of your own (or don't know anyone who has one you can use), then you need to spend the money to have a service bureau create the printout for you. If you need a high-quality printout and have a quality dye-sublimation or color laser printer at your disposal, you may be able to do the printing on your own.

If I sound as though I'm disregarding the role of inkjets in the printing process, I'm not. I've printed many photos with an inkjet printer and given them as gifts, used them as camera-ready art for brochures and business cards, and so forth. Some of my original artwork has also been printed on an inkjet, and the items look just fine in a portfolio. The printer you use depends on the printout quality you need and on whether the printer you have is capable of providing it. You might love the output that your inkjet generates, and if so, that's great. You've just saved some money, and you have a quick and easy way to create your prints!

Chapter 2: Sharing Pictures on the Web

*O*f course you can e-mail your photos to personal and business contacts, but most people are pretty tired of getting images attached to e-mail messages. They have to download the images in order to open and view them, and if they're on a dialup connection to the Internet, that can be a pain. And after the download is (finally) complete, what do they do with the pictures? If they don't need the image themselves, or if the subject of the photo isn't near or dear to them, they either throw it out (into the Trash or Recycle Bin) or squirrel the images away in a folder they'll never open again. I have a folder on my desktop called Other People's Images where I drag all the pictures that I would feel bad tossing but have no use for.

So if e-mail isn't the best way to share pictures with people who need or want to see them, what is? You have several options, including posting them on your own Web site or using one of the many image-sharing services. In this chapter, you discover what Web sharing tools are available, how to pick the one that's right for you, and how to get busy sharing photos on the Web.

Appreciating the Advantages of Web Sharing

By using the Web to share images, you eliminate the other person's need to save or throw out the images you've sent. He or she can view them, say, "Aw, isn't that cute!" or "Wow! Cool car!" and that's it. No need to download, save, throw out, or do anything with the image other than just look at it. If people want to save or print the image after they view it, that's up to them, but it isn't required or even firmly suggested. Figure 2-1 shows a page of images posted to a Web site. All people have to do to see the pictures is type the Web address into their browsers and voilà! There are the photos.

By using the Web to share pictures, you're saving your image recipients' time, hard drive space, and aggravation by creating a single repository for all the images you want to share. You're also making it much easier for yourself to keep an up-to-date selection of images available to all who want to see them, so the Web option is a win-win proposition.

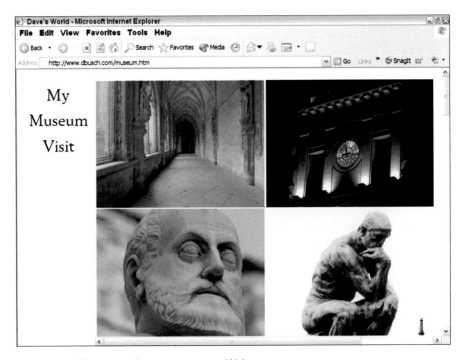

Figure 2-1: Share your photos on your own Web page.

Before you share a batch of photos with the world (remember, the Internet is international!), check the photos for anything you'd regret sharing with the rest of the population. You probably want to avoid sharing identifying features, such as addresses and people's last names, which enable strangers to make undesired contact with you. Another thing to check for is embarrassing content. Going over the images with a very discriminating eye before you share them will pay off in the long run.

Sharing personal photos with family and friends

The benefits of using the Web to share personal photos are obvious. You can share vacation photos, school pictures, shots of your new house, pool, car, bathroom tile — whatever. Through your pictures online, you can share all the stuff that you'd tell people about in a holiday newsletter. Think of the savings in postage alone! Instead of enclosing that extra sheet (or sheets) of paper, just write inside your holiday card the Web address where your photos can be found, and your work is done. If most of your friends and family have e-mail, you can alert them that way and save your wrist the strain of writing a Web address 50 times. Figure 2-2 shows an e-mail containing a Web address set up as a link. Recipients need only click the link in the e-mail and they're taken directly to your photos, wherever they're stored.

Figure 2-2: E-mail your picture link to a friend for point-and-click access.

Many e-mail programs will create such a *hot link* for you. For example, if you type anything that begins with `http://` into recent versions of Outlook, Outlook Express, or America Online's mail system, the e-mail software automatically converts the address into a hot link, colors it blue, and supplies an underline that lets the recipient know the link is live.

The recipient must also have the HTML option active for your link to be hot when the message is received. If not, the recipient can still jump to your Web page by highlighting the link, copying it (usually by pressing Ctrl+C, or ⌘+C on a Mac), and then pasting the link into a browser's address bar (by pressing Ctrl+V, or ⌘+V on a Mac).

Of course, some sharing is very targeted. If you want only your friends from college to see one batch and your family to see another, and you don't necessarily want the two camps to see each other's photos, how can you control it? By only telling certain people about certain images. Other than someone deliberately searching for your photos online, people will go and look only at the photos you direct them to, and by controlling whom you tell, you control who sees your images. Of course, if you want everyone and anyone to see all of your photos, you can store them all in the same place and use your name to identify them, making it possible for anyone to find them by searching the Web.

So where are these Web sites where your pictures can be found? They're everywhere — from the AOL Pictures feature at America Online to sites hosted by the big names in photography, such as Yahoo! and Kodak. These sites are easy to use, easy to access, and make sharing your photos with whomever you want very simple. I talk about different sites and their pros and cons a little later in this chapter.

Sharing images with business associates

So you've opened a new warehouse or have a new product to offer? Don't spend the extra cash printing up thousands of brochures or product information sheets, and certainly don't skimp and print up black-and-white flyers because printing in color is so expensive. Color is cheap online, and the cost (if any) of sharing your images online is just a tiny fraction of the cost of printing. You can even promote your goods and services with pictures, as shown in Figure 2-3.

You can put color images on your own company Web site, or if you don't have one yet, you can usually get some free Web space from the people you're already paying to provide your e-mail and Internet connection — your *ISP* (Internet service provider). Whether your ISP is an online community, like AOL or MSN, or another firm such as Earthlink or AT&T, you can take advantage of the free Web space allocated to each customer. Although you probably don't have a lot of space, it might be just enough to share a bunch of photos because photos saved for the Web (in GIF or JPG format) are much smaller in file size than photos shared in other formats. Even if your ISP gives you only 10MB of space, you can get a lot of photos in that space.

To find out if your ISP offers free Web space, you can call its support phone number or go to its Web site. Most ISPs offer either online or phone support to coach you through the process.

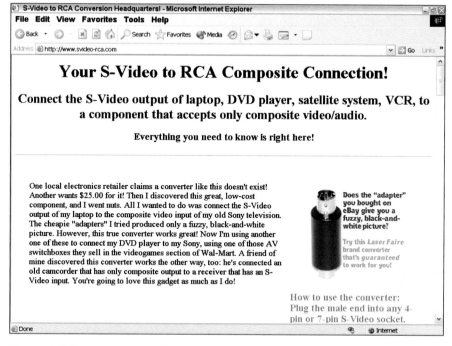

Figure 2-3: One reason for posting your photos online is to sell your company's goods or services.

Choosing a Sharing System

There are really too many free Web page hosting sites to list, and it's hard to tell which ones will remain active during the life of this book. I listed some in earlier editions and found that they were nearly *all* defunct or had changed within 12 to 18 months. Kodak, in particular, has changed the name of its photo-sharing site three or four times in the last few years, the most recent revision from Picture Center to Kodak EasyShare Gallery. You'll find an up-to-date guide to free or nearly-free hosting services at www.clickherefree.com. Of course, I'm hoping *that* service won't become defunct soon, too (but it has hung around for a couple editions of this book!).

Your best bet is your ISP or big operations like AOL, MSN, Kodak, and others, which are likely to be with us over the long haul. Of course, longevity may not be important to you. After all, when one service pulls up stakes and packs up its tent, you can always switch to another, newer free service. As a bonus, you don't have to worry about erasing all your outdated photos on the old service. They'll do it for you when they close up the shop.

You have a lot of choices. You can use an online sharing system to display your images. Most of these systems offer the space for free. You can build your own Web site in the free space that your ISP offers, or you can register your own domain and set up your own space on a host's Web server. In this case, a host offers space on its computer for you to store your pages, usually for a monthly or annual fee. You can also set up your own Web server (a computer that "serves up" Web pages to people on the Internet), but I wouldn't recommend it solely to store your images.

With all these options, choosing a sharing system is easy. The best option for you depends on what you want, how much you're willing to pay, and how much time you want to devote to setting up your images online. From simple and set up in no time to slightly complex and completely customized, your choices run the entire spectrum.

Using commercial sharing sites and services

"Commercial" normally means "for a fee," right? Well, not necessarily. Many of your sharing options are free or use something that you're already paying for. In the case of an online community, such as America Online, if you're a member, you're already paying for that membership, which enables you to send and receive e-mail, chat, surf the Web, and so forth. For AOL's monthly fee, you get access to the Internet and to its community features. One of those features, as indicated earlier, is AOL Pictures, which enables you to view your images online — and allows others to view them, too. You also get free Web space with your membership, which you can use for storing and displaying your photos.

Other commercial sharing services — Web sites known as *online galleries* — allow you to post your images for free in exchange for making you look at ads around the periphery of the Web page that displays your images. The thinking is that, by exposing you (and those you send to the site to see your photos) to the ads, the gallery's advertising partners gain exposure to a considerable customer base. Others provide free space simply because they want to be nice or to perpetuate an interest in photography. Some sell software, which they offer you throughout their site, enticing you to buy their image editing and/or photo album application. You don't have to buy, but the companies figure that many people will.

Quite a few different services are available. Your best bet for finding them is to type *Online Galleries* or similar keywords into an Internet search engine to find free or low-fee services.

If you're willing to pay to store and display your pictures, you might be better off with a service like SmugMug or PBase (www.smugmug.com and www.pbase.com), both of which offer versatile photo sharing without many of the limitations of the free services.

For example, SmugMug offers three levels of service: Standard, Power User, and Pro, for (at this writing) $39.95, $59.95, and $149.95 per year. Each service offers unlimited capacity and uses an interface that makes it easy to upload hundreds of photos quickly. With the basic service, you can track visits to your gallery, password-protect your images, organize your photos by keyword tags, and convert your images to prints and gifts. The Power User service lets you add video clips and choose your own colors and fonts for your gallery and allows much higher levels of traffic to your gallery, just in case you become hugely popular. The Pro level galleries let you sell your prints through SmugMug and even make a profit from your work.

PBase offers similar features, and some bonuses, not the least of which is a slick online magazine with gorgeous photos and useful articles. PBase charges $23 a year for 300MB of photo storage and $60 annually for 900MB of storage. You can add additional storage in 300MB increments.

Other services to evaluate (all still alive and kicking as I write this) include Yahoo!, Snapfish, Kodak EasyShare Gallery, and Shutterfly (at http://photos. yahoo.com, www.snapfish.com, and www.shutterfly.com).

Displaying images on your own Web space

Whether your ISP provides the space for free or you enlist a paid host to provide you space for your own domain, you can use your Web space to store and display photos that you want to share with friends, family, customers, and business associates. Putting the images online requires a series of simple steps:

1. **Prepare your photos for use on the Web by opening them in a photo-editing package, such as Photoshop Elements, and saving them in a Web-safe format.**

   The two formats that all Web browsers (notably Internet Explorer, Firefox, Netscape Navigator, and Opera) can deal with are .gif and .jpg. .jpg is best for photos because it supports the multitude of colors and shading within the images. Figure 2-4 shows the Save for Web dialog box in Photoshop Elements and a photo being prepared for Web use.

2. **Set up the Web page where the images will be displayed.**

   You can use a variety of graphical tools to design the page (Microsoft FrontPage, Macromedia Dreamweaver, Adobe GoLive), or you can create a page by writing HTML (Hypertext Markup Language) code. If you're using an ISP's free Web space, the ISP gives you step-by-step procedures for creating a Web page, and the software does most of the work for you.

3. **Upload the Web page and the images.**

   This is typically done with FTP (File Transfer Protocol) software, or if you're using AOL or your ISP, it may provide an Upload page that loads both the Web page you set up and the images you want to display.

Figure 2-4: Photoshop Elements' Save for Web feature creates an optimized image for Web display.

You can find free or low-cost FTP software online from sites such as www.tucows.com and www.hotfiles.com. You can also do a search for *"Free FTP Software"* at Google (www.google.com). Venerable "oldies" like WSFTP LE, shown in Figure 2-5, are very popular. "Newbies" (new online users) may prefer a program like FTP Explorer, which has a Windows Explorer–like interface, while Mac users like Transmit.

4. **Visit the page online to see how it looks.**

   You always want to check your page online to see if it's okay before you send people there to see your images. With any luck, it won't look like my page, shown in Figure 2-6.

   If you want to make changes, open the Web page file on your own computer, make the changes, and upload it again.

If you check your page online and you see red Xs (in Internet Explorer) or gray icons with a question mark (in Netscape Navigator) where images should be, this means that the browser can't locate the image that's supposed to be there. Check your Web page settings to make sure that you have the right pictures in the right places, and check to see that you've uploaded all the images to your host's Web server.

Figure 2-5: WSFTP LE is a popular FTP transfer program for uploading Web pages.

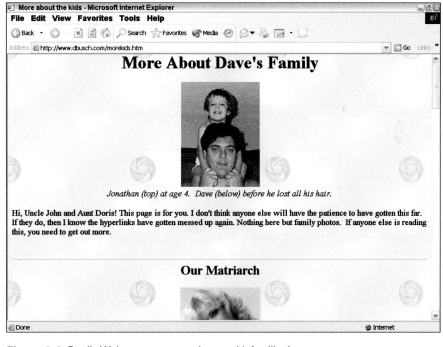

Figure 2-6: Family Web pages are popular — with families!

As time goes by, you can always expand and improve on your Web pages. Here are a few things to try:

✦ **Refreshing content:** Edit your Web pages and add new pictures. Or take down the old ones entirely and replace them with your latest shots. As you become more proficient in setting up images and designing Web pages, your site can grow with you.

✦ **Organizing pictures:** Set up multiple Web pages and use them to categorize your images. Set up a Vacations page, a Baby Pictures page, or a Graduation Ceremony page. Any category or special topic can have its own page.

✦ **Adding links:** Create links on your Web pages that take visitors to other people's sites or to online galleries where you have other pictures stored. If you're a real photography bug, you may have some of your more artistic shots stored on a gallery site. Through a link on your own page, you can direct people to your works of art.

✦ **Letting others join in:** Set up a family Web site and have each branch of your extended family post their own images to individual pages. This can help distant members of the family stay in touch (add e-mail links to the pages so people can view the images and then immediately write an e-mail to talk about them), and let everyone in the family know about new arrivals and special events like family reunions.

✦ **Advertising your business:** If you're in business, use the space to show pictures of your products, services, staff, locations — anything that will enhance your customer's interest in you and your business. Like a family site with individual pages for different branches of the family or types of pictures, businesses can also categorize their images and set up individual pages to house each group.

If you thought your only goal for that box of old photos was to put them in an album, you can now see that you can do so many more things with your images. The Internet lets you share pictures with anyone, anywhere, and it won't cost you much money or take up much of your time. Have fun!

Glossary

additive primary colors: The red, green, and blue hues used alone or in combinations to create all other colors you capture with a digital camera or scanner, view on a computer monitor, or work with in an image editing program like Photoshop, Photoshop Elements, or Paint Shop Pro. *See also* subtractive primary colors, CMY(K) color model.

airbrush: The airbrush is an image editing feature that simulates an artist's tool that sprays a fine mist of paint. It is used for both illustration and retouching.

ambient lighting: Soft, nondirectional lighting that bounces off walls, ceilings, and other objects in the scene, rather than appearing to come from a single light source.

angle of view: The area of a scene that a lens can capture, determined by the focal length of the lens. Lenses with a shorter focal length have a wider angle of view than lenses with a longer focal length.

anti-aliasing: A process that smoothes the rough edges or *jaggies* in images by creating partially transparent pixels along the boundaries that are merged into a smoother line by our eyes. *See also* jaggies.

aperture-priority: A camera setting that allows you to specify which lens opening or f-stop you want, with the camera selecting the required shutter speed automatically, based on its autoexposure system. *See also* shutter-preferred.

artifact: A type of noise in an image, or an unintentional image component produced in error by a digital camera or scanner during processing. For example, a "hot" or "dead" pixel in a digital camera sensor can show up as a white or black dot in your photos.

aspect ratio: The width-to-height proportion of an image as printed, displayed on a monitor, or captured by a digital camera.

autofocus: A camera setting that allows the camera to choose the correct focus distance for you, usually based on the contrast of an image (the image will be at maximum contrast when in sharp focus) or set by a mechanism, such as an infrared sensor, that measures the actual distance to the subject. Cameras can be set for *single autofocus* (the lens is not focused until the shutter release is partially depressed) or *continuous autofocus* (the lens refocuses constantly as you frame and reframe the image).

averaging metering: A light-measuring system that calculates exposure based on the overall brightness of the entire image area. Averaging tends to produce the best exposure when a scene is evenly lit or contains equal amounts of bright and dark areas that contain detail. Today, most digital cameras use much more sophisticated exposure measuring systems based on center-weighting, spot-reading, or calculating exposure from a matrix of many different picture areas.

backlighting: A lighting effect produced when the main light source is located behind the subject. Backlighting can be used to create a silhouette effect. Backlighting is also a technology for illuminating an LCD display from the rear, making it easier to view under high ambient lighting conditions. *See also* ambient lighting, fill lighting, and front-lighting.

balance: A property of an image that has elements of equal weight, color, size, or other attribute on all sides.

bit: A binary digit — either a 1 or a 0 — used to measure the color depth (number of different colors) in an image. For example, a grayscale 8-bit scan may contain up to 256 different tones (2^8), and a 24-bit scan can contain 16.8 million different colors (2^{24}).

black point: The tonal level of an image where blacks begin to provide important image information, usually measured by using a *histogram*. When correcting an image with a digital camera that has an on-screen histogram, or within an image editor, you'll usually want to set the histogram's black point at the place where these tones exist.

blur: In photography, to soften an image or part of an image by throwing it out of focus or by allowing it to become soft because of subject or camera motion. In image editing, to soften an area by reducing the contrast between pixels that form the edges.

bounce lighting: Light reflected from a surface, often ceiling or walls, to provide a soft, natural-looking light.

bracketing: Taking a series of photographs of the same subject at different settings to help ensure that one setting will be the correct one. Many digital cameras will automatically snap off a series of bracketed exposures for you. Other settings, such as color and white balance, can also be bracketed with some models.

brightness: The amount of light and dark shades in an image, usually represented as a percentage from 0 percent (black) to 100 percent (white).

buffer: A digital camera's internal memory, which stores an image immediately after it was taken until the image can be written to the camera's nonvolatile (semi-permanent) memory or a memory card. A buffer lets a camera capture a burst of images.

burn: A darkroom technique, simulated by most image editors, which involves exposing part of a print for a longer period, thus making it darker than it would be with a straight exposure. The term is also slang for creating a CD or DVD using writing software.

calibration: A process used to correct for the differences in the output of a printer or monitor when compared with the original image. After you calibrate your scanner, monitor, and/or your image editor, the images you see on-screen more closely represent what you'll get from your printer even though calibration is never perfect.

Camera RAW: A plug-in included with Photoshop and Photoshop Elements that can manipulate the unprocessed images captured by digital cameras. *See also* RAW.

camera shake: Movement of the camera, aggravated by slower shutter speeds, which produces a blurred image. Some of the latest digital cameras have *image stabilization* features that correct for camera shake, and a few high-end interchangeable lenses have a similar vibration correction or reduction feature.

cast: An undesirable tinge of color in an image.

CCD: Charge-Coupled Device. A type of solid-state sensor that captures the image, used in scanners and digital cameras. *See also* CMOS.

center-weighted metering: A light-measuring device that emphasizes the area in the middle of the frame when calculating the correct exposure for an image. *See also* averaging metering, matrix metering, and spot metering.

chroma: Color or hue.

chromatic aberration: An image defect, often seen as green or purple fringing around the edges of an object, caused by a lens failing to focus all colors of a light source at the same point.

chrome: An informal photographic term used as a generic for any kind of color transparency, including Kodachrome, Ektachrome, or Fujichrome.

CIE (Commission Internationale de l'Eclairage): An international organization of scientists who work with matters relating to color and lighting. The organization is also called the International Commission on Illumination. This organization's color model is based on human perception and is considered the most accurate.

close-up lens: A lens add-on, resembling a filter, that allows you to take pictures at a distance that is less than the closest-focusing distance of the prime lens alone.

CMOS: Complementary Metal-Oxide Semiconductor. A type of solid-state sensor that captures the image; used in scanners and digital cameras. *See also* CCD.

CMY(K) color model: A way of defining all possible colors in percentages of cyan (C), magenta (M), yellow (Y), and frequently, black (K). Black is added to improve rendition of shadow detail. CMYK is commonly used for printing (both on press and with your inkjet or laser color printer). A few image editors, including Photoshop, can work with images using the CMYK model.

color correction: Changing the relative amounts of color in an image to produce a desired effect, typically a more accurate representation of those colors. Color correction can fix faulty color balance in the original image or compensate for the deficiencies of the inks used to reproduce the image.

color filter array: A colored panel placed over the sensor, which keeps the sensors photosites (which are sensitive to all colors) from responding to light other than the color assigned to that pixel/photosite.

CompactFlash: A storage media commonly used in digital cameras, music players, and other devices.

composite: In photography, an image composed of two or more parts of an image, taken either from a single photo or from multiple photos. Usually, composites are created so that the elements blend smoothly together.

composition: The arrangement of the main subject, other objects in a scene, and/or the foreground and background.

compression: Reducing the size of a file by encoding using fewer bits of information to represent the original. Some compression schemes, such as JPEG, operate by discarding some image information; others, such as TIFF, preserve all the detail in the original, discarding only redundant data. *See also* GIF, JPEG, and TIFF.

continuous autofocus: An automatic focusing setting in which the camera constantly refocuses the image as you frame the picture. This setting is often the best choice for moving subjects. *See also* single autofocus.

continuous tone: Images that contain tones from the darkest to the lightest, with a theoretically infinite range of variations in between.

contrast: The range of difference in the light to dark areas of a photo.

contrasty: Having higher than optimal contrast.

crop: To trim an image or page by adjusting its boundaries.

dedicated flash: An electronic flash unit designed to work with the automatic exposure features of a specific camera. Most such devices actually measure the light reaching the sensor as a way of determining proper exposure settings.

density: The ability of an object to stop or absorb light. The less light reflected or transmitted by an object, the higher its density.

depth of field: A distance range in a photograph in which all included portions of an image are at least acceptably sharp.

depth of focus: The range that the image-capturing surface (such as a sensor or film) could be moved while maintaining acceptable focus. *See also* depth of field.

desaturate: To reduce the purity or vividness of a color, making a color appear to be washed out or diluted.

diaphragm: An adjustable component found in cameras, similar to the iris in the human eye, which expands and contracts to provide specific-sized lens openings, or f-stops. *See also* iris.

diffuse lighting: Soft, low-contrast lighting.

diffusing: Softening detail in an image.

digital single-lens reflex (dSLR): A high-end digital camera that accepts interchangeable lenses; usually used by professionals or advanced amateur photographers.

digital zoom: A way of simulating actual or optical zoom by magnifying the pixels captured by the sensor. This technique generally produces results inferior to optical zoom. *See also* optical zoom.

dither: A method of distributing pixels to extend the number of colors or tones that can be represented. For example, two pixels of different colors can be arranged in such a way that the eye visually merges them into a third color.

dock: A device furnished with some digital cameras that links to your computer or printer, allowing you to interface the camera with the other devices simply by setting it in the dock's cradle.

docking: The ability to lock an image editing program's toolbars, palettes, and other features of the interface at fixed locations, usually one edge of the application window.

dodging: A darkroom term for blocking part of an image as it is exposed, thus lightening its tones. Image editors can simulate this effect by lightening portions of an image using a brush-like tool.

dots per inch (dpi): The resolution of a printed image, expressed in the number of printer dots in an inch. You'll often see dpi used to refer to monitor screen resolution or the resolution of scanners. However, neither of these use dots; the correct term for a monitor's resolution is *pixels per inch* (ppi); a scanner captures a particular number of *samples per inch* (spi).

dye-sublimation (dye-sub): A printing technique in which inks are heated and transferred to a polyester substrate to form an image. Because the amount of color applied can be varied by the degree of heat (and up to 256 different hues for each color), dye sublimation devices can print as many as 16.8 million different colors.

electronic viewfinder (EVF): An LCD located inside a digital camera and used to provide a view of the subject based on the image generated by the camera's sensor.

emulsion: The light-sensitive coating on a piece of film, paper, or printing plate. When making prints or copies, it's important to know which side is the emulsion side so that the image can be exposed in the correct orientation (not reversed). Advanced image editors, such as Photoshop, include Emulsion Side Up and Emulsion Side Down options in its Print Preview feature.

equivalent focal length: A digital camera's focal length translated into the corresponding values for a 35mm film camera. For example, a 5.8–17.4mm lens on a digital camera might provide the same view as a 38–114mm zoom with a film camera. Equivalents are needed because sensor size and lens focal lengths are not standardized for digital cameras, and translating the values provides a basis for comparison.

EXIF: Exchangeable Image File Format. Developed to standardize the exchange of image data between hardware devices and software. A variation on JPEG, EXIF is used by most digital cameras and includes information such as the date and time a photo was taken, the camera settings, resolution, amount of compression, and other data.

existing light: In photography, the illumination that is already present in a scene. Existing light can include daylight or the artificial lighting currently being used but is not considered to be electronic flash or additional lamps set up by the photographer. Also sometimes called *existing darkness*.

export: To transfer text or images from a document to another format.

exposure: The amount of light allowed to reach the film or sensor, determined by the intensity of the light, the amount admitted by the iris of the lens, and the length of time determined by the shutter speed.

exposure program: An automatic setting in a digital camera that provides the optimum combination of shutter speed and f-stop at a given level of illumination. For example, a sports exposure program would use a faster, action-stopping shutter speed and larger lens opening instead of the smaller, depth of field–enhancing lens opening and slower shutter speed that might be favored by a close-up program at exactly the same light level.

exposure values (EV): EV settings are a way of adding or decreasing exposure without the need to reference f-stops or shutter speeds. For example, if you tell your camera to add +1EV, it will provide twice as much exposure by using a larger f-stop, slower shutter speed, or both.

f-stop: The relative size of the lens aperture, which helps determine both exposure and depth of field. The larger the f-stop number, the smaller the aperture. It helps to think of f-stops as denominators of fractions, so that f/2 is larger than f/4, which is larger than f/8, just as ½, ¼, and ⅛ represent ever-smaller fractions. In photography, a given f-stop number is multiplied by 1.4 to arrive at the next number that admits exactly half as much light. So, f/1.4 is twice as large as f/2.0 (1.4 x 1.4), which is twice as large as f/2.8 (2 x 1.4), which is twice as large as f/4 (2.8 x 1.4). The f-stops that follow are f/5.6, f/8, f/11, f/16, f/22, f/32, and so on. Most digital cameras have f-stops limited to a range of about f/2.8 to f/8.

feather: To fade the borders of an image element so that it blends more smoothly with another layer.

fill flash: A camera setting that causes the electronic flash to always fire, which produces the effect of filling in shadows in brightly illuminated images.

fill lighting: In photography, lighting used to illuminate shadows.

filter: In photography, a device that fits over the lens, changing the light in some way. In image editing, a feature that changes the pixels in an image to produce blurring, sharpening, and other special effects.

FireWire (IEEE 1394): A fast serial interface used by scanners, digital cameras, printers, and other devices. Introduced for the Macintosh and now found on all new Macs, FireWire is now becoming more popular on PCs.

flat: An image with low contrast is said to appear flat.

flatbed scanner: A type of scanner that reads one line of an image at a time, recording it as a series of samples, or pixels.

fluorescent illumination: Light produced by a tube coated on the inside with a material that glows. Mercury vapor in the tube emits ultraviolet radiation that is converted to visible radiation by the fluorescent coating. The most important aspect for photographers to consider is that fluorescent illumination doesn't have a true color temperature the way daylight and tungsten illumination does, so special filtration or white balance settings must be used to compensate for color shifts. *See also* tungsten light.

focal length: The distance between the film and the optical center of the lens when the lens is focused on infinity, usually measured in millimeters.

focus: To adjust the lens to produce a sharp image.

focus range: The minimum and maximum distances within which a camera is able to produce a sharp image, such as two inches to infinity.

focus tracking: The ability of the automatic focus feature of a camera to change focus as the distance between the subject and the camera changes. Some cameras use *predictive focus* to guess where the proper focus point will be, based on the movement direction of the main subject.

four-color printing: Another term for *process color,* in which cyan, magenta, yellow, and black inks are used to reproduce all the colors in the original image.

Four Thirds system: The Four Thirds system is a new open standard for digital SLR cameras with interchangeable lenses using a ⅘-inch image sensor. Adopted by a few manufacturers, such as Olympus, the Four Thirds system establishes a common standard for lens design and mounts, improving compatibility between lenses and camera bodies even if they are produced by different manufacturers.

framing: In photography, composing your image in the viewfinder. In composition, using elements of an image to form a sort of picture frame around an important subject.

frequency: The number of lines per inch in a halftone screen.

front-curtain sync: The default kind of electronic flash synchronization technique, originally associated with focal plane shutters, which consists of a traveling set of curtains, including a *front curtain* (opens to reveal the film or sensor) and a *rear curtain* (follows at a distance determined by shutter speed to conceal the film or sensor at the conclusion of the exposure).

Front-curtain sync causes the flash to fire at the beginning of the exposure — in the instant that the first curtain of the focal plane shutter finishes its movement across the film or sensor plane. With slow shutter speeds, this feature can create a blur effect from the ambient light, showing as patterns that follow a moving subject with the subject shown sharply frozen at the beginning of the blur trail (think of an image of The Flash running backward). *See also* rear-curtain sync.

front-lighting: Illumination that comes from the direction of the camera. See also *backlighting* and *side-lighting.*

full-color image: An image that uses 24-bit color, resulting in 16.8 million possible hues. Images are sometimes captured in a scanner or digital camera with more colors, but the colors are reduced to the best 16.8 million shades for manipulation in image editing.

gamma: A numerical way of representing the contrast of an image. Devices such as monitors typically don't reproduce the tones in an image in straight-line fashion (all colors represented in exactly the same way as they appear in the original). Instead, some tones might be favored over others, and gamma provides a method of tonal correction that takes the human eye's perception of neighboring values into account. Gamma values range from 1.0 to about 2.5. The Macintosh has traditionally used a gamma of 1.8, which is relatively flat compared with television. Windows PCs use a 2.2 gamma value, which has more contrast and is more saturated.

gamma correction: A method for changing the brightness, contrast, or color balance of an image by assigning new values to the gray or color tones of an image to more closely represent the original shades. Gamma correction can be either linear or nonlinear. Linear correction applies the same amount of change to all the tones. Nonlinear correction varies the changes tone by tone, or in highlight, midtone, and shadow areas separately to produce a more accurate or improved appearance.

gamut: The range of viewable and printable colors for a particular color model, such as RGB (red/green/blue; used for monitors) or CMYK (cyan/magenta/yellow/black; used for printing).

Gaussian blur: A method of diffusing an image using a bell-shaped curve to calculate the pixels that will be blurred, rather than blurring all pixels, thus producing a more random, less "processed" look.

GIF: Graphics Interchange Format. An image file format limited to 256 different colors that compresses the information by combining similar colors and discarding the rest. Condensing a 16.8-million-color photographic image to only 256 different hues often produces a poor-quality image, but GIF is useful for images that don't have a great many colors, such as charts or graphs. The GIF format also includes transparency options and can include multiple images to produce animations that may be viewed on a Web page or other application. *See also* JPEG and TIFF.

grain: The metallic silver in film that forms the photographic image. The term is often applied to the seemingly random noise in an image (both conventional and digital) that provides an overall texture.

gray card: A piece of cardboard or other material with a standardized 18-percent reflectance. Gray cards can be used as a reference for determining correct exposure or white balance.

grayscale image: An image that is represented using 256 shades of gray. Scanners often capture grayscale images with 1,024 or more tones but reduce them to 256 grays for manipulation by Photoshop.

halftone: A method used to reproduce continuous-tone images, representing the image as a series of dots.

high contrast: A wide range of density in a print, negative, or other image.

highlights: The brightest parts of an image containing detail.

histogram: A kind of chart showing the relationship of tones in an image using a series of 256 vertical bars, one for each brightness level. A histogram chart typically looks like a curve with one or more slopes and peaks, depending on how many highlight, midtone, and shadow tones are present in the image. Histograms can appear in camera displays or in image editing software to help judge an image. They identify the shadows, midtones, and highlights of an image.

hue: The color of light that is reflected from an opaque object or transmitted through a transparent one.

hyperfocal distance: When a lens is focused on the hyperfocal distance, the depth of field extends from half that distance to infinity. The point can be calculated or looked up in tables.

image rotation: A feature found in some digital cameras that senses whether a picture was taken in horizontal or vertical orientation. That information is embedded in the picture file so that the camera and compatible software applications can automatically display the image in the correct orientation.

image stabilization: A technology that compensates for camera shake, usually by adjusting the position of the camera sensor or lens elements in response to movements of the camera.

incident light: Light falling on a surface, as opposed to light reflected from a surface.

indexed color image: An image with 256 different colors, as opposed to a grayscale image, which has 256 different shades of the tones between black and white.

infinity: A distance so great that any object at that distance will be reproduced sharply if the lens is focused at the infinity position.

interchangeable lens: Lens designed to be readily attached to and detached from a camera; a feature found in more sophisticated digital cameras.

International Organization for Standardization (ISO): A governing body that provides standards used to represent film speed, or the equivalent sensitivity of a digital camera's sensor. Digital camera sensitivity is expressed in ISO settings. The organization has chosen the word *ISO* as its standard abbreviation because the name of the group itself varies in the different languages of its members.

interpolation: A technique that digital cameras, scanners, and image editors use to create new pixels based on the values of surrounding pixels whenever an image is resized or changed in resolution. Devices such as scanners and digital cameras also use interpolation to create pixels in addition to those actually captured, thereby increasing the apparent resolution or color information in an image. For example, in a typical digital camera, pixels capture only red, green, or blue information, so the other colors present at that image position are calculated by using interpolation.

invert: In image editing, to change an image into its negative; black becomes white, white becomes black; dark gray becomes light gray; and so forth. Colors are also changed to their complementary color: green becomes magenta, blue turns to yellow, and red is changed to cyan.

iris: A set of thin overlapping leaves in a camera lens that pivots outward to form a circular opening of variable size to control the amount of light that can pass through a lens. *See also* diaphragm.

jaggies: Staircasing effect of lines that are not perfectly horizontal or vertical, caused by pixels that are too large to represent the line accurately. *See also* anti-aliasing.

JPEG (Joint Photographic Experts Group): A file format that supports 24-bit color and reduces file sizes by selectively discarding image data. Digital cameras generally use JPEG compression to pack more images onto memory cards. You can select how much compression is used (and therefore how much information is thrown away) by selecting from among the Standard, Fine, Super Fine, or other quality settings offered by your camera. *See also* GIF and TIFF.

landscape: The orientation of an image in which the longest dimension is horizontal; also called wide orientation.

latitude: The range of camera exposures that produce acceptable images with a particular digital sensor or film.

layer: A way of managing elements of an image in stackable overlays that can be manipulated separately, moved to a different stacking order, or made partially or fully transparent.

lens: One or more elements of optical glass or similar material designed to collect and focus rays of light to form a sharp image on the film, paper, sensor, or screen.

lens aperture: The lens opening, or iris, that admits light to the film or sensor. The size of the lens aperture is usually measured in f-stops. *See also* f-stop, diaphragm, and iris.

lens flare: An optical feature of photography that is both a bane and a creative outlet. It is an effect produced by the reflection of light internally among elements of an optical lens. Bright light sources within or just outside the field of view cause lens flare. Flare can be reduced by the use of coatings on the lens elements or with the use of lens hoods. Photographers sometimes use the effect as a creative technique, and some image editors include a filter that lets you add lens flare at your whim.

lens hood: A device that shades the lens, protecting it from extraneous light outside the actual picture area that can reduce the contrast of the image or allow lens flare.

lens speed: The largest lens opening (smallest f-number) at which a lens can be set. A fast lens transmits more light and has a larger opening than a slow lens. Determined by the maximum aperture of the lens in relation to its focal length; the speed of a lens is relative: a 400mm lens with a maximum aperture of f/3.5 is considered extremely fast, and a 28mm f/3.5 lens is thought to be relatively slow.

lighten: An image editing function that is the equivalent to the photographic darkroom technique of dodging. Tones in a given area of an image are gradually changed to lighter values. *See also* dodging.

lighting ratio: The proportional relationship between the amount of light falling on the subject from the main light and other lights.

line art: Usually, images that consist only of white pixels and one color; represented in Photoshop as a bitmap.

line screen: The resolution or frequency of a halftone screen, expressed in lines per inch. The term is used within the printing industry.

lithography: Another name for offset printing.

lossless compression: An image-compression scheme, such as TIFF, that preserves all image detail. When the image is decompressed, it is identical to the original version. *See also* compression.

lossy compression: An image-compression scheme, such as JPEG, that creates smaller files by discarding image information, which can affect image quality. *See also* compression.

luminance: The brightness or intensity of an image, determined by the amount of gray in a hue.

LZW compression: A method of compacting TIFF files in image editors and other applications by using the Lempel-Ziv Welch compression algorithm, which is an optional compression scheme also offered by some digital cameras.

macro lens: A lens that provides continuous focusing from infinity to extreme close-ups, often to a reproduction ratio of 1:2 (half life-size) or 1:1 (life-size).

macro photography: The process of taking photographs of small objects at magnifications of 1X or more.

magnification ratio: A relationship that represents the amount of enlargement provided by the macro setting of the zoom lens, macro lens, or with other close-up devices.

matrix metering: A system of exposure calculation used in digital cameras that looks at many different segments of an image to determine the brightest and darkest portions.

maximum aperture: The largest lens opening or f-stop available with a particular lens or with a zoom lens at a particular magnification.

mechanical: Camera-ready copy with text and art already in position for photographing to make printing plates.

midtones: Parts of an image with tones of an intermediate value, usually in the 25–75 percent range. Many image editing features allow you to manipulate midtones independently from the highlights and shadows.

moiré: An objectionable pattern caused by the interference of halftone screens, frequently generated by rescanning an image that has already been halftoned. An image editor can frequently minimize these effects by blurring the patterns.

monochrome: Having a single color, plus white. Grayscale images are monochrome (shades of gray and white only).

monopod: A one-legged support, or unipod, used to steady the camera. *See also* tripod.

negative: A representation of an image in which the tones are reversed, blacks as white, and vice versa.

neutral color: In image editing's RGB mode, a color in which red, green, and blue are present in equal amounts, producing a gray.

noise: In an image, pixels with randomly distributed color values. Noise in digital photographs tends to be the product of low-light conditions and long exposures, particularly when you have set your camera to a higher ISO rating than normal.

noise reduction: A technology used to cut down on the amount of random information in a digital picture, usually caused by long exposures at increased sensitivity ratings. Noise reduction involves the camera automatically taking a second blank/dark exposure at the same settings that contains only noise, and then using the blank photo's information to cancel out the noise in the original picture. With most cameras, the process is very quick but can double the amount of time required to take the photo.

normal lens: A lens that makes the image in a photograph appear in a perspective that is like that of the original scene, typically with a field of view of roughly 45 degrees. A quick way to calculate the focal length of a normal lens is to measure the diagonal of the sensor or film frame used to capture the image, usually ranging around 7–45mm.

optical zoom: Magnification produced by the elements of a digital camera's lens, as opposed to *digital zoom,* which merely magnifies the captured pixels to simulate additional magnification. True optical zoom is always to be preferred over the simulated digital variety. *See also* digital zoom.

overexposure: A condition in which too much light reaches the film or sensor, producing a dense negative or a very bright/light print, slide, or digital image.

panning: Moving the camera so that the image of a moving object remains in the same relative position in the viewfinder as you take a picture. The eventual effect creates a strong sense of movement because the main subject remains relatively sharp while the background blurs.

panorama: A broad view, usually scenic. Some digital cameras also have a panorama mode used with software to stitch the images together.

parallax compensation: An adjustment made by the camera or photographer to account for the difference in views between the taking lens and the external optical viewfinder.

perspective: The rendition of apparent space in a photograph, such as how far the foreground and background appear to be separated from each other. Perspective is determined by the distance of the camera to the subject. Objects that are close appear large, and distant objects appear to be smaller.

perspective control lens: A special lens that allows correcting distortion resulting from a high or low camera angle.

Photo CD: A special type of CD-ROM developed by Eastman Kodak Company that can store high-quality photographic images in a proprietary space-saving format, along with music and other data.

Picture CD: A CD-ROM designed to hold digital images, often returned by photo finishers with a standard order of prints. The images are stored in a relatively low-resolution JPEG format of sufficient size for use for non-critical applications at home.

pixel: The smallest element of a digital image that can be assigned a color. The term is a contraction of *picture element*.

pixels per inch (ppi): The number of pixels that can be displayed per inch, usually used to refer to pixel resolution from a scanned image or on a monitor.

plug-in: A software module such as a filter that can be accessed from within an image editor to provide special functions.

portrait: The orientation of an image in which the longest dimension is vertical, also called *tall orientation*. In photography, a formal picture of an individual or sometimes a group.

positive: The opposite of a negative; an image with the same tonal relationships as those in the original scenes — for example, a finished print or a slide.

prepress: The stages of the reproduction process that precede printing, when halftones, color separations, and printing plates are created.

process color: The four color pigments used in color printing: cyan, magenta, yellow, and black (CMYK).

RAW: An image file format offered by many digital cameras that includes all the unprocessed information captured by the camera. RAW files are very large and must be processed by a special program, such as Adobe's Camera RAW plug-in or software provided by the camera vendor, after being downloaded from the camera.

rear-curtain sync: An optional kind of electronic flash synchronization technique, originally associated with focal plane shutters, which consists of a traveling set of curtains, including a front curtain (opens to reveal the film or sensor) and a rear curtain (follows at a distance determined by shutter speed to conceal the film or sensor at the conclusion of the exposure).

Rear-curtain sync causes the flash to fire at the *end* of the exposure, an instant before the second or rear curtain of the focal plane shutter begins to move, allowing background light to record when taking flash pictures under dim illumination. With slow shutter speeds, this feature can create a blur effect from the ambient light, showing as patterns that follow a moving subject with subject shown sharply frozen at the end of the blur trail. If you were shooting a photo of The Flash, the superhero would appear sharp, with a ghostly trail behind him. *See also* front-curtain sync.

red-eye: An effect from flash photography that appears to make a person or animal's eyes glow red (or among animals, yellow or green). Caused by light bouncing from the retina of the eye, red-eye is most pronounced in dim illumination (when the irises are wide open) and when the electronic flash is close to the lens and therefore prone to reflect directly back. Image editors can fix red-eye through cloning other pixels over the offending red or orange ones.

red-eye reduction: A way of reducing or eliminating the red-eye phenomenon. Some cameras offer a red-eye reduction mode that uses a *preflash* that causes the irises of the subjects' eyes to contract just before a second, stronger flash is used to take the picture.

reflection copy: Original artwork that is viewed by light reflected from its surface rather than transmitted through it.

reflector: Any device used to reflect light onto a subject to improve balance of exposure (contrast). Another way is to use fill flash. *See also* fill flash.

register: To align images, usually for lining up color separations for making printing plates. *See also* registration mark.

registration mark: A mark that appears on a printed image, generally for color separations, to help in aligning the printing plates. Many applications, such as Photoshop, can add registration marks to your images when they are printed.

reproduction ratio: Used in macro photography to indicate the magnification of a subject.

resample: To change the size or resolution of an image. Resampling down discards pixel information in an image; resampling up adds pixel information through interpolation. *See also* interpolation.

resolution: In image editing, the number of pixels per inch. Resolution is used to determine the size of the image when printed. That is, an 8 x 10-inch image that is saved with 300 pixels per inch (ppi) resolution will print in an 8 x 10-inch size on a 300 dpi printer or 4 x 5 inches on a 600 dpi printer. In digital photography, resolution is the number of pixels that a camera or scanner can capture.

retouch: To edit an image, most often to remove flaws or to create a new effect.

RGB color mode: A color mode that represents the three colors (red, green, and blue) used by devices such as scanners and monitors to reproduce color. Photoshop works in RGB mode by default and even displays CMYK images by converting them to RGB. *See also* CMY(K) color model.

saturation: The purity of color; the amount by which a pure color is diluted with white or gray.

scale: To change the size of some or all of an image. Rescaling also affects file size.

scanner: A device that captures an image of a piece of artwork, a slide, or a negative and converts it to a digitized image or bitmap that the computer can handle.

Secure Data memory card: A flash memory card format that is gaining acceptance for use in digital cameras and other applications.

selection: In image editing, an area of an image chosen for manipulation, usually surrounded by a moving series of dots called a *selection border.*

selective focus: Choosing a lens opening that produces a shallow depth of field. Usually, this is used to isolate a subject by causing most other elements in the scene to be blurred.

self-timer: Mechanism that delays the opening of the shutter for some seconds after the release has been operated.

sensitivity: A measure of the degree of response of a film or sensor to light, measured in digital cameras using ISO ratings.

sensor array: The grid-like arrangement of the red-, green-, and blue-sensitive elements of a digital camera's solid-state capture device. One vendor offers a sensor array that captures a fourth color, termed *emerald.*

shadow: The darkest part of an image, represented on a digital image by pixels with low numeric values or on a halftone by the smallest or absence of dots.

sharpening: Increasing the apparent sharpness of an image by boosting the contrast between adjacent pixels that form an edge.

shutter: In a conventional film camera, the mechanism consisting of blades, a curtain, plate, or some other movable cover that controls the time during which light reaches the film. Digital cameras can use actual shutters or simulate the action of a shutter electronically. Quite a few use a combination, employing a mechanical shutter for slow speeds and an electronic version for higher speeds. Many cameras include a reassuring shutter sound that mimics the noise a mechanical camera's shutter makes.

shutter-priority: An exposure mode in which you set the shutter speed and the camera determines the appropriate f-stop. *See also* aperture-preferred.

side-lighting: Light striking the subject from the side relative to the position of the camera; produces shadows and highlights to create modeling on the subject.

single autofocus: The camera lens focused only when the shutter release button is partially depressed, just prior to taking the picture. *See also* continuous autofocus.

single lens reflex (SLR) camera: A type of camera, often with interchangeable lenses, that allows you to see through the camera's lens as you look in the camera's viewfinder. Other camera functions, such as light metering and flash control, also operate through the camera's lens. See also digital single-lens reflex (dSLR)

slave unit: An accessory flash unit that supplements the main flash, usually triggered electronically when the slave senses the light output by the main unit.

slide: A photographic transparency mounted for projection.

slow-sync: An electronic flash technique for using the flash at a slow shutter speed, which allows background details to show more clearly.

SmartMedia: A type of memory card storage, generally outmoded today because its capacity is limited to 128MB, for digital cameras and other computer devices.

smoothing: To blur the boundaries between edges of an image, often to reduce a rough or jagged appearance.

soft focus: A diffused, unsharp image effect produced by the use of a special lens that creates soft outlines.

soft lighting: Lighting that is low or moderate in contrast, such as on an overcast day.

specular highlight: Bright spots in an image caused by reflection of light sources.

spot color: Ink used in a print job in addition to black or process colors.

spot metering: An exposure calculation system that emphasizes a small portion of the image area, usually in the center of the frame. Some cameras let you move the "spot" to other portions of the image area.

storage media: In the digital camera world, storage media most often refers to the flash memory cards used to retain images before they are transferred to your computer or another device. There are nearly a dozen different types media used by digital cameras, and the number seems to grow monthly. The most common types include two sizes of CompactFlash cards (the main difference is in the thickness); microdrives (tiny hard disks), Sony Memory Sticks, Sony Memory Stick Duo, Secure Digital (SD) cards, SmartMedia Card (generally an obsolete format today), xD Picture Card, and Reduced Size MultiMedia Card.

subtractive primary colors: Cyan, magenta, and yellow, which are the printing inks that, when mixed together equally, theoretically absorb all color and produce black. In practice, however, they generate a muddy brown, so black ink is added to preserve detail (especially in shadows). The combination of the three colors and black is CMYK. (K represents black, to differentiate it from blue in the RGB model, and is sometimes placed in parentheses to indicate that it's an optional part of the color model.) *See also* CMY(K) color model.

Tagged Image File Format: *See* TIFF.

telephoto: A lens or lens setting that magnifies an image.

thermal wax transfer: A printing technology in which dots of wax from a ribbon are applied to paper when heated by thousands of tiny elements in a printhead.

threshold: A predefined brightness level used by a device to determine whether a pixel will be represented as black or white.

thumbnail: A miniature copy of a page or image that provides a preview of the original.

TIFF (Tagged Image File Format): A standard graphics file format that can be used to store grayscale and color images plus selection masks.

time exposure: A picture taken by leaving the lens open for a long period, usually more than one second. The camera is generally locked down with a tripod to prevent blur during the long exposure.

tint: A color with white added to it. In graphic arts, *tint* often refers to the percentage of one color added to another.

tolerance: The range of color or tonal values that will be selected, with a tool like an image editor's Magic Wand, or filled with paint when using a tool like the Paint Bucket.

transparency: A positive photographic image on film, viewed or projected by light shining through the film.

transparency scanner: A type of scanner that captures color slides and/or negatives.

tripod: A three-legged supporting stand used to hold the camera steady. Especially useful when using slow shutter speeds and/or telephoto lenses.

TTL: Through the lens. A system of providing viewing through the actual lens that takes the picture (as with a camera with an electronic viewfinder, LCD display, or single-lens reflex viewing), or calculation of exposure or focus based on the view through the lens.

tungsten light: Light from ordinary room lamps and ceiling fixtures, as opposed to fluorescent illumination.

underexposure: A condition in which too little light reaches the film or sensor, producing a thin negative (one with little density), a dark slide, a muddy-looking print, or a dark digital image.

unipod: A one-legged support, or monopod, used to steady the camera. *See also* tripod.

unsharp masking: The process for increasing the contrast between adjacent pixels in an image, thus increasing sharpness, especially around edges.

USB (Universal Serial Bus): A high-speed serial communication method commonly used to connect digital cameras and other devices to a computer.

viewfinder: The device in a camera used to frame the image. With an SLR camera, the viewfinder is also used to focus the image if focusing manually. You can also focus an image with the LCD display of a digital camera, which is a type of viewfinder.

vignetting: Adding dark corners to an image; often produced by using a lens hood that is too small for the field of view, or generated artificially by using image editing techniques.

white: The color formed by combining all the colors of light (in the additive color model) or by removing all colors (in the subtractive model). *See also* additive primary colors and subtractive primary colors.

white balance: The adjustment of a digital camera to the color temperature of the light source. Interior illumination is relatively red; outdoor light is relatively blue. Digital cameras often set correct white balance automatically or let you do it through menus. Image editors can often do some color correction of images that were exposed using the wrong white-balance setting.

white point: In image editing, the lightest pixel in the highlight area of an image.

wide-angle lens: A lens that has a shorter focal length and a wider field of view than a normal lens for a particular film or digital image format.

zoom: In image editing, to enlarge or reduce the size of an image on your monitor. In photography, to enlarge or reduce the size of an image using the magnification settings of a lens.

Index

Eyedropper tool, 48, 436–437
eyeglasses
  hot spots on, 278
  viewfinders and, 104, 105,
    106–107
eyepoint, 104

F

f-stops. *See also* lenses
  defined, 91–93, 681
  in dSLR cameras, 189
  overview, 30
faxes, 152
feather, 527, 532, 681
file formats. *See* image file
    formats
fill flash. *See also* flash units,
    external
  defined, 170, 681
  for portraits, 287, 288
  when traveling, 383
fill lighting, 287, 288, 681
filling shapes with color,
    458–459
film canisters, 280
film, digital. *See* memory
    cards
film photography. *See also*
    restoring photos;
    scanning
  35mm film cameras, 194
  cleaning film before
    scanning, 633–635
  converting to digital
    using photo labs, 17, 38
    and posting to Web, 17
    using scanners, 16–17,
      35, 153
  versus digital photography,
    129
film speed, 96
  ISO ratings, 96, 191
  noise, 191
  overview, 624–625

filter holders, 176–177
filters
  accessing recently used, 588
  applying, 585, 600
  artistic filters, 594–595, 596
  Blur filters
    Blur More, 588
    versus Blur tool, 559, 588
    defined, 588
    Gaussian Blur, 588, 683
    Motion Blur, 430, 431, 433,
      588, 589, 590
    overview, 431–432, 433
    Radial Blur, 431–432, 588,
      589, 590
    Smart Blur, 586, 587
  color, scanning prints
    through, 621–622
  corrective filters
    Blur filters, 588–590
    defined, 587
    Lens Correction, 523, 524
    noise filters, 591–594
    Sharpen filters, 591
  defined, 179–180, 681
  in Effects palette, 601–603
  Filter Gallery, 586–587, 588
  Filter menu, 586, 588
  hot mirror filter, 110
  how they work, 586–587
  image editing and, 177
  low-contrast filters, 363
  neutral density filters,
    179, 180
  noise filters
    Despeckle, 591
    Dust & Scratches, 49,
      592–594
    Reduce Noise, 523, 592
  Oil Paint filter, 510–511
  Sharpen filters
    Sharpen, 428, 429, 559,
      591
    Sharpen Edges, 591
    Sharpen More, 591

  versus Sharpen tool, 559
  Smart Sharpen, 523
  Unsharp Mask, 591, 643
  using, 643–644
  single step filters, 587
  special effects filters
    distortions, 595, 598–599
    Emboss, 596–597
    Liquify command,
      595, 600
    overview, 595–596
    that stylize, 595, 599
    textures, 597
  in sports photography, 363
  third-party filters, 603–605
  tips for using, 587
  Vanishing Point filter, 522
FireWire (IEEE 1394) ports,
    34, 133–134, 681
fixed focal length lenses,
    86, 210, 211
flash techniques
  front-curtain sync, 682–683
  rear-curtain sync, 690
  slow-sync, 692
flash units, built-in
  close-ups and, 252
  defined, 108–109
  red eye and, 109, 171
flash units, external. *See also*
    digital camera
    accessories; portrait
    studio lighting
    accessories
  background cloths,
    176, 270–272
  batteries, 175, 277, 284
  brackets, 175, 280, 282,
    283
  collapsible reflectors, 176
  flash modifier devices,
    276–283
  bounce flash, 171, 172, 277
  cable connections, 172–173,
    253, 280, 285

Don't forget about these
bestselling For Dummies® books!

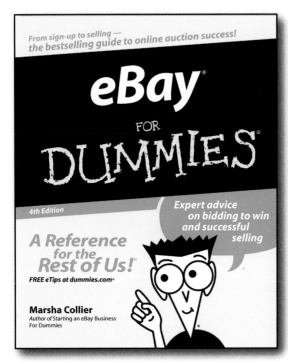

From sign-up to selling —
the bestselling guide to online auction success!

eBay®
FOR DUMMIES®

4th Edition

Expert advice
on bidding to win
and successful
selling

A Reference
for the
Rest of Us!®

FREE eTips at dummies.com®

Marsha Collier
Author of Starting an eBay Business
For Dummies

0-7645-5654-1

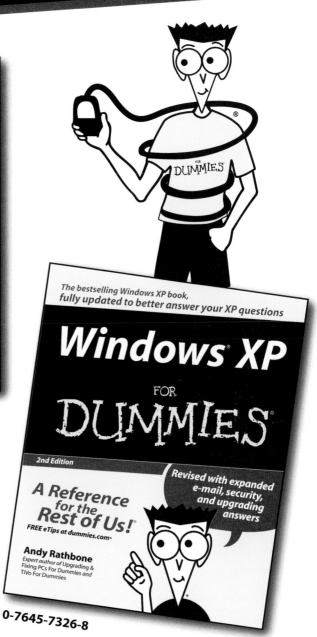

The bestselling Windows XP book,
fully updated to better answer your XP questions

Windows® XP
FOR DUMMIES®

2nd Edition

Revised with expanded
e-mail, security,
and upgrading
answers

A Reference
for the
Rest of Us!®

FREE eTips at dummies.com®

Andy Rathbone
Expert author of Upgrading &
Fixing PCs For Dummies and
TiVo For Dummies

0-7645-7326-8

Available wherever books are sold. Go to www.dummies.com or call 1-877-762-2974 to order direct.

Don't forget about these bestselling For Dummies® books!

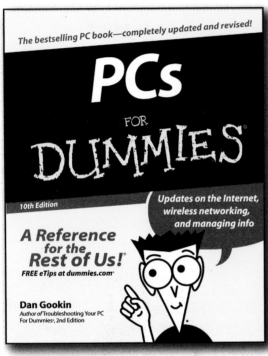

The bestselling PC book—completely updated and revised!

PCs
FOR DUMMIES®

10th Edition

Updates on the Internet, wireless networking, and managing info

A Reference for the Rest of Us!®
FREE eTips at dummies.com®

Dan Gookin
Author of Troubleshooting Your PC For Dummies®, 2nd Edition

0-7645-8958-X

Get started, get savvy, and get things done with the Internet

The Internet
FOR DUMMIES®

10th Edition

Revised to cover broadband, wireless, blogging, and more

A Reference for the Rest of Us!®
FREE eTips at dummies.com®

John Levine
Margaret Levine Young
Carol Baroudi

0-7645-8996-2

Available wherever books are sold. Go to www.dummies.com or call 1-877-762-2974 to order direct.

Don't forget about these bestselling For Dummies® books!

0-7645-7208-3

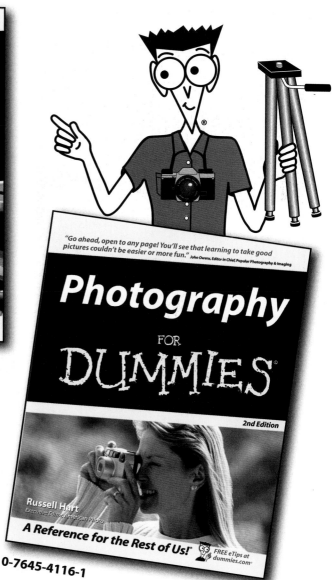

0-7645-4116-1

Available wherever books are sold. Go to www.dummies.com or call 1-877-762-2974 to order direct.

Don't forget about these bestselling For Dummies® books!

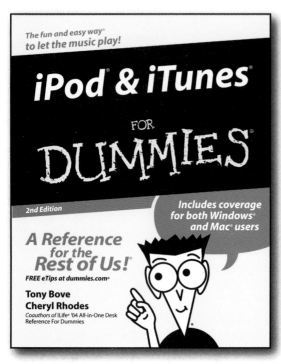

The fun and easy way® to let the music play!

iPod® & iTunes®
FOR DUMMIES®

2nd Edition

Includes coverage for both Windows® and Mac® users

A Reference for the Rest of Us!®
FREE eTips at dummies.com®

Tony Bove
Cheryl Rhodes
Coauthors of iLife® '04 All-in-One Desk Reference For Dummies

0-7645-7772-7

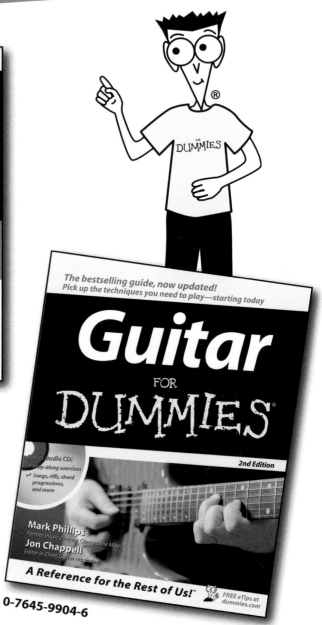

The bestselling guide, now updated!
Pick up the techniques you need to play—starting today

Guitar
FOR DUMMIES®

2nd Edition

Bonus audio CD:
play-along exercises
✓ Songs, riffs, chord progressions, and more

Mark Phillips
Former music director, Cherry Lane Music
Jon Chappell
Editor in Chief, Guitar magazine

A Reference for the Rest of Us!™

FREE eTips at dummies.com®

0-7645-9904-6

Available wherever books are sold. Go to www.dummies.com or call 1-877-762-2974 to order direct.